Decision in Normandy

Carlo D'Este retired from the U.S. Army as a lieutenant colonel in 1978, having served overseas in Germany, Vietnam, and England. Born in Oakland, California, he received his B.A. from Norwich University, an M.A. from the University of Richmond and an honorary doctorate of Humane Letters from Norwich in 1992. Also the author of three other books about the Second World War, he is completing a biography of General George S. Patton.

Decision in Normandy

by Carlo D'Este

HarperPerennial
A Division of HarperCollins*Publishers*

In loving memory of my parents
Charles and Eleanor D'Este

and

in remembrance of the American, British,
Canadian, Polish, Belgian, Dutch and French soldiers,
sailors and airmen who fought and died to liberate France

Extracts from *A General's Life* © Estate of General of the Army Omar N. Bradley and Clay Blair 1983.

A hardcover edition of this book was published in 1983 by William Collins & Sons Co. Ltd. A second edition was published in 1984 by Pan Books Ltd. It is here reprinted by arrangement with William Collins & Sons Co. Ltd. and Pan Books Ltd.

HarperCollins books may be purchased for educational, business, or sales promotional use. For information please write: Special Markets Department, HarperCollins Publishers, Inc., 10 East 53rd Street, New York, NY 10022.

First HarperPerennial edition published 1991.
Fiftieth anniversary edition published 1994.

Maps by Tom Stalker-Miller

The Library of Congress has catalogued the HarperPerennial edition as follows:

D'Este, Carlo, 1936–
    Decision in Normandy / by Carlo D'Este. — 1st HarperPerennial ed.
      p. cm.
    Reprint. Originally published: New York : Dutton, c1983.
    Includes index.
    ISBN 0-06-097312-9
    1. World War, 1939–1945—Campaigns—France—Normandy. 2. Normandy (France)— History. I. Title.
[D756.5.N6D47   1991]
940.54´2142—dc20   90-55977

ISBN 0-06-092495-0 (50th anniv. ed.)

96 97 98 **RRD H** 10 9 8 7

Contents

Introduction   13

PART I: The Great Endeavour   15
1   The Origins of the Second Front   17
2   Second Front, North Africa   23
3   The Birth of Operation Overlord   32
4   The Overlord Commanders   41
5   A Time for Decision   55
6   The Master Plan   71

PART II: Invasion   105
7   D-Day: The Invasion of France   107
8   D-Day: The Orne Bridgehead   120
9   The Field of Battle   151
10 Caen: The Search for a Strategy   160
11 Villers-Bocage   174
12 Ends and Means   199
13 The Air Chiefs   212
14 Epsom: The Battle for the Odon   232
15 The Manpower Dilemma   252
16 The Price of Caution   271
17 Caen: Too Little, Too Late   298
18 D+30: Stalemate   321

PART III: Breakout 335
19 Planning the Breakthrough 337
20 Operation Goodwood 352
21 Into the Cauldron 370
22 The Furore over Goodwood 391
23 Cobra 400
24 Turning the Corner at Avranches 408
25 The Great Encirclement 418

PART IV: Aftermath 435
26 The Falaise Controversy 437
27 The Legacy of Normandy 461
28 The Normandy Myth 476

Epilogue 503
Postscript 509
Appendix A 515
Appendix B 517
Appendix C 519
Sources 521
Acknowledgements 527
Index 531

Illustrations

Allied bombing of the French rail network
(*National Archives*)
US Army photograph, Department of Defense Archives)
Air Chief Marshal Tedder (*Imperial War Museum*)
Air Chief Marshal Leigh-Mallory (*Imperial War Museum*)
The map illustrating Montgomery's basic strategy
(*Public Record Office*)
The D-Day landings (*Imperial War Museum*)

Caen and the steelworks at Colombelles (*Imperial War Museum*)
Field Marshal Rommel, inspecting the 21st Panzer Division (*courtesy of Manfred Rommel*)
British engineers clearing Tilly-sur-Seulles (*Imperial War Museum*)
Churchill and Montgomery (*Imperial War Museum*)
Montgomery and Field Marshal Brooke (*Imperial War Museum*)
Caen (*Imperial War Museum*)
British troops pinned down near Caen (*Imperial War Museum*)
American troops in the bocage (*National Archives*)
Eisenhower with Major General Collins and Lieutenant General Bradley (*National Archives*)

British vehicles and armour crossing the Orne (*Imperial War Museum*)
American troops at St Lô (*National Archives*)

Lieutenant General Patton (*National Archives*)

Lieutenant General Dempsey with Montgomery and Bradley (*Imperial War Museum*)

American troops moving on Mortain (*National Archives*)

Part of the carnage of the Falaise Gap (*Imperial War Museum*)

German prisoners-of-war from the Argentan-Falaise pocket (*National Archives*)

Jerusalem Cemetery (*Commonwealth War Graves Commission*)

Maps

The Normandy Battlefield   *page 10–11*

Forecast of Operations,
    D + 17 to D + 90   *page 91*

The Orne Bridgehead   *page 134–135*

Situation map, 10 June 1944   *page 173*

Villers-Bocage   *page 186*

Situation map, 17 June 1944   *page 198*

EPSOM: The Odon Battlefield   *page 243*

Situation map, 30 June 1944   *page 251*

Situation map, 9 July 1944   *page 319*

Operation GOODWOOD   *page 384*

The Allied Breakout   *page 556–557*

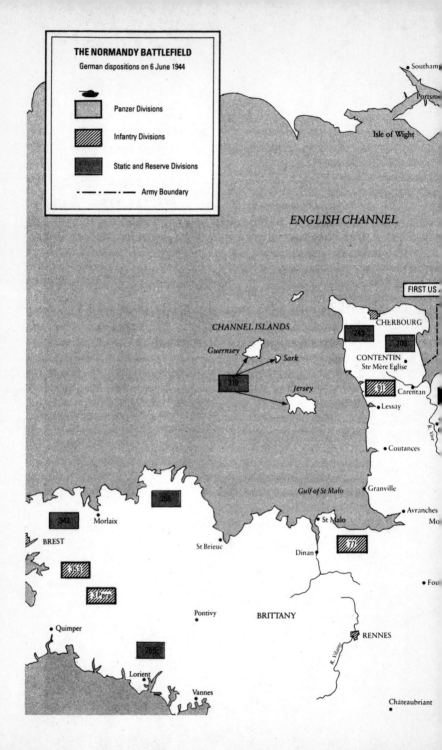

THE NORMANDY BATTLEFIELD

German dispositions on 6 June 1944

Panzer Divisions

Infantry Divisions

Static and Reserve Divisions

Army Boundary

ENGLISH CHANNEL

Southamp

Portsmo

Isle of Wight

FIRST US

CHERBOURG

243

709

CHANNEL ISLANDS

Guernsey

Sark

CONTENTIN

Ste Mère Eglise

319

91

Carentan

Jersey

Lessay

R. Vire

Coutances

Gulf of St Malo

Granville

266

Avranches

343

Morlaix

Mo

BREST

St Brieuc

77

St Malo

Dinan

353

Fou

3 Para

Pontivy

BRITTANY

RENNES

Quimper

R. Vilaine

265

Lorient

Châteaubriant

Vannes

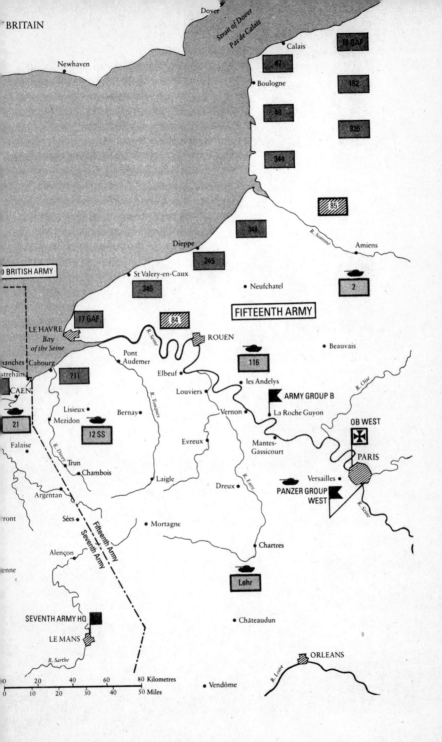

Introduction to the
50th Anniversary Edition

The great Allied invasion of Normandy on 6 June 1944 was the most complex and daring military operation in the history of modern warfare, the culmination of more than three years of conception, often contentious debate, and the most prodigious military planning ever undertaken. Its success was a testament to the cooperation of allies with fundamentally opposing military and political philosophies, as well as the indomitable courage of men called upon to fight and die on the battlefield.

Nevertheless, in the aftermath of the D-Day landings Field Marshal Erwin Rommel's army group fought tenaciously for their very survival, and when the Allies failed to advance beyond their narrow bridgehead, concern quickly turned into discord within the Allied high command. As the commander of U.S. ground forces, Lieutenant General Omar N. Bradley, later wrote, 'By July 10, we faced a real danger of a World War I–type stalemate.'[1]

There were two important aspects in the planning for Normandy: the D-Day assault and the post-invasion strategy for driving the German army from Normandy and behind the Seine, thus permitting the Allies to build up their ground armies for an invasion of Germany. Although a great many military minds were responsible for the detailed planning of Operation OVERLORD, the conception and execution of the post–D-Day plan of campaign was the brainchild of the Allied ground commander-in-chief, General (later Field Marshal) Sir Bernard Law Montgomery. As Eisenhower's designated ground force commander, it fell to him to originate and carry out the Allied battle strategy. Montgomery's so-called master plan became one of the most debated and least understood stratagems of his military career. It generated nearly endless debate and to this day still arouses fierce reaction in his critics and admirers, a fact repeatedly brought home to the author during the research and interviews for this book.

A great deal has been written about D-Day, and this work does not attempt to duplicate the excellent accounts written

[1]Omar N. Bradley and Clay Blair, *A General's Life*, New York, 1983, p. 272.

since the war. However, the Normandy campaign left a legacy of unanswered questions and bitter controversy. Post-war memoirs, campaign histories and biographies have fueled these long-standing disputes, which, inevitably, have focused on Montgomery's generalship: his failure to capture quickly the strategically important city of Caen, the manner in which the American breakout from the bridgehead came about, and the quarrel over the closing of the 'Falaise gap'. Acrimonious public exchanges between the principals have underscored the great depth of feeling which existed.

In recent years significant documentary evidence has been released by various British and American archives which reveals previously unknown aspects about Montgomery's intentions and strategy in Normandy, and reaction to them in the Allied high command. These sources give a clear and fascinating perspective on how the Normandy campaign was planned and fought, and form the nucleus of *Decision in Normandy*.

The year 1994 marks the fiftieth year since the D-Day landings, and in that half century many wars have come and gone following one of the most momentous days in history. This anniversary will be especially bittersweet: a time for remembrance, but also a time for the wounds of war to have at last healed. Although Normandy no longer bears the terrible scars of battle, the many Allied and German military cemeteries which dot the landscape offer silent affirmation of what took place in the summer of 1944. The largest is the American cemetery on the bluffs overlooking bloody Omaha beach, which an average of 1.5 million people visit annually.

As the years pass, those who fought in Normandy as young men are growing fewer. Later generations will only know of it from the pages of history. It is my sincere wish that this account will serve to shed entirely new light on what historian Max Hastings has aptly called 'the decisive western battle of the Second World War.'[2]

This is the story of one of the last great land battles ever fought, and what occurred during the eighty-day campaign which began on 6 June 1944 and ended in the greatest defeat suffered by Hitler's armies in the West.

Cape Cod, Massachusetts
September 15, 1993

[2] Max Hastings, *Overlord: D-Day and the Battle for Normandy, 1944*, London, 1985, p. 13.

PART I

The Great Endeavour

I can get home to England in my Fortress from here [Tunisia] in one night. And when I have done my share of the final business I shall come. But I want to first pay the debt I owe for the days at the end of May 1940 on the beaches at La Panne, Bray-les-Dunnes and Dunkirk. And the debt *will be paid*.

Montgomery to Brooke
15 April 1943

CHAPTER 1

The Origins
of the Second Front

It must be said to our shame that we sent our Army into that most modern war with weapons and equipment which were quite inadequate, and we had only ourselves to blame for the disasters which early overtook us in the field when fighting began in 1940.

Montgomery of Alamein

In May 1940 'The Phoney War' was shattered by Hitler's armies, who launched a lightning attack through the supposedly impenetrable Ardennes Forest against the French Army, and across the lowlands of Belgium against the British Expeditionary Force. As in the First World War the Allies were caught unprepared and thrown into disarray by the new blitzkrieg tactics of the German panzer divisions. One of the spearhead units of the German thrust was the 7th Panzer Division commanded by one of the most imaginative and daring of the Wehrmacht's commanders, Major General Erwin Rommel, later the famed commander of the Afrika Korps and the man who in 1944 was charged by Hitler with the defence of his Atlantic Wall, which included Normandy. Within days the BEF was cut off from the main elements of the French Army and trapped in a pocket around the coastal city of Dunkirk. Faced with the choice of surrendering or attempting somehow to escape across the English Channel, General Sir Alan Brooke's 2 Corps[1] fought a magnificent delaying action for the main body of the BEF while the Royal Navy hastily organized what Winston Churchill called 'the deliverance of Dunkirk'.

The successful evacuation of the British Expeditionary Force

---

[1] For ease of identification all British corps are shown by Arabic numerals, US Corps by Roman.

from the beaches of Dunkirk represented a miraculous escape from disaster. But, although a triumph of British will and courage, Dunkirk was also the first in a long series of setbacks that were to beset the British in the early days of the Second World War. The saving of the BEF was almost the only glimmer of hope in an otherwise dismal year. Not only was it the heart of the British Army but its commanders and men were the only professional soldiers capable of defending the United Kingdom against certain invasion by Hitler. More than 339,000 British and French soldiers escaped the German trap at Dunkirk. Among them was the future commander of the ground forces for the Second Front, Major General Bernard Montgomery, General Officer Commanding the 3rd British Division. With him went his future army commander, Miles Dempsey, and three corps commanders: Crocker, Ritchie and Horrocks.[1] Hitler's failure to annihilate the BEF by rapidly closing the pincers of his armies cost Germany dear in the next four years.

The salvation of the BEF was best summed up by the man who was to play a leading role in the reshaping of the British Army, Field Marshal Sir Alan Brooke:

> Had the BEF not returned to this country it is hard to see how the Army could have recovered from this blow. The reconstitution of our land forces would have been so delayed as to endanger the whole course of the war. It must be remembered that the majority of our future leaders were at that time all with the BEF – Alex, Monty, Anderson, Dempsey, Barker, Horrocks . . . and many others who played every great part in the re-raising of our forces, their training and their leading to ultimate victory. . . Had we, therefore, been deprived of the existing leaders of the Army before Dunkirk, it may be imagined how irreparable this loss would have been. ∴ Time and again throughout the years of the war I thanked God for the safe return of the bulk of the personnel of the BEF.[2]

The sorry state of the British Army after Dunkirk and the pressing need to defend the British Isles against invasion made any

---

[1] In May 1940 John Crocker was the commander of the 3rd Armoured Brigade which was engaged in attempting to stop the German offensive over the Somme. With its flanks exposed by the collapse of the French front, Crocker's unit had a narrow escape from Rommel's 7th Panzer Division, and in twenty-four hours he guided the remnants of his unit 175 miles across Normandy to escape through the port of Cherbourg only hours ahead of Rommel's pursuit.

[2] Alanbrooke Papers, 'Notes On My Life', King's College, London.

thoughts of a quick return to the continent of Europe fantastical. British priorities lay in simple survival; indeed it was evident to the new Prime Minister, Sir Winston Churchill, that immediate American aid was essential if Britain were to hold out against Hitler. To succeed in freeing Europe from the Nazi yoke not only aid but active American participation in the war was, as in 1917, a *sine qua non*. Aside from such considerations, no invasion of Europe was even remotely possible without the creation and training of an entirely new British Army. The remnants of the BEF would have to become the nucleus of a truly modern force capable of fighting the German Army on equal terms with new weapons and new doctrine.

When Britain declared war on Germany in September 1939 her army was ill-equipped and woefully unprepared for the type of warfare Hitler was about to unleash. No suitable military doctrine existed to cope with a new and revitalized German Army and its new style of warfare, first introduced against the hapless Poles that same month. The British Army of the 1930s had remained neglected and largely static in its thinking. Politicians could not decide on a proper role for the army; its leaders offered nothing constructive; and its budget all but dried up as military funds went primarily to the Royal Navy and the Royal Air Force. The potential of the tank for revolutionizing warfare was stifled by War Office penury and the traditionalists, while the new Wehrmacht was developing its own doctrine of armoured warfare called the blitzkrieg. While the Germans were developing both a new family of tanks and techniques for tank-infantry cooperation on what was envisioned as a mobile battlefield, the leaders of the newly formed Royal Tank Corps were being told that, with such a paucity of tanks, their future role was primarily to support the infantry. The British were not alone in their backward thinking: in France and the United States, de Gaulle, Patton and a few other imaginative thinkers were finding little interest in their arguments in favour of the tank as an offensive weapon of war.

The question facing Churchill was how could a Second Front, in the form of a cross-Channel invasion, ever possibly be launched? British resources were perilously strained in the first two years of the war. Military forces in the Far East were virtually on their own, half a world away and in the Mediterranean a belligerent Benito Mussolini, his courage bolstered by Hitler's backing, had declared war on Britain and France on 10 June 1940. Though Italy's military leadership was of dubious quality and her army ill-equipped, a substantial buildup of forces in Libya posed a serious threat to the British position in the Middle East, where Egypt was defended only by General Sir Archibald Wavell's tiny desert force. On the high seas the Royal Navy was fighting defensively against a powerful German Navy whose U-boats and capital ships menaced Britain's lifeline to the United States. Britain herself was under threat of imminent invasion.

There could hardly have been a more depressing atmosphere in which to conceive an offensive counterstroke. It is a tribute to Churchill's vision that he was able to look beyond the immediacy of Britain's problems and envision a Second Front.[1] He understood clearly that once the imminent threat of invasion could be neutralized and America persuaded to join the war, a Second Front was not only possible but represented the only means of defeating Germany. Fortunately the success of the RAF during the Battle of Britain in September 1940 reduced the invasion threat and helped to secure the time needed for reorganization and buildup of the armed forces. There was much to be done; doctrine and strategy for amphibious warfare were non-existent and there were no specialized vessels which could be used to land troops and equipment quickly on a hostile coast.

Shortly after Dunkirk Churchill began the first tentative steps to redress these problems when he established a Combined Operations Staff whose mission was twofold: to plan and execute commando raids against selected points in German-occupied Europe, and to begin the development and testing of suitable amphibious vehicles and equipment, along with a doctrine for their use. In so doing Churchill undoubtedly still retained vivid memories of the ill-fated invasion of Gallipoli in 1915, an operation for whose costly failure the then First Lord of the Admiralty bore a heavy responsibility. Now, for the time being the best Churchill could hope for was defiant harass-

---

[1] The post-war years have abounded with stories about Churchill's leadership but none have typified the amazing Mr Churchill better than the story told by Lord Ismay about the time after Dunkirk when Ismay's desk was piling up with notes of disaster: Then Churchill wrote, saying: 'We are stronger than ever before. Look how many extra men we have here now. Form Leopard Brigades to tear and claw the enemy.' Quoted in interview with Lord Ismay by Dr Forrest C. Pogue, 17 December 1946.

ment of the Germans, a reminder that Britain was not beaten, was still capable of striking back, even if on a small scale.

The first head of Combined Operations was a distinguished naval figure who had led the British raid on Zeebrugge in 1918, Admiral Sir Roger Keyes. He brought to the job an active and original mind and great enthusiasm, but found himself unable to cope with the internal wrangling of the Whitehall bureaucracy which did not embrace his interest in fighting an unconventional war. Within a year his relations with Churchill had soured badly; he was later to tell his successor that 'the Chiefs of Staffs are the greatest cowards I have ever met'.[1]

Churchill's relentless demands for action and progress and his growing loss of confidence in Keyes led in the autumn of 1941 to the appointment of a dynamic junior naval officer, Captain Lord Louis Mountbatten, as head of Combined Operations. In him Churchill found exactly the sort of man he was looking for, an opinionated and outspoken public hero possessed of the same sort of high-powered ideas that complemented the Prime Minister's own impetuous nature.[2]

Mountbatten recalls being summoned by Churchill in October 1941 and told:

> You are to prepare for the invasion of Europe, for unless we can go and land and fight Hitler and beat his forces on land, we shall never win this war. You must devise and design the appliances, the landing craft and the technique to enable us to effect a landing against opposition and to maintain ourselves there. You must take the most brilliant officers from the Navy, Army and Air Force to help as our planners to plan this great operation. You must take bases to use as training establishments where you can train the Navy, Army and Air Force to work as a single entity. The whole of the south coast of England is a bastion of defence against the invasion of Hitler; you've got to turn it into the springboard for our attack.[3]

Despite later charges that Churchill did not favour a cross-Channel invasion, Mountbatten never had any doubts as to the

---

[1] Quoted in *Mountbatten*, Richard Hough, London, 1980, p. 192.
[2] Not everyone agreed with Mountbatten's qualifications, among them Montgomery who once remarked: 'A very gallant sailor. Had three ships sunk under him. *Three* ships sunk under him. [Pause]. Doesn't know how to fight a battle.' Quoted in Goronwy Rees, *A Bundle of Sensations*, London, 1960.
[3] Admiral Lord Louis Mountbatten, Thames Television interview, 'The World at War, 1939–1945', Imperial War Museum (hereinafter IWM).

Prime Minister's intentions. 'He always wanted that. It may be that he got so interested in his [later] sideshow in the Mediterranean that at the last he was more interested in carrying it through than in working on [Operation] Overlord, but it was Winston who first saw the need for the cross-Channel business, and who wanted it on the proper scale... I was to have 200,000 men trained a year hence, and another 100,000 six months later.'[1]

Mountbatten was even given a seat on the British Chiefs of Staff Committee, beside Brooke, Portal and Pound. Despite his lofty position Mountbatten was frequently treated with resentment and derision, an experience which he never forgot and which still greatly disturbed him after the war. 'My job with Combined Operations was a very difficult one. I was a very junior officer and had very few men under me who weren't my junior ... the result was [the military establishment] thought I didn't know what I was doing; regarded my headquarters as made up of madmen. Refused quite often to pay attention to what we were doing. Hooted every time we suggested something. You know the Lords of the Admiralty are called "Their Lordships". They gave us so much trouble, we finally called them "Their Blockships".'[2]

The Japanese surprise attack on Pearl Harbor on 7 December 1941 was America's Dunkirk and took the United States into war. American entry into the war meant that the beleaguered British would no longer fight alone; from now on, if Roosevelt so decided, Britain would receive the necessary manpower and logistical support to launch a Second Front. But where would a Second Front be started and when? The Allies would quarrel over this point for nearly two more years before resolving their differences.

[1] Admiral Lord Louis Mountbatten, interview with Dr Forrest C. Pogue, 18 February 1947.
[2] Ibid.

CHAPTER 2

Second Front, North Africa

I am most anxious for you to know where I stand myself at the present time. I have found no one who regards SLEDGEHAMMER as possible. I should like to see you do GYMNAST as soon as possible. . . Meanwhile all preparations for ROUNDUP in 1943 should proceed at full blast, thus holding the maximum enemy forces opposite England. All this seems to me as clear as noonday.

Churchill to Roosevelt,
14 July 1942

Under the leadership of Chief of Staff General George C. Marshall, American policy by early 1942 called for holding the line against Japan in the Pacific, but for primary emphasis being given to the defeat of Germany. The first Anglo-American attempts to achieve a common strategy began in January 1942 during the ARCADIA Conference held in Washington. Churchill and the British Chiefs of Staff outlined a strategy which:

> called for tightening the ring around Germany, then stabbing in the knife when the enemy was exhausted . . . a series of operations around the periphery of Hitler's European fortress, combined with bombing raids against Germany itself . . . but no direct invasion in the near future. This represented traditional British policy, abandoned only from 1914 to 1918, an aberration Churchill was determined not to repeat.[1]

From the outset United States policy in the Second World War consistently placed direct military action above political considerations. Churchill, throughout the partnership, fought to introduce into American thinking a grand strategy which included containment of Russian ambitions. Although Russia was

---

[1] Stephen E. Ambrose, *Rise to Globalism*, London, 1980, pp. 45–6.

by now an ally in the fight against Hitler, Churchill became increasingly mistrustful of Stalin and what he perceived as the threat of Russian post-war domination of Eastern Europe.

Not surprisingly, Marshall opposed Churchill on military grounds, arguing against the tightening ring approach which he considered unsafe and wasteful of lives. He believed it would be courting disaster to leave the Red Army facing the might of the Wehrmacht unaided; indeed it would be the worst blunder in history if eight million men were lost through British-American inaction. The only answer was decisive confrontation through a cross-Channel invasion, and the quickest possible end to the war.[1]

Although ARCADIA ended in overall agreement that the priority of Allied effort should go first towards the defeat of Germany, there was no agreement on the best means of achieving it. Throughout the early months of 1942 both sides prepared their positions for further debate. The British were consistently against any early attempt at a cross-Channel invasion, while Marshall began to push hard for a plan called SLEDGEHAMMER. Originally conceived by the British as an emergency invasion of France for the autumn of 1942 if German pressure on the Red Army became intolerable, or if the German armies on the Eastern Front suddenly collapsed and Hitler's French defences became vulnerable, SLEDGEHAMMER was consistent with American desire for rapid involvement in the war, and led to Marshall's backing of what proved nothing more than a fantasy.

Marshall's chief planner was a heretofore obscure officer, Brigadier General Dwight D. Eisenhower. Under Eisenhower's direction the War Plans Division drew up American proposals which the Chief of Staff presented to Roosevelt in March. Called the Marshall Memorandum, this US strategy modified SLEDGE-HAMMER into a British-American air-ground offensive to be launched that summer of 1942, culminating in landings in France somewhere between Le Havre and Calais. The Memorandum proposed two other operations to be carried out separately: the first, codenamed BOLERO, called for a massive build-up of US troops and equipment in the United Kingdom, which would secure the bastion from which a cross-Channel invasion could be launched in 1943; the invasion itself, for the spring of 1943, was

[1] Ambrose, op.cit., p. 48.

ROUNDUP, originally a British plan for a large-scale forty-eight division operation.

Churchill fought against SLEDGEHAMMER, contending that any cross-Channel invasion in 1942 was premature and far too risky.[1] There was no disagreement at this time about the feasibility of ROUNDUP, but Churchill remained eager for American acceptance of his Mediterranean strategy, presented at the Washington conference as GYMNAST – a takeover of French North West Africa as the springboard for future operations against Rommel's Axis forces. The fundamental differences delaying agreement on a common strategy were reflected in the views of the top two Allied military chiefs:

> Brooke and Marshall saw military strategy through the eyes of very different upbringings and military experience. Like Churchill, Brooke was wedded to the traditional British maritime strategy of weakening Continental powers by blockade and peripheral operations, carried out in areas where the enemy found it most difficult to deploy and support large armies. While he accepted the probable need to cross the Channel in strength one day, his personal experiences in 1940 convinced him that this would not be practicable until German resistance was on the point of collapse.

On the other hand:

> Marshall's thinking was influenced more by organizational and logistic considerations than battle experience. Harnessing and developing the vast complex of military, political and industrial agencies responsible for the United States' war effort could only be done effectively if there was a simple coherent strategic plan which all could understand and work towards. He accepted the need to defeat Germany first but, unlike Churchill and Brooke, believed that there was only one sensible way of doing so; by direct assault across the Channel from the British Isles.[2] [*]

[1] Mountbatten warned Churchill that any invasion in 1942 was exceptionally risky; there were enough landing craft available only for 4,000 men in the first wave. At best, Mountbatten estimated the British could land only four to six divisions against some twenty-five German divisions, who could chew up the invaders without transferring a single German soldier from the Russian Front. Even worse, another defeat in France would end any chance of taking pressure off the hard-pressed Red Army. Thames Television interview, 'The World at War, 1939–1945', IWM.

[2] W. G. F. Jackson, 'OVERLORD': Normandy 1944, London, 1979, p. 46.

[*] Brooke's relations with Marshall and the other US Chiefs of Staff were always formal and rather cool. The Americans disliked Brooke's brusque and formal manner but respected his formidable intellect. Brooke, in turn, was frequently annoyed and irritated

[continued overleaf]

There was also a deep difference of opinion between Roosevelt, Marshall and Henry L. Stimson, the US Secretary of War. Roosevelt was sceptical of SLEDGEHAMMER and worried that BOLERO and ROUNDUP would effectively prevent direct American action in 1942. Despite their disagreement over strategy, Churchill was as anxious as Roosevelt to see American forces involved against the Germans soon, and told Mountbatten: 'I must find somewhere to get all these hundreds of thousands of young men into active operations.'[1] Yet Churchill had pressing reasons for dissuading his ally from a head-on clash with the Germans and, sensing that Roosevelt was open to compromise, he proposed a plan for joint action in North Africa: Operation TORCH. His forces were reaching their nadir with the fall of Tobruk in May, resulting in Rommel's drive towards the Nile Delta and, the prize Hitler craved, the oil fields of the Middle East. At home, Churchill's Prime Ministership survived a vote of censure in the House of Commons for his alleged mishandling of the war. Only in the Mediterranean did there appear to be any opportunity to reverse the long series of setbacks which had begun at Dunkirk. Stung by the audacious success of Rommel and desperately in need of a major victory to appease his critics, Churchill directed his rage at his generals. He had previously dismissed the Commander-in-Chief of the Middle East, General Wavell, in June 1941 and replaced him with General Sir Claude Auchinleck. Now it seemed that Auchinleck, too, was ineffectual and the Prime Minister was rapidly losing confidence in him.

Marshall believed that without SLEDGEHAMMER 'we were faced with a defensive attitude in the European Theater'.[2] In arguing for the retention of SLEDGEHAMMER he was in reality attempting to save ROUNDUP, which he believed was in great peril for 1943. Marshall's fear was that the British would use the advantage of TORCH to persist in peripheral operations in the Mediterranean at the expense of an invasion of Europe. Not only

[continued from previous page]
by his US colleagues, particularly the crusty Admiral Ernest J. King who, like Brooke, rarely concealed his feelings. Field Marshal Sir John Dill, Brooke's predecessor as CIGS and later the representative of the British Chiefs of Staff in Washington, was exceptionally effective in smoothing out problems between the Allied Chiefs. He was widely admired and became a great personal friend of Marshall.

[1] Mountbatten, Thames Television interview, loc.cit.
[2] Forrest C. Pogue, *George C. Marshall, Ordeal and Hope, 1939–1942*, London, 1966, p. 345.

was this seen as a setback to eventual victory in Europe, it would also delay a comeback in the Pacific, something very much favoured by the American people after the disaster at Pearl Harbour. Marshall could not accept that the British proposals would shorten the war; quite the reverse, he remained convinced that their strategy might well lengthen it. 'It was this fear of the long, tortuous approach that would leave his forces in the Pacific beleaguered and neglected for months and perhaps years that later prompted Marshall's fierce efforts to tie the British to a major offensive against the Germans.'[1]

Thus, in July 1942, during meetings with Churchill and the British Chiefs of Staff, Marshall made one final effort to save SLEDGEHAMMER, but in the face of complete British intransigence he reluctantly recommended Roosevelt accept Churchill's proposal for TORCH, an Allied invasion of French North West Africa. A depressed Eisenhower was heard to call this setback to American aspirations a day that might become 'the blackest day in history'.[2*] As it ultimately evolved, TORCH became one part of a massive Allied pincer movement in North Africa; the other was a westward offensive by the British Eighth Army, trapping Rommel's Axis forces.

Supposedly, TORCH would not set back the intended cross-Channel assault beyond 1943 and would 'blood' American forces against the Wehrmacht; but, as 1943 would show, Marshall's worst fears came true. For Winston Churchill, however, his triumph over Marshall was a masterstroke of immense proportions and changed the entire course of British-American grand strategy to favour the British view. Not only was TORCH consistent with Churchill's 'tightening the noose' policy but it committed the United States to action in an area most advantageous to Britain. Once in action there it would prove far easier to keep the United States involved in his soft-

---

[1] Pogue, *Ordeal and Hope*, op.cit., p. 349.
[2] Harry C. Butcher, *Three Years With Eisenhower*, London, 1946, p. 24.
* In later years Eisenhower changed his opinion, writing in 1960 to Ismay of SLEDGEHAMMER: 'Many of our people, *looking backward*, still believe that we would have been better off had we undertaken that operation in late 1942 in view of the fact that Hitler was so busy on the Eastern Front. *I do not share this view* and have often publicly stated that I think that the alternative, TORCH, provided us with many later advantages, not the least of which was the training opportunity, through which both sides learned how Allied commands could and should work effectively.' Quoted in letter, Eisenhower to Lord Ismay, 3 December 1960, Eisenhower Presidential Papers, Eisenhower Library.

underbelly approach and away from cross-Channel confrontation in 1942.

In August Churchill sacked Auchinleck, brought in General
Sir Harold Alexander to command the Middle East, and summoned Lieutenant General Bernard Montgomery from England
to command the Eighth Army. Churchill insisted on the soonest
possible counteroffensive to coincide with the TORCH landings in
the west, which were scheduled for October or November.

By Autumn 1942 it was evident that a cross-Channel invasion
even in early 1943 was in jeopardy. Although there was agreement in principle for ROUNDUP, there had as yet been no firm
British commitment to it. In addition, the time required to
accomplish the American buildup in England for BOLERO was
threatening the timetable for ROUNDUP: sufficient landing craft
were not available, there was no joint command or control
headquarters established, no serious discussions had taken place
about the appointment of a Supreme Commander, and few
American or British troops had been trained for amphibious
operations.

Late in 1942 Churchill had vigorously pressed for ROUNDUP
in 1943, in contradiction to his stated policy of priority of action
in the Mediterranean. Whether he seriously wanted a cross-
Channel invasion in 1943 or was merely keeping the idea alive is
still arguable. Certainly, he recognized the inevitability of the
operation one day and it can be reasoned he was doing nothing
more than keeping his options open. What soon became evident
was that ROUNDUP stood little chance in 1943, given the diversion of BOLERO resources to other theatres, and inadequate
assault craft and other shipping. As Marshall feared, TORCH had
indeed diverted attention and assets to the Mediterranean,
rendering ROUNDUP an impossibility.

A great deal has been written of Churchill's lack of enthusiasm for a Second Front. That he conceived the idea of a return
to the continent as early as 1940 and eventually came to support
an invasion is beyond question; what remains less clear is
whether Churchill's motives in 1942 and later were those of a
master politician or represented genuine fear of the military
consequences. General Sir Hastings Ismay, the Prime Minister's
personal Chief of Staff, did not believe he was fundamentally
opposed to an invasion but was simply more interested in the

Mediterranean, where he hoped to get established in the Balkans before the Russians.[1]

However, some years later Ismay admitted to Eisenhower that prior to August 1943 Churchill had been seriously concerned over the prospect of a cross-Channel invasion:

> I think you are right when you say that Winston had an ingrained dread of a return to the Continent in force until the allied strength became overwhelming, particularly in the air. One could well imagine that he was haunted by the twin horrors of the Dardanelles and Passchendaele. At the same time, I think that he definitely steeled himself to take the plunge as far back as the Quebec Conference in 1943, and that thereafter he never wavered. That is not to say that he did not continue to search for opportunities to 'nibble round the edges'.
>
> The attitude of Brookie and the General Staff towards OVERLORD was, I think, much the same as Winston's. I imagine that they recognised that the coup de grace had got to be delivered on the Continent of Europe, but they did not think that it should be attempted until the Germans were on their last legs.
>
> I am positive that neither Winston nor the British Chiefs of Staff had any intention of defaulting on their promise to go through with OVERLORD at the end of May or early June 1944, once they had given it: but I admit to being doubtful whether they would ever have agreed to so early a commitment if it had not been for Marshall's persistence.[2]

The Chief of the Air Staff, Marshal of the Royal Air Force Sir Charles Portal, has also provided a reason which may come close to the truth:

---

[1] General Sir Hastings Ismay, interview with Dr Forrest C. Pogue, 17 December 1946.
[2] Ismay letter to Eisenhower, 30 December, 1960, Eisenhower Presidential Papers, Eisenhower Library. Eisenhower had earlier written to Ismay: 'I think none of us should forget that in the winter months of February and March of 1944, when all of us were working so hard in planning Overlord, the Prime Minister himself more than once expressed his great misgivings about cross-Channel operations. You will recall his talking of the "Channel tides running red with Allied blood" and the "Beaches choked with the bodies of the flower of American and British manhood." At that time he talked in terms of two years for bringing the war to a successful conclusion, and two or three times he said to Bradley, Smith and me that if the Allied operations were successful by Christmas, in capturing his beautiful and beloved Paris, then he would proclaim to the world that this was the most successful and brilliant military operation of all times.' Eisenhower, letter to Ismay, 3 December 1960, Eisenhower Presidential Papers, Eisenhower Library. Eisenhower's highly confidential and private letters to Ismay refute the claim by some historians that Churchill never uttered words about the Channel running red with Allied blood.

> Churchill was always dying to do the Northern France show
> but he was afraid – no, he was never afraid – he hated to do it.
> He could never visualise the ability of planes to isolate the
> battlefield, so he always feared great losses ... you must
> remember that our army had met the Germans at their height,
> and after they had been pushed around, they began to feel in
> their heart that they weren't the equals of the Germans.[1]

Whatever Churchill's real feelings may have been what is clear is
that in 1942 his mind was very much on the Mediterranean
where, that autumn, his strategy finally brought a success. In
November the TORCH landings were successfully launched under
the joint command of Eisenhower. Earlier Marshall had sent
Eisenhower to London to command all US forces in the European
theatre and to implement the plans he had helped orchestrate
in Washington. To obtain American commitment for TORCH
Churchill had cheerfully agreed to Eisenhower's appointment
as C-in-C, Allied Forces in North Africa. In western Egypt,
Montgomery had restored the Eighth Army's flagging morale
and had won the first major British victory of the war by
defeating Rommel at Alam Halfa and El Alamein. The Eighth
Army was now driving west to link up with Eisenhower in
Tunisia. Nevertheless, 1942 did not end without a severe lesson
for future cross-Channel operations.

At Mountbatten's instigation the British had launched a raid
on the French port of Dieppe on 19 August 1942. The raid proved
an ill-conceived and tragic show of force against the Germans
and, in the end, was one of the war's most debated and controversial operations. The basic idea behind Dieppe had been to
demonstrate to their Russian ally that British intentions and
ability successfully to launch a cross-Channel operation were to
be taken seriously. Mountbatten was also eager to test Britain's
capabilities and admitted later that he deliberately chose Dieppe
to prove that such an operation could be achieved with proper air
cover.[2]

What Dieppe did was to bury for ever the myth that SLEDGE-
HAMMER would have been feasible in 1942, and to cast grave
doubts on ROUNDUP. It certainly did not intimidate the Germans

---

[1] Marshal of the RAF, Viscount Portal, interview with Dr Forrest C. Pogue,
7 February 1947.
[2] Mountbatten–Pogue interview, loc.cit.

or cause Hitler to order reinforcements from the Russian front. Quite the contrary, it demonstrated in stark terms to both sides the pathetic state of Allied preparations for a Second Front. The raid on Dieppe was more than a political setback, however; the cost in Canadian and British lives on that single grim day in August was frightful, with over 1,000 killed and 106 Royal Air Force aircraft lost. Thus the most telling consequence of Dieppe was further to dissuade Churchill and the British Chiefs of Staff from any commitment to cross-Channel operations, a view which was certainly correct at the time. As 1943 began, the question of where and when a cross-Channel assault would take place remained in limbo.

CHAPTER 3

The Birth of Operation Overlord

> We were forced to take what comfort we could
> derive from the last, pithy, verbal directive issued to
> me by Chief of the Imperial General Staff [Sir Alan
> Brooke]: 'Well, there it is; it won't work, but you
> must bloody well make it.'
>
> Lieutenant General Sir Frederick E. Morgan,
> Chief of Staff to the Supreme Allied Commander
> (*Overture to OVERLORD*)

In April 1942 the British Chiefs of Staff had directed Mount-batten and General Sir Bernard Paget, Commander-in-Chief, Home Forces, to begin planning for ROUNDUP. They were given three principal tasks:

(1) To study and collate the immense mass of intelligence material required; to prepare a detailed study of enemy coastal defences and of the topography of the coast of Northwest Europe.

(2) To study the techniques of assault landing as a basis for training and for decisions on the types and scale of equipment required.

(3) To prepare an outline plan which would form the basis for executive planning by commanders.[1]

It was Mountbatten and Combined Operations who first saw the potential of Normandy as an invasion site. An examination of possible invasion points had quickly narrowed the options to Normandy and the Pas de Calais region of northern France. Paget favoured the Pas de Calais, mainly because it was closest, it provided the most direct route of advance into Germany, and it would afford maximum air cover from British airfields in southern England. On the other hand, the Pas de Calais was such an obvious invasion site that the Germans had prepared strong

[1] Public Record Office (hereinafter PRO), Kew (WO 205/901).

defences and concentrated the bulk of their troops in France in this region. Moreover, other than Le Havre, its ports were far too small to accommodate the enormous flow of troops and material required in the post-invasion buildup. Mountbatten argued that invasion ought first to be based on the most favourable site and then a detailed plan developed on how best to accomplish it. He believed the most important factor in any cross-Channel operation was a rapid buildup and for this task adequate ports were imperative. In all likelihood Le Havre would be destroyed, thus creating severe problems. Normandy and Brittany, with their many excellent port facilities, looked like a far better possibility, particularly Cherbourg which had a considerable capacity. In this fashion, planning went ahead throughout the remainder of 1942 and into 1943, but without central direction it was at best a somewhat disjointed effort. With priority for 1943 shifting to the Mediterranean, no formal outline plan was produced.

In place of ROUNDUP the British proposed at the Casablanca Conference in mid-January 1943 Operation HUSKY, an invasion of Sicily. The assets for an operation against the Axis in Sicily were available and once the last German and Italian resistance in Tunisia was neutralized, attention could best be turned to mounting HUSKY. Casablanca was a major victory for Brooke and the British Chiefs of Staff, who were convinced that Allied success in the Mediterranean ought to be exploited, while preparations continued in Britain for an invasion operation. The Allies had the Axis on the run in the Mediterranean: now was not the time to provide Hitler with an opportunity to retake the initiative.

Marshall finally accepted the logic of the British position and agreed to the priority for 1943 going to Mediterranean operations. Nevertheless, he was not disposed to let cross-Channel planning lapse. Nor was Churchill:

> There had to be someone in charge of preparations who would impart a dynamic impetus to the loosely knit British and American agencies involved. They both felt it was too early to appoint a Supreme Commander, as this would need a man of high military reputation . . . and such a man could not be left in the shadows, planning what was still a hypothetical operation. They decided instead: 'That a British Chief of Staff, together with an independent US/British staff, be appointed at once for

the control, planning and training of Cross-Channel operations for 1943.'[1]

The US and British Combined Chiefs of Staff prepared a directive for the new Chief of Staff which called for the concurrent development of several operations. The most important of these was the planning for a cross-Channel operation in the spring of 1944. The old codename ROUNDUP was discarded and replaced by the now more familiar name: Operation OVERLORD.[2]

One day in March 1943 the commander of 1 Corps, British Lieutenant General Frederick Morgan, was summoned to the War Cabinet office of his old friend, General Ismay, where he was handed a bulky package of papers about everything that had been done to date about the cross-Channel invasion. Morgan was 'invited' to develop a plan for the British Chiefs of Staff about what ought to be done next. In terms familiar to anyone who has ever served the military, he was told: 'No hurry, old boy, tomorrow will do.'[3]

Morgan distilled this heap of information into specific proposals, including an outline for an British-American planning organization; the following month he was appointed Chief of Staff to the Supreme Allied Commander (Designate). The organization he put together consisted mainly of British and American planners who had previously been engaged in joint planning for BOLERO and ROUNDUP. The name given to this new organization was taken from the first letters of Morgan's new title and became known simply as COSSAC. The directive given to Morgan by his new masters, the Combined Chiefs of Staff, was to develop plans 'to defeat the German fighting forces in north-west Europe'.[4]

By 27 July 1943 Morgan and his new staff had turned what had till then been a series of loosely related proposals and plans into the first tangible outline plan for the invasion, a monumental effort and one of the best examples of British-American coopera-

[1] W. G. F. Jackson, op.cit., pp.84–5.
[2] Most accounts agree that Churchill was personally involved in the selection of the code-name 'OVERLORD' from a list maintained by the British Chiefs of Staff.
[3] Lieutenant General Sir Frederick E. Morgan, *Overture to OVERLORD*, London 1950, p.33.
[4] Ibid, p.64. Morgan also had on the COSSAC staff several former members of a now defunct organization known as the Combined Commanders, which had also been working on various projects for a cross-Channel assault.

tion of the entire war. In three months COSSAC was able to offer the Combined Chiefs of Staff a solution to the question of where and how a cross-Channel invasion could be launched. Morgan had defined his task in the following terms:

> The object of Operation 'OVERLORD' is to mount and carry out an operation with forces and equipment established in the United Kingdom, and with target date the 1st May 1944, to secure a lodgement area on the Continent from which further offensive operations can be developed. The lodgement area must contain sufficient port facilities to maintain a force of some twenty-six to thirty divisions, and enable that force to be augmented by follow-up shipments from the United States or elsewhere of additional divisions and supporting units at the rate of three to five divisions per month.[1]

The COSSAC staff had agreed with previous conclusions that only the Pas de Calais and Caen-Cotentin regions were suitable, and accepted Mountbatten's earlier conclusion that initially the Allies could not count on using captured ports which would be seriously damaged and probably blocked. COSSAC rejected the obvious advantages of the Pas de Calais in favour of Normandy, reasoning that the heavy defences and loss of ports (necessitating capture and use of alternate ports as far away as Antwerp and Rouen) made invasion there impractical and exceedingly risky.[2] Instead, COSSAC proposed a landing in the Caen sector of Normandy, followed by the early capture and development of airfield sites and the port of Cherbourg. The Caen beaches were weakly defended and excellent for both a landing and a logistic buildup. German airfields in the Caen area were limited and would be easier to neutralize, though Allied air operations would have to be conducted at virtually maximum range from southern England, thus compelling the rapid establishment of new airfields.

The landings would be a three-division assault to seize the area running from Vierville-sur-Mer in the west to Lion-sur-Mer near the River Orne in the east, a front of some thirty miles. Concurrent with the assault, an airborne force would be dropped on Caen to seize the city. Followup action would take the form of a strong thrust south and southwest to gain airfield sites and to allow sufficient depth for a turning movement toward the Coten-

---

[1] C.O.S.S.A.C. (43) 32 (Final), Digest of Operation 'Overlord', 30 July 1943, National Archives, Washington.
[2] Ibid.

tin and seizure of Cherbourg within fourteen days, by which time there would be eighteen divisions in action, along with twenty-eight to thirty-three fighter squadrons operating from fourteen airfields. After Cherbourg was captured the Supreme Commander could decide, based on the enemy situation, whether to drive east and seize the Seine ports or first to occupy the Brittany ports. COSSAC suggested the Britanny ports should probably receive first priority in order to bring in adequate divisions to force the River Seine, where it was thought the Germans would retire to form a strong defence.

In retrospect, the COSSAC outline plan seems terribly flawed. The three-divisional invasion was far too small, spread too thinly and much too vulnerable to defeat by counterattack before adequate units, ammunition and equipment could be brought ashore. A force moving from the Caen area to Cherbourg would have to fight its way across nearly seventy-five miles of enemy-held terrain. With no direct invasion of the Cotentin peninsula the Germans were being permitted far too much time to strengthen their defences or, if they chose, to cripple Cherbourg's port facilities.

Morgan and his colleagues were never under any illusions about the flaws in the plan or the size of the invasion force. They knew it was far too small; however, their directive provided no latitude: COSSAC was told to plan the assault based on available landing craft and these permitted a maximum three-division-sized attack.[1] Morgan's frustration is evident throughout his book *Overture to OVERLORD*. It did not help that his guidance from the Combined Chiefs of Staff provided no long-term political objective, nor did it provide the answers to questions which could be given only by a responsible commander.

[1] Nor were there adequate assault craft to launch immediate reinforcements. Should the assault divisions run into trouble there was no way rapidly to launch a reserve force, thus leaving the units ashore dangerously vulnerable in the event of strong resistance or counterattack. Throughout their planning COSSAC had to ensure that the Allied buildup of troops and supplies exceeded the ability of the Germans to accomplish the same. Unless the Allies could maintain the higher rate, OVERLORD was not viable as a military operation. Morgan later recalled the dilemma he had faced: 'We had worked like beavers for months. We were appalled by the volume of material and of the alternatives. I reckoned it was up to me to make a decision, yes or no. Owing to the paucity of resources we had to work with, the question was, can this be done with these resources? What is the right thing to do? I spent several sleepless nights and finally said I may as well be hung for a sheep as a lamb, and said, yes, we will do it but it would be wrong to say no. Everything pointed to the assault area we chose.' Lieutenant General Sir Frederick Morgan, interview with Dr Forrest C. Pogue, 8 February 1947.

COSSAC was essentially a committee attempting to accomplish its mission without a chief capable of making decisions: Morgan's mandate left him little room for interpretation. There was no time, either, for an in-depth study of alternatives; the British Chiefs of Staff demanded Morgan's proposals by July. Moreover, the plan could only be based on the enemy situation as it then existed, and in the summer of 1943 Hitler's so-called 'Fortress Europa' was, except for the Pas-de-Calais, a hoax. By the time the final planning measures were initiated in early 1944 the Normandy front had been greatly strengthened after Hitler appointed Field Marshal Rommel to prepare Germany's defences against a Second Front and he had begun an all-out effort to plug the weaknesses evident in Normandy. Nevertheless, despite its obvious imperfections, the COSSAC plan was an important milestone in cross-Channel planning as the first formal proposal which could be acted upon by the Combined Chiefs of Staff.[1]

As was his habit, Churchill became personally involved in the details of the planning for OVERLORD. A senior planner on the COSSAC staff, Brigadier Kenneth R. McLean, remembers how Churchill would tell Ismay:

> 'Pray let us have a certain plan by next week.' We would send something back. The PM would remark: 'I see that the Ministry of Negation has successfully marshalled bellyaches as usual.' Six out of ten of his ideas were good. If we could get the PM interested in our projects everything was fine. He would see that everything was obtained to carry through the ideas.[2]

McLean also thought the factor of revenge played an important part in Churchill's planning. 'He wanted to revenge Norway and Dakar. Churchill never suggested that we would not go to France. Helped back me up in a talk with FDR. He was determined that this plan – OVERLORD – be sold to the President.'[3]

In August 1943 the OVERLORD outline plan was one of the

[1] During the COSSAC planning there was some agitation in Washington that the signatures on all COSSAC documents were British. Brigadier McLean recalled how, in an effort to resolve this complaint, it was decided to have an American secretary sign their papers. 'We had a series of poor American captains who signed papers they knew nothing about. One of the fellows took drugs; another was mixed up with a collaborationist girl, but it stopped arguments about the British doing the planning.' Brigadier (later Lieutenant General) Kenneth R. McLean, interview with Dr Forrest C. Pogue, 11–13 March 1947, US Army Military History Institute.

[2] McLean interview, loc.cit.

[3] Ibid.

prime subjects of discussion at the Quebec Conference. Morgan's plan had already been approved by Churchill and the British Chiefs, and it soon won the same approval from Roosevelt and the US Chiefs as the major Allied ground and air effort in Europe for 1944. The suggested target date of 1 May 1944 was also approved. Yet Morgan's problems were far from over. COSSAC's plan was, after all, nothing more than an outline of proposed operations. A detailed plan was required and with time running short there were still no visible moves towards naming a Supreme Allied Commander. The need for decisions that, as a staff officer, Morgan could not make was threatening the target date yet, although COSSAC had taken gigantic steps in the evolution of OVERLORD, Morgan was left throughout the autumn of 1943 to continue his role of interim leader without the power of decision.[1]

After the war Morgan revealed the extent of his problems in his book *Overture to OVERLORD*. Privately, he wrote to Liddell Hart: 'I was never absolutely certain that the C.O.S. were behind me. Whenever one was forced to refer to them there always seemed to be an air of thinly disguised impatience with the upstart amateurs from over the way.' Morgan also observed that as the US commitment to the war grew there seemed to be signs of a developing British inferiority complex which he found 'frightening'.[2]

About the time Morgan was organizing COSSAC, Brooke was taking action to organize, equip and train a force of some fifteen divisions necessary for carrying out the British commitment for OVERLORD. Officially designated 21st Army Group, the British Liberation Army was placed under the command of General Sir Bernard Paget, who also continued in his other role as C-in-C,

---

[1] Sir Frederick Morgan remains to this day one of the lesser known figures of the war. His contributions have generally been overlooked, but he was responsible for quickly organizing a firstclass team of planners and for moving OVERLORD into the realm of the possible. Throughout the summer and autumn of 1943 he kept the planning moving ahead by dint of common sense and personal commitment, while serving two difficult taskmasters in the British and US Chiefs of Staff. As quickly as his star rose in 1943 it faded in 1944, when Supreme Headquarters Allied Expeditionary Forces (SHAEF) was created to replace COSSAC. Although his outline plan was later to receive extensive modification, it is safe to state that without Morgan and COSSAC any invasion of France in the spring of 1944 would have proven exceedingly difficult to launch. Morgan died in 1967 at the age of seventy-three.

[2] Sir Frederick Morgan, letter to Liddell Hart, 5 July 1959, Liddell Hart Papers, King's College, London.

Home Forces. Like Marshall, Brooke's great qualities included his ability to select the right man for a job and Paget, who had already established a reputation as a superb trainer of troops, was ideal. However, though he had never been told so, Paget was never a serious choice to retain command of 21st Army Group for the invasion, possessing neither the combat experience nor the reputation that Churchill and Brooke considered essential for what was to be one of the most important command appointments of the war. Even under the best of conditions OVERLORD would be fraught with risk, and the commander of this force must be the best and most experienced officer who could be found.

The TORCH landings in North Africa and the HUSKY invasion of Sicily in July 1943 provided unmistakable evidence of just how much the Allies had yet to learn about amphibious and airborne operations. TORCH was poorly executed but serious repercussions were avoided due to light resistance from the French in Morocco and Tunisia. HUSKY was less fortunate. The invasion plan called for Montgomery's Eighth Army to land on the southern coast of Sicily near Syracuse, while Lieutenant General George S. Patton's Seventh US Army landed farther to the west, near Gela. Fifteen hundred glider troops of the British First Airlanding Brigade were to support the Eighth Army by landing and securing high ground inland. Wind, darkness and inexperienced air crews turned the operation into a major fiasco. Few gliders made it to Sicily; the rest were either towed back to Tunisia or lost in heavy seas off the coast.

Colonel James M. Gavin's 505th Parachute Regimental Combat Team of the 82nd Airborne Division, which was to spearhead the American landings, fared little better, though fortunately with smaller loss of life. Again, high winds and thoroughly inexperienced aircrews resulted in Gavin's troops being scattered all over southeastern Sicily, some as far away as the British sector.[1] A number of C–47 aircraft were shot down by trigger-happy gunners of the US fleet.

Though ultimately successful, Sicily provided a disturbing example of the effects of weather, inexperience and lack of coordination during the critical beachhead phase. A further

[1] For an excellent account of the US airborne landings in Sicily, see James M. Gavin, *On To Berlin*, New York, 1978.

example came with the Salerno landings in September. Churchill and Brooke had successfully convinced their US ally that the conquest of Sicily must be followed by an invasion of southern Italy, which would, among other things, knock Italy out of the war as well as tying down large numbers of German units in Italy and thus prevent them from reinforcing other fronts. It also promised possible subsequent exploitation of Churchill's dream – his plan to attack Germany through its Achilles heel, the Balkans.

The Salerno invasion resulted in a gap of about ten miles between British and US units. The green US 36th Infantry Division was counterattacked by several of Kesselring's battle-hardened panzer units which nearly succeeded in driving the Americans back into the sea, and might have done so but for a brilliantly executed emergency drop by the 82nd Airborne Division which disrupted the Germans just enough to permit the front to be stabilized. Still, disaster was only narrowly averted at Salerno and the lesson for the forthcoming Normandy invasion was evident: assault units must land close enough together to be able to link up quickly, preventing exploitation of a gap by counterattacking defenders until a bridgehead could be established and reinforced by follow-up forces. With airborne units so important to the plan for Normandy, there could be no reoccurrence of the Sicily experience. Fortunately, the lessons of North Africa, Sicily and Salerno were not lost on the new OVERLORD commanders, who were at last announced in December 1943.

CHAPTER 4

The Overlord Commanders

> The immediate appointment of General Eisenhower to command of OVERLORD operation has been decided on.
>
> Roosevelt to Stalin,
> December 1943

> The War Cabinet desire that Montgomery should command the First Expeditionary Group of Armies. Eisenhower should have chosen Alexander but I feel the Cabinet are right as Montgomery is a public hero and will give confidence among our people, not unshared by yours.
>
> Churchill to Roosevelt,
> December 1943

From the time of the Quadrant Conference in Quebec in August 1943 it was assumed in both London and Washington to be only a matter of time before General Marshall was named Supreme Allied Commander for OVERLORD. Marshall had long desired a more active role in the war and was anxious to end his long military career with a field command. There were sound political reasons as well: Washington considered the British still lukewarm toward OVERLORD and it was thought the appointment of an American as Supreme Commander would help guarantee that Churchill and the British Chiefs of Staff did not waver in their commitment.

Although Churchill had strongly resisted Marshall's proposal for a cross-Channel invasion in 1943, he nevertheless had great admiration for what he felt were Marshall's rare qualities, even if, as his private secretary has remarked: 'He judged him more remarkable for his statesmanship than for his gifts as a military strategist'.[1] Prior to Quebec, Stimson had urged Roosevelt that

[1] John Colville, *The Churchillians*, London, 1981, p. 97.

Marshall's selection would be the best possible guarantee of OVERLORD going ahead without further British delaying tactics, and Roosevelt is believed to have told Churchill at Quebec that he would name Marshall as supreme commander.[1] Marshall himself believed he was to be selected, and had begun to think seriously about forming his new staff.

Despite the support of Stimson and Hopkins, a number of other influential men in Washington were disturbed at the prospect of Marshall leaving at such a critical time of the war. Both Admiral Ernest L. King and Admiral William D. Leahy put forth strong arguments that the United States simply could not afford to lose Marshall's powerful voice as Chairman of the Joint Chiefs of Staff, particularly in dealing with the British over strategy.[2] 'Their view was shared by General of the Armies, John J. Pershing who, as the elder statesman of the Army, warned the President in mid-September that the proposed transfer of the Chief of Staff would be a "fundamental and very grave error in our military policy".'[3]

Roosevelt desired to reward Marshall with the supreme command but was afraid of losing the one man who had proven so indispensable as the architect of American strategy, as well as the leader who kept the military machine running and inter-service rivalries under control. Unable to decide, he did nothing at all, as if, somehow, the problem would go away. Instead, he followed his politician's instinct for compromise by telling the British he was willing to have them name the Deputy Supreme Commander immediately, which was of no practical help to Morgan, who continued to press for someone to take firm charge of OVERLORD.

Certainly there was no doubt in Eisenhower's mind about Marshall's forthcoming appointment; on 1 October 1943 he had been told personally by Navy Secretary Frank Knox that Marshall had officially been named for OVERLORD.[4] As a result Eisenhower sent his own Chief of Staff, Major General Walter

[1] Forrest C. Pogue, *The Supreme Command*, Washington, 1952, p. 24.

[2] King was Chief of Naval Operations; Leahy was a former Chief of Naval Operations and now Roosevelt's personal Chief of Staff.

[3] Pogue, op.cit., p. 27.

[4] Alfred D. Chandler, Jr., (Ed.) *The Papers of Dwight David Eisenhower*, Vol. III, Baltimore, 1970, p. 1482, hereafter referred to as *The Eisenhower Papers*. Knox based his statement on the results of the Quebec Conference where Roosevelt, Stimson and Hopkins had pressured Churchill into accepting Marshall for command of OVERLORD.

Bedell Smith, to Washington to brief Marshall; and prior to the Cairo Conference in November, Roosevelt's personal advisor, Harry Hopkins, conveyed the same message to Eisenhower; he was also told he was slated to replace Marshall as Chief of Staff.

Thus by the time of the US – British meeting in Cairo in late November, prior to the Teheran Conference with Russia, there had still been no decision, neither did the Cairo meeting produce one. Stalin finally brought matters to a head at Teheran by bluntly demanding to know who was to lead the cross-Channel attack. The Russians were apprehensive and suspicious of their allies and anxious for the OVERLORD command question to be settled quickly, thus signifying a firm British-American commitment to the Second Front. Faced with pressure from both Stalin and Churchill, Roosevelt finally accepted that he could neither afford to lose his Chief of Staff nor put off a decision any longer. He summoned Marshall but in the discussion which followed found himself unable to get to the point. Marshall's recollection of their conversation reflects the President's indecision:

> [Roosevelt] . . . asked me after a great deal of beating about the bush just what I wanted to do. Evidently it was left up to me . . . I just repeated again in as convincing language as I could that I wanted him to feel free to act in whatever way he felt was to the best interest of the country and to his satisfaction and not in any way to consider my feelings. I would cheerfully go whatever way he wanted me to go and I didn't express any desire one way or the other. . . Then he evidently assumed that concluded the affair and that I would not command in Europe. Because he said, 'Well, I didn't feel I could sleep at ease if you were out of Washington.'[1]

In the months prior to Quebec it had been assumed that the supreme commander would be British, partly in return for Eisenhower's selection for command in the Mediterranean in 1942, but mainly because OVERLORD would be mounted from Britain and British forces would play a dominant role, at least initially. In July Churchill had told Brooke he wanted him to take the invasion command, only to change his mind at Quebec in what has been seen by some as a 'deal', in order to obtain the new supreme command in Southeast Asia for Mountbatten:

---

[1] Quoted in Forrest C. Pogue, *George C. Marshall, Organizer of Victory*, 1943–45, New York, 1973, p. 321.

apparently intense American pressure caused Churchill to recon-
sider his position and agree to the selection of Marshall in return
for similar US acceptance of Mountbatten, who was to be
rewarded for his contributions to Combined Operations. Churchill was known to be concerned about America's rapidly rising
influence; he may have accepted the inevitability of US dominance in Europe and therefore made the best possible compromise. Brooke was bitterly disappointed but, like Marshall, he was
far too great a soldier to let his personal feelings interfere with his
role as Britain's senior military spokesman and chief strategist.

There was no question who would be appointed in place of
Marshall. Churchill had long since made it clear that there was
only one other American officer acceptable to him: Eisenhower.
He had developed a genuine fondness and respect for this outgoing American who was so passionately devoted to the forging
of the British-American command that had been responsible for
reversing the tide of Axis domination in the Mediterranean.
Outside of General Douglas MacArthur there was no other
American with Eisenhower's experience and qualifications and
by this time Eisenhower had made it known he was not interested
in replacing Marshall as Chief of Staff; his preference was to
remain in Europe as the commander of a US army group rather
than return to Washington. The appointment Morgan had been
urging for months was at long last announced on 6 December
1943. The decision pleased Marshall, for it placed the most
important command of the war into the hands of an officer he
had been grooming for a key role since 1941.[1]

Brooke, too, was particularly pleased, believing Eisenhower a
far superior choice to Marshall, who had even less command
experience in wartime.[2] While it is true Brooke had never had
much faith in Eisenhower as a strategist, he had seen him grow in
confidence and experience in the Mediterranean, particularly in
cementing the British-American command structure into a workable and harmonious organization.

Other key American appointments for OVERLORD had
already begun. In September Major General Omar N. Bradley,
then commanding II Corps in Sicily, was told of his selection to

[1] Pogue, Marshall, Organizer of Victory, op.cit., p. 322.
[2] Alanbrooke Papers, 'Notes On My Life', King's College, London.

command all United States ground forces for the cross-Channel invasion. At Eisenhower's urging, Marshall had appointed Bradley the US invasion commander as the first concrete step in forming an American command organization in England for OVERLORD. Returning to England, Bradley set up his First US Army headquarters at Bristol. This was, however, only a partial solution to the command problem; Marshall had also decided there would eventually be a need to create an Army Group to control all US ground forces in Europe once the post-invasion buildup of forces could take place, but though Bradley was told to form the nucleus of this eventual Army Group headquarters, at this early date Marshall was not yet prepared to name him the permanent commander.

Eisenhower's appointment left only one other major post for OVERLORD unfilled. There were only two serious candidates for command of the British Liberation Army: Montgomery and General Sir Harold Alexander, commander of Allied ground forces in Italy. Alexander was Churchill's favourite general: from the earliest days of the war the Prime Minister had grown to admire the man who was affectionately known as 'Alex'. Theirs was a far different relationship from that which Churchill maintained with most of his other generals, many of whom he frequently treated with ill-concealed contempt. Despite Churchill's esteem for Alexander, even he did not completely escape such abuse, though Alexander was one of the few – Montgomery was another – whom Churchill never tried to dominate. Somehow the bulldog side of Churchill's nature never came out in his relationship with Alexander as it did with Wavell, Dill, Brooke and others. In turn, Alexander never sought to impress Churchill by currying favour, by attempting to influence his thinking or by being intimidated. Possessed of immense natural charm and without pretension, it was not in Alexander's nature ever to consider being offensive, but this in no way encumbered his relations with Churchill as it might have with other men. In Alexander, Churchill seems to have seen a reflection of the soldier he himself always wanted to be. Such was his admiration for Alexander that by the end of the war he had placed him ' . . . at the centre of his Pantheon of heroes'.[1]

[1] Colville, op.cit., p. 152.

Churchill's relations with Montgomery were quite different. Montgomery had not been his first choice for command of the Eighth Army when he had decided to relieve Auchinleck, despite Brooke's counsel that he was the best man. The PM had first met Montgomery when he visited his 3rd Division after Dunkirk. He had been impressed then with his spirit and fresh ideas, but it was not until an amazed Churchill saw what Montgomery had done to transform the Eighth Army that his feeling for him began to develop in earnest. In Montgomery, Churchill had at last found a general who won battles, the most professional soldier, in fact, that he had ever encountered: a tough, blunt, no-nonsense commander with tenacious qualities, and a near-obsession with winning the war. It was of little consequence to Churchill that he was often high-handed, arrogant and difficult to handle, perhaps because these same qualities could just as well describe the Prime Minister himself. For his part, while Montgomery deeply res-pected Churchill as a great statesman he was never afraid of him; he was respectful and admiring but, as he was to prove on several occasions, he never hesitated to say 'no' to his Prime Minister when he believed he was meddling in a general's business – and managed to escape the wrath which traditionally followed a confrontation with the strong-willed Churchill.

Just as Alexander had a strong advocate in Churchill, so too did Montgomery have a powerful backer and friend in Alan Brooke. Their relationship dated from 1926 when both men had served together as instructors at the Staff College, Camberley. When the BEF was sent to France, Brooke had been in command of 2 Corps with Montgomery as his subordinate, GOC, 3rd Division. In the months before the German invasion of France, Brooke was deeply impressed by Montgomery's training methods and the effective manner in which he prepared and trained his division for combat. The 3rd Division's superb perf-ormance at Dunkirk convinced the future CIGS that Montgom-ery was one of the outstanding commanders in the British Army and destined for higher command. Brooke was well aware of the flaws in Montgomery's character and on one occasion in France had saved his impetuous subordinate from almost certain relief by the C-in-C of the BEF, Field Marshal Lord Gort. As Brooke's star rose during the long years of the war, so his ability to influ-ence the selection of the top appointments in the army increased.

Despite a strong personal liking for the calm and competent Alexander, Brooke did have some nagging doubts about whether his sometimes excessive detachment would make him aggressive enough for the OVERLORD command. The new OVERLORD appointments would mean shifting a number of senior British and American commanders in the Mediterranean. Brooke's choice for command of 21st Army Group was Monty, and he began a series of subtle manoeuvres to ensure his selection, while at the same time taking steps to *prevent* Alexander from becoming the new Supreme Commander, Mediterranean, when Eisenhower departed.[1]

At Quebec, Churchill had been openly talking of Alexander replacing Eisenhower and Montgomery replacing Paget. However, Brooke had no faith that the Prime Minister would not eventually shift his backing from Montgomery to Alexander for the OVERLORD position. Throughout the autumn of 1943 Brooke became more concerned that Alexander lacked the requisite strategic vision to make an effective supreme commander. His diary for the period has numerous entries where he expressed doubts. In his post-war 'Notes On My Life', he commented on a diary entry he had originally made on 22 February 1943: 'Alexander . . . had many very fine qualities but no very great strategic vision. He had been carried by Montgomery through North Africa as regards the strategic and tactical handling of the situation. Monty was now far from him. . .'[2]

In late October Churchill, as Brooke suspected, had started to talk about Alexander for OVERLORD. In a note to the Secretary of State for Air, he mentioned it was his understanding that Marshall wanted Air Chief Marshal Sir Arthur Tedder as his deputy. Churchill did not consider this a prudent move inasmuch as the removal of both Tedder and Alexander from the Mediterranean would leave too great a void. The Prime Minister was even more worried by what he anticipated would be American insistence on Tedder's replacement as the head of Allied air forces in the Mediterranean by Lieutenant General A. Spaatz, who was then his deputy. Churchill thought the outspoken Spaatz a stupid and dangerous man and had little faith in him as a replacement for

[1] At this time Brooke still assumed that Eisenhower would be leaving soon to replace Marshall in Washington.

[2] Alanbrooke Papers, 'Notes On My Life', King's College, London.

Tedder. At the time, he wrote, '. . . For us it will be a question of finding someone good to sustain him.' A few days later, when the new appointments had been announced, he cabled Portal: 'I am relieved Spaatz is to command no more than the American long-range bombers.'[1]

Brooke began by suggesting to Churchill that Eisenhower be replaced in the Mediterranean by General Sir Henry Maitland Wilson, whom he considered better qualified than Alexander. There is considerable doubt about Brooke's wisdom in promoting the appointment of Wilson, whose career was thoroughly undistinguished. Known as 'Jumbo' because of his bulk, Wilson has also been described as having the hide of an elephant; Brooke would later observe that Churchill's abuse ran off him like water off an elephant's back. If Brooke felt Wilson would be less malleable than Alexander his advocacy was nevertheless a dangerous gamble, for if he were successful in convincing Churchill to accept Wilson it was probable that Alexander would be favoured over Montgomery for OVERLORD.

A near stalemate in Italy during this period did nothing to lessen Brooke's growing pessimism about Alexander. His doubts were never personal but rooted in the firm belief that Alexander was better qualified to remain a field commander. Brooke never questioned the gallant Alexander's leadership qualities, but the gulf between field and supreme command was large and required a commander of great imagination to plan and coordinate the actions of the Allied naval, air and ground forces. One can see Brooke's doubts in a diary entry for 18 November, when he wrote: 'Alexander, charming as he is, fills me with gloom. He . . . cannot see big . . . He will never have either the personality or the vision to command three services.'[2]

The CIGS did not change his opinion during an inspection trip to the Italian front in December after the Teheran Conference. He found the experience depressing, as his diary for 14 December reveals: 'Monty is tiring out and Alex fails to grip the show.' His 'Notes On My Life' later explained what he meant:

[1] PRO (PREM 3–336/1). Spaatz was selected to command all US Strategic Air Forces in the United Kingdom, the US counterpart to Air Chief Marshal Sir Arthur Harris's Bomber Command.

[2] Alanbrooke Diary, King's College, London.

There is no doubt he held some of the highest qualities of a commander, unbounded courage, never ruffled or upset, great charm and a composure that inspired confidence in those around him. But when it came to working on a higher plane and deciding matters of higher tactics and of strategy he was at once out of his depth, had no ideas of his own and always sought someone to lean on. Up to now he had fitted admirably into the various jobs I had asked him to do but looking ahead I foresaw some stormy seas with rocks, crags and sandbanks and the gravest doubts about Alex's ability to navigate such waters. Fortune favoured me and I was able to retain him in Italy.[1]

Eisenhower himself had earlier privately voiced the same misgivings Brooke had about Alexander as a supreme commander. On 19 June, the Adjutant General, Sir Ronald Adam, had reported to Brooke a conversation he had recently had with Eisenhower, who had expressed admiration for Alexander but said he did not consider him fit to take on a supreme commander's job.[1] Eisenhower, however, had no such misgivings about Alex's qualifications for OVERLORD and as soon as his opponent was announced on 6 December, Brooke had to contend with pressure from this new and quite unexpected source. Eisenhower immediately began drawing up a list of British and American commanders and staff officers he wanted to bring to England with him. Alexander's name was at the top of his list. The new Supreme Allied Commander greatly admired his cool manner and ability to get along with subordinate commanders, British

---

[1] Alanbrooke Papers, 'Notes On My Life'. Brooke was not the only senior British officer who expressed this opinion. When, late in 1944, Churchill grew frustrated with 'Jumbo' Wilson and decided to replace him with Alexander, the First Sea Lord, Admiral of the Fleet Sir Andrew Cunningham, recorded in his diary the opposition of the Chiefs of Staff to Alexander, whom he described as 'totally unfitted for the job'. Alexander was an exceedingly difficult man to understand and most who served under him did not pretend to fathom him. During the research for this book many senior officers spoke to the author privately about Alexander. Their comments ranged from 'intellectually lazy' to a commonly held belief that the real brains behind Alexander were his able Chiefs of Staff, first Lieutenant General Richard McCreery in the Middle East, and later General Sir John Harding in Italy. Criticism of Alexander was always tempered with deep respect. To suggest that Brooke's views were somehow a minority opinion would be to misrepresent the truth. Mountbatten may have best captured the essence of Alexander when he told his biographer, Nigel Nicolson: 'He had almost every quality you could wish to have, except that he had the average brain of an average English gentleman. He lacked that little extra cubic centimetre which produces genius. If you recognise that, it's perhaps a greater tribute to what he did achieve by leadership, courage and inspiring devotion in those who served under him.' Quoted in *Alex*, London, 1973, p. 280.

[2] Alanbrooke Diary, 19 June 1943, King's College, London.

and American alike, and sensed these traits would be particularly valuable in the difficult campaign ahead.

Montgomery, on the other hand, Eisenhower found abrasive and difficult to control. On 11 December, Eisenhower and Brooke met in Tunis to discuss the OVERLORD appointments and as Brooke expected, 'He would sooner have Alex with him for OVERLORD than Monty. He also knew that he could handle Alex, but was not fond of Monty and certainly did not know how to handle him.'[1] Throughout the war, relations between the two men remained on a formal and businesslike basis. There was none of the comradeship Eisenhower felt with Alexander, and the utter diversity of their characters precluded the establishment of any real warmth. Eisenhower had carefully developed his command relationships by diplomacy, tact, and the gradual growth of a spirit of Allied unity which was well suited to his personality and temperament. His modesty and friendly manner concealed a fiery temper which occasionally boiled over, in sharp contrast with Montgomery's self-assured manner which left an impression of cockiness and conceit.

Montgomery never considered Eisenhower anything other than an amateur soldier who lacked vital command experience of the sort he himself had attained. It was impossible not to like Eisenhower, with his beguiling grin and outgoing personality, but Montgomery's professionalism and dedication to the art of war had, from the beginning, left him deeply suspicious of Eisenhower's capabilities as a commander. Ability was the foundation upon which Monty judged others, with experience and performance as the acid tests of a commander's ability; in his opinion Eisenhower had not passed his rigid standard. He therefore considered it unthinkable that a man who had never commanded anything larger than a battalion in peacetime should be directing a critical operation like OVERLORD. Moreover, Montgomery tended to chafe under too tight a command rein, preferring the freedom to operate virtually independently, as he had been allowed to do under Alexander.[2]

---

[1] Arthur Bryant, *Triumph in the West*, London, 1959, p. 115.

[2] Montgomery's opinion of Eisenhower as a general never changed. His private comments in the post-war period continued to reflect this belief. It was a professional rather than a personal opinion, made without jealousy or rancour. 'When it comes to war', he once said, 'Ike doesn't know the difference between Christmas and Easter.' For

It was a great misfortune for the forthcoming campaign in Europe that Montgomery never grasped that beneath his friendly exterior, Eisenhower was a deeply resolute professional soldier. It was not his method to act in a high-handed or arbitrary manner, a trait which Montgomery unfortunately interpreted as weakness but which, in fact, was Eisenhower's strength as the commander of a multi-national force. His method of leadership was to seek the views of those concerned, to accept argument and criticism but to stand firm once he had made up his mind on a course of action. Montgomery viewed a commander's function as the making of policy and as direction in the form of simple, straightforward guidance that could be understood and implemented by his subordinates; he was apparently incapable of understanding that others might achieve the same results in a different manner. With such disparate personalities, backgrounds and methods of command it was inevitable the two men would later clash over strategy during the campaign in Northwest Europe.

Eisenhower's position was somewhat awkward. While he badly wanted Alexander, he did not want to be seen as interfering in what was, after all, a purely British appointment. As tactfully as possible he began to champion Alexander, telling Churchill he was willing to place him in temporary command of all ground forces until such time as he personally took over command of all Allied forces in Europe after the invasion.

Churchill might have made more of an issue of Alexander's selection had he not been by that time an exhausted and very sick man. Both Brooke and Lord Moran, Churchill's personal physician, were deeply worried by his condition. The intense pressures of nearly four years of war and the stress of weeks of travel to Cairo and Teheran had left him bed-ridden with pneumonia and unable to return to Britain without a long recuperation. Churchill's absence from Whitehall left him isolated from the War Cabinet, and it was evident that the British appointments for OVERLORD and the Mediterranean would have to be a matter for consultation and undoubtedly of some compromise.

his part, Eisenhower said of Montgomery during the campaign in Northwest Europe: 'Monty is a good man to serve under; a difficult man to serve with; and an impossible man to serve over.' Quoted by General Sir Miles Dempsey in a 1947 interview with Dr Forrest C. Pogue.

The War Cabinet might have supported Churchill by favouring Alexander but the unexpected announcement of Eisenhower's selection had left them somewhat shaken and very concerned about who should command 21st Army Group for, by this time, they were also aware that the appointment would not only be as commander of British ground forces but as the temporary land force commander of all Allied ground forces for the invasion. On 15 December, the Secretary of State for War, Sir James Grigg, cabled the Cabinet position to Brooke in Italy:

> The decision must of course be taken on military grounds but it was the view of the War Cabinet that public opinion here will be surprised and rather uneasy at the substitution of Eisenhower for Marshall. From this point of view they are disposed to think Montgomery would be a better choice than Alexander for Overlord. Some ministers, including myself, also prefer Montgomery to Alexander on our judgment of their military merits for this job.[1]

By mid-December Brooke began to feel quietly confident that his strategy was working. In his diary for the 13th he commented.:

> The question of the Supreme Commander for the Mediterranean is I think settling as I wanted, after many ups and downs and many tribulations. The PM has I think now pretty well settled on Wilson for Supreme Commander, Alex to command forces in Italy and Monty to come home to command land forces in Overlord. I pray and hope he does not change his mind.[2]

The next day Churchill cabled the Deputy Prime Minister, Clement Attlee, that he wanted Tedder as the deputy to Eisenhower and that the Supreme Commander was still expressing his preference for Alexander. Obviously still hesitant, he wrote: 'I have not made up my mind whether it will be Alexander or Montgomery but the CIGS is staying with Alexander now and when he rejoins me in a few days I shall be able to take a decision.'[3]

Churchill was quite mistaken in his belief that Brooke wanted Alexander. Brooke's frequent diary entries for this period, along with his post-war 'Notes On My Life' attest to his clear prefer-

[1] PRO (PREM 3-336/1).
[2] Alanbrooke Diary, King's College, London.
[3] PRO (PREM 3-336/1).

ence for Montgomery. After the war he recalled the one contradictory entry he had made on 11 December, when he had written that between the selection of Alex or Monty for OVERLORD, 'I don't mind much!' 'I certainly minded a great deal and would have had little confidence in Alex running that show!'[1]

Relations between Churchill and Tedder, the new Deputy Supreme Allied Commander, had always been frosty. Tedder had achieved his reputation in North Africa from 1941 to 1943 as the Air C-in-C, RAF Middle East, but the two men had clashed much earlier in the war when Tedder had been in the Ministry of Aircraft Production under Lord Beaverbrook, with whose methods he violently disagreed. Nevertheless, Churchill's earlier opposition to Tedder had dissipated with Eisenhower's selection and his growing realization of the strategic importance of air support in the future success of OVERLORD. Admiral Sir Bertram Ramsay and Air Chief Marshal Sir Trafford Leigh-Mallory were also confirmed as the Allied Naval and Air commanders.

Churchill did not dispute the War Cabinet's opinion, for he had perceived that Alexander's influence with the Americans could be put to good use if he remained in Italy, where the PM still nourished hopes for a major Allied thrust through the Ljubljana Gap in the direction of Vienna as part of his 'soft underbelly' philosophy of winning the war via the Balkans. As a result, Brooke's hopes were finally realized on 22 December when Churchill cabled General Ismay in London with instructions to announce the appointment of Montgomery and the realignment of the Mediterranean command. Montgomery was notified early on the morning of 24 December by a cable from the War Office ordering him to turn over command of the Eighth Army to Lieutenant General Oliver Leese and to return to London to command Allied ground forces for the invasion. Alexander was to remain in Italy.

At long last the major Allied command positions had been decided upon, though at times it had appeared that politicians in neither country would ever make up their minds. Fate had once again intervened to favour Montgomery, as it had in 1942 when Lieutenant General W. H. E. Gott, Churchill's choice to command the Eighth Army, was suddenly killed. Brooke had never

[1] Alanbrooke Diary and Papers, 'Notes On My Life', King's College, London.

deviated from his support for Montgomery, whom he considered by far the better commander than Alexander, though his insistence had brought him into conflict with his own Secretary of State, the fiery Sir James Grigg, who had a strong admiration for Paget and wanted him to retain command of 21st Army Group for the invasion. Brooke's admiration for Paget was no less than Grigg's but, as it was to do on so many occasions, his professional judgement came before his personal feelings. 'He had done a marvellous job in the training of these forces and in raising their general efficiency and I wish it had been possible to leave him in command for D-Day. I had a great personal admiration and affection for him, which made it all the more difficult to have to replace him at the last moment.'[1] Montgomery was destined to sustain his chief's absolute faith in him, but there would be times in the months ahead when that faith was put to rather severe tests.

[1]   Alanbrooke Papers, 'Notes On My Life', King's College, London.

CHAPTER 5

A Time for Decision

As at present planned, OVERLORD is not a sound operation of war.

General Sir Bernard Montgomery,
January 1944

One of Eisenhower's first actions as Supreme Allied Commander (Designate) was to summon Montgomery to his headquarters in Algiers to discuss the COSSAC outline plan. Montgomery arrived on 27 December and met Eisenhower and Bedell Smith at the St George Hotel that afternoon. Prior to their meeting Montgomery had been unfamiliar with the proposed invasion plan, but Eisenhower had been briefed about OVERLORD and given a copy of the COSSAC plan in October by a US general from the COSSAC staff who had been sent to Algiers for the sole purpose of obtaining his reaction.[1] Later Eisenhower recalled his response:

> I considered that while the plan apparently made the best possible use of the material that could be made available by the proposed target date [1 May 1944], the concept involved a plan too weak in numbers and frontage, if there were contemplated a heavy and rapid buildup with the purpose of smashing through the defending front at an early date. I had Beetle Smith come in with me during this examination and we decided, off the cuff, that a five-division attack was far more desirable.'[2]

In Eisenhower's opinion a three-divisional attack was fatally weak, and he told General Chambers that if it were his operation he would insist on broadening it to a five-division assault with two divisions in floating reserve. 'I didn't have any idea at that time it would be my operation and I gave my views for whatever

[1] Eisenhower's appointment diary shows a meeting on 27 October with General Chambers of the COSSAC staff. *The Eisenhower Papers*, Vol V, p. 134.
[2] Eisenhower, letter to Ismay, 3 December 1960, Eisenhower Presidential Papers, Eisenhower Library.

value our own lessons from the African experience would be to the COSSAC planners.'[1] Smith had first learned the full impact of the OVERLORD plan in November in Washington while attending a meeting of the Joint Staff planners with Morgan. '. . . Morgan gave the COSSAC plan. When he mentioned the puny little assault with three divisions, I nearly fell out of my seat. After all we had had more than that in all our landings. I told Eisenhower about it when I got back and he said, "My God, if I were going to do it I would want ten or twelve divisions." '[2]

At the meeting with Montgomery, Eisenhower outlined his misgivings over the size of the proposed assault force and instructed Montgomery to convey his convictions to the planners in London, along with his opinion that in order to achieve an acceptable strength he was willing to accept a delay of a month for the landings. Both Eisenhower and Smith, in separate recollections, were clear there was unanimity about the need to broaden the invasion. Smith's version is that 'We were all unanimous. You might say that on the issue of broadening the base of the attack, the addition of divisions was accepted by acclamation. Freddy Morgan wanted more but he had to work with what he had.'[3] In his *Memoirs*, Montgomery gives an entirely different account, claiming only that Eisenhower had told him 'He had only a sketchy idea of the plan and that it did not look too good.'[4]

On 31 December Montgomery flew to Marrakesh to meet with Churchill en route to London. He found the Prime Minister in bed reading the OVERLORD plan and was promptly asked for his opinion. Montgomery spent most of that evening studying the

---

[1] General of the Army Dwight D. Eisenhower, interview with S. L. A. Marshall, 3 June 1946, US Army Military History Institute.

[2] Lieutenant General Wallter Bedell Smith, interview with Dr Forrest C. Pogue, 9 May 1947. What Eisenhower meant was a beachhead large enough to accommodate up to twelve divisions, a point emphasized by Bedell Smith in an earlier interview in 1945. Eisenhower's thinking was very much in line with Montgomery's. In his *Memoirs* Montgomery wrote of the plan that was eventually adopted: 'We would need a build-up which would give us, say, eight divisions ashore by the evening of D-Day and twelve by the evening of D+2 (these figures to include the airborne divisions)' – an estimate that was exceeded. By the night of D-Day the Allies had nine divisions ashore, elements of two others, plus US and British rangers and commandos. Cf. *Memoirs*, p. 220.

[3] Eisenhower and Smith interviews, loc. cit. Eisenhower's appointment calendar reveals that he had only one other appointment on the afternoon of 27 December, which suggests that the new Supreme Commander may have spent considerable time with Montgomery that day.

[4] Montgomery, *Memoirs*, op. cit., p. 210.

plan and carefully writing out his comments. Churchill's staff had been against the idea of Montgomery seeing the plan before he could be properly briefed in London. Four days earlier General Ismay had received a cable from Marrakesh asking for an updated version of the OVERLORD plan so that the Prime Minister could show it to Montgomery. The cable included the comment that 'Colonel Warden [Churchill's personal code name] is full out on Overlord and Anvil but suspects Eisenhower and Montgomery will demand considerably heavier assaults in the full moon period.' Ismay's reply took strong exception to the idea, stating: '. . . It is most undesirable that Monty should be given an opportunity of criticizing the plan before he has discussed it with the people who prepared it. They alone can explain the reasons which have led to the adoption of the plan in its present form. We are sure it would be much better for Monty to reserve judgment until he comes home. . .'[1]

The next day Montgomery's brief written appreciation was presented to Churchill. In it he criticized the plan while carefully disclaiming any prior knowledge of it. His statement that 'Today, 1st January 1944, is the first time I have seen the Appreciation and proposed plan or considered the problem in any way' is, at best, misleading.[2] There is no doubt that the plan had been discussed in some detail with Eisenhower and Smith in Algiers and Monty's presentation to Churchill makes no reference to their misgivings, leaving the false impression that it was Montgomery himself who had originated the idea. Montgomery's later actions in London and his post-war accounts lead to the conclusion that he took sole credit for revising the plan. Although it was Montgomery who became the principal architect of the changes which were initiated, credit for recognizing the defects and insisting on alterations must go to all three men.

Marshall realized Eisenhower needed a rest before taking up his new duties and ordered him back to Washington for leave and

---

[1] PRO (CAB 120/420), ANVIL was the proposed invasion of southern France which was to coincide with the Normandy landings and was intended mainly as a diversion to draw off German attention and reinforcements from Normandy. In the months that followed, Churchill developed a vehement opposition to ANVIL; controversy over this plan was to become the most trying aspect of Eisenhower's relations with Churchill.

[2] Montgomery, op.cit., p. 211.

briefings on OVERLORD. After the meeting with Churchill, Montgomery immediately left for London to set up his new headquarters at St Paul's School, where he had been a student many years before. One of his first actions was to strip the 21st Army Group staff of Paget's men in what was nothing less than a ruthless purge. Nearly all the senior officers of the Eighth Army were brought back to England to form the backbone of the 21st Army Group staff. Headed by his able and genial Chief of Staff, Major General Sir Francis ('Freddie') de Guingand, 21st Army Group quickly became a transplant of the Eighth Army; Montgomery trusted only officers whom he knew personally and who had proved their mettle in battle. Only what he termed 'proper chaps' knew and understood his method of operation and technique of command. This purge of 21st Army Group gave rise to the comment, soon circulating London, that 'the Gentlemen are out and the Players are in'.

While Montgomery's hasty dismissal of Paget's team has been seen by his critics as yet another example of his disdain for others, it must be remembered that it was much too late to train a new staff of officers: most of Paget's had little or no combat experience. The time for niceties had long since passed. Moreover, 21st Army Group was now an Allied operational headquarters with total responsibility for planning the invasion and subsequent campaign. The lives of thousands of Allied soldiers depended on the best plan that could be devised.[1]

With Eisenhower's blessing Montgomery was now the temporary Commander-in-Chief of all Allied ground forces for the invasion. Supreme Headquarters (SHAEF) was just being formed – Morgan's COSSAC staff would shortly cease to exist – and there was an urgent need for a single headquarters to control all ground operations during the early phase of the forthcoming campaign: Eisenhower was adamant that there would be no separate headquarters created between him and his field commanders. Bradley's future Army Group headquarters was at that time only a

---

[1] Paget later admitted that Churchill thought he was far too defensive-minded and 'defeatist' for his insistence tht the COSSAC plan was deficient in resources. Churchill would say to him: 'Why can't I get someone who wants to fight?' Thus there can be no doubt that Churchill never would have accepted Paget as commander of the Allied ground forces for OVERLORD. General Sir Bernard Paget, interview with Dr Forrest C. Pogue, 6 February 1947.

skeletal operation, thus 21st Army Group became the logical headquarters to coordinate OVERLORD. Eisenhower's logic was that 'While plans called for eventual organization of American and British ground forces each under their own commander, directly responsible to me, the initial assault was foreseen as a single battle, closely interrelated in all its parts, and requiring the supervision of a single battleline commander. All were agreed on this necessity.'[1]* Eisenhower's decision was for Montgomery to retain command of the ground forces until such time as Patton's Third US Army could be landed and the US Army Group made operational under Bradley.[2] Inasmuch as no firm date could be forecast for this, the timing of the changeover was left open.

Eisenhower needed a great many new faces before he was satisfied he had assembled the best commanders and staff officers available to him. Fortunately COSSAC contained a wealth of experienced and able officers, many of whom were retained in the knowledge that their contributions to OVERLORD would be vital. Most of the principal staff positions, however, were filled by officers from Eisenhower's Allied Force Headquarters (AFHQ) in Algiers. The job of acquiring these officers and of shifting others in COSSAC who were not required was left largely to Bedell Smith. Unlike Montgomery, who obtained nearly everyone he wanted, Eisenhower had to fight a long series of bureaucratic battles to fill the large number of US command positions.[3]

In addition to overhauling the 21st Army Group staff, one of Montgomery's other priorities was to complete several senior command appointments within the Second British Army. In January the War Office, at his specific request, nominated Lieutenant General Miles Dempsey as GOC, Second Army in place of

---

[1] *Report by the Supreme Commander to the Combined Chiefs of Staff on Operations in Europe of the Allied Expeditionary Force, 6 June 1944 to 8 May 1945.*

* For the invasion 21st Army Group consisted of: First Canadian Army (2 Corps), Lieutenant General H. D. G. Crerar; Second British Army (1, 8, 12 and 30 Corps), Lieutenant General Miles Dempsey; British airborne troops (1st and 6th Divisions), Lieutenant General F. A. M. Browning; First US Army (V, VII, VIII, XIX Corps w/attached 82nd and 101st Airborne Divisions), Lieutenant General Omar N. Bradley.

[2] Originally designated First US Army Group, it was later changed to 12th Army Group to avoid confusion with First US Army. Lieutenant General Courtney Hodges was assigned to understudy Bradley and eventually command the First Army when Bradley became Army Group Commander.

[3] Eisenhower was also commander of all US forces in the European Theatre of Operations. His list included one Army Group commander, three army commanders, twelve corps commanders and, prior to end of the campaign, about fifty division commanders.

Lieutenant General Kenneth Anderson who had previously served under Eisenhower as commander, 1st British Army in Tunisia, where he had been less than inspiring and where he was disliked by the Americans. A hard-working and dedicated officer, Anderson was well known to Montgomery, who considered him lacking in the qualities he required of his army commander.

Miles Dempsey was another of the original 'Monty men' and had been a student of his at Camberley. When Montgomery had taken over the Eighth Army he requested the War Office to send him 'Bimbo' Dempsey, who arrived in December 1942 as an acting Lieutenant General in command of 13 Corps.[1] At that time 13 Corps was out of the line and Dempsey had spent the next seven months in Cairo helping to plan the invasion of Sicily. A career infantryman, Dempsey was an ardent student of military history and during the interwar period had frequently visited Europe to study its battlefields firsthand. Blessed with an active and incisive mind, a phenomenal memory and a unique skill in reading maps, Dempsey would soon leave his army staff in awe over his ability to remember everything he saw on a map, to bring a landscape literally to life in his mind even though he had never actually seen it. This talent proved particularly important during the crucial battles around Caen in June and July 1944. Dempsey was considered the Eighth Army's best expert in combined operations and, as he grew in experience, Montgomery soon recognized his potential for army command. The two men shared many qualities, including a disdain for paperwork and a determination, based on their First World War experiences, never to waste their soldiers lives'.

Of the four corps that comprised the British element of the Second Army, two had yet to be filled. 1 Corps was already under the command of Lieutenant General John Crocker, the veteran armoured corps officer who had first enlisted as a private soldier in 1915, won the MC and the DSO in France in 1917–18, and distinguished himself in 1940. A stern and humourless officer, Crocker's long experience with armoured forces made him an excellent choice as the corps commander whose units would

---

[1] Dempsey would never admit where or how he had earned the nickname 'Bimbo', and the question of its origin was said to make him blush. A deeply resolute and professional soldier, Dempsey knew it was his soldiers who were the key to success in battle, particularly his battalion commanders, whom he knew by name. 'You see, they are the important men; if they are not right, nothing can be right.'

spearhead the invasion of the Normandy beaches. Montgomery quite rightly found no reason to challenge the War Office's appointment.

The other previously confirmed appointment was that of Lieutenant General Neil Ritchie to the command of 12 Corps. Ritchie had been one of Auchinleck's unfortunate choices to command the Eighth Army. An excellent staff officer, he was totally lacking in command experience and quite unable to fight the Eighth Army effectively against the wily Rommel, a fact which Auchinleck himself belatedly remedied when he took personal command in late May 1942. For any other officer this would have meant the end of his career; Ritchie, however, was exceptionally fortunate. Brooke, who was generally ruthless with failed officers, had a soft spot for Ritchie who had served as his 2 Corps Brigadier General Staff in the BEF. The CIGS recognized that Ritchie's appointment and relief from the Eighth Army had been Auchinleck's fault and decided to give him another try: he was demoted to Major General and sent to command a division in Scotland and by 1944 had been promoted back to Lieutenant General and given command of 12 Corps for the invasion, thus becoming one of the few wartime exceptions to the long-standing tradition that failed field commanders are not given second chances.

Montgomery now appointed his old friend Lieutenant General Sir Richard O'Connor to command 8 Corps. In one of the most brilliant actions of the war, O'Connor had commanded Wavell's desert army in 1940–1 during Operation COMPASS, which had surprised and all but destroyed Marshal Graziani's Italian Tenth Army in Egypt and Libya. O'Connor's daring use of the 7th Armoured Division in a dash across the neck of the Cyrenaican Peninsula had resulted in a stunning victory at Beda Fomm and the capture of 130,000 prisoners, 845 guns and approximately 400 tanks.[1] Taken prisoner later in 1941, O'Connor had spent three and a half years as a POW in Italy. After several unsuccessful escape attempts he and several other senior British officers finally succeeded late in 1943, and he had returned to England in time to be offered 8 Corps for the invasion.

Montgomery's other corps appointment was Lieutenant General G. C. Bucknall to 30 Corps, in what was to prove one of

[1] Ronald Lewin, *The Chief*, London, 1980, p. 89.

his few poor selections, chosen despite Brooke's misgivings that he was unsuitable for a corps command. As will be seen, Brooke's judgement was correct; in August Montgomery sacked Bucknall and replaced him with the dynamic and able Lieutenant General Brian Horrocks.

During the month of January 1944 Morgan's original OVER-LORD plan was subjected to drastic revision: surgery began the day after Montgomery arrived in London. On 3 January Montgomery and Bedell Smith met with the COSSAC planners to be briefed on the invasion. Montgomery's reaction was predictably critical: calling the COSSAC plan an unsound operation of war, he outlined his ideas about what ought to be done. Emphasizing the need for an expanded frontage, Montgomery defined what he envisioned as the tasks of the US and British armies:

> The American Army will clear the Cherbourg peninsula and capture the port of Cherbourg. They will subsequently develop their operations to the south and west. The British Army will operate to the south to prevent any interference with the American Army from the east. It is hoped eventually to get a firm lodgement from Caen to Nantes with the British Army being built up through the Cherbourg peninsula and the American Army through Brittany.[1]

In the days prior to Eisenhower's arrival in London on 15 January to assume command of SHAEF, Montgomery held numerous discussions with the planners and the air and naval commanders to work out details of a revised operation. On the morning of 21 January the first Supreme Commander's Conference took place at Norfolk House in St James's Square, its subject the OVERLORD plan. When it was his turn to speak, Montgomery, with his usual bluntness and clarity, got straight to the point. He began by declaring that in view of enemy strength and the limitations on the rate of post-landings buildup, it was essential to obtain quick success against the German defenders of Normandy. The present plan would not achieve this object: the assault was far too weak and on too narrow a front, making it easier for the Germans to locate and hold the assault force and far more difficult for Allied forces to emerge rapidly and strike the enemy deep and hard.

---

[1] 'Notes on the Development of Grand Strategy', by Colonel C. P. Stacey (the official Canadian historian), PRO (CAB 44/242).

The early capture of a port was also essential to avoid total dependence on Mulberry (the artificial harbours being specially developed for the invasion). The approaches to Cherbourg provided a natural defensive barrier in the marshes and rivers at the neck of the Cotentin Peninsula. The British themselves had used this line in 1940 when elements of the BEF escaped from France through Cherbourg – then the Germans had been held off with only one brigade. Therefore any plan for the rapid capture of Cherbourg, Montgomery argued, must allow for a landing on the eastern side of this defensive barrier.[1] The existing plan would create a small bridgehead through which all subsequent operations would have to be funnelled, and it would most likely become highly congested. It was preferable, therefore, to make the widest possible landing between the areas of heavy fire from the guns of Cherbourg on the west and the Le Havre guns on the east. US forces would be placed on the right, the British on the left, with Bradley's American units given the mission of capturing Cherbourg, then pushing on to the Loire River ports and the Brittany port of Brest. British and Canadian units would deal with the main enemy forces, reinforcing Normandy from the east and southeast.

As he outlined it that day, Montgomery's proposed strategy was to concentrate in the initial stages of the operation on quickly gaining control of the main centres of road communication, followed by deep thrusts by armoured formations between and beyond these points to gain and control ground which would make it difficult for German reserves to get past them.[2] It followed that quick success necessitated an assault on a five-divisional front, plus the utilization of one airborne division.[3]

[1] Montgomery's original idea on 3 January had been to land a force either on the northern edge of the Brittany Peninsula or on the western edge of the Cotentin Peninsula around Granville or St Malo. At a second meeting on 4 January, the senior COSSAC planners convinced Montgomery that an operation so far west was not feasible.

[2] Montgomery was referring to the cities of Caen and Bayeux and the Caen-Falaise Plain, the strategically vital high ground southeast of Caen which controlled its approaches and the crossings over the Odon and Orne Rivers. All principal roads to the invasion area funnelled through Caen, whose strategic importance made it an essential objective which must be captured by the Allied armies.

[3] The use of this airborne division was envisioned on the right flank in the Cotentin. The revised plan later called for the employment of an additional US airborne division to secure the vital points in the Cotentin Peninsula and assist in capturing Cherbourg. The British 6th Airborne Division was also to be employed on the left flank to secure the Orne Canal between Caen and the sea and the high ground due east of Caen, until the assault units could secure Caen and relieve the threat of counterattack from the eastern flank.

Montgomery's proposal called for the assault to be organized under the control of two armies, one British and one American, each of which would have responsibility for a front of two corps. The area from Bayeux eastwards to the Orne River should be British and from Bayeux westwards, American.[1]

Neither the navy nor the air force was happy with the new plan. The expanded assault placed a heavy additional burden on the navy for escort and sealift, and the air commanders worried that the development of suitable forward airfields was too dependent on the early capture of Caen. Despite their dissatisfaction, though, all who were involved in the planning of OVERLORD accepted the necessity for strengthening the assault force. The US commanders were pleased with the plan since it gave them a far more important role in the invasion.

The main problem with an expanded invasion force was Operation ANVIL: there were not enough landing craft available to support a simultaneous landing in southern France. The British were dead against this operation which would drain valuable Allied manpower from Italy, arguing that the same purpose could be achieved by threat rather than by actual invasion. The ANVIL debate pitted Marshall and Eisenhower against Churchill and Brooke and occupied centre stage for the next eight months as both Eisenhower and Churchill sought to have their way. Of the many contentious issues separating the two Allies none generated more passions than this one. There followed an almost endless series of cables between London and Washington, including some of the most acrimonious exchanges of the war between Churchill and Roosevelt.

Although Eisenhower was deeply concerned over the possibility of losing ANVIL he fully supported Montgomery's other proposals, and during an afternoon meeting on 21 January, decided to submit the revised plan to the Combined Chiefs of

[1] Minutes of the Supreme Commander's Conference, 1030 hours, 21 January 1944, Eisenhower Presidential Papers, Eisenhower Library.

[2] In early August, prior to the actual landings in southern France, Churchill was still refusing to give up. In one six-hour session he attempted by every means at his command to convince the Supreme Commander to cancel ANVIL. It was one of the most trying days of the entire campaign for Eisenhower. 'Ike said no, continued saying no all afternoon, and ended saying no in every form of the English language at his command.' Quoted in Butcher, *Three Years With Eisenhower*, p. 545. The ANVIL debate did not develop completely along national, i.e. British *vs* American, lines. For example, Eisenhower's Chief of Staff, Bedell Smith, was against it, while the First Sea Lord, Admiral Andrew Cunningham, backed Eisenhower.

Staff for approval. He recognized that there would have to be a postponement of a full month in order to obtain the additional assets to support five divisions, but accepted it as the price for a properly balanced invasion force.

The 21 January meeting was extremely significant to the story of the Normandy campaign for not only did it result in the decision by the Supreme Commander to alter the original COSSAC plan but, more importantly, it brought the first pronouncement by Montgomery on the strategy he intended to follow. Throughout that day he constantly stressed the need for quick success in seizing key objectives in the British sector. It was his main reason for revising the plan and became the foundation for his post-landings strategy. As had been the case with the original plan for the battle of El Alamein, Montgomery intended to use his armoured forces to spearhead the British thrust from the beach-head to seize objectives and to keep the enemy unbalanced.[1] Only with rapid movement, combined with the hoped-for surprise of the invasion itself, could this quick success be achieved. The plan for Alamein had been to use the infantry and engineers to clear German minefields, thus allowing his armour to break loose against Rommel's defences. At Alamein Montgomery had used a massive and concentrated artillery cover to support his assault forces, and his conception of the forthcoming Normandy battles was cut from the same cloth: with heavy air and naval gunfire support, the infantry would seize the Caen-Bayeux beachhead, thus enabling the armoured brigades to land and quickly push on.

The other major change initiated by Montgomery – one which later proved to be instrumental in the success of the D-Day landings – was to insist on the use of airborne troops on both flanks to prevent interference during the early moments of the assault phase when the invaders were most vulnerable. Bradley not only concurred but fought for and eventually obtained approval for the use of not one but *two* US airborne divisions to secure the critical points in the Cotentin, and to protect the landings on UTAH beach by the US 4th Infantry Division.

---

[1] According to one of the senior COSSAC planners, Major General Charles A. West, Churchill was quoted as saying: 'Get great armoured columns and drive them in deep.' Major General Charles A. West, interview with Dr Forrest C. Pogue, 19 February 1947.

Eisenhower's support was followed by an order to the head planners to draft a signal to the Combined Chiefs of Staff outlining the revised plan and requesting their immediate concurrence. As they began their task the planners were bothered by what they viewed as several serious defects in Montgomery's plan. Would not the opportunity for quick success be prejudiced by the wide dispersal of the assault frontage which, despite Montgomery's claims to the contrary, lacked concentration at a decisive point? Deep doubts were raised in their minds about the possibility of the assault on the Caen beaches being seriously jeopardized by a simultaneous landing on the Cotentin Peninsula to capture Cherbourg at the expense of Caen. The planners concluded that the Combined Chiefs should not be asked to decide on a revised plan without prior consideration by the OVERLORD commanders of the advantages and disadvantages of Montgomery's plan and of possible alternatives.[1]

The next day, Saturday, 22 January, the SHAEF Chief of Staff directed that the signal should not be sent out until the head planners could be given an opportunity to prepare an alternative paper for consideration at the next Supreme Commander's Conference on the following Monday. That same day a compromise plan was produced which called for a four-divisional assault in the Caen sector only. The merits of each plan were compared and the planners concluded Montgomery's plan did indeed jeopardize success in the Caen sector, where the whole operation might be compromised. On the other hand, they believed their proposal would permit a proper concentration of forces and allow for decisive defeat of the Germans in that sector in seven to ten days.

The basic differences between the two plans was that the one prepared by the planners concentrated on the capture of Caen, the defeat of the German reserves and the capture of ground south and southeast of Caen suitable for airfield construction, followed by the seizure of Cherbourg; while Montgomery's plan was designed to accomplish all three at the same time by the

---

[1] Eisenhower's planning staff now included many former COSSAC officers. Montgomery's harsh criticism of the original COSSAC plan undoubtedly upset some of these officers but there is no evidence to suggest their own criticism of Montgomery's new plan for the assault stemmed from resentment. Rather, there seems to have been genuine concern over what were seen to be the flaws in his plan. Their proposed compromise plan was designed to remedy the flaws in both the original COSSAC plan and Montgomery's plan.

addition of the Cotentin landing. He saw Cherbourg and the ensuing buildup of forces as the essential ingredients for success. Operations in the Caen area were to serve as a means of anchoring the east flank while simultaneously securing airfield sites and critical terrain as a springboard for future operations by these forces. The planners conceded that Montgomery's plan would speed up the capture of Cherbourg but continued to worry about British forces being spread too thinly and the possibility of the German defenders containing the Allies in the bridgehead and then defeating the invasion force by turn. It would be of scant value, they argued, if the Cotentin landings succeeded and the Caen landings failed. Moreover, they thought the capacity of the port of Cherbourg was not nearly as great as was being suggested. At best only four divisions could be supported initially, and eight divisions after thirty days. The Cotentin was obviously unsuitable for airfields or for a troop and logistics buildup if the Caen area could not be held.

The head planners' paper was presented to Bedell Smith on Sunday evening, 23 January. Smith met with Montgomery the same night but, contrary to his earlier promise, did not wait until the next day's meeting when both plans could be thrashed out. Instead he ordered that the original signal recommending adoption of Montgomery's plan be sent out that night to the Combined Chiefs. There is no indication that Eisenhower was ever shown the compromise plan, though Eisenhower's appointment diary does show that Smith visited him sometime that night.[1] Smith's reasons for failing to wait until the following day before sending a signal may have come from this meeting with Eisenhower but it is reasonable to conclude that both Smith and Montgomery viewed the compromise plan as unsuitable and the necessity for approval by the Combined Chiefs as so pressing that further delay was intolerable. Montgomery never would have supported the compromise devised by the staff; knowing this Smith may have decided that any discussion the following day would be futile.

It is unlikely that Eisenhower would have accepted the compromise plan, particularly in view of Montgomery's opposition to it. However, in the light of subsequent events, it is worth

---

[1] The Minutes of the Supreme Commander's Conference on Monday, 24 January 1944 make no reference to the existence of a compromise plan.

noting that the planners' fears had some basis. Although Montgomery's plan was the bolder of the two in its emphasis on accomplishing three objectives simultaneously, its potential flaw was the splitting of his forces, resulting in a lack of concentration around Caen. Unfortunately the complicated logistics of mounting the massive operation did not allow for an additional option which might have overcome that particular problem. Neither during this stage of the planning nor in the final days before the landings did Montgomery ever consider his plan weak in the Caen sector. His thinking represented the views of Mountbatten and many other planners who had argued that the need for a rapid post-landings buildup was of paramount importance: the one factor which preoccupied the OVERLORD commanders was the fear of the assault being defeated before reinforcements could be landed in sufficient strength to preserve the bridgehead against a strong German counterattack. In his boldness, Montgomery was also opting for safety by taking steps to ensure the earliest possible capture of the port of Cherbourg. Admittedly both plans contained high elements of risk but it is difficult to fault Montgomery's logic in preferring an assault in the Cotentin. Ultimately, however, the fears of the head planners proved justified.[1]

There were misgivings in Washington over Eisenhower's signal. The US Chiefs of Staff still favoured Morgan's plan but did not feel able to overrule the new Supreme Commander in what would have amounted to a vote of no confidence at a time when indecision might have threatened the invasion timetable. During his two weeks in Washington earlier that month, Eisenhower had lobbied hard for a revised OVERLORD, using the same general arguments as did Montgomery in London. The British Chiefs of Staff supported the Eisenhower-Montgomery proposal, and on 1 February 1944, the Combined Chiefs of Staff gave their approval. The same day the revised plan was published as the Neptune Initial Joint Plan.[2] The invasion was now set for the end of May, with the Supreme Commander given flexibility over the final date to accommodate the weather forecasts.

---

[1] Final, revised plans would call for the capture of Caen by one British and one Canadian division.

[2] OVERLORD was the code name for the entire operation to liberate Northwest Europe; Neptune was the detailed plan for the invasion of Normandy. During the planning of OVERLORD a codename was assigned to each of the potential invasion sites in France. NEPTUNE was the designation given the Caen-Cotention sector.

Planning went ahead at full speed while the ANVIL question dragged on unsettled. Montgomery opposed ANVIL on the grounds its landing craft were essential to OVERLORD and that such an operation would weaken the Italian front at the precise time when there was a chance of beating the Russians to Vienna.[1] On 19 February, he wrote to Eisenhower arguing that ANVIL must not jeopardize 'a really good OVERLORD', and suggesting that the practicalities of the operation be cleared up at once.[2] The following day Montgomery visited Churchill at Chequers, and on 21 February despatched another letter to Eisenhower, this time urging the cancellation of ANVIL altogether. Churchill's influence was clearly contained in the letter, which concluded: 'I recommend very strongly that we now throw the whole weight of our opinion into the scales against ANVIL. Let us have two really good major campaigns – one in Italy and one in OVERLORD.'[3]

During February Eisenhower showed evidence of changing his position over ANVIL. The uncertain situation in Italy created by the Anzio landing left him of the opinion that the operation would either have to be postponed or cancelled entirely. He came under great pressure from Churchill and the British Chiefs of Staff who wanted it cancelled and from the US Chiefs of Staff who were insistent that ANVIL be confirmed. Until the matter could be resolved Eisenhower was satisfied merely to keep ANVIL alive. At the end of February Butcher noted in his diary that: 'Following Ike's representations to the British Chiefs of Staff as to the need for continued planning for ANVIL, conclusions now have been agreed by the Combined Chiefs of Staff and approved by the President and the Prime Minister. The Italian battle fronts are to have overriding priority of all existing and future operations in the Mediterranean, but ANVIL is to be planned with hope of launching it shortly after OVERLORD. . . As this action largely meets Ike's wishes, he is satisfied.'[4]

Eisenhower finally agreed that ANVIL must be postponed to insure adequate landing craft for OVERLORD but he would not agree to its cancellation. He believed Montgomery was not as

[1] Montgomery, *Memoirs*, op.cit., p. 221.
[2] Montgomery, letter to Eisenhower, 19 February 1944, Eisenhower Presidential Papers, Eisenhower Library.
[3] Montgomery, letter to Eisenhower, 21 February 1944, Eisenhower Papers, Eisenhower Presidential Library.
[4] Butcher, op.cit., entry of 26 February 1944, pp. 425–6.

opposed to the operation as was thought. After the war he spoke of Montgomery, saying 'As an individual, he had equal convictions about the probable value and practicability of ANVIL, which he expressed to me privately, but his conference and official views reflected the position of his government.'[1]

Why was Eisenhower so determined to keep the ANVIL operation even though it had to be delayed? There were numerous reasons. In addition to wanting to see ANVIL draw off German reserves and protect the southern flank of the Allied armies, Eisenhower was not at all optimistic over the usefulness of the Brittany ports, which he believed would be destroyed by the Germans before they could be captured. He may have had political reasons as well. He had seen Churchill's attitude toward capturing Vienna via Italy harden in recent months; some believed ANVIL may have been his method of guaranteeing the priority of OVERLORD against Churchill and Brooke, who still envisioned a widening of the Italian campaign. American distrust of British support for the invasion certainly had not abated, and ANVIL became Eisenhower's hole-card to ensure OVERLORD did not lose emphasis to Italy.

The problems of revising the invasion plan and gaining its adoption had occupied most of Montgomery's time and effort during the months of January and February. Free of that burden and certain of the five assault divisions he required, Montgomery now turned his attention in the time remaining to formulate a strategy for the post-landings period which would avenge the humiliation of 1940.

---

[1] Eisenhower interview, loc.cit.

CHAPTER 6

The Master Plan

> . . . Having seized the initiative by our initial land-
> ing, we must insure that we keep it. The best way to
> interfere with the enemy concentrations and coun-
> ter-measures will be to push forward fairly power-
> ful armoured force thrusts on the afternoon of
> D-Day. . . . I am prepared to accept almost any risk
> in order to carry out these tactics. I would risk even
> the total loss of the armoured brigade groups –
> which in any event is not really possible.
>
> Montgomery to Bradley and Dempsey,
> 14 April 1944

In February the ideas Montgomery had outlined to the Allied commanders began to take firm shape. While planning went ahead for D-Day in various headquarters, he met privately with Bradley and Dempsey at St Paul's School to work out the post-D-Day campaign plan. All three commanders recognized that the first few days after D-Day would be the most critical of the entire campaign. Montgomery's primary concern was how to keep Rommel's reserves, particularly the panzer divisions, away from Bradley's forces on the west flank while he drove on Cherbourg. Once the D-Day assault was successful there had to be a rapid linkup between Bradley's and Dempsey's forces into one solid beachhead in the Caen-Bayeux-Carentan area so that they could open up port facilities for the other invasion units. Immediate Allied danger lay in any gap between their forces through which the Germans could penetrate.

Once the beachhead was consolidated, speed would then be of the essence in order to create a bridgehead by seizing and holding critical terrain. Montgomery perceived the battle would be won or lost in the British sector: without a firm base on the east flank the entire assault force was perilously vulnerable to counterattack. The firepower of the German Tiger and Panther tanks, with their high velocity 88mm guns, was far superior to that of the smaller Allied Shermans which, while more manoeuverable, mounted only a 75mm gun.

A brief examination of the Normandy plan reveals that British and Canadian forces would land (on SWORD, GOLD and JUNO beaches) on the eastern (left) flank and push generally south and southeast. US forces (from UTAH and OMAHA beaches) would face south and push in that direction (except for the initial need for capturing Cherbourg, which lay northwest). The push west into Brittany would take place simultaneously with movement by the First US Army to the Loire. At some point the entire Allied force would have to realign itself to the east for the capture of the Seine crossings, the ultimate objective of the Normandy campaign. At the Seine it was anticipated that the Allies would need to regroup before continuing their offensive against Germany itself.

Some have questioned why the British were allocated the left flank and US forces the right. As Bedell Smith has related, there were no political motivations; the decision was made for military reasons. 'When the first American division came to Great Britain it was put in the southwest of England; that dictated we should come in on the right flank. The choice was dictated not by any long-range staff planning but by the availability of suitable accommodations. To have switched the flanks once these conditions were imposed would have meant an impossible criss-cross of transportation in England. There was later much altercation about changing it. We would have been glad to have it the other way, for the main effort was already set through the Low Countries and North of the Ruhr. The Low Countries were the logical route but the British were never strong enough to make the main effort.'[1]

Montgomery's previous experience against Rommel in North Africa had taught him a great deal about his opposite number. As he would elaborate in great detail in April, at the first formal OVERLORD briefing, Montgomery correctly anticipated that Rommel's strategy for defeating the invasion force would be to repel the assault on or near the beaches by heavy panzer

---

[1] Lieutenant General Walter Bedell Smith, interview with Roland G. Ruppenthal, 14 September 1945, US Army Military History Institute.

counterattacks to push the Allies back into the sea – his only hope of success lay in a rapid counterthrust *before* the Allies could gain a firm foothold. Rommel was under no illusions about what would happen if he failed. Normandy was over four hundred miles from the Third Reich at the end of a tenuous supply line and with Hitler giving the Eastern Front priority he knew he would have to make do for the most part with the forces at his disposal. Although the Allies would have difficulty with their logistics and troop buildup initially, once firmly established there was little hope of stopping them. If the might of their air, sea and ground forces could be brought to bear upon his defenders, the end result was inevitable.

Montgomery's basic problem was how to anchor the east flank securely, blocking any attempt by Rommel to roll him up and defeat the invasion or interfere with Bradley making for Cherbourg. Once the problem of Cherbourg was out of the way, attention could be directed towards an offensive to the south and, once the entire Cotentin Peninsula was secured, to a breakout into Brittany by Patton's Third US Army to secure its many potentially valuable ports.

Montgomery focused his attention on the important high ground generally southeast between Caen and Falaise. This terrain was of immense strategic importance, not only for its suitability for new airfields but, more importantly, for the fact that its occupant controlled the entire sector and the approaches to the formidable barrier of the Orne. This river rises south of Argentan and flows northwest to Thury-Harcourt, then north to Caen, and from Caen to the Atlantic, a distance of some hundred miles.

The key factor to control of this terrain was the ancient city of Caen. To gain control of the Caen-Falaise Plain the Allies would have to capture Caen and the Orne crossings, either those in the city itself or the ones due southeast as the Orne flowed toward Thury-Harcourt. If they tried to bypass Caen to gain the Caen-Falaise Plain, they would find a further barrier in the form of the River Odon, which flows into the Orne from the west at a point on the southern perimeter of the city. This meant that they would either have to cross the Orne north of the city and drive due south between Caen and Troarn or go west via the Odon and Orne crossings. If Caen were controlled by the

Germans either avenue of approach would be effectively blocked.

Caen, then, became the focal point of Montgomery's strategy. How then could it be taken? The answer, reasoned Montgomery, lay in the speed and aggressiveness with which his armour would push rapidly out of the D-Day beachhead to overrun the city and points south before Rommel could react and consolidate his forces for counterattack. Although there were known to be a number of panzer divisions in the general area of Caen, in May Allied intelligence would reveal that the 21st Panzer Division was to be the main obstacle to the British thrust. If Leigh-Mallory's tactical air forces could prevent the Luftwaffe from interfering with Dempsey's armoured forces, and also delay or disrupt any German attempt to reinforce the Caen sector, there was no reason, given a sufficiently speedy and aggressive thrust from the beaches, why Caen could not be captured quickly. As General Dempsey later recalled:

> We crawled around on the floor spreading out the maps and so far as I was concerned, looking at the Normandy terrain seriously for the first time. That day Monty stressed the fact that after the immediate reserves had been drawn in all German reserves would arrive at the battle front from the East and Southeast, thus to get across to the American sector of the bridgehead, they would have to pass across the British front around Caen. It was to be my job to make sure that they didn't move across, that they were kept fully occupied fighting us in the Caen sector. Monty also stressed that whatever happened my left flank had to be kept absolutely secure. The Eastern wall along the Orne must be held otherwise the whole bridgehead could be rolled up from that flank. He never once wavered in his determination to pursue this policy.[1]

Contrary to most later interpretations of Montgomery's master plan, his remarks then and later did not reflect a defensive posture around Caen or a ploy to use the city as a hinge. Rather, he wanted strong and aggressive *offensive* action to ensure *protection* of the critical and vulnerable British flank. As the plan unfolded and was later formally presented, the Montgomery strategy called for the Second British Army to hold and pivot at some point while US forces drove south and eventually turned eastwards when the Loire, the southern flank of the American

[1] Notes on conversation with General Sir Miles Dempsey, 4 June and Chester Wilmot, n.d. (probably 1946), Liddell Hart Papers, King's College, London.

advance, was reached. Bradley's recollection was that Montgomery's concept was not defensive and that his early orders and discussions did not contain reference to Caen as a hinge upon which the British would hold and pivot.[1] As will be seen, no one else connected with the planning or execution of OVERLORD recalls any such indication either.

On 7 April 1944, Good Friday, Montgomery called together the senior generals, admirals and airmen at St Paul's School for Exercise THUNDERCLAP, a series of briefings by the ground, naval and air commanders-in-chief. Those present included Eisenhower and, for part of the afternoon session, Churchill.

Montgomery spoke first for over an hour. Behind him on the wall was a large outline map of Normandy entitled 'Forecast of Operations from D+17 to D+90' and bearing a series of coloured phase lines. Sixteen pages of typewritten notes used by Montgomery survive and spell out in clear detail his concept of the D-Day and post D-Day operations.[2] 'This exercise,' he said, 'is being held for the purpose of putting all General Officers of the field armies in possession of the whole outline plan for OVERLORD, so as to insure mutual understanding and confidence.

'The object of OVERLORD is to secure a lodgement on the continent from which further offensive operations can be developed. . . This is an Allied operation, being carried out by British and American forces with the forces of other of our allies cooperating. It is a great Allied team and none of us could do any good without the other. . . For the initial operations I am General Eisenhower's ground force commander. . . All General Officers must understand that HQ, 21st Army Group is an Allied HQ exercising operational command and control over the land forces of the Allies, under the Supreme Commander.

'The intention,' Montgomery continued, 'is to assault simultaneously: immediately north of the Carentan estuary and between the Carentan estuary and the River Orne with the object of securing as a base for further operations a lodgement area which will include airfield sites and the port of Cherbourg.'

[1] General Omar N. Bradley, interview with Dr Forrest C. Pogue, 14 October 1946. Bradley was uncertain of the exact date but thought that Montgomery's references to Caen as a hinge did not come until early July.
[2] Copies of Montgomery's notes are in the PRO and the Eisenhower Library.

Turning his attention to Rommel Montgomery said:

'Rommel is likely to hold his mobile divisions back from the coast until he is certain where our main effort is being made. He will then concentrate them quickly and strike a hard blow, his static divisions will endeavour to hold on defensively to important ground and act as pivots to the counter attacks. By dusk on D minus 1 the enemy will be certain that the NEPTUNE area is to be assaulted in strength. By the evening of D-Day he will know the width of frontage and the approximate number of our assaulting divisions. The enemy is likely that night to summon his two nearest panzer divisions to assist. By D+5 the enemy can have brought in six panzer type divisions. If he has decided to go the whole NEPTUNE hog, he will continue his efforts to push us into the sea. We ourselves will have fifteen divisions on shore by then. After about D+8 I think the enemy will have to begin to consider a "roping-off" policy, i.e. trying to stop our expansion from the lodgement area. Some of us here know Rommel well. He is a determined commander and likes to hurl his armour in to the battle. But according to what we know of the chain of command the armoured divisions are being kept directly under von Rundstedt, and delay may be caused before they are released to Rommel. This fact may help us, and quarrels may arise between the two of them.

'The enemy buildup can become *considerable* from D+4 onwards; obviously therefore we must put all our energies into the fight and get such a good situation in the first few days that the enemy can do nothing against us.'[1]

The tasks assigned to each of the armies followed Montgomery's earlier pronouncements, with Bradley's First US Army to capture Cherbourg and then drive south towards St Lô in conformity with the Second British Army's advance. The Second British Army was to assault west of the Orne, develop operations to the south and southeast to secure airfield sites and protect the eastern flank of the First US Army during the Cherbourg operation. Subsequently they were to pivot on their left and offer a strong front against enemy movement towards the lodgement area from the east. The two followup forces were: the First Canadian Army, which was to take over the extreme left sector of

---

[1] Montgomery notes, loc.cit.

the lodgement area; and the Third US Army which was to clear Brittany and cover the southern flank while the First US Army turned east to drive toward the Seine and Paris.

Using a pointer, Montgomery next turned his attention to the map on the wall.

'You will see from the diagram on the wall how the land battle will be developed. Phase 1 is shown in GREEN. In this phase the First US Army and Second British Army secure the whole area included within the green line.[1] I estimate we may have this area by D+20 and we will fight continuously till we get it. There may have to be a pause to see how we stand administratively, if not, so much the better.'[2]

In Phase 2 Montgomery demonstrated how his armies would push out of the lodgement area to the D+35–40 lines (YELLOW), how the Third US Army would be landed and commence operations, with the US VIII Corps temporarily under the First US Army, to move into Brittany. Attainment of the D+35 line would generally align the British and American armies facing east, from Deauville in the north to Le Mans and the Loire in the south. By D+90 the Allies could hope to attain the BLACK line of the Seine. The Canadians would cross the Seine east of Rouen and operate northwards to cut off and capture the port of Le Havre in an operation dubbed AXEHEAD.

The rate of buildup would be flexible. 'The general principle on which the buildup has been planned is to land on the continent the maximum number of fighting formations in the first few days. . . Flexibility has been introduced at the earliest possible moment so that the priority of fighting formations . . . can be varied to suit operational conditions as they develop.'[3]

It was during THUNDERCLAP that Montgomery first delivered his estimate that the Normandy campaign could be over in three months. At no time that day did Montgomery emphasize or refer to a holding operation around Caen or to a deliberate policy of drawing in Rommel's reserves. What he did refer to was the same thing he had stressed earlier, and what he would later on that

---

[1] The green line marked D+17–20 ran slightly north of Avranches on the Cotentin due east to a point halfway between Caen and Falaise, and north to Troarn and Cabourg. A second line marked 'D+20' ran from south of Avranches, east to Falaise where it joined the original line.

[2] Montgomery notes, loc.cit.

[3] Ibid.

spring continue to emphasize over and over again: the need for protecting Bradley from interference. As he demonstrated on the wall map, Caen itself was never intended to be a hinge but rather the heights of the Caen-Falaise Plain would be, and only then as the first of several hinges as the lodgement area was expanded.

Two weeks after THUNDERCLAP Dempsey issued his Second British Army Operational Order No. 1, which translated Montgomery's guidance into specific tasks for his army. After the assault the intention of the Second British Army was to secure and develop a bridgehead south of the line from Caumont to Caen and southeast of Caen in order to obtain airfield sites and to protect the flank of First US Army while Cherbourg and the Brittany ports were taken. Operations were to be carried out in four phases, with maximum offensive action by mobile armoured forces. Phase 1 was the D-Day assault; Phase 2 (D+3–4) would see 30 Corps capture Villers-Bocage in the western sector while 1 Corps maintained contact and pivoted on Caen. In Phase 3 (D+7–8), 1 Corps was to secure the high ground immediately east of Argences and northeast of Bretteville-sur-Laize for the purpose of permitting airfield construction. In the final phase (D+12–17) the Second British Army would pivot on Argences and advance south to secure the remainder of the area up to Falaise and link up with First US Army at Vire.[1]

The correlation between Montgomery's presentation on 7 April and Dempsey's published plan is evident, and includes the requirement for the capture of Caen on the first day. This was the fragile reed upon which the entire campaign in the eastern sector was to be built: all future actions envisioned that day and noted in later documents and orders were predicated upon the successful capture either of Caen itself or of the Orne-Odon crossings in the west.

By all accounts the reaction to Montgomery's presentation was decidedly positive. Brooke's diary recorded it as a 'wonderful day', and Air Chief Marshal Sir Arthur Tedder's opinion was included in an entry in his desk diary which read: 'Montgomery, Dempsey and [J. Lawton] Collins [US VII Corps Commander] seemed to have learnt clearly the Anzio lesson – failure to risk an

---

[1] Second Army Operational Order No. 1, 21 April 1944 in Account of Second Army Operations, Volume I, PRO (CAB 44/261).

aggressive action while the enemy still off his balance from surprise.'[1]

Sir Arthur Tedder was no friend of Montgomery. The two men had once been close during the Alam Halfa and Alamein battles in 1942, when the RAF had provided impressive support for the Eighth Army.[2] At the conclusion of Alamein, Tedder had written to Montgomery offering the full support of the air force in the pursuit of Rommel, which he urged be undertaken at full speed. Montgomery resented receiving advice from an airman about his tactics and from that time forth relations between them cooled perceptibly. In the period before D-Day, however, Montgomery and Tedder worked together in a spirit of cooperation and relative harmony, but after D-Day things soured badly between them, with Tedder becoming Montgomery's most vocal critic at SHAEF.[3]

Admiral Sir Andrew Cunningham was also impressed but injected a note of slight pessimism in his own diary entry: 'Perhaps to me the most remarkable thing was the lip service paid to certain lessons learned in Sicily and Italy. Monty talked of withdrawing the parachutists immediately they had attained their object, a thing practically never done in the Mediterranean. He further talked of amphibious and parachute operations to prevent the battle from becoming static.'[4] Certainly, Montgomery's approach to the forthcoming battles was similar to that before Alamein when he told the Eighth Army of his determination to 'hit Rommel for six'. It was his object to crush Rommel's ability to react with a series of armoured strokes before the German commander knew what had hit him.

Churchill attended only a portion of the afternoon session at the time Montgomery summed up OVERLORD. It was not one of Churchill's better days, as Brooke noted: ' . . . The PM turned up and addressed a few remarks to the meeting. He was in a very weepy condition, looking old and lacking a great deal of his usual

[1] Diary of Air Chief Marshal Tedder, 7 April 1944, maintained by his Personal Assistant, Wing Commander (now Lord) Scarman.
[2] Tedder was responsible for all British air operations in the Mediterranean as Air Commander-in-Chief. The Air Officer Commanding the Desert Air Force was Air Marshal Sir Arthur Coningham, a New Zealander.
[3] Interviews with Lord Scarman, 1980–1.
[4] Diary, Admiral of the Fleet Sir Andrew Cunningham, 7 April 1944, British Library.

vitality.'[1] Not having heard the Montgomery presentation that morning and still deeply troubled by the Allied failure at Anzio, Churchill apparently wanted reassurance from Montgomery that the offensive would be aggressive enough to prevent any German reaction which might jeopardize the Allied foothold in France. This was yet another example of the PM's deep-rooted fears over the outcome of the invasion. It was no coincidence that a week later Montgomery sent a strongly-worded letter to Bradley and Dempsey, spelling out the lengths to which he was prepared to go in order to achieve success. Montgomery's letter provides a graphic answer to his critics who have charged him with being too tidy and over cautious. That his later actions in Normandy smacked of caution as a result of his plan failing is one thing; that his aims for Normandy were nothing less than all-out offensive action is indisputable and best illustrated here:

Comd. First US Army	BIGOT
Comd. Second British Army	TOP SECRET

In operation Overlord an uncertain factor is the speed at which the enemy will be able to concentrate his mobile and armoured divisions against us for counter-attack.

On our part we must watch the situation carefully, and must not get our main bodies so stretched that they would be unable to hold against determined counter-attack; on the other hand, having seized the initiative by our initial landing, we must insure that we keep it.

The best way to interfere with the enemy concentrations and counter-measures will be to push forward fairly powerful armoured force thrusts on the afternoon of D-Day.

If two such forces, each consisting of an Armd Bde Group, were pushed forward on each Army front to carefully chosen areas, it would be very difficult for the enemy to interfere with our build-up; from the areas so occupied, patrols and recces would be pushed *further* afield, and this would tend to delay enemy movement towards the lodgement area.

The whole effect of such aggressive tactics would be to retain the *initiative* [author's italics] ourselves and to cause alarm in the minds of the enemy. To be successful, such tactics must be adopted on D-Day; to wait till D plus 1 would be to lose the opportunity, and also to lose the initiative.

Armoured units and Bdes must be concentrated quickly as soon as ever the situation allows after the initial landing on D-day; this may not be too easy, but plans to effect such

[1] Alanbrooke Diary, loc.cit.

concentrations must be made and every effort made to carry them out; speed and boldness are then required, and the armoured thrusts must force their way inland.

The result of such tactics will be the establishment of firm bases well in advance of our own main bodies; if their location is carefully thought out, the enemy will be unable to by-pass them. I am prepared to accept almost any risk in order to carry out these tactics. I would risk even the total loss of the armoured brigade groups – which in any event is not really possible; the delay they would cause to the enemy before they could be destroyed would be quite enough to give us time to get our main bodies well ashore and reorganised for strong offensive action. And as the main bodies move forward their task will be simplified by the fact that armoured forces are holding firm on important areas in front.

Army commanders will consider the problem in the light of the above remarks, and will inform me of their plans to carry out these tactics.

HQ, 21 Army Group   B. L. MONTGOMERY
14 Apr 44   General
                                    Commander-in-Chief[1]

A copy of this letter was sent to the Prime Minister who replied on 30 April:

> My Dear Montgomery:
> Thank you very much for your letter of April 17th. For what my opinion is worth, it seems to be exactly the spirit in which the execution should proceed and I only wish that a similar course had been attempted when the forces landed at Anzio.[2]

Of all the previous major offensive actions of the war to date, perhaps none had upset Churchill more than the Allied invasion of Anzio in January 1944. In a scenario similar to that of Salerno, the Allied bridgehead had come under severe counterattack and nearly cracked under strong German pressure, but was saved in the end by support from the Allied naval and air forces. The lesson of Anzio seemed to have been uppermost in Churchill's

[1] PRO (PREM 3–339/1). The same emphasis can be found in earlier notes to his army commanders on 20 March 1944, when he stated: 'As we secure airfields and good areas for making airfields so we get increased air support – so everything becomes easier. It is very important that the area to the Southeast of CAEN should be secured as early as 2d Army can manage.' Ibid.
[2] Ibid.

mind at the first OVERLORD briefing; he viewed the near-disaster and subsequent stalemate there as a particularly bad omen. Fortunately he and Montgomery were of like mind over the need for aggressiveness and initiative as the only reasonable means of preventing an effective German reaction. Never one to underestimate Rommel, Montgomery's willingness 'to accept almost any risk in order to carry out these tactics' was a vivid demonstration of his determination not to give Rommel an opportunity to concentrate his armour for a counterthrust.

If there were still suspicions about Montgomery's attitude after THUNDERCLAP, they were certainly removed at the great dress rehearsal for OVERLORD held at St Paul's on 15 May. It was an exceptionally cold spring day in London. General Ismay recalls that the room set aside for the briefing was so chilly the participants sat in their coats to keep out the damp cold. The cast of characters who participated throughout that day in the old school in Hammersmith may have been the most glittering assemblage of Allied military leaders and senior officers ever brought together in one place: King George VI, Field Marshal Smuts, Churchill, Eisenhower, Tedder, Montgomery, Ramsay, Leigh-Mallory, Brooke and the other British Chiefs of Staff; Bradley, Dempsey, Patton, Hodges, Simpson, Crerar, the British, Canadian and US corps and division commanders; the naval and air task force commanders; and a host of other senior officers from SHAEF and Whitehall.

Few post-war accounts contain much specific detail of what transpired that day. Various diaries and memoirs contain fragmentary references to St Paul's, but fortunately one of its participants did leave a full account: Air Chief Marshal Sir Trafford Leigh-Mallory, who dictated his impressions to his personal assistant shortly afterwards. Leigh-Mallory's observations provide fascinating insight into the final OVERLORD briefing, and are contained both in a diary he left and in the notes of the official AEAF historian.[1] The AEAF account records the setting:

[1] The contributions of the Allied Expeditionary Air Force historian cannot be over emphasized. He kept an accurate, detailed record of all meetings, correspondence and activities of the senior officers of the AEAF. Of all the major commands and organizations involved in Operation OVERLORD, none kept such a complete record of its activities. Its commander, Leigh-Mallory permitted the historian to attend all of the important air conferences and frequently provided his comments for inclusion into the material being collected.

If the occasion had not been a unique and solemn one in itself, there was nothing in the setting to make it so. There was a singular absence of ceremony, and the room where the meeting took place was a dark and uninspiring lecture room in the huge barrack-like school building which Montgomery had made his Headquarters. General Montgomery himself and several of his officers wore battledress. The Prime Minister arrived smoking a cigar which he did not lay down when the King arrived. There were no cheers, no applause. The PM was wearing a black short overcoat, looking something like a frockcoat. When the King arrived the company rose to their feet, and again when he got up to make a speech before his departure. Churchill bowed in his usual jerky fashion retaining the cigar in one hand. They rose again when the Prime Minister got up to speak near the close of the proceedings. Beyond that there was no ceremony. A row of armchairs was provided at the front for the most distinguished of the company, but the rest sat out the day – from 10 to 1.45 and from 2.45 to 5 – on hard wooden forms. The audience looked down from their crescent-shaped auditorium upon a vast coloured map, on a scale of about 6 inches to a mile, of the NEPTUNE area, that portion of the north coast of France between Cherbourg and the mouth of the Seine in which the Allied invasion is shortly to be launched. It was a curious experience to see so great and vital a secret, written so large and revealed to so large a company. With the help of this great map and with charts and maps hung upon the walls, the exposition of Overlord plans went forward.[1]

The briefing was scheduled to begin promptly at nine a.m. when Montgomery ordered the doors shut; thereafter no one was to be allowed to enter. Outside the door were stationed two American military policemen to enforce Montgomery's orders. Goronwy Rees, a member of Montgomery's staff, described them as really huge men 'with their white holsters and their white hats, looking absolutely terrifying'. As the conference was about to begin Rees remembers 'an enormous hammering at the door. Monty looked round angrily . . . and again there was an enormous hammering at the door. So finally, Monty said open the door, and the doors were flung open and in marched General Patton. Even Monty couldn't prevent his being late.'[2]

[1] AEAF Historical Record (AIR 37/1057) and Leigh-Mallory, 'Impressions of the Meeting held at St Paul's School on May 15, 1944', PRO (AIR 37/784). For continuity, the comments have been combined in places.
[2] Goronwy Rees, Thames Television Recorded Interview, 'The World at War, 1939–1945', IWM.

When everyone was seated Eisenhower rose and addressed the group. His short speech, observed Leigh-Mallory, was moving in its simplicity:

> Here we are, he said in effect, on the eve of a great battle, to deliver to you the various plans made by the different Force Commanders. I would emphasise but one thing, that I consider it to be the duty of anyone who sees a flaw in the plan not to hesitate to say so. I have no sympathy with anyone, whatever his station, who will not brook criticism. We are here to get the best possible results and you must make a really co-operative effort.[1]

Eisenhower was followed by the three commanders-in-chief who each briefed their portion of Overlord, beginning with Montgomery:

> Monty was wearing a very well cut battle-dress with a knife-like edge to the trouser creases. He looked trim and business-like. He spoke in a tone of quiet emphasis making use of what is evidently a verbal trick of his, to repeat the most important word or phrase in a sentence more than once. He was occasionally interrupted by the Prime Minister, who asked questions which seemed designed to show his knowledge of strategy and tactics. Monty's most striking observation was to the effect that the plan required a very robust mentality on the part of all called upon to execute it. At one point the PM intervened, saying a trifle wryly that at Anzio we had put ashore 160,000 men and 25,000 vehicles and had advanced only twelve miles. He thought, therefore, that to take a risk occasionally would certainly do no harm. Montgomery's demeanour was very quiet and deliberate. He was not at all showy and seemed cautious, for he made no attempt to minimise the difficulties of the task. One thing he made clear, and that was his opinion that he had the measure of Rommel. He could be described as confident but certainly not complacent.[2]

As he had done at THUNDERCLAP, Montgomery again made a positive impact on his audience. General Ismay remembers that: 'Montgomery was quite first-class. His general line was: "We have a sufficiency of troops; we have all the necessary tackle; we have an excellent plan. This is a perfectly normal operation which is certain of success. If anyone has any doubts in his mind, let him stay behind." I think he must have been reading Henry V before Agincourt:

---

[1] Leigh-Mallory, PRO (AIR 37/784), loc.cit.
[2] Leigh-Mallory, loc.cit.

He that hath no stomach for this fight,
Let him depart.'[1]

Turning first to Rommel, Montgomery said the Allies could expect him to react to the menace of OVERLORD by D+2, when as many as thirteen enemy divisions might be on the move toward the NEPTUNE area, of which five were likely to be panzer. By D+5–6 a full-blooded counter-attack was likely; and by D+8 there could be a total of twenty-four divisions in Normandy opposing the invasion force. Montgomery left his audience in no doubt about what Rommel would attempt:

> Rommel is an energetic and determined commander; he has made a world of difference since he took over. He is best at the spoiling attack; his forte is disruption; he is too impulsive for the set-piece battle. He will do his level best to 'Dunkirk' us – not to fight the armoured battle on ground of his own choosing but to avoid it altogether by preventing our tanks landing by using his own tanks well forward. On D-Day he will try to force us from the beaches and secure Caen, Bayeux and Carentan. His *obsession* is likely to be Bayeux. This important nodal point splits our frontal landings in half. Thereafter he will continue his counter-attacks. But as time goes on, he will combine them with a roping-off policy, and must then hold firm on the important ground which dominates and controls the road axes in the 'bocage' country which are: the high ground east of the River Dives, the high ground between Falaise and St Lô between the rivers Orne and Vire, and the high ground west of the River Vire.[2]

In his clipped and direct manner, Montgomery went on to define the problem facing his invasion force:

> The enemy is in position with reserves available. There are obstacles and minefields on the beaches; we cannot gain contact with the obstacles and recce them. There are many unknown hazards, and after a sea voyage and a landing on a strange coast, there is always some loss of cohesion. We must time our assault so as to make things as easy as possible for the landing troops. Therefore we shall touch down so that all obstacles are dry, and so that we have 30 minutes in which to deal with them before the incoming tide reaches them.[3]

---

[1] Ismay Papers, loc.cit.
[2] Address given by General Montgomery to the General Officers of the Four Field Armies on 15 May 1944, Eisenhower Presidential Papers, Eisenhower Library.
[3] Ibid.

His prescription for success was that:

> *WE* have the initiative. We must rely on:
> (a) the violence of our assault.
> (b) our great weight of supporting fire from the sea and the air.
> (c) simplicity.
> (d) robust mentality.
> We must blast our way ashore and get a good lodgement before
> the enemy can bring sufficient reserves up to turn us out.
> Armoured columns must penetrate deep inland, and quickly on
> D-Day; this will upset the plans and tend to hold him off while
> we build up strength. We must gain space rapidly, and peg out
> claims well inland. And while we are engaged in doing this the
> air must hold the ring, and must hinder and make very difficult
> the movement of enemy reserves by train or road. The land
> battle will be a terrific party and we will require the full support
> of the air all the time, and laid on quickly. Once we can
> get control of the main enemy lateral GRANVILLE-VIRE-
> ARGENTAN-FALAISE-CAEN, and the area enclosed in it is firmly
> in our possession, then we will have the lodgement area we
> want and then can begin to expand.[1]

The development of operations up to D+90 was also the same
exposition given on 7 April. Montgomery closed his speech on a
high note, indicating his belief that the success of OVERLORD lay
in the leadership of those present:

> We shall have to send the soldiers in to this party 'seeing red'.
> We must get them completely on their toes; having absolute
> faith in the plan; and embued with infectious optimism and
> offensive eagerness. Nothing must stop them. If we send them
> into battle in this way – then we shall succeed.[2]

At the conclusion of the morning session King George made a
short speech which Leigh-Mallory described as 'conventional', in
which he said that with God's help this great operation could be
brought to a successful conclusion.[3] The afternoon was taken
up by briefings from the various task force commanders. It was
generally a sombre occasion, broken only by Major General
Elwood Quesada, Commander of the US IX Tactical Air Com-

---

[1]   Montgomery address, 15 May 1944. The lodgement area referred to by Montgomery was approximately that shown on the D+17 line in the map on p.91.
[2]   Ibid.
[3]   Leigh-Mallory, loc.cit.

mand who 'raised the only laugh of the day, when after outlining the methods he proposed to use, added dryly: "We will move like that throughout our progress over the continent of Europe."'[1]

The day's events were wound up by short speeches from Field Marshal Smuts, Churchill and Eisenhower. The South African leader was in a gloomy mood and depressed by the size of the task ahead. 'Smuts seemed almost oppressed with the difficulties and hazards of the operation as well as profoundly conscious of how very much depended on Overlord's success or failure.'[2]*

When Churchill's turn came he rose and, gripping his lapels firmly in his hands, addressed the group: 'I am hardening on this enterprise. I repeat, I am *now* hardening toward this enterprise.'[3] Churchill's turn of phrase unhappily conveyed a misleading impression to many of those present that he had previously been against OVERLORD. Eisenhower was wholly misled by the Prime Minister's meaning which was, in General Ismay's words, an expression 'you had often used to me and I had taken it to mean that the more you thought about it the more certain you were of success'.[4]

Churchill's phraseology seems to have been a purely British expression meant to convey exactly what Ismay has said. Failing to understand this, the Supreme Commander took it as a signal that Churchill hadn't previously believed in OVERLORD, that he was now only coming to 'believe with the rest of us that this was the true course of action in order to achieve the victory.'[5] Privately, Eisenhower was dismayed by what Churchill had intended as a fighting speech. 'I then realized for the first time that Mr Churchill hadn't believed in it all along and had had no faith that it would succeed. It was quite a shocking discovery. Sir Alan Brooke had been extremely pessimistic at all times about our prospect of fighting through the bocage country and I believe the PM reflected Sir Alan's tactical views.'[6]

[1] AEAF narrative, loc.cit.
[2] Leigh-Mallory, loc.cit.
* During the luncheon break, Smuts sat next to Admiral Ramsay and confessed that one of the reasons he was remaining in England to see OVERLORD through was his influence over Churchill who, he said, 'was apt to go wild now and then'. Diary of Admiral Sir Bertram Ramsay.
[3] Eisenhower interview, loc.cit.
[4] Ismay Papers, loc.cit.
[5] Eisenhower, *Crusade in Europe*, London, 1948, p. 269.
[6] Eisenhower interview, loc.cit.

Although this incident was in itself relatively minor it did, unfortunately, reflect the sort of misunderstandings that occurred during the planning and execution of OVERLORD even between Churchill and Eisenhower, who both went to great lengths to ensure each understood the other's views. Churchill's speech ended on a note of pure clairvoyance: 'Let us not expect all to go according to plan,' he told the commanders. 'Flexibility of mind will be one of the decisive factors.' Still unmistakably concerned over Anzio's near-disaster, he warned, 'We must not have another Anzio . . . where we advanced twelve miles. Risks must be taken. Rommel cannot afford to concentrate *all* his forces against OVERLORD. How does he know we will not launch another OVERLORD somewhere else? He must keep a strategical reserve.'[1]*

Eisenhower closed the meeting at 4.30 when he told the group: 'In half an hour Hitler will have missed his one and only chance of destroying with a single well-aimed bomb the entire high command of the Allied forces.'[2] On the subject of misunderstanding between Eisenhower and Churchill, it may be as well to refer to the Supreme Commander's memoirs of his relations with the PM:

> In spite of his own spirit of combativeness, it was only slowly that he could develop any genuine enthusiasm for OVERLORD. Time and time again he would express his forebodings, not in an argumentative tone but quietly as an inescapable doubt that we were wise in carrying the ground battle to Nazi Europe. At times he spoke of visions of beaches choked with the bodies of the flower of British and American youth and of the tides running red with their blood. When he was in this mood none of us tried to reply directly; General Smith and others present would merely turn the conversation to our great air strength, our naval power and other favourable factors. We would talk about the great frontage on which we would attack, the mass of special equipment, including swimming tanks and rocket ships that would surprise the enemy. Always at some point in such a conversation he would break in with an enthusiastic word of

---

[1] AEAF narrative, loc.cit.

* Churchill never ceased to be rankled by the subject of Anzio, of which he has said: 'I thought we were going to land a tiger cat and all we've got is a stranded whale.' Quoted by Sir John Colville, interview of 3 November 1982.

[2] AEAF narrative, loc.cit.

approval of our plans, proving that he was not pessimistic by nature.[1]

Churchill was not an easy convert to the idea of OVERLORD's success, but less than a month before D-Day the Prime Minister had lunched privately with Eisenhower and, with tears in his eyes, had told the Supreme Commander, 'I am in this thing with you to the end, and it if fails we will go down together.'[2] As Eisenhower later pointed out:

> Many weeks were to pass, however, before he expressed sustained confidence in the venture. One remark he frequently repeated was that if we could be sure of safe landings at most of the five beaches to be attacked, and the Allies could soon move their 30-odd available divisions to Normandy, securing the Cotentin Peninsula and a sizeable portion of the Normandy coast, he would at that point publicly say that OVERLORD had been a well-conceived and worthwhile operation. Then after outlining several hypothetical stages of progress, each of which he would speak about with increasing enthusiasm, he would add, 'And, my dear General, if by the time the snow flies you can have restored her liberty to our beautiful Paris, I shall proclaim to the world that this has been the best conceived and most remarkably successful military operation of all history.' This subject would sometimes come up in a conversation between the two of us, but just as often with others present, both American and British. My reply was always the same: 'Mr Prime Minister, I assure you that we are going to be on the borders of Germany by Christmas and if Hitler has any sense whatsoever he will see the hopelessness of his situation and surrender.'
>
> 'Ah,' he would say, 'it is well for Generals to be optimistic, otherwise they would never win a battle. But what I have just

---

[1] Dwight D. Eisenhower, unpublished manuscript, furnished courtesy of John S. D. Eisenhower. This manuscript was begun in 1967 as an informal memoir of Eisenhower's wartime relationships with Churchill and Marshall but, as John Eisenhower points out in the preface to his recent book, *Allies*, it was never completed. Eisenhower's comments are substantiated by Major General Ray W. Barker, a senior US planner on the COSSAC staff, who recalled one occasion in 1943 at Norfolk House in London when the Prime Minister was briefed on the OVERLORD plan: 'He shook his head and he said: "I wake up at night and see the Channel floating with bodies of the cream of our youth." He was worried about the losses; he thought there might have been a cheaper way of doing it and he kept proposing operations in the Mediterranean – the underbelly. But after Quebec he was into it heart and soul and so was Brooke. Occasionally there might be differences of opinion over the details but basically they were all for it and they threw themselves into it just as we did.' Major General Ray W. Barker, oral history, 16 July 1972, Eisenhower Library.

[2] Quoted in Harry C. Butcher, *Three Years With Eisenhower*, op.cit., p. 458.

said stands.' One day he gave me a hint of a possible cause for these statements, saying, 'I'd not want history to record that I agreed to this without voicing my doubts.'[1*]

While it is true there were occasions such as those described by Eisenhower when Churchill became pessimistic over the consequences if the invasion failed on the beaches, and while it was known that Churchill was keen to attack Germany through the Balkans his Assistant Private Secretary, Sir John Colville, insists it was totally untrue that the British were against OVERLORD. According to Colville, from December 1943, when the command appointments were announced, both Churchill and the military chiefs were totally behind the concept. The Prime Minister was, says Colville, enormously enthusiastic. Later, Churchill was very proud of being able to land as many British and Canadian soldiers in Normandy as the United States before the time came when American forces considerably outnumbered them.[2]

The 15 May presentation is important to the story of Normandy not only for its clear exposition of Montgomery's plans but for the controversy it generated when later misunderstandings erupted over the British commander's handling of the post-D-Day campaign. Most of the presentation and controversy focused on the use of phase lines, a device used by military planners to forecast events and ensure continuity of planning. Perhaps no other single issue of the entire campaign generated more misunderstanding than the phase lines created by 21st Army Group for the invasion briefings and perhaps it might be helpful to interrupt the campaign narrative here in order to follow this debate.

On 7 April the coloured phase lines depicted the three phases of the Normandy campaign as then envisioned. During the May briefing the same coloured lines were placed on to the huge relief map of Normandy spread across the school room floor. As

---

[1] Eisenhower, unpublished manuscript, loc.cit.

[*] Sir John Colville, in an interview of 3 November 1982, pointed out that Churchill sometimes tended to speak for effect like an actor, in this case on the great stage of history. In other instances he tended to think aloud when talking to others, often merely stating things which were not necessarily his considered view. Whatever his public views there appears to be substance to his fears that things could still go horribly wrong. OVERLORD was, after all, a one-shot operation – should it fail there would in all likelihood never be a second opportunity to attempt invasion.

[2] Colville interview, 3 November 1982.

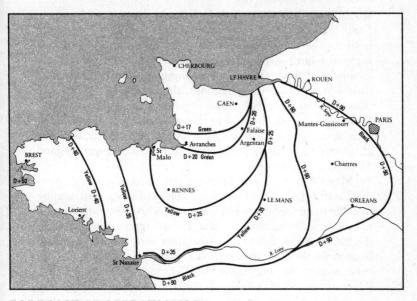

FORECAST OF OPERATIONS D + 17 to D + 90

British historian Ronald Lewin has pointed out: 'The danger of such maps is that they are essentially professional tools which, if misused, can do damage. They have two sound purposes. Every commander planning an operation must have a rough idea, at the least, of where – taking into account all possible mischances – he may get to as his attack progresses. Phase maps are thus useful for such a commander (with all the possible mischances in his mind) as a diagrammatic representation of his hopes... A phase line map in fact represents a rational estimation of a possibility, rather than a commital of a cast-iron guarantee.'[1]

Lewin is, of course, absolutely correct in his assertion that these particular phase lines were nothing more than tools used by Montgomery to illustrate how and by what estimated dates he

[1] Ronald Lewin, *Montgomery as Military Commander*, London, 1971, p. 183. The use of phase lines can be traced to COSSAC, who carried out a number of paper war games in an attempt to determine where the Germans would move their divisions during the period D-Day to D+40. According to Brigadier McLean: 'This led to phase-lines. G-2 and G-3 had maps with pins and they would move their troops back and forth.' McLean interview, loc.cit.

would carry out the post-D-Day campaign against Rommel. Some critics of Montgomery did indeed condemn his failure to hold to the dates suggested by these phase lines when the campaign later went awry. It is also true that some officers misinterpreted Montgomery's meaning and attempted to base their criticisms on these grounds alone, without taking into consideration the other, more important aspects of his plan. However, as later chapters in this narrative will demonstrate, some senior officers, including Eisenhower and Tedder, were not at all misled by these phase lines and did not misunderstand Montgomery's intentions.

Major General David Belchem, one of Montgomery's principal staff officers, has thoroughly confused anyone attempting to understand the facts behind their use. A brilliant staff officer, a master linguist and, after the war, the youngest major general in the British Army, Belchem's association with Montgomery had begun with the planning for HUSKY in the spring of 1943. At the conclusion of the campaign in Sicily Belchem was appointed BGS (Operations and Plans), Eighth Army; and when Montgomery assumed command of 21st Army Group he was summoned to London to become BGS (Operations), a position he held throughout the campaigns in Northwest Europe. After the war Belchem chose firmly to link himself and his reputation to Montgomery when he drafted the Field Marshal's two campaign accounts.[1] General Belchem, in his misguided attempts to enhance his chief's reputation became instead his apologist and rather than bolstering Montgomery's reputation he cast grave doubts upon the veracity of his and Montgomery's motives by denying responsibility for the use of phase lines. His own 1978 memoirs, *All in the Day's March*, provide the best example. While claiming that publication of the phase line map used during the OVERLORD briefings was a mistake both in 1944 and in Montgomery's 1947 *Normandy to the Baltic*, he goes on to disclaim any British responsibility whatsoever either for the map itself or for the phase lines. Responsibility, he alleges, was entirely American:

[1] Montgomery, *Normandy to the Baltic* (1947) and *El Alamein to the River Sangro* (1948). Both unofficial accounts were prepared by Brigadier Belchem under Montgomery's supervision and were originally written for the benefit of former members of 21st Army Group. Their popularity soon led to their publication for the general public.

The fact is that the phase-line map was not drawn by Montgomery's planning section, of which I was in charge. It was produced as a cock-shy by our American colleagues, because their staff planning procedures demanded such forecasts when deliberate offensive plans were recorded. All I personally ever said in this context was that Montgomery had told me that he hoped we should reach the line of the River Seine by D+90, but that this was not a definite forecast nor were we to take it as anything more than a general guide. However Colonel Muggeridge, my American deputy, asked me one day about the provision of a phase-line map, since presumably his General had requested one. I told him that we had no intention of making such a forecast, in view of the endless imponderable factors, and added that it was sufficient to tell his superiors that the assumption could be made that it was hoped to reach the Seine by D+90. Not to be outdone, Muggeridge subsequently brought me a map (the one unhappily included in *Normandy to the Baltic*), and asked me if it would be acceptable, because the Americans had to have something to put into their Planning Reports. (I still have no idea who drew it.) I replied that it was worthless, but if his General was so insistent, I would show it to Montgomery. The following day, a Sunday I recall, I was asked by Monty to join him in the flat he occupied opposite St Paul's School for tea: it was a favourite time for him to have a quiet chat with members of his entourage about the progress we were making, and the problems which were concerning us. I showed him on this occasion the map which Muggeridge had given me, and asked him what to do about it. He looked at the map, and then gave it back to me saying that it was utter nonsense and that he wanted nothing to do with it. He did add that if the Americans wanted to waste their time with such hypothetical scribbling, I was to tell them to get on with it, but to insure at the same time that they understood that he, the Operational Commander, did not wish to be associated with it. I duly put this over to Muggeridge.[1]

In *Victory in Normandy*, published shortly before his death in 1981, General Belchem sought to modify his earlier account by stating that it was not Bradley who had originally demanded the phase line map (the US Army planners attached to General Montgomery's staff all worked for Bradley), but the air force planners on the staff of Bradley's First US Army.[2]

[1]   Major General David Belchem, *All in the Day's March*, London, 1978, p. 191.
[2]   Major General David Belchem, *Victory in Normandy*, London, 1981, p. 54.

Bradley, like Montgomery, had no time for speculative fore-casts, particularly in an operation as complex as the invasion of Normandy, and consequently Montgomery's retention of the forecast maps – borne out of his overriding concern that the air force planners should not block acceptance of the invasion plan – led almost inevitably to a serious misunderstanding between Bradley and Montgomery.[1]

Victory in Normandy contains two maps representing what, Belchem alleges, are *two* separate versions of Montgomery's master plan. The first, prepared in April, reflects a pivot by the Second Army on Caen, and the second, supposedly prepared in May, shows the pivot as Argentan, thirty miles to the south. Montgomery was, states Belchem, on the horns of a dilemma:

> On the one hand, the first elements of an attractive plan pointed to an overall operation in the Normandy Lodgement area, which would pivot on Caen; on the other hand, there remained the problem of the air forces' requirements in the region of Falaise – Argentan, south and southeast of Caen. There were three Panzer Divisions in Normandy plus one astride the Seine, and if the Germans were to react as Montgomery envisaged, the question was whether the build-up of Allied forces in the British sector would be fast enough to concentrate for a thrust of some thirty-seven miles to Argentan – or even to Falaise, lying about twenty miles inland.[2]

Belchem's explanation is that Montgomery's plan for a deep thrust was too risky and, if successful, would leave both British flanks exposed and vulnerable *unless* the First US Army could match the speed of the British advance and thus protect its right flank from German interference which, in turn, would have the effect of compromising the rapid seizure of Brittany. Belchem felt that protection of the left flank of the thrust would require strong forces which would have to be diverted from the main force and inevitably weaken it.[3]

In weighing the problem, Belchem writes, Montgomery be-came convinced that the need for ports was greater than the need for airfields, and that in order to gain acceptance from the air forces he 'told me that he felt obliged to make to his colleagues a representation of his master plan which would be acceptable

[1] *Victory in Normandy*, op.cit., p. 54.
[2] Ibid, pp. 51–2.
[3] Ibid.

to the air forces without sacrificing his basic conception of the strategy to be adopted. He therefore had a second map prepared which indicated that the Second British Army would pivot on Argentan, and advance thence to the west of Paris with the US armies making a much wider swing up to the east of the city.'[1]

A major omission is his failure to point out that no matter *what* course of action Montgomery pursued there would be considerable risks, as we have seen. A slow, safe advance would provide better protection of the British flank but would also provide Rommel with too much time to react, to reinforce his defence of the Caen sector and even initiate a series of counter-attacks. Conversely, the risks inherent in a deep thrust were outweighed by the surprise and initiative this offered the invasion force. Moreover, the ultimate safety of the Allied left flank lay in the capture of this critical terrain and Montgomery never wavered in his choice of the deep thrust as the best course – there would be, at best, only a fleeting opportunity before the Germans reacted. The force which could *first* gain control of the Caen-Falaise lateral was the one most likely to hold it, a supposition later borne out by events. Montgomery's advantage lay in the Allied air forces, which had control of the skies over Normandy and would be a powerful factor in thwarting German counter-measures. As will be seen, Dempsey's recently released papers in the Public Record Office fully substantiate the concept of a quick, deep thrust by British and Canadian armour.

Belchem makes this curious statement about the presentation of Montgomery's master plan:

> One further point which must be emphasized is that the version of the battle which Montgomery had in his mind all along was that outlined in his original presentation of April 1944 and not that presented in London on 7 May, 1944 (sic).[2] He knew full well that the German Seventh Army would at all costs deny the Caen area to the invaders and that, if this supposition were to be borne out by events, the enemy would be unable to redeploy quickly enough to hold back the American forces breaking out from the western flank.[3]

Both of General Belchem's versions are suspect on examination of the evidence. If, for example, the 7 April presentation of plans

[1] *Victory in Normandy*, op.cit, p. 52.
[2] The second OVERLORD presentation was on 15 May 1944.
[3] *Victory in Normandy*, op.cit., p. 55.

is the 'correct' version we ought to believe, then Montgomery's detailed notes clearly refute Belchem's allegation that he intended only to pivot on Caen. Even though Montgomery undoubtedly recognized that he might not be able to adhere to the dates reflected by the various phase lines used, he did intend to expand the British front to the D+20 line which ran between Falaise and Argentan. This is the sector for which Montgomery told his subordinate commanders that 'we will fight continuously till we get it'.[1]

> Second British Army will push its left out towards the general line of the River Touques. *At the same time the Army will pivot on Falaise and will swing with its right towards Argentan – Alençon.* (Author's italics.)[2]

So much for the Caen pivot! Caen was unsafe as a pivot: without the Allies in possession of the Caen-Falaise Plain, their left flank remained exceptionally vulnerable both to German counter-attack and to troop movements to the west in the direction of the US flank. An examination of Montgomery's notes and maps used for the two briefings does not reveal any indication that there were two separate versions given. Moreover, it must be remembered that both briefings were given to the same commanders – two such widely different versions would surely have provoked comment and quite likely a questioning of exactly what Montgomery's proposed strategy was.

There are numerous other factors which destroy the credibility of General Belchem's two accounts. There is no record of any Colonel Muggeridge in the First US Army[3], nor was the use of phase lines ever a part of US Army doctrine during the Second World War. The American staff officers integrated into 21st Army Group for OVERLORD planning all answered to Bradley, who did not favour the use of phase lines. Belchem's statement that 'The record can now be set straight: phase-lines never at any time had any place in Montgomery's plan'[4] is refuted both by the evidence and by General J. Lawton Collins, who was present at

---

[1] Montgomery notes, 7 April 1944, loc.cit.
[2] Ibid.
[3] The officer was Colonel Gilman C. Mudgett, a Regular Army officer and 1922 graduate of West Point who was assigned to Bradley's G-3 section. Mudgett was an Armor officer who held the title of G (Ops) (US) 21st Army Group.
[4] *Victory in Normandy*, op.cit., p. 54.

the 15 May briefing and who has recounted how he witnessed an angry encounter between Bradley and Montgomery before the briefing began:

> While waiting for the audience to assemble, I witnessed a first sign, but not the last, of Bradley's irritation with Montgomery. Brad had told me that in earlier discussions of OVERLORD with Montgomery, he had refused to agree to setting any phase lines for expansion of the initial bridgehead that should be reached by certain days. He thought that Montgomery had accepted his objection, at least for the American sector. When we arrived at St Paul's School we discovered that Monty's map showed such lines. Brad insisted that the times shown, by which the phase lines were to be secured by the Americans, be removed. Monty, somewhat petulantly, finally agreed.[1]

Bradley's recently published posthumous autobiography confirms General Collins' version of events. According to Bradley, the phase line idea originally emanated from 21st Army Group and when he found out about them he objected personally to Montgomery on grounds that they made the plan too rigid and might discourage exploitation. Until the morning of 15 May Bradley thought he had persuaded Montgomery to abandon their use. He was therefore quite dismayed to find the terrain model at St Paul's School covered with phase lines: 'I was quite put out with Monty. He had unilaterally reneged on an important agreement. I did not realize it then, but Joe Collins overheard our testy discussion. . . Monty left the phase lines in the British sector.'[2]

The fact is that phase lines were produced by Montgomery's staff not only on the maps and the terrain model of Normandy, but in a series of separate maps showing each proposed phase of the operations in Normandy. These are the same maps, of which one was a summary of all phase lines, that later appeared in Montgomery's *Normandy to the Baltic*. It is not known how many copies were made but the personal papers of Mont-

[1] General J. Lawton Collins, *Lightning Joe*, Baton Rouge, 1979, p. 192. In an interview with the author in March 1980, General Collins confirmed how upset Bradley had become when he arrived at St Paul's to find phase lines laid out in tape on the Normandy terrain model. He at once raised the point with Montgomery who was loath to remove them from the American sector but was finally forced to do so at Bradley's insistence.

[2] Omar N. Bradley and Clay Blair, *A General's Life*, New York, 1983, p. 233.

gomery's late Chief of Staff, de Guingand, contain a complete set.[1]*

The idea that Montgomery would use these phase lines during the two OVERLORD briefings of his battle plan and include a copy of the same map in his post-war account, if he considered them 'hypothetical scribbling' and wanted nothing to do with them, is utterly ludicrous. It is also beyond comprehension that Montgomery would have altered his entire plan merely to accommodate the air forces or an alleged American request – particularly for a concept which Belchem claims he did not support.

The truth is that the phase lines were merely one of several methods used by Montgomery and his staff to plan strategy for Normandy. As General Belchem has correctly stated, Montgomery's master plan was 'a framework *within which* both he and his senior subordinates would conduct their detailed operations'.[2]† Montgomery's plan remained consistent from its earliest conception to its final form in May, and there is no documented validity to Belchem's claim that Montgomery changed his plan between the April and May briefings to satisfy the Allied air chiefs.

The real significance of Montgomery's use of phase lines was not the forecast of timing (which, of course, he would have been only too delighted to achieve) but their revelation of the strategy he intended to pursue in Normandy. They disclose in clear detail the *modus operandi* of that strategy. The dates cited were, in all probability, as suggested by several members of his staff to the author, also for the benefit of the logistical planners so that they would have a basis for planning the complex logistical side of the operation. What has been overlooked in all the hullabaloo over phase lines is the more important picture they present of the *means* by which Montgomery intended to execute his master

---

[1] De Guingand Papers, King's College, London.

* An examination of these maps reveal they were made in multiple copies by professional graphics experts.

[2] *Victory in Normandy*, op.cit., p. 53

† It should also be noted that General Belchem's earlier memoirs contains other errors which are cause for questioning their credibility. For example, he claims that UTAH beach was so named because General Collins 'asked me to name it after his home state in the US'. (*All in the Day's March*, p. 187), and that OMAHA beach was named after the home city of General Gerow, the US V Corps commander. As General Collins confirmed to the author, he is a native of the state of Louisiana; General Gerow was a native Virginian.

plan. The validity of the dates is arguable; the technique of accomplishing them is not.

Nor was demonstration of Montgomery's intentions confined merely to the OVERLORD presentations. For some weeks prior to the May briefing, his planning staff were hard at work on his basic strategy, which was published on 8 May by his Plans Officer, Brigadier Charles Richardson, under the title: 'Overlord – Appreciation on Possible Development of Operations to Secure Lodgment Area'.[1] External distribution of this was limited to Bradley and Dempsey and so far as is known no copy was ever sent to Eisenhower or to SHAEF.[2] In his covering letter, Brigadier Richardson included this comment: 'With regard to the outline of Action at Part IV, this represents the Commander-in-Chief's intentions as far as they can be formulated at this stage. Whether operations will develop on these lines must of course depend on our own and the enemy situation which cannot be predicted accurately at the present moment.'[3]

Richardson's seventeen-page document consisted of four parts. Parts I and II dealt with the OVERLORD mission and a terrain analysis. Part III discussed development of operations, beginning with an analysis of enemy resistance, which was expected to be in the form of efforts to defeat the Allies on the beaches and immediately inland followed by an effort to prevent the capture of Cherbourg and establishment of a safe bridgehead. If these efforts failed there would follow an effort to prevent a breakout from the bridgehead line and, failing this, attempts to stop the Allies from reaching any other large ports. Part IV was a summary of conclusions which, said Richardson, represented Montgomery's intentions as of that moment.[4]

Appended to the study was a large coloured map of Normandy upon which were superimposed a series of red arrows reflecting four possible courses of action, and one phase line marked D+14. According to the document 'The term bridgehead

[1] PRO (WO 205/118).
[2] Neither the Eisenhower Papers nor the SHAEF records in the National Archives appears to contain a copy of this document. Certainly General Belchem, the Operations Officer, knew of the document and its contents inasmuch as he was included in the internal distribution. Richardson's copy contains a handwritten comment: 'Seen by BGS (Ops).' WO 205/118.
[3] WO 205/118.
[4] Ibid.

is defined as the areas included within the present estimated Phase Line for D+14.' The D+14 line ran for approximately a hundred miles from Lessay on the west coast of the Cotentin, generally southeast to Thury-Harcourt, west to a point above Falaise (on the Caen-Falaise highway), then northeast of Argences on the edge of the Caen-Falaise Plain, to Cabourg on the Bay of the Seine.

Montgomery's planners were acutely aware of the German ability to resist the Allied advance around the D+14 line and estimated that as many as twenty-eight enemy divisions might be in action: at least twenty would be required to hold this hundred-mile front. They reasoned that both the terrain and the size and mobility of the German reserves could make further advance extremely difficult, resulting in a lengthy pause on the D+14 line. There might even be, the planners warned, local setbacks. Should these occur, the solution lay in a rapid buildup of combat strength to the point where the enemy could no longer contain intense pressure; then the Allies could slowly expand the bridgehead along its whole perimeter. The emphasis must be on never losing the initiative. 'The danger of even a temporary loss of initiative on our part is obvious, particularly if it comes after a natural reaction may have set in in the troops who have been hard-pushed for fourteen days. It is stressed again that if the enemy buildup approaches the optimum appreciation by Intelligence it may well be D+30 or even later before we can break out from the enemy's efforts to contain us.'[1]

The document spelled out a flexible plan for breaking out of the bridgehead which was designed to take advantage of enemy dispositions and weakness. Once Allied forces had gained room for manoeuvre it would become difficult for Rommel to contain them, and he would probably revert to a more elastic and mobile type of defence using strong reserves and counterattacks against successful penetrations of his line.[2]

Like the briefings, the study anticipated that the main weight of advance would come from Bradley's powerful forces who would move south astride roads from Vire to the east of Avranches in the west, with the mission of cutting off the Brittany

[1] WO 205/118, loc.cit.
[2] Ibid.

Peninsula. If German strategy was to deny access to the major ports then there was an opportunity to take advantage by striking a series of blows from each flank:

> If he accepts this strategy he must put a powerful portion of his forces to resist our move towards the Loire and Brittany. This means a consequent reduction of the operational divisions he can use to defend the Seine ... because the Seine ports are closer to the bridgehead and more convenient for buildup from England the enemy will no doubt appreciate initially that we will make for them as a first mission. Therefore until the thrust towards the Loire has become clearly evident the enemy may keep a greater proportion of his forces to defend the Seine. Once the Loire threat develops he may well redispose his forces to achieve a more equitable balance. If successful strong thrusts are kept up alternatively by us toward the Seine and Loire on a coordinated plan, we have our best chance of one or the other succeeding.[1]

Of the red-arrowed proposals for advance two were possibilities for an attack on the Seine ports. One involved a three-pronged attack due east against the Seine estuary from Le Havre to Rouen, the second a swing much farther southeast between Falaise and Argentan, then northeast to Rouen. In their analysis of these two courses the 21st Army Group staff observed that a third, combining them, appeared most likely to succeed. 'The terrain to be crossed to reach the Seine does not favour the defenders. . . The River Seine can be crossed in the face of enemy resistance more easily than can the Loire. A strong thrust towards the Seine even if it cannot reach the river, will contain enemy forces and thus aid the advance towards the Loire.'[2] One other option was considered in the form of a thrust southeast in the direction of Le Mans, which might serve as a useful diversionary operation to draw enemy forces away from the Loire and Seine ports.

The idea behind Montgomery's plan of campaign had all along been to seize the initiative and thus keep Rommel unbalanced, always dancing to a series of coordinated Allied offensives, a strategy this document outlines:

> If the enemy's will to resist does not deteriorate and he does all in his power to prevent our capturing any other major ports

[1] WO 205/118, loc.cit.
[2] Ibid.

outside the initial bridgehead, we may have great difficulty in building up our forces to the ultimate size required to defeat the German Armies in the field. The thirty divisions we can maintain through our bridgehead can be sufficient to capture additional ports only if we force the enemy to disperse his formations against us. This can best be done by making co-ordinated thrusts towards both the Loire and the Seine, so timed as to make the enemy keep moving his reserves first against one then the other. . . The major operational disadvantages of the two simultaneous thrusts is that the available air support might have to be split. By careful coordination, however, it should be possible to keep both offensives moving from bound to bound, switching the major part of the air support alternatively from one to the other. If both of these offensives are mounted, our future plans should be sufficiently flexible to permit the full and rapid exploitation of which ever one shows greatest possibilities of success even if this means considerable change in the contemplated buildup and use of US and British armies, and the development and use of ports. We have the advantage of interior lines for our operations but this advantage cannot be fully exploited unless our strength can be moved freely from one point to another in accordance with the situation as it develops.[1]

While recognizing the administrative disadvantages of switching units and reserves to mount alternative offensives against the most promising direction, the advantages were considered too great to be ignored. The timing for such thrusts was seen as:

(a) A gradual advance from the bridgehead to the line beyond which the enemy cannot hope to hold a coordinated thrust by us. This may take up to D+30. (Indicated on Map as the 'Limit of Enemy Ability to Contain Allied Forces'.)

(b) Strong offensive action by us towards Rennes. At this time the enemy may have the bulk of his forces ready to oppose action towards the Seine. If we succeed in pushing rapidly towards Rennes and begin to threaten the Loire ports and to isolate the Brittany peninsula, the enemy may redispose his forces defending the Seine. This may occur on or after D+40. We should, however, keep maximum pressure on the Seine to keep a minimum of forces in the Loire. If the enemy redisposition is affected we can then start a coordinated offensive towards the Seine. If the enemy then pulls back forces from the defence of the Loire to oppose us on the Seine, the offensive

---

[1] WO 205/118, loc.cit.

towards the Loire and Quiberon Bay should be reinforced and should be able to achieve its objective.[1]

The possibility of a pause on the D+14 line and the importance of Bradley's thrust to cut off the Brittany Peninsula had been foreseen. The document concluded that: 'Our aim during this period should be to contain the maximum enemy forces facing the eastern flank of the bridgehead and to thrust rapidly towards Rennes. . . For administrative reasons we should aim at securing the Seine ports as early as possible. By alternate thrusts towards the east and towards the southwest we should be able to retain the initiative, reap the benefit of interior lines and keep the enemy moving his reserves from one flank to the other.'[2]

Over the years Montgomery's penchant for giving oral orders and directives may have left the false impression that this held true for his Normandy master plan but the notion of such a major campaign plan being given orally is, on reflection, incomprehensible. The mass movement of four field armies without some framework in the form of a flexible plan would not, to use Montgomery's own words, 'have been a sound operation of war'.

Consequently, the 8 May planning document cannot be dismissed as merely a scenario of possibilities and options. With so much to be accomplished before D-Day, the idea of Montgomery's staff engaging in a major staff effort to prepare such a paper if it were only a 'what if' scenario is inconsistent with Montgomery's methods. The document represented a distillation of Montgomery's ideas and intentions in a clearly worded and flexible plan for the post-D-Day period. Its biggest assumption was that the Allies could quickly seize and keep the initiative. Depending upon the specific German reaction, it gave maximum latitude for expanding the initial bridgehead and for seizing port facilities in whichever direction proved most advantageous. Combined with his oral pronouncements dating back to the earliest planning sessions in January, and culminating at St Paul's School, it lays to rest the question of what really was Montgomery's true conception for winning the battle of Normandy.

[1] WO 205/118, loc.cit.
[2] Ibid, Part IV, loc.cit.

However, as the Allies were soon to discover, major flaws in the post-D-Day planning were a grave overestimation of their ability to seize quickly an initial bridgehead of the size envisioned by the D+14 line; the intense difficulties posed by the bocage country of Normandy; and, above all, the ability of the German Army savagely to resist the might of the greatest invasion armada in history.

PART II

Invasion

It meant a *great* deal to me the other day to shake hands with you again on the soil of France! It brought back floods of memories of our early times together in 1940, and all the slow and laborious work we have put in to arrive back again in a position to give the old Boche a final kick in the pants, and that day should not be too distant now!

Field Marshal Sir Alan Brooke to Montgomery

War is the last of all things to go according to plan.

Thucydides

CHAPTER 7

D-Day:
The Invasion of France

> I never want again to go through a time like the
> present one. The cross-Channel operation is just
> eating into my heart. I wish to God we could start
> and have done with it.
>
> Field Marshal Sir Alan Brooke

> Under the command of General Eisenhower, Allied
> naval forces supported by strong air forces began
> landing Allied armies this morning on the coast of
> France.
>
> BBC Broadcast,
> 6 June 1944[1]

After months of intensive planning and preparation D-Day was
set for 5 June. For nearly three months northern France had been
intensively bombed in a deliberate plan, the 'Transportation
Plan', to sever all German transportation links to Normandy
without giving away exactly where the invasion would be
launched. In one of the great achievements of the war the Allied
air forces had succeeded well beyond all expectations, and had
turned the French railways leading to Normandy into a vast
'railway desert' of smashed rail lines, bridges, depots and equipment. FORTITUDE, a massive deception operation, had succeeded
in convincing the German Supreme Command that General
Patton was to lead an invasion against the Pas de Calais region.
Now hundreds of thousands of Allied troops, ships of all descrip-

---

[1] The text of this announcement was prepared by SHAEF for release to press and radio
and first broadcast by the BBC at noon on 6 June. BBC letter to author, 21 December
1982.

tions, and masses of military hardware were crammed into the southern coastal region of England awaiting the final order to embark. The cross-Channel operation that Winston Churchill had foreseen in the dark days of 1940 was about to be transformed into reality.

The final days prior to OVERLORD were an agony of waiting. For the ordinary soldiers it was a time of virtual imprisonment in their encampments, for once the final briefings had been given and the target at last revealed no one was permitted in or out. It was no less difficult for those responsible for OVERLORD. In the minds of many senior Allied commanders there was a mood of pessimism that, in spite of all the detailed preparations, things might still go wrong on the Normandy beaches. The mood was not lightened by the Allied intelligence news that Rommel had strengthened the Normandy front by the addition of several divisions, with more possibly on the way.

Brooke's natural apprehensions were shared by Eisenhower and Churchill. Although Churchill had intended a positive attitude during his speech at St Paul's School in May for the benefit of the assembled military leaders, his private horrors over a possible failure seemed to have haunted him right up to the eve of D-Day, when he unaccountably turned almost excessively optimistic. This may have been an act. At a luncheon with the Chiefs-of-Staff on 5 June, both Brooke and Admiral Cunningham were astonished to find the Prime Minister now in an over-optimistic mood. Churchill was, Cunningham recorded, 'very worked up about Overlord and really in almost a hysterical state. He really is an incorrigible optimist.'[1]

Elsewhere the mood was decidedly ambivalent. In March Ismay wrote to Field Marshal Wavell: 'Feelings here at home are very mixed. There are a number of people who go on talking as though it is all over but the shouting. On the other hand a lot of people who ought to know better are taking it for granted that Overlord is going to be a bloodbath on the scale of the Somme and Passchendaele.'[2]

In contrast to Churchill, Brooke was still gloomy on the eve of D-Day. 'I am very uneasy about the whole operation. At the

[1] Cunningham Diary, loc.cit.
[2] Ismay, letter to Wavell, 7 March 1944, Ismay Papers, King's College, London.

best it will fall so very short of the expectation of the bulk of the people, namely all those who know nothing about its difficulties. At the worst it may well be the most ghastly disaster of the whole war. I wish to God it were safely over.'[1]*

There is evidence that the strain had begun to show on Eisenhower, the man responsible for making the final, irrevocable decision to launch OVERLORD. There were only three days available in early June upon which the operation could begin. The moonlight required by the three airborne divisions which were to go in by parachute and by glider the night before invasion to secure the vital flanks, and the low tides required for the landings and the demolition of Rommel's underwater obstacles in the forty minutes after first light, would be present together only during the period from 5 to 7 June. Any delay due to inclement weather would mean postponement for at least another two weeks – a possibly fatal delay that might threaten the Allied foothold if the notoriously bad Channel weather closed down resupply through Cherbourg and over the beaches and if winter came before a breakout could be forced.

During the first few days of June the previously fine Channel weather turned nasty and by 4 June, when the invasion force had already embarked, a full-blown storm rendered any hope of invading on the morning of 5 June impossible; it even threatened to wreck the entire invasion timetable. Eisenhower had no choice except to order a postponement of twenty-four hours while the armada waited. By late evening on 4 June the weather was still miserable. Eisenhower's Chief Meteorological Officer, Group Captain J. M. Stagg reported to the tense commanders and senior staff officers a glimmer of hope for 6 June: while the weather would remain poor, visibility would improve and the winds decrease just enough to risk launching the invasion. Stagg's

[1] Bryant, *Triumph in the West*, op.cit., pp. 205–6.

* In his 'Notes On My Life', Brooke later wrote: 'I knew too well all the weak points in the plan of operations. First of all the weather on which we were entirely dependent. A sudden storm might wreck it all. Then the complexity of an amphibious operation of this kind, when confusion may degenerate into chaos in such a short time. The difficulty of controlling the operation once launched, lack of elasticity in the handling of reserves. Danger of leakage of information with consequent loss of that essential secrecy . . . To realise what it was like living through those agonizing hours, the background of the last three years must be remembered. All those early setbacks, the gradual checking of the onrush, the very gradual turn of the defensive to the offensive, then that series of Mediterranean offensives alternately leading up to this final all-important operation which started in the early hours of the next morning.'

forecast was probably the most important weather prediction in history: a mistake forecast for D-Day could turn the entire tide of the war in Europe against the Allies. The pressure on the meteorologists was immense, and to their eternal credit they handled the problem with great courage and aplomb.

Before announcing his decision, Eisenhower took the time to consult with his subordinate commanders and quickly found that time had run out. Admiral Ramsay told Eisenhower: 'If Overlord is to proceed on Tuesday [6 June] I must issue provisional warning to my forces within the next half-hour.'[1] The air marshals, Leigh-Mallory and Tedder, were sceptical about the effectiveness of air support under such poor conditions. Turning next to Montgomery, Eisenhower bluntly asked: 'Do you see any reason why we should not go on Tuesday?' Montgomery's reply was immediate and emphatic: 'No. I would say – *Go*.'[2]

Eisenhower's historic decision came at 2145 hours that night (4 June) when he told the group: 'I don't see how we can possibly do anything else.'[3] At a second meeting several hours later in the early morning hours of 5 June, Stagg reported no change for the worse in the weather for the next day and the earlier decision was reaffirmed. Soon after, signals notified the huge SHAEF invasion force that OVERLORD was on for 6 June. There was now no turning back, but some indication of Eisenhower's remaining doubts is contained in the following message which he drafted and carried in his wallet until July, when he gave it to his naval aide, Captain Harry Butcher:

> Our landings in the Cherbourg-Havre area have failed to gain a satisfactory foothold and I have withdrawn the troops. My decision to attack at this time and place was based upon the best information available. The troops, the air, and the Navy did all that bravery and devotion to duty could do. If any blame or fault attaches to the attempt it is mine alone. June 5.[4]

During the night of 5–6 June, only hours before the amphibious landings commenced, the skies over Normandy were suddenly

---

[1] Quoted in J. M. Stagg, *Forecast for Overlord*, London, 1971, p. 114.
[2] Ibid.
[3] Quoted in Gordon A. Harrison, *Cross-Channel Attack*, Washington, 1951, p. 274, based on an account by Air Vice Marshal James M. Robb, Chief of Staff for Air, SHAEF, written immediately afterwards. Robb's account was originally furnished by Dr Forrest C. Pogue through Eisenhower, and was subsequently used in both Harrison's account and Pogue's *The Supreme Command*, the official history of SHAEF.
[4] Quoted in Butcher, op.cit., p. 525.

filled with the parachutes and gliders of the three Allied airborne divisions. The British 6th Airborne Division was dropped on the Orne bridgehead north and east of Caen by parachute and glider with the formidable task of securing intact the critical bridges over the Orne and of taking out German communications centres and strongpoints that menaced the landings on SWORD beach. In the west the 82nd and 101st Airborne Divisions landed in the marshy areas of the Carentan estuary with the mission of securing equally vital terrain to protect and support the landings on UTAH beach.

The surprise so critical to the success of the Allied plan was achieved. Soon after midnight on 5 June the alarm was spread throughout General Friedrich Dollmann's Seventh German Army as reports began to come in of the airborne landings. By 0215 the Seventh Army had ordered the highest state of alert for LXXXIV Corps which was responsible for defending the Caen-Carentan sector.[1]

By 0300 the Seventh Army Chief of Staff, Generalmajor Max Pemsel, had correctly diagnosed that a major invasion had commenced and was concentrated in the Caen and Carentan areas. The German Supreme Command in the West, at Field Marshal Gerd von Rundstedt's OB[2] West in Paris and at Rommel's Army Group B in La Roche Guyon on the Seine west of Paris, were not convinced that this was anything more than the diversionary operation long expected in Seventh Army's area prior to a main effort against the Fifteenth German Army in the Pas de Calais.[3] Rommel himself was absent in Germany, convinced that the bad weather would not permit an Allied invasion prior to his return. The German weather forecast issued for 6 June read: 'Invasion possible, but not probable because of the weather.' News of the Allied landings was passed to Hitler's Armed Forces High Command (OKW) but critical hours were lost when Hitler's Chief of Operations, General Alfred Jodl,

---

[1] Harrison, op.cit., p. 273. The German Seventh Army consisted of the LXXXIV Infantry Corps, with three static infantry divisions, two infantry divisions, and 21st Panzer Division around Caen; and the XXV and LXXIV Corps defending Brittany. The so-called static or coastal divisions manned fixed fortifications, had little mobility and were generally manned by second-rate troops, some of whom were conscripted from Russia, Poland and other conquered nations of Eastern Europe.

[2] Oberbefehlshaber West – abbreviated to OB West.

[3] Harrison, op.cit., p. 278.

refused to awaken him. Hitler did not learn of the invasion until midday on 6 June.[1]

Between 0300 and 0500 hours on the morning of 6 June over 1,000 British aircraft dumped more than 5,000 tons of bombs on the German coastal defences in the British landing sector. As soon as this preliminary bombing had ceased, the guns of Admiral Ramsay's fleet opened fire along the Normandy front. The British official history describes the scene:

> Never has any coast suffered what a tortured strip of French coast suffered that morning; both naval and air bombardments were unparalleled. Along the whole fifty-mile front the land was rocked by successive explosions as the shells of ships' guns tore holes in fortifications and tons of bombs rained on them from the skies. Through billowing smoke and falling debris defenders crouching in this scene of devastation would soon discern faintly hundreds of ships and assault craft ominously closing the shore. If the sight dismayed them, the soldiers borne forward to attack were thrilled by the spectacle of Allied power that was displayed around them on every hand.[2]

H-Hour came at approximately 0700 when the first assault units of the British 1 and 30 Corps stormed GOLD, JUNO, and SWORD beaches. The task of Crocker's 1 Corps was to take Caen and the important high ground west of the city occupied by Carpiquet Airfield, while Bucknall's 30 Corps drove inland seven miles to seize Bayeaux. Within the first two and a half hours of the assault the Second British Army had managed to land over 30,000 men, 300 guns and 700 armoured vehicles.[3] The beaches were thoroughly jammed with men and equipment and most were still under German fire, but within the first hour exits from the beachhead were forced open in the sectors of the 3rd and 50th Divisions on SWORD and GOLD beaches. On JUNO beach the 3rd Canadian Division had considerably more difficulty; it was nearly two hours after the first landings

---

[1] There is no evidence to suggest that Hitler would have acted differently had Jodl awakened him. Rommel's absence from Normandy was far more crucial.

[2] L. F. Ellis, *Victory in the West*, Volume I, London, 1962, p. 161.

[3] Ellis, op.cit., p. 194. Among the units landing in the I Corps sector was the 1st Commando Brigade under the gallant Lord Lovat. They were given the formidable assignment of landing on the extreme left flank of the British sector and knocking out the artillery batteries and garrison at Ouistreham while the main commando force moved quickly inland to link up with the 6th Airborne Division.

Above: Allied bombing of the French rail network before D-Day was enormously successful in isolating the Normandy battlefield and delaying the augmentation of German forces after the invasion.

Below left: Air Chief Marshal Tedder, Eisenhower's deputy commander, whose principal concern was the airforce operations.

Below right: Air Chief Marshal Leigh-Mallory, commander of the Allied Expeditionary Airforce, with Major General de Guingand, Montgomery's Chief of Staff.

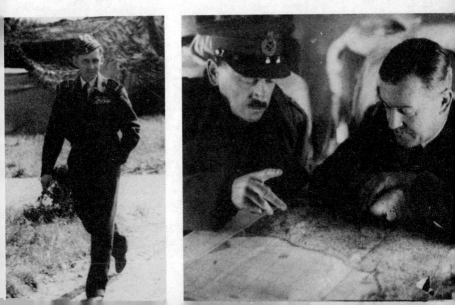

This map, prepared by Montgomery's 21st Army Group planners and published on 8 May 1944, illustrates his basic strategy for breaking out of the

Normandy bridgehead. The large figures show the various options by which the Allied armies might accomplish the breakout.

Above: The British 3rd Division landing on SWORD beach. The stormy weather just before D-Day caused an unusually high tide on 6 June which slowed down Allied disembarkation on to what were smaller than usual beaches. These quickly became blocked and remained so for some time, most of them under German fire.

Below: U.S. troops battling the tides on Omaha Beach, D-Day.

before these were opened and their advance inland could begin.[1]

In the US sector, OMAHA and UTAH beaches had been subjected to the same bombardment by the air and naval forces. The American assault began at 0630. The UTAH landings, by Major General J. Lawton Collins' VII Corps, were spearheaded by the 4th Infantry Division. They achieved complete surprise and the least opposition of any assault unit along the entire Allied front. Exits from the beach area were quickly prised open, followed by rapid movement inland to seize D-Day objectives and protect the beachhead. The landings on OMAHA beach, by the veteran 1st Infantry Division ('Big Red One') and the 29th Infantry Division of Major General Leonard T. Gerow's V Corps, were less successful. Somehow it had escaped Allied intelligence that the veteran German 352nd Infantry Division had been moved into the OMAHA sector three months earlier for defensive exercises.[2] Instead of the static 716th Infantry Division there were now two full divisions deployed around OMAHA to defend the most formidable strip of beach terrain in Normandy: unlike UTAH, which consisted of sand dunes, OMAHA was overlooked for nearly four miles by steep bluffs that ran to heights of as much as two hundred feet. The heavy cloud cover and the short time (forty minutes) allotted for the naval and air bombardment had left the German defenders here relatively unscathed. The result was nearly a disaster.

The long distance from ship to shore and rough seas swamped many amphibious vehicles; darkness and strong winds combined caused others to land in different areas from those assigned. The Germans patiently held their fire until the first wave of men hit the beaches, then all hell broke loose. Heavy fire from automatic weapons and mortars raked the beaches, inflicting heavy casualties on the confused and badly exposed troops. Worse, most of the armour to be utilized in the initial assault never made it to shore, nor did many of the demolition engineers and their

---

[1] Ellis, op.cit., p. 195.
[2] Apparently Brigadier E. T. Williams, Montgomery's 21st Army Group Intelligence Officer, had detected the movement of the 352nd Division but somehow the information was never passed on to V Corps. According to Willaims, on D-Day the First US Army Intelligence Officer, Colonel B. A. 'Monk' Dickson attempted to notify V Corps from the command vessel but was prevented from doing so by the mandatory wireless silence. Brigadier E. T. Williams, interview with Dr Forrest C. Pogue, 3–31 May 1947. There is no hint in the surviving records about where the information came from.

equipment, thus making it impossible to clear obstacles from the beach. For the first six hours the invaders held only a few yards of beach, which remained under intense enemy fire.

It rapidly became evident to the US commanders that remaining in their exposed positions was tantamount to suicide, and they began to rally their troops. Some extraordinary acts of heroism followed. The Assistant Commander of the 29th Infantry Division, Brigadier General Norman D. Cota, deliberately exposed himself to enemy fire by striding up and down the beach exhorting his men to get moving. In the 1st Division sector the commander of the 16th Infantry Regiment, Colonel George A. Taylor, performed a similar feat; he led his troops in an attack against German machine-gun positions declaring: 'Two kinds of people are staying on this beach, the dead and those about to die. Now let's get the hell out of here!'[1] Throughout D-Day the situation on OMAHA was so perilous that General Bradley seriously considered evacuating the beachhead and switching the follow-up units to the British sector or to UTAH beach.[2]

The scenes on OMAHA beach on D-Day haunted Bradley till his death; he called it a 'nightmare'. 'Even now it brings pain to recall what happened there on June 6, 1944. I have returned many times to honor the valiant men who died on that beach. They should never be forgotten. Nor should those who lived to carry the day by the slimmest of margins. Every man who set foot on Omaha Beach that day was a hero.'[3]

While Bradley agonized over what to do, reports began to filter back to the Seventh German Army that the invasion there had been repelled, reports which proved to be wrong. Precarious as the position was, some progress had in fact been made on scattered parts of OMAHA despite the disarray, congestion and strong enemy resistance, which was of the magnitude that Rommel had originally envisioned as necessary to repulse an invasion. The casualty figures graphically attest to this: on 6 June, V Corps suffered losses in excess of two thousand killed,

[1] Cornelius Ryan in *The Longest Day*, London, 1961, ascribes this now famous remark to Colonel Taylor, but in his recent autobiography, Bradley suggests it may have been Cota who said it. Cota and Taylor were among those awarded the Distinguished Service Cross for extraordinary heroism on D-Day, and their actions were mirrored a dozen times over by men of all ranks who rose to the occasion by their brave deeds on that historic day.

[2] Bradley, *A General's Life*, op.cit. p.251.

[3] Ibid.

wounded and missing on OMAHA, while the 4th Division on UTAH had losses of fewer than two hundred in what Bradley has called 'a piece of cake'.[1] Around midday, while the Americans struggled to extricate themselves from the deathtrap of OMAHA beach, the three assault divisions in the British sector were beginning their drive inland to consolidate and expand the three I Corps beachheads.

German belief that the main invasion would hit their Fifteenth Army in the Pas de Calais, a fragmented and muddled command structure within OB West which left Rommel's panzer reserves directly under the operational control of Hitler's OKW, and a failure by the German High Command to react promptly to the airborne landings on the night 5–6 June proved colossal blunders that benefited the Allies beyond measure.

As Montgomery had correctly forecast in April, there was a fundamental disagreement among the Germans over the strategy of employing the panzer divisions of General Geyr von Schweppenburg's Panzer Group West when the invasion came. Panzer Group West had been created in November 1943 by von Rundstedt to react to an invasion in either the Fifteenth or the Seventh Army sectors; it was positioned near Paris to move towards Normandy or the Pas de Calais. Von Rundstedt envisioned employing his armour in a large-scale counterattack against the expected Allied landings. Although General von Schweppenburg was ordered to cooperate with the Army Group Commanders (Rommel: Army Group B, consisting of the Seventh and Fifteenth Armies; and Blaskowitz: Army Group G, formed in May 1944 to defend southern France), there was immediate conflict.[2] Von Schweppenburg's new organization, aiming at counterattack, clashed with Rommel's strategy of defeating an invasion by employing his armour to defeat the Allies on the beaches. Without control of the panzer divisions precious time would be lost while Rommel sought authority for their employment and operational control.[3] Rommel appealed directly to Hitler for control of all armoured and motorized units. Hitler

---

[1] Harrison, op.cit., pp. 329–30, and Bradley, *A General's Life*, op.cit., p. 249.

[2] It did not help that there was a strong clash of personalities between von Schweppenburg and Rommel. Liddell Hart has commented that the former had a great prejudice against Rommel which deflected his judgement on the realities and difficulties of the Normandy campaign. Liddell Hart Papers, King's College, London.

[3] Harrison, op.cit., p. 247.

agreed at first, only to reverse his decision in March 1944 when von Rundstedt protested. As a compromise, three of von Schweppenburg's panzer divisions were transferred to Rommel's Army Group B as mobile reserves.[1][*] Four other panzer divisions located within OB West were placed under the direct command of OKW as a central mobile reserve, leaving *both* von Rundstedt and Rommel without tactical control and the means of influencing the forthcoming battles at the critical moment.[2][†]

Rommel had long recognized from his previous experiences in North Africa that he had no hope of effectively deploying the massed armour of Panzer Group West unless he also controlled the air. The decline of the once mighty Luftwaffe left him little hope they could wrest command of the skies from the Allied air forces, and therefore no choice except to reinforce the Atlantic Wall as strongly as possible and fight the decisive defensive battle along its crest. Rommel reasoned that his strategy was the only one with a reasonable chance of success:

> With the coastline held as thinly as it is at present, the enemy will probably succeed in creating bridgeheads at several different points and in achieving a major penetration of our coastal defences. Once this has happened, it will only be by the rapid intervention of our operational reserves that he will be thrown back into the sea. This requires that these forces should be held very close behind the coast defences. If, on the other hand, our principal reserves have to be brought up from well back inland, the move will not only require a great deal of time – time which the enemy will probably use to reinforce himself at his point of penetration and either organize his forces for defence or press the attack farther inland – but will also be under constant danger from the air. Bearing in mind the numerical and material superiority of the enemy striking-forces, their high state of training and tremendous air superiority, victory in a major battle on the Continent seems to me a matter of grave doubt. British and American superiority in the air alone has again and again been so effective that all movement of major formations has been rendered completely impossible, both at the front and behind it, by day and by night. . .

---

[1] Harrison, op.cit., p. 248.
[*] The three divisions were 2nd, 21st and 116th Panzer.
[2] Harrison, op. cit, p. 248.
[†] Worse still, as Harrison points out, three of these divisions were SS, trained by Panzer Group West, controlled by OKW, but administratively under the SS chain of command.

I therefore consider that an attempt must be made, using every possible expedient, to beat off the enemy landing on the coast and to fight the battle in the more or less strongly fortified coastal strip.[1]

By April 1944, in anticipation of an invasion in late spring, Rommel had continued his policy of committing his defences farther forward. The 21st Panzer Division was shifted to the Caen sector from Rennes, its panzer grenadier battalions dispersed on both sides of the Orne, its divisional artillery on the coast and the panzers held farther inland. While strengthening his defences along the coast, Rommel's decision also eliminated 21st Panzer as a mobile reserve.[2]

With his two other mobile reserve divisions placed further north to reinforce the Fifteenth Army, Rommel again appealed over von Rundstedt to Jodl for permission to move the four panzer divisions of the OKW central mobile reserve closer to the coast. An angry von Rundstedt objected to OKW, arguing that such a move prematurely committed his reserves. OKW agreed, and the last opportunity to utilize the only mobile reserves close enough to react at once to an invasion was lost.

In spite of his doubts that the action reported in Normandy in the early morning of 6 June constituted the main invasion, the size of the airborne landings clearly indicated to von Rundstedt that there would be an invasion along the Normandy coast around dawn that day.[3] He therefore deemed it imperative to commit all available panzer divisions to a counterattack as rapidly as possible that morning:

> There was therefore no time to debate contingencies . . . even if the Normandy assault were planned by the Allies as a secondary effort, it was probable that they would exploit whatever success it achieved. The attack, whatever its character, should therefore be met with all available force. [His] reasoning was clear and his action decisive. But the two panzer divisions

---

[1] Rommel is quoted in Matthew Cooper, *The German Army 1933–1945*, London, 1978, p. 498.

[2] Harrison, op. cit, p. 257.

[3] British historian Sir Basil Liddell Hart, who knew von Rundstedt well, believes that the German Supreme Commander in the West was not really hoaxed by the Allied 'cover plan' (FORTITUDE) that the real invasion would come in the Pas de Calais but rather convinced by his orthodox military training and thinking, which dictated that the best strategic course for the Allies to take was an attack at this point; a preconception which no doubt was strengthened by the 'cover plan'. Liddell Hart Papers, King's College, London.

which he ordered to move were not under his command. They were in OKW reserve. To save precious time Rundstedt issued his orders first and then notified OKW of the action, requesting approval. OKW did not approve. At about 0730 Jodl informed Rundstedt that the two divisions would not be committed until orders were received from Hitler. The 12SS Panzer Division was to hold up at Lisieux; Panzer Lehr would not move at all.[1]*

It was a critical blunder by OKW. As a field marshal, von Rundstedt had the right of appeal directly to Hitler, but the Führer was asleep and known to dislike being awakened by his subordinates. Thus von Rundstedt made no further attempt to protest at OKW's timidity or to risk ordering the movement without permission. Orders did not come until nearly 1600 hours on 6 June, when Hitler finally consented to the divisions' movement. In his own defence, von Rundstedt was later scornfully to say of his role as Commander-in-Chief in the West: 'My only authority was to change the guard in front of my gate.'[2]

The Allied invasion came at a moment when most of the senior German commanders were absent from their posts. In addition to Rommel, both the Seventh Army commander, Dollmann, and the 1 SS Panzer Corps commander, Dietrich, were away from Normandy. The only factor that could have favoured the Germans on 6 June was the weather: there was a heavy cloud cover over Normandy that morning which would have permitted movement of the two panzer divisions without risk of serious interdiction from the Allied air forces. By the time they were given permission to move the cloud cover had broken and nothing could be done before dark.[3] As will be seen, the state of affairs within 21st Panzer Division was equally bungled. Indecision at Army Group B and wretchedly slow communications between command posts cost the Germans precious hours, and with the division scattered over a wide area yet more time was lost as its commander attempted to assemble a force east of the Orne capable of dealing with the threat posed by the British 6th Airborne Division. Later, orders were received to attack across

[1]   Harrison, op.cit., p. 333.
*   Lisieux is about 25 miles from Caen; Chartres, the location of Panzer Lehr, is nearly 100 miles from Caen.
[2]   Post-war interrogation of Field Marshal von Rundstedt, originally conducted by the Canadian Army on 1 February 1946, Liddell Hart Papers.
[3]   Harrison, op.cit., p. 333.

the river to the west and further delays ensued when only one bridge in Caen could be found still intact.[1] The 21st Panzer, the only unit capable of mounting a serious threat to the invasion on the Caen flank would come into action far too late. Rommel's absence at the critical moment and the hopelessly fragmented German command structure would combine fatally to delay German countermeasures against the left flank of the Allied invasion, now tenuously held by the commandos and the airborne division.

The overcast skies had cleared away and in the bright sunshine the goal of the projected drive in the Orne bridgehead – the ancient city of Caen – was clearly visible in the distance from the high ground near the beaches, its spires shimmering in the heat. This was the place where the key part of the great plan conceived by Montgomery was to be carried out. Little did the men of the British 3rd Division know that their actions that day would be the subject of debate for many years to come.

---

[1] North of Caen the Orne runs directly to the sea east of the village of Ouistreham, while several hundred yards to the west it is paralleled by the Caen Canal. The only road crossing both obstacles ran between Bénouville and Ranville, five miles north of Caen, and was a vital target designated for early capture. Shortly after midnight a small task force of infantry and engineers landed by glider and swiftly seized both bridges intact, and held them until reinforced by elements of the 5th Parachute Brigade. With these two bridges held by the British, the 21st Panzer was forced to seek a crossing of the Orne in Caen, thus delaying their counterattack against the British 3rd Division north of Caen on the west bank of the Orne.

CHAPTER 8

D–Day: The Orne Bridgehead

The record of the 3rd British Division is the most
disappointing of all the assault sectors.

Major General David Belchem,
Victory in Normandy[1]

A successful assault on the beaches of Normandy was the essential prerequisite to the next task of the Allied armies on D–Day,
that of expanding the beachhead and carving out a lodgement
area of sufficient size to ensure a firm foothold against what was
certain to be a violent reaction by the Germans. The invasion of
6 June 1944 has been immortalized on film and in numerous
firsthand accounts since the war, which have tended to focus on
the fight for the beaches. But it was the battle for the foothold
in the Orne bridgehead which largely determined the fate of
Montgomery's master plan and the course of the struggle for
Normandy which followed.

The Orne bridgehead had been assaulted in the early hours of
6 June by the British 6th Airborne Division who now clung
tenaciously to this small piece of French soil while awaiting
reinforcements from the main assault forces the following morning. It was here that Lieutenant General John Crocker's 1 Corps
had to form the anchor of the Allied left flank. The key to the
projected D-Day advance in the Orne sector was the 3rd British
Division, whose mission was to assault SWORD beach running
from St Aubin sur Mer in the west to Ouistreham, where the Orne
empties into the Bay of the Seine, in the east – a front of some
seven miles. They were then to seize Caen and establish a
bridgehead south of the Orne.[2] Despite determined opposition in
places, the German defences at SWORD were far less formidable

---

[1] p. 109.
[2] The official language of the order read: 'The task of 3 Br Inf Div is to capture Caen
and secure a bridgehead over the River Orne at that place.' 1 Corps Operational Order
No. 1, 5 May 1944.

than those of a few miles down the beach at OMAHA. By midnight on D-Day the 50th Division, supported by elements of the 7th Armoured Division, had driven to within three miles of Bayeux and had linked up with the 3rd Canadian Division, whose farthest penetration still left it on the high ground around the village of Anisy over three miles from the western outskirts of Caen.

Since the autumn of 1943 the British 3rd Division had been training hard in the highlands of eastern Scotland as one of the three divisions selected by the War Office for the D-Day assault. Exercise followed upon exercise as they mastered the problems of combined operations in conjunction with the Royal Navy. Although not told that their mission was the capture of Caen until they had actually slipped their moorings on D-1, the division was given guidelines under the codename POLAND, corresponding to the terrain they would face on SWORD beach and in their advance on Caen.

The original divisional plan had called for the assault to be made on a two-brigade front (the 8th and 185th Infantry Brigades) with the 9th Infantry Brigade in reserve. In February 1944 the plan was modified to an assault on a one-brigade front (the 8th Brigade) which would be followed two hours later by the 185th Brigade as the Intermediate Brigade, and the 9th Brigade still the reserve. That same month the new 21st Army Group commander had visited his former unit. The 3rd Division had first gained fame under the command of a then obscure major general named B. L. Montgomery; now as a full general in temporary command of all Allied ground forces for the invasion, Montgomery told the assembled troops from the bonnet of a jeep: ' . . . that the Germans would have cause to remember the Division they pushed into the Straits of Dover in 1940.'[1]

From a steady stream of information provided by Allied intelligence, the 3rd Division expected the initial German resistance to be from the 716th Infantry Division, a static coastal defence unit. The Divisional Intelligence Summary appended to the final operations order issued on 14 May made no mention of any panzer opposition around Caen. For months Allied Intelli-

---

[1] Norman Scarfe, *Assault Division*, London, 1947, p. 49.

gence – with the help of ULTRA[1] – had been tracking the movements of all German units in France, one of which was the 21st Panzer Division. The original 21st Panzer Division had been part of the Afrika Korps but had ceased to exist when the remnants of Rommel's once powerful army were trapped at Tunis and surrendered in February 1943. The new 21st Panzer had been created from scratch in May 1943 by Lieutenant General Edgar Feuchtinger with a cadre of 3,000 men. During the next year the division was gradually formed by assembling tanks and armoured vehicles from German scrapyards, and by the spring of 1944 it was a powerful force consisting of three panzer regiments, two panzer grenadier regiments, and supporting units totalling nearly 16,000 men, of which some 4,500 were fighting troops.[2] Its famous name had been well worth preserving and the new division inherited a healthy respect on the part of their opponents in the British Army.

In April 1944 SHAEF intelligence reported the 21st Panzer in the Rennes area of east Brittany, and SHAEF continued to identify the division's presence in this region as late as 6 May.[3] A week later SHAEF reported: 'A movement of armoured elements at the end of April into the area SOUTH of Caen by road and rail from farther WEST. . . No identifications have as yet been received, but on present evidence a move of 21 Panzer Division from the RENNES area is suspected'.[4] On 20 May SHAEF again noted: 'The move of 21 Panzer Division to the area south of Caen is confirmed by details of a rail movement from the Rennes area to FLERS, BAYEUX and CAEN. It is believed to extend as far EAST as the line LISIEUX-ARGENTAN.'[5]

---

[1]   ULTRA is the term used to describe the fruits of 'breaking' any enemy high-grade machine cypher. During the operations in Northwest Europe the main sources were the Enigma cypher machine used by the Wehrmacht, and the 'Breaking' of the secret teleprinter (Geheimschreiber). In addition to 'breaking' the Enigma cyphers, some of the secret ULTRA decrypts came from American sources, primarily MAGIC, the name given to the 'breaking' of Japanese codes. As a general rule the information disclosed by ULTRA during this time was low-level and fragmentary. In the 21st Army intelligence section ULTRA was jokingly referred to as 'BBR': Burn Before Reading.

[2]   'Special Interrogation Report of General-Leutnant Edgar Feuchtinger, Comd 21 Pz Div', n.d., Liddell Hart Papers. Before the war Feuchtinger had been deeply involved in organizing the 1936 Olympic Games held in Berlin and had been responsible for the opening and closing day ceremonies.

[3]   SHAEF Weekly Intelligence Summary No. 7, 6 May 1944, PRO (WO 219/1919).

[4]   SHAEF WIS No. 8, 13 May 1944, ibid. In this same report, SHAEF noted the movement out of Caen to the St Malo sector of Brittany of a small divisional-size unit at the end of April.

[5]   SHAEF WIS No. 9, 20 May 1944, loc.cit.

The official historians were not privy to the ULTRA secret, thus neither the British nor American official histories provide the answer to the question of ULTRA's role. The US history says only that 'In April the 21st Panzer Division was moved from Rennes to Caen where its battalions were split on either side of the Orne River and its artillery committed on the coast. The disposition to all intents removed the 21st Panzer Division as a unit from the pool of mobile reserves.'[1]

Now that SHAEF had determined that the 21st Panzer Division had moved into Normandy the final intelligence summary issued on 3 June could only state: 'There are no further changes in the disposition of German divisions in the west.'[2] However, on 22 May, the Second British Army issued the most forceful warning to emanate from an Allied headquarters prior to the invasion, advising the assault divisions to prepare for up to 540 German tanks in their D-Day area: the 21st Panzer was believed to have 300 tanks, the 12th SS Panzer 160, with another 80 or so scattered throughout the 1 SS Panzer Corps, which had responsibility for the Caen sector. 1 Corps was specifically warned to expect *immediate local counterattacks by reserves and tanks of the 21st Panzer near the coast and by the 352nd Infantry Division.* [Author's italics.] By evening something stronger in armoured counterattack can be expected from 12/SS/Pz against our left flank.' The Second Army also cautioned that the 17th SS Panzer Grenadier Division, with 160 more tanks, might interfere – a fortuitously incorrect estimate, for on 6 June this unit was in its twenty-third week of training near Poitiers, south of the Loire and had no tanks, only assault guns.[3]

The final D-Day intelligence summary issued by the Second Army admitted that little was known about the organization of the 21st Panzer other than that it could be expected to attack with more than the normal two tank battalions. 'The division total may be as many as 240 tanks and 40 assault guns, including a Panther battalion and possibly some Tigers.[4] This estimate

[1] Harrison, *Cross-Channel Attack,* op.cit., p. 257. The US account makes no mention of the disposition of Feuchtinger's armour and the reader should understand that the reference to its battalions being split on either side of the Orne is intended to mean only the panzer grenadiers.

[2] SHAEF WIS No. 10, 3 June 1944, loc.cit.

[3] Second Army Planning Intelligence Summary (hereinafter SAIS) No. 23, 22 May 1944, Dempsey Papers, PRO (WO 285/3).

[4] SAIS, No. 2, 29 May 1944, ibid.

turned out to be excessively high for, as Feuchtinger later related: 'By the time it was committed on D-Day, the division consisted of 127 Mark IV tanks, 40 assault guns, a total in all of 167 armoured track vehicles.'[1]

Despite the Second Army's blunt warnings the D-Day commanders do not seem fully to have understood the situation or that the 21st Panzer had major elements already in the midst of their assault areas: their records clearly substantiate the belief that the 21st Panzer was in the Falaise area. The war diary of the 2nd Canadian Armoured Brigade, attached to the 3rd Canadian Division for the invasion, refers to the move from Rennes to Falaise and suggested that a large number of tanks might be located in the Forêt de Cinglais, some twenty miles inland near Bretteville sur Laize.[2] The 3rd British Division was told only of an unconfirmed report advising that the German division might be stationed some ten to thirty miles south of Caen. 'It could, therefore,' notes the Division historian, 'intervene against us on D-Day and we must be prepared for it.'[3]

Although ULTRA does not seem to have played a direct role in the intelligence picture of the 21st Panzer's move, it nevertheless furnished at least a hint of the shift to Normandy. On 15 May Bletchley Park forwarded to SHAEF and other commands the contents of a message from the Seventh Germany Army in the Enigma Cypher, reporting that 'The remaining elements of 21 Panzer Division . . . have arrived.'[4]* The message did not specify

---

[1] Feuchtinger interrogation, loc.cit. The Mark IV tank mounted a 75-mm gun and was more than matched by American Sherman and British Churchill tanks, both of which also mounted 75-mm guns as main armament. The division was not equipped with either Panther or Tiger tanks.

[2] War Diary, 2nd Canadian Armoured Brigade, Operations Order No. 1, 23 May 1944, PRO (WO 179/2839). The intelligence contained in this order represented what was disseminated by the 3rd Canadian Division to all assigned or attached units.

[3] Scarfe, Assault Division, op.cit. p.66. Extracted from the Divisional Intelligence Summary issued with the final operation Order of 14 May 1944. Examination of intelligence estimates contained in the war diaries of the D-Day assault units reveals a common expectation that the 21st Panzer was located in the Falaise area. For example, the last intelligence summary contained in the war diary of the 8th Armoured Brigade reported on 25 May that the 21st Panzer was based on Falaise with up to 300 tanks and self-propelled guns, and could interfere with brigade operations within four hours of 'H' hour on 6 June. (Cf., WO 171/613).

[4] The Seventh Army message was dated 5 May 1944 and contained in Message KV 3892, issued by Bletchley Park on 15 May. Cf., PRO, (DEFE 3/155).

* The gist of this signal was reproduced without a source attribution in one of the weekly MARTIAN Reports issued by the Theatre Intelligence Section which disseminated intelligence relevant to OVERLORD planning. Originally this group belonged to the British

where these elements 'arrived', but several days earlier SHAEF had obtained information, presumably from an agent, which was disseminated on 10 May to the effect that, 'At the end of April and the beginning of May armour moved into the area south of Caen from further west.' SHAEF also stated that 'Several days after this move, railway activity of armoured type was observed at Rennes.'[1] As official intelligence historian Thomas notes: 'This observation led SHAEF to interpret the move as having been carried out by 21st Panzer Division and this interpretation was confirmed by KV 3892 (Bletchley Park's message of 15 May 1944).'[2] No intelligence system is infallible and, despite ULTRA and other sources, the immense business of keeping track of some sixty enemy divisions in France was a difficult undertaking. Thomas is correct when he asserts that 'The miracle is that as much was achieved as it was.'[3]

Thus, as is now apparent, Caen had been specifically mentioned in an intelligence report available to the D-Day commanders as one of the destinations of the 21st Panzer, but there was no further evidence collected by Allied intelligence that subsequent to its arrival there elements of this division had been deployed astride the Orne around Caen. Of the four motorized infantry battalions assigned to the two panzer grenadier regiments, three were deployed around Caen: one in western suburbs, another to the east, 'while a third, together with the twenty-four 88-mm guns of the anti-tank battalion, was stationed on Périers Ridge, only three miles inland from the very beach on which the 3rd Division was to land.'[4] Moreover, the divisional flak units were also positioned in and around Caen. Feuchtinger later confirmed that the remainder of the division was dispersed over a wide area of 300 square miles, extending from Caen as far south as Falaise, and from Thury-Harcourt as

Home Forces, eventually passed to COSSAC via 21st Army Group and, in the early months of 1944, became part of SHAEF G-2. The intelligence contained in these reports was obtained from all sources except ULTRA. Official historian Edward E. Thomas points out that the yield from non-ULTRA sources was appreciated in the MARTIAN reports against an ULTRA background.

[1] MARTIAN 95, 10 May 1944, PRO (WO 219/1942).
[2] Edward E. Thomas, letter to the author, 9 November 1982.
[3] Edward E. Thomas, letter to the author, 28 November 1982. Not only were there some 60 divisions in France to keep track of, but there were also between 200 and 250 divisions throughout the operational area of the German Army which were of concern to Allied intelligence.
[4] Chester Wilmot, *The Struggle for Europe*, London, 1952, pp. 299–300.

far east as Mézidon on the River Dives (approximately fifteen miles southeast of Caen).[1]

As we have seen, Rommel's growing frustration over the inadequacy of panzer reserves near the Normandy coast had led him sometime in April to order these movements. His Chief-of-Staff, Lieutenant General Hans Speidel later explained: 'Rommel had known that every hour would matter in the struggle to destroy the first enemy lodgements and prevent him reinforcing and increasing his foothold. He had therefore practised the 21st Panzer Division stationed south of Caen in its May training at exploiting the momentary weakness of the enemy just after landing by going over automatically to the counterattack. Every possibility had been thought of and tried out in manoeuvres. The 21st Panzer Division had been stationed by Rommel at this vital point, but he had not been allowed more panzer forces than this one division.'[2]*

The disagreement between the senior German commanders in France led to 21st Panzer being given a dual role. The purpose of concentrating the motorized infantry around the Orne was to support the 716th Infantry Division against any Allied invasion along the coast of this sector of Normandy, while the panzers were held further to the rear to act as a tactical reserve. The problem, Feuchtinger later complained, was that this dual role resulted in neither being effectively carried out. This was certainly not the method envisaged by Rommel for defeating an invasion; in other circumstances he would probably have left the division intact as a powerful mobile counterattack force. However, the paucity of German forces stretched across Normandy forced him into all but emasculating the 21st Panzer's striking power and mobility. The mobile flak units, for example, were dispersed as far as the coast near Ouistreham and in the event of invasion were to come under the control of the Caen flak command instead of Feuchtinger.[3]

The fact that no Allied intelligence-gathering activity was

---

[1] Feuchtinger interrogation, loc.cit.

[2] Lieutenant General Hans Speidel, *We Defended Normandy*, London, 1951, p. 94.

* Speidel's account is faulty on the question of panzer reserves. Rommel had, in fact, been given two additional divisions: the 2nd and the 116th Panzer, neither of which was stationed in Normandy prior to the invasion. Rommel was given operational control while Geyr von Schweppenburg retained responsibility for their training and organization. Cf., Harrison, *Cross-Channel Attack*, p. 248.

[3] Feuchtinger interrogation loc. cit.

able to pinpoint and confirm the actual dispersal of major elements of the 21st Panzer around Caen itself is balanced by the steady stream of warnings which ought to have been sufficient to alert the assault units to this possibility.[1] The series of general warnings issued by SHAEF caused the Second Army intelligence to forewarn of possible massive German panzer interference in the assault area. As it turned out, SHAEF had otherwise accurately predicted the disposition of the 21st Panzer; moreover, its very dispersal ought to have suggested that Rommel had in mind more than its use as a mobile striking force to counter any invasion in the Caen sector. It is thus difficult to escape the conclusion that 1 Corps ought to have anticipated anti-tank and armoured interference from the 21st Panzer from the outset.

Less easy to explain is the apparent lack of attention paid by the various Allied headquarters to German dispositions in the assault area around Caen. There seems to have been a preoccupation with German units in the Cotentin, where the two US airborne divisions were to be dropped in support of the UTAH beach sector. .

Even more curious is the apparent disinterest displayed by Montgomery in the planned operations in the Orne bridgehead. Once he had declared the intentions of the master plan to his subordinates he appears to have forgotten about it – instead he turned his full attention to the task of motivating the troops of 21st Army Group for the forthcoming invasion.

Montgomery's intelligence officer, Brigadier E. T. Williams, has noted that Montgomery did occasionally show an odd sense of detachment from situations when he ought to have been deeply involved.[2] For the THUNDERCLAP exercise Montgomery had grilled his subordinates on every conceivable type of contingency or mishap and, given the critical importance of the British

---

[1] These warnings were no doubt issued in the realization that moves by German units could have taken place within Normandy that had not been reflected in intelligence reports. Moreover, the fact noted by SHAEF on 20 May that the 21st Panzer was dispersed over a wide area should have alerted the intelligence staffs of the Second Army and 1 Corps that some units might be found around Caen itself. The deployment of the 21st Panzer to Normandy occurred at the same time as a general reinforcement of Normandy by OKW, Hitler and Rommel. It is appropriate, as a consequence, to question why the movement of the 21st Panzer was not probed more deeply. We cannot be certain what aerial reconnaissance missions were flown over the Orne Sector prior to D-Day nor what the results disclosed. What is known is that the panzer grenadier battalions and divisional artillery of the 21st Panzer managed to evade detection prior to the invasion.

[2] Interview with Sir Edgar Williams, 8 April 1983.

operations in the Orne bridgehead, it would have been expected that he would assure himself that Dempsey, Crocker and the assault commanders were fully prepared for every possible situation on D-Day: what, for example, would Crocker do if panzer interference occurred sooner than expected? How would the thrust towards Caen be carried out if German resistance could not be overcome quickly?

Williams believes that his chief carefully avoided getting too close to an operational situation in order to ensure that he did not lose his way by getting bogged down in details. His failure to involve himself fully in the planning for the airborne operation at Arnhem in September 1944 is the best known example.[1]

While it would have been difficult, if not impossible, to have altered the basic 3rd Division assault plan at the last moment, more attention to the intelligence estimates might have at least alerted General Rennie and General Crocker that the thrust toward Caen would be likely to run into more immediate interference from the 21st Panzer. Instead, Rennie and his two lead brigade commanders landed on the morning of 6 June mistakenly anticipating a less formidable enemy force blocking their advance toward Caen.

The division plan called for the 8th Brigade to seize a beachhead and drive inland as quickly as possible to capture and hold positions on Périers Ridge some three miles south of the beaches. Meanwhile, Brigadier K. Pearce Smith's 185th Brigade would land and commence operations to secure Caen. Lieutenant Colonel Nigel Tapp, who commanded the 7th Field Regiment, Royal Artillery, was in support and he recalls that Brigadier Smith's plan was quite simple. It was 'To land, to form up in the Hermanville area and to advance with the KSLI [the 2nd Battalion, The King's Shropshire Light Infantry] on the centre axis Hermanville-Lebisey-Caen, supported by the Staffordshire Yeomanry [one of three regiments,[2] the 27th Armoured Brigade] and my regiment, with the remaining field artillery regiments of the Division to call on for fire support. The Warwicks [the 2nd Battalion, The Royal Warwickshire Regiment] on the right and slightly back, and the Norfolks [the 1st Battalion, the Royal

---

[1] Williams interview, loc.cit.
[2] A British 'regiment' was in reality only a battalion-sized unit. An armored 'regiment,' for example, consisted of thirty-six officers and six hundred thirty enlisted men.

Norfolk Regiment] on the left. The KSLI were to mount the tanks of the Staffordshire Yeomanry and advance along the main axis to secure Caen as quickly as possible. The Norfolks on the left and the Warwicks on the right were to mop up and secure objectives captured by the mobile column.'[1]

Brigadier Smith remembers wishing his three battalion CO's 'Good hunting' moments before disembarking. Based on the intelligence reports, 'I did not expect on my race to Caen, to confront 21st Panzer Division or any other Armoured Division. . . Information concerning the strength and dispositions of 716th Division was somewhat nebulous and what with the speed of my advance and with the expected support of the Staffordshire Yeomanry tanks, 7th Field Regiment, Royal Artillery, I did not anticipate much opposition.'[2]

By 1100 hours Smith's three battalions had assembled near Hermanville as planned and were ready to commence operations when things began to go wrong. First, the tanks of the Staffordshire Yeomanry had not been able to get off the beaches due to the tides and heavy traffic congestion, and the situation was growing worse by the minute as the tide continued to come in. The weather had caused an unusually high tide on the morning of 6 June which slowed down and seriously restricted the entire disembarkation process of the Staffordshire Yeomanry on QUEEN beach.[3] Where normally there would have been a width of thirty yards at high tide, there was this day *less than thirty feet*, leaving the tanks precious little room to manoeuvre laterally. The exit routes were still under German fire and the result was 'a most unpleasant pile-up of vehicles'.[4] The War Diary of the Staffordshire Yeomanry was more explicit: 'A terrible jam on the beach where no organization appeared to be operating and no marked exits were to be seen. The majority of our tanks remained stationary for approximately 1 hour . . . and even after leaving the beach, vehicles remained head to tail for long periods on the only available routes.'[5] Clearance of the beach exits, noted the

---

[1] Major General Sir Nigel Tapp, letter to the author, 22 March 1982.
[2] Brigadier K. Pearce Smith, letter to the author, 27 August 1982.
[3] One of the sub-beaches of SWORD.
[4] 'Notes on the Work of 101 Beach Sub Area During the Normandy Operation', copy furnished by Norman Scarfe. In order to clear the congestion, the beachmaster was forced to hold up further landings for thirty minutes.
[5] War Diary, The Staffordshire Yeomanry, June 1944, PRO (WO 171/863).

divisional history, 'proved to be about the hardest and most heart-breaking job of the invasion.'[1]

The bottleneck on QUEEN beach posed an even more serious problem for Brigadier Smith. As the division historian relates: 'The Brigadier was in an unhappy dilemma: whether to launch the assault on foot or wait for the tanks. [Rennie's] order was that "This advance will be carried out with speed and boldness so that the enemy's local reserves can be overcome quickly and the Brigade established on its objective ready to meet counter-attacks by reserve formations which may develop towards evening on D-Day." The question was whether more speed might not be attained by waiting for the tanks than by committing the troops to an attack on foot.'[2] By noon less than two squadrons of the Yeomanry had managed to form up off the beaches, and these were confined to the road network because of a large minefield directly across the planned route of advance. At 1115 Smith and the KSLI commander, Lieutenant Colonel F. J. Maurice, both riding bicycles, met outside Hermanville to discuss the problem of the missing tanks. At noon Maurice returned from a recce to report the extent of the problem. Smith at once ordered the KSLI to proceed towards Caen on foot and the tanks to marry up with them as soon as possible.[3]

While the 185th Brigade was adjusting plans for the advance on Caen, Brigadier E. E. E. Cass's 8th Brigade was experiencing the most serious problem encountered by the 3rd Division on D-Day: a formidable German fortress, codenamed 'Hillman', which stood on high ground on the northern edge of Périers Ridge, squarely in the path of the 185th Brigade's route of advance to the south. Responsibility for neutralizing 'Hillman' belonged to Cass.[4] Both 'Hillman' and another nearby fortress named 'Morris' were problems of unexpected proportions. 'Morris' was taken without incident around 1300 hours by the

---

[1] Scarfe, *Assault Division*, op.cit., p. 80.
[2] Ibid, p. 79.
[3] War Diary, 2nd Bn, KSLI, 6 June 1944, PRO (WO 171/1325).
[4] 'Hillman' was a maze of deep concrete bunkers and pillboxes, all connected by trenches. Much of the complex was underground and well camouflaged from aerial observation. Intelligence reports had been unable to do justice to this formidable fortress whose outer defences of wire, anti-personnel and anti-tank mines covered nearly three-quarters of a square mile. The 3rd Division had been warned of the existence of a German strongpoint in the area but had been led to believe that it would be neutralized by a combination of air strikes and naval gunfire.

1st Battalion, The Suffolk Regiment, after naval and artillery fire had convinced its sixty-five occupants that surrender was in their best interest. However, when 'A' Company of the Suffolks attempted to storm 'Hillman', they were greeted by a murderous hail of machine-gun fire. D-Day was not the time to discover that 'Hillman', like 'Morris' in fact, was the local German coastal HQ. The occupants of 'Hillman' were unscathed and determined to resist. A bitter confrontation between the Suffolks and the German gunners ensued.

The original intent had been to support the assault on 'Hillman' with fire from a nearby Royal Navy cruiser but the FOB[1] attached to the 8th Brigade had been killed earlier and there was no one else trained to take over his function. Thus the Suffolks were forced to attack 'Hillman' without the benefit of a preliminary bombardment and fire support. During the first attempt both protective wires were breached but those who survived could not get close to the machine-gun cupola sweeping that sector of 'Hillman'. Until this obstacle could be reduced it proved impossible and suicidal for the infantry to get close enough. Soon a tank of the Staffordshire Yeomanry was brought up and it lumbered through the gap with infantry crouched behind it, but its armour-piercing shells had no effect on the cupola. As one of the participants, Corporal R. L. Lawson has related: 'Yet another stalemate developed. . . Any movement from [our] section brought machine-gun fire and more casualties.'[2]

The deadly battle for 'Hillman' went on throughout the afternoon and into the evening and eventually required the support of more tanks of the Staffordshire Yeomanry and of the 13/18 Hussars. Unfortunately 'Hillman' could not be easily bypassed and left for later mopping up, as the Norfolks had found out when they suffered nearly 150 casualties while attempting to evade its fire during the afternoon. The difficult task of eradicating 'Hillman' involved breaching the minefield and neutralizing each concrete emplacement one by one, many of whose defenders chose to fight on until blown up by explosives. In addition to creating problems for the advancing 185th Brigade,

[1] Forward Officer Bombardment.
[2] Unpublished account of Corporal R. L. Lawson, 'A' Company, 1st Battalion, The Suffolk Regiment. Furnished by Norman Scarfe.

the delay at 'Hillman' tied up two squadrons of tanks, one of which should have been supporting the KSLI.

The Suffolks have been severely criticized by Chester Wilmot for spending too much time planning their attack on 'Hillman' at a time when speed was of the essence. Calling such preparations 'a luxury which the invaders could not afford', Wilmot suggested 'The need of the hour was for speed and action, almost regardless of casualties. The way had to be cleared or the initiative would be lost. And yet the Suffolks spent most of the afternoon organizing their attack and they do not appear to have proceeded with the urgency the occasion demanded.'[1]

The leadership of the 3rd Division was later criticized as too conservative and disinclined to develop their advantage quickly enough. Wilmot, for example, has described Rennie as a dogged and able Scot who was well suited to plan and launch the assault but temperamentally unable to push his advantage. The assault brigade commander, Brigadier Cass, was 'stolid to the point of being ponderous, and his troops tended to take their cue from his own measured gait'.[2] As Wilmot saw it, 'The personalities of these two men had inevitably made their mark upon the battalions, and in assault exercises they had shown the same tendencies to dig in prematurely. When Crocker returned from North Africa to take over the corps, he had done what he could to cure this characteristic, but it was too deeply rooted in the men and their commanders, and in the general training of the forces which had remained in Britain since Dunkirk. For months these men had known that they would be part of an assault division in the invasion of Europe. With this prospect they had lived too long, studying every aspect of the enemy's defences and weapons, rehearsing interminably for the crucial moment of their landings. They had steeled themselves for this hour but in all their training their attention had been fixed upon the strip of sand which would lie ahead, when the landing ramps went down.'[3] When the assault proved to be less costly than expected, Wilmot charges, the brigade dropped the momentum of their attack before the other brigades were ready to pick up the slack.[4] Yet Rennie was

[1] Wilmot, op.cit., p. 310.
[2] Wilmot, op.cit., p. 304–5.
[3] Ibid.
[4] Ibid.

so highly respected by Montgomery that he was selected in mid-July to command the 51st (Highland) Division when this veteran unit performed so poorly its commander was summarily relieved and sent home.[1] If Brigadier 'Copper' Cass was 'stolid', he was also, says the division historian, 'a tremendously pugnacious and fiery old red-head: very alarming to subalterns and good cause for alarm in the enemy. He was a martinet, a shade like Monty himself, reassuring to have on one's own side.'[2]

What Wilmot's account overlooks is the fact that the Suffolks simply had not expected such a difficult obstacle and were not initially organized for the type of attack eventually required to overcome it. The battalion had other tasks that day, the first of which had been the reduction of nearby 'Morris'. The first attempt against 'Hillman' was made by a single infantry company augmented by a breaching platoon and three mine clearance teams. Had the divisional leadership known of the true extent of 'Hillman's' defences, the problem would undoubtedly have been approached far differently. Urgency notwithstanding, to have continued the assault against 'Hillman' without reorganization and planning would have proved utterly senseless.[3]

Further, the idea that the division was somehow 'overtrained' is absurd. Previous experience in earlier amphibious operations in the Mediterranean had all too clearly confirmed the precise opposite. While any training is by its very nature repetitive, there is simply no evidence to suggest the 3rd Division had gone 'stale' by D-Day. General Tapp disputes any suggestion the division was overtrained, pointing out that: 'I do not believe a formation can ever be overtrained for such a complicated operation as an assault landing.'[4] A number of men lost their lives during the OVERLORD training and the landings the morning of 6 June were accomplished through heavy machine-gun, small arms, mortar and artillery fire.

Divisional historian Scarfe comments that: 'While we had been warned that casualties could be as high as 80% and so tended not to look forward with any great personal cocksure-

---

[1] See Chapter 16. On D+7 General Rennie was wounded when his jeep hit a mine; he was evacuated to England and replaced by Major General L. G. Whistler.

[2] Norman Scarfe, letter to the author, 15 February 1982.

[3] When the German defenders of 'Hillman' emerged the following morning to be taken prisoner, there were 270 officers and men, including a full colonel.

[4] Major General Sir Nigel Tapp, loc.cit.

JUNO

Third Canadian Division

le Hamel
Asnelles sur Mer
50 Brit Div
Mont Fleury
la Rivière
Vaux
Meuvaines
Ver sur Mer
Graye sur Mer
Courseulles sur Mer
Bernières sur Mer
St Aubin sur Mer 48Cdo
7 Brit Div (elts)
Crépon
Ste Croix sur Mer
Langrune sur Mer
8 Cdn
51 Brit Div (elts)
Banville
8 Cdn
Taillville
Bazenville
Tierceville
Reviers
2 Cdn
736
Villiers le Sec
Colombiers sur Seulles
Bény sur Mer
Douvre
Creully
Third Canadian Division
R. Seulles
St Gabriel
Fontaine Henry
Basly
69 Brit
7 Cdn
9 Cdn
21 Panzer Division
Rucqueville
le Fresne Camilly
Colomby sur Thaon
Anguerny
Coulombs
Thaon
Anisy
Bayeux
Villons
les Buissons
R. Mue
Cambes
736 Ger
Secqueville en Bessin
Galmanche
Buron
Loucelles
Bronay
Bretteville l'Orgueilleuse
St Contest
Putot en Bessin
Authie
716 Ger Div
Cristot
Norrey en Bessin
la Villeneuve
CAEN
St Mauvieu
Fontenay le Pesnel
Carpiquet
Airfield
R. Odon
R. Orne
0 1 2 3 4 5 Kilometres
0 1 2 3 Miles
12 SS Panzer Div (elts)
(Night – 6 June)

THE ORNE BRIDGEHEAD

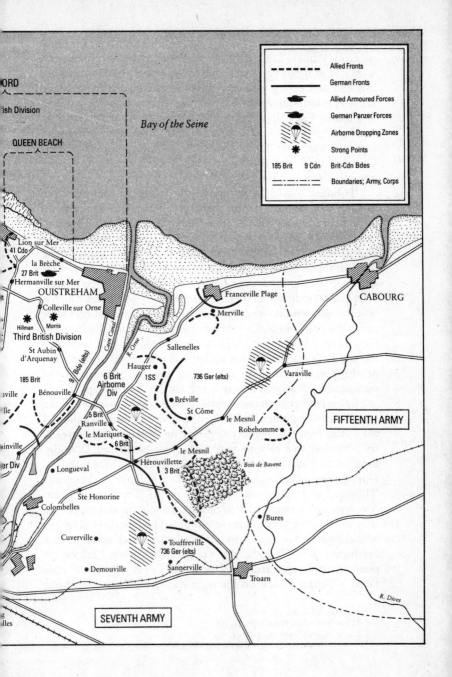

Bay of the Seine

QUEEN BEACH

ORD

ish Division

| Allied Fronts |
| German Fronts |
| Allied Armoured Forces |
| German Panzer Forces |
| Airborne Dropping Zones |
| Strong Points |
| 185 Brit 9 Cdn Brit-Cdn Bdes |
| Boundaries; Army, Corps |

Lion sur Mer
41 Cdo
la Brèche
27 Brit
Hermanville sur Mer
OUISTREHAM
Colleville sur Orne
Hillman   Morris
Third British Division
St Aubin
d'Arquenay
185 Brit
Bénouville
5 Brit
Ranville
le Mariquet
6 Brit
Longueval
Ste Honorine
Colombelles
Cuverville
Demouville

Franceville Plage
Merville
CABOURG

Sallenelles
Hauger
1SS
736 Ger (elts)
Varaville

6 Brit
Airborne
Div
Bréville
St Côme
le Mesnil
Robehomme

FIFTEENTH ARMY

le Mesnil
Hérouvillette
3 Brit
Bois de Bavent

Bures

Touffreville
736 Ger (elts)
Sannerville
Troarn

R. Dives

SEVENTH ARMY

Cam Canal
R. Orne
9 (Bde (elts)
elts)

inville
r Div
ville
le

ness, this is not to suggest that in our thinking and our training we were not properly equipped to carry on after D-Day. Moreover, this had no bearing whatever on the exercises, training and the familiar plans – all of which specifically embraced moving inland and taking Caen. In addition, the two follow-through brigades had been given no such warnings. Our feelings were that if we did not take Caen on D-Day, we'd surely take it on D plus 1. Certainly we felt pretty disappointed and frustrated NOT to have got into Caen as planned on D-Day.'[1]

'Hillman' was by no means the only complication to befall the 3rd Division on the afternoon of 6 June. The Norfolks ran into pockets of German resistance around St Aubin D'Arquenay and were held up: an area east of St Aubin had been chosen as the glider landing site for 6th Airlanding Brigade due to reinforce the 6th Airborne bridgehead that evening. The Warwicks were detached to clear the area of enemy fire. As General Tapp relates: 'The glider landing area was dotted with telegraph poles which it was thought would wreck the gliders. The Royal Engineers were to cut the posts but could not begin on this task until the area was clear of enemy fire. The thought seems to be logical but I watched the whole operation and the gliders either snapped off the poles or the poles sheared off a piece of the wing. None of the occupants appeared to be any worse for this contretemps.'[2]

By early afternoon the division learned of the presence of the 21st Panzer when the 185th Brigade ran into the 2nd Battalion of the 192nd Panzer Grenadier Regiment on Périers Ridge. 'Already the Division was face to face with the 21st Panzer Division, thought to have been from 10 to 30 miles south of Caen.'[3]* During their advance that afternoon the KSLI managed to evade 'Hillman' and made solid progress in the direction of Caen. Along the way, one squadron of tanks caught up and supported the capture of Bieville. From the vicinity of Bieville the KSLI made a bold dash for Caen, only to be forced to fall back under intense fire from Lebisey Wood about a mile further south. Lacking the planned flank and armoured support, Colonel Maurice now faced a panzer attack on his right flank; with no other force

---

[1] Norman Scarfe, loc.cit.
[2] Major General Sir Nigel Tapp, loc.cit.
[3] Scarfe, *Assault Division*, op.cit., p. 83.
* Why this impression persisted in the face of the Second Army warning is not clear.

nearby to assist he was unable to deal with both problems simultaneously and was forced to withdraw to Bieville. General Tapp comments that 'Although the KSLI got two companies into Lebisey Wood the battalion was in a very exposed position – no protection on the right or left flanks and nothing coming up behind. There were sounds of German tanks milling about on the ground between Lebisey and Caen, and other German tanks burning to the west of Lebisey Wood. Furthermore, the Lebisey ridge is very 'flat' and the corn was high, so visibility was poor. In the circumstances the Battalion commander decided to consolidate his position round Bieville and Beuville. During the night the Germans heavily reinforced Lebisey with elements of 21 Panzer and 12 (SS) Panzer – it was to be six weeks before they were ejected.'[1]

The performance of the KSLI on D-Day was brilliant but not without a high price in casualties: 113 officers and men either died or were wounded, mainly in and around Lebisey Wood.[2] Brigadier Smith revisited the scene after the war and has called it the key to Caen. Lebisey was, notes Smith, 'A long, straggly village with narrow, heavily wooded lanes and commanding views of the whole area, north, south, east and west and with a small tributary of the Orne and marshy land on both sides; it was a very formidable obstacle. But it was not so revealed in the air photographs as I found to my cost on D-Day and D plus 1. The companies of the KSLI reaching Lebisey had a tough reception; both company commanders were killed and the decision was rightly made to retire to Bieville.'[3] Lebisey Wood sits less than three miles from the centre of Caen and only slightly over a mile from its northern suburbs. It was the closest any element of the 3rd Division got to Caen on D-Day or, for that matter, until the second week in July.

At the close of D-Day the 3rd Division occupied a salient running from Blainville-sur-Orne, on the Orne Canal, west to

[1] Major General Sir Nigel Tapp, loc.cit. At 1800 hours the KSLI commander realized that further progress was hopeless and, with casualties already running high, he ordered the lead company to withdraw after dark to Bieville, which it successfully did around 2315 hours. War Diary, 2nd Bn, KSLI.

[2] Scarfe, *Assault Division*, op.cit., p. 91. Casualties to the KSLI equated to 14% of the unit strength. The 8th Brigade infantry battalions suffered similar losses: 1st Bn, The East Yorkshire Regiment: 65 killed, 141 wounded; 1st Bn, The South Lancashire Regiment: 107 killed or wounded.

[3] Brigadier K. Pearce Smith, loc.cit.

Bieville and thence north to Lion-Sur-Mer on SWORD beach. There had as yet been no linkup with the 3rd Canadian Division, leaving the Germans in nominal control of a four-mile-wide gap caused, in part, by the only attempted German counterattack of the day.

As effective as the hot reception the KSLI received from the Germans in the Lebisey Wood was the action of the 21st Panzer, part of which was emplaced around Périers Ridge where, late in the afternoon, the first panzers appeared and the first counterattack of the day was launched. D-Day had been one of the most frustrating of Feuchtinger's life; he later claimed that from the first notification of British paratroop landings around the Orne, which came in shortly after midnight, until 0730 hours the morning of 6 June, he received no orders to counter the invasion: the alarm system supposed to take effect in the event of invasion was never used.[1] The lack of flexibility existing in the German command structure was never more in evidence than now. Feuchtinger insisted that he had explicit instructions from Army Group B not to move his division. In the absence of new orders the 21st Panzer sat in place.

At 0500 hours Army Group B passed control of the 21st Panzer to the Seventh Army but Feuchtinger relates that he was not aware of this until 0700 hours, and even then he received no guidance. Yet 'By 5.30 a.m. on D-Day Feuchtinger had a clear picture of the 6th Airborne positions in Ranville and on the Bois de Bavent Ridge. He telephoned Army Group B to ask permission to attack and recapture the Orne River and Caen Canal bridges, but it was refused.'[2] At 0630 he could bear the indecision no longer and ordered two of his panzer grenadier battalions to attack the airborne forces. Finally, at 0730 he telephoned the Seventh Army and Speidel at Army Group B to seek permission for a full-scale counterattack to drive the British from the Orne bridgehead, but received authority only for the limited attack by the grenadiers. '21st Panzer now learned that its anti-aircraft units, deployed to protect the likely routes forward of the division, were being smashed by air attacks. For Feuchtinger this was the last straw. Deciding that he must attack the airborne division landings without waiting for anyone's permission, he ordered his

---

[1] Feuchtinger interrogation, loc.cit.
[2] Napier Crookenden, *Dropzone Normandy*, New York, 1976, p. 234.

division to move forward to concentration areas in the Chicheboville Woods south of Cagny as a preliminary to a full-scale attack on Ranville and the Orne bridges. By 7.30 22nd Panzer Regiment was at last on the move after a five-hour wait beside their tanks.'[1] Sometime after 0900 hours Feuchtinger was placed under the command of the LXXXIV Corps which was already over burdened with the attempt to direct the efforts of the infantry divisions along the invasion front.[2]

Rommel's earlier decision to split the division and Speidel's indecision on the morning of 6 June combined to produce a delayed reaction that had grave consequences for the Germans. Precious hours were wasted at the precise moment when the invaders were the most vulnerable to a counterattack. Once they did begin to move, it was found that the only bridge north of Caen was under British control and it was necessary to detour through Caen itself in order to mount an attack against the 3rd Division. Thus it was mid-afternoon before Feuchtinger was able to assemble and move a panzer regiment to the west bank of the Orne to deal with the British advance south of Périers Ridge towards Caen.

Early that evening a battlegroup of about fifty panzers and an infantry battalion were on the move into the gap between the Canadians and the British. When this force attacked a British strongpoint manned by a squadron of Lieutenant Colonel J. A. Eadie's Staffordshire Yeomanry which was then anchoring the 3rd Division's right flank, they received a sharp rebuff. Instead of catching the British by surprise, thirteen panzers were quickly knocked out of action. The swift parry of this panzer thrust was no stroke of good fortune, for Colonel Eadie had predicted back in May exactly what the Germans would do. General Tapp vividly recalls a tactical discussion during which Eadie stated: 'I know what the German armour will do. They will drive their command tanks onto an eminence effectively out of range of my six pounders [about 1,000 yards], make a quick plan, get back

---

[1] Crookenden, op.cit., p. 234.
[2] Feuchtinger interrogation, loc.cit. An unresolved question concerns Feuchtinger's whereabouts the night of 5–6 June. David Irving in *The Trail of the Fox* states that he was away in Paris and blames Rommel's Chief of Staff, General Speidel, for refusing to release the 21st Panzer earlier, despite the frantic pleading of General Marcks, the LXXXIV Corps commander. Rommel's naval advisor, Admiral Friedrich Ruge, says he heard the same but cannot substantiate it. Feuchtinger claims he was at his post during the critical hours beginning at the time of the airborne landings.

into their tanks before any effective field artillery concentration can be brought to bear, and withdraw behind the ridge. They will form up their squadrons, give out their orders, then drive straight for their objective. What they do not know is that I have three troops of 'Fireflies' [Sherman tanks with 17 pounder guns – a well kept secret] which I will station on Hermanville ridge and leave as a backstop.'[1] This is precisely what happened the afternoon of 6 June and Feuchtinger later effusively praised the excellence of the British anti-tank defences which stopped his counterattack dead in its tracks.[2]

Despite this setback, a small tank-infantry force slipped through the gap and reached the coast at Lion-sur-Mer. Finding the defences there intact the Germans were about to begin reinforcing when by a sheer coincidence of timing nearly 250 gliders accompanied by heavy fighter cover flew overhead and landed near the Orne at St Aubin, in the area cleared by the Warwicks earlier that afternoon. This was the 6th Airlanding Brigade reinforcing the Orne bridgehead exactly as scheduled. Mistakenly believing that this powerful force was landing in the same area and would certainly trap them, this 21st Panzer taskforce hastily abandoned their attempt to hold open the gap. It was yet another German blunder. 'This was the time for a counter-stroke. The assault forces were tired and strung out in a series of hastily-prepared positions. The weather had so delayed the unloading that tanks, anti-tank guns and artillery had not been brought forward in the strength which had been planned. The line was thin and there were gaps which cried out for exploitation. But the Germans were not in a position to take advantage of the opportunity which was offered that night and that night alone. Too many hours had been wasted while the Supreme Command was making up its mind.'[3]

Although they had withdrawn from the gap by dark, the 21st Panzer was still able to block the approaches to Caen. The division had been largely ineffective on D-Day, losing over fifty tanks; nevertheless, it had still managed to prevent forward elements of the 3rd Division from gaining Caen. Moreover, by this time the 12th SS Panzer Division was on the move toward

[1] Major General Sir Nigel Tapp, loc.cit.
[2] Feuchtinger interrogation, loc.cit.
[3] Wilmot, op.cit., p. 314.

Caen from the vicinity of Lisieux and by nightfall some units had reached the Odon southwest of the city, while other divisions were also beginning to move on Caen from south and east. Belatedly, orders for countermeasures came in from OKW and OB West to destroy the enemy in the bridgehead. The two divisions defending Caen (the 21st Panzer and the 716th Infantry) were switched to control of 1 SS Panzer Corps whose veteran commander, SS General Joseph 'Sepp' Dietrich, was ordered by von Rundstedt to 'throw the enemy landed near Caen back into the sea'.[1][*] By that evening Rommel had returned to his headquarters at La Roche Guyon after a headlong all-day dash by automobile from his home near Ulm, and was once again in command of the German Front.

The events which took place on D-Day in the Orne bridgehead were, for the most part, a series of unexpected situations and missed opportunities. The Germans bungled a rare opportunity to interfere with the consolidation of the twin bridgeheads on both sides of the Orne, and later the chance to exploit the dangerous gap between the Canadians and the British. The 8th Brigade was behind schedule and unable rapidly to overcome 'Hillman', the 185th Brigade was fragmented in unforeseen tasks, and the leading elements of the 27th Armoured Brigade were trapped on the beaches and the roads leading south toward Caen near 'Hillman', and in defending the gap between the two divisions. Only by committing the reserve 9th Brigade did the 3rd Division retain any hope of attaining its D-Day objectives. That brigade had successfully landed shortly after midday and had the mission of pressing straight down the right flank to capture Carpiquet Airfield and, if possible, the western edge of Caen. The brigade commander, Brigadier J. C. Cunningham, went immediately to Hermanville where to his amazement he found Rennie and Crocker conferring over a map by a broken orchard wall. Reporting to his superiors, Cunningham exclaimed: 'I've never seen anything like this. I've been in half a dozen campaigns

---

[1] 'I SS Panzer Corps in the West (1944)', Manuscript C-024, German Report Series Foreign Military Studies, US Army Military History Institute.

[*] This order was received by telephone at 1500 hours, 6 June, shortly after 1 SS Panzer Corps was assigned to Army control. The Corps was part of Geyr von Schweppenburg's Panzer Group West and had thus been outside the control of Army Group B and the Seventh Army prior to this assignment.

but never before have I been beaten onto the battlefield, not only by my Divisional but my Corps Commander!' Matters became more serious as the two generals instructed Cunningham to disregard his original mission and move the 9th Brigade to cover the approaches to Pegasus Bridge, the only crossing over the Orne and Orne Canal north of Caen between Benouville and Ranville. The Corps commander was growing increasingly concerned over the state of the beleaguered airborne. Until reinforced by the 6th Airlanding Brigade that evening, Gale's toehold east of the Orne was extremely tenuous, but of particular concern to Crocker was the security of Pegasus Bridge. If that were lost all British forces east of the Orne would be trapped. With this thought in mind Crocker ordered Cunningham to cancel his original mission and move immediately to the bridge. Cunningham half-seriously remonstrated with Crocker by saying: 'I'm all teed up to capture Caen after [securing] Carpiquet and know exactly what to do. I must stick to my objective.' 'Sorry,' he was told, 'we know it's bad luck but you will have to go and help them.'[1]* Crocker's decision was made shortly after 1300 hours and set the final seal to British hopes of capturing Caen on D-Day.

The necessity for Crocker's decision is not difficult to understand; his task was to capture Caen and Carpiquet Airfield while at the same time ensuring the left flank of the bridgehead held firm against any counterattack the Germans might throw at his units. Crocker's operational order had been issued on 5 May and reflected exactly Montgomery's demand for speed and initiative on D-Day: 'The task of the assaulting divisions is to break through the coastal defences and advance some 10 miles inland on D-Day. Great speed and boldness will be required to achieve this. It will be necessary to forestall the action of the enemy's local reserves quickly, to overcome minor resistance met during the advance, to get set before the arrival of reserve formations, and be ready to meet the enemy's first counter attacks,

---

[1] Unpublished account by Brigadier J. C. Cunningham, IWM.
* Moments after his returning to HQ a mortar bomb seriously wounded Brigadier Cunningham and either killed or wounded most of his staff. The 9th Brigade ended D-Day split in three separate locations: the 1st Battalion, The King's Own Scottish Borderers was sent to reinforce the area between St Aubin d'Arquenay and the bridge at Bénouville; the 2nd Battalion, The Ulster Rifles were inserted between the other two brigades on the right flank around Périers; and the 2nd Battalion, The Lincolnshire Regiment remained in the brigade assembly area near Plumentot.

which must be expected to develop by the evening of D-Day.'[1]

In line with Montgomery's requirements Crocker ordered that: 'As soon as the beach defences have been penetrated, not a moment must be lost in beginning the advance inland. Armour should be used boldly from the start. Such action will forestall the enemy's reaction, confuse him, magnify his fears and enable ground to be made quickly. All available artillery must be ready to support the advance.[2] If opposition is met which cannot be overcome by these strong advance guards, simple plans embodying the full resources of artillery and armour must be employed to dislodge the enemy quickly and certainly.'[3]

The plan Crocker developed, in addition to capturing Caen, called for a deep and rapid thrust approximately fifteen miles due south by the 2nd Canadian Armoured Brigade to secure the high ground around the town of Evrecy which controlled the approaches to the Odon and Orne from the southwest. With control of the Orne bridgehead, Caen, Carpiquet Airfield, and the high ground around Evrecy, 1 Corps would dominate the most important terrain features in the Caen sector and make it difficult for the Germans to interfere with the buildup taking place on the beaches. In the event of counterattack, Crocker's specific instructions to the 3rd Division were to 'before dark on D-Day, have captured or effectively masked Caen.'[4] When he had issued this order in May, Crocker was unaware of the presence of the 21st Panzer and there is no evidence that he knew differently prior to 6 June. Yet Crocker's operational order is the real culprit: it provided a grossly misleading picture of the Orne bridgehead by suggesting that there would be only minor resistance during the attack on Caen – the impression given to Brigadier Smith and the other D-Day commanders was that of a lightly-defended sector. Although German armour was always a serious problem, the 21st Panzer contained no Tiger tanks and the British Shermans would be capable of dealing with the threat.

[1] 1 Corps Operational Order No. 1, 5 May 1944, PRO (WO 171/258).

[2] Critics of the 3rd Division are more than likely unaware that immediately after landing on the morning of 6 June, Lieutenant Colonel Tapp's 7th Field Regiment moved so quickly inland to deploy their guns in the fields south of Hermanville that for a time they were actually the leading element of the division and were in front of the southernmost infantry in that sector of the 3rd Division front (Cf., Assault Division, p. 79).

[3] PRO (WO 171/258).

[4] 1 Corps Operational Order No. 1, loc.cit.

The real menace, however, were the powerful German anti-tank guns, which were capable of stopping a British advance by knocking out the tanks supporting the infantry. The general faults on the part of the British senior commanders on D-Day are well illustrated not only by their failure to heed their intelligence – which suggested a far different picture of the potential German reaction – but also by their failure to probe more deeply into the nature of the German defences in this part of the Orne bridgehead.

Could Caen have been captured by the 3rd Division on D-Day? More importantly, could the city have been held once captured? The answer to these questions can, of course, only be speculative, but on the basis of what is now known the answer to both questions appears to be 'no' – not with the 21st Panzer prowling the flanks around Caen, its overall command ineptness notwithstanding. General Tapp agrees: 'I am sure the Division could not have reached Caen without the armour.' The divisional historian supports this view, adding: 'But the question Chester Wilmot and the others didn't seriously ask was whether, even with the planned marry-up between the KSLI and Staffs Yeomanry, and the dash for Caen by these two battalions at midday on D-Day, they would have been able to take Caen with 21st Panzer Division already ensconced there. I doubt it. I think that if they got in, they'd have been ambushed and probably very badly mangled and lucky to pull back in any order. To have taken, according to plan, a bridgehead across the Orne in Caen would have needed, in the existing circumstances, some sort of miracle. Given the presence of 21st Panzer it was *not* reasonable for us to expect – or be expected – to take Caen on D-Day.[1]

Brigadier Smith believes Caen could have been taken only if four prerequisites had been met:

(1) That the 8th Brigade capture 'Morris' and 'Hillman' fairly quickly.

(2) That the supporting armour disembark in time fully to support the drive on Caen by the 185th Brigade.

(3) That the 185th Brigade and the Staffordshire Yeomanry reach Caen *before* 21st Panzer arrived on the scene.

[1] Norman Scarfe, letter to the author of 15 February 1982.

(4) That there was no unexpected opposition – particularly around Lebisey.

'None of these four provisos materialized and that is why Caen did not fall on D-Day.'[1]

Thus, while Rennie's original plan to capture Caen was certainly ambitious it was not unreasonable, provided the German defences were limited to the 716th Division and provided other circumstances did not arise to cause unnecessary delay. The merits of the British plan for the Orne bridgehead will be long debated but it is unfair to pin responsibility for the failure to secure Caen on the 3rd Division. If the divisional leadership at times erred on the side of caution the reasons seem justifiable, and it must be remembered that it was General Crocker who made the decision to remove the 9th Brigade from the drive on Caen. None of this has prevented some stinging criticism of the 3rd Division, most recently by Major General Belchem, who disapproved of virtually every aspect of their D-Day performance.[2]

However, any assessment of this unit can only be made on the basis of all factors and on D-Day, as we have seen, almost nothing other than the assault on the beaches went according to plan. The important independent armoured brigades were missing. Each of the three assault divisions had been assigned an armoured brigade to land as a follow-up element providing firepower and mobility, protection for the assault battalions, and additional strength for the deep thrusts inland envisioned by Montgomery. The slower than anticipated progress of the lead infantry and delays in landing these armoured units left them little opportunity to penetrate the German defences and establish themselves on key objectives. By midnight on D-Day the entire 27th Armoured Brigade was ashore, but except for the Staffordshire Yeomanry (whose role turned out to be essentially defensive because of the appearance of the 21st Panzer), it had not played any major role in the attempt to capture Caen.[3] In assessing the role of the

---

[1] Brigadier K. Pearce Smith, loc.cit.
[2] Belchem, *Victory in Normandy*, op.cit., pp. 109–10.
[3] Due to stiff German resistance the 3rd Canadian Division fell far short of its D-Day objectives. The 9th Canadian Infantry Brigade on the left flank ended up over four miles north of Carpiquet Airfield, while the 2nd Canadian Armoured Brigade was not only unable to push to Evrecy but never came close to its alternative objective of the Odon River. The armoured cars of the Inns of Court Regiment had been given the special mission of driving quickly and deeply behind German lines to destroy all crossings over

independent armoured brigades it is important to understand the mobility and firepower each represented to the divisions they supported. Each brigade consisted of three tank regiments and possessed an overall strength of approximately 190 medium (Sherman) tanks and 33 light tanks. The powerful armoured fingers that Montgomery had intended to run deep into the German vitals were: the 27th Armoured Brigade to support the 3rd (Br) Division drive on Caen; the 2nd Canadian Armoured Brigade who were to secure the high ground around Evrecy[1]; and the 8th Armoured Brigade Group which was to dominate the area around Villers-Bocage with the object of holding up German forces moving toward the bridgehead.[2]

If the results in the Orne bridgehead were less successful than planned, the Allied landings had nevertheless been a phenomenal success despite the perilous position in the OMAHA sector and even though it had not been possible to consolidate the five assault areas into one contiguous front. In general, the three essential conditions for success had been met. The *surprise* of the operation had been beyond all expectations; the deception that Normandy was merely a feint continued until early August when the Germans finally realized that they had been hoaxed and that there never would be a second invasion in the Pas de Calais. Allied *mastery of the air* was total. The Luftwaffe was hardly to be seen and most aircraft showing an inclination to fight were shot down. An example of the pitiful state of the once elite and powerful Luftwaffe was seen in the British zone. During the first twenty-four hours of OVERLORD a meagre thirty-six enemy aircraft were observed.[3] The timidity of the Luftwaffe (some Germans called it cowardice) during the campaign was to prove the greatest adverse morale factor to the Germans defending

---

the Orne from St Andre-sur-Orne to Thury-Harcourt in order to prevent or delay the movement of enemy reserves. 'C' Squadron lost some of its vehicles during the assault landing and others on the beaches, and was unable to begin its dash for the Orne due to heavy beach congestion. On 6 June its armoured cars attained neither the primary objective of the Orne crossings nor the alternative objective of the Odon.

[1] War Diary, 2nd Canadian Armoured Brigade, PRO (WO 179/2839). After capturing Evrecy the brigade was intended subsequently to seize and dominate the high ground between the Odon and the Orne; push forward patrols to the Orne, and to take over the mission of blowing the Orne crossings in the event that 'C' Squadron, Inns of Court Regiment failed to do so.

[2] War Diary, 8th Armoured Brigade Group, PRO (WO 171/613).

[3] Ellis, op.cit., p. 212.

Normandy. As Rommel had feared, lack of airpower also doomed German hopes of defeating the Allies.

Preventing the buildup of enemy land forces proved, for the most part, to be successful. Allied domination of the air made any movement on the ground a living hell and German units moving toward Normandy soon found reason to curse the missing Luftwaffe. Over the long term the success of the Transportation Plan which had decimated the French rail and road networks into Normandy was the single most important factor in the Allied gains.

For the German Army in France, D-Day was disastrous. Of the many mistakes in evidence that day the greatest seems to have been Rommel's unfortunate absence in Germany to visit his wife, Lucie, whose birthday fell, ironically, on 6 June. The following day he was to have journeyed to Berchtesgaden to make a final attempt to convince Hitler of the foolishness of the German defensive posture in Normandy. According to Speidel: 'Rommel wished once more to expound to Hitler the military and political facts of the situation and demand a change in the top-level organization and bringing up of reserves of all three arms of the Wehrmacht.'[1]

Rommel's forceful presence on 6 June could substantially have changed events. One who believes this is General Siegfried Westphal, von Rundstedt's able and respected Chief-of-Staff, who has remarked: '[Rommel] would not have put up with the holding back of the Panzer divisions by the OKW in the hinterland, as was the case. In my opinion High Command West and Army Group B yielded too readily on the 1st day of the landing. Rommel, most probably, would have tackled Hitler personally on the telephone.'[2]

Aside from the failure promptly to commit the 21st Panzer, the other great German mistake on D-Day was the unnecessary absence of the 12th SS Panzer Division from Caen. Its commander was a battle-hardened and exceptionally able panzer leader, SS Major General Kurt Meyer, who had learned his craft in the bloody campaigns of Roumania and Russia. Although Meyer was still a colonel in command of a regiment on D-Day, he took

---

[1] 'OB West, A Study in Command', Manuscript B-308, German Report Series, Foreign Military Studies, US Army Military History Institute.
[2] German Generals' Collection, Liddell Hart Papers, King's College, London.

over command of the division within days as the youngest major general in the German Army. Meyer was a determined and fanatical commander who was not deterred by adversity.[1] There had been a heavy cloud cover the entire morning of 6 June and the 12th SS could have moved for some six hours untroubled by Allied aircraft. As it was, when finally told by OKW to move into Caen, the cloud cover had gone and the division took a pounding when it began its move from Lisieux later that afternoon. Throughout the battle for Normandy, Meyer and the young toughs of his 'Hitler Jugend' division proved a deadly thorn in the Allied hide. It was nothing less than a stroke of Allied good fortune that kept them from being a major threat on 6 June.

On that momentous day over 130,000 Allied ground troops and over 23,000 airborne were landed in Normandy. In spite of the unexpected setbacks at OMAHA, where the toehold around the beaches was still slender but gradually improving, the invasion had been a stunning success. Wilmot has suggested that Montgomery was perhaps not totally serious about his plan to thrust his armoured brigades deep into the Normandy country-side to peg out claims as far south as Evrecy (1 Corps sector) and Villers-Bocage (in the western sector of 30 Corps near the boundary between Dempsey's Second British Army and Brad-ley's First US Army), and that the Allied ground commander had deliberately left this idea in the plan. 'This bold, indeed impudent aspect of the plan was included by Montgomery (and retained on his insistence even after the palpable strengthening of the Ger-man defences in Normandy during May) so that his troops would have a star to strive for, and would not miss opportunities of exploitation for lack of orders as had happened at Gallipoli.'[2]

[1] More so than any other German commander in Normandy, Meyer embodied the conception of the fanatical Nazi who would fight to the death for his beloved Führer. Few German officers could claim more combat experience than Meyer, who had begun his service with the SS in 1933 as a member of Hitler's elite bodyguard. In 1939 he fought in Poland and in 1940 in Holland and France. As a regimental commander he played a leading role in the Greek campaign. According to his interrogation report, when Hitler invaded Russia he was at the forefront of the drive to the east. 'For three years he fought in Russia reaching almost the furthest point to be achieved by German forces, deep into the remote Caucasus. Three times he was completely encircled by Russian forces during the retreat, and fought his way out with a handful of survivors. . . To him the battle of Caen-Falaise was magnificent in the best Wagnerian tradition. As he described his actions and those of his men, it seemed as though he liked to consider himself as Siegfried leading his warriors to their death.' Interrogation of SS Major General Kurt Meyer, n.d., German Generals Collection, Liddell Hart Papers, King's College, London.

[2] Wilmot, op.cit., p. 291.

To rationalize this aspect of Montgomery's plan as merely a leadership device is to understate his motives. As we have already seen, Montgomery's intentions, while admittedly audacious, were conceived in the light of his previous experience and in the firm belief that Rommel's forces would be an exceedingly tough nut to crack if they were given time to recover their wits and organize strong defensive measures and possible counterattacks. Montgomery's reasoning lay in the strategic importance of the objectives assigned to his assault units. If the primary element of surprise could be achieved there was certainly a reasonable prospect of these objectives being attained quickly. Moreover, it was his perception that once attained these strategic points would not only give him the whip hand, but would threaten the entire German hold on the eastern flank of the bridgehead. In short, this aspect of his plan was entirely consistent with the overall master plan. While it certainly proved overly ambitious in the end, it was a risk well worth the taking and, if achieved, would probably have turned the tide of the campaign in his favour at once.

The story of Normandy as it eventually evolved established beyond doubt the correctness of Montgomery's thinking: had events turned out differently he would have been hailed for a boldness and audacity that rivalled the achievements of Patton in August. As it was, the plan fell far short of expectations and the result was abuse and criticism from his critics, foremost among them Omar Bradley, who accused him of being the same old, overcautious Monty, of promising much and delivering little. In turn, much of the blame has unfairly fallen upon the 3rd Division. They were asked to achieve what turned out to be the impossible. The very boldness of Montgomery's plan ensured that the price of failure would be serious consequences and, as we shall see, Montgomery unfortunately helped to perpetuate the problem by his own actions and denials.

On the night of 6 June Winston Churchill addressed an excited and packed House of Commons, telling the assembled MPs of the great Allied achievement: 'This vast operation is undoubtedly the most complicated and difficult that has ever taken place . . . and the whole process of opening this great new front will be pursued with the utmost resolution both by the commanders and by the United States and British Governments whom they serve.'[1] Churchill had always privately predicted that the campaign in Normandy would be difficult but not even he could foresee the onerous series of battles against a determined foe that would eventually reach near-stalemate before being decided during the long, hot days of August.

All this was in the future; for the moment Montgomery had more important matters on his mind. Bayeux fell on 7 June and earned the honour of being the first French city to be liberated. Caen, a tantalizing four miles away, continued to elude capture and remained in German hands for a considerable time. During the following days the failure to secure Caen and the nearby critical terrain provoked sharp controversy within the Allied High Command and altered the course of the entire campaign.

D-Day was over and the difficult and bloody battle for Normandy had begun.

[1] Winston S. Churchill, *Triumph and Tragedy*, Boston, 1953, p. 6.

CHAPTER 9

The Field of Battle

Gate to the Continent, this is the rich and varied
province of Normandy – with its apple trees which
dot the spring meadows with their white flowers,
wooded hills and shaded vales, forests, corn crops,
and abundant pastures and celebrated sand
beaches.

Recent French Tourist Guide

Unable adequately to defend three thousand miles of Atlantic
coastline and successfully hoaxed over the site of the invasion,
the German Army in the west never had any real hope of
deterring the Allies for long. As we have seen, German bungling
on D-Day precluded all but the crudest countermeasures. Only
the presence of 21st Panzer Division prevented Montgomery's
leading assault elements from securing Caen and its approaches
from the east; by the morning of 7 June the British grip on their
left flank remained extremely tenuous. The absence of the
armoured brigades had robbed Montgomery of the vital initiative required to make his bold plan work and henceforth the
German Army would make the Allies pay a high price for every
foot of ground in Normandy.

Throughout the battle of Normandy both von Rundstedt and
Rommel were severely restricted in the deployment of their forces
by Hitler, who imperiously dictated a policy of 'no withdrawal'.
After the war von Rundstedt recounted how a piecemeal commitment of the panzer divisions around Caen in a defensive role was
a 'great mistake'.[1] 'I wanted to relieve them with infantry divisions but they were always too closely engaged and anyway were
under fire from the Navy. I wanted to establish the infantry
behind the Orne, get them properly dug in, but I wasn't allowed

---

[1] Post-war interrogation of Field Marshal von Rundstedt, Liddell Hart Papers, Liddell
Hart Centre for Military Archives, King's College, London.

to yield ground [by Hitler].'[1] Hitler's orders had been issued before the invasion when he had demanded that 'Every leader, every commander of a strongpoint, of an island, of a fortress, or of a ship must pledge to me his honour that he will never surrender, that he will continue the struggle to the last fighter, to the last grenade, to the last cartridge.'[2] Shortly after D-Day Hitler repeated his orders, telling the Seventh Army: 'There can be no question of fighting a rearguard action nor of retiring to a new line of resistance. Every man shall fight or fall where he stands.'[3]

On 17 June von Rundstedt and Rommel were summoned to a meeting with Hitler at Soissons to review the situation in France. A grim Rommel 'relentlessly described the seriousness of the situation.'[4] Hitler was told: 'how impossible were the conditions under which the German soldier was being forced to fight. With von Rundstedt's support, Rommel asked Hitler to come to the front and get an accurate picture of the situation for himself by talking direct to the field commanders.'[5] He urged that no effort be made to clean up the front around Caen by offensives which would reduce the strength of the panzer divisions. Rommel and von Rundstedt were in agreement on the need to reinforce the Orne sector with infantry divisions, with the panzer divisions assembled on the flanks. It was Rommel's intention to carry out a limited withdrawal out of range of Allied naval gunfire and then launch an armoured counterstroke into the flank of Montgomery's Second British Army.[6]

Rommel's entreaties fell upon deaf ears and Hitler stuck to his policy of no withdrawal; any other solution was 'defeatism'. That night Rommel told his naval advisor, Admiral Ruge, that 'Hitler was very optimistic and calm, [and] judged the situation differently. . .'[7] Nor would Hitler accede to the requests by his two field commanders for authority to make decisions and move their forces freely in response to Allied offensive measures. The Führer never visited Normandy and nothing was changed as a result of the conference. As Rommel recorded it, victory was to be

[1] Von Rundstedt interrogation, loc.cit.
[2] Matthew Cooper, op.cit., p. 505.
[3] Ibid.
[4] Friedrich Ruge, *Rommel in Normandy*, San Rafael, 1979, p. 190.
[5] *The Rommel Papers*, ed. by B. H. Liddell Hart, New York, 1953, pp. 478–9.
[6] Ibid, p. 479.
[7] Ruge, op.cit., p. 190.

gained by 'holding fast tenaciously to every square foot of soil'.[1]

Rommel's unfinished Atlantic Wall and lack of adequate forces provided no opportunity for a strong defence; in fact without the panzer divisions to rope off the invasion area and strike a killing blow, his defences were left in tatters. Now that the invader had penetrated his beach defences, the problem became one of organizing some kind of fluid defence capable of repelling Allied penetration until such time as countermeasures utilizing the strength of the panzer divisions could be initiated.

Rommel was therefore required to improvise in order to cope with Montgomery's tactics; certainly the evolution of German defensive strategy in Normandy bore no signs of having been deliberately planned. The measures adopted by Rommel's veteran field commanders evolved from their precarious situation in the immediate post D-Day period. The set-piece battle was impossible without the strong support of the largely absent Luftwaffe, and the resulting Allied air superiority provided no opportunity to establish a proper defence in depth. Thus, as Montgomery himself would soon find, improvisation and innovation were the only viable substitutes.

The ensuing battles were not engagements between an invader and a well prepared defender able to fight a conventional land battle. Instead, the campaign in Normandy rapidly turned into a series of vicious, smaller unit actions, a classic confrontation at close quarters with no holds barred. As it is in most wars, the dirty business of winning battles fell to the infantryman. Despite the vast array of sophisticated and deadly weapons of war available to both sides, success or failure in Normandy ultimately became the ability of the foot soldier to take or hold *ground*. It was obvious to the German commanders they could now no longer win a head-on confrontation with Montgomery, so with great skill they turned the terrain to their advantage in order to minimize Allied air and artillery superiority.

Unlike North Africa where two opposing forces could manoeuvre freely, the close, confined terrain of Normandy provided a natural advantage to the defender – a terrain dominated by the bocage over some fifty miles, generally between the Orne and Vire Rivers. The bocage is a series of small fields ringed by

---

[1] *The Rommel Papers*, op.cit., p. 479.

earthen banks three or four feet high and overgrown with dense shrubbery, making it impossible to see beyond a single field at a time. Dirt tracks criss-crossed the bocage around the edges of these small fields, permitting troops and equipment to move relatively free from observation either from the air or the ground. Thousands of such fields each became a battleground which the Germans cleverly turned into a death trap. The soldiers who fought there remember the battle of Normandy as a never-ending series of firefights for the right of possession.

The bocage also includes a series of streams, rivers, and steep hills and valleys, all of which favoured the defender. In the middle of Normandy, some twenty miles due south of Bayeux, stands Mont Pinçon, the highest point in the region, 1200 feet above sea level astride a vast plateau. This particular region is even denser and more difficult to fight in than the other parts of the bocage: roads virtually disappear and forests abound; in tourist books this region is so much like that of Switzerland including dense fog in summer and winter alike, that it is called *la Suisse Normande*. Indeed, the first-time visitor to the bocage finds a region of France almost untouched by time and a modern world.

The British sector extending east from Bayeux to the Orne was part bocage and part rolling farm land punctuated by small farming hamlets and small woods. Several important terrain features dominate the approaches to Caen from east and west: the Caen-Falaise Plain, Carpiquet Airfield five miles due west of Caen, and Hill 112, five miles southwest of Caen between the Orne and Odon Rivers. East and southeast of Caen the countryside turns from farm land into a series of steep, wooded hills and ridges to the east of the River Dives, forming a natural defensive barrier. The Germans had created a further obstruction by flooding the lowlands of the Dives between Troarn and Cabourg. In the west the bocage disappears and is replaced by the reclaimed marshlands of the Cotentin Peninsula – a difficult area for the deployment of armoured forces, which were generally restricted to the road network. In anticipation of an invasion Rommel had ordered that the Vire estuary be flooded and potential landing sites covered with long steel or wooden spikes known as *Rommelspargel* (Rommel's asparagus), many of which were cleverly booby-trapped with mines or artillery shells. The flooding of the

Vire created yet another obstacle to a linkup with American forces from OMAHA and UTAH beaches.

It was this combination of terrain and the unforeseen presence of the 21st Panzer Division which held up Montgomery's D-Day advance around Caen. The key to defending Normandy lay in blunting the effectiveness of Montgomery's armoured formations and his air support. Unable to employ their forces as they would have liked, the Germans rapidly developed new measures to elude devastation from the air. A post-war analysis revealed how the Germans had brilliantly used the bocage to the best possible advantage and in the process reduced the effects of Allied air attacks by up to 75%. The Germans tended to dispose their defences throughout the disorderly maze of copses, woods and hedgerows, thus making them unprofitable targets for artillery and air. The result was that most of the time the air forces were less effective as an offensive weapon than imagined. As the study noted, the heavy bomb attacks against Caen and its surrounding villages were used as substitutes for heavy assault-tank attacks, but German dispersal tended to blunt their effectiveness. Thus, 'The air weapon in Normandy proved more effective as a defensive weapon against the enemy attack than as a means of attacking an enemy deployed in defence.'[1]

The author of this study, Arthur Davies, pointed out how the bocage with its combination of open spaces and woods invited tank operations yet provided a marked advantage for a defender:

> [The bocage] proved the most dangerous terrain of the whole campaign for tanks in the attack. The bocage was first-rate country for the employment of infantry anti-tank weapons and the light machine gun (Bren or Spandau). Here determined infantry, armed with rocket tubes or bazookas can remain hidden until a tank is within 50 yards and can destroy all but a very heavy tank with one shot. By defending Normandy rather than establishing the main defence line along the Seine, the Germans pinned the invaders down to the shortest possible front and protected the whole of France.[2]

The most deadly weapon in the German arsenal was the 88-mm anti-aircraft gun, first used to great effect by Rommel in North Africa. In Normandy a refined version was in use as a dual-

[1] Paper by Arthur Davies: 'Geographical Factors in the Invasion and Battle of Normandy', Liddell Hart Papers, n.d., King's College, London.
[2] Ibid.

purpose weapon: in addition to its capability against aircraft it could knock out any Allied tank at ranges of up to 2,000 yards and proved lethal as an anti-infantry weapon when it fired fused shells to create airbursts.[1] Easily concealed in the bocage or a fortified village, this formidable weapon was ideal for use in Normandy. No less effective was the German strategy for stalling the British advance around Caen by taking every advantage offered in the more open farm country. Here the numerous small villages were in such close proximity that they formed exceedingly difficult obstacles to an attacking force. The Germans utilized these villages to provide mutual support and create natural fortresses that covered a sector in great depth.[2]

> In most nucleated villages in western and central Europe there are near the houses garden patches which are generally surrounded by hedges, trees and walls. Outside the village are large, open communal fields, generally devoid of cover... Trees, hedges and buildings form a strong defence locality with adequate cover from air and ground observation and the open, cultivated fields between villages can be swept by machine-gun and artillery fire. Such a village is a hedgehog in a grid of hedgehogs and defensible by a small mixed force of infantry, artillery and three – four tanks.[3]

However, such defences were not without a flaw:

> A village grid of this kind has one fatal weakness. It is never deep enough and as successive villages are captured it becomes thin and ultimately cracks. To remedy this, German defensive tactics relied on quick counter attack by tanks to re-take villages before Allied troops had had time to consolidate their defences. This cost the Germans many tanks but preserved the village grid in depth.[4]

On the British front the Germans had an additional helpful terrain advantage in the form of the Orne and Odon Rivers which formed a barrier round the Caen sector east and southwest of Caen. The effect of these features was to canalize Allied operations within an area favourable to the Germans, where each natural obstacle could be used to maximum effect.

Nevertheless, Caen was a problem. Rommel could not afford

---

[1] W. J. K. Davies, *German Army Handbook, 1939–1945*, London, 1973, pp. 104–5.
[2] Arthur Davies, loc.cit.
[3] Ibid.
[4] Ibid.

to let Montgomery capture the city and the important terrain surrounding it. To do so would have meant loss of that flank, permitting the Allied armoured divisions to rampage unhindered toward the Seine and Paris, thus leaving the German position in Normandy untenable and his forces effectively trapped. The alternative was to pull back out of range of the Allied fleet and establish a strong line with far more reinforcements than were being sent to Normandy. However, Hitler's crippling 'no withdrawal' policy left Rommel no choice except to fight to hold Caen. Even without Hitler's interdict the alternative of retreating behind the Seine was equally unpalatable as Montgomery could not be permitted to build up his forces unhindered for a massive operation either to rupture the Seine defences at his leisure or to envelop them from the south.

In spite of the defensive talent displayed by his troops, Rommel was never under any illusion over the ultimate fate of his forces in Normandy. At best he might buy time and even create a temporary stalemate, but any hope of defeating the invasion was wishful thinking. His ragged and hasty defensive tactics proved formidable but strategically, unless he somehow could find the means of establishing a strong defensive line somewhere and unless he was granted the freedom to manoeuvre, his armies faced eventual annihilation.

Had the Germans opted to reinforce Normandy rapidly with divisions from the Fifteenth Army and the OKW reserve in the early days of the battle before Montgomery could complete his own buildup, they might have turned the tide in their favour. Near the Seine and within a hundred miles of Caen were three panzer and two field infantry divisions.[1] However, as we now know, Rommel, like the other senior German commanders, believed – and would continue to believe for some time yet to come – that the main Allied blow in the form of a second invasion would come in the Pas de Calais, and that Normandy was merely a diversionary operation. The German fixation on the Pas de Calais was not aided by their intelligence which was ineffectual

---

[1] Cf., Ellis, op.cit., German Army dispositions map, pp. 10–11. These figures do not include the nine static infantry divisions guarding the coast of Northern France between the Seine and the Belgian border. Two of the panzer divisions were north of the Seine and the third (Panzer Lehr) was at Chartres. A fourth mobile division, the 17th SS Panzer Grenadier, was near Poitiers.

and never deduced that there were insufficient forces remaining in England to mount a second invasion.[1]

Moreover, Rommel was in no position to repeat the brilliant tactics he had displayed in North Africa where he had had the freedom to manoeuvre and could dictate the employment of his forces. In Normandy he had to contend with restrictive if also helpful terrain, an unyielding Hitler, Geyr von Schweppenburg, who opposed the rapid employment of the panzer divisions and his nominal superior, old von Rundstedt – their agreement on the Orne sector defence was a rare one. To add to his woes, the paucity of air support from Hermann Goering's Luftwaffe made movement of German units difficult and exceedingly costly.

According to Speidel, Rommel considered a minimum of five panzer divisions necessary for the defence of the Normandy coast, later quoting Rommel as saying: 'Elements which are not in contact with the enemy at the moment of invasion will never get into action, because of the enormous air superiority of the enemy... If we do not succeed in carrying out our combat mission of warding off the Allies or of hurling them from the mainland in the first 48-hours, the invasion has succeeded and the war is lost for lack of strategic reserves and lack of Luftwaffe in the west.'[2]

Geyr von Schweppenburg never conceded the validity of Rommel's strategy. Even after the war he refused to change his opinion, arguing: 'The Atlantic Wall was an outpost position. Therefore, the whole defence theory of Hitler, Jodl, and Rommel was unjustified. Since Hannibal, decisive battle had not been fought in outpost positions. With their theory, Hitler, ignorant of military matters [and] Rommel, the pure tactician ... stamped themselves as indistinguishable from the trench-war soldiers of 1918.'[3] His contention was that panzer divisions cannot fight with mass and shock effect within range of great enemy battle

[1] The Allied deception plan – FORTITUDE – succeeded far beyond the expectations of its planners. On the orders of Hitler and OKW the main elements of the Fifteenth Army were retained in the Pas de Calais until late July (Cf. Pogue, *The Supreme Command*, pp. 193–4). One of Rommel's biographers, David Irving, has shown that Army Group B was warning their commanders in late June of large forces massed in southern England. (cf, *The Trail of the Fox*). Ruge's account of *Rommel in Normandy* details visits by the Field Marshal to the Fifteenth Army sector despite the increasingly dire situation in Normandy.

[2] Post-war interrogation of Lieutenant General Hans Speidel, German Report Series, Foreign Military Studies, Manuscript B-720, US Army Military History Institute.

[3] Commentary by Geyr von Schweppenburg, in Manuscript B-720, loc.cit.

fleets in restrictive terrain. While von Schweppenburg's beliefs may have been tactically correct in historical terms, what he utterly failed to grasp was that time was the greatest factor, and that once firmly established ashore the combination of Allied air supremacy and sheer weight in men and material simply would not permit the countermeasures he envisioned. Nevertheless, he stubbornly placed the blame squarely upon Rommel: 'History will not absolve him from responsibility for having been the strongest motive behind an inept use of the entirely battle-fit German panzer command. By turning part of it into mobile coastal pillboxes and having another part follow hesitatingly, because of a suspected later enemy landing on the Channel Coast or for other reasons, he wasted its concentrated force. He had been warned sufficiently; emphatically by the unusually far-sighted General von Falkenhausen, among others.'[1]

As bleak as the long-term outlook for the German Army in France may have been to its leaders, defeat in Normandy was at this early stage far from a *fait accompli*. The German field commanders viewed matters far differently from Hitler. But what was the truth? From Hitler's perspective, if Normandy was indefensible then so too was France and at that moment in the war the western borders of Germany itself were undefended. Hitler viewed the defence of Normandy in strategic terms and, mistrusting his commanders in the field, did the only thing he could – as he had so often done in Russia he insisted on counterattack to blunt the enemy offensive and buy time until powerful reserves could be assembled. The real question was: given the rapid rate of the Allied buildup, how much time was there to buy?

The answer to this question would largely be determined by the outcome of the forthcoming battle for Caen.

---

[1] Geyr von Schweppenburg commentary, loc.cit.

CHAPTER 10

Caen: The Search for
a Strategy

I never expected 3rd Division to get Caen on the
first day and I always said that if we didn't get it the
first day it would take a month to get it afterwards.

Lieutenant General Miles Dempsey,
Commander, Second British Army

The triumph of the D-Day landings was shortlived on the eastern
flank as the Second Army set about the task of carving out a
bridgehead of sufficient size to accommodate the first of the
followup units which began landing on D+1. The main objective
remained the capture of Caen but the events of 6 June in the Orne
bridgehead foretold the difficulty that faced Crocker's 1 Corps.

The first days of combat in Normandy set the course for the
remainder of the battle for Caen. The morning of 7 June found
the Second Army locked in a struggle with German panzer and
infantry units. Montgomery's first order to Dempsey after coming ashore was 'to proceed relentlessly with the original plan' by
establishing his left flank on the River Dives, to capture Caen and
then, pivoting on Caen, to swing his right flank forward.[1] Bradley
was told to press his attacks around OMAHA beach, attain the
original objectives for D-Day, and capture the towns of Isigny
and Carentan in order to link up the US V and VII Corps. VIII
Corps was to ensure this linkup held firm before attacking to
sever the Cotentin Peninsula near La Haye du Puits and isolate
Cherbourg from further German reinforcement.

On 7 June there was already evidence of German intentions;
the 12th SS Panzer Division, which was now arriving in force,
launched the first of several unsuccessful counterattacks during

---

[1] Montgomery's instructions to Dempsey were in accord with the Second Army's
mission as first presented in the Second Army Operational Order No. 1, 21 April 1944.
Cf., C. P. Stacey, *The Victory Campaign*, Ottawa, 1960, pp. 141–2.

the next two days against the Canadian 3rd Division, causing the front west of Caen to stabilize on the Caen-Bayeux highway, which would remain the line of demarcation for the next several weeks. Meanwhile, the US V Corps did establish a firm bridgehead in the OMAHA sector when the defences of the German 352nd Division finally broke under the heavy American pressure. By the night of 8 June, when the US 1st Infantry Division made contact with elements of 50th Division near Port en Bessin, the entire Allied front was linked up.

Caen was never seriously threatened in the week after D-Day. In the Orne bridgehead the 3rd Division, the 6th Airborne Division and Lovat's Commando Brigade were still far too weak in numbers and armour to accomplish much more than a holding operation until the 51st (Highland) Division and the 4th Armoured Brigade could land. Neither Gale nor Lovat had been told prior to D-Day the length of time he would be expected to hold his bridgehead.[1] The lightly equipped airborne were under particularly heavy pressure and fought commendably in resisting a determined series of German probes against their positions. The slow development of the battle in the first few days convinced the corps commander, Crocker, that the 6th Airborne Division must continue its role in the Orne bridgehead for an indefinite period. Gale vividly remembers Crocker visiting him on D+2 or D+3 to ask how long he could stay in his position. Gale replied that they could stay as long as the German effort against the airborne remained as battlegroup attacks, but that if it developed into a properly planned offensive then they would be most vulnerable.[2]

Despite fresh attempts to renew their attacks against Caen neither the British nor Canadian 3rd Divisions was able to advance on the city. On 7 June the British 3rd Division had initiated a new attack to capture the high ground around Lebisey, but, still lacking adequate strength, they were beaten off with heavy losses from automatic weapons fire from entrenched German positions in the Lebisey Wood. The main accomplishment of both divisions was to plug the dangerous gap between them and establish a contiguous front. Crocker, who had been

---

[1] General Gale, letter to the author, 17 February 1982, and Lord Lovat, letter to the author, 1980.
[2] General Gale, loc.cit.

cautioned by Montgomery to place the security of his left flank before any renewed offensive action, made no further attempt to press attacks on Caen without the additional support from his followup units.[1]

30 Corps had not even come close to attaining its D-Day objectives, which had called for the capture of Villers-Bocage by the 8th Armoured Brigade who were to operate as the corps advance guard. The armour encountered the same problem on GOLD beach as the 27th Armoured Brigade had on SWORD beach: 'The main trouble was from congestion. The beach at high water was extremely narrow and the exits inadequate . . . By last light practically none of the forces for the proposed mobile column had been landed. No tanks of 24 L[ancers] due on the second tide came in. The Brigade at last light on D-Day had two Regts committed and no reserve force landed.'[2] Thus, instead of moving quickly inland to 'dominate' the area around Villers-Bocage, the 8th Armoured Brigade was unable even to advance beyond the Caen-Bayeux highway. Most of the day had been spent in clearing out stiff pockets of resistance in the hamlets near GOLD beach.

Beginning on the morning of 7 June the armoured and infantry forces of Bucknall's 30 Corps met far less organized resistance in the western sector of the British front and had made excellent progress south of Bayeux and were in the Seulles Valley when on 9 June they ran into advance elements of the Panzer Lehr Division, which had been ordered into the area by von Rundstedt to seal the gap on this flank. Air Marshal Coningham's 2nd Tactical Air Force had constantly harried the reinforcing panzers.[3] The experience of Panzer Lehr was typical. One of the best divisions in the German Army (led by the able Lieutenant General Fritz Bayerlein, who had been Rommel's Afrika Korps chief-of-staff) Panzer Lehr was savaged during its move on 7 June

---

[1]   Crocker had already prepared for such an occurrence in his Operational Order of 5 May. The 3rd Division was told: 'Should the enemy forestall us at Caen and the defences prove to be strongly organized thus causing us to fail to capture it on D-Day, further direct frontal assaults which may prove costly, will not be undertaken without reference to 1 Corps. In such an event 3 British Div will contain the enemy in Caen and retain the bulk of its forces for mobile operations inside the covering positions.'

[2]   War Diary, 8th Armoured Brigade Group, 6 June 1944, PRO (WO 171/613). The 24th Lancers, due to land during the second tide, did not land until late afternoon and were not ready for action until midnight.

[3]   The 12th SS, and Panzer Lehr.

from the Chartres area to the Seulles Valley to block the 30 Corps thrust toward Villers-Bocage. His objections overruled, Bayerlein had been ordered by the Seventh Army commander (Dollmann) to move his division in daylight; as a result Panzer Lehr suffered serious losses before their nightmare journey ended.[1]

Montgomery's first priority was to renew the assault against Caen without delay, and time was already working against him. His ability to mount a major attack capable of capturing the city and its strategically vital terrain features southeast and southwest was limited to the rate of his post-D-Day buildup. This buildup was already running behind schedule due to miserable weather in the English Channel, which delayed the arrival of the Highland Division and 4th Armoured Brigade. A direct assault on Caen could still succeed, but not without the firepower of these two units. Thus by D+2 Montgomery's dilemma was to find some method of securing Caen before the Germans heavily reinforced their defences.

The inability of 1 Corps to continue attacks capable of taking Caen and Carpiquet airfield to the west had indeed provided Rommel with vital time. Despite air harassment the 12th SS were now in possession of the terrain west from Carpiquet to the vicinity of Audrieu, about three miles south of the Caen-Bayeux highway.[2]

Montgomery's military philosophy was to conceive and execute a simple, workable plan which could be easily understood by all concerned. Soon after assuming command of 21st Army Group he had told his staff: 'I will not get bogged down in details . . . I will give orders to the next lower commanders. Nothing will be in writing either in the first place or for confirmation. I never read any papers. Half of all papers are not read and the other half are not worth reading.'[3] He did not like having to alter his tactical plans unless compelled to do so; not only was it not his method but he saw such changes as harmful to the order and cohesion he

---

[1] Panzer Lehr lost more than 130 trucks and fuel tankers, 5 tanks and 84 self-propelled guns, half-tracks and prime movers. Prior to this disastrous move it had been the only German division in Normandy at full strength. Apparently Dollmann was merely carrying out an order from von Rundstedt that Panzer Lehr should move by daylight.

[2] The arrival of the 12th SS effectively blocked any further threat to Caen from the Odon sector by the 3rd Canadian Division.

[3] Notes for Staff Conference, 21st Army Group, 13 January 1944, PRO (CAB 106/1037).

considered essential to success in battle. 'Once principles and normal, sound methods had been established satisfactorily, he was prepared to depart from the "normal" if necessary; but his instinct was to see the latter as a danger, a "groping in the dark", which as a trainer [of men] he fundamentally mistrusted.'[1]

Yet by D+3 a reconsideration was unavoidable. On D+2 he had ruled out a frontal attack on Caen. 'The Germans are doing everything they can to hold onto Caen,' he wrote to his former Brigade Major and now Military Secretary in the War Office, Major General Frank 'Simbo' Simpson, 'I have decided not to have a lot of casualties by butting up against the place. So I have ordered Second Army to keep up a good pressure at and to make its main effort toward Villers-Bocage and Evrecy, and thence southeast toward Falaise.'[2]

Moreover, Montgomery was aware that a German counter-attack was certain. Rommel would never be satisfied at merely defending Caen but would attempt a counterstroke at the earliest possible moment to crush the invasion on this flank before Montgomery could strengthen his assault units and continue his own offensive.

The first steps in the evolution of an alternative plan were taken on 10 June in a field outside Port en Bessin where Bradley and Dempsey met with Montgomery. The new plan called for encircling Caen simultaneously from the east and west. With a mapboard balanced on the bonnet of his Humber staff car, Montgomery outlined the genesis of a new strategy to outflank Caen.

Unwilling to risk a frontal assault, Montgomery decided to squeeze Caen in the jaws of a double envelopment. His left pincer would be a short hook executed due east of the city via the Orne bridgehead, using the 51st Division and the 4th Armoured Brigade as the main assault force. Immediately upon landing these two units would cross into the Orne bridgehead and attack

[1] Nigel Hamilton, *Monty: The Making of a General, 1887–1942*, London, 1981, p. 172.
[2] Montgomery, letter to Simpson, 8 June 1944, furnished by Nigel Hamilton. Simpson knew Montgomery well and had served as his Brigade Major in 1937–8 when Montgomery had commanded the 9th Infantry Brigade. In his present position as Secretary to the CIGS in the War Office, Simpson became a conduit for Montgomery to pass on his private thoughts to Brooke. This confidential channel also permitted Montgomery to try out ideas on Simpson, knowing Brooke would see them without the information getting into official channels.

south in the direction of the hamlet of Cagny, astride the Caen-Lisieux highway, thus effectively cutting the German communication link to the east. In the west 30 Corps would form the right pincer by continuing their attack straight down the Seulles valley to capture Villers-Bocage, then turn east where they would link up with the British 1st Airborne Division which would be dropped in the Odon valley around Noyers and Evrecy. The right hook would be spearheaded by the veteran 7th Armoured Division (the 'Desert Rats') of Eighth Army fame.[1] Once Cagny and Evrecy were secured Montgomery intended to employ the British 1st Airborne Division behind the Orne between these two villages, thus blocking any German escape to the south and trapping Caen's defenders. This plan called for the attacks to begin simultaneously that same day: 10 June.

However, Montgomery's daring plan to drop the 1st Airborne Division ran into immediate opposition from Air Chief Marshal Leigh-Mallory, who refused to sanction the use of aircraft to carry out the scheme on the grounds that it was far too hazardous for his air crews. Leigh-Mallory contended that a night operation was impossible owing to the threat of friendly fire from the Allied fleet; nor, he said, would Admiral Ramsay agree to a ceasefire as he believed it would leave his ships too vulnerable to air attack by the Luftwaffe. A daylight drop was also impossible, said Leigh-Mallory, since his unarmed aircraft would have to run the gauntlet of Caen's heavy anti-aircraft defences.[2] Leigh-Mallory's refusal infuriated Montgomery and in a letter to his Chief-of-Staff, de Guingand, on 12 June, he castigated the air chief for his failure to support the airborne operation:

> I sent you a wire last night, re: Leigh-Mallory and his refusal to drop 1st Airborne Division. The favourable conditions I am working up to are that the DZ [Drop Zone] would be within range of the artillery of the 7th Armoured Division in the Villers-Bocage area. If we then drop the airborne division in the

[1] The 7th Armoured Division was the first followup force of 30 Corps to land on D+1. Noyers and Evrecy were D+2 objectives of the 3rd Canadian Division and dominated the approaches to Caen from the southwest. The advanced armoured element (the 2nd Canadian Armoured Brigade) was to have taken Evrecy on D-Day.

[2] AEAF Historical Record, (AIR 37/1057), PRO. Despite their ineffectual role in Normandy the Luftwaffe was still potent enough to cause Admiral Ramsay grave concern for his fleet if there were a ceasefire to permit Leigh-Mallory's aircraft to drop the 1st Airborne. He was therefore not disposed to accept such an arrangement.

Evrecy area we would be very well placed and might get a 'big scoop'. The real point is that L-M, sitting in his office, cannot possibly know the local battle form here and therefore he must not refuse my demands unless he first comes over to see me. He could fly here in a Mosquito on one-half hour, talk for one-hour and be back in England in one-half hour. Obviously he is a gutless bugger who refuses to take a chance and plays for safety on all occasions. I have no use for him.[1]

Montgomery, who normally got along well with Leigh-Mallory, had a point. Shortly before D-Day Leigh-Mallory had expressed similar reservations about the US airborne operation in the Cotentin and had urged Eisenhower to cancel it on grounds that the casualties would be unacceptably high. Eisenhower quickly overruled him and after D-Day Leigh-Mallory sent a profusely worded apology to the Supreme Commander for having doubted the success of the operation. Leigh-Mallory's refusal to support Montgomery's proposal was indicative of his scepticism toward all airborne operations. Despite his frustration, Montgomery took no action to bring the matter to Eisenhower's attention and seek his support. In this instance it was perhaps as well for, as we shall see, other factors prevented the airborne plan from being carried out.

As Montgomery surmised, the Germans were now planning to strike back; coincidentally, their operation was timed to commence at approximately the same time as Montgomery's proposed offensive. Ordered by Rommel to organize an armoured counterattack designed to split the British between Caen and Bayeux, General von Schweppenburg, whose Panzer Group West was now located in an orchard about twenty miles south of Caen, was preparing to launch the three panzer divisions located around Caen against the Second Army. On 9 June Montgomery had written to de Guingand: 'The bad weather is a great nuisance as what we want now is to be able to take quick advantage of our good position by striking deep before the enemy can build up strength against us. However, we are not doing too badly.'[2] But the delay in landing 51st Division and 4th Armoured

---

[1] 21st Army Group Papers, (WO 205/5D), PRO. For some time after the invasion the Main HQ of 21st Army Group remained in England; Montgomery sent daily messages or letters to de Guingand to keep him informed of events in Normandy. Montgomery's anger with Leigh-Mallory was only momentary; by 27 June he was writing to Brooke that Leigh-Mallory 'is a very genuine chap and will do anything he can to help with the war'.   [2] PRO (WO 205/5D).

Brigade prevented his attack from jumping off on 10 June and before they could begin their operation the Germans struck east of the Orne that same day against the 6th Airborne Division.

Two days of bitter fighting took place, necessitating diversion of part of the 51st Division to assist Gale's badly depleted force. The German attack was finally snuffed out during the night of 12 June when Gale daringly launched a sudden counterattack to plug a dangerous gap in his lines around Breville. With a pitifully understrength parachute battalion, reinforced by a company of infantry and a squadron of tanks from the Highlanders, Gale's surprise attack routed a regiment of the 346th Division and restored the British line. Gale's inspired decision was the turning point in the battle for the Orne bridgehead and, as he later wrote: 'Neither in the North or the South were we ever seriously attacked again.'[1]

Other than this one abortive attack against the airborne, the intended German counterstroke never materialized. When Rommel met with von Schweppenburg on 10 June he recognized that the moment was not right for such an attack, due to the problem of getting reinforcements into position and the necessity to relocate some units to the Cotentin to meet the American threat against Cherbourg. Moreover, new attacks by the Canadians northwest of Caen were putting additional pressure on his defenders.

Von Schweppenburg was a stubborn commander and still determined to initiate the counterattack, but on 11 June his Panzer Group West was destroyed by the RAF after he had foolishly failed to order his mobile HQ to be camouflaged. He was wounded and escaped with his life but his staff were less fortunate; most were killed and immediately thereafter German plans for a counterattack were suspended. Contrary to some accounts, it was not a lucky target of opportunity which caused the demise of Panzer Group West but a deliberate attack by the RAF who had been notified of its whereabouts by British intelligence the day before, following receipt of an ULTRA intercept from Bletchley Park.[2]

---

[1] Richard Gale, *With the 6th Airborne Division in Normandy*, London, 1948, p. 101. Gale's parachute battalion suffered 141 casualties out of some 160 officers and men who had begun the counterattack.

[2] Cf. Ralph Bennett, *ULTRA in the West*, London, 1979, the first account of ULTRA in the campaign for northwest Europe.

With von Schweppenburg now out of the picture and his HQ a shambles, SS General Dietrich took over command of the German defence of the Caen sector. Dietrich was a longtime Nazi comrade of Hitler who had been rewarded earlier in the war for his service to the Party by being given a high rank in the SS. His qualifications as a field commander were gravely doubted by both von Rundstedt and Rommel; neither man was ever happy as long as Dietrich was in command but fortunately he made no attempt to carry out von Schweppenburg's plan correctly suspecting that the British were about to commence a new attack.[1]

We now know that during the pre-D-Day planning Dempsey was deeply concerned by the problem of what action should be taken if the Second Army operations failed to develop along the lines planned for the advance inland. His personal notes used to brief his subordinate commanders repeatedly refer to this point and to his plans for dealing with such a situation. Churchill had not been the only one concerned by the results of the Anzio landings:

> The landing at Anzio has shown that if our front remains stationary for a period of even three or four days, there is grave danger that it will congeal, and that great difficulty will be experienced in breaking out. The problem of build-up, which immediately follows the assault in an invasion, precludes the possibility of a sustained and continuous assault. Main bodies must halt on bounds for periods of three or four days in order to allow sufficient strength to be built-up. The main force cannot be allowed to spreadeagle itself and get unbalanced.[2]

Dempsey was also aware that the mobile forces assigned to take the deep objectives on D-Day might fail: 'If the enemy is in strength, these mobile columns will not only fail to carry out any worthwhile penetration – they will be driven back onto the main body. And if that happens, and it is more than probable that it will, we shall be up against the same Anzio difficulties when the day comes for the advance of the main bodies to continue.'[3] Dempsey reminded his commanders that 'in France there will be

---

[1] It would be weeks before Panzer Group West was again a factor in the Normandy campaign. Its location and destruction was directly attributable to ULTRA which was able twice to report its location with great accuracy. It was the first of such ULTRA intercepts, which were to have an impact on the campaign.

[2] Dempsey Papers, PRO (WO 285/1).

[3] Ibid.

no sea flank to help the advance of Second Army. *We will use airborne forces instead.*' (Author's italics.) His intent was to employ the airborne as his army reserve in a manner that would permit a main force to reach it before it became a liability as a result of what would be certain violent reaction by the Germans.

Inasmuch as the official British history maintains that Montgomery carried out his master plan as originally conceived, there has been no discussion of alternative plans or the fact that they even existed. There may not have been such alternatives considered at Montgomery's headquarters but they most certainly were of prime concern to Dempsey and his Second Army staff. Whether Dempsey was merely being prudent by preparing for any eventuality or whether he believed Montgomery's plan had little prospect of success is not known.

As his reserve Dempsey had Major General R. E. Urquhart's 1st Airborne Division and the Polish Parachute Brigade which it was hoped would be ready for employment by June. The airborne were to be used either to exploit success or to assist the main force in the event of the advance stalling. Dempsey's overriding fear: 'We must concentrate all our efforts during the early weeks of the invasion to ensure that we do *not get pinned down*. We must retain our ability to keep the operation fluid. We must hold 1st Airborne Div in reserve until it is clear that we may be unable to break out of the ring without their assistance. Then we must use them in conjunction with the main attack to *make sure that we do* break out.'[1]

Plans called for the 1st Airborne Division to be prepared to undertake an airborne landing anytime from the night of D+6–7 onwards. In anticipation of such an operation Dempsey in late April assigned to Lieutenant General Sir Richard O'Connor the task of preparing a detailed scenario for employment of the division in conjunction with a corps offensive in the area between Caen and Falaise. For several weeks the 8 Corps staff studied the problem in an exercise codenamed WAKE.[2] O'Connor focused on an advance by 8 Corps on the axis Evrecy–Falaise with two infantry divisions and one armoured division. Included in his

---

[1] Dempsey Papers, PRO (WO 285/1).
[2] A complete copy of the 8 Corps outline plan, dated 13 May 1944, is contained in Dempsey's papers in WO 285/1.

study was the employment of the 1st Airborne Division astride the Caen–Falaise highway near Bretteville-le-Rabat. O'Connor's conclusions were accepted by Dempsey and envisioned the 1st Airborne Division being used in conjunction with the initial or secondary infantry attacks as a means of what Dempsey termed 'breaking through the ring'. The airborne would land between 10,000 and 20,000 yards behind the front where it could link up with the main force within twenty-four hours.[1*]

By D-Day the Second Army planners foresaw the need for an airborne operation in the Odon valley around Evrecy and Noyers. Originally the idea was to employ the division in this sector to prevent any German withdrawal from Caen to the west. Codenamed WILD OATS, the operation would come under the command of 30 Corps and was due to commence on 13 June. However, when the Second Army drive on Caen stalled after D-Day the plan was amended to coincide with Montgomery's planned thrust by the 7th Armoured Division toward Villers-Bocage, which was the first objective in linking up the armour and the airborne. On 10 June a planning team from the 1st Airborne Division flew to France to meet the Second Army and 30 Corps planners to work out a detailed plan for WILD OATS.[2]

Despite Leigh-Mallory's refusal to carry out the operation, the 1st Airborne Division was still held in readiness to initiate WILD OATS at short notice, and on 12 June Montgomery told de Guingand that he still considered an attack by the Second Army against Villers-Bocage, Evrecy and Noyers the highest priority in Normandy.[3] Leigh-Mallory's opposition notwithstanding, WILD OATS was still not feasible as long as 30 Corps remained stalled in its offensive south of Bayeux. The pre-invasion plan called for 30

---

[1] WO 285/1, loc.cit.

* O'Connor's plan envisioned the Second Army front generally along the line of the Orne and Odon. The object of WAKE was to deny the Germans the use of the road network emanating from Falaise by capturing and controlling the entire Caen-Falaise Plain and establishing a new front line running from Conde-sur-Noireau in the east, to the south of Falaise, and running northeast of Falaise to join with 1 Corps, who would advance to the area astride the River Dives. The operation would be carried out in five phases, starting the night of D+13, with the 1st Airborne Division to be employed two nights later to gain control of the Caen-Falaise highway and to disrupt enemy communications until relieved by the 11th Armoured Division, who would continue south, capture Falaise and establish themselves firmly in control of the area south of the town so as to block all German movement toward the front via Falaise.

[2] War Diary, 1st Airborne Division, June 1944, PRO (WO 171/392).

[3] Montgomery, letter to de Guingand, 12 June 1944, PRO (WO 205/5D).

Corps to capture Villers-Bocage by D+2, preparatory to a renewed offensive south to gain control of Mont Pinçon. It is evident from Dempsey's diary that at the same time Montgomery was altering his thinking about how to capture Caen, the Second Army commander too was formulating fresh ideas for the deployment of 30 Corps to capture or isolate Caen. Not surprisingly, nowhere in Dempsey's diary or notes for this period is there any mention whatsoever of a British strategy of attracting and pinning down Rommel's reserves.

In fact, Montgomery's revised strategy may well have been influenced by Dempsey. The day before Montgomery formally announced his new plan for capturing Caen, Dempsey's diary reads:

1100 hours: Saw C-in-C at HQ, 21 Army Group. I asked him to impress on 5 American Corps the importance of their driving SOUTH to get, first DODIGNY and then CAUMONT. I gave him my future intentions with 7th Armd Div, 51 Div and – possibly – 1 Airborne Division.

1200 hours: Saw Commander 1 Corps ... I gave him my intention regarding 7 Armd Div who will start operating tomorrow morning – and the probability that I will get him to employ 51 Div EAST of the two rivers in order to isolate CAEN from the EAST and South-East. He is to be prepared to carry out this operation on 11 June. If the attacks of 7 Armd Div and 51 Div went well, the landing of 1 Airborne Div to the South of CAEN might well be decisive.

1300 hours: I discussed with [Lieutenant General] Browning during the day the possibility of employing 1st Airborne Division SOUTH of CAEN on the evening of 11 June or later. He set in motion the machinery for planning and carrying it out.[1]

The British offensive commenced on 10 June on the western flank just as the German attack began against Gale's force. When the 51st Division began the left hook the following day, some easy gains were made on their left flank, but a brigade-sized attack on the main objectives of Ste Honorine, Cuverville and Demouville was strongly repulsed, with heavy losses, by a battlegroup of the 21st Panzer Division. The Highlanders were forced

---

[1] Dempsey Diary, 9 June 1944, PRO (WO 285/9).

to withdraw to the Orne, forcing Montgomery temporarily to abandon his plan to envelop Caen from this flank. The success of the plan was now dependent upon the right pincer aimed at Villers-Bocage.

However, the offensive in the Seulles Valley also fared poorly and within hours became stalled as Panzer Lehr counterattacked the 8th Armoured Brigade, preventing clearance of the roads around Tilly sur Seulles for the 7th Armoured Division, who were to advance south along the axis of the Bayeux-Tilly road. The 'Desert Rats' found their first experience of combat in the bocage stifling and unlike anything they had previously experienced. Despite reorganizing their forces on 11 June to cope with Panzer Lehr's defences, the division made little progress and could not advance beyond Tilly. That night they were strongly counterattacked and suffered considerable casualties.[1]

After the failure of the left pincer, the slow progress of the offensive on the right flank spelled serious trouble for Montgomery's new plan to unhinge the Germans from Caen, but there now occurred an unexpected opportunity which, had it been exploited, would have broken open the whole German defence there. If Panzer Lehr could be held in place by the 50th Division, there was evidence that the German front was weakly held west of the River Aure, about three miles west of Tilly. The British–US inter-army boundary was just west of the Aure where the US 1st Infantry Division was pushing rapidly toward Caumont virtually unopposed.

On the morning of 12 June Dempsey went to the HQ of the 7th Armoured Division to find out for himself what could be done to speed up their advance: the division commander, Major General 'Bobby' Erskine, briefed Dempsey on the possibility of outflanking Panzer Lehr and driving on Villers-Bocage from the west. This was good news indeed for Dempsey, who was very concerned that 30 Corps was losing the initiative at the worst possible moment. Fifteen minutes after leaving Erskine, Dempsey met with the corps commander, Bucknall. 'I told him to switch 7 Armd Div from their front immediately, to push them behind 11 H[ussars] and endeavour to get VILLERS-BOCAGE that way. Prov-

---

[1] The 56th Infantry Brigade attached to the 7th Armoured suffered some 150 casualties and the 2nd Battalion, the Essex Regiment were forced to call their own artillery fire on their own positions, in order to drive off the Germans. Cf. Ellis, Chap. XII.

ided this is carried out with real drive and speed, there is a chance we will get through before the front congeals.'[1] After the war, Dempsey told Chester Wilmot that he had ordered Erskine to move the 7th Armoured without waiting for instructions from 30 Corps and that he would personally inform Bucknall of his decision.[2] There is conflicting evidence whether the order to disengage 7th Armoured came during Dempsey's visit or shortly afterwards from Bucknall. According to Bucknall: 'I issued the orders myself verbally to General Erskine,' and his diary notes the order coming at noon.[3] Erskine's diary records receiving the order to move at 1230, 12 June.[4] Regardless of where the order came from, the machinery was now set in motion for what would prove to be one of the most potentially decisive and controversial British operations in Normandy .

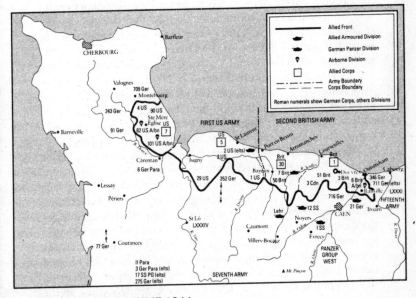

SITUATION MAP, 10 JUNE 1944

[1] Dempsey Diary, 12 June 1944, PRO (WO 285/9).
[2] Unpublished interview with Chester Wilmot, 1946, Liddell Hart Papers, King's College, London.
[3] The Papers of Lieutenant General G. C. Bucknall, IWM.
[4] Diary of General Sir George Erskine, IWM.

CHAPTER 11

Villers-Bocage

The whole handling of that battle was a disgrace.

Lieutenant General Miles Dempsey

The order for the 7th Armoured Division to disengage and initiate a right hook aimed at the crossroads town of Villers-Bocage came none too soon for General Erskine who, according to one of his former operations officers 'thought that he should have been given the opportunity to go for Villers-Bocage twenty-four hours earlier'.[1] Erskine later claimed that the idea for the renewed right hook was his: 'After some unsuccessful stabs at Tilly, I suggested the use of the Division's mobility round the right flank of 50 Division. I was sure there was a soft spot here and had in fact reconnoitred routes and had a cut and dried plan for a swoop on Villers-Bocage. The plan was eventually accepted but after much delay. It could have been carried out 24 hours earlier and those 24 hours were vital...'[2] Just how vital was borne out by the events which followed on 13 and 14 June.

When asked about the operation after the war by Chester Wilmot, Bucknall insisted that the decision was the result of a plan developed at 30 Corps. 'It was vital to develop some means of breaking out of the exasperating stagnation now threatening on 30 Corps' front. So by evening on 11 June I had decided to get the Corps as early as possible on to a two Inf Div front (the best for proper punching), disengage 7th Armd Div, and use it in its proper role round our right flank in a right hook, which I hoped would carry the element of surprise with the object of securing the Villers-Bocage feature. This would incidentally crack up the

---

[1] Major General G. T. A. Armitage, letter to the author, 29 April 1982. Erskine had taken command of 7th Armoured Division in North Africa in early 1943 after the former commander, Major General A. F. Harding, was wounded, and was highly regarded by his officers and men.

[2] General Armitage, letter to the author, 16 June 1982.

opposition in front of 50 Div and enable us to get forward. My staff got to work on the planning, arrangements for US 5 Corps, etc., and warning was given to Comd 7th Armd Div and others concerned to be prepared for the move round.'[1]

While the idea had most certainly been under consideration at 30 Corps, the problem was that Bucknall had done absolutely nothing to implement it until Dempsey arrived on the scene and, immediately grasping the urgency of losing no further time, spurred the corps commander to action. The idea had first been discussed on the afternoon of 10 June as the 30 Corps war diary notes: 'Corps Commander held conference with GOC's 7 Armd Div and 50 Inf Div to discuss future operations and directed Comd 7 Armd Div to consider transferring his axis further west.'[2] Two more days were to elapse before the idea was translated into reality by Dempsey.

As the 7th Armoured implied by breaking contact with Panzer Lehr and beginning their drive in less than four hours, far too much time had been spent in making plans: Erskine was delighted by the order and, understanding at once the urgency conveyed by Dempsey, promptly ordered Brigadier Robert Hinde's 22nd Armoured Brigade to spearhead the drive.[3] As far as Erskine was concerned the order was long overdue. Hinde's Brigade Major recently recalled that the pre-D-Day planning clearly specified that the 7th Armoured was to take Villers-Bocage almost immediately and then push quickly south to seize Mont Pinçon.[4] During the afternoon the brigade successfully disengaged from Panzer Lehr and by 1600 hours was on the move toward Villers-Bocage.[5] Hinde had acquired a reputation in North Africa as a fearless commander, so fearless in fact that he was known as 'Looney'. His former brigade major has described him as 'One of the most colourful personalities I came across in the Army. He believed in leading from the front but against that

[1] Bucknall, letter to Chester Wilmot, 29 March 1947, Bucknall Papers, IWM.
[2] War Diary, 30 Corps, June 1944, PRO (WO 171/336).
[3] The 22nd Armoured Brigade was the main fighting element of the 7th Armoured Division and consisted of an armoured regiment (4th County of London Yeomanry), two tank battalions of the Royal Tank Regiment, and a motorized infantry battalion. This veteran unit had earlier gained fame for its splendid performance at Alam Halfa and El Alamein.
[4] Interview with Lieutenant Colonel S. F. T. B. Lever, 19 April 1983.
[5] War Diary, 22nd Armoured Brigade, June 1944, PRO (WO 171/619).

he had little regard for staff work and administration which he regarded as a responsibility of others.[1]

The predicted gap west of the Aure was indeed there in the disorganized German lines and by late evening of 12 June leading elements of the 22nd Armoured Brigade reached the Caumont-Villers-Bocage road five miles west of the town. After meeting light resistance, Hinde wisely decided not to continue further movement against Villers-Bocage that night, as it was not known what German opposition might be encountered there and a reconnaissance in force might prematurely disclose British intentions. In the early morning hours of 13 June the drive resumed and within a short time a tank-infantry force stormed virtually unopposed into Villers-Bocage at 0800 hours, led by the 4th County of London Yeomanry (Sharpshooters) and 'A' Company, 1st Battalion The Rifle Brigade.

After being so effectively contained by Panzer Lehr, the men of the London Yeomanry found the easy capture of the important crossroads town an exhilarating experience, perhaps too exhilarating in the light of what shortly transpired. In eighteen hours they had advanced to an objective which the day before had seemed unattainable. 'In the words of Captain Pat Dyas (who commanded one of the RHQ tanks) it seemed unbelievable that, after being contained for so long, the Sharpshooters, after breaking out, were allowed to drive unmolested through villages of welcoming French people until, approaching from Tilly-sur-Seulles (via Caumont) they reached their first objective – the road junction in the town of Villers-Bocage – where little resistance was found. Some German billeting parties seen to be marking up French houses were more surprised to see the British tanks than the Sharpshooters were to see them.'[2]

A lieutenant of the Rifle Brigade later wrote of the astonishing welcome given the British by the townspeople. 'Once in the main street of Villers-Bocage we were amazed at the terrific reception which we received from the dense crowd of gaily dressed civilians who thronged the pavements. Everything seemed normal and

---

[1] Quoted in Armitage letter to the author, 16 June 1982.
[2] Unpublished account of 'Villers-Bocage, 13 June 1944', prepared by Major W. H. J. Sale, 1980. Major Sale's account was pieced together by interviews with surviving members of the 4th CLY. Some German infantry were trapped in Villers-Bocage by the unexpected arrival of the British, causing sniper fire on the streets to become a problem.

even the gendarmes had turned out in their khaki and blue uniforms to guide us through the town.'[1] This mutual joy was shortlived.

Villers-Bocage had strategic importance to both the British and the German armies. Situated at the head of the Seulles valley, the town was the gateway to Mont Pinçon ten miles to the south and to the Odon valley and Caen in the east. The road network for the entire area originated from Villers-Bocage and, as with another famous market town – Bastogne – the force controlling the town and its environs controlled this network.

Brigadier Hinde knew that Villers-Bocage could not remain effectively in British hands without control of the high ground northeast of it on the Caen-Villers-Bocage highway, known as Point 213, less than a mile from the edge of town. 'A' Squadron was ordered to continue northeast to seize Point 213, followed shortly thereafter by the motorized infantry of 'A' Company of the Rifle Brigade which parked along the highway nearby while two troops of 'A' Squadron deployed around the high ground. From the moment it was captured, the veteran regimental commander, Lieutenant Colonel (Viscount) Arthur Cranley, was apprehensive about advancing beyond Villers-Bocage until a reconnaissance could be made of the area to the east. Several German armoured cars were seen in the distance observing the Sharpshooters and Cranley knew this information would quickly be passed to all German units operating in the area.[2] Hinde's brigade major, Major Lever, observed that Cranley 'was undoubtedly cautious in his progress. I seem to recall that my operations map had as many reports of German 88-mm guns than perhaps ever existed at the time. . . Hinde was right up with Cranley urging him on as fast as possible.'[3] Cranley made his misgivings known to Hinde but his requests for additional time to conduct a more thorough reconnaissance were, according to eyewitnesses, 'repeatedly refused and [he] was ordered to continue his advance to secure the high ground beyond Villers-Bocage. . .'[4] Obviously still troubled by the unknown situation

---

[1] 'Villers-Bocage, Normandy, 13th June 1944' by Lieutenant Bruce Campbell, June 1945. Account furnished by Major Christopher Milner.
[2] Major Sale, loc.cit.
[3] Quoted by Armitage, 16 June 1982, loc.cit.
[4] Major Sale, loc.cit.

around Point 213, Cranley left the four tanks of his Regimental HQ parked on the main street of Villers-Bocage while he went forward in his scout car to inspect the new 'A' Squadron positions.

In anticipation of a British flanking movement aimed at Villers-Bocage, the 2nd Panzer Division had been alerted to move from its position north of the Seine near Amiens to Normandy, to establish blocking positions in the Villers sector. Unknown to the British, two companies of the 1st SS Panzer Corps panzer reserve had already arrived and were in position outside Villers-Bocage the morning of 13 June. One of these units, No. 2 Company, 501st Heavy Tank Battalion, was commanded by a young SS Obersturmführer (captain) named Michael Wittmann, who had already achieved fame as a panzer ace and who, that day, would earn the plaudits of friend and foe as the most acclaimed tank commande in history. This Tiger force now lying in wait for the 7th Armoured was the first of the German reinforcements hastily ordered up to help plug the dangerous gap in the German defences on the left flank of 1 SS Panzer Corps. Not far behind advance elements of the 2nd Panzer Division would later reinforce Panzer Lehr in the Villers-Bocage area. Their hasty forced march across the Seine had been completely undetected by Allied intelligence, so that their presence, along with the Tigers, was a complete surprise to the British.[1] Certainly, the 22nd Armoured Brigade had no inkling of what awaited the London Yeomanry. Major Lever recalls that 'Intelligence indicated enemy forces along the way including armour but with absolutely no suggestion that these included Tiger or Panther tanks.'[2] As a post-war German account of 1 SS Panzer Corps' operations was to relate:

> Panzer Lehr Division was not able to establish a continuous front, and we had to consider the possibility of enemy tanks breaking through along the road Villers-Bocage–Caen. The weak reconnaissance elements of this division's reconnaissance battalion committed in this gap on the flank of adjacent LXXXIV Corps reported advancing United States forces, which as it seemed, intended to capture the mountainous terrain west of Tilly... By 10 June the appearance of British tanks on the left wing of Panzer Lehr Division and of United

---

[1] The 2nd Panzer had begun its move on 9 June via Paris where it crossed the Seine. The division had escaped detection by moving only at night.
[2] Lieutenant Colonel S. F. T. B. Lever, letter to the author, 2 August 1982.

States forces within this gap made it appear probable that the enemy had discovered few German troops were in the area of Tilly – south of Bayeux-Balleroy. Early on the morning of 12 June [sic], the commander of the five tanks [Tiger], which had been placed in readiness north of Villers-Bocage sighted an enemy motorized column, including tanks, on the march from Tilly toward Villers-Bocage.'[1]

What is now known is that Wittmann and his company of four other Tigers and a Mark IV Special had a similar mission to the 4th CLY – that of occupying the commanding terrain around Point 213 – and of doing whatever possible to stem any British advance to the east into the Odon valley. 'From the evidence of his executive officer his objective was the same as the British – the road junction [northeast] of town. He must have been surprised to see a squadron of British armour leave Villers-Bocage and advance to occupy positions to its south. Wittmann's first throughts are now known to be that he must endeavour to stop the British and protect the flanks of Panzer Lehr.'[2]

One of the most amazing engagements in the history of armoured warfare was about to begin near Point 213. From various published and unpublished accounts, the encounter between Wittmann and the 22nd Armoured Brigade can be reconstructed.

At 0800 'A' Squadron, 4th CLY and 'A' Company, 1st Battalion The Rifle Brigade pass through Villers-Bocage. At 0905 lead elements of the Yeomanry reach Point 213 accompanied by an advance party of the infantry from 'A' Company. The main tank-infantry column consisting of some twenty-five half-tracks and tanks of both units halt several hundred yards behind on a hedge-lined section of the highway awaiting instructions before moving forward to deploy with 'A' Squadron around Point 213. The infantry is summoned forward at the same moment that two or three Tigers are spotted running parallel to the column, screened by a hedge. The Tigers swing around and face the column whose crews have just dismounted. Wittmann, who has observed the column halt from a position on the wooded high

---

[1] Major General Fritz Kraemer, '1 SS Panzer Corps in the West (1944),' Manuscript C-024, 1948, German Report Series, US Army Military History Institute. Kraemer was a regular German Army officer attached to the Waffen SS as Chief of Staff of 1 SS Panzer Corps. His reference to 12 June should read '13 June'.

[2] Major Sale, loc.cit.

ground several hundred yards north of the highway, recognizes its extreme vulnerability and decides to attack at once on his own without waiting for the other Tigers to assist.[1]

Wittmann was in the better tactical position. He paused only to explain his intention which was, without waiting for support, to attack the British column using

> speed and fire-power to block the road and thus prevent the British vehicles from being reinforced or from withdrawing. He knew that the high hedge banks were too thick to be pierced by the light-armoured vehicles and that there was too little room on the road to allow the enemy machines to turn round and escape. Running to the left of, and parallel to, the road on which the British column lay there was a narrow cart track. This led from the high ground to the road at a point almost at the crest of 213. Wittman decided to approach the column via this track and to destroy, as his first victim, the personnel carrier r ar the road and track junction. The high velocity gun was laid, aimed and fired. The half-track, swung across the road by the force of the impact, caught fire and began to pour out dense clouds of black smoke . . . the heavy Tiger thundered towards the British, shuddering only slightly as the heavy gun fired shell after shell into the mass of machines. Half-tracks, carriers and tanks were smashed by 8.8cm shells, and then with a final burst of speed the 55-ton steel monster, destroying in its rush a British tank which it met on the narrow path, crashed through the junction, was swung in a tight arc onto the roadway and began its descent upon the vehicles lined up outside the village and along the narrow high street.[2]

Wittmann's Tiger entered the main street where it immediately encountered the RHQ tanks whose crews were also caught dismounted and unable to react to the menacing sight of a lone Tiger roaring unexpectedly into view. What happened next is recounted by several of the participants:

> [The Tiger] immediately knocked out Colonel Arthur's tank, then that of the Regimental second in command, Major Carr, whom he seriously wounded, followed by the Regimental Sergeant-Major's tank. Captain [Pat] Dyas in the fourth tank, reversed and backed into the front garden of a nearby house.

---

[1] According to the German account, Wittmann and his men were surprised by the astonishing degree of unconcern displayed by the British. One of the German gunners was heard to complain: 'They're acting as if they'd won the war already.' Wittmann replied: 'We're going to prove them wrong.' Quoted in Paul Carell, *Invasion – They're Coming*, London, 1962, p. 155.

[2] Matthew Cooper and James Lucas, *Panzer*, London, 1976, pp. 144–5.

His own gunner was at that moment out of the tank, so he had to watch helplessly as the tank commander, with his head well out of his turret, presented the vulnerable side of his Tiger tank as he continued through the main street towards the road junction [on the western edge of Villers-Bocage].[1]

The Tiger had so far been unmolested during its destructive sally through town but at the road junction it encountered the leading tanks of 'B' Squadron:

He exchanged shots with Sergeant Lockwood in a Cromwell and was hit at least once which was possibly the cause of his missing the British tank. The road junction was effectively in British hands. The Tiger had seen enough and done enough to stop the British advance. The main danger to Panzer Lehr was still 'A' Squadron. He must have reversed away to disengage from Sergeant Lockwood, who was somewhat handicapped by the part of a house which he had demolished because it contained a German sniper. On his return through the main street [the Tiger] came face to face with Pat Dyas in his Cromwell, still bent on stalking him. He knocked out Dyas and killed two of his crew, one by machine-gun fire whilst escaping. Dyas, although wounded, succeeded in getting away, as did the other member of his crew.[2]

After creating havoc within the town, Wittmann prudently withdrew into the woods southeast of Villers-Bocage. With the aid of a French girl, Captain Dyas managed to reach the commander of 'B' Squadron. 'From the latter's tank he spoke to Viscount Cranley still in his Scout car on the high ground and told him of the events within the town. In reply Colonel Arthur said he realised the situation was desperate and that 'A' Squadron was at that moment being heavily attacked by German Tiger tanks. No further messages were received from him.'[3]

Within the space of some *five minutes* a single Tiger had devastated Cranley's force and left behind a trail of wrecked and burning vehicles, the shattered leading element of the 22nd Armoured Brigade. It was only the beginning. Wittmann now

[1] Major Sale, loc.cit. According to Major Sale, the RHQ was merely carrying out normal practice when protected by its forward squadrons. 'The fact that some tank crews were dismounted would have been due to the fact that much useful information can be gained by talking to the local population. . . Previously in Italy and certainly later in the war, normal civilian telephones were still in operation. By getting the locals to use them one could often telephone around and find out the exact location of enemy troops ahead.'

[2] Ibid.

[3] Ibid.

withdrew and returned to his unit to re-arm and re-fuel his Tiger. In the early afternoon, this time with four other Tigers and the Mark IV Special, and possibly three other tanks plus infantry in support, he returned to Point 213 to renew the attack against the remnants of Cranley's outgunned and outnumbered tank-infantry force.[1] It was a total mismatch and what was left of 'A' Squadron was soon overwhelmed. Cranley, along with many others, was captured. From what is known, apparently only one survivor managed to escape the debacle at Point 213. 'He, although wounded, got back to Villers-Bocage where a French butcher hid him until, three days later, after surviving the Allied bombing of the town, he escaped back to British lines.'[2] This survivor told of the tank crews attempting to escape but being killed, wounded or captured by the German infantry supporting the Tigers. All attempts to reinforce the isolated squadron were rebuffed by other German elements which were now engaging the British in and around Villers-Bocage.

After dealing with Cranley at Point 213 the Germans returned to mop up the remaining infantrymen of the Rifle Brigade. Individual acts of heroism by the infantrymen were in vain. One corporal, for example, bravely charged the Tigers with only a Sten gun. British casualties were high. The 4th CLY lost 4 killed in action, 5 wounded and 76 men missing. Accounts vary as to the material losses but at least 20 Cromwell tanks, 4 Fireflys, 3 light tanks, 3 scout cars and a half-track were knocked out.[3] 'A' Company lost some 80 infantrymen including 3 officers killed.[4] By early afternoon both British units had virtually ceased to exist. Nearly 30 infantrymen managed to escape and the first safely to reach British lines on 14 June was Captain Christopher Milner, who had made a dramatic escape after being stalked along a hedge by a German officer who kept shouting at him: 'Englishman, surrender! Englishman, surrender!'[5] The remainder of the 4th CLY now came under the command of 'B' Squadron, whose commander tightened his defences within the town and attempted – in vain – to learn the fate of his sister unit, 'A' Squadron.

Wittmann, however, had not yet finished performing his task

[1]   Major Sale, loc. cit.
[2]   Ibid.
[3]   Regimental History, County of London Yeomanry, p. 181.
[4]   R.H.W.S. Hastings, *The Rifle Brigade in the Second World War, 1939–1945*, Aldershot, 1950, p. 352.
[5]   Unpublished account of Major Christopher Milner.

of giant killer. With the same force he returned to Villers-Bocage later that day, along with fresh tank support from the first arriving units of the 2nd Panzer Division. This time he pushed his luck too far, for the Sharpshooters were prepared and had baited a trap. In the ensuing engagement the Mark IV Special and three Tigers were knocked out, including Wittmann's, which was hit by a six-pounder anti-tank gun situated on a side street. Wittmann, his crew and those of the other tanks got away on foot: most of the British supporting infantry had been lost at Point 213, so there was no way to prevent their escape. The four German tanks were set on fire to prevent their later recovery.[1]

Almost single-handedly, this one audacious and brilliant German tank commander had crushed the British advance around Villers-Bocage and forced the 7th Armoured Division on to the defensive. The Germans were greatly relieved by Wittmann's stunning accomplishment. 'The idea of placing in readiness the five Tiger tanks which had been left intact during the enemy air attacks had produced good results, preventing an enemy attack and a probable rolling up of the entire corps front at least on 12 June or the day following.'[2]

The loss of 'A' Squadron and 'A' Company not only stopped the 7th Armoured offensive dead in its tracks, but the arrival of other tanks and infantry of the 2nd Panzer now threatened the entire divisional grip on Villers-Bocage itself. A series of engagements during the remainder of 13 June left British retention of Villers-Bocage a risky proposition without additional infantry support. Hinde's command was split into two forces, one holding Villers-Bocage, the other Tracy-Bocage, several miles west on the Caumont road and protecting the only line of communication open to the west. As Major Lever has said, 'At this stage the Germans had spotted an obvious weakness and were reinforcing their positions with a view to a major kill. It would therefore have been sheer folly to have left an armoured regiment in an exposed position without proper infantry support.'[3]

A 7th Armoured Division intelligence summary issued later that day estimated that a force of up to 40 Tiger tanks from the

---

[1] Major Sale, loc.cit.
[2] Major General Fritz Kraemer, loc.cit.
[3] Lieutenant Colonel Lever, loc.cit. According to Lever, Hinde was shattered by the loss of 'A' Squadron at Point 213.

2nd Panzer were in the Villers area and now engaging the hard-pressed 22nd Armoured Brigade.[1] Erskine grew increasingly concerned about a German attack from the south as probing actions began to the west of Villers-Bocage. Earlier in the day both Erskine and Hinde 'reckoned the Brigade Group could hold both Villers-Bocage and Tracy-Bocage, but as the day wore on it became apparent that more infantry would be needed to keep both positions'.[2]

The 50th Division was failing to make progress against a determined Panzer Lehr around Tilly and were certainly not in any position to assist the 7th Armoured by the time darkness fell. If the 2nd Panzer or Panzer Lehr were to cut the roads between Villers-Bocage and Caumont, 'B' Squadron would be trapped and probably suffer the same fate as 'A' Squadron. Armitage recounts that 'Erskine therefore ordered Hinde to pull back after dark, to hold Tracy-Bocage in strength, a move entirely agreed to by the Brigadier.'[3] With 'B' Squadron surrounded on three sides and the Brigade stretched too thinly and without adequate infantry support, this was a sound decision. In the early evening hours of 13 June the Brigade withdrew to new positions a mile west of the town between Tracy-Bocage and Amaye-sur-Seulles, with the main force concentrated around Hill 174, where Hinde intended to defend the high ground until reinforced.

Erskine had now committed his last available infantry battalion to Hinde and that night he made it clear to the corps commander that the 7th Armoured was at considerable risk unless the 50th Division got forward quickly with additional infantry to reinforce the 22nd Armoured Brigade. According to the war diary, Erskine told 30 Corps:

> 22d Armd Bde are between Lehr Div on north and 2 Pz on south. Position resembles a bee's nest. You know our strength. For this reason I decided to tighten up 22d Bde locality and withdraw from V–B. – Corps Cdr entirely agrees with this decision. I have made it clear to Cdr, 22d Armd Bde to hold tight where he is. Will corps cdr agree to this no matter what it costs? Answer: 'Yes'.[4]*

[1] War Diary, the 7th Armoured Division, PRO (WO 171/439).
[2] Major General Armitage, 29 April 1982, loc.cit.
[3] Major General Armitage, loc. cit.
[4] War Diary, the 7th Armoured Division, 13 June 1944, loc.cit.
* In a report given to the 30 Corps Liaison Officer at 1945 hours, Erskine reiterated his intention to hold Villers-Bocage the following day.

Erskine was confident of holding the new positions but only if Bucknall provided reinforcements. He reminded corps that 'The Line of Communications has been cut in several places, but I consider 22d Bde have sufficient in hand to stand and fight where they are even if supplies cannot get through.'[1] Erskine's decision to give up Villers-Bocage had been made with obvious reluctance, and when he spoke with Brigadier Hinde at 1650 hours he made it clear that the 22nd Armoured Brigade was 'to hang onto the high ground at all costs.'[2]

There is no doubt that during the night of 13 June Erskine's intentions were to retain his hold on Villers-Bocage. In view of the later harsh criticism that he had given up the 7th Armoured's advantage too easily, Erskine's telephone and wireless communications with 30 Corps that night are important. The wireless log of the 7th Armoured records that Erskine was quite explicit about standing and fighting, and included this entry: 'I intend to bomb and harass routes through Villers-Bocage in support of 22d Bde. The comd is quite clear that this must be held at all costs.'[3] As Armitage has observed: 'Erskine's role, in short, was to represent to Bucknall that his Division was out on a limb, had encountered unexpected opposition and was headed for a hiding unless reinforced or pulled back. This Erskine did with exceptional clarity and there can be no excuse for misunderstanding by his higher headquarters.'[4]

Although Hinde's new positions around Hill 174 were defensively sound, the one at nearby Tracy-Bocage was perilous. As Armitage recalls: '\[Erskine] had visited Hinde at Tracy-Bocage and recognised that it was not a sound position to hold unless 50 Division could close up. Hinde was concerned about the large number of vehicles on the position; the tanks could not find many good hull-down sites, there were thick woods close on three sides, ideal for infiltrating infantry to approach and he was overlooked from higher ground.'[5] Colonel G. P. Gregson, commander of the 5th Regiment, Royal Horse Artillery which was in direct support of the 22nd Armoured Brigade, remembers that

---

[1] War Diary, the 7th Armoured Division, 13 June 1944, loc. cit.
[2] War Diary, the 22nd Armoured Brigade, 1650 hours, 13 June 1944, loc.cit.
[3] War Diary, the 7th Armoured Division, 13 June 1944.
[4] Major General Armitage, 29 April 1982, loc.cit.
[5] Ibid.

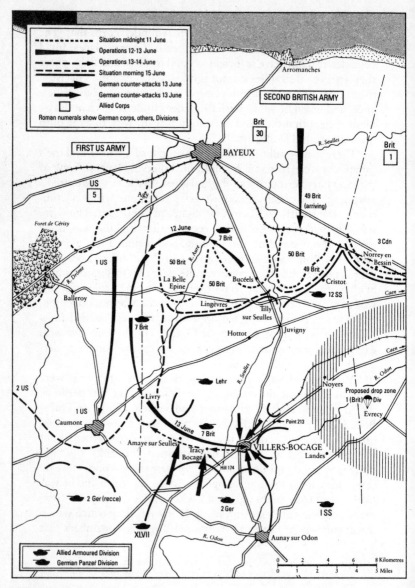

Situation midnight 11 June
Operations 12-13 June
Operations 13-14 June
Situation morning 15 June
German counter-attacks 13 June
German counter-attacks 13 June
Allied Corps
Roman numerals show German corps, others, Divisions

SECOND BRITISH ARMY

FIRST US ARMY

Arromanches

Brit
30

Brit
1

BAYEUX

R. Seulles

US
5

Agy

49 Brit
(arriving)

3 Cdn

Norrey en
Bessin

Foret de Cérisy

1 US

12 June

7 Brit

50 Brit

50 Brit

49 Brit

Cristot

12 SS

Caen

R. Aure

La Belle
Epine

Bucéels

50 Brit

R. Drôme

Balleroy

Lingèvres

Tilly
sur Seulles

Juvigny

7 Brit

Hottot

Caen

2 US

Lehr

R. Seulles

Noyers

R. Odon

Proposed drop zone
1 (Brit) ✈ Div

1 US

Livry

Evrecy

Caumont

13 June

7 Brit

Point 213

Amaye sur Seulles

Tracy
Bocage

VILLERS-BOCAGE

Landes

Hill 174

2 Ger (recce)

2 Ger

I SS

XLVII

R. Odon

Aunay sur Odon

0   2   4   6   8 Kilometres
0   1   2   3   4   5 Miles

Allied Armoured Division
German Panzer Division

VILLERS-BOCAGE

after the withdrawal from Villers-Bocage, Hinde's perimeter had to be shortened due to enemy pressure in the thick bocage where observation was very difficult. On the morning of 14 June one artillery battery came under very accurate fire from a German 210-mm gun and though this fire subsided, tank and infantry pressure began to increase. Corps artillery attempted to help out but was hampered by the difficulty of target location.[1]

With the 7th Armoured intent on recovering from its setback, it was now the corps commander, Bucknall, who determined the outcome of the battle. Instead of reacting quickly to Erskine's request for support by detaching an infantry force from 50th Division to reinforce the 22nd Armoured Brigade, Bucknall elected to continue the offensive by the 50th Division against Panzer Lehr, in the hope that the division could advance to Villers-Bocage and relieve Hinde. With Panzer Lehr fully engaged around both Tilly and Villers-Bocage and the 2nd Panzer only beginning to occupy the Villers sector in strength, it was probable that the original gap along the Aure River was still unplugged by the Germans.

Bucknall seems to have misunderstood the urgent need to reinforce the 7th Armoured while there was still time. Certainly, the losses at Point 213 and the subsequent need to withdraw from Villers-Bocage were severe setbacks, but they were by no means irreversible: the division still posed a substantial threat to the German flank but *only* if immediate steps were taken to press what remained of their advantage before the 2nd Panzer could close up in strength and block further movement toward Caen. At that time Hinde's positions astride the Caumont-Villers-Bocage road at Hill 174 were defensible against anything the Germans could throw at him, but what concerned both Hinde and Erskine was the possibility of a concentrated attack by the main elements of the 2nd Panzer Division. Erskine told corps: 'I consider that 2 Pz Div were taken by surprise but they can be expected to react fairly violently. Can you give me an indication of what the corps commander intends if their reaction is violent?'[2]

Bucknall's plan was for 50th Division to attack toward Hottot on the Caumont-Tilly road, and in reply to Erskine's

---

[1] Major General G. P. Gregson, letter to the author, 8 August 1982.
[2] War Diary, 13 June, loc.cit.

sitrep he optimistically told the 7th Armoured: 'Since 1,000 tons of bombs will precede attack, 50 Div will attack in narrow front with full arty spt. I think it will be successful. This attack should fully occupy Lehr and thus help you.'[1]

This was grossly misplaced optimism on Bucknall's part, for Panzer Lehr's defence in this sector had stiffened considerably and remained as unyielding as it had been against earlier attacks. Moreover, Bayerlein was aware of the 7th Armoured's withdrawal from Villers-Bocage and the arrival of the 2nd Panzer, and was not in the least intimidated by the superior British air and artillery support. The end result was a butting match in which 50th Division failed to gain any substantial new ground, and never managed to advance anywhere near the village of Hottot.

By the morning of 14 June it had become evident that the 50th Division attack would fail to relieve the 7th Armoured and at this point Bucknall's resolve to back Erskine's decision to hold the Tracy-Bocage salient evaporated. In his book, *The Struggle for Europe*, Chester Wilmot suggests Bucknall lost his nerve but the truth seems to be that the corps commander was now paying for his decision made the previous night. What was now certain was that the 7th Armoured was in some danger without infantry reinforcements and, although reinforcements were available in the form of two infantry brigades of the recently landed 49th Division, Bucknall never considered seeking permission from Dempsey to divert one or more of these units from their originally planned commitment on the eastern flank of 30 Corps. By midday Bucknall's concern about Erskine's line of communication and the growing threat posed by the 2nd Panzer and Panzer Lehr led him to order – with Dempsey's permission – the withdrawal of the 7th Armoured to new positions east of Caumont. Without support, Erskine had no choice but to concur.

A written order, codenamed Operation ANISEED was issued that afternoon, but before the 22nd Armoured Brigade was able to commence its withdrawal the 2nd Panzer launched a heavy attack which was effectively crushed, largely as a result of timely artillery fire from US artillery units supporting the 1st Infantry Division around Caumont. Colonel Gregson remembers the effects of this support: 'I had with me a US liaison officer –

[1] Message, 30 Corps to the 7th Armoured Division, 13 June, War Diary, loc.cit.

Captain Chuck Babcock and he called for a "Serenade"[1] – the target was only some 300 meters in front of us . . . I remember Babcock said: "If we get out of this I'll be court-martialled – only Commanding Generals can order a 'Serenade'." The "Serenade" duly arrived in minimum time and very accurate. I don't ever again wish to be so close to such a volume of fire. The effect was devastating and we knocked out some 11 tanks and completely broke up the attack – all was quiet except for snipers in the trees outside our positions.'[2]

Despite firmly repulsing this attack, there was still no other viable option left to the 7th Armoured except withdrawal. Nevertheless, when the order finally came, Hinde's war diary recorded the reason given: '1600 hours – Bde Comd to GOC for conference. Receives orders for withdrawal (Op ANISEED). The main reason for this withdrawal was the slow progress made by 50 Div in the TILLY–LINGEVERES area.'[3]

With Hinde involved in working out a strategy for the withdrawal, the direction of operations for 22nd Armoured Brigade was left to Major Lever, the brigade major. 'It is very clear in my mind,' wrote Lever, 'particularly as I was personally conducting operations . . . that the situation was extremely precarious. Without reinforcements the situation could have become untenable after say 24 hours. . . There is no doubt Bayerlein commanding the German forces sensed a local victory and was determined to exploit it.'[4]

During the night of 14–15 June Bucknall's order to withdraw was carried out, covered by accurate and continuous fire from American artillery and the RAF which flattened Villers-Bocage. Thirty-six hours earlier the town had been liberated; now it lay in ruins and back under German control. The price of Bucknall's withdrawal order was to concede the battle of Villers-Bocage to the Germans by default.

Bucknall's timidity and apparent desire to fight a conventional, orderly infantry battle had, in a single stroke, forfeited the initiative successfully to continue the offensive and maintain the British threat to Caen from the west. What might have occurred had Bucknall acted quickly and decisively can, of course, only be

---

[1] A term used to denote a concentration of all available artillery fire upon a specific target.   [2] Major General Gregson, loc.cit.
[3] War Diary, the 22nd Armoured Brigade, 14 June, loc.cit.
[4] Lieutenant Colonel Lever, loc.cit.

speculation. However, there is little reason to doubt that a reinforced 7th Armoured – despite later charges which questioned the resolve of the Division – could not only have held the area around Tracy-Bocage but eventually resumed the offensive toward the Odon valley. General Armitage believes Bucknall's decision was unnecessary if the corps commander had elected to reinforce Erskine. '7th Armoured could have held on *with* reinforcements. Without any, despite the "bloody nose" given to 2nd Panzer around Villers-Bocage and Tracy-Bocage, their chances were less certain.'[1] Dempsey had promised the 33rd Armoured Brigade by 17 June, and with one or more additional infantry brigades Erskine would have been in a position to hold out indefinitely with these forces and the supporting fires of the air forces and the artillery which had already accounted for the destruction of eleven German tanks.

Bucknall later defended his decision by claiming that 'General Erskine did not ask me for infantry reinforcements. We put all the artillery support available at his disposal. His picture made it clear to me that we could not maintain 7 Armd Div on the AMAYE spur with its axis continually interrupted by Boche armour and detachments of panzer grenadiers without heavy loss in armour and infantry. After discussion between us I decided it would be best, as our true object had failed, to get the Army Commander's permission to withdraw 7 Armd Div to suitable ground covering the approach to our junction with 5 US Corps and right of 50 Div. I did not urge General Erskine to stay and I did not offer to send reinforcements.'[2]

By his own admission, General Bucknall apparently never seriously considered attempting to hold the Tracy-Bocage positions. 'I have no doubt at all that 7 Armd Div could have held the AMAYE spur position for at least another twenty-four hours. Even had further reinforcements of infantry been available, I would not have considered holding the position then worthwhile.'[3] Moreover, even Bucknall admitted 'There was no fear of a counter-attack on 50 Div front. They were opposed, we knew, by small pockets of panzer grenadiers and tanks and there was no sign of buildup.'[4]

[1] Major General Armitage, letter of 29 April 1982.
[2] Bucknall, letter to Chester Wilmot, 29 March 1947, loc.cit.   [3] Ibid.
[4] Bucknall, letter to Chester Wilmot, 15 April 1947, Bucknall Papers.

Bucknall did not believe the 151st Infantry Brigade (50th Div), then in corps reserve, could have been sent to Villers-Bocage in time to affect the fight there, or that the two brigades of the 49th Division could prepare for battle in time. 'They were destined in the Army plan in any event for the Fontenay front on the East flank of the Corps. Moreover, 49 was a young Div with no recent battle experience and it was important to launch them nicely into their first fighting in a properly coordinated battle, and not bundle them helter-skelter into hot armoured scrapping like that round V–B and Amaye. In my opinion, only a most favourable situation would have justified upsetting the Army plan, or further stripping the stretched and strained formations of 30 Corps in order to carry out what you might call a heavy "parry" once this lightning attack was held.'[1] Inexperienced or not, the 49th Division had trained for months to enter combat and *could* have been utilized had Bucknall elected to insert them into the Villers-Bocage sector.[2]

Less easy to explain is the complete absence of Montgomery's and Dempsey's influence during the critical moments of the battles on 13 and 14 June. The importance of the 30 Corps offensive was obviously on Montgomery's mind when he wrote to Brooke on 14 June: 'When 2nd Panzer Division suddenly appeared in the Villers-Bocage–Caumont area it plugged the hole through which I had broken [and] I had to think again [and be careful] not to get off balance... So long as Rommel uses his strategic reserves to plug holes that is good.' But Montgomery 'had not got sufficient strength to be offensive on both flanks of Second Army', resulting in a decision 'to be defensive in the Caen sector on the front of 1 Corps, but aggressively so', concentrating his offensive punch in 30 Corps. 'I shall hold strongly and fight offensively in the general area Caumont–Villers-Bocage, i.e., at the junction of the two armies.'[3]

---

[1] Bucknall, letter of 29 March 1947, loc.cit.
[2] The leading brigade of the 49th Division was committed to the 50th Division sector northeast of Tilly-sur-Seulles on the night of 13 June.
[3] M501, Montgomery to Brooke, 14 June 1944, Alanbrooke Papers. Twenty-four hours earlier Montgomery had confirmed to Brooke that his object had been to swing the right wing of the Second Army behind Panzer Lehr, and using the 7th Armoured Division seize Evrecy and Aunay-sur-Odon and the Orne River crossings as far south as Thury-Harcourt. The 49th and 50th Divisions were to reinforce by swinging southeast using Tilly-sur-Seulles as a pivot.

While Bucknall clearly lacked the aggressiveness and determination to retain the initiative, both Montgomery and Dempsey must share responsibility for failing personally to take a firmer grip on the battle and, if necessary, to order Bucknall to beef up his defences around Villers-Bocage. The situation on the 1 Corps front had been stagnant for days and Montgomery's decision on 14 June to concentrate his efforts on the western flank came far too late. When 30 Corps renewed its offensive on 17 June they found themselves in much the same situation as 1 Corps. Ironically, at the very moment Montgomery was telling Brooke of his shift in priority to the west, Dempsey was working out a scheme with Leigh-Mallory whereby 'I would attack with the LEFT of 1 Corps and take CAEN.'[1]*

Bucknall's misreading of the importance of maintaining the 7th Armoured as a threat to the German flank is shown by his reluctance to reinforce Erskine, and his argument that operations on the 30 Corps front were merely a local effort to break up the opposition until seized upon by Dempsey as the key to threatening Caen and permitting the employment of 1st Airborne Division was a complete misunderstanding of the army commander's intentions. As Bucknall wrote after the war: 'The 30 Corps effort over these few days was not regarded, in the absence of provision, as anything but subsidiary to the Main Ops, and its possibilities were, I am convinced, only latent in the Army Commander's mind for use *if we get a good break*.'[2] Written as this was in 1947, it is likely that Bucknall's reasons had much to do with Montgomery's proclamations that he had always intended to use the Second Army in the role of pinning down the German reserves to the Caen front. However, as will be seen, there was no evidence of such a strategy at this early date.

While the 7th Armoured was not responsible for Bucknall's indecisiveness they certainly were fully accountable for the debacle at Point 213. Armitage believes 'They took too many risks and their local tactics were poor.'[3] Unaccustomed to the tactics employed by the Germans and mentally unprepared for a sur-

[1] Dempsey Diary, 14 June 1944, loc.cit.
* See Chapter 13.
[2] Bucknall, letter to Chester Wilmot, 29 April 1947, loc.cit.
[3] Major General Armitage, letter of 29 April 1982

prise attack, the 4th CLY appear to have been over-confident as a result of their achievements in capturing Villers-Bocage so easily. In a post-mortem written shortly afterwards Hinde noted two major problems: inadequate tank-infantry cooperation and poor dispersion. 'The main lesson is of course the closer co-operation of tanks and inf in BOCAGE country – much closer than had been considered normal previously . . . I do not think that our Armd Regts react quickly enough to the requirements of dispersion when held up on a road. Yet no comd would disperse his Sqn or Regt off the road without orders.'[1] Erskine accepted full responsibility for the disaster at Point 213 and after the war wrote: 'I will not try to excuse what was undoubtedly poor local tactics but we had been pushing along at great speed and taking many risks. The damage to 4th CLY was as much my fault as anybody's for urging the speed of advance. . .'[2]

Bucknall's performance in Normandy surely came as no surprise to Brooke, who had never concealed his disappointment at his selection by Montgomery. The Sandhurst-trained Bucknall had commanded the 5th Division in Sicily and Italy and had so impressed Montgomery that he was brought back to England to take command of 30 Corps. After the first OVERLORD briefing in April a disturbed Brooke told Montgomery that Bucknall lacked the experience to command a corps, commenting in his diary: 'Bucknall was very weak and I am quite certain unfit to command a Corps.'[3] Later, in his 'Notes on My Life', he was to write: 'On listening to Bucknall that afternoon I was convinced he was not of the calibre to handle a corps in such an important operation. I told Monty so but was informed by him that he knew him well and that although he had not shown up well, he had full confidence in him. Monty does not often make mistakes so I said no more but it was not long after the commencement of operations that Monty found out I had been right and was forced to replace him.'[4] There is some doubt over whether Bucknall even attended the final OVERLORD briefing on 15 May for, according to his personal diary, his entry for that date mentions 'shopping

---

[1] War Diary, the 22nd Armoured Brigade, June 1944.
[2] Quoted in Armitage letter of 16 June 1982.
[3] Alanbrooke Diary, loc.cit. Bucknall had been allocated seven minutes to speak at THUNDERCLAP, and after speaking for nearly seventeen minutes was unceremoniously told to sit down.
[4] Alanbrooke Papers, loc.cit.

in London' and in the afternoon talks with members of the 1 Corps staff.[1]

By temperament and experience Bucknall was too conventional and cautious, and unable to adapt his thinking to the type of battles his corps was now fighting in the difficult bocage against the more experienced Germans. As his Chief-of-Staff, Brigadier Pyman, was diplomatically to put it later: 'He had done a great deal for the Corps and he was a fine D-Day commander. But the open warfare was not nearly so much up his street. He kept getting out of position.'[2] 30 Corps HQ was one of the most battle-experienced in the British Army and had developed a very strong personality of its own. Its veteran staff officers were accustomed to a firm and inspirational type of commander, and strong leadership such as was provided by their former commander, Lieutenant General Oliver Leese. They found Bucknall lacking in inspiration and his tenure as corps commander has privately been described as a 'non-event'. The problem was that he never managed to get himself known throughout the corps, where a firm hand was required with the veteran 50th Division and the 7th Armoured. A more forceful commander might have cured the tired 'Desert Rats' of their casual approach to training during the all-important pre-invasion period.[3]

To some extent Bucknall's weaknesses were balanced by the efforts of the brilliant Brigadier Harold E. 'Pete' Pyman who, as Brigadier General Staff, brought great experience and ability to the task of coordinating the work of the corps staff. However, no staff officer, no matter how talented, can fill a leadership void, and the battle of Villers-Bocage, one of the most decisive moments in the battle of Normandy, literally cried out for a firm and forceful leader. The potential rewards offered by determinedly retaining a grip on the Villers-Bocage positions demanded boldness and resourcefulness, qualities Bucknall simply did not possess. He was a good officer but simply out of his depth as a corps commander and if blame is to be assigned for the failure at Villers-Bocage, it properly belongs with Montgomery who misjudged his ability to move up to higher responsibility. Bucknall's

---

[1] Bucknall Diary, 15 May 1944, Bucknall Papers.
[2] General Sir Harold E. Pyman, *Call to Arms*, London, 1971, p. 74.
[3] According to Lever, one of the units which took this attitude was Cranley's 4th County of London Yeomanry. Interview, 19 April 1983.

major misjudgement was in failing to recognize the importance of taking advantage of the gap in the German defences along the inter-army boundary. The opportunity had been recognized as early as the afternoon of 10 June, and had the 7th Armoured begun its movement toward Villers-Bocage even a day sooner, by the time the 2nd Panzer arrived in the area, the division, and possibly the remainder of 30 Corps, would have been firmly established on the high ground with adequate anti-tank defences. The opportunity had always been brief and now that it was lost the British threat of a continuation of the right hook disappeared, leaving Villers-Bocage in German hands where it remained until August.

The official British history is a marvel of obfuscation in its narration of the battle for Villers-Bocage, and sets a facile gloss over the significance of the setback to British aspirations, suggesting that the fault was mainly with the 7th Armoured Division and as a result of the timely presence of the two German panzer divisions. Villers-Bocage raised some important and unpleasant questions, not only about the impact it had on Montgomery's battle plans but the initiative of the 30 Corps commander.

As we shall see in Part IV, the British official history is not forthright in its discussion of important issues, particularly of those which might in any way reflect unfavourably upon Montgomery's generalship. Bucknall's role in the decision to withdraw the 7th Armoured Division is not mentioned, and the attack by the 50th Division against Panzer Lehr is discussed as if it were the best and only option open to 30 Corps:

> In reaching these decisions the divisional and corps commanders were influenced by the knowledge that while the 7th Armoured Division was outstretched deep in country held by the Panzer Lehr Division, the 2d Panzer Division was in turn coming into action against it from the south. Until the 50th Division made headway and the (7th) armoured division was strengthened by the addition of the 33d Armoured Brigade, its precarious positions at Tracy-Bocage and the near-by Amaye sur Suelles were only a *liability*.'[1] (Author's italics.)

The problem was that for some months afterwards the 7th Armoured Division did not perform particularly well, and for

---

[1] Ellis, op.cit., p. 255.

this reason tended to take the brunt of the criticism over Villers-Bocage. Unfortunately, the sanitized and misleading interpretation in the official account placed a stamp of truth and authenticity on to this battle without any real discussion of the implications of the events of 13–14 June. Calling the results of the operation 'disappointing', the senior official historian, Major Ellis, wrote: 'With Panzer Lehr still holding up the advance of 50th Division and with a second armoured division coming up unexpectedly against them, the 7th Armoured Division could hardly have achieved full success. As it was, the immediate result of these operations was disappointing.'[1]

These and other statements have undoubtedly influenced many people into accepting that Villers-Bocage and certain other events in Normandy were of no great significance. What Ellis failed to reveal was that the defeat at Villers-Bocage was a humiliating and quite probably a needless defeat to British aims at rapidly expanding the Caen bridgehead. Publicly, General Dempsey defended the withdrawal, maintaining that the 30 Corps offensive had contributed to drawing German panzer reserves on to the Second Army's front. In fact, Dempsey was irate and dismayed at the outcome. In an unpublished post-war interview he revealed his true feelings:

> This attack by 7th Armoured Division should have succeeded. My feeling that Bucknall and Erskine would have to go started with that failure. Early on the morning of the 12th [June] I went down to see Erskine – gave him his orders and told him to get moving and that I would tell the corps commander what he was doing. If he had carried out my orders he would never have been kicked out of Villers-Bocage but by this time 7th Armoured was living on its reputation and the whole handling of that battle was a disgrace. Their decision to withdraw [from Villers-Bocage on 13 June] was made without consulting me; it was done by the corps commander and Erskine.[2]

---

[1] Ellis, op.cit., p. 256.
[2] 'Notes on conversation with General Dempsey', by Chester Wilmot, n.d. Liddell Hart Papers. Wilmot elected not to use Dempsey's unflattering comments in his book. Dempsey chose not to relieve Bucknall after the battle of Villers-Bocage but by early August, after a disastrous start to Operation BLUECOAT, he realized the time had now come and asked Montgomery to sack him. Erskine and Hinde were similarly relieved. Viscount Cranley survived captivity and died some years after the war. By the end of July 1944 it was decided to merge the 4th County of London Yeomanry with the 3rd CLY under the control of the independent 4th Armoured Brigade. The new unit was designated by the 3rd/4th County of London Yeomanry (Sharpshooters). Michael Wittmann, the 7th

Although Dempsey's criticism of the decision to abandon Villers-Bocage on 13 June appears to be excessively harsh, it does fairly reflect his utter disenchantment over what he considered a needless surrender of the initiative. Even had Bucknall been able on 13 June to reinforce Hinde speedily – which he was not – withdrawal was necessary. Dempsey was later quoted as saying that as a result of the failure to hold Villers-Bocage there was 'no chance now of a snap operation with airborne troops either to seize Caen or to deepen the bridgehead on XXX Corps front. It is clear now that Caen can be taken only by a set-piece assault and we do not have the men or ammunition for that at this time.'[1]

The gravity of the threat posed by the 7th Armoured had never been lost upon the Germans. As General Kraemer has revealed, not only was there a strong possibility of the 1 SS Panzer Corps' flank being rolled up from the west, but until the arrival of the 2nd Panzer there was little, other than Wittmann's small panzer force, to stop the British. The Germans never understood why Montgomery failed to press his advantage. Of the period around 10 June, Kraemer wrote: 'It was still incomprehensible why the enemy exerted himself with assaults in the direction of Caen and did not make a powerful drive to exploit the open gap on either side south of Bayeux.'[2] The arrival of advance elements of the 2nd Panzer had helped relieve the growing anxiety over the gap. 'A later attack by this division was not successful, but the enemy had let a favourable opportunity slip. On 13 June contact was established between 1 SS Pz Corps and LXXXIV Corps. Thus the gap which might have enabled the enemy to make an easy breakthrough almost without losses was sealed off.'[3]

By 17 June – D+11 – Dempsey's worst fears had come true: the front had congealed. The situation on the British front had changed little in over a week except in the 30 Corps sector. To the east, neither the 3rd Canadian nor the 3rd British Divisions had gained any significant new ground. What made the failure of the

Armoured's nemesis that grim day, was already something of a legend for his previous heroic exploits on the Eastern Front. His deeds at Villers-Bocage confirmed the legend which made him the most successful tank commander of the entire war. Prior to his death near Falaise in early August, he was responsible during the Second World War for the destruction of 138 tanks and self-propelled guns, and the disablement of 132 anti-tank guns. Cf., James Lucas and James Barker, *The Killing Ground*, London, 1978.

[1]   Quoted by Chester Wilmot in *The Struggle for Europe*, p. 340.
[2]   '1 SS Panzer Corps in the West' (1944), loc.cit.
[3]   Ibid.

right hook by 30 Corps so important was that in Normandy there were no open flanks which could be turned. For a brief moment the German weakness along the Aure had presented the closest thing to an open flank that was to occur during the period before the breakout. At the most propitious moment so far in the Normandy campaign the British, in what was ultimately to prove one of the costliest Allied mistakes in the liberation of France, lost their one great opportunity to break open and exploit Rommel's still unsettled defences around Caen.

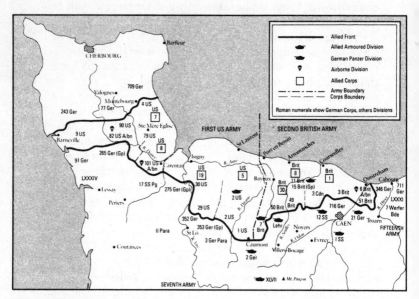

SITUATION MAP, 17 JUNE 1944

CHAPTER 12

Ends and Means

> I never once had cause or reason to alter my master
> plan.
> > Montgomery

The British setback at Villers-Bocage forced Montgomery to abandon, at least for the moment, the plan to envelop Caen. In a full week of battle after the D-Day landings there had been little tactical and no strategic success on the British front. Historically, the argument offered by Montgomery and his adherents was always optimistic, and maintained that the role of the Second British Army was – and always had been – to attract and contain the major elements of Rommel's infantry and panzer reserves to the Caen front in order to ease the way for Bradley in the west.[1]

The goal of the pincer movement against Villers-Bocage was *never* designed merely to attain such limited goals. The Second Army operations had been carefully planned before D-Day to maximize surprise and initiative, mainly through aggressive action by the armoured units, not to be a defensive strategy. Yet, not surprisingly, most British officers and men who participated in the abortive offensive against Villers-Bocage believed – and no doubt still believe – that their primary mission had been to attract German panzer strength to the Caen front. One example is provided by Major Sale, who states in his unpublished account of the battle: 'The British high command obviously intended to make contact with the German tanks in such strength in order to divert them from continuing to move toward the Americans. The British plan was successful but hard luck on the Sharpshooters, for many of them were the sacrifice on that day, 13 June 1944.'[1]

They would have been dismayed had they known that Montgomery's true aim was for them to act as the dagger against Caen by tearing an irreparable hole in the German flank, capable of

---

[1] Sale account, loc.cit.

further exploitation into the Odon valley. Possession of Noyers and Evrecy would have left the 12th SS in the jaws of a trap between the 3rd Canadian Division and the 7th Armoured Division and possibly other elements of 30 Corps. To exploit this success Montgomery would have been justified in demanding – and getting – the 1st Airborne plan reinstated. While the 'Desert Rats' would have been vulnerable to attack by the 2nd Panzer, they could have called upon naval gunfire and air support to retain their grip on these new positions until reinforced. Moreover, the suddenness of this thrust might well have forced Rommel to abandon the Caen salient to avoid annihilation, despite Hitler's uncompromising orders to stand firm.

Having come so soon after D-Day, the failure of this second of Montgomery's plans against Caen was a severe blow. When asked about it by Chester Wilmot after the war, Montgomery replied that he had not been worried when Dempsey withdrew. 'The thrusts had served their purpose. They had drawn the armour on to the right flank. Having achieved that there was no point in incurring useless casualties just to hold the ground.'[1] In his own unofficial account, *Normandy to the Baltic*, Montgomery retold the events of 13–14 June but failed to comment on their implications, stating only that 'the exposed position of 7 Armoured Division became untenable.'[2]

In addition to the loss of an excellent opportunity, the other major result of the failure at Villers-Bocage was further to limit Montgomery's options of when and where he could attack Rommel. A frontal attack had been ruled out soon after D-Day and now the envelopment of Caen had likewise failed. The Caen bridgehead was already far too small and though the buildup of British forces was continuing, albeit unsatisfactorily, it was still necessary to keep pressure on the Germans to prevent them from gaining time to organize and mount a counteroffensive.

In the US sector the approaches to Cherbourg were being stoutly defended. Bradley now had four corps committed (V, VII, VIII and XIX) and held a fairly wide salient running from Caumont to the west coast of the Cotentin Peninsula, which had been cut in half and isolated by VIII Corps. Nevertheless, the

[1] Interview with Chester Wilmot, 18 May 1946, Liddell Hart Papers.
[2] Montgomery, *El Alamein to the River Sangro and Normandy to the Baltic* (as one volume), op.cit., p. 222

offensive against Cherbourg by VII Corps was proving difficult in the marshlands of the Merderet River.

The buildup of Allied forces and supplies over the beaches was running behind schedule due to poor weather and bottle- necks, and a noticeable shortage of artillery ammunition was beginning to be felt.[1] But the real problem was this: Bradley's primary effort was to secure the western bridgehead and capture Cherbourg. Until this was done there would be insufficient forces to begin an offensive to enlarge the American bridgehead to the south of the Cotenin.

Time was the principal factor. So far the deception plan was still confusing the Germans, who were reinforcing Normandy piecemeal but immobilizing the main forces of their Fifteenth Army in the Pas de Calais for what their leaders thought would be the main invasion. The FORTITUDE planners had never imagined that the deception plan would work for an extended period, believing that the German High Command would sooner or later realize they had been the victims of a gigantic hoax.[2] When that moment came there would be a massive and immediate enemy reinforcement of Normandy. Such a prospect was not reassuring, especially if it occurred before the Caen bridgehead was enlarged. While it was premature to speak of stalemate, the prospect could not be ruled out. Clearly, Montgomery must employ fresh tactics to circumvent Rommel. But what would these be? A fundamental precept of Montgomery's strategy had been, from the very beginnings of his OVERLORD planning, to ensure that the left flank was firmly anchored and Bradley left free from major German interference while the Cotentin and Cherbourg were secured. The strategy was to have been accomplished by the capture of Caen and its vital nodal points, *not* by the employment of what were essentially defensive tactics. However, until VIII Corps (the first of the followup corps) could be landed and

[1] Ammunition expenditures were far in excess of availability; mixups in priority of landing for supplies apparently caused less essential items to be landed first. However, the need for heavy artillery support to help break the bottleneck around Caen was the prime reason for these growing shortages.

[2] Even in mid-July the German High Command was not fully convinced that the Normandy landings had been the main Allied effort, and still visualized a landing in the Pas de Calais where most of the Fifteenth Army was still being retained. Cf.: Records of the US Army European Theater, Study: 'Strategy of the Campaign in Western Europe, 1944–45', Eisenhower Library, and SHAEF G–2 Weekly Report, Enemy Order of Battle in the West, 22 July 1944, PRO.

committed, Montgomery lacked the offensive punch required for a third sustained thrust against Caen.

Montgomery was thus forced to consider a new strategy: the Second Army must divert the reinforcing German divisions (mainly the panzer) away from Bradley's front by keeping them fully occupied defending Caen until such time as Dempsey was strong enough to mount an offensive capable of capturing or encircling the city. By attracting the panzer and infantry reinforcements en route to Normandy Montgomery was astutely taking advantage of a bad situation and was, in fact, able to salvage some benefit from the Villers-Bocage debacle which had at least resulted in the commitment of the 2nd Panzer division to his front. With Panzer Lehr, the 12th SS and the 21st Panzer already in place, a total of four panzer divisions were now opposing the Second Army.

Given the present tactical situation, there was nothing wrong with Montgomery's new strategy; the problem was that he never admitted it was any such thing. Quite the contrary, he always insisted his original master plan called for holding on the left, forcing Rommel to commit his reserves there, thus permitting Bradley to capture Cherbourg and break out on the right. However, it was not until *after* D-Day that this conception became his strategy and, as we have already seen, nothing whatsoever in his pre-D-Day plans, notes or speeches ever alluded to such methods.

In his *Memoirs*, as he had previously in *Normandy to the Baltic*, Montgomery continued to maintain that his plan unfolded exactly as intended:

> Briefly, it was so to stage and conduct operations that we drew the main enemy strength on to the front of the Second British Army on our eastern flank, in order that we might the more easily gain territory in the west and make the ultimate breakout on that flank — using the First American Army for the purpose . . . in the Caen sector, the acquisition of ground was not so pressing; the need *there* was by hard fighting to make the enemy commit his reserves, so that the American forces would meet less opposition in their advances to gain the territory which was vital on the west . . . I was convinced that strong and persistent offensive action in the Caen sector would achieve our object of drawing the enemy reserves on to our eastern flank: this was my basic conception. From the beginning it

formed the basis of all our planning. . . I never once had cause
or reason to alter my master plan.[1]

As he had in North Africa, Montgomery had indeed changed his
plan and his concept of the battle; his post-war insistence that
everything had gone according to plan may have convinced
gullible audiences, but his colleagues and senior subordinates
were never in any doubt that his claims were concocted after the
fact, and were grossly untrue.

Little has ever been said publicly to dispute Montgomery for
reasons which will be explored later. However, in post-war
interviews, personal correspondence, reports and personal
diaries, many of those who were closely associated with Montgomery have revealed the facts about his true actions and intentions in Normandy. Let us briefly examine some of what has been
said.

Other than his Chief-of-Staff, de Guingand, few were ever
closer to Montgomery or understood him better than his able and
trusted intelligence officer, Brigadier Edgar 'Bill' Williams. A
brilliant scholar and Oxford don, Bill Williams rose from the
rank of 2nd lieutenant in 1939 to brigadier at the age of thirty-
one in 1944. For nearly three years he was Montgomery's senior
intelligence officer and one of only several men permitted frequent access to his Tactical HQ. Both as a trusted confidant and
his intelligence officer, Williams was privy to all Montgomery's
plans and thinking. By nature, Williams was inclined to speak
frankly with Montgomery in order to obtain guidance or to press
home a point. One of his tasks was to condense the daily flow of
intelligence to 21st Army Group – including the immensely
important ULTRA intercepts from Bletchley Park – and present
the results to his chief. There are some who credit Bill Williams
with being the real brains behind Montgomery, credit he would
be quick to deny. After the war he spoke candidly with Dr Forrest
Pogue about a wide range of subjects, including Normandy. Of
Montgomery he has said:

> Monty was a wonderful Intelligence man's Master. You never
> had to repeat to him. He was all business while you were
> reporting to him, and then afterwards you could pull his leg. As
> the war grew on, he spent less time with his seniors. He was less

[1] Montgomery, *Memoirs*, op.cit., pp. 254–5.

willing to accept direct criticism and was somewhat inclined to be lordly. His substitute family of young subordinates was a great relief to him. But he suffered from the disadvantage of remoteness from people who could stand up to him.[1]

Williams himself was never nonplussed over his chief's intentions in Normandy:

> We did not expect the bulk of the [German] armour against 21st Army Group. Monty tries to change the story. Shortly before D-Day I produced a memo which Monty could use in briefing of his four generals. We knew Caen would call for a reaction. We also knew that certain armour – 21st Panzer – was there. The best way into the bridgehead for armour in the Orleans Gap was towards Caen. We felt that the Germans would use armour as a stopgap and then put in the infantry, pulling out the armour for another job. We knew they could not pull it all out. [We] thought 17th SS Panzer Division would be used against First Army.[2]

Had Monty always intended to 'hinge' on Caen, he would surely, Williams noted, have increased the defensive capabilities of the Second Army in the Caen area. And as Pogue noted, Williams did not 'recall that 21st Army Group increased its anti-tank elements in the Caen area. To say that the bulk of the armour would be at Caen would not fit into the pre D-Day idea.'[3] Williams explained how he would deal with Montgomery during their discussions:

> My habit was to try and get an idea of what the enemy would do by trying out certain things on Monty. I would say if I do this what will the enemy do. However, the enemy might have something to say about that. It was difficult for me – difficult to know Monty's plan. I had to fix the earliest and latest times the enemy would know about our actions. You must remember there could be a discrepancy between my appreciation and Monty's decision.[4]

However, Williams was never in doubt about Montgomery's offensive intentions regarding Caen:

> [Williams] remembers that Monty took stuff from his appreciation [Monty's notes on St Paul's speech comes from this].

---

[1] Interview with Dr Forrest C. Pogue, 30–31 May 1947, loc.cit.
[2] Ibid.
[3] Ibid.
[4] Ibid.

Drew rivers in red pencil to pull out on map. Will be in Monty's papers. No doubt we wanted Caen – a D-Day objective.[1]

In fact, Williams himself briefed the intelligence officers at Bletchley Park about Montgomery's intentions, and later pointed out to Dr Pogue that:

> Three to four days before D-Day I briefed [that the] armoured brigades [were] to peg out claims – [and that they] must be regarded as expendable. I didn't speak officially but said what I thought was necessary. Indicated that I didn't like to have to say it, because my brother was in one of the brigades. Dempsey described how he expected to get his brigades forward to Tilly-Harcourt. Was to sneak one column through to Caen, another to Tilly-Harcourt.[2]

Montgomery's post-war claims are firmly refuted by Williams, who noted:

> In my first intelligence summary – issued on D-Day – I wouldn't mind betting that I said: 'We have Bayeux but not Caen'. We had four worries: (1) causeways on UTAH (2) OMAHA (3) Bayeux (4) Caen. These things I carried as targets. You don't develop private targets at a headquarters. I carried them as targets because Monty and Freddie [de Guingand] did. When you get the build-up around Caen you see the value of it . . . Monty wanted Caen the first day. Expected to get it quickly. When he saw coagulation he said this will make a good pivot. He was trying to take not hold the enemy. Wanted to utilise his advantage.[3]

Brigadier Williams was certainly not the only knowledgeable officer to dispute Montgomery's version of events. Others have spoken off the record, among them Eisenhower's chief-of-staff, Lieutenant General Walter Bedell Smith:

> Very simple to answer the question on Caen. Monty now gives the erroneous picture. Caen is the gateway to a broad, long, flat plain from Caen southeast towards Paris. It becomes wider and wider towards Dreux-Evreux where the chalk streams flow and where I'm going to do some fishing when I am through

---

[1] Interview with Dr Forrest C. Pogue, 30–31 May 1947, loc.cit.
[2] Ibid.
[3] Ibid. After the war Brigadier Williams worked with the UN Secretariat, and then returned to Oxford to resume his interrupted academic career. He served as a Fellow of Balliol College and held a number of other posts within the University prior to his retirement in 1980, including Warden of Rhodes House. In 1973 he was knighted by Queen Elizabeth II.

with this. Monty intended to make his main effort in this good tank country coupled with the swing to the right by the Americans. Monty has always planned his big battles for direct penetration (he likes direct attacks, which is why he is good for assaults and no good on envelopments), but he wins his battles by envelopments he never planned. He won them all by wide envelopments, but he never planned them. Monty wins his battles afterwards. At Alamein the Freyberg attack was the payoff. He was on the flank and Monty was trying to push through. Alex became nervous and sent [Lt-Gen Richard] McCreery (he told me this) up to sit with Monty in case a break came, so Monty would be sure to exploit the break.

Brooke was confident we couldn't go through the bocage. Thought it was a fantastic plan. Said he had retired through there. Had contempt for the plan... Germans thought the Caen attack was the chief attack. They kept their armor there in front of them.[1]

Even Montgomery's close friend, Sir James Grigg, the Secretary of State for War, was not misled:

Of course Montgomery's original idea was to break out of the bocage country around Caen into the open in the first few days after landing – it would be idle to deny that... At Caen I am sure he soon came to the conclusion that to break-out would cost more casualties than with his shrinking British manpower he could afford and I know he adjusted his ideas so as to preserve his main purpose. This was to use the Anglo-Canadian Army as a hinge which should bear the brunt of the enemy counter-attacks, and especially to attract to that flank the bulk of the German armour and so to facilitate and accelerate the American breakout and double wheel which was the essence of his strategy.[2]

Montgomery's claims were also hotly disputed by one of the senior OVERLORD planners, Captain J. Hughes-Hallett, Royal Navy, who was closely involved in the cross-Channel planning, first under Mountbatten, and later with COSSAC. Hughes-Hallett bluntly contradicts Montgomery:

Monty's talk of his original intention to hinge on Caen is absolutely balls. Monty is a great operational commander. When he was checked in his original intent of taking Caen he had the idea of doing the other operation. I believe the second

---

[1] Interview with Lieutenant General Walter Bedell Smith by Dr Forrest C. Pogue, 9 May 1947, US Army Military History Institute.
[2] P. J. Grigg, *Prejudice and Judgment*, London, 1948.

thing shows greater insight and don't see why he doesn't tell the truth. [A reference to Montgomery's revised strategy of attracting and containing Rommel's panzer reserves to Caen].[1]

Chester Wilmot, one of Montgomery's most eloquent advocates, demonstrated his own uncertainties in a letter to Liddell Hart during the preparation of his book *The Struggle for Europe*:

> There is no doubt that the intention to hold on the left and break out on the right was the basis for his conception and appears in the very first documents in February. For instance the 2d Army outline plan dated February 21st defines the Army's objective in these words: 'The ultimate object of 2d British Army is to protect the flank of the United States Armies while the latter capture Cherbourg, Angers, Nantes and the Brittany ports. There is no intention of carrying out a major offensive until the Brittany ports have been captured.' And yet the Chief Historian of the RAF said to me yesterday – 'Of course Montgomery's original intention had been to break out to the East and capture Le Havre,' and went on to say that this policy was only changed after D-Day.
>
> However, I can find nothing in the early documents about any deliberate plan to compel the enemy to commit all his armour against the British. In his two main speeches to his Commanders he speaks in rather negative terms of 2d Army's task, declaring in one case – 'The army will pivot on its left and offer a strong front against any movement towards the lodgement area from the East.' At this stage he seems to have thought of Dempsey's role as that of blocking rather than attracting and destroying the enemy's armour.[2]

Wilmot's book was published well before release of the war documents and his uncertainties are reflected in his book. While generally believing that Montgomery followed his original intentions, he wrote that his policy was to harry the Germans all along the Allied front, keeping them unbalanced and eventually snapping their defences. 'This policy of attrition was the antithesis of Montgomery's approach. He was an equally firm believer in the employment of superior power; indeed he had become notorious for his refusal to commit his troops to the offensive without it.'[3] Although accepting the premise that Montgomery

[1] Interview with Captain J. Hughes-Hallett, RN, by Dr Forrest C. Pogue, 11–12 February 1947, US Army Military History Institute.

[2] Chester Wilmot, letter to Liddell Hart, n.d., Liddell Hart Papers, King's College, London.

[3] *The Struggle for Europe*, op.cit., p. 372.

never wavered in the pursuit of this main strategic purpose, Wilmot wrote that:

> . . . he did modify and change the means by which he sought to achieve it. After the war, however, over-anxious to defend himself against American criticism, he asserted that 'the operations developed in June, July and August exactly as planned'. In making this claim, Montgomery does himself less than justice, for his real genius as a commander was shown in the way he varied his day-to-day policy to meet the unpredictable situations caused by bad weather, by Hitler's suicidal policy of fighting for every yard, and by tactical failure or slowness on the part of both British and American troops.[1]

Brigadier E. J. Foord, the respected deputy G–2 of SHAEF, was another who disagreed with Montgomery's post-war claims. Thought by many to be the brightest intelligence officer on the SHAEF staff, Foord, too, was well placed to understand the plans and intentions of the 21st Army Group, and maintained daily contact with Bill Williams to discuss intelligence matters. In 1946, Liddell Hart recorded these comments after a discussion with Foord:

> Foord does not share the view that there was no change of plan. He says that the original intention was that the Germans should be forced back by the application of the main weight on the Caen flank . . . it being reasoned that once the British had broken out into the Caen-Falaise Plain the Germans would have to pull back in the bocage country [to the west]. Foord thinks that it was only when Monty failed to make progress in the Caen sector that he determined to make the main effort with the Americans through the Bocage. There was, it is true – he says – no intention of breakout with 2d British Army and swanning towards Paris, but it was intended that the British should make the main effort. He says that he had never heard of the theory of containing the German armour on the right [German] flank until after D-Day. It had always been realised the bulk of the German forces would tend to be drawn into the Caen sector but he never heard of any theory to draw them in there deliberately.[2]

Yet another officer who well understood the significance of Montgomery's change of plan was Group Captain T. P. Gleave,

---

[1]   *The Struggle for Europe*, op.cit., pp. 272–3.
[2]   'Notes of a Discussion with Brigadier E. J. Foord of G–2, SHAEF', Liddell Hart Papers.

who served on the COSSAC and AEAF planning staffs, and later with SHAEF. In 1947, Dr Pogue recorded these comments in an interview with Gleave:

> Says without doubt Montgomery has shifted ground in his story about Caen. On 2 April [1944], Gleave, Leigh-Mallory and others talked to Monty. He said yes, he understood the importance of Caen – and the airfields beyond. Caen was not the important point – it was always the airfields around Lisieux. . . He knew that the important thing was to hold the hump beyond Caen, so that the German push there could be blunted, and German guns near Ouistreham would quit hitting our beaches. Because he failed to take the airfield sites, we were unable to stop movements around Le Mans both towards Monty and towards the American front. It is true that Monty took the bulk of German armor. They didn't intend for him to get out of Caen, and after he started beating against that city they kept sending up tanks.[1]

Gleave disputes Montgomery's contention that this strategy was included in the original pre-D-Day planning:

> It is true he helped the attack to the west and he deserves credit for that, but when he says that was his plan, he is stating *his second reconsideration*. As a result of his failure to take Caen his area became very congested. . . Original plan was to run out great armored fingers around Caen. When the Germans came in they would be enfiladed. [We] were to get the humps beyond Caen so as to control the terrain. Montgomery made the mistake the Russians never made by failing to by-pass Caen after he didn't take it. If he had by-passed it they would have withered gradually. [Montgomery] repeated Rommel's error in North Africa when he kept hitting away at certain points instead of by-passing.[2]

At this point it would be useful to examine another of Montgomery's pre-D-Day briefings, one given to his own senior officers within 21st Army Group. Montgomery's preparations for the battle of Normandy repeated the pattern he had established when he assumed command of the Eighth Army, and this

---

[1] Interview with Group Captain T. P. Gleave by Dr Forrest C. Pogue, 9 January 1947, US Army Military History Institute.

[2] Gleave is correct when he asserts Montgomery's strategy of containment was his 'second reconsideration'. When the original plan broke down immediately after D-Day, Montgomery's *first* reconsideration was the attempted double envelopment of Caen; when this too failed, his second reconsideration became the strategy he continued to pursue throughout the battle(s) for Caen in June and July.

briefing was carefully designed, as indeed were all his actions, to ensure that each of his officers understood exactly what was expected of him in Normandy. Montgomery spoke at some length about the absolute need for offensive eagerness and how this was expected to influence the battle:

> Great energy and 'drive' will be required from all senior officers and commanders. I consider that once the beaches are in our possession, success will depend largely on our ability to be able to concentrate our armour and push fairly strong armoured columns rapidly inland to secure important ground or communication centres. Such columns will form *firm bases in enemy territory* from which to develop offensive action in all directions. Such action will tend to throw the enemy off his balance, and will enable our build-up through the beaches to proceed undisturbed; it will cut the ground from under the armoured counter-attack. . . Inaction and a defensive mentality, are criminal in any officer – however senior.[1]

The official history followed the Montgomery dictum without dispute but in total contradiction of the facts. Summarizing the British position in mid-June, the official history states, rather defensively:

> The enemy's success in holding Caen was indeed handicapping the planned expansion of the British lodgement area. Nevertheless the Second Army's achievement and the general military situation ought not to be measured chiefly by that fact. . . For General Montgomery had always foreseen that the enemy's strongest opposition might well be encountered on the eastern flank of the Second Army and had planned to hold it there so as to facilitate advance in the American sector. Taking a long view, he was justified in feeling that Rommel was now playing his game. We *had* established 'a firm left wing', even though it did not yet include Caen or extend to the Dives. . . It is difficult to discern in this 'the makings of a dangerous crisis.'[2]

What Ellis fails to point out is that after over a week of battle Rommel was no longer fighting for Caen by choice but upon Hitler's orders. Defensive strategy after invasion was precisely what Montgomery had hoped at all costs to *avoid*. From a defensive point of view his left wing was indeed firm, but after

---

[1] Extracted from Montgomery's 'Notes for my Address to Senior Officers Before Overlord', PRO (PREM 3–339/1). Prior to the invasion he personally briefed every senior officer from the rank of lieutenant colonel upwards.
[2] Ellis, op.cit., p. 266.

Villers-Bocage Montgomery had no workable *offensive* strategy for capturing Caen and enlarging his bridgehead.

The question which must be asked is: how long could Montgomery get away without accomplishing this without also adversely affecting the Allied buildup and timetable for securing Normandy before the winter weather cut off resupply? What the first week of the campaign brought home to Montgomery in stark terms was that until 8 Corps was ready for deployment to break the Caen logjam, there was no suitable alternative to a defensive strategy of keeping Rommel temporarily occupied so that Bradley would not face the same dilemma.

The new strategy which Montgomery now began to employ had one fatal flaw, a flaw which would be exposed time and time again in the coming weeks – the more German divisions attracted to and pinned down holding Caen, the more difficult would be the task of defeating them for, sooner or later, Montgomery must attack Rommel in strength.

Although battered and harassed day and night by the Allied airforces, naval gunfire and the Second Army artillery, the Germans had so far fought with great skill and tenacity to retain their hold on Normandy. As Montgomery had made clear before D-Day, Rommel was a determined and resourceful opponent despite his near-crippling problems. Neither side had reason to be satisfied with the present situation. Rommel was quite unable to mount a counterstroke and so was forced to take what little satisfaction he could by disrupting Montgomery's drive on Caen and in making the British and American armies pay heavily for every gain. Caen was not Alam Halfa and Montgomery cannot have been satisfied with yet another change of plan, indeed the idea of switching plans not once but *twice* in the space of little over a week can only have appalled the man whose very success as a field commander was based upon good, sound planning. In this sense it was Montgomery who would for the next several weeks be dancing to Rommel's tune. Even if the holding strategy proved successful, it must in the end eventually be abandoned in favour of a strong new offensive.

It was at this uncertain moment that the air force, in the person of Air Chief Marshal Leigh-Mallory, came forward to offer an alternative solution.

CHAPTER 13

The Air Chiefs

Air Marshal Coningham asked for a greater sense
of urgency from the Army and a frank admission
that their operations were not running according to
plan.

Minutes of the Allied Air
Commanders' Conference,
16 June 1944

Without the navy and the air force Montgomery's armies could
not have landed on the beaches of Normandy, and it soon became
apparent that without the help of the navy and the air force, his
forces would not break out far beyond them. The Allied Air Force
had provided round-the-clock support to Montgomery in the
form of interdiction of enemy troop movements and also direct
air support of ground operations following the invasion.

But within the first week of the campaign cracks had begun to
appear in relations between air and ground commanders. Leigh-
Mallory had flatly turned down Montgomery's plan to employ
the 1st Airborne Division behind Caen, and this was followed by
stinging criticism from Air Marshal Coningham that progress on
the British flank was far too slow as a result of the failure by
Montgomery to capture Caen quickly. Throughout the remainder of the campaign the cool, sometimes frigid relations between
Montgomery and the powerful air chiefs would have a strong
influence on events. Matters became even more difficult because
of the unwieldy command structure, for not only did the air chiefs
frequently disagree with Montgomery, they just as frequently
disagreed amongst themselves.

Three airmen formed the nucleus of the air structure in
Normandy: Air Chief Marshal Trafford Leigh-Mallory, com-
mander of the Allied Expeditionary Air Force; Air Marshal
Arthur Coningham, commander of the 2nd British Tactical Air

Force; and, behind the scenes, Air Chief Marshal Arthur Tedder, Deputy Supreme Commander. Together they controlled the air forces used to support Montgomery's ground operations.

When he was appointed commander of the AEAF, Leigh-Mallory was given authority only over the two British and US Tactical Air Forces supporting Montgomery and Bradley: he had no control whatever over the strategic air forces of Air Chief Marshal Arthur Harris's Bomber Command and Lieutenant General Carl A. Spaatz's US Strategic Air Force. A quiet and dignified airman, Leigh-Mallory was not popular with the other air commanders or within SHAEF; his reserved manner and dry, sometimes inarticulate performances at high-level meetings caused some to dismiss him as a lightweight, pro-British, figure-head commander. Yet no Allied commander was ever handed a more difficult, if not impossible task, than Leigh-Mallory.[1]

Soon after taking command of the AEAF, Leigh-Mallory had encountered an obstacle in the form of POINTBLANK, a June 1943 Anglo-American directive which called for a priority commit-ment of the strategic air forces against the German Air Force and those industrial targets sustaining the Luftwaffe. The subsequent creation of SHAEF and the AEAF were seen by Harris and Spaatz as threats to their POINTBLANK authority. Clearly OVERLORD would require some form of support from their bomber forces, but with the development early in 1944 by the AEAF of a strategic plan to bomb and destroy the French railways and their communications network into Normandy, the threats became real. In particular, the strong-willed Harris became a determined and formidable opponent of OVERLORD, opposing any diversion of Bomber Command from the task of destroying Germany's industrial base, which he mistakenly believed could destroy Hitler's ability to wage war and thus bring the Third Reich to its knees. Once committed to OVERLORD, Harris believed his Bom-ber Command would fall under Eisenhower's control and, even worse, under the direction of Leigh-Mallory and Tedder, for neither of whom does he seem to have had any great fondness.

Relations between the Air Ministry and Bomber Command had always been uneasy; Harris resented interference in bomber

[1] Not only was his task to support Montgomery, but he was also responsible for the air defence of the United Kingdom. Like Air Chief Marshal Dowding in 1940, he had to consider the possibility of military failure on the continent of Europe and ensure that an adequate and balanced air force remained in Britain to protect her shores.

operations and was quick to take offence at directives emanating from the air staff. Chief-of-Staff Portal found Harris a stubborn and often troublesome subordinate who was in many ways a virtual law unto himself, but on the question of support for OVERLORD Portal was steadfast, at least initially. In reply to a memorandum arguing against Bomber Command involvement in OVERLORD, Portal told Harris: 'The extent to which the support of Bomber Command will be required in the various phases of OVERLORD will be determined by the Combined Chiefs of Staff after they have considered General Eisenhower's recommendations.'[1]

The original AEAF bombing plan for OVERLORD was found faulty and revamped by Professor Solly Zuckerman, a renowned zoologist who had become an expert in devising bombing policy. Brought back from the Mediterranean by Tedder to serve as his scientific advisor, Zuckerman foresaw the immense benefits to be gained from isolating the Normandy battlefield by destroying the French rail network. Thus the Transportation Plan became the object of the most intense opposition from Harris and Spaatz, who were now backed by the Air Ministry which had suddenly reversed course and decided to oppose it. 'But it was Harris and Spaatz who unleashed the most formidable revolt against the Transport Plan, or indeed against any tactical employment of the heavy-bomber force at all. Even at this late stage, neither officer had renounced his private conviction that Overlord was a vast, gratuitous, strategic misjudgement, when Germany was already tottering on the edge of collapse from bombing'[2]

Of the two, Harris proved by far the more cooperative. As Zuckerman noted in his private journal: 'The amazing thing is that Harris, who was even more resistant than the Americans to the idea of AEAF domination, has in fact thrown himself whole-heartedly into the battle, has improved his bombing performance enormously, and has contributed more to the dislocation of enemy communications, etc, than any of the rest. At no point has he hesitated to throw himself into the tactical battle when asked.

[1] Denis Richards, *Portal of Hungerford*, London, 1977, p. 316. Much of Harris's power came from the protection afforded him by Churchill who had been persuaded to support POINTBLANK. Churchill in turn was strongly influenced by his own scientific advisor, Lord Cherwell, who was a strong advocate of the principle of mass bombing of German industrial targets, an idea which he embraced as his own.

[2] Max Hastings, *Bomber Command*, London, 1979, p. 327.

The Americans, on the other hand, are terrified lest they be asked, and never offer. What the battle in the West gets from them is what is left over from pre-planned operations againt oil, the aircraft industry and ball bearings.'[1]

The American attitude was embodied in Spaatz's entirely negative attitude to both Leigh-Mallory and support of OVER-LORD. According to Zuckerman: 'The whole situation arose out of the primary fear of the Strategic Air Forces that they were going to be taken over by L-M and forced to engage in operations in connection with Overlord, instead of being allowed to continue their own way and to win the war by long-distance bombing. As Spaatz put it to me a long time ago, there were two factors involved in this. One was a question of prestige. As he put it, he might sink sufficiently low to accept orders from Tedder; he certainly was not going to accept any from anybody else since he had the biggest Air Force. The second point was the fear that if they did come under the cloak of the AEAF they would be subordinated to Army operations and in that way the fight for independence would be set back.'[2]

It was bad enough that Leigh-Mallory and the AEAF were the victims of the power struggle between the strategic air forces on the one hand, and SHAEF on the other, but the problem was exacerbated by American disdain and suspicion of the British, including both Tedder and Portal. There were not only fundamental disagreements over bombing strategy, with the Americans favouring daylight bombing and the British night bombing, but with the industrial might of the United States now at its peak, the US air forces in Europe outnumbered the RAF in strategic bombers by more than two to one. Long accustomed to taking a back seat to the more established RAF, the Americans were determined not only to demonstrate their independence but they also seemed to believe they no longer had anything to learn about air warfare from the British. The requirement to support ground operations in France was considered by Spaatz and others a very unwelcome intrusion and a misuse of the strategic bombers, which Spaatz, backed by General H. H. 'Hap' Arnold, Chief of Staff of the US Army Air Force, believed could win the war against Nazi Germany single-handedly.

[1] Journal of Professor Solly Zuckerman, 9 July 1944.
[2] Ibid.

The task Eisenhower, Tedder and Leigh-Mallory faced in gaining backing for their plan was indeed formidable. All were convinced of the value of a deliberate campaign against the railways and the significant impact it would have on German ability to augment their forces in Normandy when the invasion came. A series of tense, heated meetings took place early in 1944 and the wrangling dragged on into the spring, threatening the plan and ultimately the very success of OVERLORD itself. With great reluctance Churchill finally gave his assent to the use of the strategic bombers to carry out the plan, but only after pressure from Washington.[1]

Zuckerman knew the air chiefs well and saw the result of the disagreements between them at firsthand. Bomber Command and its representatives viewed Leigh-Mallory as a tactical air commander who simply did not understand the significance of the air war against the enemy's homeland.'[2] Leigh-Mallory failed to take a firm stand against his opponents, which caused them to view his inaction as a sign of weakness. In truth it was not so much weakness as a sense of helplessness which beset him: his mandate was vague, the other air chiefs resented him, and his personality did not leave him equipped to deal with the vicious in-fighting which ensued.

At no time was Leigh-Mallory ever given command or even authority over the strategic air forces, which were the preserve of Tedder. 'On the rare occasions when the heavy bombers undertook operations in connection with OVERLORD, they did so on the authority of Tedder, Eisenhower's Deputy, not on that of Leigh-Mallory ... From Leigh-Mallory's point of view, everything depended on his close cooperation with Tedder.'[3]

Leigh-Mallory was viewed by his subordinate Air Marshal Coningham with no great affection, and relations between Leigh-Mallory and Tedder were always strained. In his memoirs Tedder made no secret of his disdain for the AEAF Chief, whom he refers to as earnest, brave and zealous but lacking in inspiration as C-in-C and too prone to interfere with his subordinate

---

[1] To avoid revealing Normandy as the site of the invasion it was necessary to bomb the entire French railway network. For every bombing mission against the Normandy network, the Allies launched two missions against targets in other regions, particularly the Pas de Calais.
[2] Solly Zuckerman, *From Apes to Warlords*, London, 1978, p. 229.
[3] Ibid. p. 347.

commanders.[1] The gulf between the brilliant, intellectual but brittle personality of Tedder and the dedicated, somewhat stolid Leigh-Mallory was too great ever to be bridged. Consistently undercut by Tedder, who had been given full responsibility for coordinating air matters by Eisenhower, rarely shown support by Eisenhower himself, never enthusiastically supported by Portal, and sniped at from the sidelines by the bomber barons who were loath to see their aircraft employed in support of OVERLORD, Leigh-Mallory found himself an unwanted cog in the air chain of command.[2]

Zuckerman has summed up Leigh-Mallory's plight in these words: 'Poor Leigh-Mallory, he could not have derived much pleasure or satisfaction from being Commander-in-Chief of the AEAF. He did not stand a chance either in the jungle where Commanders brought in from the Mediterranean knew all the call-signs, nor in the higher, more rarified atmosphere where the Commanders of the heavy bombers mused about the destruction of Germany. His job seemed to me lonely and friendless... I always felt that L-M bore himself with dignity in the adverse currents of the impossible situation to which he had been appointed. It simply was not his world.'[3]

Leigh-Mallory's two greatest obstacles were his personality, which was far better suited to the direct action of a fighter commander, and his poorly defined command role. Although Montgomery may not have appreciated Leigh-Mallory's efforts to assist him, evidence of the air chief's good intentions is abundant, including this diary entry made in early July: 'I want to help the Army all I can, because that is what I am convinced the

[1] Lord Tedder, *With Prejudice*, London, 1966, pp. 564–5.

[2] Eisenhower's original intent had been for Tedder to command all OVERLORD air operations and leave Leigh-Mallory to command the fighter aircraft, but the AEAF organization and mission, as they eventually evolved, fell between two stools – SHAEF, and the RAF and USAAF. Bedell Smith thought the AEAF unnecessary and believed it ought to have been consolidated within SHAEF. 'Leigh-Mallory,' said Smith, 'was difficult at first but we found him after a time to be extremely able and honest and loyal. He stood for what he wanted. Had the interest of the RAF very much at heart. After he got to working with us we couldn't have asked for more. He was just fine.' Smith interview, loc.cit. Nevertheless, other than Montgomery, no one on the Allied side could rile Eisenhower quicker than Leigh-Mallory, whose personality and manner rubbed the Supreme Commander the wrong way. Leigh-Mallory's acute frustration was best summed up by this diary entry made in mid-July: 'Here I am with the biggest Air Force the world has ever seen, and I do not think more than 20 per cent of it has been in operation since the start [of OVERLORD].'

[3] Zuckerman, op.cit., pp. 348–9.

Air Force should now do. I have always been of that opinion . . . we must do our utmost as an Air Force to give them every possible assistance and to try and unstick them.'[1]

The tactical air commander in Normandy responsible for support of the Second British Army was Air Marshal Coningham, a veteran fighter pilot and former commander of the Desert Air Force. A native New Zealander, Coningham had acquired the nickname 'Mary' (derived from Maori) in the First World War where he had served with the New Zealand Expeditionary Force. Behind a soft-spoken exterior and an intensely charming manner, the tall yet burly Coningham was ambitious and ruthless, rarely bothering to conceal his contempt for certain other of the air commanders. Once during the Sicily campaign he mockingly presented flowers to Spaatz – his superior – in a gesture designed to indicate that 'he had nothing to learn from an American general' who had been in the war less than a year. 'It was,' wrote Zuckerman who was present, 'the first occasion on which I saw personal Anglo-American relationships go wrong at that level.'[2]

The real focus of Coningham's venom, however, was Montgomery, whom he believed had stolen recognition away from himself and his air force after Alamein. In the desert the two men had worked in close harmony, living side by side in caravans and closely coordinating air-ground actions. When Montgomery gained fame and massive publicity for his victory over Rommel the ambitious Coningham felt slighted and from that time forth relations deteriorated to the point where Montgomery in Normandy would deliberately bypass Coningham; this only intensified their bad relations as the frustrated air marshal constantly criticized Montgomery's actions.[3]

Tedder had brought Coningham back from the Mediterranean to fill the tactical air command position, wanting an experienced commander fully versed in air-ground operations and coordination, and for this task Coningham was certainly one of

[1] Leigh-Mallory Diary, loc.cit. His diary abounds with similar examples.
[2] Zuckerman, op.cit., p. 204.
[3] Montgomery's feelings were summed up in a letter of 26 August to Brooke: 'Coningham is violently anti-army and is disliked and despised by all soldiers; my army commanders mistrust him and never want to see him . . . For my part I am very distressed about the air set-up. I have laboured long and hard to establish friendly relations with the RAF; it looks now as if the whole of one's work is to be wasted.' Alanbrooke Papers.

the best qualified of the senior RAF commanders. Tedder also seems to have deliberately picked Coningham as a foil to Montgomery in the belief that Montgomery might be induced to make better use of the air forces with Coningham in charge.[1] The original intent had been to appoint Coningham as Leigh-Mallory's deputy but this met with what Zuckerman describes as 'violent opposition' from the US tactical air commander, General Lewis Brereton (9th USAF) 'who flatly refused to serve under Coningham'.[2] In a compromise move Coningham was given a role similar to Montgomery's, with command of both the 2nd Tactical Air Force and the Advanced AEAF until Leigh-Mallory was able to establish his HQ in France.[3]

This arrangement never worked. Leigh-Mallory refused to accept it despite Eisenhower's ruling that Coningham should be Montgomery's opposite number, and Montgomery himself doomed it to failure by dealing directly with Leigh-Mallory on heavy bomber support and with Air Vice Marshal Harry Broadhurst on tactical air matters.[4]

Harry Broadhurst was one of the most colourful officers in the RAF; he was also an experienced fighter pilot who had fought in the Battle of Britain, and in North Africa, Sicily and Italy.[5] After he rose to higher command the resolute Broadhurst refused to ride a desk, preferring instead to set the example by spending as much time as possible in the air. In North Africa he acquired a captured German Storch observation aircraft and later had it sent back to England and painted bright yellow; eventually it ended up in Normandy as his personal aircraft. Broadhurst felt Coningham's personal and vehement anti-Montgomery attitude was adversely affecting air operations and resented being placed in the middle of a personal squabble.[6] For his part, since inter-service loyalty was taken for granted, Coningham as Broadhurst's superior, resented the excellent relationship which existed between him and Montgomery. Just as Leigh-Mallory and Montgomery did not want Coningham, Coningham did not

[1] Both Tedder and Coningham had long felt Montgomery had failed to make good use of the air forces in the pursuit of Rommel across North Africa after Alamein.
[2] Zuckerman, op.cit., p. 348. Another example of the in-fighting between senior airmen.   [3] Ibid.
[4] Interview with Air Chief Marshal Sir Harry Broadhurst, 22 November 1979.
[5] Broadhurst was Senior Air Staff Officer to Coningham in 1942, and Commander, Allied Forces, Western Desert in 1943.
[6] Broadhurst interview, loc.cit.

want Broadhurst but was equally powerless to prevent his appointment.

Broadhurst had supported Dempsey's 13 Corps in Italy where relations had developed serious strains as a result of several errors in coordination by Dempsey's staff. Montgomery continued to have great faith in Broadhurst; he was Dempsey's opposite number, was consulted as frequently and on at least one occasion Montgomery gave Dempsey a severe 'rocket' after talking to Broadhurst.[1] When he was posted to 83rd Group as Dempsey's chief airman Broadhurst was naturally apprehensive, but whatever differences which may have existed in Italy were soon forgotten and, as he recalls: 'We never made a move without talking to each other.'[2]

Broadhurst provides a vivid example of the bad feeling which existed against Montgomery. On one occasion in Normandy Tedder greeted Broadhurst with the comment: 'How's your bloody Army friend today?' Broadhurst replied: 'Well, what do you expect him to be, my enemy? It's difficult enough when he's supposed to be friendly,' and walked angrily away.[3]

These were difficult days for the Allied commanders. Eisenhower and Tedder were beginning to show frustration and apprehension over what was happening in Normandy, as was Leigh-Mallory, and there was no doubting that they had good reason. Coningham's growing hostility towards Montgomery – a hostility which had turned into an obsession – was not helpful at a time when the outcome of the battle for the bridgehead was still in doubt.

Coningham's feelings did not abate with the conclusion of the war and in 1947 he gave an interview to Dr Pogue which revealed a good deal about his state of mind. Pogue noted that he found Coningham 'the bitterest critic of Montgomery I have heard speak.'[4] The entire interview amounted to a virulent diatribe

[1] Broadhurst interview, loc.cit.

[2] Ibid. After barely being on speaking terms in Italy, Broadhurst and Dempsey became great friends in Normandy and their friendship continued until Dempsey's death. Broadhurst feels the earlier misunderstandings in Italy were primarily a result of Dempsey's inexperience with the Air Force, and it was a tribute to Dempsey's fairness and realization he was in the wrong that permitted their once cool relations to be forgotten in Northwest Europe where they worked smoothly together as a team.

[3] Ibid. Broadhurst recalls that he was livid at Tedder's remark and later wondered about getting sacked for his angry riposte. However, Tedder was too great an airman to let his feelings get out of hand over a minor incident of justifiable insubordination.

[4] Pogue interview with Air Marshal Sir Arthur Coningham, 14 February 1947.

against Montgomery and his post-war 2nd TAF despatch was similarly critical. So critical in fact, that the Air Ministry refused to publish it.[1] Coningham was a fine airman but he never grasped that in Normandy, unlike the desert, he was not Montgomery's equal. Thus it was no surprise that Montgomery turned more frequently to Broadhurst who did not share his superior's attitude. The entire business, recalls Broadhurst, was 'very unpleasant':

> The way I looked at it was, the Army in this particular situation, had to occupy the ground. They had to supply us and we couldn't pretend to be the main arm of the thing. You could almost say they could go on without us. So we were definitely subordinate to the Army's planning. You could influence the planning but you were subservient to it in that they had to hold the ground and they had to occupy it. . . They had to have the major say in the whole thing. So it was no good someone like Coningham saying they had to be equally important. His job was to support the Army plan, and influence it as much as he could to suit the air force's ability to do their best.[2]

Montgomery's quarrels with various associates has tended to implant the idea that he was at fault in the dissension with the air chiefs. Nothing could be further from the truth. While there was no love lost between him and Tedder and Coningham, Montgomery was well aware of the necessity for maximum cooperation between air and ground forces. He also knew that a definite gulf existed between the two arms before D-Day and in an effort to put the matter right Montgomery set about impressing the point upon his three army commanders. On 4 May he wrote to Bradley, Dempsey and Crerar outlining the problem and the steps he considered essential to achieve the smoothest possible working relationships: 'I feel very strongly on the whole matter,

[1] Air Marshal Coningham's 'Report of Operations, 2d TAF', (1945) is in the PRO (AIR 37/876). It can best be described as scathingly critical of Montgomery and 21st Army Group.

[2] Broadhurst interview, loc.cit. In his unpublished autobiography, Kingston-McCloughry notes that not one officer of air rank in the AEAF received a decoration in the large honours list published after D-Day, which caused considerable resentment when it was seen how well the army was represented. Kingston-McCloughry also alleges that Montgomery tried to ensure that Broadhurst received a knighthood for his services, believing he would never obtain the recommendation of Coningham. Montgomery took Broadhurst's case to the Air Ministry and Tedder but neither would agree to an immediate award; instead they put it 'in the bag' to be awarded at some unspecified future date. Montgomery continued to press his case and eventually the KBE was awarded to Broadhurst in 1945.

and I know that we can achieve no real success unless each Army and its accompanying Air Force can weld itself into one entity. . . The two HQ have got to set themselves down side by side, and work together as one team; that is the only way. I wish Army Commanders to give this matter their personal attention. There is much to be done and not too much time in which to do it. We must not merely pay lip service to a principle; we must put into practice the actual methods that will achieve success.'[1]*

Most of the senior airmen of the Second World War had been the flying aces of the First, but the only two to achieve high status in the Second were Portal and Tedder. Others, like Broadhurst, were products of the Second World War and better able to adapt to the changing requirements of aerial warfare.

Montgomery's problem was that, unlike the North African operations, these present plans meant that the army was baulking some RAF intentions. He had to attempt to restore the balance between air and ground forces that had worked so well in the desert; unfortunately, as he recognized only too clearly, that harmony had been severely strained by the ill-feeling generated since then. Nevertheless, even if the restoration of equally good relations seemed impossible, he was still determined to seek some improvement.

Coningham's attitude stemmed mainly from a severely bruised ego; with Tedder the reasons were entirely professional and originated from what he sincerely believed were the potentially serious repercussions of failing to expand the Caen bridgehead quickly and, above all, obtaining new airfield sites on the Caen-Falaise Plain.

The root of the air-ground controversy in Normandy hinged on this point. As early as 20 March Leigh-Mallory began urging Montgomery to include a provision in his plan to ensure the early capture of airfield sites.[2]

Sensibly, Montgomery refused to make promises he could not be certain of keeping and gave Leigh-Mallory no firm commitment on this point, then or later. Leigh-Mallory continued to press Montgomery in the belief that the airfields would be

---

[1] Montgomery, letter to Dempsey, 4 May 1944, Dempsey Papers, PRO (WO 285/2).

* The complete text of Montgomery's letter is in Appendix A.

[2] Minutes of the Chief of Staff's Meeting, 21st Army Group, 20 March 1944, PRO (WO 205/19B).

essential to support ground operations near the Seine. As we have already seen, General Belchem has argued that the prime reason for the inclusion of this airfield terrain in the master plan lay in satisfying the demands of the air force. In reality their requirements coincided nicely with Montgomery's own strategic aims of rapidly driving his armour beyond Caen to seize the same critical terrain. Belchem has even suggested Mongtomery responded to this air command pressure by preparing a second phase-line map showing the Second Army pivoting on Argentan and US forces making a far wider swing along the Loire, an unsupported intimation.[1]

Tedder's growing anxiety was that the failure of the Second Army to capture the Caen-Falaise airfield sites was keeping the major part of the air forces in England. Tedder wanted Coningham in Normandy, to better control the air support. However, as long as these forces remained in England, it was not considered feasible for Coningham to move his HQ. 'I also feared that our delay in attacking, for whatever reasons, would allow the enemy to assemble a reserve and thus to overcome the good effects of the Transportation Plan.'[2] It was Coningham, however, who soon emerged as the most vocal critic of the army. On 16 June he unleashed a savage attack at the Air Commanders' Conference at Stanmore by disputing the assessments of Montgomery's Plans Officer, Brigadier Richardson, and demanding that Montgomery admit his plan was not working. Behind his rhetoric was the contention that the air force could not provide proper support without the additional airfield terrain. Broadhurst, the commander who would have benefited the most from it, thought too much emphasis was placed on its capture for that purpose, explaining later that though it certainly would have been nice to have, in the event it became less essential as good use was made of captured German airfields. 'I never felt myself short of any airplanes; we could call on enormous reinforcements if we wanted them.'[3]

Evidence of the growing concern on the part of the air chiefs had first surfaced at the Allied Air Commanders' Conference on 14 June when the minutes recorded Tedder saying:

[1] Cf., David Belchem, *Victory in Normandy*, p. 52, and chapter 6.
[2] Tedder, op.cit., p. 554.
[3] Broadhurst interview, loc.cit.

... that though he did not want to panic, the situation in the Eastern sector was such that it might become critical at any moment, and he felt that they ought to be prepared to hold the Air Forces in readiness to give all-out assistance as and where necessary. Later in the day he refused to sanction the programme of the 8th Air Force for a heavy attack on Berlin for the 15th, and ruled that they should be held ready for employment in the battle area.[1]

The minutes for the following day reflect an agenda which included 'discussion of air assistance to the Army in the "stalemate", North of Caen'.[2] Present at this meeting was General Arnold, who candidly asked,'What was the trouble at Caen?' Later Arnold said he 'hoped this was not going to be another Cassino'.[3] Leigh-Mallory, who had been to see Montgomery the day before, attempted to inject some balance by telling his associates that he thought Coningham's views too gloomy and that 'General Montgomery regarded Caen as the most vital objective and since the situation around Caen was static, he was looking for assistance from the Air Force in loosening up the positions.'[4] This did little to deter Coningham, who the following day demanded that the army press forward with a greater sense of urgency.'[5] Coningham was right but for the wrong reasons; the plan had indeed failed but it was not from a lack of urgency, although he could perhaps be forgiven for feeling that a sense of urgency had initially been lacking in the 7th Armoured Division at Villers-Bocage. Their precipitous withdrawal from the town had been the spark which ignited the airmen's criticism.

Well aware of what was happening in Normandy, Leigh-Mallory had been anxious to find some method whereby the air force could assist Montgomery in breaking loose around Caen. The night of 13 June de Guingand had telephoned to say that Montgomery might want him to fly to Normandy the next day to discuss the employment of the 1st Airborne Division, but after learning of the withdrawal at Villers-Bocage Montgomery abandoned that plan and had de Guingand cancel the meeting. On his

[1] Minutes of the Allied Air Commanders' Conference, 14 June 1944, PRO (AIR 37/1057).
[2] Ibid, 15 June 1944.
[3] Ibid.
[4] Ibid.
[5] Ibid. 16 June 1944.

Above: Caen in the distance and the huge steelworks at Colombelles in its north-east sector, from which the Germans could observe all Allied movement in the fight for the city.

Below: Rommel *(left)* inspecting Lieutenant General Feuchtinger's 21st Panzer Division. Rommel's strategy for defeating the invasion was correct; its failure resulted from the absence of the Luftwaffe and a German command set-up which denied him control of the panzer divisions.

Above: British engineers clearing the centre of the hotly contested village of Tilly-sur-Seulles.

Below left: Winston Churchill and Montgomery, during one of the Prime Minister's flying visits.

Below right: Montgomery and Field Marshal Brooke, CIGS and architect of British military strategy during the Second World War.

Above: Caen, the city which the Allies failed to bypass and had to take the hard way. Almost miraculously, William the Conqueror's eleventh-century Abbaye aux Hommes remained unscathed.

Below: British troops pinned down during the struggle for the city.

Above: American troops in the bocage country: small fields ringed by earthen banks densely overgrown, making it impossible to see beyond a single field at a time. It was terrain which greatly favoured the defender against the Allied forces, who were not adequately trained to fight in such country.

Below: A grim-faced Eisenhower, Supreme Allied Commander, with Major General Collins *(left)* and Lieutenant General Bradley at VII Corps HQ, 4 July 1944, during the first abortive and costly attempt to break out of the Cotentin peninsula.

own initiative Leigh-Mallory decided to visit Montgomery to propose a new form of assistance that could, he believed, break open the static situation. On 14 June he flew to Normandy with de Guingand and that afternoon they met with Montgomery and Dempsey. His proposal appears in the AEAF historical record:

> General Montgomery had been very dissatisfied with his opposition to the scheme for employing the 1st Airborne Division in the battle for Caen, but had eventually been persuaded to drop the idea of using airborne troops to loosen up the static situation before Caen, and agree to the idea of a heavy air bombardment that would clear an opening for our troops to advance. General Montgomery did not regard the situation in the Eastern sector as in any way a critical one, but shortage of artillery ammunition had led to something like a stalemate around Caen, and he felt compelled to keep a strong holding force north of the town to meet any attempt of the enemy's armour to break through to the sea which was very close. This had prevented him reinforcing the attacking forces to the East and West as much as he had wished. The Air C-in-C proposed that to 'unfreeze' the situation an air bombardment might be launched by medium and heavy bombers on a front of say 5,000 yards, behind which the Army might advance. He also proposed that some of his planning staff should fly to France tomorrow [June 15th] to discuss aiming points for such a bombardment. This was agreed.[1]

In his diary Leigh-Mallory reflected on the day's events. 'Monty,' he wrote, 'was not in a good temper for I had sent him a signal shooting down an airborne operation he wanted mounted.[2] When I met him, therefore, he was not very kindly disposed. However, he brisked up a bit when I offered him, in exchange for the operation I was not prepared to carry out, a much more attractive proposal. . . When I made it he just swallowed it up, though even now I am not sure that he will choose the right area. We shall see.'[3]

What bothered Leigh-Mallory was the army's apparent lack of resolve:

> As an airman I look at the battle from a totally different point of view. I have never waited to be told by the army what to do in

[1] PRO (AIR 37/1057).
[2] The plan to drop the 1st Airborne Division on 13 June in the right pincer of Montgomery's second thrust for Caen.
[3] Leigh-Mallory Diary, 14 June 1944, loc.cit.

the air, and my view is not bounded, as seems to be the case with the army, by the nearest hedge or stream. I said as much, though in different words, to Monty and tried to describe the wider aspects of this battle as I see them, particularly stressing the number of divisions which he might have had to fight had they not been prevented from appearing on the scene by air action. He was profoundly uninterested. The fact of the matter is, however, that we have reduced the enemy's opposition considerably and the efficiency of their troops and armour even more so. In spite of this, the army just won't get on. It looks to me as though if they catch a prisoner or see a tank belonging to a particular enemy division they at once assume that the whole of that division is intact and moving against them. I may be doing them an injustice, but they don't appear to me to realize that, due to our action, that division has certainly been disorganized and is probably very much below strength. So we have a bog, but I hope my scheme will unstick things. Nevertheless, the fact remains that the great advantage originally gained by the achievement of surprise in the attack has now been lost. I hope my scheme will loosen things up, but I can't be sure.[1]

After returning to his HQ at Bentley Priory, Leigh-Mallory met with Zuckerman and Air Commodore E. J. Kingston-McCloughry, his Head of Operational Plans and Deputy Chief of Operations. His solution to Montgomery's problem was unique in that it was only the second time anyone had proposed the use of strategic bombers in *direct support* of a ground operation.[2] This idea had originated with Zuckerman and Kingston-McCloughry who saw a rare opportunity to use bomber support to influence a ground operation. Zuckerman's recollection of their meeting is that Leigh-Mallory said Montgomery was 'fairly confident but ready to admit that the original plan to encircle Caen from the east and west had broken down.'[3] Kingston-McCloughry makes the same statement in an unpublished autobiography, adding that 'Montgomery was most enthusiastic over the plan.'[4]

Next morning both men flew to Bayeux. Montgomery himself did not attend the meeting but was represented by Dempsey, Crocker and a number of other general officers. Dempsey opened

---

[1] Leigh-Mallory Diary, 14 June 1944, loc.cit.
[2] The bombing of the Abbey of Monte Cassino on 15 February 1944 and the town of Cassino on 15 March 1944 were the first occasions strategic bombers were used in such a role.
[3] Zuckerman, *From Apes to Warlords*, op.cit., p. 268.
[4] Kingston-McCloughry Papers, IWM.

the meeting in an atmosphere Zuckerman found a little theatrical. 'A depressed Dempsey wearing riding breeches walked up and down in front of the row of desks at which we sat, tapping his boots with a riding crop while he explained the disposition of our forces and that of the Germans. He told us that his troops were weary, and that if the combined operation we had in mind was too hazardous, he dared not take the risk of his men being killed by our own bombs.'[1] Kingston-McCloughry recorded a sense of impending gloom when he saw Montgomery was not present and within moments his fears came true; the meeting was quickly broken up by the arrival of Tedder, accompanied by Coningham and Broadhurst.

> Together with Dempsey and Crocker they moved to a side room where they remained for some ten minutes, after which our party was called in – the two generals having withdrawn – and firmly told the matter was none of our business. Any air support Monty needed would be dealt with by the tactical air forces under Coningham. Taking advantage of my special relationship with Tedder, I argued back, pointing out that while we were no doubt dealing with a land battle, a new factor had to be considered; namely, the weight of bombs that could be accurately put down by the strategic as well as the tactical air forces. Kingston also wanted to know why the army was stuck if the Tactical Air Command could give adequate air support. This remark was also brushed aside and the class, as it were, dismissed.[2]

In reality, Leigh-Mallory's ambitious plan was doomed from the beginning for several reasons, among them military protocol. After meeting Leigh-Mallory the night before Kingston-McCloughry had tried without success to locate Coningham in London to tell him of the plan, but he was dining out and had failed to leave his address with his HQ. When he later learned of the proposal and meeting, Coningham was furious at Leigh-Mallory's arrangement with Montgomery.[3] Tedder did not learn

---

[1] Zuckerman, op.cit., p. 269.
[2] Ibid. The meeting was held in an old schoolhouse which was serving as Dempsey's headquarters.
[3] According to Leigh-Mallory's diary Coningham was not bypassed: 'On my return from seeing Monty, I rang up Air Marshal Coningham. He was out at dinner and I could only get his deputy [Air Vice-Marshal] Strafford, to whom I explained the ideas of Monty and myself. My views were communicated to Coningham late at night when he returned from dining, and he at once made immediate arrangements to go to France the next day with Air Chief Marshal Tedder. . .' Entry of 8–10 July 1944, loc.cit.

of the plan officially until the next morning when Leigh-Mallory telephoned him and seems to have used that omission as one of his reasons for scuttling the Bayeux meeting. Nevertheless, the outcome would probably have been the same had protocol been followed to the letter. Tedder's own version is that:

> ... on arrival at General Dempsey's Second Army head-quarters I found in session a joint Army/Air conference. The purpose was to consider the tactical use of heavy bombers on the lines that Leigh-Mallory had agreed. Neither Spaatz nor Coningham was represented. I was much disturbed at these developments, and found Coningham, who happened to be in Normandy that day, incensed. I agreed with General Dempsey that Coningham and his staff should consider the proposal for this use of the bombers, and report back. This was speedily done and the operation was cancelled.[1]

Tedder's account ignores the fact that Coningham's presence in Normandy that day was no coincidence and that both Harris and Spaatz were represented, although neither command favoured supporting the operation.[2] Leigh-Mallory took the rebuff as a direct repudiation of his authority and had to be dissuaded by his staff from immediately resigning his command in protest.[3]

Even had Tedder not given the plan the coup de grace it is difficult to see how it could have been carried out. The larger problem was the terrain around Caen, which did not lend itself to such an operation. There were insufficient distinguishable ground features upon which to create an identifiable bomb line and aiming points, nor were there sufficient targets provided by the Second Army thus leaving the fundamental requirements of bomber employment unfulfilled. Both Bomber Command and the US Strategic Air Force opposed the operation, contending that their accuracy was too questionable to prevent friendly casualties.

This incident was not an example of Leigh-Mallory duping

---

[1] Tedder, op.cit., p. 552 and Tedder Diary. Tedder had learned of the meeting direct from Coningham the night of 14 June, and from this point on the plan was doomed.

[2] Kingston-McCloughry, loc.cit.

[3] Ibid. Leigh-Mallory was well aware that his idea was bound to generate continued controversy. On 26 June he wrote: 'I foresee a first-class row on this issue, but I am prepared for it. When I originally propounded this scheme of full air support to the Army, Air Chief Marshal Tedder was not present, but General Marshall was. He thoroughly agreed with it. If the present attack on Caen is not successful I shall raise the scheme a second time, and I believe that Ike will back me.'

the army into accepting an operation, the significance of which within the air command they did not fully understand. On the contrary, 21st Army Group had for some time anticipated such a role for the bombers, and as de Guingand has revealed: 'Back in the planning days at St Paul's School the Army was giving a great deal of thought to this subject. We fully appreciated the primary role of the strategic air forces, but nevertheless we considered that we should on occasions harness their great power to the immediate support of the land battle.'[1] According to de Guingand, extensive investigations were undertaken in conjunction with the RAF before D-Day to try to solve the problems of accuracy, safety measures and interference with friendly operations.[2] When this opportunity arose in mid-June the army was eager to test out its feasibility. De Guingand blames the failure on the army: 'In the first place, the [1] Corps had not prepared their case sufficiently, and we had to admit that the tasks appeared to be within the scope of the Tactical Air Forces. I was very disappointed, however, for we were most anxious to try out the machinery.'[3] In contrast to de Guingand's frankness, neither Montgomery nor Belchem refer to the idea in their accounts. Evidently both men felt any reference to the plan might have implied the real plight of the army at that moment, something Montgomery was certainly not prepared to admit after the war.

However, the real significance of the entire incident is that it prepared the way for the eventual employment of bombers in a completely new role. At this particular moment the circumstances were inappropriate but it would not be long before the idea would surface again.[4] Instead, the air force agreed to work out a plan of renewed close air support whereby medium and fighter bombers would attack individual strong points,[5] which in the event did little to influence the advance against Caen.

The collapse of the bomber plan, the increasingly poor weather developing over Normandy, and the inability to mount a

[1] Major General Sir Francis de Guingand, *Operation Victory*, London, 1947, p. 400.
[2] Ibid, pp. 400–1.
[3] Ibid, p. 401.
[4] According to Brigadier McLean, the SHAEF operations staff had been thinking along the same lines as Leigh-Mallory. Dr. Pogue recorded the following in a 1947 interview: 'When [the] fight slowed at Caen we worked up a paper on congealment in the bridgehead. Suggested use of bombers to blast a hole through the enemy.'
[5] AEAF Historical Record, PRO (AIR 37/1057).

strong attack against Caen without 8 Corps placed Montgomery in the position of having to continue his holding action until a new offensive could be mounted. Now another complication arose further to hinder the Allied armies. On 19 June the worst storm in nearly forty years unexpectedly lashed Normandy. Allied shipping sustained heavy losses in the fierce seas: some eight hundred ships of all sizes were beached or lost. The Mulberry harbour being erected on OMAHA beach was totally destroyed and never replaced; the British Mulberry at Arromanches was damaged but fortunately not lost. For three days the storm raged. Few men or supplies could be landed during this period and, as one account points out, the 'Great Storm' had in three days destroyed more vessels than the Germans had managed to harm during the entire campaign.[1] There were now a total of twenty Allied divisions and supporting forces in Normandy (approximately 500,000 men) requiring a huge daily infusion of supplies. The losses in material amounted to over 140,000 tons and 'seriously interfered with the planned buildup of the Allied strength in Normandy.'[2] The effect on manpower ashore was even more serious; when the storm broke, the Second Army was already two brigades behind schedule and this figure had increased to three divisions by 22 June when the storm finally abated.[3]

Offensive operations ground to a near halt as well. Bradley's final push against Cherbourg had to be delayed for two days at the very moment when his operations were going well. The most troublesome aspect of the great storm, however, was its effect on Bradley's operations. It had been Montgomery's intention to have Bradley begin his offensive to the south concurrently with operations against Cherbourg. On 19 June he issued a directive which stated: 'It is important that the [First] Army should not wait till CHERBOURG is actually captured before extending its operations to the south-west. As soon as they can be organized, operations will be developed against LA HAYE DU PUITS and against COUTANCES. Later, as more troops become available,

---

[1] Eversley Belfield and H. Essame, *The Battle for Normandy*, London, 1975.
[2] Ellis, *Victory in the West*, op.cit., p. 274. It was not until the end of June that the buildup regained its daily average prior to the storm.
[3] Ibid.

these operations will be extended towards GRANVILLE, AVRAN-CHES and VIRE.'[1] The storm put paid to this idea, delaying the arrival of VIII Corps and causing several of his battered divisions to need additional time to prepare for a new offensive.

In the British sector, other than to maintain pressure around Caen there was no cohesive plan yet in being for the Second Army after the setback at Villers-Bocage. In Montgomery's mind was another plan to envelop Caen from both flanks, this time using 8 Corps to attack out of the Orne bridgehead in an operation similar to the one previously aborted by the 51st Highland Division on 11 June. By 19 June, however, Montgomery had abandoned the idea of launching 8 Corps out of the Orne bridgehead and in a directive to Dempsey and Bradley he out-lined his reasons:

> Detailed examination of the problem has revealed that the difficulties of forming up 8th Corps in the bridgehead east of the R. Orne, and of launching it from that bridgehead as the left wing of the pincer movement against Caen, are very great. The enemy is strongly posted on that flank and certain preliminary operations would be necessary; these would take time and we do not want to wait longer than we can help. It has therefore been decided that the left wing of the pincer movement, from the bridgehead over the Orne, shall be scaled down and be only of such a nature as can be done by the troops of 1 Corps already there. 8th Corps will be switched to form part of the right, or western wing of the pincer movement. . . The above operations will be begun at or about dawn on 22 June. 8 Corps will be launched on its task on the morning of 23 June.[2]

Montgomery's aim was to mount a major offensive across the Odon River to seize Hill 112 and the other high ground domina-ting the west bank of the Orne southwest of Caen. It was his third attempt to capture or isolate Caen and it was to this operation, codenamed EPSOM, that he now turned his full efforts.

---

[1] 21st Army Group Directive M-504, 19 June 1944, Dempsey Papers, PRO (WO 285/2).
[2] Ibid.

CHAPTER 14

Epsom: The Battle for
the Odon

Blitz attack of 8 Corps goes in tomorrow, and once
it starts I will continue battling on the eastern front
until one of us cracks, and it will not be us.

Montgomery to Eisenhower,
25 June 1944

In late June the struggle for dominance of the Caen bridgehead
was much like that of two wrestlers tussling for position, neither
of whom was yet capable of defeating the other. There was little
question that once Montgomery obtained a full buildup of his
forces success would be only a question of time and tactics, nor
was there any question of the ultimate futility of the German
position in Normandy, which could be measured by their failure
to utilize the bad weather interlude to launch the long intended
counterstroke against the Second British Army.

Rommel was in the process of assembling a powerful panzer
force for this purpose but the success of the Allied air effort was
generally continuing to thwart these efforts. On 11 June Hitler
had ordered the 2 SS Panzer Corps, consisting of the 9th and 10th
SS Panzer Divisions, from the Eastern Front to Normandy; after
a rapid movement to France they were delayed by the necessity to
detrain in Lorraine and complete their move to Normandy by
road. Other units were also on the move: the 1st SS Panzer
Division was somewhere between Paris and Normandy and the
2nd SS Panzer Division had completed a lengthy journey from
southern France and was now positioned around St Lô, opposing
Bradley.

With Montgomery forced to delay mounting his new offensive and the air forces largely grounded during the storm, it would
have been the ideal moment for Rommel to strike. Unable to do
so without the benefit of three of the SS Panzer divisions then en

route to Normandy, he was thrown back in the interlude on strengthening his patchwork defensive line. The storm was definitely advantageous to the Germans: they were aware that Montgomery was preparing a fresh offensive and the hiatus provided time to strengthen the Caen sector, including the defences along the Odon. The bad weather was also one of the few times during the campaign during which the new panzer divisions could move with relative freedom towards Normandy.[1]

After Villers-Bocage Montgomery returned to the idea of a more powerful offensive east of the Orne, this time utilizing Lieutenant General O'Connor's 8 Corps. The extreme eastern point of the Orne bridgehead had always been the most logical place from which to strike at Caen. A strong penetration to the vicinity of the Caen-Lisieux highway could still isolate Caen from the east and thus create the favourable circumstances needed for an exploitation southeast on to the Caen-Falaise Plain. To be successful, such an offensive required a corps-sized force but the delay in landing 8 Corps would necessitate postponement of the attack for a week or longer, time Montgomery did not have. ULTRA was telling him of the movement of the additional panzer divisions to Normandy, and to retain the advantage it was imperative that offensive pressure be kept up.[2]

Dempsey has recorded that the plan 'to push 8 Corps down past Caen from the 6th Airborne Division bridgehead was never intended to achieve more than expansion of the bridgehead down to the high ground between Caen and Falaise. We wanted to get that so our presence there would be a standing threat which the Germans could not afford to ignore. It would also provide us with a wonderful "killing ground". This was, however, never considered as a jumping-off ground for the break-out. We were

[1] An exception was the 2nd SS Panzer Division (Das Reich) which had been in Army Group G reserve at Toulouse, and was bombed, strafed and harassed throughout its move by the Resistance and Allied air. This division had earned notoriety for one of the most shameful acts of brutality committed during the Second World War: the annihilation of the village of Oradour-sur-Glane, near Limoges, in reprisal for suspected concealment of explosives. The entire population of the village had been rounded up, the men locked in barns and the women and children in the church. Six hundred and forty two people were then machine-gunned or burned to death and the village burned to the ground. Only remnants of this once elite division arrived intact in Normandy. Like Lidice, the village was never rebuilt and stands today as a reminder of this atrocity. Cf., William L. Shirer, *The Rise and Fall of the Third Reich*, New York, 1960; also a book by Max Hastings, *Das Reich*, London, 1981.

[2] Cf., Ralph Bennett, *Ultra in the West*.

going for this ground in the Odon attack at the end of June.'[1]

Unfortunately, this idea had to be abandoned before it could be carried out. The shallow Orne bridgehead was already beginning to become very congested with troops, supplies and airfields. Moreover, without 8 Corps there really was little hope for a successful offensive from this direction and the storm further set back their arrival. On 19 June Montgomery outlined his reasons in a directive to Dempsey and Bradley: 'Detailed examination of the problem has revealed that the difficulties of forming up 8 Corps in the bridgehead east of the R. Orne, and of launching it from the bridgehead as the left wing of the pincer movement against Caen are very great. The enemy is strongly posted on that flank and certain preliminary operations would be necessary; these would take time and we do not want to wait longer than we can help.'[2]

Like it or not, Montgomery's options of where to launch his next offensive had been severely reduced after the loss of Villers-Bocage. An offensive in this sector was no longer practical now that Panzer Lehr and the 2nd Panzer firmly blocked a renewed attempt at a right hook. It was also perhaps questionable whether Montgomery would have been prepared to entrust this task to 30 Corps after their precipitous withdrawal of the 7th Armoured Division.

As we already know, Montgomery had long since ruled out a frontal attack against Caen and by about 18 June, with the German defences far stronger, he had no reason to change his mind about the drawbacks of a head-on confrontation. With the odds against success, and time and terrain restricting the assembly of 8 Corps to strike the massive blow against the city, Montgomery's options were reduced to an attack in the Odon River sector west of Caen. Here, there was ample space for preparing an offensive and for manoeuvre by 8 Corps.

The Odon flows generally northeast toward its confluence with the Orne in the southern suburbs of Caen. North of the river is rich, rolling farmland and numerous small hamlets, from which the ground slopes gently downhill to become heavily wooded around the Odon. To the south the woods give way to

---

[1] Chester Wilmot interview with Dempsey, 1946, Liddell Hart Papers, King's College, London.
[2] 21st Army Group Directive M-504, loc.cit.

far more open farmland which quickly rises to a deceptively high elevation shown on the map as Hill 112, from which on a clear day Caen and the entire region can be viewed. Hill 112 was a natural springboard for a deeper penetration south toward the high ground around Bretteville-sur-Laize, which dominates the western approaches to the Caen-Falaise Plain. A successful attack in this direction also offered the option of cutting the Orne southwest of Caen and capturing the Caen-Falaise Plain, thus isolating the city and leaving the entire German right flank exposed. If successful, the Odon attack could become the jumping-off ground for further operations to seize control of the Caen-Falaise Plain, and Falaise.

After the fiasco at Villers-Bocage Montgomery intended to take no chance on another failure, and his new offensive, code-named EPSOM, was a return to his preferred tactics of a direct penetration by a powerful and well prepared force. For EPSOM he intended to deploy the full combat power of the Second Army into the strongest attack yet launched by the British in Normandy. All three corps would participate, with O'Connor's 8 Corps the spearhead, by means of an attack between Carpiquet airfield and Rauray on a four-mile wide front, supported by 30 Corps in the west and 1 Corps in the east. 8 Corps consisted of three divisions (the 15th Scottish, 43rd Wessex and 11th Armoured) plus augmentation by the 4th Armoured Brigade and a tank battalion, raising the corps strength to some 60,000 men and over 600 tanks. In addition, 8 Corps artillery was augmented by the guns of the other two corps, providing O'Connor with an awesome firepower consisting of over 700 guns plus the naval gunfire of three Royal Navy cruisers. Air support included both fighter cover and fighter-bomber support from the 2nd TAF.

Montgomery not only respected O'Connor's brilliance as a commander but had a deep personal regard for him as a friend whom he had known since the 1920s when both men were instructors at Camberley. Their friendship had resumed when each commanded a division in Palestine in 1939. After O'Connor's capture and internment, Montgomery sent a touching letter to Lady O'Connor: 'I was so glad to hear from you and to get news of Dick. I have a very great regard and real affection for Dick. To me he is the salt of the earth and definitely one of the elect. You probably do not know this and few people would guess it, as outwardly I suppose we are very different. I don't suppose he knows it but I love your Dick and it is dreadful to think of him a prisoner in Italy.'[1]

O'Connor's accomplishments in the western desert had marked him as one of the outstanding armoured commanders of the British Army and after his daring escape from an Italian POW camp in late 1943, he was delighted to be selected by Montgomery for command of 8 Corps. A product of The Cameronians, the exceptional Scottish regiment that has consistently generated successful leaders, O'Connor was a natural choice for a corps in Normandy. EPSOM would be his first battle since Beda Fomm in 1941. Although 8 Corps was untested in combat, O'Connor's presence was reassuring and inspired confidence, especially with the air chiefs. His arrival in Normandy caused Leigh-Mallory to comment '[O'Connor] is a tower of strength, and when h~ gets cracking I should not be surprised at anything.'[2]

Shortly after taking command of 8 Corps, O'Connor quickly demonstrated the exceptional strength of his character and his independence of mind. On 19 February 1944 Dempsey wrote advising that he and Montgomery wanted one of his armoured division commanders relieved on the grounds that the officer lacked the drive to lead his unit into combat. O'Connor was directed to sack the officer and prepare an adverse fitness report. O'Connor flatly refused to submit the report and declined to sack his new subordinate on the reasonable grounds he could hardly remove an officer whom he did not know. The officer went on to lead his division with distinction through the entire campaign in Northwest Europe.[3]

Montgomery's original timetable called for the EPSOM offensive to commence on the morning of 23 June but the delay in landing 8 Corps and the fact that the men were weary and seasick when they finally landed left the C-in-C thoroughly frustrated and with no choice except to postpone the operation until the morning of 26 June. When he wrote to General Simpson in the War Office on 20 June he made no secret of his concern:

---

[1] O'Connor Papers, Liddell Hart Centre for Military Archives, King's College, London.
[2] Leigh-Mallory Diary, loc.cit.
[3] O'Connor Papers, loc.cit. Lest an erroneous conclusion be drawn, the 11th Armoured Division was not part of 8 Corps at the time of this incident.

My Dear Simbo:

This weather is still the very devil. A gale all day yesterday; the same today. Nothing can be unloaded. Lying in ships off the beaches is everything I need to resume the offensive with a bang. In particular I must have 43d Division complete and more artillery ammunition. If I can unload these by tomorrow night then I am OK. If I cannot do so I shall have to postpone the attack which would be a great nuisance as every day's delay helps the enemy. I am now five days behind my estimated build-up, all due to bad weather. . . The real point is that the delay imposed on us by the weather is just what the enemy needs, i.e. time to get more divisions over here and we know some more are on the move. It is all a very great nuisance.[1]

Preliminary operations were to commence on 25 June by a 30 Corps attack to seize both the high ground around the village of Rauray and eventually Noyers on the Caen-Villers-Bocage highway, one of the objectives of their abortive operation in mid-June. With 30 Corps protecting its right flank and 1 Corps its left, 8 Corps would launch its attack through the 3rd Canadian Division which held that sector of the front. As Montgomery later wrote: 'The operation was planned in two phases, the first culminating with the seizure of the Orne crossings. . . In the 1 Corps sector the intention was to ensure the security of the bridgehead, and prepare to eliminate the enemy salient north of Caen and clear the city, as the 8 Corps thrust took shape.'[2]

The task given to O'Connor was formidable. For nearly three weeks the Germans had been busily strengthening their defences along the Odon. Blocking O'Connor's advance was the tough 12th SS Panzer Division, reinforced on both flanks by elements of the 21st Panzer (to the east) and Panzer Lehr (to the west), all of whom were now intimately familiar with the terrain they were defending. There is no doubt that Montgomery's decision to switch 8 Corps from the Orne to the Odon was largely influenced by the flow of intercepted German wireless signals provided by ULTRA, particularly those revealing the movements of the 1st SS Panzer to Caen to replace the 716th Division and 2 SS Panzer Corps, thus making it imperative for the new offensive to begin

---

[1] Nigel Hamilton, loc.cit.

[2] Montgomery, *El Alamein to the River Sangro and Normandy to the Baltic*, op.cit., p. 228.

before their arrival further strengthened the German defence of Caen.[1]

As was his custom before a major operation, Montgomery summoned the general officers of the Second Army to review past and future operations on 23 June. Also attending was Lieutenant General H. D. G. Crerar, whose First Canadian Army was scheduled to assume responsibility for the extreme left flank of 21st Army Group. Crerar's War Diary records Montgomery's lengthy review of the situation:

> . . . the first phase of the recent operations, i.e. the assault, had already been won. The Allied armies had got their lodgement area, had kept the initiative and had thrown the enemy off balance. Following this, a pause was required in order to deal with the second phase. This second phase called for a building up of our strength, and ability to deal with enemy counter-attacks and forcing the enemy to 'plug holes' instead of building up an important tactical reserve. This phase had also been won. A third phase entailed, firstly, the capture of Cherbourg and Caen and, secondly, snapping his 'roping off' dispositions and the smashing of the enemy troops so engaged. This third phase was now to commence. It was most important to exploit any advantages so gained in order to make the enemy's future still more difficult. The Allied Armies have had bad luck as regards weather and 'build-up' programme was now at least six days behind. This delay has enabled the enemy to bring up, and build up, reserves amounting to 3 divisions. It was, there-fore, not going to be so easy to accomplish as it would have been had circumstances been more favourable to us.[2]

Montgomery went on to outline his four principles for fighting the battle:

> The first was to keep the initiative. This had been accom-plished. The second object had been rapidly to improve our build-up. This, owing to the weather had not been successful. The third object had been to damage and delay the enemy build-up. This, generally speaking, had been successful. His fourth intention had been to pull the main enemy weight on the British Army, in order to ease the pressure against the First U.S. Army. In this, the object had been attained. This last aim had been in accordance with the strategy of the campaign which

[1] Bennett, op.cit., pp. 83–4.
[2] War Diary of Lieutenant General H. D. G. Crerar (CAB 106/1064), PRO. Montgom-ery's actual notes for this conference called the storm and its delay to a resumption of the offensive a 'tragedy' and 'exactly what the enemy needed as it has given him time to collect reserves'. Cf., letter Montgomery to Simpson, 23 June 1944, loc.cit.

was to get early possession of the Cherbourg and Brittany peninsulas. To succeed in this, the main German forces required to be brought against the British Army, holding the eastern sector of the bridgehead, and that Army must hold firm.[1]

'Now we are absolutely safe,' said Montgomery, 'under no conditions can we be pushed into the sea unless we make some frightful mistake which we shall not do.'[2] Once again he emphasized the effects of the weather which 'has put us back badly. We should have started Phase 3 yesterday but we have four divisions on the sea and it is too rough to unload; we are five days behind.'[3] Summing up, Montgomery said: 'The general picture is the enemy is firming up in front of the Second Army. . . He now has three panzer divisions in reserve. . . He obviously means to hold us in the Caen sector. . . We have now reached the showdown stage.'[4] 'The 'showdown' began the morning of 25 June when 30 Corps attacked with the 49th Division toward Rauray with heavy air support, and tore a gap some three miles wide and just over a mile deep, but despite heavy losses Panzer Lehr refused to surrender Rauray.

Bad weather marked the beginning of the 8 Corps attack the next morning, and virtually no aircraft left England to lend support.[5] The plan called for the 15th Division to lead the advance and capture the Odon bridges five miles to the south; with the Odon open, Major General G. P. B. 'Pip' Roberts's 11th Armoured Division would pass through and drive southeast to seize the Orne bridges and expose the high ground leading to the Caen-Falaise Plain to further exploitation.

Following a lengthy artillery bombardment the Scots[6] made rapid headway through the corn fields but this was not to last. When they reached the hamlets and the bocage the Germans

[1] Crerar War Diary, loc. cit.
[2] Montgomery, letter to Simpson, 24 June, 1944.
[3] Ibid. Phase 3 refers to the capture of Caen and Cherbourg.
[4] Ibid.
[5] Broadhurst's 83rd Group managed to fly nearly 500 sorties despite a heavy ground mist and low cloud cover.
[6] The 15th (Scottish) Division was generally considered to be the most effective and best led infantry division in 21st Army Group. The famous regiments represented in this proud division included the Cameronians, The Royal Scots Fusiliers, The Gordon Highlanders and The Argyll and Sutherland Highlanders. The GOC, MacMillan, was severely wounded in August and had to give up command of the division, which was taken over by Major General C. M. Barber, another Scot.

recovered to defend gamely the series of fortified villages blocking the British approach to the Odon. Vicious hand-to-hand
fighting took place in most, with the villages of Cheux and
St Mauvieu the focus of the most intense combat. Twice St
Mauvieu was counterattacked by panzers and infantry, and
twice these attacks were repulsed, largely as a result of an
accurate and concentrated curtain of supporting artillery fire.[1]

By noon, with progress only modest, O'Connor decided to
attempt a thrust by the 11th Armoured to seize the Odon bridges,
but they fared little better at cracking the heart of the 12th SS
strong points south of Cheux. This was miserable terrain in
which to employ armour and unfortunately, in the 12th SS they
were up against one of the most formidable German divisions,
who fought skilfully and resolutely, extracting the maximum
price for each small gain by the British.

The first day of EPSOM ended in a sea of rain and mud a mile
short of the Odon. The 15th Division had pushed their left flank
to Colleville, some four miles south of their start line. On their
right, 30 Corps was still short of Rauray. Despite superiority in
artillery, armour and air support, German defensive skill, the
weather and the close confines of the bocage had combined to
give the British a less than satisfactory start to their offensive.

Bradley reported far more encouraging news that the fortress
of Cherbourg had finally fallen to Collins's VII Corps after a
massive air, naval and artillery bombardment. The German
commander, General von Schlieben, was captured but having
been ordered by Hitler to fight to the death, he refused Collins's
demand to order the surrender of the remainder of the Cherbourg garrison. Collins taunted von Schlieben by suggesting that
he had saved himself at the expense of his men and could not
justify allowing them to continue fighting, but the German
remained defiant.[2] Although resistance in Cherbourg itself ended

---

[1] This was but one outstanding example of the contribution made by the gunners of
the Royal Artillery. When it came to mastering the art of concentrated fire power the
Royal Artillery stood second to none. Within minutes the nearly 300 guns of a corps
artillery could be brought into action against a target. One corps commander, Sir Brian
Horrocks, paid this tribute: 'Although I am an infantryman, in my opinion, the arm of the
service which did most to win the last war was the Royal Regiment of Artillery.' Cf.,
Corps Commander, London, 1977, p. 36.

[2] Collins, op.cit., p. 323. After hearing of the capture of von Schlieben, Bradley
pondered whether to invite the German commander to dinner. A visiting friend said 'no',

the next day, mopping up action continued until 1 July when the last remnants of the German defences around the city were cleaned out. The port area was found to be a tangled mess and despite immediate action to open the port to Allied shipping, it was a month before Cherbourg began to function.

SS General Dietrich, the German commander on the Odon front, appealed to the Seventh Army Commander for reinforcements to stop the British advance, specifically for General Paul Hausser's newly arrived 2 SS Panzer Corps. Rommel was reluctant to commit 2 SS which he intended to use as his counterattacking force against the British, but agreed to bring up reinforcements in the form of battlegroups from the other panzer divisions in the vicinity, including one from the 2nd SS Panzer at St Lô.

A German armoured counterattack was decisively repulsed on the morning of 27 June and by the same evening lead elements of 8 Corps had penetrated to the northern banks of the Odon. A bridge was taken intact, permitting the 11th Armoured to pour across on the morning of 28 June to begin movement towards the Orne crossings. Dempsey feared the consequences of another German counterattack and refused to commit the 11th Armoured across the Orne until the still tenuous Odon bridgehead could be expanded and reinforced. This decision was taken on the basis of known German countermeasures obtained from ULTRA which included the movement of two new German panzer divisions into the Odon valley.[1]

At yet another critical moment, however, the principal German commanders were absent from their posts. Rommel and von Rundstedt had been ordered back to Germany to meet Hitler and on 28 June they were en route to Berchtesgaden. Dollmann had been steadily losing his nerve since the fall of Cherbourg and, after learning that the British had captured the bridge over the Odon, he ordered an immediate counterattack by 2 SS Panzer Corps. Hausser asked for time to organize his attack but was

---

causing Bradley to comment: 'I might have asked him in for dinner if the bastard surrendered four days ago instead of killing my soldiers. But I won't now.' Cf., Diary of Lieutenant Colonel Chester B. Hansen (Bradley's aide-de-camp), US Army Military History Institute.

[1] ULTRA had pinpointed the movements of the 9th and 10th SS Panzer which were now in the vicinity. Cf., Ralph Bennett, Ultra in the West.

overruled by the now frantic Dollmann, who killed himself several hours later.[1]

With no direction available from above Hausser was left to carry out Dollmann's ill-conceived order. The final two days of EPSOM on 29 and 30 June were the most savage of the offensive. On 29 June the 11th Armoured captured Hill 112, the same day that Hausser counterattacked. The plan he had hastily cobbled together called for the combined efforts of both 1 and 2 SS Panzer Corps, with the main thrust aimed at Cheux from the west. The 9th and 10th SS Panzer were to form the main force, supported by elements from the other three panzer divisions already there.

Alerted to his attack by the capture of an SS officer who was carrying a description of Hausser's battleplan, the 15th Division not only beat off the counterattack that night but turned it into a rout.[2] Apparently this valuable intelligence was never transmitted to Dempsey who, not realizing that this had been the main German effort, concluded that the main attack had not yet been launched and would come elsewhere. Dempsey's understandable but unfortunate decision was the turning point of EPSOM. He ordered O'Connor to pull the 11th Armoured back behind the Odon to meet the expected threat to 8 Corps which at that moment lacked sufficient depth to defeat a strong armoured counterattack.[3] The 11th Armoured had represented the main threat to the Germans and their voluntary withdrawal permitted the Germans to recapture Hill 112 the following day.

When the battle for Hill 112 resumed it became one of the most gruesome horrors of the Normandy campaign, a series of vicious engagements reminiscent of the warfare of 1914–18. The Germans were unable to retain control of this deathtrap which was hereafter a 'no-man's land' occupied only by the dead. After five days both sides were equally spent and with the 11th Armoured badly positioned behind the Odon and casualties

---

[1] Long after the war rumours continued to circulate that Dollmann had not died of a heart attack as had been reported at the time. Historian David Irving has disclosed that the Seventh Army Chief of Staff, Major General Max Pemsel, revealed to him (and later publicly) that his superior had poisoned himself. Cf., *The Trail of the Fox*.

[2] Ironically, Hausser was shortly thereafter named as Dollman's replacement as the Seventh Army Commander.

[3] According to the 8 Corps war diary, the order to consolidate their position and withdraw the 29th Armoured Brigade of the 11th Armoured Division came from the Second Army at 2100 hours, 28 June, and specified the withdrawal of the armour north of the Odon. War diary, 8 Corps, EPSOM, PRO (WO 171/286).

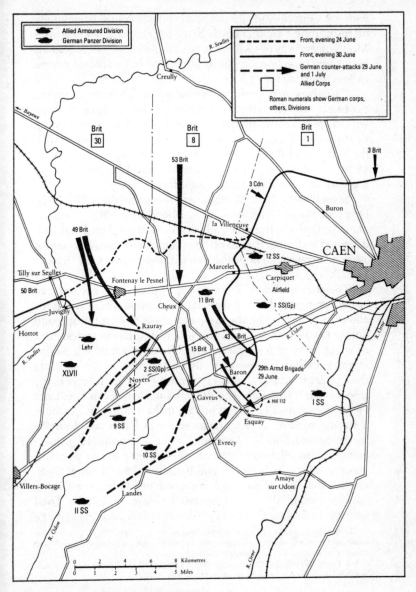

EPSOM: THE ODON BATTLEFIELD

within 8 Corps already unacceptably high, a continuation of the offensive meant another costly battle for Hill 112. It was a price Montgomery was not willing to pay and, with the ultimate goals of the operation now obviously unattainable, he ordered EPSOM to be terminated on 30 June.

Casualties on both sides were indeed starkly high; according to one account the narrow Odon had at one point been dammed with corpses.[1] An examination of their war diary shows that 8 Corps suffered 4,020 casualties in the five-day campaign, with the 15th Division bearing the brunt of these losses: 2,331 – over 58%.[2] By comparison the 11th Armoured and the 43rd Division together accounted for 1,256 casualties (31%).[3]

Several days later Montgomery wrote to the GOC, 15th Division, Major General G. H. A. MacMillan: 'Please congratulate the Division from me and tell all officers and men that I am delighted with what they have done. I am sending you a present of 180,000 cigarettes. I hope the men will enjoy them. Good luck to you all.'[4]

The grievous losses suffered by the gallant 15th Division can be best understood by the fact that the division was in action for about 325 days during the campaign in Northwest Europe, and during EPSOM suffered about 25% of their total casualties, most of which were to the infantry arm.[5] Total strength of a British infantry division is approximately 18,350 men; of this total less than 50% are infantry, and only about 25% actually serve in the rifle companies (about 4,600 officers and men). Casualties from EPSOM thus ran well in excess of 50% in the infantry and, without a steady infusion of reinforcements, such losses could not be sustained indefinitely. This was a major reason for Montgomery's cancellation of EPSOM. The example of one battalion was typical: on 26 June the 2nd Battalion, The Glasgow Highlanders lost 12 officers and sustained nearly 200 casualties, mainly around the hotly contested village of Cheux. Total strength of this battalion was approximately 35 officers and 786

[1] Belfield and Essame, The Battle for Normandy, op.cit., p. 115. Meyer's 12th SS lost some eight hundred men in the Odon battle. In several instances his men tied explosives round their waists and jumped on to British tanks.

[2] 8 Corps War Diary, 'A' Branch (WO 171/291), PRO. Figures include killed, wounded and missing, computed as of 0600 hours, 2 July 1944.

[3] Ibid.

[4] MacMillan Papers, IWM.

[5] Belfield and Essame, op.cit., p. 116.

other ranks; thus *one day's* losses amounted to 34% of their officers and nearly 25% of the entire rifle battalion.[1]

What did EPSOM really accomplish? The official history suggests that the British had somehow won a major victory, yet records this success in purely defensive terms: 'Our own casualties had been considerable but *our position was unshaken.*' (Author's italics.)[2]. While it is true that 'The enemy had suffered a sharp defeat,'[3] this defeat was purely in terms of men and material. Tactically, the British had gained little ground and had achieved none of their objectives. The suggestion by the official historians that ' . . . EPSOM had in fact forestalled and spoiled the last German effort to break the Allied front that could be made while there were still some fresh armoured divisions with which to attempt it,'[4] befuddles the fact that this result was a fortuitous by-product of an operation of immense intentions which were not attained.

No amount of pretence can conceal that the real object had been a short pincer movement to outflank Caen from the west and, like the Villers-Bocage ploy, it was a dismal failure. In their final positions astride the Odon on 30 June, 8 Corps posed no serious threat to Caen. Once again, the only major achievement from an operation with far-reaching goals was defensive. For the second time in two weeks an armoured division had been voluntarily withdrawn, and both times the decision to do so cost the British dearly.

There is little doubt that Montgomery considered time and the weather the predominant factors in preventing his plans from progressing satisfactorily. Commenting on the situation existing on the last day of June, Montgomery later wrote: 'In fairer conditions the build-up of formations and stores might have been kept to schedule; with greater weight and increased resources the American operations could have proceeded more rapidly, and 8 Corps operations might have succeeded in taking Caen before the flower of the SS Panzer formations had become available in its defence.'[5]

---

[1] Cf. Ellis, *Victory in the West*, op.cit., p. 278 and Appendix IV.
[2] Ibid., p. 286.
[3] Ibid.
[4] Ibid.
[5] Montgomery, *El Alamein to the River Sangro and Normandy to the Baltic*, op.cit., p. 233.

However, Montgomery has grossly exaggerated the extent to which his holding action in drawing off the panzer divisions actually succeeded. By attacking the Odon when he did, Montgomery most certainly put paid to Rommel's plan to launch a decisive counterstroke by forcing the hasty commitment of Hausser's panzer corps, and his jabbing tactics at Caen certainly disrupted and weakened Rommel's 'roping-off' policy. The combination of these attacks and the effects of Allied air and artillery did severely reduce the fighting effectiveness of the German divisions. Nevertheless, it must be remembered that the Germans never intended to use the newly arrived panzer divisions against Bradley (with the exception of the badly mauled 2nd SS Panzer). They were positioned around Caen for purely *offensive* reasons of their own: to initiate a counterstroke aimed at Bayeux.

As crippled as most of the panzer divisions were, they were able – repeatedly – to prevent the Second Army from capturing or outflanking Caen. One must then ask what was intended by each of these British operations and in each case the various operational orders and other war documents state quite clearly their aims, yet never has more historical nonsense been perpetuated then over the question of Montgomery and his Caen strategy. The *sine qua non* of all this debate becomes non-existent upon careful examination of the first three weeks of the Normandy campaign, especially of EPSOM. Dempsey clarified the issue when he revealed: 'Monty had originally intended that Second Army should only be required to fight its holding battle for two or three weeks – just long enough to cover the period while the Americans were taking Cherbourg and were regrouping to attack southwards.'[1] And the means by which this 'holding action' was to be accomplished, as we have seen, was by maximum aggressiveness in the first days of the campaign to *seize* and *hold* the critical terrain surrounding Caen.

EPSOM's failure delayed the commitment of the First Canadian Army which upset Crerar, who was told by Montgomery that the problem was too little space in the overcrowded Caen bridgehead to accommodate another army – a statement which demonstrated the inaccuracy of his claim to his general officers on 22 June that he had now attained the lodgement area required.

[1] Dempsey interview, loc.cit.

For the near future Montgomery proposed to bring in Lieutenant General Ritchie's 12 Corps and, following this, 2 Canadian Corps would be sent to Normandy as soon as practicable. However, Montgomery refused to make any promise to Crerar about when the First Canadian Army would become operational: '. . . Owing to the delay, caused by the weather, in the "build-up" and in the capture of Caen, and the securing of the line of the River Dives to the east, it was necessary to phase back the arrival of the Canadian Army until this situation had been attained. The first essential was the completion of the Second British Army to full strength and securing the necessary "elbow room" in which to concentrate another Army.'[1]

The Second Army task of protecting Bradley had been carried out with great success but Eisenhower was perfectly aware that the real objects of the British attacks had not been achieved, and with Dempsey stalled before Caen he could see that the options open to Montgomery were few. According to Eisenhower's biographer, the Supreme Commander was unhappy about the implications of this new holding strategy. Montgomery ' . . . was preparing to settle into what amounted to a siege of Caen, hoping to draw off German strength and thus make it possible for Bradley to break out on the right. Eisenhower had expected the breakout on the left, on the shortest road to Paris, and regarded Montgomery's program as a change in the basic plan, brought on by his unsuccessful attempt to get Caen.'[2]

A senior member of the SHAEF staff and former COSSAC planning officer, Brigadier Kenneth G. McLean is quoted as calling Montgomery a 'big cheat' in his claims: 'For Montgomery to say that he was holding the Germans so Bradley could break out was absolute rubbish and a complete fabrication that only developed after he was stopped outside Caen.'[3]

As matters stood at the end of June a breakout was only possible from the American sector. Bradley, however, made it clear to Eisenhower that he was not yet ready to mount an offensive to secure the southern half of the Cotentin Peninsula.

---

[1] Crerar War Diary, loc.cit.

[2] Stephen E. Ambrose, *The Supreme Commander*, London, 1971, p. 428.

[3] Ibid. McLean was one of the key OVERLORD planners and was well versed on this subject. He was the officer who presented the first COSSAC briefings to Montgomery when he assumed command of 21st Army Group in January 1944.

Furthermore, the original plan called only for American forces to break out into the Brittany Peninsula. Future operations, including realignment of US and British armies so that both were facing east, were dependent upon the attainment of a suitable lodgement area from which a breakout could be executed on *either flank*.

In a letter to Eisenhower on 29 June, Bradley recorded his need for a slight delay. The storm had postponed the arrival of VIII Corps from England and his 4th Infantry Division had sustained nearly 6,000 casualties in the drive on Cherbourg, and needed additional time to refit before being committed to a new offensive.[1] With Bradley unable to jump off quickly and 8 Corps halted far short of its goals in the Odon, Montgomery was compelled to continue the search for a workable strategy of capturing or isolating Caen.

Not only was Eisenhower growing deeply concerned over the obvious discrepancies between what Montgomery had originally planned and what the ground C-in-C was telling him in letters and messages, but he was equally unhappy over the poor state of relations between Coningham and Montgomery. Tedder's diary for the latter part of June contains numerous references to the problem. On 30 June, for example, he wrote: 'Saw Eisenhower who is worried about Army-Air cooperation. Monty has suggested to Ike's mind Coningham is being too critical and a little uncooperative. The matter will not be settled till, as in Africa, the Army and Air commanders live side by side.'[2] Eisenhower decreed that there must be more effort to improve air-ground relations and instructed Tedder on 21 June to involve himself personally in the matter to ensure that Montgomery received whatever air support was requested and 'to see that they have asked for every kind of air support that is practicable and in maximum volume that could be usefully delivered.'[3]

Repetitive as it may have been, the question of 'What next?' had to be asked yet again. What was certain was that another delay was unavoidable before a new offensive could commence against Caen after two failures to outflank it. Despite Eisenhower's fears, Montgomery was still loath to consider the un-

[1] Bradley, letter to Eisenhower, 29 June 1944, Eisenhower Papers, Eisenhower Library. Bradley was forced to delay his offensive until 1 July.
[2] Tedder Diary, loc.cit.
[3] Alfred D. Chandler (Ed.), *The Papers of Dwight David Eisenhower*, The War Years, Volume III, p. 1952.

pleasant alternative of an all-out siege of Caen, and on 30 June formally announced in a written directive what had in reality been his new strategy for over two weeks, namely that of holding on his left flank while drawing the bulk of the German reserves on to the Second Army front while Bradley continued offensive action on the right flank.[1] EPSOM had been an attempt to eliminate the necessity for this unsatisfactory strategy but this second major offensive failure obliged Montgomery to continue what he had never intended.

At this moment Montgomery faced another knotty problem. His manpower resources, particularly the precious infantry, had suffered heavy casualties. He had to avoid incurring similar losses. Throughout most of June battle losses had actually been *fewer* than the manpower planners had forecast, but the high cost of EPSOM made another such operation without Lieutenant General Ritchie's 12 Corps risky.[2]

In an unpublished post-war interview with Chester Wilmot, Montgomery defended his Caen strategy:

> Of course we would have liked to get Caen on the first day and I was never happy about the left flank until we had got Caen. But the important thing on the flank was to maintain our strength so that we could not only avoid any setback, but could keep the initiative by attacking whenever we liked. On this flank ground was of no importance at all. I had learnt from the last war the senseless sacrifice that can be made by sentimental attachment to a piece of ground. All I asked Dempsey to do was to keep German armour tied down on this flank so that my breakout with the Americans could go more easily. Ground did not matter so long as the German divisions stayed on this flank. If I had attacked Caen early in June I might have wrecked the whole plan.[3]

Apparently Wilmot, an ardent admirer of Montgomery, recognized the hollowness of these claims for he never used the interview. Then, in a moment of inadvertent and rare candour to an outsider, Montgomery admitted for perhaps the only time the true seriousness of his problems:

[1]   21st Army Group Directive M–505, 30 June 1944.
[2]   Although 12 Corps HQ was established in Normandy at the end of June, its units were not, and their first commitment to battle did not come until 16 July, during Operation GOODWOOD.
[3]   Interview with Chester Wilmot, 18 May 1946, Liddell Hart Papers, King's College, London.

We were short of ammunition, we were short of troops, the enemy had brought in two very strong divisions to hold Caen. At best, it would have been touch and go whether we could take it or not. If we had failed, we would have been forced on the defensive. We might have had such losses that we could not even hold the ground we had, and we certainly could not have attacked again for some time. That would have given the Germans the opportunity to switch their armoured divisions to the American sector. You must remember that the British Army was a wasting asset. We had not the manpower to replace heavy casualties. The War Office told me before D-Day that it could guarantee replacements only for the first month. After that I would have to break up divisions or ancillary troops. Consequently there was no sense in incurring casualties to gain ground when we were doing our job on this flank anyway. It would have been very easy for me to yield to the public criticism and the American pressure and to have made greater efforts to gain ground on this flank. It might have helped my immediate reputation but it would have crippled the British Army.[1]

The only alternative was for Montgomery to proceed exactly as he now did by maintaining continued pressure on Caen with a series of limited small attacks by 1 and 8 Corps, while Bradley carried the burden in the west. It was clearly not the strategy Montgomery preferred and certainly no part of his original plan, but despite his known dislike of improvisation, he was employing the only tactics that made sense in the circumstances. It would be incorrect to argue that conditions had reached stalemate but that day was not far off, and if the Germans no longer possessed any hope of winning the battle of Normandy, the plain fact was they had not only proved their capability to resist stubbornly but had succeeded in thoroughly blunting the Second Army's offensive operations. In these unsettled conditions Montgomery still faced the problem of finding some means of breaking open the Caen flank – and soon.

At the end of June there was turmoil of a different kind within the German High Command. After the collapse of the Odon counterattack by 2 SS Panzer Corps, Geyr von Schweppenburg prepared an exceptionally pessimistic assessment which recommended that the Caen bridgehead be abandoned and a new defensive line be re-established further back, out of range of the guns of the Allied fleet in the Bay of the Seine. Hausser submitted

[1] Wilmot interview, 18 May 1946.

a similar report to von Rundstedt. Both von Rundstedt and Rommel agreed with these gloomy appraisals; von Rundstedt submitted them to OKW and asked to be given a free hand immediately, and discretion to conduct his own battle – which, by implication, meant freedom from Hitler's pervasive interference. Hitler was predictably incensed and directed OKW to inform von Rundstedt to hold his present positions. He also ordered von Rundstedt's immediate dismissal and named Field Marshal Gunther von Kluge as his replacement. For his temerity Hitler also ordered von Schweppenburg's removal several days later. In a telephone call to OKW on the night of 1 July, von Rundstedt warned Keitel, the chief of OKW, of the gravity of the German situation in the west. 'What shall we do? What shall we do?' asked Keitel. 'Make peace, you idiots,' said von Rundstedt. 'What else can you do?'[1]*

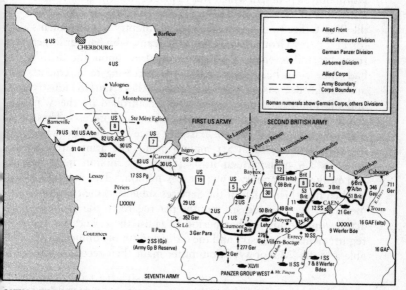

SITUATION MAP, 30 JUNE 1944

[1] Quoted by Sir Winston Churchill in *Triumph and Tragedy*, Boston, 1953, p. 23.
* Ostensibly von Rundstedt was being allowed to retire voluntarily for reasons of health and age, an assertion the Field Marshal vehemently denied after the war. Geyr von Schweppenburg's replacement was General Heinrich Eberbach, a veteran armoured corps commander.

CHAPTER 15

The Manpower Dilemma

> The good general must not only win his battles; he
> must win them with a minimum of casualties and
> loss of life.
>
> Montgomery

By early July the British were in serious trouble as a result of a
rapidly growing shortage of trained infantry reinforcements in
Normandy, a problem which was to plague Montgomery for the
remainder of the war. Well before D-Day he had been warned by
the War Office to expect a shortage of infantry reinforcements
for 21st Army Group. Unlike the Americans, who had far larger
resources and reserves of manpower to draw upon, the British
had since 1939 been confronted with increasing requirements
and steadily decreasing manpower assets. Allocations to industry
and the military services were rigidly controlled by the War
Cabinet and were based upon approved annual forecasts. These
manpower limits had been in existence since March 1941, when
the army was allocated 2.1 million men.[1] The army strength
grew to 2.6 million men in 1943, to 2.7 million in 1944
and peaked in January 1945 at 2.9 million.[2] The procedure
worked like this: 'Each of the Services submitted their requirements for the ensuing six months per regard to the probable
actions/operations in that period. Against these were set the
requirements of industry and the estimated supply of men available and the [Manpower] Committee made their recommenda-

[1] 'As early as 1941, 94 out of every 100 males in the United Kingdom between the ages
of 14 and 64 had been mobilized into the services or industry, and of the total British
working population of 32,000,000 approximately 22,000,000 were eventually drafted
for service either in industry or the armed forces.' See Roland G. Ruppenthal, *Logistical
Support of the Armies*, Vol. 1, Washington, 1953, p. 60.
[2] Major General A. J. K. Pigott, *The Second World War, 1939–1945, ARMY:
Manpower Problems*, App B, The War Office, 1949. This was one of a series of restricted
documents prepared by the War Office to record selected subjects.

tions to the Government with whom the final decision lay.'[1]

The General Staff of the War Office was responsible for drawing up the Orders of Battle and for creating the units to fill them, a never-ending process which had to be adjusted constantly to meet the rapidly fluctuating edicts imposed by the strategy makers. Faced with greater requirements than available assets, the army staff were frequently forced to convert or break up units to satisfy higher priority needs. For example, when the war began 50% of the British Army consisted of infantry units; this quickly rose to 60% after Dunkirk, when the threat of German invasion was still great. Towards the middle of the war this figure had dropped to 20%, and the Royal Artillery became the largest arm with 22%.[2] Given the rigid ceiling on total manpower the only means of increasing the strength of one arm was at the expense of others – hence the constant shuffling of units and personnel.

The army's 1944 requirements were drawn up by the War Office in the summer of 1943 and included sufficient manpower for 21st Army Group to mount OVERLORD with sixteen British and Canadian divisions. Little was left over for long-term reinforcements; the task of satisfying OVERLORD requirements had left available manpower reserves dangerously low, and the War Office was predicting that at least two infantry divisions and several separate brigades might have to be disbanded by the end of 1944 for lack of reinforcements.[3]

The officer charged with the unenviable responsibility for providing reinforcements was General Sir Ronald Adam, the Adjutant General, and he went to unusual lengths to find solutions. He recalls being stranded on Gibraltar in late 1943 when, by chance, he met the Canadian Defence Minister, Colonel J. L. Ralston. Adam succeeded in persuading Ralston to transfer two hundred young Canadian officers to the British Army for use as first replacements in 21st Army Group during the forthcoming invasion. These officers proved to be of such high quality that they were absorbed directly into British units and taken on the D-Day landings, leaving a like number of British officers to be used as first replacements.[4] While this may appear trivial along-

---

[1] Major General A. J. K. Pigott, op.cit., p. 17.
[2] Papers of General Sir Ronald Adam, King's College, London.
[3] PRO (CAB 78/21).
[4] Adam Papers, loc.cit.

side the total numbers participating in OVERLORD, it amply illustrates how acute the problem had become.

The British had known since the summer of 1943 that they would have a worldwide shortage of infantry in 1944 and the War Office forecast made it clear that in all likelihood the cannibalization of existing units to fill shortages would become essential. As OVERLORD drew closer, the manpower forecast was refined. At a manpower meeting on 30 May 1944, chaired by the Deputy Prime Minister, Clement Attlee, the War Office presented a memo from the Secretary of State for War, Sir James Grigg, which specifically referred to the anticipated infantry problem:

> Estimate of infantry casualties and normal wastage needing replacement between April and December 1944 based on latest forecasts of operational activity, taking into account wounded returning to duty, amounts to 102,250. Taking account of sources of reinforcements the year end shortage 1944 will still be 30,000 with a peak period at the end of September when the shortage may be as high as 35,000.[1]

Grigg went on to outline measures taken to reduce these shortages which would still make the infantry position 'precarious'. The army's solution was to have 35,000 additional men transferred to the infantry for retraining.[2]

It would be logical to conclude that the estimated shortage of 35,000 and the transfer of 35,000 new men to fill those shortages would eliminate the problem. In theory it ought to have worked but in practice it succeeded only in averting a calamity. The estimated shortages were based on the casualties predicted for OVERLORD, and despite the best of intentions the War Office planners bungled when they computed the casualty rate for Northwest Europe. They computed the *total numbers* of reinforcements required fairly accurately, but where the blunder occurred was in their estimation of *infantry* losses. The official British history whitewashes the entire issue and one has to look to the official Canadian account for the truth. As the Canadian history explains:

---

[1] PRO (CAB 78/21).
[2] Ibid.

Casualties in the infantry arm in Normandy had been heavier, and those in the other arms lighter, than had been anticipated in Allied planning... All had grossly miscalculated ... 'the rates of wastage' used by the British War Office ... were undoubtedly based mainly on the fighting in North Africa, and they proved inapplicable to Northwest Europe. To state the matter in its simplest and starkest terms, the War Office had predicted that in periods of 'intense' activity 48% of the casualties would be suffered by the infantry, 15% by the armoured corps and 14% by the artillery... But down to 17 August in Normandy the infantry had 76% of the Canadian casualties, the armoured corps only 7% and the artillery 8%.[1]

It is evident from available data that the Canadian experience was mirrored in British units whose infantry casualty rate was running as high as 80%. Nor was the growing problem of infantry reinforcements limited to the British Army, for Canada too faced a similar crisis brought about by reliance on the British casualty estimates. Until late 1944 the Canadian contribution to the war was entirely through the use of regular soldiers, augmented by volunteers. Since the summer of 1943 the Canadians had accepted the War Office figures and used them as a basis for providing reinforcements to all overseas based units.[2] By December 1943 warning signals began emanating from Italy which questioned the accuracy of North African casualty rates in a European theatre. Those on the scene in Italy could see from the emerging statistics a disturbing rise in infantry losses, particularly amongst officers.

Despite these warnings the Canadian Military Headquarters

---

[1] Colonel C. P. Stacey, *The Victory Campaign*, op.cit., p.284. With the British history so unhelpful, the only logical place to find out how the manpower crisis was dealt with inside the War Office is the records of the Adjutant General in the Public Record Office (Class W.O. 162). However there are no such records for the Second World War – all are missing. For some years they were kept in the Cabinet Office Historical Section but in 1968 they were returned to the Ministry of Defence records repository outside London, and eventually ought to have been transferred permanently to the Public Record Office. The entire collection – approximately 164 boxes – has disappeared and despite two years of fruitless butting against a bureaucratic wall, the Ministry of Defence records experts deny any knowledge of the Adjutant General records or what may have happened to them. This despite the fact that the Cabinet Office Historical Section retains a receipt for their transfer. Although information about the manpower problems can be found from other sources, the loss of these valuable records leaves an unfortunate gap in the British history of the Second World War. If the indifference shown during the author's attempts to locate these records is any example, there is scant hope that they will ever become available to future historians.

[2] Colonel C. P. Stacey, *Arms, Men and Governments*, Ottawa, 1970, p. 425.

(CMHQ) in London chose to continue relying on the War Office data.[1] In the months before D-Day there developed a considerable difference of opinion between CMHQ and Ottawa, complicated by a misunderstanding of the data furnished by the War Office. The Canadians in London had estimated 1944 casualties at 75,000, of whom 50% might be returned to their units after six months. In April they discovered that the War Office did not consider that all of these men would recover and be re-employed in active operations.[2] There ensued a disagreement over the acceptable replacement rate; CMHQ proposed a rate of 5,000 reinforcements per month during the summer of 1944 to allow for unforeseen contingencies, but Ottawa stuck to their own projection of 4,000 per month, which actual experience proved to be totally inadequate.[3] Thus, despite the anxiety of some knowledgeable officers in the Canadian headquarters, they entered the Normandy campaign with a considerable infantry deficit which was recorded on 31 May as being 3,337 troops.[4]

What emerges from this tangle is that no one in the War Office seemed to have questioned the validity of using North African casualty rates in Northwest Europe, nor did the planners grasp the implications of the tricky and difficult bocage and the strong defence which would be offered by the Germans. As they tended to do throughout the war, the British severely underestimated German fighting ability and determination.

By March 1944, 21st Army Group had perceived that the casualty rate for OVERLORD could be expected to exceed the War Office projections. On 17 March Montgomery personally warned CMHQ of a potential shortage of infantry and suggested that steps be taken to prepare for this by retraining additional personnel.[5] However, lack of conscripts and an unsuccessful campaign to recruit volunteers failed to make up the shortfall prior to D-Day. Although Canadian participation in the early weeks of Normandy was small, by mid-July when more units were engaged the earlier warnings of higher than estimated losses became reality. Actual infantry casualties were running nearly

[1] Stacey, *Arms, Men and Governments*, Ottawa, 1970, p. 425.
[2] Ibid.
[3] Ibid, p. 426.
[4] Ibid, pp. 432 and 434.
[5] Ibid, p. 427.

80% *higher* than forecast.[1] So serious did this situation become that the Canadian First Army commander, General Crerar, cabled his concern to CMHQ on 4 August:

> Am concerned about infantry general duty deficiencies which approximate 1900. Our ability to continue severe fighting or to exploit a break out would be seriously restricted through lack of replacement personnel... I consider this the most serious problem of Canadian Army at the moment and to require most energetic handling.[2]

Crerar's prognosis was correct and Canadian casualties steadily rose during August and hit their peak at the end of the month, when infantry shortages reached 4,318.[3] After Normandy this situation improved for a short time but the costly battles in the Scheldt Estuary around Antwerp, continuing casualties in Italy and the near-stalemate which halted the Allied armies along the German border made it unmistakable that the war would continue well into 1945.

The Canadian Government was forced to resort reluctantly to conscription in order to meet its manpower needs. Their experience in Normandy having convinced them of the unreliability of British casualty estimates, they initiated in September their own new system based on actual battle losses.[4] The new figures demonstrate quite clearly the serious underestimation of infantry losses and the overestimation in other arms. For periods of intense combat the infantry figures jumped by 80% for officers and 50% for other ranks, while those of the armoured corps and the artillery decreased by 25% for officers and 50% for other ranks.[5]

The crisis facing Montgomery in July was no sudden accident. He was well aware of the longstanding War Office projection of a potential infantry shortage of 35,000 by September[6]; indeed this knowledge can be related to his master plan for Normandy. Quick results might mean heavy initial casualties but

---

[1] Stacey, *Arms, Men and Governments*, p. 435. Statistics for the period 6 June – 10 July reflect total infantry casualties of 4,105 versus a forecast of 2,282.

[2] Ibid, p. 437.   [3] Ibid, pp. 438–9.

[4] Ibid, pp. 438–9.   [5] Ibid, p. 453.

[6] On 19 May he wrote to Brooke: 'The implications of the manpower situation on 21 Army Group are going to be very serious. We are already short of over 13,000 men of our WE plus authorized reinforcements even before we commence fighting, and the situation will deteriorate and not improve.' Alanbrooke Papers.

in the longer term it meant the saving of lives and the conserving of his infantry assets. The situation in early July obliged Montgomery to take his infantry strength into consideration when planning future operations. While 21st Army Group was still a very powerful fighting force, it was not capable of remaining so for long without a steady infusion of reinforcements. He could count on much higher casualties and some difficult battles before the Normandy campaign was concluded, and the inevitable result would be to have fewer fighting units, for the time was close at hand when he would be forced to cannibalize several of them. The problem facing Montgomery was this:

> For D-Day itself and for approximately ten days afterwards, losses had been pleasantly lower than estimated; and from then on, as the panzer divisions of the German reserve were drawn in, they had jumped to the alarming ratio of 2:1. That is, for every man who became a casualty, and for whom a replacement had been provided, and was standing by in the reinforcement holding units, two men were becoming casualties; and there was only one man to replace them both. The time was rapidly arriving – it was less than two weeks away, in fact – when there would be no more infantry reinforcements. They had all been fed to the units and had themselves become casualties in their turn. There simply was no way out except feet first or two feet under; and the infantry themselves knew it better than anybody else. That fact was becoming very obvious. And the only way now, to keep divisions up to strength, was to break-up an existing division, already bled and shaken, and distribute the survivors piecemeal throughout the armies.[1]

In fact, Air Chief Marshal Harris did complain that Bomber Command's losses in May and June exceeded those of the entire 21st Army Group since D-Day. British and Canadian killed as reported on 30 June totalled 3,356, while those of Bomber Command were approximately 3,500.[2] In April and May the Allied air forces had lost nearly 12,000 men and over 2,000 aircraft in pre-OVERLORD operations.[3]

Post-war British accounts of the Normandy campaign have not given sufficient emphasis to the seriousness of either the reinforcement problem or the effects it produced on Mont-

---

[1] Alexander McKee, *Caen: Anvil of Victory*, London, 1965, p. 249. McKee's observations are based on firsthand experience in a reinforcement unit in Normandy.
[2] Ellis, op.cit., p. 307, and AEAF Historical Record PRO (Air 37/1057).
[3] Ibid, p. 112.

gomery's strategy after D-Day. He has been savagely criticized for overcaution and lack of imagination in his direction of the British Army around Caen, yet what has never been understood is the dilemma he faced in using 21st Army Group at maximum fighting strength while still avoiding unnecessary casualties – a paradoxical impossibility! How much of this was really overcaution and how much a commonsense need to employ his dwindling combat strength judiciously is a matter of personal opinion. However, the lesson of EPSOM and the other early battles does seem to point to the necessity for Montgomery's compromise strategy of drawing in and containing the majority of the German reserves to the Caen front instead of the all-out attacks and deep penetrations originally envisaged.

The only alternative was to request assignment of US units to 21st Army Group from Bradley, an alternative that was unacceptable and would have been firmly rejected. In any case, there were not enough US divisions available in Normandy to permit this course of action. In early July Montgomery did ask for the US 3rd Armored Division to be assigned to him but Bradley, remembering Pershing's problems during the First World War, evaded having to tell Montgomery 'no'. He compromised by expanding the US front so that the responsibility was taken over by a US corps, leaving the division under his control.[1]

The casualty and reinforcement reports provide stark testimony to the seriousness of Montgomery's problem. On 29 June, 21st Army Group reported a total of 22,460 casualties since D-Day.[2] By the following day, when EPSOM ended, losses had jumped by another 10% to 24,698,[3] and by 17 July – on the eve of Operation GOODWOOD – casualty figures had risen 60% over those of 29 June to 37,563. By comparison, on 29 June there were a total of 7,335 infantry reinforcements of all ranks available in the five 21st Army Group reinforcement groups, of which two were located in Normandy.[4] During the same period (29 June–17 July) the availability of infantry reinforcements dropped to

---

[1]   Omar N. Bradley, *A Soldier's Story*, New York, 1951, pp. 327–8.

[2]   War Diary, 21st Army Group, 'A' Section, SITREP No. 25, 1 July 1944, PRO (WO 171/139). These figures are cumulative and include killed, wounded and missing.

[3]   Ellis, op.cit., p. 307, also cumulative from 6–30 June. Ellis quotes German losses up to 30 June as 80,783, not including losses resulting from the capture of Cherbourg.

[4]   War Diary, 21st Army Group, 'A' Section, PRO (WO 171/139). (480 officers and 6,885 other ranks.)

6,654.[1] After GOODWOOD the casualty figures rose to 52,165 (an increase of 132% since 29 June) while infantry reinforcements continued to decrease dramatically by 117%, to a figure of 2,837 immediately available.[2] The full impact of the War Office's miscalculations is evident from the great imbalance between reinforcements for the infantry and those available for the other arms. On 28 July when these figures were reported, infantry reinforcements represented only 14.7% of the total reinforcements within 21st Army Group (2,837 vs 19,324), yet the infantry continued to absorb upwards of 70% of *all* casualties.[3]

From the outset of war in September 1939 to the end of June 1944 the infantry had absorbed 54% of the total battles casualties of the British Army. Of 326,877 men lost, the infantry arm sustained 177,709. By comparison the Royal Artillery had lost 62,591 men (19%), and the Royal Armoured Corps 19,457 (6%).[4]

In early July the problem was serious enough for the War Office to send General Adam to Normandy to warn Montgomery and Dempsey personally. Dempsey later recorded that 'Bill Adam came out on a visit to Normandy about the second week of July, and in a talk in my caravan he warned me that if our *infantry* casualties continued at the recent rate it would be impossible to replace them, and we should have to 'cannibalise' – to break up some divisions in order to maintain the rest. For we had put almost all our available manpower into Normandy in the first few weeks.'[5]

The British regimental system further complicated the difficulty of providing adequate numbers of infantry reinforcements. The system made it difficult – sometimes impossible – to send reinforcements who came from one section of the United Kingdom to a division representing a different geographical area. For example, the practice was to send Highlanders only to a Highland regiment, Durham 'Geordies' to the Durham Light Infantry, and so forth. This, of course, took no account of

---

[1] PRO (WO 171/139).   [2] Ibid.   [3] Ibid.

[4] These battle loss statistics included prisoners-of-war, and a shocking 42% of the total since 1939 (137,000) was attributable to this one category. Of the infantry losses, 37% (66,319) were POWs, mainly from Dunkirk, Singapore and North Africa. Source: War Office casualty figures contained in 'General Return of the Strength of the British Army', 30 June 1944, PRO (WO 73/161), pp. 180–1.

[5] Liddell Hart Papers, loc.cit. Dempsey's recollection is confirmed by General Adam in a letter to the author dated 28 February 1979.

requirements which fluctuated according to the casualty rate. Consequently, the numbers of reinforcements available at any given moment were not necessarily a valid indicator: a Durham battalion might require reinforcements but if none was available the system did not provide for the substitution of Highlanders.[1]

Montgomery's seeming reluctance to mount a successful attack against Caen was the basis for the growing criticism. American commanders began to question why their casualty rate was nearly 50% higher than Montgomery's when the balance of forces was generally equal. As recorded on 30 June these figures were 24,698 British and Canadian casualties, and 34,034 Americans.[2]

While aware of the criticism, Montgomery made no effort to discuss his problems with Eisenhower except to insist repeatedly that his strategy was to keep German reserves pinned to the Caen front. Eisenhower, whose own frustrations were increasing daily, openly complained to Churchill when the latter paid him a visit in early July,[3] triggering a monumental row between Brooke and the Prime Minister. Brooke had found Churchill in a foul and critical mood the night of 6 July and had reacted by demanding to know why the Prime Minister would not trust his generals for five minutes instead of continuously belittling them.[4] As far as Brooke was concerned, Montgomery had his full backing and Eisenhower's complaint had no impact in Whitehall except to anger the CIGS.

Grigg's May projections eventually proved accurate, with the actual infantry shortages by the end of September amounting to some 32,000 men, or about 3,000 fewer than forecast.[5] It was fortunate that the War Office had foreseen the shortage and taken steps to alleviate the problem insofar as was possible but, as Colonel Stacey has shown, estimates of the actual casualty rates

---

[1] There were exceptions to this policy, particularly in the Scottish divisions where the high infantry casualty rate made it impossible to generate adequate numbers of Scots reinforcements. Eventually it became a joke within the 15th (Scottish) Division that it ought to be renamed the '15th Scotsmen' as that was the total number of Scots left in the division. Letter, A. C. Jenkins to the author, 9 November 1983.

[2] Ellis, op.cit., p. 307.   [3] Eisenhower, unpublished manuscript, loc.cit.

[4] Alanbrooke Diary. This incident took place between 10 p.m. on 6 July and 2 a.m. on 7 July.

[5] PRO (WO 216/101). Grigg's forecast was for the entire army; the figures for 21st Army Group were not given but the majority of these shortages were attributable to Northwest Europe, which was designated the priority effort for 1944.

were so severely understated that had the War Office *not* foreseen a problem the results for 21st Army Group could well have been twice the original estimate. If the early June casualties had not been less than anticipated it is indeed frightening to contemplate their effects during the remainder of the Normandy campaign.

The War Office had also predicted that by the end of 1944 21st Army Group would have to disband two infantry divisions and three independent armoured brigades, and redistribute their remaining assets.[1] In the actual event, two divisions and a number of independent armoured battalions and regiments were either broken up or transferred to other units. Throughout July Montgomery managed to avoid any disbandment of units but as his casualty figures continued to rise steadily during the battles for Caen and the breakout in July and early August, he found no other option. On 14 August he cabled Brooke:

> Regret time has now come when I must break up one infantry division. My infantry divisions are so low in effective rifle strength that they can no – repeat NO – longer fight effectively in major operations. The need for this action has been present for some time but the urgency of the present battle operations forced me to delay decision. Can now do so – NO – repeat NO – longer. Request permission to break up at once 59th Division. 56th Infantry Brigade will be retained as an independent brigade for the present. Request matter be treated as urgent – repeat – urgent – and authority sent tomorrow.[2]

Permission was immediately forthcoming and Montgomery wrote a difficult letter to the divisional commander, Major General L. O. Lyne, telling him that the division had to go because of the acute shortage of infantry. The 59th Division had been selected because it was the junior division in 21st Army Group and not as a result of its performance in battle. Later, Montgomery visited the division to speak personally with its senior officers, and Dempsey and Ritchie sent letters of appreciation. By the end of the month – under the greatest secrecy – the division had disappeared.[3]

The 59th Division was followed in late November by the 50th Division, which produced a furious outburst from the Prime

---

[1] PRO (WO 216/101).
[2] Montgomery cable (M-92), to War Office, PRO (CAB 106/1066).
[3] Unpublished autobiography of Major General L. O. Lyne, IWM.

Minister who angrily demanded the Chiefs-of-Staff find some means of procuring enough physically qualified men to fill the shortages in Montgomery's combat units.[1] Other units were also disbanded or transferred in August. The independent 56th Infantry Brigade became part of the 49th Division when its 70th Brigade was disbanded; the 33rd Armoured Brigade lost two battalions; the 8th and 34th Tank Brigades each lost a regiment, and the 27th Armoured Brigade was disbanded.[2]

British knowledge that the size of 21st Army Group would be limited by the numbers of reinforcements that could be made available had been the basis of their original concept that sometime after the initial assault, the main effort would have to be made with US forces which, once a suitable lodgement area was attained, would be far larger. By the end of the Normandy campaign British-Canadian and US fighting strength looked like this:

	US	British–Canadian[3]*
Army Groups	1	1
Field Armies	2	2
Corps	7	5
Armoured Divisions	7	6
Infantry Divisions	14	9
Airborne Divisions	2	1
Independent armoured/tank Brigades.	-	8

During the remainder of the campaign in Northwest Europe the American commitment rose to become eventually nearly three times that of 21st Army Group:

[1] Churchill, memo to Chiefs-of-Staff, in PRO (WO 216/101). The Chiefs-of-Staff replied by reminding Churchill that this action had been anticipated and nothing could be done about it, and even if sufficient men could be found, considerable training was necessary before they could become qualified as infantrymen.

[2] Ellis, op.cit., App. IV.

[3] Ibid.

* A tenth infantry division – the 59th – had already been disbanded by the end of August, along with the 27th Armoured Brigade. The battered 6th Airborne Division was detached at the end of August for a well-earned rest. Originally scheduled to remain in Normandy only a few weeks while the bridgehead was established, the 6th Airborne Division fought the entire campaign. Losses were 821 killed, 2709 wounded and 927 missing. The armoured division figures include the 79th Armoured which never fought as a division and whose mission was to provide specialized equipment and units to other elements of 21st Army Group in support of various operations.

	US	French	British–Canadian[1]
Army Groups	2	-	1
Field Armies	5	1	2
Corps	14	2	7
Airborne Corps	1	-	1
Armoured Divisions	15	3	7
Infantry Divisions	42	9	12
Airborne Divisions	3	-	1
Independent Armoured Brigades	-	-	6
Independent Infantry Brigades	-	-	1

Montgomery's strength increased slightly during the latter stages of the war when three Canadian units (I Corps, the 1st Infantry and the 5th Armoured) were transferred from Italy. Montgomery was also given the 52nd (Lowland) Division, a highly trained mountain division. The 1st British Airborne Division was in combat only during the period of Operation MARKET-GARDEN, the disastrous airborne operation at Arnhem in September 1944. During the ten days of that battle the 1st Airborne Division lost 1,300 killed, over 1,700 seriously wounded and 3,800 captured.[2] The division ceased to exist except in name and never fought again during the war.

Ever since the United States had actively entered the war in 1942 the British had shared an equal role in determining grand strategy, but with the invasion of France British influence was on the decline. Ever mindful of this decline, Churchill saw any reduction in the British commitment in political terms. There is no indication that Montgomery ever discussed his growing man-power problems with Eisenhower or that he was instructed by London to avoid discussion of the subject. However, there is ample evidence that Eisenhower and the SHAEF staff were aware

[1] L. F. Ellis, *Victory in the West*, Vol 11, London, 1968, App. IV. General Jean de Lattre de Tassigny's First French Army fought under the control of General Jacob L. Devers' 6th US Army Group which had become operational in mid-August when the invasion of southern France (Operation DRAGOON) was finally launched, despite the continued objections of Churchill and the British Chiefs-of-Staff. In addition to the loss of the 1st Airborne Division, the 50th Division was lost in November due to cannibalization, as previously noted.

[2] Ibid, p. 55.

of the problem. SHAEF grew concerned over the British reinforcement shortage and with the two utterly different methods of computing casualty estimates. The British system was termed in a 1 July memo 'intelligent guesswork', while the US system was cited as being more realistic. The American system employed greater coordination, with the operational side providing the battle picture to the medical staff who calculated casualties from formulae contained in an army field manual.[1]

In mid-May 1944 a SHAEF planning memo warned of the expected British shortages and suggested that it would be prudent not to count on any German collapse in Normandy 'lest we may be caught with our trousers down'.[2] On 24 July, Eisenhower's naval aide recorded in his diary this comment about British manpower:

> ... Friends at Naval Headquarters said they felt that Monty, his British Army Commander, Dempsey, the British corps commanders, and even those of the divisions are so conscious of Britain's ebbing manpower that they hesitate to commit an attack where a division may be lost. To replace the division is practically impossible. When it's lost, it's done and finished. Even naval ratings, Air Force personnel, and nondescripts are being 'cannibalised' for replacements.[3]

A full and frank admission of the plight of British manpower would clearly not have been welcomed by Churchill who was anxious to avoid any reduction in the strength of 21st Army Group during the final victory over Germany. The PM was under no illusions about the powerful influence his American ally would have upon post-war Europe. Late in 1944, when the reinforcement problem again became acute, Churchill cabled Montgomery that: 'I greatly fear the dwindling of the British Army is a factor in France as it will affect our right to express our opinion upon strategic and other matters.'[4]

[1] SHAEF Papers, PRO (WO 219/3937).
[2] Ibid (WO 219/2506).
[3] Harry C. Butcher, *Three Years With Eisenhower*, London, 1946, pp. 534–5. Butcher was the keeper of Eisenhower's unofficial war diary but when his naval aide's book was published Eisenhower strongly denied in private correspondence to his British wartime colleagues that he had ever authorized Butcher to keep the diary.
[4] Churchill, telegram to Montgomery, 12 December 1944, PRO (WO 216/101). Churchill's preoccupation with this problem is evident in the minutes and cables available in the Public Records Office. Most of Churchill's wartime papers are contained in his private papers which are under the control of the Churchill Trust. Although these papers

Churchill's concern over casualties and manpower caused him to intervene directly with Eisenhower on at least one occasion, when he telephone from London directly to the Supreme Commander's quarters in France:

> Churchill's request was that if possible Eisenhower should avoid too many British casualties; British losses had been severe, and Britain was being assaulted by the V-weapons. Eisenhower understood the point at once but [told Churchill] if Britain wished to be in the van of the battle, as Montgomery had suggested, British casualties could not be avoided.[1]

After peaking in September as predicted, the infantry position improved considerably during the pursuit of the remnants of the German Army in Normandy to the West Wall of the Third Reich. Except for the Battle of Arnhem, casualties were exceptionally light but throughout the winter months of 1944, while the Allies were stalled near the Siegfried Line, a series of cables were exchanged between Montgomery and the War Office about how to deal with infantry losses, which were again growing. The disbandment of 50th Division in November was a direct result of these exchanges.[2]

Churchill can have had no doubt about what would happen; when he visited Normandy in July he was given a note by Montgomery which read:

> Casualties are slowly mounting. As the war proceeds the manpower situation will necessitate that some units and formations have to be disbanded. I am in very close touch with the War Office on this matter and when it becomes necessary to disband units the policy will be to take first the war formed units. No regular or territorial unit will be disbanded; if the men of any such units are required, the units would be reduced to cadre basis and 'kept in being'.[3]

The Chief Administrative Officer of SHAEF, Lieutenant General

have been deposited in the archives of Churchill College, Cambridge, they will not be available to historians until well after his official biographer, Martin Gilbert, completes his monumental task. Thus, the full impact of Churchill's concern over the manpower drain can only be glimpsed through examination of those records available in the Public Record Office and other archives.

[1] Major General Sir Kenneth Strong, *Intelligence at the Top*, London, 1968, p. 149. Strong was Eisenhower's chief intelligence officer (G–2).

[2] See PRO (WO 216/101).

[3] Papers of Sir James Grigg, Churchill College, Cambridge.

Sir Humfrey Gale, wrote candidly on the subject in a letter of 8 August:

> As you know we have practically come to the end of British manpower and consequently 21st Army Group has to maintain its units up to strength by cannibalisations of other units within the Group. They find that the demand is, as it is in the case of the US Army, about 80% for infantry, and that of this 80% approximately 75% is for 'riflemen'. They are meeting this demand by reduction to cadre and in some cases complete disbandment of nine battalions which were outside divisional organization and were earmarked for special duties in the early stages. This works out very closely to the original estimate that one infantry division or its equivalent would have to be cannibalised by about the end of July. To meet further demands they are now reducing the size of their light AA units and are re-training the men so released for duty in infantry units.[1]

Bradley too had his own infantry replacement problems when US casualties in the bocage in July ran at approximately 90% of all casualties versus a planning figure of about 70%. The great difference was that these losses could be filled fairly quickly with only temporary imbalances, and the crisis was shortlived.[2]

Both the US and Canadian official war histories were candid in discussing their reinforcement problems. Not so the British history, which evades the question entirely except for several brief generalized references, such as: 'At the beginning of July . . . it was not even certain that the British manpower situation would make it possible to maintain all these [divisions] if the war continued for long.'[3] There is no attempt to present the serious impact this problem created for Montgomery and its effect on his tactical employment of British forces. In later chapters we shall see how the tactical decisions by both Montgomery and Dempsey during operations in mid-July were largely influenced by the urgent need to conserve the precious infantry assets of 21st Army Group.

---

[1] General Gale, letter to Lieutenant General J.C.M. Lee, 8 August 1944, papers of Lieutenant General Sir Humfrey Gale, King's College, London.

[2] Ruppenthal, op.cit., pp. 458–63. The US problem was, however, compounded by the fact that experience thus far had shown a need for 95% of all infantry replacements to be rifle and heavy-weapons trained, rather than the figure of 76% calculated by the War Department in May. As Ruppenthal states: 'To make matters worse, only 39.7% of the infantry replacements arriving in the theater [in July] were rifle trained.'

[3] Ellis, op. cit., p. 308.

Shortly before this book went into production new evidence was uncovered which casts serious doubt on the legitimacy of the infantry reinforcement shortage. That 21st Army Group was desperately deficient in infantry reserves is indisputable, but according to British Army records there were more than ample trained infantry personnel available in the United Kingdom to fill Montgomery's shortages and prevent the disbanding of line units. Each month the army published a detailed breakdown of its forces in a document entitled 'General Return of the Strength of the British Army'. The summary dated 30 June 1944 shows some astonishing figures. Within the United Kingdom the infantry assets totalled 12,113 officers and 210,000 other ranks actually serving with infantry units. Of this total, only 48% were serving in or committed to 21st Army Group as reinforcements.[1]

The shortfall within 21st Army Group had been projected at 35,000 and within the uncommitted regiments and battalions located in United Kingdom – the majority of which were Territorial Army units – were 3,152 officers and 56,335 rifle infantrymen. Within the twenty-five infantry training centres were another 1,442 officers and 35,293 other ranks. In addition, there were also the following other types of infantrymen in various units: 1,184 armoured foot guards; 5,173 motorized infantry (357 officers and 4,816 other ranks); and 8,955 Machine-Gun and Support infantry (525 officers and 8,430 other ranks).[2]

Altogether, the infantry picture looked like this:

	Officers	Other Ranks
Infantry Regiments and Battalions	3,152	56,335
Infantry Training Centres	1,442	35,293
Infantry Depots	1,031	10,921
Misc. & Infantry Training Units	748	6,702
TOTAL	6,373	109,251

[1] 5,128 officers and 100,756 other ranks were assigned to 21st Army Group per the 'General Return of the Strength of the British Army', 30 June 1944, PRO (WO 73/161), p. 43. These were all rifle infantry. There were several other categories of infantry serving in 21st Army Group: Motorized: 282 officers, 3,870 other ranks; Machine-Gun and Support: 470 officers, 7,420 other ranks; Armoured Foot Guards: 491 officers, 6,069 other ranks; and Motorized Foot Guards: 37 officers, 888 other ranks.

[2] PRO (WO 73/161).

While these units[1] were undoubtedly committed to the defence of the United Kingdom and other tasks, and some of the personnel were possibly reinforcements for 21st Army Group, the majority of these men were apparently not considered as a means of alleviating the grave infantry deficiency in Normandy. Moreover, the strength return for June 1944 had not changed appreciably from the figures shown in the summary issued on 31 December 1943. There is no reason to doubt that there would have been ample time to programme all or some of these infantrymen to fill the projected losses in Normandy.

The evident availability of vast numbers of uncommitted infantry poses several disturbing questions. Why was none of these troops used in Normandy? Why were United Kingdom-based infantry units not disbanded instead of line infantry units of the Second Army? Were they deliberately withheld and, if so, on whose authority? Churchill's penchant for steeping himself in the most minute details of British military forces is well known, and with manpower always a critical problem – both politically and militarily – it is inconceivable that he should have been unaware of the availability of over 100,000 infantry within the United Kingdom itself. Did Churchill, perhaps, so mistrust the eventual success of OVERLORD – and his military commanders – that he was simply unwilling to commit them to Montgomery and to the other theatres of war where the infantry shortages were equally grim? Or did the Prime Minister place limitations on the numbers of men he was willing to sacrifice at this stage of the Second World War?

The answers to these and other questions can only be resolved by further study of this complex subject when the relevant policy documents and War Office working papers can be located and studied by historians. In the meantime, the evidence at present available suggests that the infantry shortage which plagued

---

[1] Ibid. A total of 110 rifle battalions were located in the UK, some at or near full strength. Among the regiments represented were: the Royal Warwicks, the Royal Welch Fusiliers, the Cameronians, the Royal Scots Fusiliers, the Black Watch, the Worcestershire Regiment and the Sherwood Foresters. Total infantrymen in the British Army on 30 June 1944 came to: 38,269 officers and 501,009 other ranks. Excluded from these figures were prisoners-of-war, Army Reserves, the Indian Army, Colonial, Local Colonial, Dominion Forces, and the Home Guard, which constituted an additional 5,149 officers and 1,727,095 enlisted men.

Montgomery and other senior commanders for the remainder of the war was in fact a myth.

Unfortunately British reinforcements and manpower problems were not the only ones to contend with; the senior British commanders in Normandy also encountered an unexpected and disheartening problem with some of their veteran combat divisions.

CHAPTER 16

The Price of Caution

No good trying to fight a first class enemy unless the
soldiers are absolutely on their toes. They must
have a 'stomach for the fight'. They must have the
light of battle in their eyes. They must look forward
to a good fight. They must be full of 'binge'.

Montgomery[1]

Montgomery's troubles were not confined to a shortage of
infantry reinforcements. Two of his three veteran divisions from
the Eighth Army were not performing satisfactorily in Normandy. He had deliberately included three combat-tested divisions in 21st Army Group and had given them important roles in
the belief that he needed experienced units to balance the untested divisions which comprised most of his command, the
soundness of which decision was and still is under debate. The
50th (Northumbrian) Division was one of the three D-Day
assault units; the 7th Armoured Division (the famous 'Desert
Rats') and the 51st (Highland) Division were brought into battle
immediately after D-Day. Bradley employed the same approach
in the First US Army and chose the 1st Infantry Division ('Big Red
One') to land on OMAHA beach. Whereas American employment
of experienced divisions paid handsome dividends throughout
the entire campaign in Northwest Europe, the British experience
was not always happy.

Neither the Highlanders nor the Desert Rats seem to have
been prepared for the difficult fighting in the bocage, where they
appeared weary and frequently over cautious. Many of their
troops were the same men who had fought bravely and well
during nearly four years of war and had managed to survive.
With no large turnover of personnel before Normandy, these

---

[1] Quoted in *Monty: The Making of A General, 1887–1942*, op.cit. p. 441.

divisions contained too many men who had again been ordered to put their lives on the line. Time and again they had been asked to perform difficult tasks and none was to prove more difficult than Normandy, where they found themselves in a strange environment that offered none of the freedom of manoeuvre they had enjoyed in the desert. Instead they found a hostile land and an even more hostile enemy who was determined to fight to the bitter end, and the rude reception they found in Normandy must have shattered the mood of cockiness, even arrogance, in which they had entered the campaign. They seem to have been mentally unprepared for close combat in the hedgerows where the enemy could not even be seen.[1]

Erskine, the 7th Armoured commander, whose performance at Villers-Bocage had so angered Dempsey, was relieved in early August, along with the corps commander, Bucknall. The new commander was Major General G. L. Verney, whose observations about the division are unflattering but honest:

> The division had been formed from the forces who were in Egypt at the time when the Italians came into the war, and the bulk of the Division had taken part in all the Western Desert campaigns. After that they had served for a short time in Italy before being brought home about Christmas time 1943, preparatory to taking part in the Invasion, where they landed on the second day. A great many of the officers and men were war-weary by the time they got home and unfortunately there was no large-scale system of relief; in fact, very few left the Division, and it was owing to this that they made a very poor showing in Normandy.
>
> Looking back, it is quite easy to see that there ought to have been considerable changes; whole units, particularly in the Infantry Brigade, should have been exchanged for fresh troops who had spent the last few years training in England. The fighting that the Division had had to do in the Desert had generally been fluid, and, since the battle of Alamein in October 1942, had consisted in pursuit of a retreating enemy. Normandy, where they met an enemy who had no intention of

---

[1] Major General Roberts has commented: 'I think there can be no doubt whatsoever that Monty's principle of including experienced formations and units in the invasion force was unsound; much better results would have been achieved if fresh formations, available in England, had been used in their place . . . I noticed . . . on several occasions the differences in dash between formations which had been fighting a long time and those who were fresh.' Letter to Liddell Hart, 28 March 1952, Liddell Hart Papers, King's College, London.

retreating and on the contrary was determined to drive them back into the sea, came as a very nasty shock.[1]

Verney traced the 7th Armoured's problems to their earlier experiences:

There is no doubt that familiarity with war does not make one more courageous. One becomes cunning, and from cunning to cowardice is but a short step. The infantryman who does not want to 'have a go' can find opportunities for lying low at the critical moment; the tank man can easily find a fault in his engine or his wireless, and thus miss taking part in the battle. This is a disease that spreads rapidly. The commander who finds his men getting 'canny', soon loses his confidence and becomes nervy himself. If he happens also to have done a lot of fighting, and especially if he has been 'brewed up' in his tank himself once or twice, he gets slow and deliberate; and is quite unable to take advantage of a situation that requires dash and enterprise. This is a most important point in an armoured division, which exists to exploit a favourable situation quickly.[2]

The problems Verney encountered in the 7th Armoured were not limited to fatigue but included what, in his opinion, was a tendency to live too much on their past reputation:

A further factor added to my difficulties. From the time that General Montgomery had taken over the Eighth Army in 1942, that Army had had a great deal of advertisement. No doubt this was well deserved, but as they had much more of it than the rest of the Army there was a good deal of jealousy. Even more important, however, is the fact that two of the three divisions that came back from Italy at the end of 1943, the 7th Armoured and 51st Highland, were extremely 'swollen-headed'. They were a law unto themselves; they thought they need only obey those orders that suited them. Before the battle of Caumont, I had been warned to look out for the transport of the 7th Armoured on the road – their march discipline was nonexistent. Both these divisions did badly from the moment they landed in Normandy. They greatly deserved the criticism they received, and it was a very severe shock to the 7th Armoured

---

[1] Unpublished diary of Major General G. L. Verney, courtesy of Major Peter Verney.
[2] Verney Diary, loc.cit.

when their Commander, General Erskine, was removed and given a non-fighting appointment.[1]*

Montgomery was even more displeased with the performance of 51st Division. As Verney has noted, they had no sooner landed than it became evident that the Highlanders had not adequately prepared themselves for Normandy. There was evidence of too much jollity and insufficient attention to tactical training before D-Day. The commander, Major General D. C. Bullen-Smith, a Lowland officer, was not nearly firm enough with his subordinates, and tended to accept that they knew better on matters concerning training and tactics. In the vernacular of the army, what the 51st Division needed was a hard-driving 'arse-kicker'. Instead, they were given far too loose a rein, and when they went up against the Germans they proved too slow, overly cautious and unwilling to take risks in the early battles around Caen. By mid-July a thoroughly disgusted Montgomery had seen enough and despatched a 'for your eyes only' cable to Brooke which read:

> Regret to report it is considered opinion Crocker, Dempsey and myself that 51st Division is at present not – NOT – battleworthy. It does not fight with determination and has failed in every operation it has been given to do. It cannot fight the Germans successfully; I consider the divisional commander is to blame and I am removing him from command. Bullen-Smith has many fine qualities but he has failed to lead Highland Division and I cannot – repeat, cannot – therefore recommend him to command any other division. I consider he would be able to perform the duties of Dep. of Infantry but you may consider that an unsuccessful divisional commander is not – repeat, not – the man for that job. He would command a District or a Training Division; I consider best man to put in 51st Division in its present state is [Major General T. G.] Rennie, and I have confidence he would bring it up to its former fine state. Can you send Rennie over at once to report to me on arrival?[2]

[1] Verney Diary, loc.cit.

* According to his diary, Erskine was relieved by Dempsey on 3 August after Operation BLUECOAT got off to a very poor start. The corps commander, Bucknall, was also relieved and, according to Brigadier Pyman: 'The dismissal of Bucknall and Erskine was fully justified – they made no effort to push hard or carry out their orders.' Cf. Pyman Papers, King's College, London.

[2] Montgomery, cable (M/54), to Brooke, 15 July 1944, PRO (CAB 106/1092). Montgomery thought this performance so poor that he considered sending the entire division back to England for retraining. Montgomery also admitted to Brooke that he could not fathom the reason but correctly surmised that 'they must have a Highlander'.

Divisional histories have generally tended to be self-serving and uncritical in describing their exploits but in the case of the 51st Division there was a rare admission of its early troubles in Normandy. Of the period up till mid-July when Bullen-Smith was relieved, the divisional historian wrote candidly:

> But it was obvious all was not well with the Division. They had long been accustomed to thinking of themselves as invincible, and second to none – British or German; and now the proud division which had been acclaimed 'most to be feared' by the Germans in the whole British Armies in 1917, had for the first time since High Wood in 1916, met failure – not in the splendid isolation of St Valery, but in the sight of other formations, formations too which had never aspired so high – 'and that was the bitterest pill of all'. Deep down, the officers and men of the 51st knew what they could still do, and remembered what they themselves had done in battle in the 8th Army, while other divisions, now fighting, had been resting and training at home; and so as the inevitable price of failure in battle, changes in command were made.[1]

Rennie immediately demonstrated that he was the right commander to revitalize the Highlanders. In early August before the Division faced its first big test under its new commander, he issued a message to his troops which struck exactly the right chord:

> The Highland Division is about to take part in a battle under command of the 2d Canadian Corps. This may well prove to be the decisive battle in France. The Division has an enterprising part to play, well suited to its particular characteristics. The battle also bears a strong resemblance to some of those great battles in North Africa in which the Division added laurels to its reputation of the last war. In Africa we fought side by side with Australians and New Zealanders. Now we are with Canadians and it is a coincidence that during the closing stages of the Great War we were also fighting beside a Canadian Corps. The Highland Division fought at El Alamein, which great victory was the turning-point in our fortunes. . . The success of the battle depends on the determination and offensive spirit of every Commander and Soldier in the Division. . . Good luck to every one of you.[2]

[1] J. B. Salmond, *The History of the 51st Highland Division, 1939–1945*, Edinburgh, 1953, p. 149.
[2] Salmond, op.cit., p. 155.

As the divisional history recounted, 'If ever a message contained sound battle psychology, that one did. Let it be remembered that there were, even in high places, those who were whispering that the Highland Division was now "punch drunk" – and it had, it was said, fought too many battles since Alamein. It had been admittedly a very great fighting Division, but now its star had waned. It now contained, so it was said, too many men who had crossed the starting-line once too often.'[1]

Rennie, an experienced and astute commander, was all too aware that it was most important to utilize the carrot as well as the stick:

> Steeped in the tradition of a very great regiment of the Highland Brigade, Rennie knew of what his famous fighting regiments were capable, and what they had done under Wolfe and Wellington, under Colin Campbell and Harper. With all the concentration of a brain trained to the selection of essentials and to decision, the Divisional Commander made absolutely sure that for this battle, so critical in the fortunes of the 51st, his Division would be launched to a fair start.[2]

While the 51st Division's performance improved greatly under Rennie, who had commanded the 3rd Division but had been wounded shortly after D-Day and was only now fit for a return to duty, these were problems which vexed the senior British commanders.[3]

What went wrong? Numerous reasons have been suggested, nearly all of them privately, for this was a subject no one has wanted to talk about in public: once the war ended it became an unpleasant subject that few were even willing to admit had existed. Certainly the British were not the only army to experience such problems. The American public has never been told, for example, the real truth about the behaviour of certain units during the early stages of the Ardennes counteroffensive in December 1944, when hundreds of American troops fled to the safety of the rear in sheer panic.

One of the few to comment on the British problem was

---

[1] Salmond, op.cit., p. 155.
[2] Ibid, p. 156.
[3] Rennie was killed in 1945 during Operation PLUNDER – the crossing of the Rhine River – and was the only British divisional commander to lose his life during the campaign in Northwest Europe.

Lieutenant General Sir Brian Horrocks, who took over command of 30 Corps from Bucknall:

> I was sad to learn that during this bitter fighting in the Bocage my old friends of the desert, both infantry and armoured, had been rather 'sticky' and had not shown the drive and initiative of the formations which had been training in the UK since 1940. I have always felt this was a natural phenomenon. Those 'desert warriors' had been doing all the fighting to date; but then they should have been removed to the depths of the country, where the terrain resembled what they might expect in Normandy, and put through some really tough training.[1] This did not happen, and the Bocage could hardly have more differed from the open desert and mountainous country of North Africa to which they were used. As a result, they suffered unnecessary casualties, particularly in Tank Commanders, who were used to fighting with their turrets open and were easily picked off by the hidden German snipers in the thick hedgerows.[2]

Horrocks offers these further observations on the problem:

> I have always felt that this aspect of divisional psychology was never properly studied during the last war. After a longish period of fighting, the soldiers, though capable of looking after themselves, begin to see all the difficulties and lack the *elan* of fresh troops. They begin to feel it is time they had a rest and someone else did some fighting. No doubt this is what happened in Normandy to these veteran divisions from the Middle East. It is to their eternal credit that they soon regained their old form and ended the war among the best troops we possessed. In a curious way my absence from the recent fighting proved an advantage to me; we had served together in the days of their desert victories and I had not seen them during their sticky Bocage period, so, unlike some of the other Generals, I was delighted to have them under my command.[3]

Neither division had been adequately rested since the early days of the desert campaign, nor had the third of the veteran divisions

---

[1] Lieutenant Colonel Lever has also commented on the absence of suitable terrain and the morale problems within the division when it trained in England. In Normandy ' . . . tank commanders found themselves in totally unfamiliar conditions – the Thetford training area in East Anglia had little resemblance to Normandy Bocage conditions. . . You may incidentally recall we had a few problems of doubtful morale in the division just prior to embarkation for the Normandy landings and it was necessary for Montgomery, at the request of Erskine, to come up to East Anglia and give us all a pep talk. I may say a highly successful one.' Quoted in letter to the author of 9 June 1982.

[2] Sir Brian Horrocks, *Corps Commander*, London, 1977, p. 28.

[3] Ibid, pp. 28–9.

to be employed in Normandy, the 50th (Northumbrian) Division. Although this unit performed without encountering the problems of its two sister divisions, its officers and men were not convinced that there was a sound need for them to be in Normandy as one of the assault divisions. As an impartial New Zealand observer remarked on 21 June:

> There was a strong feeling among the men while in England that the Div should *not* be asked to do the assault on D-Day. It had been intended that 49 Div would do it. But General Montgomery rescinded that and determined to use tried troops. There was a lot of resentment especially in 69 Bde. They call the CinC 'Fling em in Monty'. Absence without Leave became very prevalent in the New Forest Area amounting to well over 1,000 and there was considerable unrest. When operations commenced all this died down – but the heavy losses in officers and NCO's has given rise to new grumbling. The real fact is that the Div is tired – a few days rest would work wonders.'[1]

On the same day that these comments were being written, the Second Army was recording that since D-Day the 50th Division had suffered 312 officer and 3,662 other rank casualties, the highest of any division in Normandy.[2]

With losses difficult to replace and formations being broken up or transferred to other units, the need to avoid large casualties seems to have filtered down to the lower-level commanders, who tacitly accepted this as a desired course of action. From the early days of the planning for OVERLORD, the need to keep down British-Canadian casualties had become an accepted part of Montgomery's philosophy. On 19 March 1944, for example, he wrote to Lieutenant General Sir Ronald Weeks, the Deputy CIGS:

> The situation re reinforcements is not good, as you say. But we must take things as they are and find the best answer. . . We have got to try and do this business with the smallest possible casualties. If we play our cards properly, I believe we could do it fairly cheaply. There are so many conflicting interests involved,

---

[1]   Notes by Brigadier James Hargest, New Zealand observer with 30 Corps, 6 June–10 July 1944, PRO (CAB 106/1060).

[2]   Dempsey Papers, PRO (WO 285/13). Total casualties for this veteran division for the entire Normandy campaign numbered 474 officers and 6,156 enlisted men, the highest of any British division except for the 3rd Division.

but things are slowly working out the way I want them and I have great hopes that all will be well.[1]

As is so often the case in war, things had not worked out as Montgomery had hoped. Along with the steady wasting-away of the infantry in the bocage there was yet another problem confronting the British commanders. This was a noticeable decline in the performance of their junior leaders – mainly in the noncommissioned officer ranks – where the best of these leaders had already become officers. Some had also become casualties in this or earlier campaigns.

This, in turn, triggered another problem: junior officers were forced to take up the leadership slack, often by their personal presence, by performing jobs which ought to have been performed by the NCOs. As a consequence the junior officer casualty rate rose dramatically in the infantry arm, particularly among infantry company commanders, a trend repeatedly observed in the operational records of 21st Army Group and the Second Army. On 30 June, for example, the 21st Army Group War Diary recorded: '2d Army urgently request a further 14 coy cdrs be despatched.'[2]

The loss of so many junior officers was mainly due to the hazards of the infantry but in some instances these losses were the result of carelessness. One of the most illuminating documents to emerge from Normandy was the notes of Brigadier James Hargest, a New Zealand observer attached to 50th Division (30 Corps) until nearly the end of the campaign when he was tragically killed on his farewell visit to the division. Hargest had a brilliant record as an infantryman in the First World War and had participated in some twenty actions including Gallipoli, rising from 2nd Lieutenant to Lieutenant-Colonel. During the Second World War he commanded the 5th New Zealand Infantry Brigade in Greece, Crete and Libya. In November 1941 he was captured and later incarcerated in the same senior officers' POW camp as General O'Connor. Like O'Connor, Hargest eventually escaped and made his way to sanctuary in Switzerland. In the words of distinguished New Zealand commander, Major Gen-

---

[1] Dempsey Papers, PRO (WO 285/2).
[2] War Diary, 21st Army Group, 'A' Section, PRO (WO 171/139).

eral Sir Howard Kippenberger, Hargest, had he survived the war, 'would probably have been the present Prime Minister.'[1]

Hargest's observations of British combat tactics were candid, honest and written by an officer remarkably well qualified to write about the infantry soldier and the operations which he observed not from the comparative safety of a rear headquarters but up at the sharp end with the men about whom he wrote. Some examples from Hargest's notes will illustrate the problems he observed:

> The casualties among officers is high in percentage. I believe this is due to the closeness of the country permitting snipers to get close in and to the fact that men lie down in such country and are only urged forward by the personal example of their officers, and by the fact that officers carry map boards with talc coverings that flash in the sun. I witnessed an attack by the 8 D[urham] L[ight] I[nfantry] [50th Division] where from about 600/800 yards I could pick out almost every officer by his map board shining. In the 9 D.L.I. on 14 June all four coy cdrs were hit.[2]

Later in the campaign he noted:

> The high percentage of officer casualties is due to the necessity of them being *always* in the front to direct advances in the difficult country. Since D-duy the [50th] Div has lost 2 Brigadiers and 12 Commanding Officers . . . and a great number of Coy Cmdrs and Senior NCO's.[3]

Major General G. P. B. Roberts has echoed these observations, writing in 1952 to Liddell Hart: 'I think it would be fair to say that casualties in Company Commanders and their equivalent were probably the most serious loss that units suffered during this phase of the war. A tremendous amount depended upon this level of officer; provided he was of the right calibre the whole of his Company could be carried forward. The replacement of these Officers became more and more difficult until one got to the stage where the C.O. had to try and carry the Regiment forward which

---

[1] Major General Sir Howard Kippenberger, letter to Brigadier H. B. Latham, Cabinet Office Historical Section, 9 May 1951, (CAB 106/1060), PRO. Latham placed a covering note on the Hargest report which read: 'Lt-Col Warhurst: I think you might like to know of the attached report *before* it goes into our rivals (?) It seems to me quite first class.' None of Hargest's report ever appeared in the British Official History.

[2] Notes by Brigadier James Hargest, loc.cit.

[3] Ibid.

was almost beyond his powers. On the German side, on the other hand, since they were fighting in somewhat different circumstances to ourselves and as you say had more reason to fight desperately, they were capable of carrying out their tasks without the continued pressure of immediate leadership.'[1]

Hargest offered this comment on the insistence by the British soldier for leadership by example from his officers:

> The English soldier . . . differs from the soldier in the dominions. I notice that as soon as men lose their officers in the thick growth they lose heart. Today [16 June] I met several Bren gun sections coming back and in reply to my enquiries why! they said the fire was heavy and they had got out of touch. It did not occur to them to go on. Result – great loss of firepower. This is not suggesting that they lack courage, they don't.[2]

Unfortunately, as Hargest observed, this general lack of independence created another serious problem – bunching together. The results were often unnecessary misfortune:

> This morning 16 June at a German road block which the enemy had obviously registered 8 men were killed or wounded by one mortar. . . [Battle notes, 13–16 June 1944]: Bunching was as bad as ever. One other failing of the Tommy is his liability to sudden panic – not when he is attacking, but when he has gained his objective and is consolidating or has consolidated. On one occasion [10 June] at Saint Pierre the 8th D.L.I. captured the village with the aid of tanks (8 Armd Bde) with very little loss. That night they held it but at 0700 hours next morning while under mortar fire they panicked and some of them went right back to their previous day's start line – result very heavy casualties. They retook the place that day with little loss. . . On Thursday 22nd June 30 men were gathered around a carrier getting food. Three mortar bombs fell on them causing 22 casualties. Such a waste and great amount of unnecessary suffering. . . The old trouble of not relying on their own weapons is prevalent among infantry here. They call for supporting fire always and often when held up whereas they might well get on alone. The guns are well served and bring

---

[1] Major General G. P. B. Roberts, letter to Liddell Hart, 28 March 1952, Liddell Hart Papers. The same observation was made in 1952 by Brigadier Pyman who noted that the 43rd and 50th Divisions had lost a number of their best COs in the first month. The infantry leaders were very tired and easily rattled by mortaring.

[2] CAB 106/1060, loc.cit.

down accurate fire at short call and in great volume. They are rather splendid.[1]

How serious was the problem? We can begin to gain a perception by focusing on the 50th Division. On 25 June Hargest wrote:

> The men are tired after 18 days of unrelieved strain. They are supposed to infiltrate the enemy's position – first by patrolling, then by moving on from one firm base to another. They achieve nothing – only sustain grave casualties. Their advances have no impetus. The moment the enemy spandaus or mortars open fire the troops go to earth and stay there; lose men and morale. Its all wrong. Had we young officers of spirit and training to *push* these patrols we might achieve something. The English [UK] soldier will accept losses without losing morale provided he sees some results – but this niggling is hard on him.[2]

Even worse, Hargest's evaluation of the state of British morale was not optimistic:

> Speaking with other officers I come to these conclusions. The morale of the infantry officer and soldier is not high. This applies to new troops as well as Veterans. Officers are not keen on patrol work as an example. Even senior officers grumble about being too long in line and have opinion that they are being 'used'. . . Last week I saw 15 (S) Div in action 26th [June]. They began their battle on Monday and by Saturday 1st July they were relieved – used up . . . *I wonder is it the long strain under discipline?* The troops have not that spirit essential to Victory. It appears to me that the Higher Comd will do well to depend on air, artillery and tanks. I realise that the enemy's morale is lower but ours frightens me.[3]*

---

[1]　PRO, (CAB 106/1060), loc.cit. In his autobiography, Lord Lovat comments on the bunching by the men of the 2nd Battalion, The East Yorkshire Regiment on Red Beach near Ouistreham on D-Day. He quotes Cornelius Ryan's *The Longest Day* in which one of his commandos remarked that their 'bodies were stacked like cord wood. They had been knocked down like nine pins.' Cf., *March Past*, London 1978, p. 310.

[2]　Ibid.

[3]　Ibid.

*　A vivid example of what Hargest meant was the case of the 6th Battalion, The Duke of Wellington's Regiment, part of the 49th Division. The 49th Division had first entered combat operations with 30 Corps on the night of 13 June, but by the end of the month the morale and efficiency of this unit was in tatters. There had been very heavy losses – 23 officers and 350 other ranks – and only 12 of the original officers were left, none of them company commanders, who were all either dead or casualties. In a confidential report the CO wrote: '75% of the men react adversely to enemy shelling and are "jumpy". 5 cases in 3 days of self-inflicted wounds – more possible cases. Each time men are killed or wounded a number of men become casualties through shell shock or hysteria. In addition to genuine hysteria a large number of men have left their positions after shelling on one pretext or another and gone to the rear until sent back by the M.O. or myself. The new

Other problems contributed to the often unsatisfactory performance of the infantry units. The manpower demands of the RAF, the signal corps, the artillery, the tank regiments, the REME and ordnance services, and elite units like the airborne and commandos all tended to drain off those with the greatest leadership potential. The infantry was thus left with whatever remained. As a consequence, infantry training was geared to the lowest common denominator. Weapons training, especially with machine-guns, tended to cater for every possible contingency and left little room for exploitation, initiative or variations from the plan. Brigadier Shelford Bidwell recalls what an experienced infantryman said to him in 1944: 'Look, all that I can do with my men, the sort of men I have, is to persuade them to get out of their holes in the ground, march up to the objective, dig a hole there, and get into it.'[1]

It was not that the men of the infantry lacked courage – they did *not* – but realism among infantry officers dictated that there were definite limits to what they could expect from their men. As Hargest has so vividly observed, the preferred method of fighting was to gain a piece of ground which invited a counterattack, and then use their machine-guns. These were the tactics of attrition not unreminiscent of the later phases of the Battle of the Somme. Moreover, as Bidwell notes: 'We had the great disadvantage of having to train under the jealous eyes of a civil population who were looking out for any severity or injustice, and journalists, MP's and local busy-bodies were perpetually discovering abuses. Discipline was therefore lax and if discipline is lax the soldier is encouraged to avoid the difficult options.'[2]

Constraints on discipline in turn led to an avoidance of really tough training for battle, such as that practised by the airborne

drafts have been affected, and 3 young soldiers became casualties with hysteria after hearing our own guns. The situation has got worse each day as more key personnel have become casualties. State of discipline is bad although the men are a pleasant cheerful type normally . . . NCO leadership is weak in most cases and the newly drafted officers are in consequence having to expose themselves unduly to try and get anything done . . . 6 DWR is not fit to take its place in the line.' When this information reached Montgomery he reacted by calling the battalion commander – a regular officer – 'defeatist' for his suggestion that the unit either be re-equipped and re-trained or disbanded and split among the other units of the division. 'If it is not possible to do either . . . I request that I may be relieved of my command.' By 6 July the 6th DWR had been disbanded and replaced on the line by the 1st Battalion, The Leicestershire Regiment. Cf., 'Report on State of 6th DWR, 49th Div, 30 June 1944', PRO (WO 205/5G).

[1] Brigadier Shelford Bidwell, letter to the author, 25 November 1982.
[2] Ibid.

and commandos. When schemes did exist to teach civilian soldiers to attack in an aggressive manner they sometimes misfired because they contained 'hate' propaganda which was thought to excite blood lust, and this was quenched by the chaplains and bishops.

British infantrymen fought bravely in Normandy but not always to the best advantage and if the performance of infantry units was sometimes less than satisfactory, responsibility can be traced to the generally inadequate battle indoctrination in England before D-Day, which failed to prepare the men for combat in the bocage against a determined and experienced enemy.[1] Obviously both the level of training and performance varied from unit to unit, but on balance there were far too many examples for it to have been an isolated phenomenon. Liddell Hart has criticized the lack of forceful and bold leadership, but this was only one symptom of the deeper malaise which manifested itself in Normandy. The all-too-frequent end result in battle were situations at the squad level where the men were simply inadequately indoctrinated *not* to wait around for an officer or NCO to tell them what to do next, but to close with the enemy, firing every weapon available and for the next-in-line to take command at once if their leader was hit.

Cooperation between divisions and corps was not always what it ought to have been. Brigadier Hargest closely observed a disturbing trend:

> I can't understand why there is so little cooperation between British formations simply because they are in different corps or divisions. Perhaps it is that quality in the Englishman which refuses to allow him to interest himself in anything outside his own circle. Minding one's own business. In war it can be dangerous.[2]

A specific example occurred during EPSOM which illustrates the point:

[1] The British were forced to learn the hard way the fundamental difference in battle philosophy between them and their enemy. The Germans were thoroughly imbued with what Brigadier Bidwell notes as the ancient tradition of responding to leadership, no matter what the source and, if lacking, personally to provide it. For the Germans, being on the defensive meant *attack*. 'The basic [German] defensive tactic was a counter-attack. British troops were to learn quickly, albeit painfully, that their fight only started *after* they had thankfully reached their objective.' Cf., S. Bidwell and D. Graham, *Firepower: British Army Weapons and Theories of War 1904–1945*, London, 1982, pp. 215–6.

[2] PRO (CAB 106/1060), loc.cit.

I came across a specific case this week. The 49th Div of 30 Corps attacked and captured Fontenay and Tessel Wood on Sunday. It is 30 Corps' left division and worked along the Corps Bdy. The 8 Corps attacked Cheux on Monday and moved up along the 30 Corps Bdy with units of 50 Div plus tanks on its right flank. In any other army there would have been the closest liaison between the two corps and the two neighbouring divisions. But no! 8 Corps knew what transpired in 30 Corps only from LO's. The units side by side knew little or nothing of each other. On *Wednesday* evening 60 hours after the 8 Corps attack I desired to pass along the road between the two Corps. I sought information as to whether it was safe. No one on 8 Corps HQ could tell me. I proceeded along it from the East enquiring from each unit of the 8 Corps as I passed. Infantry artillery and tanks – no one knew. I passed from one to the other until I found myself within half a mile of the village of Fontenay so decided to try it. When I reached there I found the outskirts of the village full of 49 Div troops. They were within 40 chains of their neighbours and neither side knew anything of the other. The aftermath – on Thursday evening the enemy seized on the weakness and is reported to have driven a wedge between the two formations nearly 2 miles deep.[1]

What, in fact, operations in Normandy were beginning to demonstrate was the war-weariness of the British Army and the greatest strains were upon the infantry, who bore the brunt of the brutal Normandy battles. Major General H. Essame, a veteran infantry commander and an exceptionally observant commentator on the war has written:

> Only those who have some first-hand knowledge of it can begin to appreciate the incessant dangers and discomforts, as well as the cumulative stresses and strains, which the front-line soldier is called upon to endure for weeks or months on end, often without proper rest. The demands made upon the fighting troops proved so heavy that few men over 40 could withstand the burden, and the average age for commanding officers in the 'teeth arms' units was only 35.
>
> In the Second World War, as always before, the heaviest battle casualties occurred amongst the infantry soldiers and few of them managed to survive a year in action without being wounded. Such a steady drain on their fighting manpower kept nearly all infantry battalions permanently under strength as battle formations. They were further handicapped by the fact

[1] CAB 106/1060, loc.cit.

that many of their men, sent as replacements, tended to be imperfectly trained, and were new to the conditions. All these factors put further strain on those who remained to carry on. Of this problem, which universally plagued all infantry battalions, Eric Linklater wrote: 'However rapidly reinforcements may arrive, reinforcements cannot restore a battalion to its previous efficiency without a period of rest and training during which its new-comers can be absorbed into and identified with their fighting teams.' In Normandy such periods of rest and training were infrequent, and the record for continuous fighting was probably held by the Commando Brigade who spent 83 consecutive days in action. When judging any lack of enthusiasm displayed in action, especially by the veterans of the 8th Army, it must also be remembered that, for most of the front-line soldiers, the bleak rule was that you normally continued to fight on; either until you were killed, or so severely wounded as to be unfit for further active service in the line.[1]

In November, Major General Lyne, the former commander of the now disbanded 59th Division, replaced Verney in command of the 7th Armoured after the latter was unable to cure the division's bad habits well enough to satisfy Montgomery and Dempsey. Lyne observed that their heart was certainly in the right place and that a feeling existed within all ranks that things had not been going right for them. The 7th Armoured had not been spared the serious drain that years of heavy fighting had produced, which not even the introduction of complete new units at various times had cured.[2]

As Verney had before him, Lyne saw a tendency in some quarters to regard the division as so veteran and battleworthy that re-training to meet new conditions was considered unnecessary, a trend which the new commander quickly stamped on.[3]

In a post-war essay titled 'Lessons of Normandy', Liddell Hart found it 'disturbing and depressing' how poorly some units performed in the attack:

Time after time they were checked or even induced to withdraw by boldly handled packets of Germans of greatly inferior strength. But for our air superiority, which hampered the Germans at every turn, the results would have been much worse. Our forces seem to have had too little initiative in

[1] Belfield and Essame, op.cit., p. 166.
[2] Lyne Papers, loc.cit.
[3] Ibid.

infiltration, and also too little determination – with certain exceptions. Repeatedly one finds that big opportunities were forfeited because crucial attacks were stopped after suffering trifling casualties. That was particularly marked with the armoured formations. Moreover, it all too often appears that a 'divisional' attack was in fact merely carried out by a tiny fraction of the available strength, and that the real burden was borne by a few squadrons. Backing up was very poor and slow.[1]

Liddell Hart suggested these causes: general war-weariness accompanied by a prevalent feeling that the end of the war was near, that risks should not be taken needlessly; the Allied penchant for using mechanical weapon-power which induced the tendency to 'let the machine win the war rather than taking risks'; a decline in NCO quality and the rising casualties in the ranks of commanders and potential commanders.[2]

His sharpest criticism was reserved for what he saw as the failure of the British training system to develop bold and resourceful leadership and 'the ill effects of side-tracking, before or early in the war, the ardent and experienced tank leaders who had shown the best grasp of armoured mobility – and were best qualified to bring up a new generation in the faster operational tempo required.'[3] Finally, he cited what he saw as a 'growing reluctance to make sacrifices in attack as compared with defence.'[4]

Liddell Hart was not the only one who believed that some units did not perform with a sufficient sense of urgency. US general James M. Gavin relates an example: During Operation MARKET-GARDEN, his 504th Parachute Infantry made a costly and daring attack to seize the Nijmegen Bridge. His men braved the fast-rushing waters of the River Waal and the intense fire of German guns to seize the bridge intact. Following this, tanks of the Grenadier Guards poured across to link up with the hardpressed airborne. Instead of pressing on, the British unit stopped for tea, causing Gavin's angry battalion commander to demand: 'What in hell are they doing? We have been in this position for

---

[1] Liddell Hart Papers, King's College, London.
[2] Ibid.
[3] Ibid.
[4] Ibid.

over twelve hours, and all they seem to be doing is brewing tea. Why in hell don't they get to Arnhem?'[1]

The impressions left in the minds of many American commanders was that the British sometimes tended to be far too conservative. General Gavin has related a conversation he had with the Airborne Commander, Lieutenant General Sir Frederick ('Boy') Browning after the operation:

> As my time with Airborne Corps was coming to an end, and they were going back to some other assignment, Browning had a few of us in for cocktails at his house in Nijmegen – good Dutch gin and hot tea, ideal cocktails for those living in the open in Holland in the fall. As it came to an end, he walked me through the garden and allowed as how I gave too much freedom of action to my subordinates. I couldn't believe it. Freedom of action! The Germans had us outnumbered in each of the tactical fights we got into, when we were scrambling for our lives, and we won all of our engagements. That has always stuck in the back of my mind, for I couldn't understand it by American standards at all. We give our subordinates, and that includes division and corps commanders, as well as small unit leaders, a great deal of freedom of action so that they can take advantage of unexpected surprises that arise from time to time.[2]

Browning's comments to Gavin were not representative of the British philosophy of command, which taught that commanders should control their subordinates with the lightest of reins and allow full freedom as to method in carrying out a mission. In the view of many, there was far too much freedom and senior commanders often proved reluctant to step in when things were obviously going wrong. The British tended to retain unsatisfactory commanders too long before relieving them, while the exact opposite occurred in the US Army, where senior commanders were frequently relieved for the slightest transgression, often without adequate time to grow into a job. This practice greatly disturbed Gavin who has written: 'I have a haunting memory that does not diminish with the passage of time of how unfairly and thoughtlessly we treated some of our senior officers.'[3]

---

[1] Gavin, op.cit., pp. 181–2.
[2] Lieutenant General James M. Gavin, letter to the author, 2 September 1980.
[3] Gavin, *On to Berlin*, op.cit., p. 232.

The British had no Pattons and too few senior commanders like John Harding and Gerald Templer who breathed fire down the necks of laggards. In Normandy both Montgomery and Dempsey were altogether too considerate in retaining commanders who did not measure up. Perhaps time had mellowed him but Montgomery, whose reputation was based in no small part on his ruthlessness in removing failed commanders, was too inclined to retain such officers in Normandy. Dempsey, for example, admits to being disenchanted by the performances of Bucknall and Erskine at Villers-Bocage yet waited until August to remove them.

Both Gavin's and Liddell Hart's comments are echoed by one of the most notable military figures in post-war Britain, Field Marshal Lord Carver, a former CIGS, and Chief of the Imperial Defence Staff. As the commander of the independent 4th Armoured Brigade in Normandy, Carver, a colonel in 1952, wrote to Liddell Hart:

> I find it less easy to answer your comments on Normandy. I do not deny your main criticism. I think that the causes were complex and various, leading to a cumulative effect which was perhaps most marked at about the time of the final collapse at Falaise. One of the contributory causes was, I think, the emphasis placed before the campaign on the expected fierceness of the battle on the beaches. There was a tendency to build up a climate of feeling that, once ashore, it would all be fairly easy and merely a matter of build-up. In the early days in the beachhead it was fairly easy to get people to take exceptional risks, whether they were old sweats or keen young chaps, eager to win their spurs. Progressively both became disillusioned, either because opportunities, created by bold action were not exploited – like Villers-Bocage – or because boldness did not create the opportunities, but only led to certain casualties, particularly in the thick bocage. One was so often being told that the coming battle was the one that was going to break through and that no losses must deter one. Then the whole thing would come to a grinding halt, and instead of being told one had failed, one was told that one had served one's purpose in containing the enemy.[1]

But the main problem, observed Carver, was British tactics:

---

[1] Carver, letter to Liddell Hart, 8 May 1952, Liddell Hart Papers, King's College, London.

The failure of our tactics of attack to deal with the German layout of defence was one of the reasons for everything coming to a halt so soon. Our plans so often laid on an immense fire-plan to carry the leading battalions about 1,000 yards into the enemy position. In fact, as the Germans were always prepared to sacrifice their first line, not very strongly held, but strongly enough to demand a proper attack, including mine-clearing, this attack came to a halt just on their main position. The immense fire-plan gave them warning and the time to move up to the clearly defined objective the number of tanks and SP anti-tank guns necessary to hold it quite strongly and certainly to hold it at a considerable advantage against the attacking tanks, which then (probably about dawn) were moving forward.[1]

'I had constant fights,' noted Carver, 'with the divisional commanders:

I supported to try and get them to design the fire-plan to deal with the anti-tank gun defence primarily, leaving it up to the tanks to get the infantry up. This involved a fire-plan in much greater depth and no preliminary bombardment or barrage for the infantry. I was never successful, and it was General Simonds[2] who first broke away from the 1914–1918 standard tactics of attack.'[3]

As a consequence:

During all the earlier dog-fight battles therefore, tank soldiers became pretty disillusioned about the prospects of boldness being rewarded. Too often they were exhorted to dash forward when everything else had gone wrong and the main enemy defence had hardly been touched. The result was that when opportunities really did occur and when the opposition really was weak, the infantry commanders were not prepared to put their trust in exploiting tactics, preferring to plod on with successive 'well laid-on' attacks and many of the tanks soldiers by that time were chary of doing it anyway.[4]

Of the veteran combat units of the desert Carver commented: 'In the regiments which had been in the Middle East, as many as half and often more than that had been doing it for four years. Many who had been brave as lions and still were prepared to be on

---

[1] Field Marshal Lord Carver, loc.cit.
[2] Commander, 2nd Canadian Corps.
[3] Field Marshal Lord Carver, loc.cit.
[4] Ibid.

occasions, either had lost their nerves – they usually went fairly soon – or had a pretty shrewd judgement as to what risks they could take and still have a fairly good chance of surviving.'[1]

A related problem was a lack of understanding and cooperation between the armoured and infantry commanders. During the desert campaign the British had nurtured some bad habits which were carried over into Normandy. As Carver has pointed out, battle plans too often called for predictable, setpiece tactics better suited to earlier wars. Tank commanders were frequently not allowed to employ the sort of tactics which might have turned the typical Normandy slogging matches into genuine exploitation.

The problem of tank-infantry cooperation, let alone between corps and divisions, had plagued the British Army for too long for it to have been cured even by 1944. In the desert tanks and infantry had tended to operate independently, with generally far from satisfactory results, and in the early days of Normandy the armoured and infantry commanders often failed to grasp opportunities.

American units generally had no such problems with tank-infantry cooperation. From the earliest days of the war[2] the armoured divisions were loosely organized into combat commands where units could be quickly switched back and forth into mobile task forces capable of tackling a specific problem. The enormous success enjoyed by Patton's Third US Army would never, for example, have been possible without this cooperation and the outstanding relationships which developed between infantry and armoured commanders. Unlike the Americans, the British were too bound by tradition and it was not until they received some sharp lessons in fighting in the bocage from the Germans that they began to refine their tactics to deal with them.

Without infantry support in the bocage the tank became an exceptionally vulnerable target for German anti-tank weapons. Military doctrine generally holds that an offensive superiority of at least three to one is required to defeat a well-placed defender. In Normandy the Germans found they could accept a ratio of nearly five to one. There were numerous instances where British

---

[1] Field Marshal Lord Carver, loc.cit.
[2] In the United States prior to 1940 tanks had also been regarded as support only for the infantry.

armour would actually overrun German anti-tank gun positions, but without proper infantry support they were unable to knock them out. The Germans developed a remarkable ability to recover and hit tanks in the back before they could react and complete their task.

The long-standing problems of cooperation were at the heart of the situations now found in Normandy by the British. As Liddell Hart has remarked, this was partly due to an insufficiency of bold and aggressive commanders but it also stemmed from the old and seemingly never-ending jealousies inspired during the interwar period when the Royal Tank Corps was considered nothing more than a support arm of the infantry.

During the latter stages of the First World War tanks were first used on the battlefields of France and the results were less than spectacular. The interwar period saw little momentum for developing an armoured vehicle capable of dominating a modern battlefield. Only in Germany was there any real impetus: the fledgling Wehrmacht emerged with forceful leaders and a new and potentially powerful panzer force.

The notion that the doctrine of panzer employment developed by the German Army was a result of the ideas of Liddell Hart is a myth. The German panzer concept of fighting in combined arms groups owed little to Liddell Hart or J. F. C. Fuller, but was the result of the advancement of their own ideas and philosophy of war. While Liddell Hart envisioned deep armoured strokes and no doubt provided considerable food for thought to panzer leaders such as Guderian, it is also true that it was the Liddell-Hart Fuller school of thought which invented the heresy of fighting with whole brigades of tanks, leaving the infantry and artillery merely to hold firm bases and only take over the ground after the tanks had captured it.

When the Royal Tank Corps (later redesignated the Royal Tank Regiment) was created in the 1920s there was little enthusiasm except in the breasts of Fuller, 'Hobo' Hobart, C. M. F. Broad and a few others. These men represented what might be termed the blitzkrieg school of British armoured warfare. However, even within this elite circle there was disagreement over the future role of the tank. Some argued that it was an armoured support gun to be used in conjunction with the infantry who remained the dominant partner. But as Brigadier Shelford Bidwell has observed, unlike the Germans, none could get round to the conclusion that the tank in reality 'was a highly versatile form of *artillery* – of fire-power – combining the properties of an assault gun; "infantry tank"; assault weapon in its own right; mobile, armoured anti-tank gun; and weapon for pursuit'.[1]

The Germans had no such problems when they created the panzer division, which was built round the concept of a combined arms team capable of solving the problems likely to be encountered on the battlefield. The panzer division, in the hands of determined and ambitious younger commanders like Rommel, became the most deadly and effective element in Hitler's Wehrmacht. In short, whereas the British endlessly quarrelled amongst themselves over the role of armour, the Germans approached the problem from the purely practical point of view of how to make the most effective use of what they had.

When the Royal Armoured Corps (RAC) was created after the outbreak of the Second World War, it was staffed with many ex-cavalry officers who had no great desire to serve in this new force and consequently none of the dash of their counterparts in the new German panzer divisions. To make matters worse, this problem was magnified by the lack of a suitable doctrine. The problem with the Royal Armoured Corps was that it never really existed except as a fiction. The Corps itself never progressed beyond a Directorate in the War Office. It was originally created with the intention of becoming a large corps, like the Royal Regiment of Artillery, with its own common doctrine and a common promotion system. In practice each cavalry regiment remained distinct and exclusive. The officers of the Royal Tank Regiment were deemed outsiders unworthy of admission to this exclusive club, an attitude borne out by the fact that no officer from the RTR was ever promoted to the command of a cavalry regiment.

One of the reasons the RAC never worked was its composition as four separate elements:

(1) The original Royal Tank Corps became the Royal Tank Regiment, consisting of a number of tank battalions. The personnel in these units were interchangeable and com-

---

[1] S. Bidwell and D. Graham, op. cit., p. 214.

manders were picked from the best of the field of those
eligible for promotion to Lieutenant Colonel.

(2) The original horse cavalry regiments which had been
converted to armour were self-contained closed circles
who found their commanders from their own officers. The
result was an uneven standard: some COs were very good,
others downright bad. Occasionally, a regiment was so
bad that the Military Secretary was forced to intervene and
refuse a recommendation for command. Only then was
there a cross-posting but *only* from another cavalry regiment or, occasionally, from the Royal Horse Artillery.

(3) Former units of the Territorial Army which had been
converted to tanks, such as the 4th CLY. Generally, these
units tended to perform well.

(4) Purely wartime raisings, such as the Reconnaissance Regiments, and units designated as regiments of the Royal
Armoured Corps.

The justification for preserving these disparate elements was the
retention of esprit de corps, but the disadvantages greatly outweighed this factor: their very exclusiveness militated against
good inter-arm cooperation. Too many officers belonged to the
establishment and consequently were difficult to discipline or
remove from command. The traditions of the British regimental
system thus worked against acceptance of the new Royal
Armoured Corps, where regular officers were more concerned
with the prestige of belonging to a 'proper' regiment than with
being posted where they were needed. This attitude was far from
being corrected by the time of Normandy.

Montgomery had found to his dismay that there was a lack of
cooperation between armour and infantry within the Eighth
Army. His use of a *corps de chasse* had proved such a failure at El
Alamein that he vowed never again to use an all-armoured corps,
a pledge he reiterated soon after assuming command of 21st
Army Group. Thus, as Field Marshal Lord Carver has noted, the
British Army, tied as it was to outdated traditions and doctrine,
were painfully slow to learn the lessons of combined arms. The
North African desert became littered with examples of this
failure.

In the early days of Normandy Brigadier Hargest observed this trend repeatedly, along with a gnawing inconsistency in performance: sometimes cooperation was excellent and the results satisfactory, but where it was missing the results were all too often unhappy and too frequently this was the case. An example took place on 11 June in the drive against Tilly-sur-Seulles by 7th Armoured Division. The leading tanks:

> were in contact with the enemy at Bucéels . . . they could not locate the enemy opposition which was well hidden and so could not get on. Although they had an infantry Bde under command – the 131st Bde – there was no supporting infantry coy within three miles of the front. The tank officers complained to me that they were in need of infantry and in this they were right. The advance which had begun well ended rather dismally by being halted though there was little opposition.[1]

Attempts to persuade a change in tactics failed:

> On the way back I met the Div Comdr Gen Erskine and respectfully suggested that infantry were necessary to consolidate immediately and to mop up. They could prevent lateral movement by the enemy and if they entered a position with the tanks they could take it with little loss. As it was the enemy lay down and peppered the rear after the tanks had passed. The GOC replied that he preferred to go on alone. The pace was too hot for the infantry. I suggested that they could be lorried up to the front by a shuttle service. He said that they would suffer casualties. At any rate he had advanced 6 miles – if he could maintain that for 30 days that would be 180 miles. The answer came the next day. The 7th Armoured Div advanced about a mile. On the 3d day it withdrew nearly the whole of that mile and then was disengaged [to execute the right hook against Villers-Bocage].[2]

After ten days of combat Hargest came to the conclusion that:

> Our tanks are badly led and fought. Only our superior numbers and our magnificent artillery support keeps them in the field at all. They violate most of the elementary principles of war. They bunch up – they are the reverse of aggressive – they are not possessed of the will to attack the enemy . . . My opinion is that a great deal of their failure is due to the retention of the absurd Regimental system. Because there is no work for cavalry the Cavalry Regts were given tanks. The officers are

[1] CAB 106/1060, loc.cit.
[2] CAB 106/1060, loc.cit.

trained in armour not because they like armour, but because they are cavalry men. They are in armour because [tanks are] like horses in other units. An airman is a good airman because he loves being in a plane. Not so with Armour. The Royal Corps is sound and every unit in armour should belong to the R[oyal] T[ank] C[orps]. At the moment we suffer because of incompatibility and the lack of the 'will to fight' in the Armoured Corps.[1]

Fortunately there were a number of superb younger commanders in Normandy who were products of the Royal Tank Corps – men like Carver and 'Pip' Roberts – but there were far too few such officers to overcome the problems noted by Hargest and others. Moreover, even when the armour were performing well there still remained the apathy of some infantry commanders.

During the training for OVERLORD there does not seem to have been an adequate appreciation of the problems that the bocage would create or of the tactics the Germans would employ at the small unit level. Montgomery, as we know, correctly gauged their strategy for coping with the invasion, but such strategy on a grand scale had precious little to do with the business of battalions and companies ruthlessly pitted against one another in the bocage. The early results in Normandy demonstrated the inadequacy of armour–infantry teamwork, and it was too late effectively to begin practising what ought to have been strongly indoctrinated during the invasion training.

It took some nasty knocks in the bocage before many British units awoke to the realization there would be no success without teamwork. However, old concepts and ideas die hard and the end result was all too often setbacks of the sort which occurred at Villers-Bocage, setbacks which were both costly and unneces-

---

[1] CAB 106/1060, loc.cit. Hargest subsequently saw little evidence of improvement sufficient to cause him to change his opinion. Two examples will suffice: 'On 12 June I came across a whole squadron of tanks in a field supported by SP guns. They told me that there was a Tiger tank in Verrière about 1,000 yards to the left front and in reply to my query as to why they did not attack they said it was very powerful.' On 17 June a tank of the 8th Armoured Brigade (another veteran desert unit) sat passively at a British roadblock while several German scout cars and an SP gun moved down a straight road. 'The tank did not fire although the target was a perfect one. Neither did it call on the tanks in its troop nearby for support. The infantry Bde Comd sent down a message asking that the gun and cars be taken on. The reply was "If I do he will reply to my fire." After a delay of fully 20 minutes and only after an infantry anti-tank gun had come into action beside it, did the tank fire. Its third round got what looked like a direct hit on one vehicle – after a few shots it relapsed into silence and was only persuaded to fire again later. It was armed with a 25 pdr and a Besa MG which was also in range of the target.'

sary. Opportunities for exploitation were bungled, lives were needlessly lost and the troops involved became overly cautious and reluctant to take unnecessary risks.

By the time these various problems had surfaced, well into the campaign, there was little anyone could do to rectify them, although efforts at cooperation tended to improve in later campaigns. What Carver has so damningly pointed out is that Montgomery's tactics in Normandy were a major factor in the cautious attitude which pervaded 21st Army Group. The boldness that Montgomery had so confidently predicted before D-Day was impossible to generate in a strategy which lauded the defensive role his Second Army was playing on the eastern flank. Caution has never bred boldness and, although it was the alternative chosen after the failure to attain the D-Day objectives, the price that had to be paid came high. To the detriment of the British Army, this defensive mentality continued for the remainder of the Normandy campaign.[1] In 1952 Liddell Hart wrote: 'Seven years have passed since the war ended, yet the significance of the comparative odds in Normandy, in relation to the results, has never been brought out in any official report, history, or training manual. . . There has been too much glorification of the campaign and too little objective investigation.'[2] Since this essay was written over thirty years ago Normandy is still viewed through rose-coloured glasses and, with the possible exception of Operation GOODWOOD, few perceptible lessons were learned from the experience.

By 6 July 1944 exactly thirty days had passed since D-Day, yet objectives targeted for capture that first day or shortly thereafter were no closer to being attained. Amidst a growing tide of criticism, the time had arrived when the capture of Caen could no longer be put off despite Montgomery's plethora of problems. In frustration, he finally returned to the idea Leigh-Mallory had advanced three weeks earlier.

---

[1] The British Army has been singled out for a detailed examination in this chapter because the effects of morale, leadership and tactics played an important part in the early failures in Normandy. This is not to suggest that the US forces had no problems of their own. For a discussion of these subjects as they affected the American Armies the reader may wish to consult Russell F. Weigley's *Eisenhower's Lieutenants*, Bloomington, Indiana, 1981.
[2] Liddell Hart, loc.cit.

CHAPTER 17

Caen: Too Little, Too Late

CAEN FALLS, NAZI LINE UNHINGED
Stormed by British and Canadians

Daily Mail
10 July, 1944

The beginning of the fourth week in the battle for the Caen bridgehead saw Montgomery revert to his more traditional tactics of the frontal assault – an inevitable but necessary alternative after his earlier attempts to pinch off Caen from the west had failed. The feasibility of another envelopment was long past, resulting in the development of a new plan for all-out siege against the city, though by this time Caen itself had lost its strategic value to Montgomery. What was so important was the vital Bourguébus Ridge farther southeast from which to launch an Allied breakout. However, since Caen could no longer be bypassed to secure this ground, it would have to be taken the hard way. The increasing congestion in the bridgehead continued to hinder the deployment of the Second Army: it was scarcely one-fifth of the size required.[1] Ironically, the congestion prevented the First Canadian Army and 12 Corps from landing, thus denying Montgomery the use of their offensive potential needed to clear the bridgehead to help break the German hold on Caen once and for all. So, quite clearly, Caen would have to be taken with the forces at his disposal or not at all. After EPSOM the Second Army expected a major German counterattack, particularly in the Odon sector and in preparation for this, they reverted to a defensive holding posture. But, exhausted as some of the

---

[1] By the afternoon of 2 July over 900,000 troops had been landed across the Normandy beaches and this figure reached one million several days later. One vehicle was landed for every 5.3 men and .62 short tons per man. Cf., AEAF Commanders' Conference notes, 4 July 1944.

British units were, the Germans were in far worse shape. As a consequence the counterattacks never materialized except on a limited scale in early July, and these were easily rebuffed.

Montgomery's directive of 30 June instructed the Second Army to hold the main enemy force between Villers-Bocage and Caen while developing operations for the capture of the city as the 'opportunity offers – and the sooner the better'. Meanwhile Bradley would launch his previously delayed offensive to secure the entire Cotentin Peninsula and, when its base was reached, around Avranches, VIII Corps would press into Brittany while the remainder of his forces began an envelopment south of the bocage towards Laval, Mayenne, Le Mans and Alençon.[1] Montgomery firmly emphasized that his policy was: (1) to keep the initiative and (2) to have no setbacks. Left unsaid was an equally important third policy: to hold down the casualties of the British and Canadian forces. This new directive was issued after a meeting that day with Bradley and Dempsey at which Montgomery outlined his plan. He asked Bradley to take over the front presently occupied by the 7th Armoured Division near Caumont. According to Bradley, Montgomery was apparently deeply concerned over the number of panzer divisions opposing the Second Army and, in particular, by the bulge on the Odon front left by 8 Corps during EPSOM.[2]

This new policy did nothing to assuage the anxieties of the other senior commanders. When he learned of it, Leigh-Mallory was infuriated and considered it 'perfectly bloody'. 'It misses the boat in every possible direction and will, I think, if adapted, sow discord between us and the Americans. It also makes 2d Army look deplorable. We had our chance in the early days and missed it.'[3] Leigh-Mallory was right; the outrage and frustration felt by many American officers then remained long after the war had ended. Unable to understand the reasons for Montgomery's action and suspecting that US forces were being used as sacrificial lambs while the British dallied round Caen, American critics began to voice their opinion that the campaign was being badly mismanaged by the British commander who ought to be replaced

---

[1] 21st Army Group Directive, M-505, 30 June 1944.
[2] Bradley Papers, US Army Military History Institute.
[3] Leigh-Mallory Diary, 3 July 1944, loc.cit.

as Allied ground force commander at once by Eisenhower, as originally planned.[1]

Leigh-Mallory was but one of many who feared that Montgomery's Caen strategy was over cautious and destructive. Eisenhower's concern had been building for several weeks and, despite Montgomery's words of assurance that his operations were developing satisfactorily, the Supreme Commander remained unconvinced. According to his Chief-of-Staff, Bedell Smith, when Eisenhower had visited Bradley on 24 June it was evident that the First Army would soon capture Cherbourg and with that would come a pressing need for more elbow room on the US front. Smith relates that it was at this point that 'The Supreme Commander had already made up his mind that the full weight of U.S. strength should be used to break out into the open on our right.'[2] Smith was adamant that it was not until his 30 June directive that Montgomery first showed 'an intention of holding on the left and breaking through on the right. He directed the British forces to contain the greatest possible part of the enemy forces. This was a correct evaluation, brought about by the German reaction at Caen. Bradley and the Supreme Commander agreed in a conference that if an early breakout was in the cards, U.S. forces would have to do it. They were sure it could be done.'[3] However, as Smith relates, 'As late as July 7th, Montgomery, in a letter to the Supreme Commander, was uncertain at which point our main effort would have to be made. He rightly figured that the enemy action would have something to do with the final decision. This is something to be remembered by those that are so fond of using the phrase "according to plan". The press began to call the operation "stalemate". Criticisms began to pile up, but all commanders kept their heads, and went about their business.'[4]

The possibility of stalemate had always bedevilled Churchill and there was considerable concern within SHAEF and in London that the possibility of stalemate now existed. The experience of the Great War had left the British with a deep-rooted dread of

---

[1] The most stinging attack against Montgomery's policy came in a 1946 book, Top Secret, by a member of Bradley's staff, Ralph Ingersoll, which is discussed in Part IV.
[2] Memo by Lieutenant General W. B. Smith, 22 February 1945, Eisenhower Library.
[3] Ibid.
[4] Ibid.

the effects of static warfare. Their ghastly losses in the trenches of France from 1914–18 had never been forgotten and, with their manpower reserves having dwindled through over four years of war to a precarious point by the summer of 1944, such concern was legitimate. At this point in the war the Prime Minister, never a patient man even in the best of circumstances, evidenced growing concern not only about the stagnating drive against Caen but also over ANVIL, the proposed landing in southern France recently renamed DRAGOON. Churchill pleaded and cajoled with Eisenhower to cancel this operation on the grounds that it was totally unnecessary. While a series of harshly worded cables were being exchanged with Washington, Churchill doggedly and in vain argued against pulling troops away from Alexander at the very moment when victory in Italy was at hand. Uppermost in Churchill's mind were the political benefits he foresaw from a successful thrust towards Vienna before the Russians, a ploy which Marshall and Roosevelt stubbornly refused to accept. By the end of June Churchill had more or less resigned himself to the *fait accompli* of DRAGOON, although characteristically he refused to let Eisenhower off the hook and persisted in pestering the Supreme Commander in a final but futile attempt to sway his intentions.

Compounding British concern was the initiation of a new German terror tactic, the V-1 weapons, the first of which struck London from sites in Holland on 13 June. The subject of the V-1s and what to do about them became a major topic of discussion at meetings of the War Cabinet. While air action would be directed at destroying the V-1 sites it was recognized that the Germans had not only cleverly hidden these but in most cases were operating from hardened sites that were difficult to destroy by air action alone.[1] The present situation in Normandy meant that Allied ground forces would be of no immediate help in eliminating the V-1 menace.

Communications between Montgomery and Eisenhower mostly consisted of frequent exchanges of messages or letters,

---

[1] The codename CROSSBOW was given to the Allied measures taken to deal with the V-1 and later V-2 weapon sites. One of Brooke's great concerns was to prevent any impetuous decision by Churchill, who was considering savage reprisals against German cities, including the use of poison gas, a strategy which Brooke considered very counterproductive.

generally the result of none-too-subtle attempts by Eisenhower to spur on his ground force commander to greater action. Eisenhower's obvious unease in Montgomery's presence and the British general's desire for maximum freedom to follow his own designs, account for their lack of face-to-face communication. This approach, though, did little to promote understanding and harmony between the two generals or between their respective headquarters. During the entire campaign Eisenhower and Montgomery met a mere nine times, with de Guingand generally acting as Montgomery's go-between with the Supreme Commander and SHAEF.[1] Eisenhower was far more comfortable with the outgoing de Guingand, who shared his love of good company and friendly conversation; in fact, had it not been for de Guingand's efforts, relations between SHAEF and 21st Army Group might well have been far worse.

It is generally accepted that Eisenhower's anxiety about Montgomery's dilatoriness led him to complain directly to Churchill in an effort, as one account put it, to 'persuade Monty to get on his bicycle and start moving.'[2] However, in his unpublished manuscript Eisenhower revealed that it was Churchill who first came to him to express his deepening concern over Normandy. '. . . after we were ashore in Normandy but not at once achieving the advances that Montgomery had erlier predicted on his maps, Mr Churchill expressed unhappiness at our lack of progress. He was especially disappointed by the failure on our left to capture Caen. He came to see me one day, accompanied by General Brooke. He pointed out that at the final pre-invasion briefing the seizure of Caen within 24 hours had been assumed. Our failure, after many days of fighting to seize this key city strengthened his fear that we were descending into a bitter "trench-warfare" situation similar to that of World War I or, at best, were experiencing on a larger scale the early results of Anzio.'[3]

Eisenhower attempted to reassure Churchill that matters were not quite so gloomy: 'I told him I had personally never paid any attention to predictions that envisioned specific geographical gains at specific times. If it were possible to keep rigidly to such

---

[1] *Eisenhower Papers*, V, op.cit.
[2] Ambrose, *The Supreme Commander*, op.cit., p. 435.
[3] Eisenhower, unpublished manuscript, loc.cit.

schedules it would be only because the enemy was so weak or so inefficient as to make our progress a mere march. I emphasized we were successfully pursuing our basic purposes and I saw no reason for pessimism.'[1] Nevertheless, Eisenhower did tell Churchill 'that while certain tactical operations had not turned out as planned, yet the Allies were attracting German reinforcements to the Caen sector and it looked now as if the breakout would be made through the difficult "bocage" country on the West. I emphasized my confidence that all would turn out well.'[2]

According to Eisenhower, 'That meeting was the occasion for a most significant statement by Mr Churchill. He referred to General Marshall's delegation to me of absolute authority to transfer or to send out of my Theater any American I thought was not measuring up to the standards that should be expected of him. Because administrative authority over His Majesty's forces could not be given to an American he said, he and General Brooke did want me to know that, should I have any dissatisfaction with a British subordinate, no matter what his rank, I had merely to let the CIGS know and the individual would be promptly removed from the Allied command. I thanked the Prime Minister and General Brooke for their confidence but told them I had no present intention of recommending anything of the kind; if some future emergency arose, I would notify them.'[3]

Inasmuch as no other British commander had come under fire from the Prime Minister, Churchill's statement could only have been a reference to Montgomery and a subtle reminder to the Supreme Commander that even the most senior British commander was not immune from removal should this prove to be in the best interests of Allied unity. Eisenhower's attempts to reassure Churchill were obviously not entirely successful. The Prime Minister's strong feelings about Montgomery and Caen led to open and hostile criticism of the British general at a meeting of the Chiefs-of-Staff on the night of 6 July, causing an angry Brooke to record that Churchill ' ... began to abuse Monty because operations were not going faster, and apparently Eisenhower had said he was over-cautious. I flared up and asked him if he could not trust his generals for five minutes instead of continuously

[1] Eisenhower, unpublished manuscript, loc.cit.
[2] Ibid.
[3] Ibid.

abusing them and belittling them.'[1]* Brooke later recalled: 'I think what infuriated me most was that there had not been a single word of approval or gratitude for the excellent work Monty had done. I lost my temper and started one of the heaviest thunderstorms that we had had. He was infuriated, and throughout the evening kept shoving his chin out, looking at me and fuming at the accusation that he ran down his generals.'[2]

Military operations which might result in defeat or stalemate were one of the Prime Minister's fixations throughout the war but never more so than over the liberation of France. Earlier reverses in other theatres of war had left a lingering fear that his generals might once again lose the initiative, resulting in either stalemate or in permitting the Germans to snatch victory. Politically, stalemate in Normandy was a worrisome possibility: it would have given Hitler a huge bargaining chip in any negotiations to end the war and would have left all of western Europe vulnerable to conquest by the Red Army. Churchill in fact was sufficiently troubled to ask for a personal briefing on Normandy. Brigadier McLean, one of the original COSSAC planners and now with SHAEF G–3, had already briefed him on several occasions and thought that the Prime Minister's 'experiences in the last war made him want to avoid any stalemate. He, like Smuts, visualized a long fight in France.'[3] In July, McLean was summoned to England to brief Churchill again personally, and these are the notes taken by Dr Pogue of that event:

> In July when we were congested in the bridgehead, the P.M. asked for someone to come and tell him the plans. I went to Chequers. We talked for hours. Every time the P.M. got past his second glass he talked about his battalion in the last war. After dinner we went out into the orchard – the P.M. stopping to take a pee against the hedge. He was wearing his zip suit and a straw hat. At intervals he sent in for whiskies and soda. At 6 (P.M.) he said: 'I suppose you are one of those damned people who have to have their tea.' So I had tea while he had whisky. His

[1] Alanbrooke Diary, loc.cit.

* This was perhaps the most savage encounter between the two men during the war. The strains of nearly five years of war were obviously taking their toll on both men, and during the summer of 1944 Brooke's diary records a series of confrontations between the Prime Minister and the Field Marshal. Brooke had not lost his respect for Churchill, merely his patience.

[2] Bryant, *Triumph in the West*, op.cit., p. 230. At Brooke's instigation, Montgomery later briefed Churchill on his strategy during a visit to Normandy at which the PM pronounced himself well satisfied that his field commander knew what he was doing.

[3] Interview with Brigadier Kenneth R. McLean by Dr Forrest C. Pogue, loc.cit.

arguments were irrelevant to SHAEF. He insisted that we were stuck. Said that he didn't like ANVIL; we will have a disaster. I said we should bring divisions around and launch through the north. He said 'NO – go on in Italy.' . . . McLean told him of plans to cross the Seine. He said, 'Oh, that is next season's campaign.' He thought it would take much longer than it did. Didn't believe in a killing battle to take places. Couldn't forget the long dragged out battles of the last war. Thought we would be in the fight for months. [You] must remember that in trying to understand his views on the European campaign.[1]

Despite the setbacks of June, nothing which had transpired since D-Day had swayed Montgomery from his original idea that once a firm bridgehead was established across the entire Allied front, priority must be given to the capture of additional ports in Brittany. In his mind the logistical priorities of the Allied armies came before any major attempt at a breakout: once this task was accomplished, Bradley's forces were to expand their front beyond the bocage and swing to their left so that a concerted drive could be mounted to push the German Army toward the Seine. Successful accomplishment of this required the Second Army to act as the hinge while the Allied door slammed shut to pin the Germans against the Seine but in their present positions, the Second Army had not yet attained the ground required for the execution of this task: the Caen-Falaise Plain.

Within a day or two of his 30 June directive, Montgomery had recognized that he could no longer avoid a frontal assault against Caen. With the success of future operations dependent upon attainment of the Caen-Falaise Plain, he directed Dempsey to execute the first step, an assault to capture Caen by 1 Corps who would utilize the 3rd British Division on the left, the 59th Division in the centre and the 3rd Canadian Division on the right, assisted by two armoured brigades and heavy fire support by the artillery and naval guns. This new offensive was scheduled to jump off on the morning of 8 July and was given the codename CHARNWOOD.

The mission given to Crocker's 1 Corps was to secure Caen and to establish bridgeheads south of the Orne while O'Connor's 8 Corps would prepare to renew the offensive against the Odon flank at short notice.[2] As a preliminary, the 3rd Canadian

---

[1] McLean interview with Pogue, loc.cit.
[2] Stacey, *The Victory Campaign*, op.cit., p. 157.

Division would attack on 3 July to secure Carpiquet Airfield and the approaches to Caen from the west. The Canadians succeeded in capturing Carpiquet village but the airfield was heavily fortified and strongly defended by elements of Kurt Meyer's 12th SS, so that the Canadians were able to secure only a portion of the airfield against fierce German resistance during a two-day battle which left heavy casualties on both sides. That same day Bradley was able finally to launch his offensive across the entire First Army front which had as its preliminary object the capture of the St Lô–Periers–Lessay road. Although modest gains were made in the next five days, the offensive gradually but inexorably ground to a halt in the dense bocage north of St Lô and in the marshlands of the Cotentin far short of its objective. Despite Montgomery's later claims of pinning the panzer divisions to his front, two of them had already slipped away to reinforce the German left flank and participate in a series of counterattacks against the First Army.[1] The Germans possessed all the advantages offered by the terrain and, as Montgomery later said ' . . . there were very few good roads [most of which tended to run parallel to the US advance] across the extensive marshlands and floods; the bocage country was extremely thick; the weather was atrocious and not only restricted mobility and caused great discomfort to the troops, but seriously limited any attempts to give them support from the air; and owing to maintenance difficulties, ammunition remained in short supply.'[2]

Privately, Montgomery was somewhat disillusioned by the American tendency to attack on too broad a front, thus losing the advantage of concentration of forces at a decisive point. Although he himself had conspicuously failed to practise his own doctrine in the battle for Caen, Montgomery believed that Bradley had lost all chance of success by his insistence in attacking across the entire First Army front. Although relations between the two commanders would later disintegrate into open antipathy on the part of Bradley, during the Normandy campaign their association was generally cordial. Montgomery went to

---

[1] Panzer Lehr and 2nd SS Panzer. Against the First Army there were now approximately 70 battalions of infantry, and 250 tanks to support them. Stacey, *The Victory Campaign*, op.cit, p. 165.

[2] Montgomery, *El Alamein to the River Sangro and Normandy to the Baltic*, op.cit., p. 237.

great lengths not to offend the US commander, and was tactful and exceptionally diplomatic whenever he dealt with Bradley.[1]

Patton, who had secretly moved his Third Army HQ to Normandy in preparation for exploitation after the First Army cleared the Cotentin, was privately critical of Montgomery's tactics. The two generals had been fierce rivals ever since Montgomery had usurped a major role for the Eighth Army during the planning for the invasion of Sicily in the spring of 1943. During Operation HUSKY and later Patton had demonstrated his intense dislike of the British in general and of Montgomery in particular. Patton's own genius for command had been largely obscured in the past year by his penchant for publicly opening his mouth and putting his foot in it and by the two deplorable slapping incidents in Sicily which had ultimately cost him command of the Seventh Army and very nearly a role in OVERLORD.

Patton had been selected to command the Third US Army but by the spring of 1944 was again in trouble over what came to be known in April as the 'Knutsford incident' when he was quoted in the press as suggesting that it was the evident destiny of the British and Americans to rule the post-war world. Furious over the public tumult resulting from this new indiscretion, Eisenhower appeared strongly inclined to dismiss Patton but torn between his need for Patton's experience and his weariness in attempting to control his controversial subordinate, Eisenhower waffled and wrote to Marshall for guidance. Marshall assured Eisenhower of his full backing whatever the decision, suggesting

---

[1] Although there was cordiality in their face-to-face contacts, there is evidence that Bradley, in the privacy of his entourage, sometimes tended to deride Montgomery. His close friend and subordinate, Major General J. Lawton Collins, provides an example in his autobiography. During a visit to Collins on 25 June, Bradley said with a chuckle: 'Joe, you will love this. Monty has just announced, "Caen is the key to Cherbourg." I said: "Brad, let's wire him to send us the key." In the interest of Allied amity we did not do it.' (*Lightning Joe*, p. 220). Bradley's aide, Chester Hansen, maintained a detailed diary for his chief which was later utilized in the preparation of *A Soldier's Story* which was ghostwritten by Hansen. Hansen reflected the growing disdain within the First Army for Montgomery. His diary contains numerous uncomplimentary references, among them this one, written on 30 June: 'Went to tea with Monty and found him oppressive. Monty is beginning to believe in the Monty legend, and that he is a great man of history, fully convincing him of his godlike role. Asked me what my insignia was. "I say, how do you have a major for an ADC? Simply a dog's body, you know, a whipping boy. I would not have an ADC who is more than a captain."' Cf., the Hansen Diaries, US Army Military History Institute.

that the choice be governed strictly by the Supreme Commander's needs for OVERLORD. Eisenhower could ill afford to lose a commander of Patton's calibre and so elected to retain him in command of the Third Army. It was a decision Eisenhower never had cause to regret. Between them, 'Marshall and Eisenhower had made it possible for Patton to fight another day.'[1]

While Patton never successfully curbed his impetuous tongue, he was at this time keeping a very low profile while quietly preparing himself for a role he desperately craved in the battle of Normandy. He had been closely following events in Normandy and was not impressed by the progress of the battle. He thought it his destiny to lead an army against the Germans in Europe and now, with both Bradley and Montgomery halted far short of their goals after major offensives, it was evident that his Third Army would, after all, play an important role in the liberation of France. The day before departing for France Patton confided his contempt for Montgomery to his diary: 'Went to see Ike at 1500. He was just back from France and seemed cheerful but a little fed up with Monty's lack of drive. . . His current plan is [eventually] for four American Armies, with one small American Army for Montgomery, as the British have reached their limit of 14 divisions. . . Why an American Army has to go with Montgomery, I do not see, except to save the face of the little monkey.'[2] After his arrival in Normandy he wrote on 7 July: 'I had lunch with Bradley, Montgomery and De Guingand. After lunch, Montgomery, Bradley and I went to the war tent. Here Montgomery went to great lengths explaining why the British had done nothing. Caen was their D-day objective, and they have not taken it yet.'[3]

A lengthy trip to Normandy in early July had done little to reassure Eisenhower. Other than one brief visit to Montgomery's HQ on 2 July, the Supreme Commmmander spent most of his time with Bradley, and he returned to England on 5 July deeply concerned over the divisiveness of the Montgomery-Coningham feud and the stagnation on the British front and, as his naval

[1] Pogue, *Marshall: Organizer of Victory*, op.cit., p. 386.
[2] Martin Blumenson, *The Patton Papers*, Volume 11, Boston, 1974, p. 472.
[3] Ibid, p. 479.

aide's diary recorded, 'smouldering' over the whole business.[1] After discussing the problem with Tedder and Bedell Smith, the Supreme Commander drafted a letter 'tactfully telling Monty to get a move on'.[2] By design Eisenhower abhorred interfering in the operations of his subordinates; consequently his letter was less a directive than an exhortation to speed up the pace of his operations. 'It appears to me,' wrote Eisenhower, 'that we must use all possible energy in a determined effort to prevent a stalemate or of facing the necessity of fighting a major defensive battle with the slight depth we now have in the bridgehead. We have not yet attempted a major full-dress attack on the left flank supported by everything we could bring to bear.'[3]

British criticism of Eisenhower in the post-war years – led by Montgomery – has tended to focus on his preference for constant attack on a broad front, and has been justified by pointing to the post-Normandy strategy which, they argued, cost the Allies a golden opportunity of ending the war in 1944. However, Eisenhower's approach of acting like a football coach running up and down the line with encouragement to attack, attack, attack, emanated less from his strategic concept of war than from his belief and understanding that this was precisely the manner in which Montgomery had planned his campaign. In fact, Montgomery's plan constantly to hammer at the Germans from both flanks coincided nicely with Eisenhower's own concept of fighting the battle of Normandy.

Eisenhower's letter of 7 July arrived too late to have any impact on Montgomery's plans for CHARNWOOD. However, sometime on 6 July Montgomery made a decision to seek heavy bomber support for the operation: what Leigh-Mallory had suggested three weeks earlier was suddenly and quite unexpectedly requested by 21st Army Group. The German defences blocking the British advance were known to be exceptionally strong and had in the days leading up to CHARNWOOD been heavily reinforced. Thus, during the daily Air Commanders' Conference held at Leigh-Mallory's AEAF HQ at Stanmore, a request was submitted for Bomber Command to blast a path open for the advancing ground forces by heavy saturation bomb-

---

[1] Butcher, op.cit., p. 520 and Tedder Diary.
[2] Tedder Diary, 6 July 1944.
[3] *Eisenhower Papers*, III, 7 July 1944, p. 1982.

ing of the northern approaches to Caen and its suburbs. Eisenhower was present at the 7 July meeting – a most unusual circumstance, for never before or, for that matter, during the remainder of the Normandy campaign did the Supreme Commander ever attend one of these meetings. The conference notes in the AEAF Historical Record do not explain the reason for his presence that day, but it is reasonable to conclude that Eisenhower was there to provide his full backing for Montgomery's request, and to ensure that the matter was not ignored by the air chiefs, particularly the sometimes reluctant Air Chief Marshal Harris. In the event, the plan was quickly accepted and Harris proved cooperative. The conference notes reveal little debate or discussion about the decision to employ some 450 heavy bombers for the Caen operation that night.[1]

Tedder played no part in the decision to bomb Caen. Having previously turned down Leigh-Mallory's proposal in mid-June, Tedder did not appear to welcome the plan but he did not attempt to interfere with Montgomery's request. According to the AEAF Historical Record for 7 July: 'ACM Tedder believed that the heavy bombers should not be used in the battle except in exceptional circumstances to prevent a crisis, to break up an enemy attack, but not to prepare for an attack by our own troops.' What worried Tedder was his suspicion 'that this attitude would encourage the Army to ask on every occasion for heavy bomber support, and that the strategic bombers would thus be unduly diverted from their proper tasks'.[2]

Montgomery's rather sudden decision to seek this support may have derived in part from a visit by Air Commodore Kingston-McCloughry and Air Vice Marshal Wigglesworth (the Senior Air Staff Officer) of the AEAF. According to Kingston-McCloughry, Montgomery was enthusiastic and replied 'yes' to

[1] AEAF Historical Record, July 1944, PRO (AIR 37/1057). Tedder was the officer responsible for coordinating and approving air operations which concerned SHAEF and was usually present at these daily meetings as the senior SHAEF representative.

[2] Ibid. Tedder's attitude undoubtedly emanated from his conviction that Montgomery was too cautious and was unwilling to take necessary risks. When presented with a paper from Zuckerman proposing the use of the strategic bombers in a carefully planned direct support role of the army, Tedder acidly replied that 'he was not interested as "he was neither concerned with Cassinos nor with agriculture"'. Zuckerman confirms the AEAF version: 'It was apparent that the decision was in a sense outside T's hands, and it did not look as though he liked the proposal – although he did not object to it.' Zuckerman Journal, 9 July 1944.

the question of whether he desired heavy bomber support.[1] He also alleges that Churchill had a great deal to do with Montgomery's decision. In his unpublished autobiography he states: 'One Friday Winston Churchill intervened to say to Montgomery, you take Caen by Monday or you are out. Monty's reply was, but I will take it tomorrow if you will only give me what I require. What is that? queried Churchill. The heavy bombers, said Monty. You shall have them, was the answer. Thus after all the delay and opposition this is how Bomber Command began its support to help the Army break through the bridgehead.'[2] In early July there was suspicion within Montgomery's HQ that one of his aides had hand-carried a secret letter from the Prime Minister telling the British general to 'get Caen or get out'. Kingston-McCloughry unfortunately failed to reveal the source of his information but, given Churchill's previous habit of communicating directly with his generals in the field, it is conceivable that his frustration in early July may have led him to threaten Montgomery, in the hope that it would spur the sort of action Eisenhower had been urging but to date had been unable to induce. Certainly, any action to relieve Montgomery was unthinkable: not only would such an action have greatly embarrassed Churchill and the Allies but it would have given the Germans new resolve to resist, and also have generated considerable unease in Moscow. However, as a motivational tactic such a letter would have been consistent with the Prime Minister's past behaviour. Montgomery never hesitated to tell Churchill whenever he thought him meddling in military matters but both his respect and wariness of the Prime Minister were such that he would have taken very seriously indeed any admonition to speed up his operations.

Still, despite the attractiveness of this idea as the reason why Montgomery hastily requested the bombers, there are greater reasons to doubt that the incident took place. Sir Ian Jacob, one of Ismay's deputies, believes that meddlesome as Churchill could sometimes be, he would in these circumstances have worked through Eisenhower rather than directly with Montgomery.[3] Nor is there even a hint of such an incident in any of the unpublished papers of those, like Brooke, who were privy to

[1] Kingston-McCloughry Papers, loc.cit.
[2] Ibid. The same allegation is contained in a 1955 book, *The Direction of War*.
[3] Interview with Sir Ian Jacob, 16 May 1979.

everything that took place at Number 10, Downing Street. Churchill's private secretary, Sir John Colville, was temporarily serving with the RAF during the Normandy campaign but he, like Jacob, believes that any action of this nature by the Prime Minister most certainly would have come to light. Colville is clear, however, that Churchill was distressed over Montgomery's handling of the campaign and was heard to be critical on several occasions during the summer of 1944.[1] There is no indication that Kingston-McCloughry had some ulterior motive or any prejudice against Montgomery to exorcise by revealing Churchill's alleged involvement. Although his unpublished autobiography is critical of Montgomery in places, his close friend and wartime associate Lord Zuckerman notes that Kingston-McCloughry greatly admired the Field Marshal.[2] Whether or not Churchill was involved – directly or indirectly – the strange circumstances surrounding the last-minute decision to bomb Caen raise questions which may well be answered only when Churchill's wartime papers are made public.

At the time, Zuckerman noted in his journal that there appeared to be an ulterior motive behind the sudden military decision made on 7 July. The initiative for the bombing came from the Chief of Plans and Operations of the Advanced AEAF,[3] Air Vice Marshal Stephen C. Strafford. 'It was perfectly plain that L-M knew nothing about it till the moment Strafford put up the suggestion.' Moreover, as Zuckerman wrote: 'There can be little doubt and Strafford indicated this very strongly to me that the whole decision was a political one and that Caen had to be captured over the weekend.'[4]

The evidence points to the bombing request coming from

[1] Sir John Colville, letter to the author, 6 June 1982.
[2] Zuckerman, op.cit., p. 270.
[3] Overall command and control of the AEAF came from Leigh-Mallory's HQ in the London suburb of Stanmore where air policy and plans were developed and coordinated. The operational arm of the AEAF was vested in an organization known as the Advanced AEAF. Based in Uxbridge, the Advanced AEAF was under the command of Air Marshal Coningham who retained operational control of both the US and British tactical air forces. Strafford was actually Coningham's man rather than Leigh-Mallory's, which explains the AEAF Chief's surprise when Strafford proposed the Caen bombing operation. Although Montgomery, as we have seen, tended frequentely to bypass Coningham to deal directly with Leigh-Mallory, in this instance the request for the Caen bombing appears to gone through established channels.
[4] Zuckerman Journal, 9 July 1944.

21st Army Group via the Advanced AEAF.[1] What is known is that in the twenty-four hours preceding the operation there was considerable high-level discussion taking place in Normandy and London. After returning from his early July inspection tour of the front, Eisenhower conferred with both Tedder (5 and 6 July) and with Leigh-Mallory (6 July). Patton's diary confirms Eisenhower's evident distress with Montgomery. On 7 July Portal met Montgomery in Normandy and the employment of the strategic bombers would have been an obvious subject of discussion.

That the bombing request had political overtones was made clear to Zuckerman by an influential American officer on the AEAF staff who apparently reported directly to General Arnold in Washington. Zuckerman recorded in his journal that the officer had 'made it perfectly plain, too, that he frequently has information which nobody in the place has got. For example, in this Caen battle he knew before anybody else that the calling-in of the heavy strategical forces had been ordered from the highest political level – almost before anybody in AEAF knew that this was going to be called for at all.'[2]

The concept of the bombing scheduled for the night of 7 July appeared similar to the one previously proposed by Leigh-Mallory and originally devised by Zuckerman in early June.[3] On schedule, at approximately 2200 hours, the first wave of Bomber Command heavies began dropping one-thousand-pound-bombs, most of them fused to explode six hours later when the ground advance was to commence. Zuckerman, who witnessed the bombing, says that the main operation lasted about an hour, during which Bomber Command dropped some 6,000 bombs in a narrow area of northern Caen.[4] Broadhurst also witnessed the bombing and offers an unusual and interesting account of this event:

[1] The AEAF minutes for 7 July 1944 attribute the request to 21st Army Group. The AEAF entry reads: 'The Army asked on July 7th for a bombing attack that night on certain strongpoints north of CAEN in preparation for an attack due to be launched on July 8th.' Cf., AEAF Historical Record, 7 July 1944, PRO (AIR 37/1057).

[2] Zuckerman Journal, 9 July 1944. The young officer referred to by Zuckerman – a Lieutenant Colonel Burt – was evidently one of the young Turks Arnold was fond of placing in headquarters outside his control, in order to keep him fully informed. According to Zuckerman, Colonel Burt had previously been a member of Arnold's air staff in Washington.

[3] The earlier plan had seven main aiming points; the 7 July plan contained only two. Cf., Zuckerman, p. 272.

[4] Zuckerman, op.cit., p. 273.

On the bombing of Caen, Dempsey [when told Broadhurst was going to watch the bombing from his Storch aircraft] said, take me with you. I said OK. We'd been having a lot of trouble with suppressing the [friendly] ground ack-ack. Shooting at everything with these new divisions coming in. I'd had a lot of trouble because I was responsible for the air defence and I'd grounded the flak because they wouldn't take any bloody notice. So off we go. We circle over Y11, the field right on the edge of the enemy line, and watched this extraordinary thing in which the British gunners took on the German flak guns. German gunners were shooting at our guns, and the German flak were shooting at the bombers. You've never seen such a sight! Every gun in the district was shooting and we were circling around watching.[1]

Broadhurst went on to recount how he and Dempsey nearly lost their lives:

Suddenly Dempsey said to me, 'Harry, Harry! For crissake put her down, we're being fired at!' I looked back and even though we were doing eighty miles per hour, the guns were all behind, and puff-puff. Well, you try and put a Storch down and it's not easy because of the high lift. So I dived for the ground and by the time we got down to the ground there were all these chaps machine-gunning us as well. Everybody was shooting at us. . . We landed in a cornfield. Troops came rushing across headed by a captain and I said to Dempsey, for heaven's sake, get out and wear your red hat! If I get out in my blue uniform they'll shoot us. Well, he got out and waved his hat, looking the bloody fool. This Canadian came up and he realized something had gone wrong somewhere. He said: 'I demand your identity card!' Bimbo Dempsey said: 'Don't be a bloody fool, I'm your commanding general.' We had been hit eleven times and I said to Bimbo, look, I can get it out of here, if you like, and push for home. We can keep it low down. He said: 'I'm going with this chap!' After I got back he rang me up and said: 'I can assure you no ack-ack is going to fire a bloody gun other than horizontally in my sector!'[2]

In the two days of hard fighting that followed the bombing, the northern half of Caen was entered and secured by 1 Corps, whose units reached the banks of the Orne where it passes through the city. On 9 July they were halted by stiff resistance from the remnants of Caen's German defenders, who had moved into new

[1] Broadhurst interview, loc. cit.
[2] Ibid.

positions on the south bank of the river, preventing any further advance for the moment.

Montgomery later praised the assistance rendered by Bomber Command in the capture of Caen. 'Investigation showed the tremendous effect of the heavy bombing on the enemy. . . The Bomber Command attack played a vital part in the success of the operation.'[1] Montgomery's optimistic assessment appears to have been more fantasy than fact. In reality the devastation wreaked upon the ancient and once beautiful city of Caen did little materially to assist in its capture. Quite the contrary, the bombing in some instances inhibited the progress of some 1 Corps units attempting to traverse the bombed-out ruins: there were huge craters and piles of rubble the size of small hills; in places what had once been streets were now gaping holes.

On 6 and 7 June Caen had already been severely bombed and the efficiency of the CHARNWOOD bombing completed the task of destruction. Most of the city had been evacuated after the invasion but even by the time of the final assault on 8 July there were still several thousand civilians trapped there. Many sought sanctuary in the great cathedral, the Abbaye-aux-Hommes in the city centre, and in the Hôpital du Bon Sauveur, both of which were miraculously spared. The cathedral was only slightly damaged and proved a stunning sight to the Allied troops amidst the rubble of what had once been the hub of Caen.

How necessary was the bombing of Caen to its capture? Zuckerman and Kingston-McCloughry conducted a survey immediately afterwards in an effort to determine its effectiveness. What they found totally contradicts the official version and Montgomery's attitude. Their report stated that there was virtually no sign of enemy gun positions, tanks or German dead in the target area. They interviewed a number of officers and men of the 3rd Division, who expressed bewilderment over why the bombers had even been employed.[2] Although the bombing had been extremely accurate, Zuckerman and Kingston-McCloughry reported that no targets of military value had been attacked. They

---

[1] Montgomery, *El Alamein to the River Sangso and Normandy to the Baltic*, op.cit., p. 240.

[2] Air Commodore E. J. Kingston-McCloughry and S. Zuckerman, 'Observations on Bomber Command Attack on Caen, 7 July 1944', PRO (AIR 37/1255), and Zuckerman, op.cit., pp. 273–7.

found from their interviews that there were a number of worth-while targets but none of these had been included within the area selected by the army. According to Zuckerman, 'Apart from the enormous lift to their morale which the appearance of the heavy bombers had given, their view was that the bombing had made no material difference to the whole operation. They could not understand why heavy bombing had been called for and . . . said that not a single dead German or any enemy equipment had been found in the area that had been bombed.'[1]

Zuckerman noted in his journal that: 'The incredible part of the performance was that the aiming points given for the attack were the same as those which had been turned down three weeks ago because there was nothing there for the bombers to hit, and turned down by Coningham and Tedder.'[2]

An eyewitness confirms that the effect of the bombing on the Allies was a tremendous boost to morale. Major General Sir Nigel Tapp's 7th Field Regiment was still in support of the 185th Infantry Brigade, and he recalls: 'The psychological effect on the [185] Infantry Brigade my Regiment was supporting was elec-trifying – you must remember that we had been stopped for a month in front of Lebisey Wood – we had lost two commanding officers and a significant number of casualties from mortaring and shellings – consequently the noise and sight of the bombard-ment was a tremendous morale boost. Officers and soldiers were jumping out of their slit trenches and cheering.'[3]

The effect of the bombing on vehicular movement was mixed. In some instances the rubble greatly hindered movement into Caen. Major General Tapp remembers little interference to his regiment. 'I remember as soon as practicable driving into Caen, and although the devastation resembled some areas of London after the Blitz, I did not find any particular hindrance to move-ment by military vehicles.'[4]

The overall ineffectiveness of the bombing was evident from the savage resistance put up by the Germans. Casualties during the two-day battle for Caen were staggering. Within the infantry

[1] Zuckerman, op.cit., p. 276, quotes an RAF officer saying that there had been no enemy guns in the target area and many artillery battalions adjacent to it were still active the following day.
[2] Zuckermann Journal, 9 July 1944, loc.cit.
[3] Major General Sir Nigel Tapp, letter to the author, 1 July 1982.
[4] Ibid.

battalions losses of 25% were the rule rather than the exception. As one account comments: 'The Normandy slaughterhouse was swallowing up the infantry. The expenditure of flesh and blood in the present battle for Caen was cause for alarm, for Germans as well as British. In this lovely summer weather it was not unusual for an infantryman to wonder at each sunset whether he would ever live to see another, and at each dawn whether that would be his last.'[1]

General Tapp thought the bombing of little material value to ground operations, pointing out that 'Unless they are closely coordinated with ground attacks . . . the determined defender (like the German) emerges, shakes himself and resumes his resistance.'[2]

The hasty decision to employ the bombers had left no time for close coordination and Zuckerman and Kingston-McCloughry judged the CHARNWOOD bombing as merely a frill to an already established ground plan. They argued that if bomber support was to be effectively employed the entire fire plan had to be integrated at the start of planning and not at the last moment.[3] Their report was presented to Tedder a few days later but the Deputy Supreme Commander refused to sanction its wide circulation on the grounds, as Zuckerman put it, that 'He had never read a more demoralising document.'[4]

The other important question which must be asked is whether Bomber Command was mistakenly employed as a means of sparing Montgomery further criticism for his direction of the campaign. There is little doubt that the last-minute decision to bomb Caen had few tactical benefits. What remains unanswered is whether Leigh-Mallory's original proposal was hastily grasped by Montgomery as an attractive method of lessening the intense pressure upon him to break the stalemate by any possible means. Even if Churchill was not involved in the decision, only further revelation will determine whether Caen became a sacrificial offering to enhance Montgomery's position as ground commander.

The capture of the northern half of Caen was of no immediate

---

[1] Henry Maule, *Caen*, London, 1976, p. 66.
[2] Major General Sir Nigel Tapp, loc.cit.
[3] Bombing Report, loc.cit.
[4] Zuckerman, op.cit., p. 277.

tactical benefit to Montgomery. For the moment all he had possession of was a ruined city and a symbolic victory. As long as the Germans continued to hold a line along the Orne, Caen itself was useless without occupation of the heights of Bourguébus Ridge, some four miles southeast. Also, the Germans still occupied the eastern suburb of Colombelles; their observers in the huge steelworks there could observe all enemy movement from its tall towers. More important than the capture of Caen was the fall of Carpiquet Airfield and the terrain leading to the banks of the Odon around Bretteville-sur-Odon.

The British press trumpeted the seizure of Caen as a great victory; had it been captured early in June it would indeed have been a significant one, but by now the capture of this once great prize was largely a hollow victory – too little, too late. The key to success had always been its rapid seizure and, failing this, its bypassing and isolation. Except as a means of delaying the British, Caen had long since lost its value to the Germans: what was important to them now was to continue to hold a line along the Orne, thus blocking any further attempt by Montgomery to advance southeast toward Falaise.

Despite the questionable tactical benefits of the bomber raid, the operation did serve to convince the ground commanders of the value of such operations. Broadhurst recounts how the bombing affected Dempsey: 'That bombing of Caen shook him. I think that converted him. He saw some 800 odd aircraft go through the worst flak he had ever seen, going up in flames, chaps bailing out, planes coming down and blowing up. They just came in a stream. . . It was the first time anyone had ever seen one of these bomber raids at the sharp end.'[1]

For the Germans, the decision to hold Caen to the bitter end was Hitler's and the price of this strategy came steeply. The 12th SS lost a great many of its remaining tanks and anti-tank guns (including some 20 tanks on 8 July) and had seen its infantry strength reduced to that of a battalion, while the 16th Luftwaffe Field Division (defending the northeast sector of Caen) suffered 75% casualties.[2]

Even with the dreadful German losses, Hitler remained determined to keep the bridgehead to its present size and to yield no

[1] Broadhurst interview, loc.cit.
[2] Stacey, *The Victory Campaign*, op.cit., pp. 163–4.

further ground to the Allies. A directive to OB West on 8 July anticipated that the Allies would now launch 'a thrust forward on both sides of the Seine to Paris. Therefore, a second enemy landing in the sector of Fifteenth Army, despite all the risks this entails, is probable; all the more so, as public opinion will press for elimination of the positions for long-range fire on London.'[1] This was clear evidence of the success of the Allied deception plan, and in his directive Hitler decreed that the reserves of the Fifteenth Army should remain in place until it could be determined whether Patton's phantom army group would land on the Pas de Calais or in Normandy.[2]

While Montgomery unquestionably improved his position by CHARNWOOD, the mere possession of the northern half of Caen, Carpiquet and Bretteville was hopeless as a hinge for support of

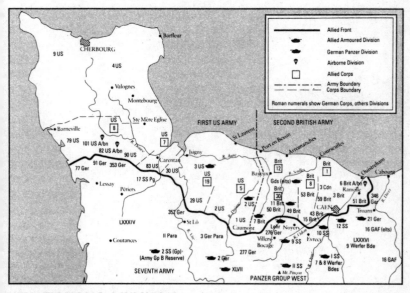

SITUATION MAP, 9 JULY 1944

[1] Quoted in Stacey, *The Victory Campaign*, op.cit., p. 164. Hitler's reference is to the German V-1 weapon sites and the effect he believed his terror tactics were having on the British.

[2] Ibid. pp. 164–5.

future operations on either flank. The elusive high ground of the Caen-Falaise Plain still lay in German hands, the Caen bridge-head remained unsatisfactorily small, high casualties to the infantry had left the manpower problem more acute than ever and, to add to Montgomery's problems, Bradley's offensive was stalled in the mud and bocage of western Normandy. Time remained the critical factor; it was essential that the Allied commanders develop and execute a concerted plan for a break-out that would snap Rommel's 'roping-off' policy once and for all. During the 10 July meeting between Montgomery, Dempsey and Bradley two plans were approved to break out of the Normandy bridgehead.

CHAPTER 18

D+30: Stalemate

The problem is Monty who can be neither removed
nor moved to action.

Diary of Air Chief Marshal Tedder,
8 July 1944

Montgomery's fame and remarkable success had largely been
achieved by consistency of purpose and dogged determination in
the execution of military operations. The word 'improvisation'
was not really part of his vocabulary despite the fact that this trait
is a generally accepted characteristic of any successful commander. There is, however, a wide gulf between the exercise of
necessary tactical improvisation and Montgomery's hollow
claim that the battle for Caen was all part of a pre-conceived
strategy rather than a post-D-Day exigency which, by D+30, had
already begun to tarnish his reputation.

Omar Bradley was quite right when he bluntly said: 'By July
10, we faced a real danger of a World War 1–type stalemate in
Normandy. Montgomery's forces had taken the northern outskirts of Caen, but the city was not by any means in his control.
The airfield sites still lay beyond his grasp. My own breakout had
failed. Despite enormous casualties and loss of equipment, the
Germans were slavishly following Hitler's orders to hold every
yard of ground.'[1]

What Montgomery absurdly attempted to portray as the end
result of a deliberate master plan was, in reality, one of the most
untidy series of operations he ever conducted. Later, he sought to
deflect criticism of his generalship by suggesting that his enemies
at SHAEF took advantage of the controversy by attempting to
discredit him.[2] The main culprits were alleged to have been
General Morgan and the airmen, while Eisenhower was dis-

[1] Bradley, *A General's Life*, p. 272.
[2] Montgomery, *Memoirs*, p. 256.

missed as merely too amateur and inexperienced to comprehend the true intent of the master plan. What Montgomery refused to acknowledge was that his plan had long since been derailed and that the Second Army now found itself in a virtual cul-de-sac, a situation the capture of the northern half of Caen had done little to alleviate. We have already seen how the strategy on the left flank had become transposed from one of boldness to a series of vicious engagements with Rommel's panzer divisions. The Second Army had indeed carried out its task of protecting Bradley but in a manner vastly different from that envisaged. General Dempsey's notes for the 15 May St Paul's School briefing have been preserved. Based on Montgomery's guidance given in April, they reflect a vastly different scenario from that which took place around Caen. The Second Army commander had cited its four immediate tasks:

(1) To get ashore on a front sufficiently broad and in adequate strength to provide a base for development and buildup of the invasion force.

(2) To penetrate sufficiently far inland to overcome all enemy coastal defences and to gain space for the buildup through the beaches.

(3) To secure the important tactical features and centres of communication in order to deal with counterattacks and

(4) 'To be all set by D+3 or D+4 to develop operations in the way we wish.'[1]

Only later, said Dempsey, would operations be developed south and southeast to secure airfields and to protect the eastern flank of the First US Army:

> It is clear that having once secured the initial bridgehead the Army must face both east and south, and that for every mile it advances south, it prolongs its eastern flank by that same distance. It is in effect continually doing a left or half-left turn, and I have got to be quite certain that there is *a very firm left marker for this operation*. I must have an absolutely secure pivot on my EASTERN flank on which the operations of Second Army will turn.
> *I must have* CAEN.
> Once I have got Caen, and the water-line from Caen to the sea,

[1] Dempsey Papers, PRO (WO 285/1).

securely held, I can safely develop the swing with the bulk of the Army.[1]

British armour was earmarked to perform the key role of protecting the invasion force and smashing local counterattacks:

> Then comes their *mobile* role, on the success of which a great deal depends. Having secured the *initiative*, we must on this D-Day take the fullest advantage of it, and we have planned to *thrust three strong armoured forces* well into the enemy's territory. I have marked on the map the areas which it is hoped these armoured troops will reach – VILLERS BOCAGE on the front of 50 Div, EVRECY on the front of 3 Cdn Div, and an area to the EAST OF CAEN on the front of 6 Airborne Div. There is no doubt that, if we can achieve this, we will go a long way toward dislocating the enemy's power of resistance and counterattack.[2]

Of Montgomery's four goals set in May, only the first could be said to have been fully attained by 10 July. Moreover, according to Dempsey's notes, he did not feel that the Second Army could adequately protect Bradley until the remaining three were completed. Having repeatedly failed to gain this terrain, there would be no real means of stopping Rommel from shifting panzer divisions to the west did he choose to do so. The only alternative thus left to Montgomery was to mount a series of limited offensives to ensure that these divisions were compelled to remain in the vicinity of Caen – not so much Montgomery's new strategy of forcing Rommel to retain the bulk of his armour there as Rommel's own strategy of 'roping off' the British around Caen to prevent a critical breakthrough.

The concept of 'hitting Rommel for six' had turned into a strategy of attempting to grind the German Army into oblivion by the application of overwhelming Allied air and firepower. However, what Montgomery consistently evaded was the point that Rommel still could *not* afford to shift the bulk of his panzer divisions to the American sector: had Rommel or von Kluge done so, there was no reason why a breakthrough attempt could not have been made on the eastern flank, particularly as this option had been retained as part of the original plan. It was becoming more and more obvious with each passing day that a major

[1] Dempsey Papers, loc.cit.
[2] Ibid.

confrontation southeast of Caen or along the Odon-Villers-Bocage-Caumont sector was unavoidable. As far as the US forces were concerned, it had been equally obvious for some days to both Bradley and Eisenhower that 21st Army Group was incapable of implementing the original scheme of hard jabs at the Germans from both flanks until their defences cracked and a breakthrough could take place.

Capture of the remainder of the Cotentin remained the essential American task: it was necessary to expand the First Army's front at least to Avranches, so that Patton's Third Army could be actively employed in its planned role of liberating Brittany and the valuable ports there. Montgomery's first priority remained the security of his logistical position so that the huge number of Allied forces which were due ashore by D+90 could be accommodated. By D+30 nothing had changed to dissuade him from this. On 8 July, in reply to Eisenhower's letter of the previous day, he was firm on the point that 'We must get the Brittany peninsula. From an administrative point of view this is essential; if we do NOT get it we will be greatly handicapped in developing our full potential.'[1] Still insisting that his main priority in the British sector was to attract and keep the enemy reserve divisions pinned to the Caen flank, Montgomery indicated that he would continue this strategy for the immediate future.

The problems created by a continuation of this strategy were many. For several weeks the inadequate size of the British bridgehead had threatened dire consequences, and now, even after CHARNWOOD, it was literally choking with troops and supplies. As time passed and more units arrived, so the problems multiplied as more and more supplies and equipment were required to support them, though the remainder of Crerar's First Canadian Army was long overdue and sat anxiously in England awaiting the summons to Normandy and their promised role in the campaign. The war of attrition resulting from Montgomery's change of strategy had sapped the core strength of the infantry divisions and clouded the future of several, while two of the three veteran divisions had performed so unsuccessfully that both of their commanders were about to be sacked.[2] By the conclusion of

[1] Montgomery, letter to Eisenhower, M-508, 8 July 1944, Eisenhower Papers.
[2] Erskine of 7th Armoured and Bullen-Smith of 51st Highland.

CHARNWOOD on 9 July the British front was a jagged line running from east of the Orne, through the centre of Caen and along the configuration of the Odon to the north of Evrecy, where it curved back toward Bayeux in a large semi-circle as far west as the inter-army group boundary at Caumont. The original thrust at the German flank around Villers-Bocage had turned into a large bulge currently occupied by the 2nd Panzer, the 9th SS Panzer and several infantry divisions.

As Montgomery had explained it to Eisenhower, CHARN-WOOD would be launched in order 'to set my eastern flank alight, and to put the wind up the enemy by seizing Caen and getting bridgeheads over the Orne; this action would, indirectly, help the business going on over on the western flank.'[1] Montgomery's prognosis for future operations by the Second Army was for more of the same and reflected uncertainty when he told Eisenhower: 'Having got our eastern flank on the ORNE, I shall then organise the operations on the eastern flank so that our affairs on the western flank can be got on with the quicker. It may be that the best proposition is for the Second Army to continue its effort, and to drive southwards with its left flank on the ORNE; or it may be a good proposition for it to cross the ORNE and establish itself on the FALAISE road. Alternatively, having got Caen and established the eastern flank on the ORNE, it may be best for Second Army to take over all the CAUMONT area – and to the west of it – and thus release some of Bradley's divisions for the southward "drive" on the western flank. Day to day events in the next few days will show which is best.'[2]

The great success being trumpeted in the press after CHARN-WOOD had not been in evidence on 7 July when Montgomery's BGS Plans, Brigadier Richardson, presented his chief with a rather gloomy assessment which reflected the uncertain state of affairs throughout the Allied front. Noting that in the British sector 8 divisions held a front of 77,500 yards, while in the American 9 divisions held some 108,000 yards, this document showed the Second Army outnumbering the Germans two to one in infantry and four to one in tanks, while the First Army's superiority was three to two in infantry and eight to one in

[1] M-508, loc.cit.
[2] Ibid.

tanks.[1] Richardson's appreciation warned that should the Allied deception plan (FORTITUDE) collapse, the enemy buildup would soon rise to alarming proportions. 'The period during which the enemy was completely dancing to our tune, throwing in panzer formations piecemeal to stop penetrations and operating on a hand to mouth policy is beginning to come to an end. We still have sufficient superiority particularly if we use our tanks boldly and risk the resultant losses to upset the enemy's plans and carry on with our own: to drive south until we get out of the bocage. On a very long term view time is on our side with the effects of Anvil and the Russian front coming into play. During the next two months we shall have great administrative difficulties and the volume of the American build-up will have to be diminished.'[2]

Two circumstances, one real, the other likely, troubled the 21st Army Group planners. First, the unsatisfactory configuration of the British bridgehead formed a crazy quilt pattern which '. . . with its two salients east of the Orne and across the Odon requires an extravagant use of holding units to make it secure. Three divisions alone are concerned with the Orne bridgehead, one of them an airborne division which should have been withdrawn weeks ago.'[3] However, it was the possible collapse of FORTITUDE which was seen as the gravest threat, and this was considered a far greater possibility now that Field Marshal Gunther von Kluge had arrived to take command of OB West in place of the deposed von Rundstedt. Von Kluge, they reasoned, would be more active than his predecessor in pressing the tactics of attempting to rope-off the Allied advance in the bocage:

> As regards the future there are certain disquieting possibilities, including possible re-appreciation of the situation by the new German C-in-C and abandonment of the cautious policy which has retained so many divisions north of the Seine. Were these divisions committed to Normandy a temporary stalemate would not only be possible but probable. The delay in our advance towards Brittany and the risk that we shall not obtain sufficient port capacity before the bad weather sets in. . . For

---

[1] 'Review of the Situation at D+30', Appreciation by 21st Army Group BGS Plans, 7 July 1944, (WO 205/644), PRO. US superiority in armour was of no consequence until the First Army could escape the confines of the marshy terrain of the northern Cotentin.
[2] PRO (WO 205/644).
[3] Ibid.

the next month we shall be passing through a lean period as regards the Allied build-up particularly in view of the fact that such divisions as will land are mostly armoured divisions and the pressing need is for infantry divisions.[1]

Von Kluge did, in fact, arrive determined to turn round the situation in Normandy and was quite scornful of Rommel's attitude. As Liddell Hart related it: 'Von Kluge had already been influenced against Rommel at the Führer's H.Q. by Hitler, Jodl and Keitel, who had spoken of him as independent, defeatist and disobedient. In addition, the military situation had been represented to von Kluge as not unfavourable. Consequently, he arrived at Rommel's H.Q. full of that exaggerated optimism which was shown by most Eastern front commanders on the day they first entered the Western theatre, and administered a severe censure to Rommel'[2] for his 'defeatist' attitude.

The new German C-in-C was a stern, no-nonsense 'Prussian' Junker who had acquired the nickname of 'clever Hans'. Speidel, who witnessed the first bitter encounter between the two field marshals, described von Kluge as tough, cool, energetic, quick of grasp, courageous and hardy but inclined to pose. 'He was,' said Speidel, 'remorseless in insisting on the last ounce of effort from his subordinates... He gave the impression of freshness and vigour. Kluge had just passed a fortnight in Berchtesgaden, and had not only taken instructions from Hitler on his new task; he had also let himself be convinced that the disasters in the West were the results of bad leadership and the mistakes and omissions of the armies in the field.'[3]

According to Speidel, von Kluge told Rommel imperiously: '"The recall of Field-Marshal von Rundstedt is the outward sign of Hitler's dissatisfaction with the leadership in the West. Rommel, too, does not enjoy the absolute confidence of the Führer. At Supreme Headquarters, it is thought that Rommel allows himself to be too easily impressed by the allegedly overpowering effect of the enemy weapons and is too inclined to pessimism. Rommel is also displaying an obstinate self-will and not carrying out the intentions of the Führer wholeheartedly. Field-Marshal Rommel," Kluge concluded, "you must obey unconditionally from

[1] PRO (WO 205/644), loc.cit.
[2] Liddell Hart, *The Rommel Papers*, op.cit., pp. 480–1.
[3] Lieutenant General Hans Speidel, *We Defended Normandy*, op.cit., p. 121.

now on. It is good advice that I am giving to you."[1] Stung by von Kluge's harsh criticism, Rommel sent the new C-in-C a lengthy memorandum outlining the problems encountered in attempting to defend Normandy. Rommel was especially critical of the refusal of his request before D-Day to move the 12th SS into position in the Cotentin to counterattack any Allied landings in this sector.[2]

After a sceptical von Kluge had toured the Normandy front he realized that Rommel was right. While the two men, now in general agreement with one another over the inevitable results of the German position in Normandy, attempted to work out some means of gaining more time, Montgomery's planners were citing two priority tasks for the Allied ground forces: an American breakthrough from the Cotentin south to Avranches, so that Patton could be sprung loose into Brittany; and the expansion of the British sector, not only to reduce the risk of German counter-attack but to relieve the burgeoning administrative congestion and to create sufficient space to accommodate the First Canadian Army.

On one side of the battle, Rommel was still in Hitler's doghouse for his 'defeatist' attitude while on the other, Montgomery, although he had been receiving enormous press publicity as the architect of the Allied ground campaign, found that the first thirty days had done little to enhance his reputation at the highest political and military levels. The doubts already evident in Churchill and Eisenhower had spread to Bradley's HQ, where there was growing disbelief and disgust over Montgomery's inaction and his claims to be adhering to his master plan. A number of senior officers there were appalled by what was seen as British impotence at American expense. A good deal of their ire was directed at Eisenhower who they felt should be exercising firmer control over his subordinate, Monty.

This reaction was soon exhibited at the highest level of the US War Department. In mid-July Secretary of War, Stimson toured Normandy and returned to Washington openly distressed by what he had seen there. He questioned why the ground armies

---

[1] Lieutenant General Hans Speidel, We Defended Normandy, op.cit., p. 121.
[2] Liddell Hart, The Rommel Papers, op.cit., pp. 481–4.

had made so little progress despite the almost total Allied air supremacy and the absence of the Luftwaffe. Of major concern to the War Department was the increasingly hostile attitude of the US press, who were beginning seriously to question what was going on in Normandy. The Assistant Secretary for Air, Robert A. Lovett, recorded the extent of the problem in a letter to Spaatz. After giving a press conference in July he wrote: ' . . . it became apparent that both the press and the people over here were beginning to wonder why in the heck the Ground armies didn't get rolling. I naturally avoided the question, mumbling into my beard about the difficult terrain, the ditches and hedgerow character of the countryside, etc. My evasive tactics shook them off my tail but left me convinced that this subject was a burning one. This conviction was strengthened by a blast in the *Washington Post* a few days later at the Army. . .'[1] As Lovett noted, 'The General Staff doesn't like such questions and I think was rather rudely shocked when the Secretary returned and asked what could be done to accelerate our progress, pointing out that the program was scheduled for a very much faster rate and that it had never been met at any stage in spite of the superb coverage given by the Air and the complete lousing up of all the German communication systems.'[2]

The focus of War Department unrest was not so much Montgomery as Eisenhower, who was faulted for not exercising greater control over the campaign. Even so, Montgomery was not well thought of in Washington; Marshall had developed an unfavourable impression as far back as the spring of 1943, during the planning for HUSKY and nothing he had seen during the intervening year had caused him to change his mind. Apparently even Roosevelt was expressing displeasure at the turn of events, and 'began complaining to Marshall that Montgomery was hogging all the credit and that the sooner Ike moved across the Channel and took over personal command, the better for public (and British-American) relations.'[3]

According to Lovett, 'The Secretary immediately on his return, called a War council meeting and laid it right on the line

---

[1] Robert A. Lovett, letter to Lieutenant General Carl Spaatz, 25 July 1944, Spaatz Papers, Manuscript Division, Library of Congress.
[2] Ibid.
[3] Leonard Mosley, *Marshall*, New York, 1982, p. 285.

... he recommended very bluntly that General Eisenhower be told to get his advance headquarters into France at once and the American armies know that he is the Commander-in-Chief.'[1] Marshall was equally unhappy with events in Normandy and, despite his rule for not interfering with commanders in the field, he rather bluntly told Eisenhower that it was time for him to grasp the reins of command more firmly by taking personal charge of the ground campaign. 'Marshall was nettled first of all by reports that the Press was talking of Montgomery's victories, Montgomery's forces' advance – when the troops in most cases were American. Apparently, the specific reason for his cable to Eisenhower to the effect it was time for him to take over came from a [Washington] *Post* editorial about Montgomery's slowness. There was considerable grousing by American commanders on Ike's tendency to be too easy on Montgomery.'[2] In fairness to Montgomery, there is no evidence that he actively courted the attention he was getting in the press and, as the ground commander, it was natural that press reports should credit him with both the Allied success as well as blame him for the stagnation into which the campaign was falling.

Despite the contretemps within the War Department there was no discernible change in Normandy; Eisenhower declined to be pressured into any sudden reversal of his original plan not to replace Montgomery until the Third Army was committed and Bradley elevated to the command of 12th Army Group. SHAEF had grown to such enormous proportions and had become such a cumbersome headquarters (felt by many to be grossly overstaffed) that any early move to Normandy would prove a major logistical and communications problem.

No plans had ever been laid to create a small tactical headquarters from which the Supreme Commander might have directed the campaign,[3] and day-to-day control of the ground forces from SHAEF's advance HQ at Portsmouth was simply not feasible. Marshall had conceived of SHAEF as a small strategic headquarters which would make high-level decisions and, had

---

[1] Lovett, loc.cit.
[2] Dr Forrest C. Pogue, letter to the author, 21 October 1980.
[3] Eventually a small tactical HQ called SHELLBURST was established in Normandy for Eisenhower, but this came too late to enable the Supreme Commander personally to take over control of the campaign.

he become Supreme Commander, would undoubtedly have implemented the concept. The prime architect of a large SHAEF staff was Bedell Smith, who argued (no doubt correctly) that any small HQ would inevitably expand into a big one. 'So I decided we should start out with a big staff. Besides I was tired of the concept which was growing up in the Mediterranean to the effect that Eisenhower was a political commander, while other people handled the fighting. So I argued for a full staff and got Eisenhower to see it my way.'[1]

Thus, despite Marshall's broad hints, Eisenhower remained unruffled by the critical comments filtering back to him from Washington. The Supreme Commander was clearly displeased with Montgomery but he was nevertheless simply not prepared to tinker with the structure of the Allied ground command at this critical moment when the cure might prove worse than the disease.

The earlier capture of Cherbourg and now the partial fall of Caen signalled the need for serious thought beyond the mere attainment of sufficient elbow room by expanding the Allied bridgehead. The failure of Bradley's operation to break through German defences in the Cotentin was a foregone conclusion – some new and dramatic plan had to be devised that would work. Likewise, the Second Army bridgehead had to be tidied up quickly, either as part of a concerted plan to seize control of the Caen-Falaise lateral or by means of a separate operation.

Until now the use of armour in the bocage had been limited and ineffectual, but in his 7 July report Brigadier Richardson recommended the inevitable: the use of British armour in a key role. He told Montgomery that a large armoured operation was not only desirable but absolutely essential. 'Our tank superiority is sufficient to enable us to take big risks provided a plan can be formulated to use tank superiority on ground of our own choosing.'[2] Two possibilities existed for offensive action in the near future: an infantry attack through the thick bocage around Villers-Bocage to erase the bulge that so worried Montgomery, or an armoured stroke aimed at Falaise. An infantry attack was

---

[1] Smith interview, 9 May 1947, loc.cit.
[2] PRO (WO 205/644).

bound to be of limited gain and would inevitably generate more high casualties in the ranks of the already badly depleted infantry divisions but, as the planners analyzed it, 'a thrust towards FALAISE provides an opportunity to use tanks en masse and hence to assert our great superiority in numbers. The enemy is fully alive to this, but unless we are prepared to fight him with our tanks it seems that no further progress on the British sector is likely for many weeks to come. With our great artillery superiority coupled with air supremacy it is felt that we should be justified in risking battle Southeast of CAEN but this should be done only when the weather is suitable for air action. Having fought this battle and pushed the bridgehead SOUTH as far as the FORET DE CINGLAIS, the VILLERS-BOCAGE pocket finds itself in a rather insecure position. Then should be the time to concentrate our infantry divisions for a thrust Southeastwards to straighten up the line bet‿een CAUMONT and the FORET DE CINGLAIS.'[1]

Brigadier Richardson's recommendations were, in effect, a repudiation of Montgomery's holding strategy and served as a blunt reminder to his chief that the Second Army simply could no longer avoid an all-out confrontation with Rommel: it was that or stalemate. Dempsey's later plan for Operation GOODWOOD would also necessitate great use of tanks, something Montgomery never relished.

At the same time that Richardson was presenting Montgomery with future options, Bradley was formulating a plan that he had been desirous of attempting for some time but which was only now feasible. This was for a major operation to spring the First and Third Armies free of the Cotentin once and for all. Meanwhile Dempsey, too was mulling over the possibility of a major operation by the Second Army toward Falaise. What seems clear is that by D+30 both generals were showing evidence of growing frustration over the current state of affairs on their respective fronts, and both were determined to present Montgomery with viable alternatives.

On 10 July the three commanders met at Montgomery's TAC HQ near Bayeux for one of their most important conferences of the campaign. That morning Montgomery had summoned Dempsey to his caravan. As Dempsey recalled the events of that

[1] PRO (WO 205/644).

day, ' . . . Monty rang me in the morning and indicated that the American attack was not going well and asked me to come to his TAC HQ. When I went there he said to me, "I'm afraid Brad is barely off his start-line. It'll take him another two or three weeks to organise enough strength to break out. You'll have to continue your holding battle on the left." A few minutes later Bradley arrived and we discussed the whole problem.'[1]

Their discussion opened with a review of Bradley's difficulties. Dempsey remembers Bradley saying 'that because of the flooded ground the Germans had been able to establish a strong defence line and that the forcing of this had taken all his effort. He didn't think that he could hope to launch the break out attack until he had got a good firm start-line along the St Lô-Periers-Lessay road and was well clear of the flooded ground.[2] 'Monty quietly replied: "Never mind. Take all the time you need, Brad." Then he went on to say: "If I were you I think I should concentrate my forces a little more" – putting two fingers together on the map in his characteristic way.'[3]

> Monty was wonderful. There were no recriminations – although Bradley had obviously made his own task the more difficult by trying to buck the whole line right along instead of concentrating and punching a hole in one important sector. Monty told him not to worry and not to hurry and – without Bradley realizing it – got across to him the idea that he must concentrate his forces for a solid punch at one point. Bradley probably now thinks that he thought of this himself because Monty was careful to put the suggestion very tactfully. The upshot was that Monty had ordered me to continue our battle around Caen and to keep the German forces committed there.[4]

Montgomery's order to continue making a show of force around Caen was not quite what Dempsey had in mind, as he later revealed: 'My main job now was to stop the Germans relieving their armour with the infantry divisions which were just beginning to arrive from other parts of France, and I had also at all costs to make them believe at Rundstedt's HQ and in Berlin that Caen was regarded by us as the key to the whole situation and

---

[1] 'Operation Goodwood', paper prepared by Liddell Hart based on discussions with Dempsey, 1952, Liddell Hart Papers (see also chapter 20). Bradley's offensive ended after two weeks at a cost of nearly 40,000 casualties.
[2] Ibid.
[3] Dempsey interview, loc.cit.
[4] Ibid.

that we intended to break out from Caen. I realized I would have to make the greatest possible show of force around Caen so as to keep Hitler's attention concentrated upon it. One way to do this of course would have been to continue to put in the kind of attack we put in on the Odon. But these infantry battles were very costly and I had already been warned by the War Office that my resources were limited and that I must keep a close eye on the casualties. Consequently I decided that the best way to focus attention on Caen was to make not only a major attack but a major demonstration with the Air Force.'[1]

The fact was that Dempsey had become weary of the essentially defensive role his army had been playing and was now convinced that there was an alternative method whereby he could comply with Montgomery's instructions and still achieve far-reaching results. After Bradley had departed, Dempsey proposed to Montgomery that the Second Army be permitted to make a breakthrough on the eastern flank. He argued that the operation he had in mind would effectively kill two birds with one stone: satisfy Montgomery's insistence on continued pressure on the left, and at one and the same time achieve a breakthrough in the direction of Falaise. The codename given to this proposed operation was GOODWOOD – like EPSOM, named after a famous English race course. With Richardson's report undoubtedly fresh in his mind, Montgomery gave Dempsey permission to begin planning for GOODWOOD which was tentatively scheduled for 17 July.

Bradley had discussed with Montgomery his plans to spring the First Army free of the bocage and the marshlands, which would begin on 20 July. The wheels were now set in motion for the two greatest offensives yet initiated in Normandy, one of which was finally to prove the beginning of the end for the German Army in the west.

---

[1] Dempsey interview, loc.cit.

PART III

Breakout

The hour of the great American break-out under General Omar Bradley came at last.

Winston S. Churchill

CHAPTER 19

Planning the Breakthrough: Cobra

By 11 July General Bradley had conceived the idea; two days later the idea became the First Army's plan. It was called COBRA.

Martin Blumenson[1]

The most important point to be understood about the break-through from the Normandy bridgehead is that it had little to do with the original concept laid down in Montgomery's master plan. It is true that his plan called for US forces to push south out of the Cotentin bridgehead as part of the general Allied advance, but the plans now being developed by Bradley and Dempsey were designed to accomplish decisive breakthroughs in both sectors of the Normandy front. Both plans were conceived mainly out of frustration caused by the failure of American and British armies soon after D-Day to capture certain objectives as intended and which by early July were still under German control. The attempt to break the German hold on the Cotentin had produced near-stalemate and it was this unsatisfactory situation which led Bradley to the conclusion that he must devise some means of ensuring that US forces did not fail a second time. Operation COBRA was the name given to the operation to free the Americans from the difficult bocage country round St Lô and Coutances, and its concept was specifically Bradley's.

There was no question that grievous losses in men and material had gravely weakened Army Group B and that it was only a matter of time before it would crack under pressure applied at the right time and place. The problem facing the Allied commanders was how to bring this about. A point generally

[1] *Breakout and Pursuit*, Washington, 1961, p. 187. See pp. 350–1 for a brief definition of 'breakthrough' and 'breakout'.

overlooked in the debate about Normandy has been illustrated by Martin Blumenson:

> The Germans massed their forces [around Caen] ... not because Montgomery drew them there but because they were trying to fulfill a purpose of their own. Traditional German military thought and doctrine stressed the attainment of victory by a decisive act rather than by strategy of gradual and cumulative attrition. As a consequence, throughout the month of June, the Germans sought to launch a bold and massive counterattack that would destroy the Allied beachhead and drive the Allies back into the sea. They concentrated their forces and their efforts for that decisive action in the terrain around Caen, for that was the only place they could do so – not only because, as Montgomery had calculated, the communications network converged toward that point, but also because the ground itself favored that deployment.[1]

Containment was not a strategy preferred by the Germans who for some time had nurtured hopes of launching a counterstroke powerful enough to shred the Allied front before the fateful breakthrough took place. But, given Hitler's inflexibility and the continuing success of FORTITUDE, containment was the last and only hope the battered German Army possessed. As we have seen, even von Kluge's initial arrogance and misunderstanding of the true situation soon turned into a realistic assessment that it was clearly only a matter of time before a breakthrough occurred. Time and time again his men had found a way to hold against overwhelming odds and parry what might have been a decisive breakthrough, but on each occasion the casualty lists grew alarmingly.

Bradley's operational methods bore a remarkable similarity to Montgomery's. Both generals preferred the calm isolation of their tactical field headquarters where they could ponder a terrain map and determine the course of future operations. Bradley called himself his own G–3: 'Well, I make the decisions, draw up the general plan but then turn it over to G–3 [Operations] to issue orders and go into details.'[2] His staff had constructed for Bradley a large map of Normandy covered by acetate. As he later described it, Bradley would retreat alone to

---

[1] Martin Blumenson, 'Some Reflections on the Immediate Post-Assault Strategy', in *D-Day: The Normandy Invasion in Retrospect*, Kansas, 1971.
[2] Hansen Collection, US Army Military History Institute.

his map, which was initially located in a tent and later moved into a specially designed caravan similar to Montgomery's: 'and with my colored crayons, outline various operations and would soon find out that one wouldn't work because of the road net. That's the way I made the study to find this particular place. Then after having decided on the place I still continued to draw the lines of advance using the various road nets for various divisions and worked it out to where I could visualize the divisions, which direction they would take and exactly where I wanted the concentration of bombing and firepower, and it wasn't until I had the thing quite well outlined that I brought in a corps commander that I had picked to carry out the operation, General Joe Collins.'[1]

The place picked by Bradley for a breakthrough was the St Lô-Périers-Lessay road, the only artery running roughly parallel to the route of advance towards Avranches, where the 'corner' could be turned and a breakthrough exploited.

> 'It was some time – I would guess in early July – when I began to study the terrain, the road net. Particularly, you had to look for a place where you would not be hung up by swamps or river crossings. You wanted a terrain where there was a good road net so that you could use maximum troops and one from which you could break out on the other side and have a good road net to go in different directions after you had broken through the crust of German resistance.'[2]

Given the nature of the terrain in the northern Cotentin, with its poor road network, swamps and marshes, this technique had not been attempted during his costly try at a breakthrough in early July.

For Bradley's new brainchild to succeed it was essential that certain preliminary operations be carried out. Specifically, he had to gain control of the terrain north of the long, straight Périers road; this was the vital element in fulfilling his requirement for a place where he could concentrate Collins's VII Corps on high, firm ground and avoid the swampland which would hinder an advance. This need to 'punch' his way out of the Cotentin was what Montgomery had advocated during their 10 July meeting. However, Bradley was convinced that even this approach was

---

[1] Bradley, oral history, US Military Academy Library, West Point, NY.
[2] Ibid.

hopeless until firmer ground farther south was taken where his armour could be effectively set loose. To attain this ground, located some five to ten miles south of the St Lô-Périers road, by another slow grinding offensive was no longer tactically sound; moreover, it would be too time-consuming and costly when a breakthrough was needed now.

Before the start of his earlier, abortive offensive, Bradley had made it clear that he hoped for a breakthrough then and there: 'I am very anxious that when we hit the enemy this time, we will hit him with such power that we can keep going and cause him a major disaster. I want to keep going without any appreciable halt until we turn the corner at the base of the peninsula.'[1] Instead, this massive operation was a dismal failure and never came close to a breakthrough, but it did convince Bradley that some new method had to be found.

How much influence Montgomery may have had on Bradley during the 10 July conference the latter never revealed. British and American thinking on the subject of offensive action was so divergent that any similarity between the two generals with regard to planning ended when it came to tactics. Bradley viewed Montgomery's battle tactics with some disdain: 'When Montgomery prepared to attack he dragged up everything he had for an all-out campaign – he called it "squaring up for an attack". We Americans, on the other hand, constantly nibbled away at key positions of an enemy and sought to prevent him from entrenching himself in position. We constantly kept him knocked off balance.'[2] In comparing himself to Montgomery Bradley later reflected that, 'Yes, Montgomery is conservative, far more so than I am.'[3] Yet even Bradley had to admit that his nibbling tactics did not always work, and that perhaps he had something to learn from Montgomery. Although he disliked the sort of slugging match that inevitably led to high casualties, Bradley's early July offensive had turned into just that.[4] It was not,

[1] Bradley, letter to Eisenhower, 29 June 1944, loc.cit.
[2] Hansen Collection, loc.cit.
[3] Hansen Diary, 16 July 1944, US Army Military History Institute.
[4] Weigley reminds us that: 'High as it is, the figure of 40,000 does not adequately express the cost of the campaign. It does not include the especially heavy toll of psychologically wounded imposed by the Bocage, the victims of combat fatigue severe enough to cause at least temporary disablement, who numbered an additional 25 to 33 per cent of 40,000. Some 90 per cent of the casualties were concentrated among the infantrymen'. *Eisenhower's Lieutenants*, op.cit. p. 143.

however, the last time he was to employ such tactics; in the winter of 1944 a misguided attempt to take the Huertgen Forest resulted in a gruesome butcher's bill.

To attain the terrain north of the St Lô-Périers road from which to launch VII Corps meant a good deal more close-in bocage combat. In mid-July his aide Chester Hansen, recorded Bradley saying of COBRA: 'I said I didn't want to stand up and slug but I also said that at one time we were going to have to and this is it. While in this bocage, canalized by swamps we can do nothing else. No room for maneuver. We've got to stand here and slug it out with him. Afterwards we can make the breakthrough and run deep.'[1]

What Bradley and the other Allied commanders had discovered to their dismay was how much more formidable the bocage had turned out to be in reality than had ever been anticipated in England. As Bradley candidly admitted: 'The necessity for a very concentrated punch became apparent as soon as we had established our beachhead because the German resistance was very tough. There were days when we wouldn't move, other days when, if we gained a thousand yards, we were doing pretty well, and it was slow going. You remember we were fighting through the hedgerows, the so-called bocage country and you can't appreciate that country until you have seen it. I hadn't visualized it at all as much as I had studied photographs and maps before I went in.'[2]*

One of the great unanswered questions about Normandy is why Bradley and Eisenhower so easily accepted the task of

---

[1]   Hansen Diary, 16 July 1944, loc.cit.

[2]   Bradley, oral history, loc.cit.

*   Bradley was certainly not alone in his inability fully to comprehend the problems of the Normandy bocage, a point emphasized by Bedell Smith who commented in 1945: 'All commanding officers were theoretically aware of the hedgerow terrain, but none had seen it. You cannot imagine it when you have not seen it. I had seen air photos of it but I could not imagine what it was like. None of us actually appreciated what the bocage country was really like. Field Marshal Brooke, who had fought there, was very pessimistic about our chances . . . Morgan had also fought in the country and was equally pessimistic. England had no terrain suitable for training for hedgerow tactics, though it was much discussed. Commanders did not realize the difficulties and our men could not imagine what it was like.' Interview with Bedell Smith and Major General H. R. Bull, 14 September 1945 by Roland G. Ruppenthal, US Army Military History Institute. Other commanders have told the author that the difficulties had not been adequately understood in England during the training period before D-Day, where it was not in any case possible to simulate the dense conditions later found in Normandy. See also Chapter 16 for discussion of this point.

making a major Allied effort through the dreadful terrain of the
Cotentin Peninsula? Neither has ever directly addressed this
question, although Bradley briefly mentions the problems in his
unpublished oral history transcripts. If Bradley was as surprised
by the difficulty of the Cotentin as he has admitted, so too were
his subordinate commanders. One of them, Lieutenant General
James M. Gavin, may well have been speaking for Bradley when
he wrote in his memoirs: 'Although there had been some talk in
the U.K. before D-Day about the hedgerows, none of us had
really appreciated how difficult they could turn out to be . . . the
hedgerows played a far more significant tactical role than either
the Americans or British had anticipated.'[1] The one major over-
sight in the pre-OVERLORD planning seems to have been the lack
of a suitable terrain study of the Normandy bocage and its
implications. If such a study was made by SHAEF or 21st Army
Group, it had little impact in preparing the Allied commanders
and units for what lay ahead.[2] Certainly, its favourable aspects
for German defence were not foreseen by any of the senior
commanders.

Bradley, in his desire to achieve a knockout punch that would
spring loose a strong force into the more open country of the
southern Cotentin, had to find a method of executing COBRA that
offered a strong probability of success. The solution he devised
was the saturation bombing of a narrow sector of the front,
followed by an immediate and concentrated ground attack to
penetrate the gap thus created. Russell F. Weigley's excellent
account has recently described the planning for COBRA:

> The desperation of the Bocage deadlock had driven Bradley
> and his staff to a plan uncharacteristic of the American army
> both in its emphasis on concentrated power on a narrow front
> for a breakthrough, and in its vision of the indirect approach
> and a possible envelopment of enemy strongpoints as eventual

[1] Gavin, On to Berlin, op.cit., pp. 121–2. During the invasion of Normandy Gavin was
the assistant division commander of the 82nd Airborne Division, and in August became
its commander.

[2] Lieutenant Colonel Lever, the Brigade Major of 22nd Armoured Brigade recalls
vividly that his unit had no concept whatever of the bocage. His unit trained in the
relatively open country in and around the Thetford Forest area of Suffolk, and its
commanders and men expected to find the terrain in Normandy similar to that of East
Anglia. It was not until the brigade began actual combat operations in Normandy that the
realization was graphically brought home exactly what the bocage meant. Interview of
19 April 1983.

dividends of American mobility. Adversity indeed has its uses; it had pushed Bradley to contrive an excellent plan.

The key to the initial breakthrough, to bursting the infantry stalemate, was to be partly Collins's heavy attack on a narrow front, the concentration unusual in American planning. Still more, air power was to provide the key. As Collins came into the planning, he and Bradley together called on their memories of the air strike preceding the entrance into Cherbourg. If the object was to escape a deadlock reminiscent of the First World War, they could call on a weapon never available in 1914–1918, a truly massive aerial bombardment that could exceed by many orders of magnitude any artillery preparation possible on the old Western Front.[1]

The idea for COBRA was not a result of Leigh-Mallory's concepts or of the example of CHARNWOOD but, according to Bradley, was a logical consummation of ideas which he had held from as far back as 1939. Immediately after investigating the effects of the bombing of Caen, Zuckerman and Kingston-McCloughry had been invited to a conference at Bradley's HQ to discuss the plan. Bradley and his tactical air commander, Major General Elwood 'Pete' Quesada, wanted help in setting the bomb line correctly. Zuckerman's account of this meeting is clear about Bradley's determination to break loose, with Patton poised to exploit the hole created in the German line. 'Even if they expressed little interest in Monty's operations, the Americans knew that the support provided him by the air had not helped to get him through Caen. They were determined to do better.'[2]

Bradley had picked the St Lô-Périers road for two reasons; it was a terrain feature easily identifiable by the air force who would first pinpoint and then smash the German positions by means of a saturation bombing. The other important factor in Bradley's reasoning was that the bombers could fly *parallel* to the highway and thus not mistakenly bomb portions of the US front.[2] Once a gap of some three and a half miles was opened by the bombers, Bradley intended to utilize two infantry divisions to hold open the shoulders of the bulge while two armoured divisions blitzed through towards Avranches, and a motorized infantry division drove on Coutances.

[1] Weigley, *Eisenhower's Lieutenants*, op.cit. pp. 137–8.
[2] Zuckerman, op.cit., pp. 278–9.

Bradley was determined to avoid the problems of cratering which Montgomery had recently experienced at Caen, and for this reason it was decided to use only fighter-bombers for COBRA. As Bradley recounted it: 'for several weeks prior to planning COBRA I had been hunting for an enemy concentration where strategic air might be used to wipe out a division. It was while searching for this target that this thought occurred to me one day: Why not combine this mission with the breakout, first smash a division from the air, and then tramp right on through it.'[1]

In his account of the war, Bradley argues that the use of such tactics was not a novel idea. However, the fact remained that the tactics of carpet bombing with friendly troops close by had never been successfully accomplished (Caen was still too recent to be deemed a successful example). Why did Bradley believe he could succeed with COBRA using what were – in reality – untried tactics? As explained by the US official history: 'That COBRA stirred hope of more than a limited advance – indeed, of a dissolution of the stabilized condition of OVERLORD – was attributable to the planners' belief that they could eliminate two factors that had hampered the Caen operation: the obstructions that bomb craters and debris had placed in the path of ground troops and the long time interval between the air bombardment and the ground jump-off.'[2] The history points out: 'Optimistically assessed, if COBRA could co-ordinate the blast effect of a heavy air bombardment with an overwhelming ground attack, the Americans might smash the German ring of containment. Even if COBRA achieved only limited success, the ground gained would give the Allies additional maneuver room. The operation seemed worth a trial. It at least offered a prospect of relief from the painful type of advance that characterized the battle of the hedgerows.'[3]

It will be recalled that as late as 8 July Montgomery was still uncertain about future operations and the focus of his attention was a breakthrough in the western sector which would attain the 'corner' at Avranches for the purpose of attaining Brittany. Montgomery's official documents for this period confirm this fixation on Brittany and its extreme importance logistically.

---

[1] Omar N. Bradley, *A Soldier's Story*, New York, 1951, p. 330.
[2] Blumenson, *Breakout and Pursuit*, op.cit., pp. 187–8.
[3] Ibid, p. 188.

Exploitation was not then in his mind, but the security of the Normandy bridgehead and its ability to be resupplied most certainly was. Bedell Smith made the point bluntly in 1947 when he said: 'The breakout was not planned by Monty. I remember when Eisenhower and I went to see Bradley and he made the proposal. He said we are inching forward but we will soon be up here where we can break out. I recommend we swing around. Ike said, I approve and went to Monty's H.Q. He approved and passed the word on to Bradley.'[1]

Bradley's idea was undoubtedly made more urgent by the apparent inaction on the British front and the growing belief that the Second Army would never get out of its rut. Eisenhower was rapidly losing confidence in Montgomery, as was Bradley, and the result was their solid belief that whatever breakthrough operation eventually succeeded, it would be American-inspired.

At about this same time the planners at SHAEF were deeply involved in a series of staff studies known by the codename Operation LUCKY STRIKE. By early June they had begun developing a series of scenarios which might be applied if German resistance crumbled faster than anticipated. Under Plan B of LUCKY STRIKE it was assumed that no significant enemy forces remained in Brittany nor in the area between the Loire River and the line Laval-Le Mans-Chartres, and that no strong mobile forces existed south of the Loire, i.e. an open flank.[2] Simultaneously an informal plan was also being developed which visualized a breakthrough in the west which might allow Patton's Third Army to get loose in the Loire Valley with a completely open flank to the south.

Colonel Charles Bonesteel III had been involved in the cross-Channel operations since 1942 in a variety of key planning assignments, including one of Bradley's G–3 representatives at 21st Army Group. After the war he revealed:

> No one had an idea of envelopment until after D-Day. It was about the first couple of weeks after D-Day that we worked up a plan – inner circle meeting with de Guingand, Bill Williams, Belchem and myself. We worked into the idea when British

---

[1] Smith interview with Pogue, loc.cit.
[2] Report of US Forces European Theater, 1942–6, Study No. 1, n.d. Eisenhower Papers. This study was prepared by the post-war US occupation headquarters and was probably completed some time in 1946.

action up here [round Caen] got kind of sticky; began to get the idea of getting Patton loose in the Loire valley when we could get loose. . . There wasn't anything clearly defined from standpoint of a breakout. You could do it by penetrations or increased pressure all around. Monty wanted the planned attack – like El Alamein or Mareth. I think he never realized what the bocage country meant. After things stabilized on the D plus 4 line, British tactics consisted of mounting one major attack after another. However, they were for limited objectives. Great excitement prior to the first Caen [the operations which took place immediately after the D-Day landings] when there was a feeling that they might be able to go ahead. De Guingand excited at the possibilities.[1]

This was Plan B, and its concept was this: 'The Allied plan of action contemplated a straight drive east with 21 Army Group and a portion of the U.S forces, and simultaneously, a wide sweep with a strong U.S. armored force along the north bank of the Loire to block the Paris-Orleans gap and thereafter cooperate with the other armies in the destruction of German armies west of the Seine. At the same time operations in Brittany would proceed with a minimum of troops.'[2]

As will be seen, it was essentially the LUCKY STRIKE plan which was later implemented after COBRA. There is no clear evidence of Montgomery's reaction to the plan but given that it involved three key members of his staff, it cannot have escaped his attention. What is known is that there was nothing ever mentioned by Montgomery in any of his communications at the time nor in his post-war account or memoirs. Bonesteel says only that: 'I took it personally to show Bradley about the time of Cherbourg. LUCKY STRIKE plan was very well liked in 21 Army Group and at SHAEF. Monty and de Guingand brought out the idea that it would require a single command. I explained to Bradley that there was no need for 21 Army Group to continue its control. They had developed specious arguments to the effect

---

[1] Interview with Dr Forrest C. Pogue, 18 June 1947, US Army Military History Institute. Bonesteel's experience and common sense were greatly respected by the senior British staff officers in 21st Army Group. Their trust in him made him the ideal officer to represent Bradley's views to them. Sir Edgar Williams recently recalled that Bonesteel had been 'on top of the situation' since well before D-Day. Interview with Sir Edgar Williams, 8 April 1983.

[2] USFET Study No. 1, loc.cit.

that we couldn't get Mosquitos without this control.'[1] Bonesteel also makes an astonishing revelation: 'I saw Bradley at 11 one night. Ike came visiting. I was caught in the back of the caravan while they talked. Ike was sold on the British view of single command at the time. (To fix time, this was just about the time of the attack south on the western side of the Peninsula) . . . Ike didn't change that night. One of the few times I have seen Bradley angry. Bradley argued.'[2]

Thus, while there were obviously several options being discussed in the weeks after D-Day about how a breakthrough operation might be undertaken and exploited, it is important to note that nothing was ever put forward by Montgomery himself in the form of a plan or directive. By the time Montgomery got round to outlining his future options to Eisenhower on 8 July, he was still firmly focused on capturing Brittany with the Third US Army.

Bradley himself has made it clear that Montgomery played no part in the conception and development of COBRA. In a 1946 interview with Dr Pogue he stated emphatically that: 'Montgomery did not help to plan the breakout. . . The real breakout near St Lô was not planned before the invasion. The two original plans did not have this idea. The original COSSAC plan called for a cutting of the [Cotentin] peninsula along the St Lô-Coutances line and then a swing back to Cherbourg. The other plan, which came after the front was widened involved a drive beyond St Lô and then a turn towards Brest and towards the east.'[3]

The 'other plan' referred to by Bradley was a directive issued to the army commanders on 10 July by Montgomery. In this directive he began by restating his policy of continuing to draw off the main German forces to the eastern flank. In order of priority his goals were:

(a) *First*
We must gain possession of the Brittany peninsula. From an administrative point of view this is essential; if its capture is long delayed we will be greatly hampered in developing our full potential.

---

[1] Bonesteel interview, loc.cit.
[2] Ibid.
[3] Interview with Dr Forrest C. Pogue, 14 October 1946, US Army Military History Institute.

(b) *Second*

Having captured CAEN and thus secured a sound position on our eastern flank, we must now gain depth and space in our lodgement area. We require space for manoeuvre, for administrative purposes, and for airfields.

(c) *Third*

We must engage the enemy in battle unceasingly; we must 'write-off' his troops; and generally we must kill Germans.[1]

At the time Montgomery issued this directive he was apparently not prepared to heed Brigadier Richardson's warning of the necessity for staging a major operation southeast of Caen with his armour. He had that same day heard Dempsey's arguments for GOODWOOD and, although he had given his Army Commander permission to begin planning the operation, his mind was at that moment fixed on the western flank of the Second Army which was given the following mission:

> CAEN will be held securely, and our positions in the bridgehead east of the R. ORNE to the north of CAEN will be maintained, and improved as the opportunity offers. The FAUBERG DE VAUCELLES, lying on the south side of the ORNE opposite CAEN, will be secured and a bridgehead thus gained, if this can be done without undue losses; I am not prepared to have *heavy* casualties to obtain this bridgehead over the ORNE, as we shall have plenty elsewhere. To the south of CAEN the Army will immediately operate strongly in a southerly direction, with its left flank on the ORNE.
> Objective: the general line THURY HARCOURT – MONT PINÇON feature – LE BÉNY BOCAGE.
> The Army will retain the ability to be able to operate with a strong armoured force east of the ORNE in the general area between CAEN and FALAISE. For this purpose a Corps of three armoured divisions will be held in reserve, ready to be employed when ordered by me.[2]

The First US Army was directed to pivot on its left and to swing south and east on the line from Le Bény Bocage-Vire-Mortain and Fougères. When Avranches was reached, VIII Corps was to turn west into Brittany with three infantry divisions and one armoured division. As for the remainder of the First Army,

---

[1] 21st Army Group Directive M-510, 10 July 1944, Eisenhower Papers.
[2] Ibid.

Montgomery instructed Bradley: 'Plans will be made to direct a strong right wing in a wide sweep, south of the bocage country towards successive objectives as follows:

(a) Laval – Mayenne; (b) Le Mans – Alençon.[1]

This was one of the strangest directives ever issued by Montgomery, for it directed *both* armies directly into the worst of the bocage where casualties were bound to be high and the going slow. While retaining the option of employing the all-armoured corps in the open country of the Caen-Falaise Plain, Montgomery made it clear that he would use this force only in the right conditions. 'The opportunity for the employment of this Corps may be sudden and fleeting; therefore a study of the problems involved will be begun at once.'[2] The LUCKY STRIKE option clearly had been rejected, as this directive ignored Patton's army as the instrument for a wide sweep to the Loire.

Bonesteel contends Montgomery's 10 July plan was issued without the benefit of his staff's advice, and that it 'perturbed Bradley and scared hell out of me. Based on the view that Monty had fly-trapped the Germans in the area opposing the British. I went back to get that cancelled. Got Richardson, Williams and Belchem to get them changed.'[3] As will be seen in Chapter 20, this directive did die stillborn. Three days later the Second Army operational directive for Operation GOODWOOD was issued and bore no resemblance whatsoever to Montgomery's 10 July instruction.

Montgomery's version of these events is entirely inconsistent. In *Normandy to the Baltic* he states:

> It has been made abundantly clear that the role of Second Army was to contain the main enemy strength and to wear it down by sustained offensive action. Thereby I was creating the opportunity to launch the break-out by First United States Army under the best possible conditions. Second Army was succeeding in its role because the enemy was determined to ensure that we were prevented from exploiting our armoured resources and superior mobility in the better country south-east of Caen. Once we became established in strength on the high ground south of Bourguebus, with lateral routes south of Caen, and with our eastern flank up to the sea secure, we would be able to

---

[1] 21st Army Group Directive, M-510, 10 July 1944, loc. cit.
[2] Ibid.
[3] Bonesteel interview, loc.cit.

launch attacks in strength to the south and south-east.[1]

To accomplish this object:

> It followed, as I have already remarked, that the key to
> retaining strong enemy forces on the eastern flank was the
> establishment of strong forces in the area south-east of Caen,
> and the violence of the enemy's reaction to our operations in
> the Caen sector had amply shown the measure of his deter-
> mination to prevent our progress in that direction. We were
> thus achieving our immediate object. Meanwhile I had in mind
> also the longer term aspect of our eastern flank operation. It has
> been shown that my intention was to swing the main break-out
> thrust from the west flank eastwards to the area Le Mans-
> Alençon. It would then be necessary for Second Army to wheel
> south and east to come into line with the American forces, so
> that the whole front would face east and north-east. While the
> American right flank closed the routes from Normandy to the
> gap between the Loire and Seine, the rest of the Allied strength
> would drive the enemy back against the Seine below Paris,
> while the air forces kept the bridges out and harassed the
> ferries.[2]

It cannot be over-emphasized that both before and after D-Day
the Allied commanders were not thinking in terms of a 'breakout'
except as it pertained to the seizure of Brittany. The phrase
'breakout' is one which was coined after the fact and is intended
to describe the events later precipitated by COBRA. Bradley's
concept of COBRA was to get loose of the dreadful bocage and
spring VIII Corps under Patton into Brittany whose importance
he, like Montgomery, had always understood:

> More fearful than Montgomery that the front was stabilizing,
> Bradley also showed more concern about the race for the
> buildup. No other officer outside the services of supply was so
> consistently mindful as Bradley of the Breton ports. To Brad-
> ley, Brittany was the necessary foundation on which to build
> the American army group he would soon command and the
> logistical strength to carry the Allies out of stalemate and into
> victory. COBRA took for its purpose a breakthrough and break-
> out to the Breton ports.[3]

Martin Blumenson has clearly defined the distinction between
the two concepts in the official US history:

[1] Montgomery, *El Alamein to the River Sango and Normandy to the Baltic*, op.cit.,
p. 241.
[2] Ibid, pp. 241–2.
[3] Weigley, *Eisenhower's Lieutenants*, op.cit., p. 137.

The word *breakthrough*, frequently used during the planning period, signified a penetration through the depth of the enemy defensive position. The word *breakout* was often employed later somewhat ambiguously or as a literary term to describe the results of COBRA and meant variously leaving the hedgerow country, shaking loose from the Cotentin, acquiring room for mobile warfare – goodbye Normandy, hello Brest.[1]

As it was with so many other aspects of Normandy, the popular conception has been that COBRA was somehow conceived as a brilliant masterstroke and designed to achieve spectacular results. However, the truth is far more mundane; neither Bradley, Montgomery nor their staffs ever viewed COBRA in terms other than to attain a *breakthrough* which would enable the First and Third Armies to operate in country far more favourable to exploitation than the bocage where it was presently an impossibility.

> During the twelve days that separated the issuance of the plan and the commencement of COBRA, command and staff personnel discussed in great detail the possible consequences of the attack. 'If this thing goes as it should,' General Collins later remembered General Bradley saying, 'we ought to be in Avranches in a week.' Certainly it was reasonable to hope that COBRA would precipitate a breakthrough that might be exploited into what later came to be called the breakout, but a justifiable hope did not prove a firm intention – particularly when considered in relation in the stubborn German defense in the hedgerows.[2]

Blumenson could find no reliable evidence of such a hope and none exists except as a fantasy; this is confirmed by General Collins in his autobiography when he reveals that Bradley did not tell even him during the early planning phase of COBRA of his plans for employing Patton and VIII Corps.[3] 'Perhaps in their most secret and wildest dreams American planners had visions of a COBRA that would slither across France, but as late as 18 July there were "still a few things that [First] Army has not decided yet." One of those "few things" was that COBRA was to be synonymous with breakout.'[4]

While Bradley was putting the finishing touches to COBRA, Dempsey and his Second Army staff were doing the same to a nearly identical operation – GOODWOOD.

[1] Blumenson, *Breakout and Pursuit*, op.cit., p. 197.
[2] Ibid, pp. 197–8.
[3] Collins, *Lightning Joe*, op.cit., p. 236.
[4] Blumenson, *Breakout and Pursuit*, op.cit., p. 198.

CHAPTER 20

Operation Goodwood

What I had in mind was to seize all the crossings of
the Orne from Caen to Argentan.

Lieutenant General Sir Miles Dempsey

Lieutenant General Sir Miles Dempsey, personally knighted in a
Normandy field by King George VI, found himself in an unhappy
position. Although he bore the title of GOC, Second British
Army, he had good reason to wonder what his true role really
was. Having served Montgomery since shortly after Alamein he
well knew his chief's penchant for immersing himself in the
business of running an army. But in Normandy Montgomery was
an army group commander and the Allied ground C-in-C. Yet
little had changed; Montgomery thought of himself as an army
group commander but, as Sir Edgar Williams has observed, he
acted more like an army commander. He still involved himself
closely in the affairs of the Second Army, dictating precisely what
was to be accomplished and leaving precious little initiative to his
army commander, with the result that Dempsey was treated
more like a corps commander than an army commander.[1] The
role thus given to Dempsey was one Montgomery himself would
never had accepted but it was a measure of Dempsey's loyalty
that he served in this diminished capacity without protest.

Some senior officers have questioned whether Dempsey was
little more than a colourless figurehead commander deliberately
put there by Montgomery – an impression undoubtedly height-
ened by his frequent habit of bypassing Dempsey to give orders
directly to his own subordinate commanders. O'Connor, for
example, recalled how Montgomery would frequently visit him
to ask: 'What's the form? Can you do this or that in the future?'
Sometimes new orders would come at once and on other occa-

[1] Interview with Sir Edgar Williams, 8 April 1983.

sions they would be issued to Dempsey.[1] While this practice was not altogether unusual in the British Army, it did mean that Dempsey had to formulate a role for himself. His assiduous avoidance of publicity of any sort didn't help, and even though occasional newspaper articles appeared about him in the British press, they tended to be lost in the flood of publicity which attended Montgomery. Eventually Dempsey became so frustrated that he would deliberately sit up as high as possible in his staff car so that his troops would recognize him.[2]

Few knew Dempsey well and to ask about the man is to generally draw a blank response even from those in fairly senior positions who saw a good deal of him. One of his senior staff officers, Selwyn Lloyd, later wrote of Dempsey that 'Wherever he went he inspired confidence and was a most welcome visitor to any harassed commander of a subordinate formation. Time and again he realized the tactical opportunity and saw it was exploited. . . I have never known anyone who got to the point quicker.'[3] General Richardson has called him a 'thinker' and the most intellectual general then serving in the field;[4] Brigadier Pyman, who served him as his Chief-of-Staff later in the campaign, provides an example of the cryptic manner in which Dempsey went about the business of commanding an army. In early September 1944 he sent the following order to 30 Corps: Dear Horrocks – You will capture (a) Antwerp (b) Brussels. Signed M. C. Dempsey.'[5]

Dempsey has left few personal papers, but from what is available to the historian a far stronger personality can be deduced than that suggested by his public image. He was an exceptionally loyal subordinate and neither by word nor deed ever took issue with the decisions made by Montgomery, but one can sense in several of his unpublished interviews his deepening sense of frustration at the stagnating situation the Second Army had encountered during the first month after D-Day. The need to gain an adequate foothold and the limited options open for offensive action left him with little flexibility as long as Mont-

[1] Interview with General Sir Richard O'Connor, 13 August 1979.
[2] Interview with Sir Edgar Williams, 8 April 1983.
[3] The Times, 10 June 1969.
[4] Interview with General Sir Charles Richardson, 13 November 1979.
[5] Pyman, Call to Arms, op.cit., p. 74. Horrocks replaced Bucknall on 4 August 1944.

gomery was planning the Second Army's battles. Too bright and able to continue as a figurehead, it was not surprising that by mid-July 1944 Dempsey decided that the time had come to assert his authority with Montgomery, whose tactics had not been particularly productive. Dempsey wanted to propose a viable alternative, and the means by which he chose to do so took the form of Operation GOODWOOD.

He recognized that there was little he could do about Montgomery's dictum that his main mission was to continue pinning the main German panzer force to the Caen sector, but it was not necessary to carry out his new orders by means of the tactics of limited operations which had promised so much, and had, so far, failed. Dempsey's personal notes reveal his acute awareness that the desperately needed early breakthrough would not be met by a renewal of infantry attacks. At last a ready-made opportunity existed to employ the under-used armoured divisions to deliver a killing blow on the eastern flank and, at a single stroke, crush the German hold on Caen.

By mounting a powerful armoured stroke directly into the good tank country of the Caen-Falaise Plain, the British, for the first time in Normandy, would be permitted to make effective use of their burgeoning armoured forces. The bridgehead now contained three armoured divisions (the 7th, the 11th and the Guards) as well as five independent armoured brigades and three independent tank brigades – a massive force totalling approximately 2,250 medium and 400 light tanks.[1] As Broadhurst has revealed, Dempsey had been deeply impressed by the effects of the bomber attack on Caen preceding CHARNWOOD and, like Bradley, had concluded that another operation by Bomber Command on German strong-points, blocking the approaches to the Caen-Falaise Plain, could pave the way for efforts by his armoured divisions to exploit any temporary advantage. Indeed, there was no longer any justification for this tank force not to be employed in the open country southeast of Caen.

Dempsey also wanted to limit the mounting casualties to his infantry. Daily statistics kept by his staff were not encouraging, nor was he reassured by the visit of General Adam, the Adjutant

---

[1] Ellis, op.cit., Appendix IV.

General, who came to Normandy specifically to warn Dempsey of the War Office's inability to replace infantry losses beyond the end of July. Faced with the unpleasant prospect of cannibalizing one or more of his infantry divisions to generate reinforcements, Dempsey determined to devise a new offensive which would, temporarily at least, delay the moment when such action would be necessary. He declared that: 'By contrast, our strength in tanks was increasing all the time – tank reinforcements were pouring into Normandy faster than the rate of tank casualties. So we could well afford, and it was desirable, to plan an operation in which we could utilize that surplus of tanks and economise infantry.'[1]

All previous operations by the Second Army had been master-minded by Montgomery but GOODWOOD was the brainchild of Dempsey, who not only conceived the idea of an all-armoured stroke but eventually sold the idea to his C-in-C. Given the previously unsatisfactory performance of British armour in North Africa and the constraints now imposed by the terrain of Normandy, the prospect of employing an armoured corps did not please Montgomery. Before Alamein he had faced a near-mutiny, as his authorized biographer has noted, when General Lumsden, the commander of his *corps de chasse*, had baulked at using his armour to make the breakout from the Eighth Army positions around Miteiriya Ridge.[2] In the end, Montgomery so mistrusted his own armoured commanders that he withdrew the *corps de chasse*, leaving his infantry divisions and armoured brigades to break Rommel's Afrika Korps and win the battle of Alamein.

Soon after taking over 21st Army Group Montgomery had assembled his senior staff officers to outline his philosophy of command. Mindful of his previous unhappy experience with armour, he had this to say:

---

[1] 'Operation Goodwood', Liddell Hart Papers, loc.cit. In 1952, Liddell Hart persuaded Dempsey to talk at length with him about GOODWOOD. He put together a set of notes which were amended by Dempsey with the comment: 'In general, your notes do most faithfully record what I tried to convey . . . but I would like them back one day because they put it all so clearly.' When the Cabinet Office Historical Section learned that Dempsey had spoken with Liddell Hart, they sent one of the official historians to interview him about GOODWOOD. None of what Dempsey had to say was used in the official history and the transcript (CAB 106/1061) remains closed to researchers.

[2] Nigel Hamilton, *Monty*, Part Five, Chapter 12, op.cit.

The battle fighting comes under two heads: (1) fighting (2) frigging around . . . you must keep the initiative to win; it is the easiest thing in the world to lose in battle. . . The grouping of forces is a battle winning factor. However, it cannot be done until the plan has been laid and you have decided how you want to fight. There are no such things as permanent armies or corps; only the division is set. Divisions are grouped according to this employment in the plan. I will never employ an armoured corps.[1]

Although Montgomery's tactics in Normandy tended to dismay the Americans and alarm his critics, it should be understood that they were rooted in his North African experience. His lack of confidence in both his *corps de chasse* and his mistrust of exploitation with such a force had coloured Montgomery's thinking from the beginning. One of his strongest virtues – one never appreciated by the American generals – was that he was, above all else, a realist. He knew what his troops could do and what they could not. British and Canadian troops were rock solid in the defence but, as we have seen, were less dependable in the offensive and disinclined to take advantage of opportunities – a tendency fostered by the harsh bocage of Normandy. By this stage Montgomery seemed finally to have learned that if he did not exercise caution when attacking the Germans they were very dangerous and capable of inflicting serious reverses upon his troops. The use of phase lines was a graphic manifestation of his distrust of exploitation as much as it was of his recognition that his men functioned best with specific goals laid out for them. It was all the more distressing that his plans for Normandy had gone awry in the early days and now necessitated the employment of tactics he preferred to avoid. Exploitation by his armoured forces in the period immediately following the invasion was one thing; the employment of a *corps de chasse* under present conditions was quite another.

Yet the plan outlined to him by Dempsey on 10 July was not based on these principles; instead it was a plan to employ massed armour around which a course of action was then determined. Despite his long-standing disdain of utilizing such a force, Montgomery acceded to Dempsey's proposal, doubtless feeling that it was the best option open to him. It was certainly a measure of the

[1] Notes from 21st Army Group staff conference, 13 January 1944, PRO (CAB 106/1037).

unacceptability of his present situation that Montgomery consented to the use of an all-armoured force but, as Dempsey reminds us: 'Prior to Goodwood, our position on the left flank remained dangerous, for the ground we had gained east of the Orne on D-Day gave us a very shallow bridgehead there. It barely sufficed to prevent the enemy having our beaches under observation. From the high ground near Bréville, just inside our front, the whole stretch of the beaches west of the Orne could be clearly seen. The Germans, rather surprisingly, never made a serious attack here to gain the commanding ground, but it always remained a risk until we expanded the bridgehead.'[1]

On 12 July Dempsey recorded in his diary: '1630, saw C-in-C at my HQ and told him of the plan I had formed for the use of 8 Corps next week. He approved.'[2] The plan that Dempsey had developed called for the combined resources of four corps to be employed. The three armoured divisions were to be regrouped under the command of 8 Corps and assembled east of the Orne in the small bridgehead being held by the 6th Airborne Division and 51st Highland Divisions – the same place from which Montgomery had wanted to launch EPSOM. After a thorough saturation bombing, this massed armoured force of some 750 tanks would rapidly tear open a hole in the German defensive line and outflank Caen from the east. It was expected that the shock of this blow would so shred German defences that the force could gain the heights of Bourguébus Ridge overlooking Caen and then exploit their success in the good tank country beyond.

At the same time, Crocker's 1 Corps and Lieutenant General Neil Ritchie's recently arrived 12 Corps could launch subsidiary infantry attacks, supported by armour, along the flanks, while Lieutenant General Guy Simonds's 2 Canadian Corps would attack directly south from their present positions in Caen to secure the southern half of the city – Faubourg de Vaucelles – and protect the rear of 8 Corps. Preliminary operations would begin on 15 July with diversionary attacks from the Odon sector by 12 Corps to gain a firm base and with a view to a subsequent advance towards Aunay sur Odon or Thury-Harcourt 'as the situation may indicate'. 30 Corps was meanwhile to secure the Noyers area and be prepared to exploit to the high ground

---

[1] 'Operation Goodwood', loc.cit.
[2] Dempsey Papers, PRO (WO 285/9).

north-east of Villers-Bocage 'if a favourable opportunity presents itself'.[1]

Shortly before the attack the air forces would commence a huge aerial bombardment along the lines of CHARNWOOD. The object was twofold: to clear the way for the armour to make a rapid penetration and to neutralize German positions farther to the rear. In an attempt not to repeat the mistake made during CHARNWOOD, when the bombing had preceded the ground attack by about five hours, the aerial attack in support of GOODWOOD was to be launched less than two hours prior to the movement of the lead armour. As with EPSOM, additional support was to come from over 700 guns plus naval gunfire. Plans for aerial support called for the use of both tactical aircraft and strategic bombers, making it the largest operation of its kind ever attempted in direct support of a ground operation.[2] Originally planned to commence on 17 July, but later changed to the 18th, GOODWOOD was timed to precede COBRA by two days.

In conformance with Montgomery's directive that the Second Army continue to pin down Rommel's panzers in order to leave Bradley unhindered for COBRA, Dempsey devised his plan to ensure that there would be no sudden German inclination to shift these divisions:

> The primary consideration in the 'Goodwood' plan was the necessity of hitting hard; attracting the enemy's armour to the eastern flank; and wearing down his strength there so as to weaken his capacity to resist a renewed break-out effort on the western flank. But another consideration was the need to expand the bridgehead, which was becoming overcrowded as reinforcements and supplies were pouring in all the time. To gain more room it was necessary to capture Caen, which blocked our expansion and was an awkward wedge in our flank. Its capture would loosen the enemy's hinge, and provide us with a firm hinge ('Get a firm hinge' was a term I constantly used to impress the point.) There was also an increasing need for new airfields, and the best area for these was around Caen – particularly on the Bourguébus plateau. To gain that airfield area had been a feature of our planning before D-Day. By striking first on one side of the Orne and then on the other, we should force him to bring divisions across, and be able to hit them with our air force in the process of crossing, when they

[1] Ellis, op.cit., p. 334.
[2] Ibid, p. 335.

were particularly vulnerable. I called this 'tennis over the Orne'.[1]

While Dempsey had conceived GOODWOOD as such a powerful armoured threat that the Germans must move their reserves to meet it or run the risk of a complete breakthrough, he had also chosen a sector fraught with potential difficulties.

Firstly, the area chosen for 8 Corps to assemble was not suitable for surprising the Germans. One of the drawbacks was the Colombelles steelworks in the eastern suburbs of Caen; from as far away as the Odon battlefield nearly ten miles to the southwest, its enormous towers were clearly visible like massive fingers pointing at the sky. The Germans still controlled Colombelles and thus possessed the priceless advantage of unhindered observation from the towers of the entire Caen area. Any attempt to move the three armoured divisions – all of which were then located well to the west of the city – to their start-line east of the Orne would be detected at once, and so any such movement was impossible until immediately prior to the operation.

The terrain stretching south and southeast of Caen is open, rolling agricultural land, consisting mostly of cornfields punctuated by an occasional copse. The fields slope gently up towards the heights of Bourguébus Ridge. Though this high ground is a mere hundred yards above sea level, it nevertheless provides a defender with a virtually unobstructed view back over Caen and its suburbs to the south and east. Nearby, the Caen-Falaise road runs in a straight line to Falaise, twenty-one miles to the southeast, while about three miles east of this highway run the two main rail lines linking Caen with the rest of France. The entire area between Caen and Falaise is honeycombed with small, nondescript farming hamlets, most of which had been converted into fortified German strongpoints.

GOODWOOD's success was in large part dependent upon the air force neutralizing the guns sited on Bourguébus Ridge and in the nearby villages of Bras, Soliers, and Hubert Folie, all of which provided excellent fields of fire directly into the proposed British route of advance. The two railway embankments were also natural barriers and would be dangerous obstacles for approaching tanks: while they offered momentary protection

---

[1] 'Operation Goodwood', loc.cit.

they could be breached only through small road tunnels which were obvious targets for the German gunners.

Still, the most serious problem facing the British was how to retain the element of surprise. The plan was bold but for boldness to succeed the armour must move nearly 12,000 yards from their start-line to gain Bourguébus Ridge. As long as the eastern and southern sections of Caen remained in German hands, the necessity of having to initiate GOODWOOD from the east bank of the Orne was a severe complication. How then to prevent detection of a huge armoured force approaching within sight of the German observers in the towers of Colombelles? O'Connor's solution was to order his three armoured divisions to proceed by blackout night movement under the cover of friendly artillery fire. While this might not eliminate detection, O'Connor hoped by this means to reduce that possibility. Once near the west bank of the Orne only the leading division – the 11th Armoured – was to be permitted to cross the river on the night of 17–18 July. The Guards and the 7th Armoured were to be held back there until the start of the operation. 8 Corps was presented with a traffic problem of monumental proportions, for there were only *six* available crossing sites over the Orne. A British armoured division in 1944 consisted of 286 tanks, 261 scout cars, 100 armoured cars, and 2,098 lorries of assorted sizes: a total of 2,745 vehicles; thus for the three divisions, the total came to well over 8,000 vehicles.

If there was any real key to success Montgomery and Dempsey considered it to be the preliminary bombing, especially since there were problems in providing adequate artillery support after the first few hours: there was a shortage of 25-pounder ammunition but, more importantly, the area chosen for GOODWOOD was totally unsuited for the constant artillery support required to keep the Germans off-balance. To put the artillery within supporting range meant moving the guns into the narrow salient east of the Orne and this could be accomplished only *after* the tanks had cleared the area. Moreover, if all went according to plan the leading elements would soon be out of range, so the solution lay in heavy air support, which would minimize the need for artillery by taking out enemy strongpoints, guns and tanks.

Having decided on a need for full air support, Montgomery and Dempsey next faced the problem of how to ensure that it would be approved without the protest and procrastination which had occurred in the past. Montgomery was well aware of the prolonged and often vicious infighting over the use of strategic bombers to attack railway targets in France prior to the invasion. 'Bomber' Harris had never made a secret of his opposition to using Bomber Command in support of ground operations, and despite their previous employment only days before, Montgomery suspected that the idea of diverting large numbers of strategic aircraft in support of GOODWOOD would be accepted only if he could convince Harris and the other air chiefs of the benefits to be derived from their support.

Montgomery had written to Eisenhower on 12 July: 'Grateful if you will issue orders that the whole weight of the airpower is to be available on that day to support my land battle. . . My whole eastern flank will burst into flames on Saturday. The operation on Monday may have far-reaching results. . .'[1] To emphasize the importance of the operation, Montgomery asked Eisenhower to keep all visitors away from his TAC HQ for the time being. The same thing had been said prior to CHARNWOOD, but despite his growing misgivings about Montgomery, Eisenhower took the bait and replied with an equally exaggerated letter: 'I am confident that it will reap a harvest from all the sowing you have been doing during the past weeks. With our whole front acting aggressively against the enemy so that he is pinned to the ground, O'Connor's plunge into his vitals will be decisive. I am not discounting the difficulties, nor the initial losses, but in this case I am viewing the prospects with the most tremendous optimism and enthusiasm. I would not be at all surprised to see you gaining a victory that will make some of the "old classics" look like a skirmish between patrols.'[2] Eisenhower added that Bradley would 'keep his troops fighting like the very devil, twenty-four hours a day, to provide the opportunity your Armoured Corps will need, and to make the victory complete.'[3]

Eisenhower's enthusiasm for GOODWOOD and his high expectations quickly infected even the sceptical Tedder, who wrote to assure Montgomery: 'All the Air Forces will be full out to support your far-reaching and decisive plan to the utmost of their

---

[1] Quoted in Pogue, *The Supreme Command*, op.cit., p. 188.
[2] Ibid.
[3] Ibid.

ability.'[1] As recorded by his PA, Wing Commander Scarman, Tedder's diary for 14 July records that both he and Eisenhower were 'immeasurably happier at this turn of events. Chief [Tedder] anxious to move Army to action, even if weather makes full air support impossible. Monty seems to have accepted this view.'[2]

Not only was GOODWOOD seen as a major step away from what SHAEF viewed as Montgomery's excessive caution and defence-mindedness, but it also seemed to create a new mood of goodwill and confidence after the disappointments over the rate of advance. Sadly, this mood soon degenerated into the exact opposite and relations worsened beyond repair throughout the remainder of the war in Europe. However, all that was in the future; for the moment SHAEF's optimism was intensified by the receipt of Dempsey's operational order on 13 July, which assigned the following tasks to 8 Corps:

> On 18 july will cross R. Orne North of Caen, attack south-wards and establish an Armd. Div. in each of the following areas:-
> BRETTEVILLE SUR LAIZE – VIMONT – ARGENCES – FALAISE.[3]

The mention of Falaise ignited the imagination of Eisenhower and Tedder. If Montgomery intended to drive that far, GOODWOOD would certainly not be another of the by now familiar battles for position. The Second Army plan signalled only one thing: *breakthrough*!

Montgomery lost no time in pressing his request for full air support, presenting it to Coningham, who passed it to the air commanders at the daily AEAF conference at Stanmore on 15 July. According to Leigh-Mallory: 'Coningham has changed his attitude. At this morning's conference he laid before me in detail exactly what the Army wanted, and then left it to me to take the necessary steps. Tedder listened and said nothing. I think he has been told by Ike to leave things to me.'[4] The trouble was that Leigh-Mallory could not be forceful enough, with the result that while there were no objections from the other air chiefs neither was there any firm decision. These discussions continued the

---

[1] Quoted in Pogue, *The Supreme Command*, op.cit., p. 188.
[2] Tedder Diary, 14 July 1944.
[3] Second Army Operational Instruction No. 2, 13 July 1944, War Diary, Second Army, PRO (WO 171/196).
[4] Leigh-Mallory Diary, 15 July 1944.

following morning; the AEAF historical record suggests that there was some concern about the weather and the possibility that it might force a delay. There certainly seemed to have been agreement in principle to support GOODWOOD but the cumbersome command structure of the air forces was never more clearly evident than in this plethora of talk and complete absence of decision.

Montgomery was committed to postponing GOODWOOD unless he received a guarantee of support by the strategic air forces, and with less than forty-eight hours left he needed a firm decision at once. Understandably apprehensive, he ordered his BGS Plans, Brigadier Richardson, to England on 16 July with the assignment of breaking the impasse at Stanmore before it was too late. Richardson was well equipped for this task, having previously represented 21st Army Group there. The experience left him with vivid memories:

> I was invited to speak at the conference, and so I said what General Montgomery wanted, and this thing was kicked around and no decision of any sort was arrived at. At the end of it I went up to Tedder and said I've got to get a decision on this, either it's on or not. What do I do next? And he said, 'You'd better go and see Air Marshal Harris.'[1]

Tedder played a curiously detached and minor role in this affair. As the coordinator for all major air operations in support of SHAEF, a responsibility he had usurped from Leigh-Mallory, he was the one person capable of breaking the logjam of procrastination by exerting pressure on Harris and on Spaatz, whose 8th US Air Force would also be involved. Instead, he left the problem to a junior army officer to resolve. His earlier promise to Montgomery was now showing itself to be rather hollow.

Several hours later Richardson was ushered into Harris's office in the massive underground complex at Bomber Command HQ outside High Wycombe. Harris's first words were: 'Richardson, what do you want?' After listening to the army requirements, Harris pressed a bell and said: 'Send me Air Vice Marshal Bennett – the Pathfinder!'[2] With Bennett present, Harris demanded: 'Tell Bennett!' And for the third time that day Richardson repeated his story; when he finished Harris turned and said

---

[1] Richardson interview, loc.cit.
[2] Air Vice Marshal D. C. T. Bennett, AOC, the Pathfinder Force of Bomber Command.

'Bennett, can you do it?' Bennett replied, 'Yes, sir,' and Harris announced: 'It's on! Richardson, you go and fix up the details with Bennett.'[1]*

While the question of air support was being resolved, Montgomery was making crucial and unexpected alterations to the GOODWOOD plan. Dempsey's original operational order had been published on 13 July, but by the 15th Montgomery had doubts about Dempsey's intent to drive on Falaise. Apparently worried that his two subordinate commanders might have misinterpreted their mandate, he went to O'Connor's HQ at noon where, in their presence, he sat down and wrote out a revised directive. Dempsey describes how Montgomery said to him: '"Let's be quite clear about this" – and wrote out a personal directive for me, headed "Notes on Second Army Operations". It was the first time, and the last, that he gave such a written directive.'[2]

These 'Notes' radically changed the 8 Corps mission to that of establishing *all three* armoured divisions in the area, Bourguébus – Vimont – Bretteville-sur-Laize. The only mention of Falaise was that armoured cars should push far to the south in the direction of Falaise, spread alarm and despondency and, as Montgomery put it, discover 'the form'. Little was said about future operations other than a vague comment of 'cracking about' as the situation permitted.

Two things now happened which were to prove a later source of trouble. First, knowledge of Montgomery's new directive to the Second Army was confined to those involved, and not even Main HQ, 21st Army Group was aware that there had been a change in the plan. Second, a revised operational order was issued by the Second Army on 17 July but the copy destined for SHAEF never arrived. Thus, as the date for GOODWOOD drew near, SHAEF still believed that the main object of the operation was to capture Falaise.

Various explanations have been offered for Montgomery's

---

[1] Richardson interview, loc.cit.

* Harris is portrayed as difficult and stubborn when it came to the support of ground forces, but in this instance he willingly acceded to Montgomery's request. Richardson got quicker action from Harris in a few minutes than all the talk at Stanmore had produced in two days. The removal of this final obstacle came none too soon, for there were barely forty hours left before H-hour.

[2] 'Operation Goodwood', loc.cit.

action. The official history argues that he feared that COBRA would probably not follow immediately after GOODWOOD, so it might prove necessary for the German armour to be held there for some days until Bradley could launch his attack: 'The first and most important task therefore was to win a stronger position from which to fight the German armour on the Caen flank.'[1] This argument is suspect on several counts. Even though Montgomery was suggesting breakthrough to SHAEF, there had never been any misunderstanding between Montgomery and Dempsey over what the Second Army commander was to accomplish, nor did Dempsey need reminding that it would be impossible to establish an armoured division in the Falaise area without first capturing Bourguébus Ridge. Furthermore, it would have been impossible for the Germans to detach their armour and move it clear across the Allied front in time to hinder Bradley: to have done so would have been suicidal and left the way open for the British to breakout to the east – the Seventh Army, defending in the Cotentin, would then have faced the choice of possible encirclement from the east or withdrawal to the south.

ULTRA was providing unmistakable evidence that the German High Command was expecting major attacks in both the Caen and Cotentin sectors. Of particular concern was an expected drive by the British on the Caen-Lisieux-Evreux axis, combined with an expected landing between the Somme and the Seine by the First US Army Group, the non-existent force in England 'created' by FORTITUDE.[2] Thus to argue that the Germans would even consider moving their armour away from Caen is absurd.

None of this was any concern to the harried O'Connor, whose problems were more immediate as he and his staff struggled with the problem of how to mount an extremely complex operation on short notice in an unfamiliar area. O'Connor had argued that Crocker was far better qualified to direct GOODWOOD and knew the terrain intimately but Dempsey would not change his mind. An example of the extraordinary problems faced by 8 Corps took place on 16 July when it was discovered that a British minefield which lay directly across the initial axis of advance could not be cleared before H-Hour without sacrificing secrecy. This minefield had been hastily laid some days earlier by

[1] Ellis, op.cit., p. 330.
[2] Bennett, *Ultra in the West*, op.cit., pp. 92–3.

the 51st Division and had not been properly charted. Now the entire minefield was overgrown with corn and the best that could be done was to clear a few narrow lanes through which it would be necessary to funnel the three armoured divisions.[1*]

Post-war accounts differ about how much Montgomery and Dempsey confided in O'Connor over the aims of GOODWOOD. Dempsey said he did not discuss his idea of GOODWOOD as an exploitation. 'The idea of such an exploitation was in my mind but I did not discuss it with, or disclose it to, my subordinates. In framing the plan, I confined it and the orders to the opening phase – of securing the high ground south of Bourguébus – in strict accordance with Montgomery's instructions.'[2] O'Connor did not remember Dempsey ever mentioning GOODWOOD as an exploitation and in his orders to his division commanders he did not specify anything other than the initial objectives.[3] Nevertheless, another account reveals that: 'The divisional commanders were told that it was hoped that Falaise would be reached, and this objective was provisionally assigned to the 11th Armoured Division. Major General Roberts related that "We had discussed in conference with Dick O'Connor what should be done after we were firmly established on the high ground beyond Bourguébus and I am quite sure that Falaise was in everyone's mind as a point to be aimed for." When [Major General] Hobart went up to 8th Corps HQ before the battle, O'Connor consulted him as to "the best formation in which the three armoured divisions should move once they had broken through into open country".'[4]

In spite of Montgomery's more conservative orders, Demp-

---

[1] Extracted from Engineer Report by Major Geoffrey Galloway, CRE, 51st Div, Liddell Hart Papers.

[*] Up to three nights before GOODWOOD the 51st Division had been told to hold defensively against a possible German armoured attack. The mines had been laid over a ten-day period; now suddenly the division was ordered to lift them all in two days *by night* to avoid German detection. The task involved both anti-personnel and anti-tank mines; the area had been heavily shelled, resulting in some being detonated, buried or displaced; recording had not been accurate due to the hasty laying, enemy interference and bad weather. The Highland engineers did the best they could in the two nights given them but it was futile; the best that could be done was to clear fourteen gaps the width of a tank plus ten yards on either side, with three more being added at the last moment. After GOODWOOD, when the task could be done by day, it took three companies of Royal Engineers *five days* to clear this minefield.

[2] 'Operation Goodwood', loc.cit.

[3] O'Connor interview, loc.cit.

[4] Paper by Liddell Hart, 'The Aims of Operation GOODWOOD'. Liddell Hart Papers.

sey remained optimistic that a breakthrough was possible. On the eve of GOODWOOD he moved his TAC HQ up to 8 Corps:

> I said to myself: 'As it's more than possible the Huns will break, I will move my TAC HQ up to 8th Corps' HQ. By 1200 hours we may get a report from the leading armour that there are no more enemy in sight – and then what are we going to do? I must be prepared for that.' I felt that the decision couldn't be left to the Corps Commander – I must be up forward myself, so that I could take over and direct the exploitation. What I had in mind was to seize all the crossings of the Orne from Caen to Argentan – the nearer ones with the Canadians, and the further ones with the armour – thus shutting off the enemy's main force, which lay west of the Orne. The air, too, would have been concentrated on the crossings. I had these all marked. What would the Germans have done? First, probably they would have tried to strike eastward over the Orne. If blocked there, as was probable, they would have had to retreat southwards – the only course left open to them. I felt fairly confident of being able to check any eastward attack on their part, once I had secured the crossings.[1]

It was not until nearly 0200 hours the morning of 18 July that the operation was finally confirmed for the coming dawn. Expectations were varied: Dempsey evidently foresaw the opportunity for a complete breakthrough; Montgomery had refused to commit himself beyond the capture of Bourguébus Ridge; and SHAEF was confidently expecting big results. What none of them had grasped was the strength and depth of the German defences in the GOODWOOD sector. Despite the night movement of the armour the Germans had long since detected this shift and were expecting a major attack. In the days prior to GOODWOOD the Second Army's daily intelligence summaries, while admitting some uncertainties about the location of several of the German panzer divisions, provided no evidence that they were aware of a strong defensive buildup across the Orne. The final summary issued on 17 July contained an ominous hint that the enemy might have as many as 230 tanks east of the Orne, but inexplicably dismissed this possibility by suggesting that the attacking force would probably not encounter more than three divisions, totalling 120 tanks.[2]

---

[1] 'Operation Goodwood', loc.cit.
[2] Second Army Intelligence Summary No. 43, 17 July 1944, Dempsey Papers, PRO (WO 285/3).

This intelligence lapse unfortunately coincided with a definite lull in the interception of German signals by ULTRA. In the week prior to GOODWOOD few intercepted signals emanated from Bletchley Park to Allied intelligence officers, and those that did provided no warning of what was occurring on 'the other side of the hill'.[1] Nevertheless, ULTRA did suggest that the Germans were not in the dark about Allied intentions. Shortly after midnight on 15–16 July ULTRA intercepted a signal from Field Marshal Hugo Sperrle, commander of Luftflotte 3, forecasting a largescale attack that would be ' "*decisive for the course of the war to take place south eastwards from Caen about the night of 17–18th*". [Author's italics.] By midday – that is, thirty-six hours before GOODWOOD was launched – this forecast was in the hands of those who were at that moment putting the finishing touches to the plan of attack.'[2] This was the best ULTRA could provide and it was evidently insufficient to shake the confidence or cause undue alarm within 21st Army Group. As they would discover, it would have been wise to question whether tactical surprise could be attained.

What the British did not know was that the Germans, under the direction of the new commander of Panzer Group West, General Heinrich Eberbach, had prepared the strongest defensive line yet mounted in Normandy to counter this new threat. The next day was to demonstrate yet again the seemingly endless habit of the Allies to underestimate the tenacity of their opponent.[3]

17 July was a day of misfortune for the German Army. Early that evening Rommel's staff car was attacked by two RAF Spitfires near the village of St Foy de Montgomery as he was returning from the front to his Army Group B headquarters at La Roche-Guyon: his open-topped Horch crashed into a tree, spewing its three occupants on to the road. Rommel was taken to a nearby hospital unconscious and with grave head injuries, so serious in fact that there was no question of his returning to Army Group B. He was later invalided home to Germany, his last battle

---

[1]   Bennett, op.cit., p. 108.

[2]   Ibid, pp. 108–9.

[3]   On 17 July Dempsey recorded in his diary: '1430 hours – Saw Commander 8 Corps at his Headquarters. I gave him the enemy dispositions as known to us this morning. They are at present very favourable to tomorrow's operation.' Dempsey Diary, PRO (WO 285/9).

Above: British vehicles and armour waiting to cross one of the six congested bridges over the Orne during the start of Operation GOODWOOD, 18 July 1944.

Below: After savage fighting, the important crossroads town of St Lô fell on 18-19 July during the buildup for Operation COBRA.

Above left: Lieutenant General Patton checking the disposition of German forces during the drive towards the Seine in August (*left*, Major General Gaffey).

Above right: Lieutenant General Dempsey, Commander, British Second Army (*center*) with Montgomery and Bradley.

Below: American infantry moving up to Mortain in August. The fights for Mortain and Hill 317 nearby were two of the outstanding Allied small-unit actions of the Second World War.

Part of the carnage of the Falaise Gap, where what had been the most modern army in the world was largely reduced to using horse-drawn transport in an attempt to escape the Allied trap.

Above: Some 10,000 German soldiers died in the Argentan-Falaise pocket. An estimated 50,000 were taken prisoner and were for a time kept in temporary prison camps.

Below: An indelible image of twentieth-century European war: Jerusalem Cemetery, one of sixteen British military cemeteries in Normandy and the smallest. All Allied military cemeteries remain to this day beautifully maintained by the Commonwealth War Graves Commission and the American Battle Monuments Commission.

fought. It was ironic that Rommel's removal from the war should come near a village bearing the name of the general who kept his picture displayed in a prominent place in his mobile office. Rommel had done his best to defend Normandy against the overwhelming forces of the Allies but his task had been hopeless from the beginning. His quarrels with von Rundstedt and von Schweppenburg over strategy, and the implacability of Hitler, doomed his task to one of futility. Within months he would die by his own hand as a result of his involvement in the 20 July plot against Hitler. In one of the more perfidious actions of his rule, Hitler personally ordered an elaborate State funeral for the hero of the Reich he had murdered.[1]

Dawn comes early in the high summer of Europe and on the morning of 18 July it was evident that this would be an exceptionally clear day over the battlefields. Three armoured divisions were poised on both banks of the Orne, and the infantry of three corps anxiously awaited the coming of the bombers: in the distance, from the direction of the Bay of the Seine, could now be heard the unmistakable sound of massed aircraft. Bomber Harris was about to make good his promise of all-out support for Montgomery. The great showdown on the eastern flank was about to begin.

[1] Rommel's involvement in the anti-Hitler plot was never more than indirect, but there were too many links from the plotters to the Field Marshal, including his own Chief-of-Staff, Speidel, who was an active conspirator and was arrested by Gestapo. As was his custom, Hitler left his dirty work to others, and on 14 October 1944 two senior Army officers from Berlin visited Rommel at his home near Ulm. He was given the choice of returning with them to Berlin to face one of Hitler's kangaroo 'People's Courts' or to commit suicide by swallowing a poison capsule. In the ultimate act of perfidy, Hitler had arranged for von Rundstedt to deliver the funeral eulogy and the old field marshal did so in the belief that Rommel had died of his wounds from Normandy, which had been the 'official' version.

CHAPTER 21

Into the Cauldron

> The attack we put in on July 18th was not a very
> good operation of war tactically, but strategically it
> was a great success, even though we did get a
> bloody nose. I didn't mind about that. I was pre-
> pared to lose a couple of hundred tanks. So long as I
> didn't lose men.
>
> Lieutenant General Sir Miles Dempsey

At 0530 hours on the morning of 18 July Panzer Group West found itself the target of one of the most awesome air attacks ever launched against ground troops. The first wave alone dropped six thousand tons of bombs on German positions along the Orne from Colombelles to Manneville, on Cagny and in the area from Touffreville to Emiéville. A preliminary analysis compiled by the AEAF shortly afterwards reported that the entire drop had been approximately 6,000 one-thousand-pound bombs and 9,600 five-hundred-pound bombs on the three target areas.[1] A second bombing attack began at 0700 by medium bombers of the Eighth and Ninth US Air Forces, but by this time there were such thick clouds of smoke and dust over the battlefield that many aircraft could not find their targets and had to return to base without dropping their bombs. At 0830 more bombers of the Eighth Air Force completed the task by dropping nearly 13,000 hundred-pound and over 76,000 twenty-pound fragmentation bombs in the area of Bourguébus Ridge. Before the day ended more than 4,500 Allied tactical and strategic aircraft had been in action against the Germans east of the Orne. As with EPSOM three weeks earlier, the Bomber Command attack had been followed up by the massed artillery fire of three corps, supported by naval

---

[1] 'Preliminary Analysis of Air Operations – "GOODWOOD"', July 1944, PRO (AIR 37/762).

gunfire, which together hurled nearly a quarter of a million rounds on to the GOODWOOD battlefield. De Guingand was one of those to witness the attack:

> I drove out with Air Marshal Coningham to see the bombers attack. It was a perfect opal summer morning. . . We climbed up into a haystack from which we could see the factory area of Caen [Colombelles] and waited for things to happen. Before long we could hear a drone, and almost immediately the northern and eastern skies were full of aircraft. It looked just like a swarm of bees homing upon their hive. I thought how terrible it must be to suffer under the Harris technique in a German town. . . One appreciated the great bravery of those pilots and crews as they flew straight into the most ghastly looking flak. Every now and then an aircraft would burst into flames and usually shortly afterwards a few parachutes could be seen making their way to earth.[1]

Theoretically everything and everyone in the target areas should have been destroyed but in fact the bombing was not completely successful. Leutnant Freiherr von Rosen, the acting commander of 3rd Company, 503rd Heavy Tank Battalion, was positioned with his unit in the orchards outside Emiéville when the bombing began. This sector was pounded for nearly two and a half hours, first by the heavies of Bomber Command and later by medium bombers and artillery fire. The noise was so deafening that all he could remember saying to himself was 'Will there never be an end to these explosions?' Suddenly, the bombardment stopped and there was an eerie silence across the battlefield. When von Rosen emerged from his tank he found that where the bombing had been accurate the devastation was nearly total; some of his Tiger tanks had been literally buried and others turned upside down as if their 58-ton weight had been no more than playing cards. Some of the men who had survived were dazed and demoralized, others were crazed from the incessant bombing and shelling, describing the experience as a vision of hell.[2]

Somehow, though, the bombardment had failed to knock out all of the anti-tank guns and tanks situated in and around the hamlets of Cagny, Emiéville and Bourguébus, which covered the British avenues of approach down the corridor from the Orne

[1] De Guingand, *Operation Victory*, op.cit., p. 403.
[2] Quoted in film 'Operation GOODWOOD', produced for the Directorate of Army Training, Ministry of Defence.

bridgehead. The artillery behind Bourguébus Ridge was untouched and a battery of four German 88s survived unscathed in Cagny. Moreover, the bombing had once again caused severe cratering in some sectors, rendering many roads impassable and leaving an enormous cloud of dust over the battlefield.[1]

As was to be expected, there was great congestion at the six crossings over the Orne where, as far as the eye could see, the roads were choked with slowly moving vehicles and dust. Despite the monumental task facing the traffic controllers the movement was orderly as units patiently waited their turn to cross the Canal de Caen and the river. The most serious problem was still the minefield: the need to funnel all vehicles and tanks through the narrow passages in the 'friendly' minefield made movement deliberate and difficult, and greatly hindered the deployment of the Guards and 7th Armoured Divisions. Dempsey had anticipated the problems O'Connor would face in deploying his armour at the last minute and when he gave the 8 Corps Commander a copy of Montgomery's 15 July 'Notes' his guidance was: 'What we want over there are tanks. It doesn't matter about anything else . . . Don't worry about your infantry or your sappers or field ambulances or any of your [administrative] tail. Just get the tanks and the motor battalions over.'[2]

Despite the immense obstacles the ground attack was launched promptly at 0730 hours as the lead armour of the 11th Armoured Division – the 29th Armoured Brigade – began its dash into the narrow corridor of the GOODWOOD battlefield. After a rapid advance, which brought leading units to the vicinity of Cagny, the attack began to slow noticeably at about 1100 hours. German 88s and Tigers which should have been knocked out by the air attack suddenly and unexpectedly came into action and began engaging British tanks, many of which were caught like sitting ducks in the open.

Commanded by the highly regarded Major General G. P. B. 'Pip' Roberts, the 11th Armoured was generally considered the

---

[1] After GOODWOOD, Professor Solly Zuckerman made a study of the bombing and found that there had been extensive cratering in many places. It was not unusual to find craters up to forty feet across and twelve feet deep.

[2] Interview with Chester Wilmot, loc.cit. Dempsey's guidance to O'Connor arose from the fact that he realized the sheer impossibility of getting the three armoured divisions through the bottleneck in sufficient time and thus attempted to alleviate the problem by having O'Connor push the tanks across first. As will be seen, this was only partially successful.

best British armoured division to fight in Northwest Europe. Roberts was a veteran of the Eighth Army where his 22nd Armoured Brigade had played a pivotal role in the battle of Alam Halfa. Later, he had briefly commanded the 7th Armoured Division as a brigadier and the 56th Armoured Brigade of the 6th Armoured Division, before assuming command of the 11th Armoured in 1943. In 1944, at the age of thirty-seven, he was the youngest divisional commander in the British Army. The 11th Armoured had previously been commanded in England by the legendary 'Hobo' Hobart, and, as Roberts has related, the division had been trained exceptionally well in fundamentals – communications, wireless discipline and drills for movement.[1] O'Connor considered Roberts the best armoured division commander in the theatre, and years later recalled that no one had ever had a bad word to say about him. 'He was quite first class.'[2]

One of the missions assigned to Roberts by O'Connor was the capture of the villages of Cuverville and Demouville, both of which were directly along the route of the 11th Armoured advance. Roberts was not happy with this task, believing that their capture would divert too much of his infantry from the more important responsibility of supporting the rapid advance of the 29th Armoured Brigade before the Germans could recover from the shock of the bombing. Before the operation began he remonstrated with O'Connor that this mission ought to be assigned to the 51st Highland Division, who were to support the left flank of the Canadian advance down the east bank of the Orne during their attack to capture the Faubourg de Vaucelles. As Roberts later recounted the story, 'It meant that half the division was engaged on the front lines. . . I not only spoke to Dick O'Connor about it but I wrote to him and said that this is a grave disadvantage to my division, and I was told that if I didn't like the plan because of my experience and so forth, then one of the other divisions could lead.'[3] At the time Roberts never understood what he considered to be O'Connor's excessive caution, and it

---

[1]   Interview with Major General G. P. B. Roberts, 9 January 1980.
[2]   Interview with General Sir Richard O'Connor, 13 August 1979. The men of the 11th Armoured have never forgotten their exceptional commander. In 1979, while the author was touring the Normandy battlefields during the anniversary of the D-Day landings, a group of former 11th Armoured troopers were overheard to comment on the quality and inspiration of their general and how sorry they were that he had been unable to make the reunion that year.
[3]   Roberts interview, loc.cit.

was only after the battle that he learned of Montgomery's 'Notes', which he believes was the reason. In his instruction to O'Connor and Dempsey, Montgomery had written that 'The eastern flank is a bastion on which the whole future of the campaign in N.W. Europe depends; it must remain a firm bastion; if it became unstable the operations on the western flank would cease.'[1] According to General Roberts:

> I never knew the reason until I saw the 'Notes' by Monty which said that this must be a bastion and therefore, the existing front troops (i.e., the 51st Division) were held there in case anything went wrong with the breakout... It was still carrying that instruction too far because with the Canadians attacking on our right, with the 3d [Br.] Division attacking on our left, and with us in the middle, it would have been impossible for the Germans to have laid on a counter attack if the people sitting in the trenches had moved forward two miles. It was an absurd idea. But it was necessary for them to remain in their trenches until somebody else had taken Cuverville and Demouville.[2]

O'Connor refused to budge and the best that Roberts could accomplish before GOODWOOD was to strike a compromise with the corps commander. Another of Roberts's tasks was to capture the fortified hamlet of Cagny on the division's left flank near the Caen-Vimont railway line. Inasmuch as he already had responsibility for Cuverville and Demouville, Roberts asked O'Connor to be relieved of this task. 'It was agreed that I would go to take Cuverville and Demouville but that I would only *mask* Cagny until the Guards [Armoured Division] came forward; and that was a very unfortunate decision because there was nothing in Cagny except four 88's ... and those four 88's knocked out our sixteen tanks which were masking Cagny until the Guards arrived. Knocked them all out in a matter of minutes. So I quite wrongly but perhaps understandably advised the Guards when they arrived that Cagny was strongly held. It took the Guards until 4 P.M. to enter the place.[3]

[1] Roberts interview, loc. cit.

[2] Ibid.

[3] Ibid. Roberts relates that Tiger tanks and anti-tank guns had moved in to help defend Cagny from the north as well as the battery of 88s, but believes that the hamlet was relatively undefended from the south and might have been captured far more easily from this direction. Another reason for the long delay occurred because the leading elements of the Guards had been ordered not to attempt to take Cagny if it was strongly held but instead to bypass it and drive on Vimont. This strategy caused untold problems as Cagny held and the Guards' advance stalled.

The German 88s in Cagny were part of the 16th Luftwaffe Field Division and had miraculously escaped the bombardment. Oberst Hans von Luck was the commander of the 21st Panzer Division's 125 Panzer Grenadier Regiment and the senior German army officer responsible for that area of the front. He had returned only that morning from a three-day rest in Paris, arriving at his headquarters just after the bombing had ceased. In an attempt to pull together the pieces of his shattered defences, von Luck journeyed to Cagny, where the first thing he observed were some fifty to sixty British tanks advancing toward the railway embankment and the heights of Bourguébus Ridge beyond. To his surprise he also found the four Luftwaffe 88mm guns still intact, along with a Tiger and an 88mm anti-tank gun. The Luftwaffe guns were still pointing skywards but von Luck had a more important task in mind and promptly ordered the Luftwaffe officer in charge to move them to the northwest corner of Cagny, to ignore the tanks round the Caen-Vimont railway line and to fire instead at the British tanks following from the northeast down the corridor. The officer refused, stating that his mission was air defence, not shooting at tanks. Von Luck had no time for debate; he drew his pistol, calmly asking the officer 'if he would like to be killed immediately or cooperate. He decided the latter.'[1] The tanks von Luck had first observed near the railway were those of the leading armour of the 29th Armoured Brigade, the 3rd Battalion, Royal Tank Regiment, which had been ordered to move at full speed toward Bourguébus. It was the unit following, the 2nd Fife and Forfar Yeomanry, the one ordered by Roberts to mask Cagny, which caught the full brunt of von Luck's brilliant gambit. Not only did the lethal fire take an immediate toll of some sixteen British tanks but, more importantly, it held up the advance of the units following the 3rd Tanks and the advance of the Guards Armoured. It had been at this point that the Guardsmen were to have pivoted slightly to their left and driven through the orchard and hedgerow country to Vimont and the Caen-Falaise Plain beyond: the plan that O'Connor had fashioned was designed to enable a breakthrough to take place either on the left flank, by the Guards Armoured shredding the German defences round Vimont, or by the combined weight

---

[1] Quoted in film 'Operation GOODWOOD'.

of the 7th Armoured and 11th Armoured through Bourguébus Ridge.

General Roberts had assigned the clearing of Cuverville and Demouville to the 159th Infantry Brigade, which spent most of the morning at this task, and as a result they were unable to provide badly needed infantry support to the 29th Armoured Brigade. The armour was forced to carry on with only the infantry of their support battalion (the 8th Battalion, The Rifle Brigade) towards Bourguébus and the villages of Verrières and Rocquancourt to the east of the Caen-Falaise highway. Not only were the guns of Cagny proving to be a deadly thorn but now anti-tank guns and Tigers east of Cagny also came into action and began taking a toll of British tanks attempting to converge on the Caen-Vimont railway embankment; those advancing beyond the embankment toward Bourguébus became excellent targets for the German guns and tanks which had escaped the bombardment.

The 11th Armoured had experienced little difficulty in breaching the Highland minefield but the Guards Armoured and 7th Armoured were less fortunate. A monumental traffic jam built up at both ends of the minefield as units of both divisions attempted to follow the 11th Armoured into the corridor. The axis of advance was much too narrow for effective fire and manoeuvre by three armoured divisions competing for the space that, in normal circumstances, would have been allocated to a single armoured *brigade*. By midday, when the Germans had begun to react with growing intensity, the 7th Armoured Division was nowhere to be seen. Their mission had been to follow 11th Armoured, to provide security to their left flank and capture Bourguébus Heights, but the congestion round the start line prevented their commitment until late in the afternoon when an armoured regiment was finally brought into action.

What 8 Corps was running into late that morning was really topclass German defence. The inadequacy of British intelligence about German strength east of the Orne was unhappily demonstrated by the presence of perhaps the best defensive structure they had yet been able to prepare in Normandy. Other than Sperrle's warning of 15 July, which had failed to shake British complacency, ULTRA had been of little help to the Allies during the period leading up to GOODWOOD. 'The last few days of June and the first three weeks of July turned out to be one of the few relatively lean periods for ULTRA in the west. The volume of traffic dropped when the front became temporarily stabilized soon after the fall of Cherbourg, and was slow to pick up again until Cobra brought about a resumption of mobile warfare a month later. . .'[1] Under Eberbach, Panzer Group West had anticipated the GOODWOOD offensive and had disposed the forces of 1 SS Panzer Corps and LXXXVI Corps in four defensive belts nearly ten miles deep, with a fifth as the reserve. Within the axis of the GOODWOOD advance were two infantry divisions in the first belt and two panzer grenadier regiments of the 21st Panzer Division in the second. The third belt was a series of villages heavily fortified with anti-tank guns and infantry and some 270 *Nebelwerfers* – the six-barrelled heavy mortar known as the 'Moaning Minnie' – whose fire was used to support the second belt. The fourth belt was the area running from Bourguébus Ridge in the west to Troarn in the east. Finally, there was the armoured reserve of the fifth belt, well out of range of the British guns, consisting of a battalion of Panther tanks of the 1st SS Panzer Division and two battle groups of infantry and Tigers of the 12th SS Panzer. All told, Eberbach held some sixty to eighty tanks as his mobile reserve.

The advance of the 29th Armoured Brigade, without the support of either the 7th Armoured Division or the infantry of 159th Brigade, slowed to a crawl about noon, having advanced nearly 12,000 yards. With the leading elements of Major General A. H. S. Adair's Guards Armoured Division pinned down by 88mm fire from Cagny and the nearby Tigers, the British lost the initiative. This fact was not lost on O'Connor, who understood that the ultimate success of GOODWOOD lay in the speed and shock which the mass of his armour would have on the demoralized Germans. What neither O'Connor nor any of the other British commanders knew was that the Germans had so effectively anticipated the new offensive. A German intelligence summary of 15 July had warned of an impending attack east of the Orne:

> According to information derived from photographic reconnaissance of the lodgement area, the enemy command is planning to start a major operation across the Orne towards the

[1] Bennett, op.cit., p. 100.

southeast from about 17 July onwards. It is worthy of note that this date coincides with the period most favourable for new landing operations.[1]

This prediction was followed on 17 July by a similar warning from Army Group B that the Second British Army was expected 'to push foward across the Orne in the direction of Paris'.[2] The commander of 1 SS Panzer Corps, SS General Dietrich, claimed to have known of the concentration of British armour east of the Orne by lying down and pressing his ear to the ground, which carried the sound of tracked vehicles moving, an expedient he had learned on the Eastern Front.[3]

As strong as the German defences turned out to be, they were nevertheless a mere fragment of what they might have been had the battle-weary divisions been reinforced with fresh men and equipment. By 16 July German casualties in Normandy had climbed to over 100,000, including 2,360 officers.[4] When Dietrich was interned after the war, he told his Allied interrogators that during the GOODWOOD battle the only factor that had enabled the 1st SS and 12th SS Panzer Divisions to keep their armour in the battle had been the excellence of the German tank workshops located in the nearby Fôret de Cinglais, where, despite primitive conditions, skilled mechanics had made extensive repairs in as little as three to four days. So important was their work that Dietrich went there to decorate these men personally with the Iron Cross (Second Class), an honour not given lightly in the German Army.[5]

With the advance of the 11th Armoured stalled on the slopes of Bourguébus Ridge, the critical moment in the battle had arrived. It was essential that the initiative should not be lost but there was little O'Connor could do, with most of the 7th Armoured stuck back at their start-line and the 159th Infantry Brigade fully occupied in Cuverville and Demouville awaiting relief. O'Connor's first option was to request another saturation bombing of Bourguébus in the hope that it would knock out the

---

[1] Quoted in Ellis, op.cit., p. 333.

[2] Ibid, pp. 333–4. Both warnings were contained in written intelligence summaries and thus not detectable by ULTRA.

[3] Interrogation of Colonel General Joseph 'Sepp' Dietrich, Liddell Hart Papers.

[4] Bennett, op.cit., p. 103. The German casualty figures were established through ULTRA.

[5] Dietrich interrogation, loc.cit.

remaining 88s and artillery. An urgent request was sent to the Second Army for another bombing that afternoon, with percussion bombs to avoid cratering. According to O'Connor, his request was promptly denied. Though he was never told why it may be concluded that the Allies would have found it impossible to mount another operation on such short notice.[1]

The situation had become very sticky for Roberts and his men. In the early afternoon Dietrich committed part of his reserves when it became clear that the main British attack was aimed at Bourguébus: the Panther battalion of the 1st SS was moved there where it at once launched a series of counterattacks against the 29th Armoured Brigade. The German commander had not intended to commit the Panthers quite so soon, but once they had reached Bourguébus and made sudden contact with the advancing British armour it proved impossible to disengage. The remainder of the afternoon and evening of 18 July turned into the biggest tank battle of the entire campaign, a virtual shootout between the outnumbered but superior German Tigers and Panthers and the massed but more vulnerable British Shermans and Cromwells. Had it not been for repeated attacks by rocket-firing RAF Typhoons, matters would have gone worse for the British than they did.

With another major air strike ruled out, O'Connor recognized that his one final hope of renewing the advance lay in getting at least part of the 7th Armoured forward to assist the sorely pressed 29th Armoured Brigade. At 1350 hours O'Connor met Roberts and Erskine, and between them they devised a joint plan which called for a two-pronged attack against Hubert Folie and Bourguébus, with Roberts's armour on the right and Erskine's 22nd Armoured Brigade on the left. The only unit of the 22nd Armoured Brigade to get clear of the mess around the Orne had been the 5th Battalion, Royal Tank Regiment and O'Connor ordered this unit to move out at once, without waiting for the rest of the brigade. But, despite the repeated exhortations of 8 Corps during the afternoon, it became evident to the frustrated O'Connor that his gamble was not going to work: by 1500 hours the 5th Tanks had only reached the Caen-Troarn highway, and when the regiment arrived at Grentheville, at about 1700 hours, they were

---

[1] O'Connor interview, loc.cit.

too late to be of much help to the 29th Armoured Brigade. The remainder of the 7th Armoured was strung out back to the Orne bridges; the 131st Infantry Brigade did not begin crossing until after 2000 hours that night.

There seems to have been a good deal of dismay at 8 Corps that the 7th Armoured had been needlessly slow in closing up on 18 July; it was felt to be one more example of their poor performance in Normandy. However, there really does not seem to have been much that could be done to speed up their movement.[1][*] Not only was the congestion too great but there was a good deal of German interference with units running the gauntlet of the corridor, as some of the recovered Tigers operating in the area of Emiéville initiated counterattacks. By the time the 22nd Armoured Brigade had finally assembled, at about 1800 hours, and begun the thrust toward La Hogue that O'Connor had directed early that afternoon, they were indeed too late, as the Germans continued to stiffen and repulse any further advance against Bourguébus Ridge. Furthermore, the 29th Armoured Brigade was by this time too spent to begin a new drive: nearly half its tanks had been lost — two of its three regiments each had only about twenty tanks still operational. One hundred and twenty-six tanks of the 11th Armoured were put out of action that day, nearly ninety of them from enemy fire. Some were disabled, recovered and put back into service, only to be knocked out again, while many others were destroyed outright, although a good many crews escaped and also returned to fight another day.

---

[1]   GOODWOOD is one of the best documented battles ever fought. In addition to the unit war diaries, there is a detailed unpublished account prepared after the war by the British Army of the Rhine, which for a number of years conducted annual battlefield tours. Shortly after the operation concluded, O'Connor wrote an appreciation of GOODWOOD and several years ago several of the key participants, including General Roberts and Oberst von Luck, were brought together to participate in the film about GOODWOOD, which is still used as an historical example in discussions of current military doctrine. See, for example, the RUSI Journal, March 1982.

[*]   After discussing GOODWOOD with General Hobart in 1947, Liddell Hart came to the conclusion that Erskine did display undue caution, in no small part as a psychological consequence of the Italian campaign which had left its mark on the 7th Armoured. In Italy the division had frequently run into German traps during its advance, and since Villers-Bocage had proved so disastrous, this tendency had perhaps increased. The success of the main thrust of GOODWOOD depended upon rapid reinforcement by the 'Desert Rats' for the initial gains made by the 11th Armoured. It was Liddell Hart's opinion that the only way to overcome Erskine's caution would have been to have O'Connor alongside him to spur him on. 'Notes for History, Talk with General Hobart, 19.8.47', Liddell Hart Papers, King's College, London.

On the left flank the Guards Armoured Division lost sixty tanks, most of them around Cagny and Emiéville.

Thus ended any possibility that day of securing Bourguébus Ridge or of breaking through to the Caen-Falaise Plain beyond. Had the Guards succeeded in driving through to Vimont, the German positions around Bourguèbus would have been vulnerable to a flank attack; but with both divisions at a virtual standstill the turning point in the GOODWOOD battle had passed without the British being able to press their advantage. Since about 1100 hours that morning the 11th Armoured had been unable to capture any new ground. Now that the initiative was lost it would never be regained.

This fact was understood by Dempsey who undoubtedly conveyed it to Montgomery when the two commanders met at Second Army HQ at 1800 hours on the evening of 18 July.[1] Nevertheless, less than two hours earlier Montgomery had elected to send Brooke a grossly misleading signal that suggested the exact opposite. 'Operations this morning a complete success,' wrote Montgomery. 'The effect of the air bombing was decisive and the spectacle terrific . . . situation very promising and it is difficult to see what the enemy can do just at present. Few enemy tanks met so far and no (repeat) no mines.'[2]*

In truth, not only had the air strikes failed to dent the anti-tank defences of Bourguébus, but a similar failure on the left flank had missed Touffreville and created extensive cratering south of the village: as a result, the 3rd Division had not made much headway. Why Montgomery elected to send such a wildly overoptimistic evaluation is a mystery, but it was the first of several blunders he committed during GOODWOOD that were to damage his credibility. Whatever his motive Montgomery could not claim ignorance, for reports had been flowing in throughout the day. While it is true that there had been a good deal of misleading information put forth during the early hours of the battle, when the situation was still very confused, by late afternoon on the 18th it was sufficiently clear for Montgomery not to

[1] Dempsey Diary, 18 July 1944, PRO (WO 28/59).
[2] Quoted in Ellis, pp. 344–5.
* Montgomery also told the CIGS that the Guards Armoured Division had passed Cagny and were in Vimont, and that 11th Armoured had reached Tilly la Campagne. Neither village ever came close to being captured during the entire operation.

have misunderstood it. A Second Army sitrep for the period from 0001 to 1200 hours that day had, for example, given a false impression that the main enemy defences had been broken,[1] but this was well before the true extent of problems facing 8 Corps could have filtered back. Dempsey, however, was in close touch with 8 Corps throughout the day and he grasped what was happening round Cagny and Bourguébus. Moreover, barely ten minutes after Montgomery had cabled the CIGS, Dempsey had met de Guingand, although his diary does not reveal the extent of their discussion.[2]

This was not Alamein, where Montgomery could keep hammering away at the Germans until they cracked, but a very delicate operation where timing and speed were of the essence. Despite what appeared to be significant gains, GOODWOOD could not be termed a complete success until Bourguébus fell and as of the evening of 18 July this was still far from a certainty, as Montgomery himself would soon discover. It was bad enough for him to have misled Brooke but he foolishly compounded the mistake by reading a communiqué for the BBC implying similar gains which had not in fact taken place.

While false hopes were being raised at SHAEF and in London, Dempsey seems to have been the only senior commander to sense that the battle was far from decided and that the fleeting opportunity for a breakthrough had vanished. Too much crucial time had been needlessly lost while Robert's infantry struggled to clear villages which ought to have been bypassed and left for followup units to deal with; and the strongpoint of Cagny had held out for long enough to blunt the advance of the Guards Armoured Division. By the night of 18 July most of Caen, except for the still contested Colombelles, was under Canadian control but, important as this was, it had little to do with the main object of GOODWOOD, which was to drive a wedge deep enough to gain access to the German strongpoints blocking further movement on to the Caen-Falaise Plain. Instead of three armoured divisions placing intolerable pressure on these defences, the 11th Armoured had been forced to carry the burden alone. The other grave mishap to befall the British on 18 July was the inability of

---

[1]   PRO (CAB 106/1085).
[2]   Dempsey Diary, 18 July, loc.cit.

the 7th Armoured to get forward in time to influence the action. Any doubt about the meaning of what transpired on 18 July was later put in perspective by Dempsey, who said:

> Once it was evident that the armour were not going to break-out, the operation became an infantry battle – and it was no part of the GOODWOOD plan to get drawn into a costly struggle of that kind. So I really lost interest (only to the extent that I saw there was no chance of it developing into that enthralling battle which I had thought possible) in the operation by evening, and was ready to call it off – except for trying to get onto the initial objectives, which were necessary if we were to obtain a satisfactory tactical position.[1]

During the night of 18 July the Germans moved swiftly to reinforce the Bourguébus sector with fresh troops and tanks of the 1st SS Panzer Division and by the next morning the villages forming the bulwark of their defence – Bourguébus, La Hogue, Four, Soliers, Hubert Folie and Bras – were all strongly defended. The 12th SS was also ordered forward to plug the German right flank between Frénouville and Emiéville but did not arrive until the daylight hours of 19 July, leaving a gap in the defences south of Cagny which might have been exploited had the British commanders known of it.

In addition to the loss of nearly two hundred British tanks, casualties for the first day of GOODWOOD numbered approximately fifteen hundred for the 1st, 8th and 2 Canadian Corps.[2] During the final two days, 19 and 20 July, the struggle continued with tank losses and casualties mounting on both sides. The British could claim to have taken only one of the objectives assigned in the revised directive of 17 July, and even that was a near run thing. The 7th Armoured and the 1st SS Panzer shared Bourguébus Ridge, while the Guards Armoured had succeeded only in penetrating a few hundred yards south of Frénouville – nearly two miles short of Vimont. The third objective, the area of Bretteville sur Laize, lay nearly four miles south of St Martin de Fontenay, where the 2nd Canadian Division was halted on 20 July.

---

[1] 'Operation GOODWOOD', loc.cit.
[2] Ellis, op.cit., p. 345. 8 Corps losses were 521 killed and wounded – the heaviest were to the 11th Armoured (236) and the lowest to the 7th Armoured (48). Throughout GOODWOOD tank losses became difficult to document accurately.

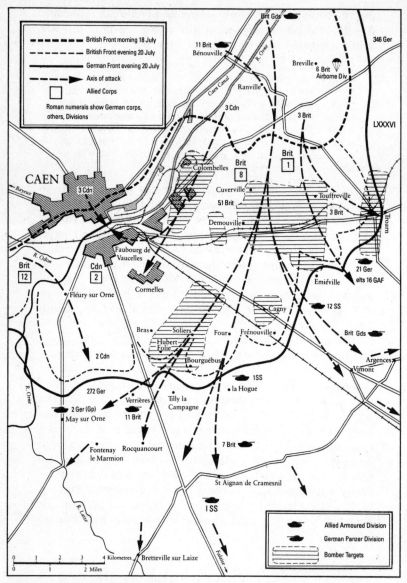

Legend:

- ▬ ▬ ▬ British Front morning 18 July
- – – – British Front evening 20 July
- ——— German Front evening 20 July
- ▬ ▬ ➤ Axis of attack
- ☐ Allied Corps

Roman numerals show German corps, others, Divisions

Brit Gds
11 Brit
Bénouville
346 Ger
Breville
6 Brit
Airborne Div
Ranville
3 Cdn
3 Brit
LXXXVI
CAEN
3 Cdn
Colombelles
Brit
8
Brit
1
Cuverville
Touffreville
51 Brit
3 Brit
Troarn
Demouville
R. Odon
Faubourg de
Vaucelles
21 Ger
elts 16 GAF
Brit
12
Cdn
2
Cormelles
Emiéville
Fléury sur Orne
12 SS
Cagny
Bras
Soliers
Four
Frénouville
Brit Gds
Hubert
Folie
2 Cdn
Bourguébus
Argences
Vimont
R. Orne
1 SS
la Hogue
272 Ger
Verrières
Tilly la
Campagne
2 Ger (Gp)
11 Brit
May sur Orne
Fontenay
le Marmion
Rocquancourt
7 Brit
St Aignan de Cramesnil
R. Laize
1 SS
0 1 2 3 4 Kilometres
0   1   2 Miles
Bretteville sur Laize

Allied Armoured Division
German Panzer Division
Bomber Targets

OPERATION GOODWOOD

As Dempsey had suspected, regaining the initiative was impossible. O'Connor's task was made more difficult by a lack of artillery and air support. Nearly all the artillery was still west of the Orne and what few supporting aircraft were standing by were grounded by heavy rains which swept across Normandy on 20 July. Most of the Allied aircraft were now diverted to support of COBRA, which had been due to commence that day but was itself postponed because of bad weather. With the battlefield a quagmire, further offensive action seemed futile. Montgomery recognized that there was little to be gained by continuing GOODWOOD and officially terminated the offensive that had, for all practical purposes, ended the day it had begun.

One of Dempsey's objects had been to minimize his infantry losses, and even in this he was not completely successful. From 18 to 22 July (when the figures were complete) casualties within the four corps directly involved were:

1 Corps	1,656
8 Corps	1,818
12 Corps	449
2 Canadian Corps	1,614
Total	5,537[1]

Losses within 30 Corps, which played no direct role in GOODWOOD, were 631 for the same period. The Second Army casualties since D-Day now stood at 45,795, of which 6,168 occurred during the period 18–22 July, or nearly 14% of the total British losses since 6 June.[2] On the surface, therefore, there did not appear to be much to show for GOODWOOD, which one account later aptly termed 'the death ride of the armoured divisions'.[3] 'On the map, the results looked unimpressive. After three days of battle, the British had just reached the edge of parts of Bourguébus Ridge to which they were clinging precariously. South and east of Caen, the great offensive had penetrated nowhere more than seven miles and this on a very narrow front. To achieve

---

[1] War Diary, 21st Army Group, 'A' Branch, PRO (WO 171/139). Figures are for killed, wounded and missing between 0600 hours 18 July and 0600 hours 22 July.
[2] Ibid.
[3] Alexander McKee, *Caen: Anvil of Victory*, London, 1965.

this the British had lost over 400 tanks, but many were later recovered and repaired.'[1]

Strategically, Montgomery could argue that GOODWOOD had indeed been successful. The enlargement of the bridgehead virtually precluded any further German counteroffensive threat on the eastern flank. He finally had *all* of Caen, and the three major obstacles to his advance – Caen and the rivers Odon and Orne – were now at his back. Moreover, the new positions occupied by the Second Army posed a grave threat to the entire German right flank: their anchor was lost and the severe battering they had taken during GOODWOOD ensured that they lacked the strength to take it back.

GOODWOOD shattered the false optimism that had been implanted in von Kluge by OKW and Hitler, and even he was forced to accept that the fighting ability of his forces had been sapped to the point of desperation. Strategically, the new positions he was forced to defend with Panzer Group West were hopeless. There was little left with which to reinforce Eberbach, and if this line cracked the entire flank would collapse. Had Rommel been permitted to build a new defensive network weeks before when his panzer divisions still retained most of their strength, it might have been a different matter. Now, however, the only unanswered question in von Kluge's mind was how much longer Army Group B could continue to hold out.

Even though the panzer and infantry units had taken a fearful pounding they had managed the almost impossible task of stopping a truly massive Allied offensive, and had left the Second Army in a rather poor position from which to renew an offensive towards Falaise. The Guards Armoured Division had certainly learned a lesson in their first taste of combat in Normandy. As the recent GOODWOOD film pointed out the Guards, who were new to tanks, having been formed from the regiments of the Foot Guards, and anxious for battle, 'had been led to believe that between them and breakout lay "only a few old men and boys with spandaus"'.[2] Before GOODWOOD, Rommel had told Hitler that his ability to hold out was nearing an end and that it was only a matter of weeks before the German Army must pull back or face annihilation. His warning had fallen on deaf ears, and now

---

[1] Belfield and Essame, op.cit., p. 145.
[2] Quoted in film, 'Operation GOODWOOD'.

Rommel himself lay close to death in a French hospital, leaving von Kluge to inherit command of Army Group B in addition to his post of C-in-C, OB West. Though stretched nearly to breaking point, they had once more staved off defeat in Normandy, but it was clear to the German commanders that they simply could not continue to absorb punishment of this magnitude.

GOODWOOD typified the German genius for defence. Despite the heaviest tactical bombardment of the war and open countryside which was not particularly suited for defensive operations against a powerful enemy who controlled the air, Panzer Group West had not only prevented a British breakthrough but had turned the battlefield into a massive scrapyard of broken and burnt-out British armour. As one British officer described it in his diary: 'It was a scene of utter desolation. I have never seen such bomb craters. Trees were uprooted, roads were impassable. There were bodies in half; crumpled men. A tank lay upside down, another was still burning with a row of feet sticking out from underneath. In one crater a man's head and shoulders appeared sticking out from the side. The place stank.'[1]

Dempsey's reaction was ambivalent:

> The attack we put in on July 18th was not a very good operation of war tactically, but strategically it was a great success, even though we did get a bloody nose. I didn't mind about that. I was prepared to lose a couple of hundred tanks. So long as I didn't lose men. We could afford the tanks because they had begun to pile up in the bridgehead. Our tank losses were severe but our casualties in men were very light. If I had tried to achieve the same result with a conventional infantry attack I hate to think what the casualties would have been.[2]

Montgomery would doubtless have agreed, for not only had he belatedly obtained strategically important new ground but could claim to have firmly tied down four corps of panzers and infantry during the moment when Bradley was about to launch COBRA, although it must still be noted that had the Germans elected to move away any of their main forces, GOODWOOD would probably have succeeded as Dempsey had originally envisioned. Still, serious flaws in the plan had prevented what might have been far more rewarding results. Had Montgomery, for example, not

---

[1] Quoted in Belfield and Essame, op.cit., p. 145.
[2] Dempsey interview with Chester Wilmot, loc.cit.

tampered with the plan by placing such stringent restrictions upon 8 Corps in his 15 July directive, O'Connor might have been disposed to take greater risks on 18 July.

The boldness originally suggested in the GOODWOOD plan seems to have been needlessly sacrificed by an overemphasis on security. Montgomery's mandate that O'Connor should give first priority to the security of his flanks was inconsistent with the premise that the three armoured divisions must strike quickly after the bombardment while the Germans were still disorganized. As General Roberts has pointed out, it was completely unrealistic to imagine that the Germans could have mounted any sort of counterstroke after the awesome bombing and against the combined might of three attacking corps. Was it a lack of confidence by Montgomery in his armoured units, bred by his previous experience in the western desert, or was it a healthy respect for his enemy? The answer is not clear, but certainly Montgomery seemed to have displayed excessive caution which was not justified and which, in turn, was most forcefully brought home to O'Connor.

The casualty figures do not bear out Dempsey's contention that his casualties were low. Most of the 6,100 losses were again to the infantry, who had been given the unenviable task of rooting out German resistance in the suburbs of Caen and in the fortified villages east of the Orne. Losses in 1 Corps, whose task it was to protect the left flank of 8 Corps, were equal to those of the Canadians and only slightly lower than for 8 Corps itself.

Neither Montgomery nor Dempsey seemed to have grasped the conflicting position in which they had placed O'Connor: on the one hand, security was overemphasized and on the other, O'Connor was told to get his armour forward quickly. Perhaps too much was anticipated from the bombardment, but O'Connor was forced to employ unsound tactics in an effort to accomplish a Herculean task. How different the outcome might have been had Dempsey ordered a combined tank-infantry thrust down the corridor to Bourguébus, where there would have been sufficient infantry available to deal with problems such as Cagny. What the British Army terms 'thrustfulness' had been absolutely essential on 18 July, and the spearhead of the 11th Armoured Division under the command of the most battle-experienced divisional commander in 21st Army Group was the perfect instrument to accomplish this, provided the tanks and infantry were permitted to work in unison instead of being forced to accomplish entirely separate tasks.

Roberts more than fulfilled the requirement for thrustfulness and it was absurd to have expected him to sustain the advance with his main infantry force tied down miles to the rear in Cuverville and Demouville. Here was the first real instance of the infantry shortage directly influencing the tactical thinking of both Montgomery and Dempsey – by deliberately attempting to mould his tactics to a pre-conceived organization of his forces, Dempsey was defeating his plan beyond salvage. Of the many flaws inherent in the GOODWOOD plan, it was this one which did more than anything else to ensure that the offensive would eventually bog down. It was a mistake the Germans would not have made in similar circumstances.

O'Connor's failure was to ensure that the confusion around Cagny was cleared up when his 'masking' instruction showed obvious signs of creating serious problems for both Roberts and for Adair's Guards Armoured Division. It was one of the few occasions in the battle where he possessed the ability to influence the outcome. Thirty-five years later he was able vividly to recall the dilemma he faced then. In many ways, O'Connor was a general far ahead of his time. For example, before GOODWOOD began he had anticipated the need for the infantry to keep up with the tanks (his disagreement with Roberts notwithstanding) and at the same time be protected from small-arms fire which made movement by lorry unsatisfactory. O'Connor found a solution by ordering that a number of the self-propelled gun-carriers of the artillery be turned over to the infantry for use as armoured personnel carriers. There were predictable howls of outrage at this temerity to violate the hidebound organizational structure of the army, and the order was soon countermanded by Dempsey, who was not convinced of its merit.[1] O'Connor's protests to Dempsey fell on deaf ears but in his postmortem on GOODWOOD, the resolute little general again made his point by insisting: 'The difficulty experienced by the infantry was in keeping up with the tanks, which was due to the lack of a suitable armoured vehicle in which they could be carried forward. The introduction of some

[1] O'Connor interview, loc.cit. In 1979 O'Connor still had regrets that he had not pursued the matter more forcefully with Dempsey.

such vehicle, it is felt, is of the utmost importance.'[1] The postwar evolution of infantry tactics, of course, saw exactly what O'Connor had envisioned in 1944, when such an idea was clearly considered revolutionary.

The rain and heavy cloud cover that had settled over Normandy on 20 July had forced a postponement of COBRA, and the day when the air forces would again demonstrate their awesome powers remained uncertain. While Bradley and the American commanders anxiously awaited a break in the weather, a storm of another sort was building within the Allied High Command. Its target was Bernard Montgomery.

---

[1] PRO (CAB 106/1085).

CHAPTER 22

The Furore Over Goodwood

Ike said yesterday that with 7,000 tons of bombs
dropped in the most elaborate bombing of enemy
front line positons ever accomplished only seven
miles were gained – can we afford a thousand tons
of bombs per mile?

Diary of Captain Harry C. Butcher[1]

Eisenhower was described as 'blue as indigo' over what he
considered a lost opportunity; he was also angry at Montgomery's deception. But the angriest and most frustrated were the air
chiefs, over what they believed was Montgomery's duplicity in
promising decisive results and then failing to press his advantage.
Unaware of the problems encountered by 8 Corps, they viewed
GOODWOOD as the clearest example yet of Montgomery's
unwillingness to take risks.

The air chiefs could be forgiven their distress over this latest
turn of events for they had, in fact, been entirely misled by
Montgomery. In addition to promising conclusive results from
GOODWOOD when he requested air support, he had not bothered
to inform SHAEF of his change of orders to O'Connor on 15 July.
His revision of the original Second Army operational order was
written in only two copies: one was given to Dempsey, who
passed it to O'Connor; the other Montgomery retained himself.
When the revised Second Army instruction went astray, SHAEF
was left in ignorance of Montgomery's intentions, as was his own
headquarters. Montgomery's message to Brooke during the
afternoon of 18 July had been similarly misleading; so was a press
conference he gave that evening, during which he read an optimistic communiqué suggesting that 8 Corps had achieved a

[1] Butcher, *Three Years With Eisenhower*, op.cit., p. 531.

breakthrough.[1] Brigadier Williams later commented: 'Monty built up 8 Corps under Dick O'Connor trying to break through. Then had a terrible press conference. Talked to them like children. Bloody stupid communiqué he read to them. We hadn't advanced an inch. That night Dietrich smashed a bunch of our tanks.'[2]

In 1952 Tedder was to comment: 'There is no question to my mind but that we in SHAEF were quite clear that the intention of that Operation was to push right through to the South. We did in particular welcome the fact that O'Connor was to be given command of all the armour in view of his magnificent courage and leadership when he drove through to Beda Fomm and cleaned up the Italians in the Western Desert. Moreover a drive through to Falaise would at long last have begun to give us the airfield country south of Caen, which had been one of the original objectives.[3] Even General Belchem was later forced to admit that Montgomery had overstated his case for GOODWOOD, but he blames Eisenhower for misinterpreting his chief. 'When the plans were announced to Eisenhower, there arose a complete misunderstanding between him and Montgomery. Eisenhower announced that *both* the British and American armies were about to make a break-through and that the British offensive was to be exploited towards Paris.'[4] After Montgomery's 15 July written directive Belchem admitted that 'Montgomery took no steps to correct Eisenhower's misunderstanding, lest the massive air support even for the limited attack were denied him.'[5] Still later, Belchem asserted that Montgomery did not do so out of fear that the strategic air forces would be denied him for 'a relatively "local" operation which amounted to a battle for position.'[6] Privately, however, he told Dr Pogue that 'Monty shouldn't talk to the press. He tries to do the proper thing, always gets it mixed

---

[1] Reports being passed to SHAEF were also highly misleading. The afternoon of 19 July a SHAEF G–2 intelligence summary was still proclaiming GOODWOOD a surprise: 'Our breakthrough into plain south and southwest of CAEN has taken enemy by surprise.' SHAEF Cable Log, 19 July 1944, 1718 hours, Eisenhower Papers.

[2] Pogue interview with Brigadier Williams, loc.cit.

[3] Tedder, letter to Liddell Hart, 28 April 1952, Liddell Hart Papers. In this letter Tedder stated that his conclusions were made only after consultation with several colleagues who were knowledgeable about GOODWOOD.

[4] Belchem, *All in the Day's March*, op.cit., p. 204.

[5] Ibid.

[6] Interview with Dr Pogue, 20 February 1947.

up and is misquoted. He felt he had to give the interview because there was a view in Britain and the United States that the British and Canadians were doing nothing while the U.S. were doing everything.'

In his *Memoirs* Montgomery replied to his critics by admitting that: 'This was partly my own fault, for I was too exultant at the Press conference I gave during the GOODWOOD battle. I realise that now – in fact, I realised it pretty quickly afterwards. Basically the trouble was this – both Bradley and I agreed that we could not possibly tell the Press the true strategy which formed the basis of all our plans. As Bradley said, "We must grin and bear it." It became increasingly difficult to grin.'[1]* What Montgomery consistently neglected to mention was that there was nothing to stop him from telling the press 'off the record' of his intentions: not only were all press despatches censored but the men of the fourth estate had an excellent record of not betraying secrets harmful to the war effort. That Montgomery chose not so to talk to them can only have been deliberate. Moreover, nothing precluded Montgomery from being candid with Eisenhower except the mistaken belief that the Supreme Commander had never grasped his intentions in Normandy. The cost of his failure to be frank with his superior was further to strain not only his relations with Eisenhower but his credibility with the air chiefs, who now mistrusted him more than ever. To make matters worse, Montgomery, whose tact was never one of his virtues, foolishly sent a private signal to Eisenhower on the night of 19 July, rejoicing over his alleged gains east of the Orne.

Excerpts from Tedder's diary illustrate the extent of the concern of the air commanders. Wing Commander Scarman, who maintained his diary, observed:

19 July: It is now clear the Germans have succeeded in holding our attempt to break through. Chief very concerned. . . [More on Montgomery and air commanders] Montgomery will not

---

[1] Montgomery, *Memoirs*, op.cit., p. 257.

* Bradley knew very little about GOODWOOD and now has made an admittedly speculative assessment by claiming that Montgomery oversold the operation to SHAEF in order to take advantage of a possible breakout and claim full credit for winning the battle of Normandy. Such a spectacular victory, asserted Bradley, would enable him to retain his post as Allied ground C-in-C and stem the mounting criticism. *A General's Life*, p. 273. There is no evidence whatsoever to support Bradley's interpretation.

deal with Conginham, but only with L-M [Leigh-Mallory]. This entails Broadhurst, Coningham's subordinate, dealing *direct* with L-M... L-M has even moved his own personal caravan ... with Monty. L-M seems to be cashing in on the discomfiture of his own subordinate.

20 July: CAS [Portal] most concerned about the Army failure, the Chief regards Monty as the cause.

21 July: [At a high-level SHAEF meeting Tedder remarked]: 'Unless we get the Pas de Calais quickly, southern England will have a bad time.' [A reference to the V-1 weapon menace.] When Bedell [Smith] replied we would not get there at all soon, Chief said 'Then we must change our leaders for men who will get us there.'[1]

According to Eisenhower's biographer, he was 'livid' over GOOD-WOOD. 'He thundered that it had taken more than seven thousand tons of bombs to gain seven miles and that the Allies could hardly hope to go through France paying a price of a thousand tons of bombs per mile.'[2] There was also talk, unfounded as it turned out, that Eisenhower was considering Montgomery's replacement. Butcher recorded in his diary: 'Anyway Ike is like a blind dog in a meat house – he can smell it but he can't find it. How he will handle the situation remains the principal suspended interest of the diary, at the moment.'[3] Tedder was deeply concerned that Eisenhower was not prepared to deal firmly with Montgomery and was on the verge of taking independent action on his own. According to his diary, 'Eisenhower agreed and is preparing a paper to dispatch to Monty. Chief intends, if SAC will not act, to put his views in writing to British Chiefs of Staff. Chief also told Eisenhower frankly "YourownpeoplearethinkingyouhavesoldthemtotheBritish if you continue to support Montgomery without protest".'[4]

Despite Churchill's offer that he was free to relieve any British commander who did not measure up – including Montgomery – Eisenhower showed no intention of asking for the 21st Army Group Commander's removal. He did, however, realize that he must take some action, and on the afternoon of 20 July Montgomery and Eisenhower met privately at 21st Army Group. Nothing has ever been revealed about what transpired during

---

[1] Tedder Diary.
[2] Quoted in Ambrose, *The Supreme Commander*, op.cit., p. 439.
[3] Diary of Captain Harry C. Butcher, 20 July 1944, Eisenhower Presidential Papers.
[4] Tedder Diary, 21 July 1944.

their conversation, but the following day Eisenhower chose to formalize his feelings in one of the many interminable letters the two generals exchanged during the campaign.

Eisenhower's letter of 21 July had as its stated purpose 'to assure myself that we see eye to eye on the big problems'. However, its real purpose was clearly to convey his dissatisfaction to Montgomery. Of GOODWOOD he wrote: 'Then, a few days ago, when Armored Divisions of Second Army, assisted by tremendous air attack, broke through the enemy's forward lines, I was extremely hopeful and optimistic. I thought that at last we had him and were going to roll him up. That did not come about.'[1] Tactfully, but quite firmly, Eisenhower reminded Montgomery that 'the recent advances near Caen have partially eliminated the necessity for a defensive attitude, so I feel that you should insist that Dempsey keep up the strength of his attack. Right now we have the ground and air strength and the stores to support major assaults by both armies simultaneously. . . The enemy has no immediately available major reserves. We do not need to fear, at this moment, a great counter offensive.' The letter concluded with a sharp admonition that 'eventually the American ground strength will necessarily be much greater than the British. But while we have equality in size we must go forward shoulder to shoulder, with honors and sacrifices equally shared.'[2]

This was the sternest rebuke of Montgomery by Eisenhower during the Normandy campaign, but it did not satisfy Tedder, who complained of not seeing the letter before its despatch. It was 'not strong enough. Montgomery can evade it. It contains no *order*.'[3] As far as Tedder was concerned Eisenhower was irresolute, and Montgomery's reply of 22 July telling of plans for a new offensive and a new directive to his army commanders did nothing to reassure him that Montgomery appreciated the vital importance of time which had been emphasized in the Supreme Commander's letter.[4]

---

[1] Eisenhower, letter to Montgomery, 21 July 1944, *Eisenhower Papers*, III, op.cit., pp. 2018-9.

[2] Ibid. On this point Brooke agreed with Eisenhower, writing to Montgomery on 28 July: 'I feel personally quite certain that Dempsey must attack *at the earliest possible moment* on a larger scale. We must not allow German forces to move from his front to Bradley's front or we shall give more cause than ever for criticism.' Alanbrooke Papers.

[3] Tedder Diary, 21 July 1944.

[4] Tedder, *With Prejudice*, op.cit., p. 568.

Tedder has been accused of a personal vendetta against Montgomery, based mainly on his failure to capture airfield sites on the Caen-Falaise Plain. However, this is a misrepresentation of Tedder's motives – the truth was that he honestly believed that Montgomery was not aggressive enough and must either be persuaded to change his tactics or be replaced by someone who would. Tedder's distrust and dislike of Montgomery are well known, but it is a disservice to assert that he would wreck the Allied command structure for personal reasons – he was far above such personal vanity.

GOODWOOD caused endless controversy in 1944 and is still being debated. Several years ago the Directorate of Army Training produced a two-hour film about GOODWOOD. One of the major conclusions drawn from the film was: 'It is felt that General Montgomery did not plan GOODWOOD as the breakout but that he hoped that a breakthrough might result. This enthusiasm permeated to General Dempsey who, misled by over-optimistic intelligence, was more confident than circumstances warranted.'[1]

This conclusion seems inaccurate. From its first conception, Montgomery was sceptical of GOODWOOD and what it might accomplish. More probably he considered Dempsey's optimism fanciful and decided on 15 July that the time had come to ensure that both Dempsey and O'Connor understood exactly where their priorities were to be directed. Certainly he was quite prepared to turn 8 Corps loose in an exploitation, but the experience of six weeks of intense combat against the resourceful and determined German Army must have convinced him that a breakthrough was doubtful. Yet Montgomery was guilty of conveying to his superior the same false optimism he had taken steps to curb in his own army commander, a fact not lost on his critics, who suspected that he was protecting himself against any eventuality.

As if his troubles with GOODWOOD were not enough, Montgomery had another, even more pressing problem to solve: how to pacify a very angry Winston Churchill. The Prime Minister was irate over what he believed to be a deliberate snub by Montgomery to his proposed trip to the Normandy battlefield.

---

[1] 'A War Study of Operation GOODWOOD,' booklet to accompany the film, n.d., prepared by the Directorate of Army Training, Ministry of Defence.

Montgomery had asked Eisenhower to keep all visitors away during GOODWOOD and, inasmuch as Churchill had been contemplating another visit to Normandy at about this time, the Prime Minister interpreted this as a wilful attempt to keep him at home. A perplexed Brooke was summoned to Churchill's bedside on the night of 19 July; he found him in a rage. 'What was Monty doing dictating to him; he had every right to visit France when he wanted? Who was Monty to stop him?'[1] So incensed had Churchill become over the matter that the same day he had sent Eisenhower a petulant letter defending his decision. 'I have no intention of visiting General Montgomery's Headquarters, and he should not concern himself about me in any way, except that he should provide a Staff Officer who could show me about. . . If however, General Montgomery disputes about it in any way, the matter will be taken up officially, because I have both a right and a duty to acquaint myself with the facts on the spot.'[2]

The next day a worried Brooke flew to Normandy and instructed Montgomery to write a note to the Prime Minister stating that he had been unaware of his desire to visit Normandy, and extending an invitation to do so. Shortly after Brooke's return to London the same night Churchill rang him to express delight, and 'felt rather ashamed of himself for all he had said!! And well he might feel ashamed of himself! What a storm in a china cup! All for nothing!'[3] As he later described the episode in his 'Notes on My Life', Brooke related that 'Winston had never been very fond of Monty; when things went well he put up with him, when they did not he at once became "your Monty".'[4] Throughout their long relationship, both during and after the war, Montgomery was careful not to place himself on the wrong side of Churchill – or, for that matter, of Mrs Churchill. On more than one occasion Clementine Churchill had firmly reprimanded Montgomery when he misbehaved. The first known example of her displeasure with him occurred when Montgomery flew to Marrakesh on 31 December 1943 to discuss OVERLORD with the Prime Minister, accompanied by his aide, Captain Noel Chev-

---

[1] Bryant, *Triumph in the West*, op.cit., p. 234.
[2] Churchill, letter to Eisenhower, 19 July 1944, Eisenhower Papers.
[3] Alanbrooke Diary, 20 July 1944, loc.cit.
[4] Bryant, *Triumph in the West*, op.cit., p. 235.

asse. Churchill was still bedridden with pneumonia and shortly after their arrival Lady Churchill said to the two officers: 'Well, it's time we all dressed for dinner. Why don't you go and change, Captain Chevasse.' Montgomery interrupted to reply, 'That won't be necessary; I never have my ADCs dine with me.' Lady Churchill bristled: 'Who are you to tell me whom I entertain in my house! Captain Chevasse is *my* guest and will dine with us!'[1] Although Montgomery was later more careful to avoid incurring her wrath, this was not the only occasion when Mrs Churchill put him firmly in his place for his sometimes loutish behaviour in the Churchill household.

At one a.m. on 25 July Eisenhower was awakened by a telephone call from Churchill. Butcher summoned the Supreme Commander to the phone and he responded 'with a lusty "God damn"'. Eisenhower was heard to say to the Prime Minister, 'What do your people think about the slowness of the situation over there?' 'This morning Ike said he had talked more than a half hour to the P.M. and that during the P.M.'s recent trip Monty obviously had sold Winston a "bill of goods". The P.M. was supremely happy with the situation. Then de Guingand phoned Ike, to assure him that Monty had "fattened up" the attack, and that one was on today in the British sector, as well as in the American. Ike said he had started to be alarmed at Monty's hesitance 10 days ago, had confided in Tedder his fears, and now Tedder is just reaching the phase of irritation in which Ike found himself several days ago.'[2]

Both Brooke and Montgomery were extremely angry at Eisenhower's comments to Churchill. Brooke's irritation was confided to his diary. 'My God, what psychological complications war leads to. . . I am tired to death with and by humanity and all its pettiness. Will we ever learn to "love our Allies as ourselves"??!! I doubt it . . . it is equally clear that Ike knows nothing about strategy and is *quite* unsuited to the post of Supreme Commander as far as any of the strategy of the war is concerned!'[3] Montgomery was stung by Eisenhower's remarks and never forgave him. In his *Memoirs* he took his revenge by

---

[1]   Related by Sir John Colville, interview of 2 November 1982.
[2]   Butcher Diary, 25 July 1944, loc.cit.
[3]   Alanbrooke Diary, 27 July 1944, loc.cit.

castigating Eisenhower for failing to understand the situation in July.[1]

Quite clearly, the nerves of those concerned with winning the battle of Normandy were stretched thin after the disappointment of GOODWOOD, and no one was reassured by the news coming out of Germany on 20 July, the date of the abortive attempt on Hitler's life by a group of German Army plotters led by Colonel Count von Stauffenberg, who had planted a bomb in a briefcase placed under the table of the Führer's war conference room at Rastenberg, East Prussia – the 'Wolf's Lair'.[2] When the news reached the Allies the following day, there was concern at SHAEF that GOODWOOD had lost a momentous opportunity to exploit the obvious disarray within the German High Command. What no one knew was that the many weeks of frustration and concern since D-Day were about to come to an end with COBRA.

[1] Montgomery, *Memoirs*, op.cit., pp. 260–2. New evidence uncovered since publication strongly suggests that both Eisenhower and Dempsey had good reason to react as they did. While Montgomery did not foresee a 'breakout' he *did* intend the Second Army to attain full control of the Caen–Falaise Plain as far south as Falaise itself. On 14 July he sent Brooke a detailed letter outlining his objectives for GOODWOOD. 'The time has now arrived to deliver terrific blows, designed to "write off" and eliminate the bulk of his holding troops. I doubt if he can collect more troops to rope us off again *in the west*, and it is in the west that I want territory, i.e., I want Brittany . . . The general aim in this battle will be to destroy all possible enemy troops in the general area Caen–Mezidon–Falaise–Evrecy.' Appended to this letter was a large map with coloured arrows depicting that the aim of 8 Corps in GOODWOOD was to thrust the 7th Armoured Division through the shoulders of the penetration opened by the Guards Armoured Division around Cagny to the east, and the 11th Armoured Division, who would clear Bourguébus Ridge to the west. The armoured cars were to dash ahead and form a screen along the front Mezidon–Falaise–Condé-sur-Noireau while the Desert Rats drove to the south and seized Falaise. Despite his change of heart barely twenty-four hours later, Montgomery left Brooke in *no doubt whatsoever* this his territorial aim for GOODWOOD was Falaise. M511, Montgomery to Brooke, 14 July 1944, Alanbrooke Papers.

[2] Hitler's life was saved when one of the officers sitting at the heavy oaken table moved the offending briefcase to the far side of the table support – away from where Hitler was standing – moments before it exploded. Hitler was wounded but survived and extracted sweeping reprisals on anyone connected with or even suspected of being a part of the plot.

CHAPTER 23

Cobra

> It's a madhouse here. . . You can't imagine what it's
> like.
>
> Field Marshal von Kluge

The same miserable weather that had terminated GOODWOOD
had prevented COBRA from being launched on 20 July. After
savage fighting the long-sought prize of St Lô fell to Corlett's XIX
Corps on 18–19 July and subsequent preliminary operations had
been successful in establishing VII Corps north of the St Lô-
Périers road, where three infantry divisions were poised to push
wide the shoulders of the gap to be blown open by the bombers of
Eighth and Ninth US Air Forces. Several miles to the rear was the
exploitation force of two armoured divisions and a motorized
infantry division. Defending against the Americans was Hausser's Seventh Army, consisting of LXXXIV Corps in the COBRA
sector, and II Parachute Corps, whose zone extended east to the
vicinity of Caumont – nearly 30,000 German troops, considerably more than the Americans estimated. Bradley's anxiety was
noted by Chester Hansen, who recorded in his diary for 23 July:
'No chance of Cobra today, the weather was misty and the sky
grey. General looked at the sky with a mildly profane "Dammit".
Said, "I'm going to have to court-martial the chaplain if we have
much more weather like this."'[1]

Since COBRA was dependent upon the support of the air forces
the final decision was left to Leigh-Mallory, who rescheduled the
operation for the afternoon of 24 July, when it appeared that the
skies would finally clear. 'We tried to lay on a battle for the 24th,
for the Met. said there was more than a 50/50 chance of it coming
off. The Commander of the 8th American Air Force [Spaatz]

[1] Hansen Diary, 23 July 1944.

400

agreed with ill grace, but at the very last moment the weather died on us. . .'[1]

Operations for 24 July were cancelled but not before some 1,600 bombers had taken off. They were hastily recalled but too late to prevent nearly seven hundred tons of bombs from being dropped on the target area. A bombing error killed 25 and wounded 131 soldiers of the US 30th Division. Bradley was dismayed, not only by the accident but by the fact that the bombers had not made their bomb run parallel to the St Lô-Périers road but *at right angles*, which was contrary to his understanding of what had been agreed with the air force. Bradley regarded this as a serious breach of good faith in planning by the air forces but was unable to talk the air chiefs into making their bombing runs parallel to the road. Faced with the unpleasant choice either of cancelling COBRA or postponing its start indefinitely he concurred, and the operation was rescheduled for the next morning – 25 July.[2]

Although far from ideal the weather improved sufficiently, and COBRA commenced as a virtual repeat of GOODWOOD: wave after wave of American Ninth Air Force fighter-bombers attacked the target area, followed immediately by 1,500 heavies of the Eighth Air Force, disgorging some 3,400 tons of bombs. Sadly, COBRA was again off to a calamitous beginning; there was another 'short' bombing which again struck the hapless 30th Division and a unit of the 9th Division. Casualties were severe and included the highest ranking Allied officer killed in Northwest Europe – Lieutenant General Lesley J. McNair, Commander of Army Ground Forces, who had gone up to the front lines to observe the bombing, despite warnings that he ought to remain further back.[3]

For the American troops on the ground this was a dreadful and frightening experience as thousands of bombs rained indis-

---

[1] Leigh-Mallory Diary, 22–5 July 1944.

[2] Bradley, *A Soldier's Story*, op.cit., pp. 347–8. The air force claimed that they were unable to funnel down the St Lô-Periers road in less than two and a half hours and, inasmuch as only a few hours remained before the bomber crews were briefed, it was too late to plan such a major alteration.

[3] Casualties numbered 111 killed and 490 wounded by the American bombing error. McNair had been designated the commander of the phantom army group in England to replace Patton, whose presence in Normandy could not be kept a secret much longer. McNair was buried in the strictest secrecy, attended only by general officers, in order to avoid any compromise of FORTITUDE.

criminately upon American and German alike. Soon afterwards Hansen recorded the reaction of the commanders on the scene: 'General Hobbs [CG, 30th Division] said afterwards it was horrible. The ground belched, shook and spewed dirt to the sky. Scores of our troops were hit, their bodies flung from the slit trenches. Dazed and frightened our troops especially since yesterday's operation where shorts were serious. [Major General Clarence] Huebner [CG, 1st Division] who is an old front line campaigner said it was the most terrifying thing he had ever seen. Remote feeling of helplessness when you see bombs falling. Doughboys were quivering in their holes.'[1] Bradley's reaction was pure anguish: '"Oh Christ," I cried, "not another short drop?"'[2]

Panzer Lehr Division was dug in along the edge of the target area and General Bayerlein's account of the bombing was all too familiar:

> It was hell . . . The planes kept coming overhead like a conveyor belt, and the bomb carpets came down, now ahead, now on the right, now on the left. . . The fields were burning and smoldering. The bomb carpets unrolled in great rectangles. . . My front lines looked like a landscape on the moon, and at least seventy percent of my personnel were out of action – dead, wounded, crazed or numbed. All my front line tanks were knocked out. Late in the afternoon, the American ground troops began filtering in. I had organized my last reserves to meet them – not over fifteen tanks, most of them from repair shops. The roads were practically impassable. Then next morning the bombing began all over again. We could do nothing but retreat. Marshal von Kluge sent word at six that afternoon that the line along the St. Lô-Périers road must be held at all costs. It was already broken. But a new SS tank battalion was coming in with sixty tanks to drive to the Vire River and cut off the Americans. They arrived – five tanks, not sixty.[3]

The Air Force refused to accept responsibility for the tragic 'short' bombings on 24 and 25 July. Their investigation con-

---

[1] Hansen Diary, 25 July 1944. The front-line troops were positioned only 1,200 yards outside the target area.

[2] Bradley, *A Soldier's Story*, op.cit., p. 348.

[3] Post-war interrogation of General Leutnant Fritz Bayerlein, n.d., Liddell Hart Papers. Bayerlein was highly respected on both sides. After the war he cooperated willingly and energetically in the preparation of the US Army's 'European Report Series' which was a detailed collection of accounts of German military actions in Northwest Europe.

cluded that no agreement was ever made to bomb parallel to the St Lô-Périers road, and that 'The bombs which fell outside the target area during the 25 July operation were within the normal expectancy of errors.' Moreover, they argued that the necessity to concentrate 1,500 heavy bombers in a narrow target area in a minimum of time further complicated the problems. 'This resulted in a great deal of maneuvering on the bombing run and the rapid sequence of the attacking waves did not permit smoke and dust from bomb bursts to clear, thereby complicating the problem of target identification for following units.'[1]*

Thus, COBRA began in depressing circumstances and the rapid penetration Bradley had envisioned did not occur – the advance on 25 July was less than two miles. As acute as Bayerlein's situation was, the 30th Division found Panzer Lehr 'doing business at the same old stand with the same old merchandise – dug-in tanks and infantry'.[2] Indeed, German artillery fire was in some instances untouched by the bombing and able to rain heavy fire in front of the advancing American troops.

What no one was able to comprehend at the end of the first day of COBRA was that what appeared to be continued stiff German resistance was in fact a brittle façade which would soon crack under renewed pressure by VII Corps. The pessimism within the US Command was observed by Hansen: 'We talked of the lesson to be learned from it. Apparently heavy bombers cannot be used in tactical support. Cassino seemed to substantiate that. Yet airmen were enthusiastic about this. Leigh-Mallory and others in it.' Eisenhower was quoted as saying: 'I look upon heavies as an instrument for strategic attack on rear installations. I don't believe they can be used in support of ground troops. That's a job for artillery. I gave them a green light on this show but this is the last one.'[3]

The following day was indecisive with excellent progress in some sectors and negligible gains in others. VIII Corps initiated

---

[1] Eighth Air Force, 'Special Report of Operations, 24–25 July 1944,' Spaatz Papers, Manuscripts Division, Library of Congress. The air force also argued that had the ground troops been positioned 3,000 yards back as they had recommended, the friendly casualties would have been negligible. Bradley had rejected this on grounds that his troops must be closer in order to be able to exploit the gap created by the bombs.

* According to Bradley the Air Force report was little more than a whitewash, 'The Air Force brass simply lied.' *A General's Life*, p. 279.

[2] Quoted in Weigley, *Eisenhower's Lieutenants*, op.cit., p. 154.

[3] Hansen Diary, 25 July 1944.

its offensive on the right of VII Corps and ran into a stone wall of resistance, but by 27 July it became evident that German opposition was crumbling fast. What spelled the difference was a daring gamble by General Collins to deepen his penetration in the target area by committing two of his mobile armoured columns before the time was ripe for an exploitation. The possibility existed that the armour might cause congestion on the front, but his decision proved to be a correct one. On the left flank the 2nd Armored Division broke through the German lines at the important crossroads town of St Gilles in what turned out to be the beginning of the exploitation phase of COBRA[1].* VIII Corps suddenly found their progress virtually unimpeded. Bradley recognized that with this sudden turn of fortune it was time to turn Patton loose. The Third Army was to become operational on 1 August but in the interim Patton was given immediate control of VIII Corps.

For weeks Patton had been anxiously waiting in the wings for an opportunity to redeem himself after the humiliation of his relief in Sicily; he was determined not to bungle whatever chance he got. Bradley was not pleased to have him as a subordinate. The campaign in Sicily, where Bradley had been Patton's subordinate, had highlighted the strong differences in their characters and their approach to command. The volatile Patton was given to sudden fits of anger; his profane manner was often his undoing and a source of embarrassment to both Eisenhower and Bradley, as it was to Marshall. Bradley was repelled by Patton's tendency to swear at his troops and could never understand his need for crudeness. More importantly, Bradley felt Patton had not been sufficiently familiar with the planning details for HUSKY, that he had left far too much to his deputy commander, and had not involved himself deeply enough in the logistics and enemy situations. He viewed Patton's insistence on capturing Messina before Montgomery as an ego trip at the expense of his troops. Though he remained a loyal subordinate, Bradley had nevertheless grown more and more disenchanted with Patton, and found

---

[1] Blumenson, *Breakout and Pursuit*, op.cit., pp. 252–5.
* Bradley remembers that, 'Slowly it came to me that Cobra had not failed. It had succeeded; we had broken through. Joe Collins, absolutely justifying our faith in him, enlarged the rupture in the German lines and kept right on moving south, mile after mile.' *A General's Life*, p. 281.

serving under him a great strain, so that by the time he was appointed by Eisenhower to command the First Army for the invasion Bradley was delighted to be out from under. 'I disliked the way he worked, upset technical plans, interfered in my orders. His stubbornness on amphibious operations and his parade plans into Messina sickened me and soured me on Patton.'[1] Above all else, two events that did most to sour Bradley on Patton occurred on 3 August 1943 and again on 10 August, when the furious Seventh Army Commander slapped a soldier thought to be malingering in separate incidents at two field hospitals. For a disgusted Bradley, this was the last straw.

COBRA admittedly made an awkward situation for both men, with the one-time superior now the subordinate, but although their journey together to the end of the war was not always without difficulty, Bradley was soon to have ample reason to be pleased with Patton's presence in Normandy. Patton had already told Bradley: 'I must get in and do something spectacularly successful if I am to make good.'[2] Just how spectacularly successful Patton would be, even he could not perceive at that moment.

On 28 July Bradley began to visualize more sweeping results from COBRA and stated privately that he would not be surprised if his forces were in Rennes within two weeks. 'We shall continue attacking, never give him a chance to rest, never give him a chance to dig in. . . We shall never stop until the [German] army is beaten and until the army knows it is beaten. I shall never discuss terms. I shall insist on an unconditional surrender immediately.'[3]

That same day Bradley wrote to Eisenhower: 'To say that personnel of the First Army Headquarters is riding high tonight is putting it mildly. Things on our front look really good. I told Middleton to continue tomorrow morning [with VIII Corps] toward Avranches and go as far as resistance will permit. As you can see we are feeling pretty cocky.'[4]

By 29 July there was a frenzy of movement across the south Cotentin as four armoured divisions began to pour south of Coutances. The gains had been spectacular and threatened com-

---

[1] Hansen Papers, US Army Military Institute.
[2] Hansen Diary, 27 July 1944.
[3] Hansen Diary, 28 July 1944.
[4] Bradley, letter to Eisenhower, 28 July 1944, Eisenhower Presidential Papers, Eisenhower library.

plete dismemberment of the German left flank in Normandy. But it was by no means a simple task; the advancing armour and infantry fought a series of bloody battles with the retreating Germans. One particularly bloody engagement took place near St Denis-le-Gast between a force of the 2nd SS Panzer and 17th SS Panzer Grenadier Divisions and the 2nd Armored Division. After the battle one American officer described the carnage as 'the most Godless sight I have ever witnessed on any battlefield.'[1]

The long-standing dream of mobile warfare was now a reality; what had been planned as a penetration followed by an envelopment had turned into exploitation, supported superbly by Quesada's IX Tactical Air Force. 'From the beginning of COBRA to the end of July, fighter-bombers in the VII Corps zone alone claimed 362 enemy tanks and assault guns destroyed and 216 damaged, 1,337 other vehicles destroyed and 280 damaged. The number of burned-out vehicles along the roads confirmed that these claims suffered relatively slightly from the airmen's usual vice of exaggeration.'[2]

By 30 July the 4th Armored Division, the VIII Corps spearhead, had driven clear to Avranches and, finding two bridges intact over the River Sée, had entered the city unopposed. Situated at the base of the Cotentin between the Rivers Sée and Sélune, Avranches was the gateway to an Allied advance into Brittany and southern Normandy and 'in the summer of 1944 was a prize beyond compare.'[3] However, to ensure that this corridor to the south and west was held open, it was vital that the town of Pontaubault, four miles south of Avranches, should be captured as well. At Pontaubault the road network led south, east and west. American good fortune held during the afternoon of 31 July when the Pontaubault bridge over the Sélune was also captured intact by Combat Command A of the 4th Armored Division.

Six days earlier COBRA had begun as an attempted breakthrough in an atmosphere of despair, but what had been a faint hope of a breakout turned into reality when the last barrier at

---

[1] Quoted in Weigley, *Eisenhower's Lieutenants*, op.cit., p. 160.
[2] Weigley, op.cit., pp. 165–6. The reader interested in a detailed account of combat operations during COBRA is advised to consult Martin Blumenson's *Breakout and Pursuit* and *Eisenhower's Lieutenants*.
[3] Blumenson, *Breakout and Pursuit*, op.cit., p. 314.

Avranches-Pontaubault fell. For the first time since 6 June the German defences had not only been bent but broken by an Allied attack. Now, with the combined forces of VII and VIII Corps descending upon Avranches like a torrent, the moment was at hand for an offensive into the Brittany Peninsula and a pursuit of the remnants of a shattered Seventh Army.

German desperation on the western flank was reflected in this anguished exchange between a stunned von Kluge and his OB West Chief-of-Staff, General Gunther Blumentritt, on 31 July:

> It's a madhouse here. . . You can't imagine what it's like. . . So far, it appears that only the spearheads of various [American] mobile units are through to Avranches. But it is perfectly clear that everything else will follow. Unless I can get infantry and anti-tank weapons there, the [left] wing cannot hold. . . Someone has to tell the Führer that if the Americans get through at Avranches they will be out of the woods and they'll be able to do what they want. . . It's a crazy situation.[1]

A German attempt to secure the Pontaubault bridge before the 4th Armored arrived was unsuccessful. What von Kluge has described as a *Riesenauri* – 'one hell of a mess' – was about to turn into a nightmare as the Allied general the Germans most feared, George Patton, moved in to fulfil his destiny.

---

[1] Quoted in Blumenson, *Breakout and Pursuit*, op.cit., p. 323.

CHAPTER 24

Turning the Corner
at Avranches

Let's take a chance now that we have the ball.
Let's forget those fine firm bases in the dreary shell
    raked spaces.
Let's shoot the works and win! Yes, win it all.

George S. Patton[1]

August 1944 marked the turning point in the fortunes of Lieutenant General George S. Patton Jr. A firm believer in divine
providence, he knew himself very lucky indeed to be in command
of the Third US Army.[2] Had it not been for the foresight of
Eisenhower and Marshall, who had instinctively understood that
the Allies would one day badly need his unique dash and genius in
Europe, Patton might have been cooling his heels in obscurity
somewhere in the United States.

At noon on 1 August Patton's army officially became operational; in a move planned before the invasion. Bradley went up
to command 12th Army Group, which also became operational
that day. Lieutenant General Courtney Hodges, who had been
understudying Bradley, assumed command of the First Army.
Patton attempted to find something suitable to drink in celebra-
tion of the event but the best his staff could come up with was a
bottle purporting to be brandy. 'We tried to drink this, but
gagged.'[3] He was relieved to be back in command and eager to
prove his mettle. His first order was to Major General Troy
Middleton to thrust his VIII Corps towards Brest and Rennes.
'The waiting was pretty bad . . . but now we are in the biggest

---

[1] Extracted from poem, 'Absolute War', quoted in Blumenson, *The Patton Papers*, II,
p. 492.
[2] The codename Patton personally selected for the Third Army was 'LUCKY'.
[3] George S. Patton, *War As I Knew It*, London, 1946, p. 98.

battle I have ever fought and it is going fine except at one town we have failed to take... I am going there in a minute to kick someone's ass.'[1] The machinery was now in motion to finish what COBRA had started.

By the afternoon of 1 August, Major General John S. Wood's 4th Armored Division had become the first American unit to enter Brittany, and by early evening they had advanced forty miles to the outskirts of Rennes. During the following days American units poured through the neck of the funnel at Avranches-Pontaubault; indeed the movement of so many units over a short period of time became a traffic control problem reminiscent of GOODWOOD. Patton's immediate priority was to pass his two corps – Middleton's VIII and Major General Wade Haislip's XV – through this major bottleneck without delay. It was, said Patton, 'one of those things which cannot be done, but was. It was only made possible by extremely effective use of veteran staff officers and by the active part taken in it by corps and division commanders who, on occasion personally directed traffic. It was very evident that if a jam occurred, our losses, particularly with truck-borne infantry, would be terrific, and I had to say to myself, "Do not take counsel of your fears".'[2]

Instead, with two armoured divisions loose in Brittany – the 6th Armored to the north, driving on St Malo and ultimately, Brest; and the 4th Armored, preparing to assault the well garrisoned Rennes – Patton had good reason to be pleased. In the days that followed these two divisions moved so quickly that they outran their communications and became very difficult to control: VIII Corps and the Third Army actually lost track of their locations on several occasions.[3]

Patton's assigned mission was to liberate the Brittany Peninsula and seize the ports of St Malo, Brest and the area of Quiberon Bay, where the Allies intended to construct a large port facility. VIII Corps was given this task, with XV Corps to assist if needed. Patton's plan was to first isolate Brittany, cutting the peninsula at the base by sending two divisions south to Rennes

---

[1] Quoted in Blumenson, *The Patton Papers*, II, p. 494.
[2] Patton, op.cit., p. 98. Patton's primary concern was the Luftwaffe.
[3] So chaotic was the American communications network, which had never been designed for such far-flung operations, that it frequently took in excess of thirty-six hours for messages to be sent and acknowledged.

and then on to Quiberon Bay, while two divisions, led by the 6th Armored, drove due west on Brest. Only when Brittany and the ports were secure could Patton turn eastwards 'where the decisive battle of the European campaign would obviously be fought'.[1]

However, no one had thought that the battle for Brittany would be anything more than a deliberate, controlled advance of the sort which had occurred in the bocage. When the breakout at Avranches quickly developed into very mobile warfare, Patton was the first to grasp the immense possibilities open to the Third Army. 'What emerged was a concept quite different from that which had governed operations in the Cotentin. Patton saw his immediate objectives far in advance of the front, for his intent was to slash forward and exploit not only the mobility and striking power of his armored divisions but also the German disorganization. . . There seemed little point in slowly reducing Brittany by carefully planned and thoroughly supervised operations unraveled in successive phases.'[2]

Moreover, Patton soon came to the conclusion that operations in Brittany could be minimized while the rest of the Third Army was turned eastward to drive towards the Seine through the unprotected underbelly of Normandy – the Orleans gap. The immense possibilities of a drive to the east were not lost on Bradley either, and on 3 August he made a decision which, as the US official history records, was to change the entire course of the campaign. Patton was to leave only 'a minimum of forces' to secure Brittany. 'The primary American mission was to go to the forces in Normandy who were to drive eastward and expand the continental lodgment area.'[3] Montgomery immediately concurred, for he too saw that the spectacular success of COBRA had radically changed the entire conception of how operations would develop. Within hours the original Allied strategy of OVERLORD was abandoned. To his credit, Montgomery resisted pressure from the logisticians to divert more forces to Brittany when Brest was found to be heavily defended, telling Brooke: 'The main business lies to the east.'[4]

---

[1] Blumenson, *Breakout and Pursuit*, p. 348.
[2] Ibid, p. 349.
[3] Ibid, p. 431.
[4] Montgomery, cable to Brooke, 4 August 1944, quoted in Blumenson, p. 432.

Montgomery has since implanted the notion that what ensued was a direct result of his master plan coming to fruition.
There, were, however, some important differences between his
version and the truth. As we have already seen, Montgomery's
conception was to turn the First US Army eastwards once
Avranches was breached and, in a series of deliberate advances
by Canadian, British and American forces, push the Germans
back to the Seine. In his *Memoirs* he fails to acknowledge that
COBRA came about from Bradley's initiative and not as a direct
result of his master plan. Instead he states unequivocally that:
'The strategy of the Normandy campaign was British, and it
succeeded because of first class team-work on the part of all the
forces engaged – British and American.'[1] General Belchem later
fuelled the controversy by alleging that Montgomery had planned an envelopment by the Third Army to the Seine that coincidentally duplicated the actual events of August 1944. He offers
in evidence a map purporting to show the Third Army driving on
the axis Laval-Le Mans, and on to the Seine north and south of
Paris.[2] If such a map ever existed it has mysteriously disappeared;
there are no copies in the records of 21st Army Group, de
Guingand's papers, the Eisenhower archives, or any other known
historical source, nor does it resemble any of the known phase-
line maps in existence. In fact, until 3 August the Third Army's
mission had been to secure Brittany. Its later mission was to
provide Allied flank security along the Loire River as the other
Allied armies drove east.

That Montgomery developed the framework of Allied
strategy in Normandy is beyond dispute, but to mislead by
suggesting that the operations now developing on the American
front were that framework come to fruition is stretching the
point. Assuredly it was the result of Anglo-American cooperation, but it must be pointed out that prior to COBRA Montgomery
was directing the Third Army on Brittany while the First
Army swung east through the bocage. It was only after COBRA
had succeeded that Montgomery, too, began thinking in terms
of a long, sweeping envelopment to the Seine and Paris by

[1] Montgomery, *Memoirs*, op.cit., pp. 261–2.
[2] Belchem, *Victory in Normandy*, op.cit., p. 51.

US forces emerging from the confines of the bocage.[1]

At this decisive point in the campaign it can be said that Montgomery, Bradley and Eisenhower (who was present with Bradley when the decision was made to drive towards the Orleans gap on 2 August) were all in agreement over current Allied strategy.[2] With this crucial decision the last remnants of the original plan had been modified to the point where it made little difference – except perhaps to certain British-American egos – where the credit went. What can be said is that the success now being enjoyed by the Allied armies was the product of *both* Montgomery's and Bradley's planning and improvization.

The post-war battle of egos has obstructed the search for the truth, and nothing could have been more unhelpful than Montgomery's claim in his *Memoirs* that this was his plan. Bradley had planned what was now a breakout and exploitation; what was now about to occur was, in fact, Plan B of LUCKY STRIKE which, it will be recalled, was developed on the premise that:

(a) There were no appreciable enemy forces left in the Brittany peninsula.

(b) Few enemy forces were in the area between the line Le Mans-Chartres, and the Loire River.

(c) No strong mobile German forces were south of the Loire.

In short, for all practical purposes an open flank existed south of the bocage.[3] Montgomery's master plan had envisioned a slower, more deliberate move to the Seine rather than the exploitation of

---

[1] As late as 28 July Montgomery was still proclaiming Brittany as his first priority objective. At a conference with his corps commanders on that date, Dempsey's notes record: 'C-in-C's object remains the same – BRITTANY. *This is the only geographical objective.* It is First Army's task to get it. Second Army's task is: (a) to draw onto itself the maximum German strength, particularly armour, and weaken it. (b) To hold the pivot secure. . . (c) to help First Army in every way possible to get Brittany.' Dempsey Papers, Second Army Orders of Battle – Notes and Directives, June–Jul, PRO (WO 285/8).

[2] Eisenhower was clearly infected by Bradley's plans for exploiting the breakout at Avranches. That same day – 2 August – he wrote to Montgomery urging boldness by armoured and mobile columns against the enemy flanks. *The Eisenhower Papers*, IV, pp. 2047–8 and Pogue, *The Supreme Command*, p. 204. Eisenhower also cabled Marshall an optimistic assessment, foreseeing 'a chance for the Allies to win a tactical victory and create virtually an open flank. If this happened he proposed to send only a small part of his forces into Brittany while using the bulk of the Allied units to destroy the enemy west of the Rhine and exploit as far to the east as possible.' Quoted in Pogue, *The Supreme Command*, p. 204. The complete text of Eisenhower's cable, S–56667, 2 August 1944, is in *The Eisenhower Papers*, IV, pp. 2048–51.

[3] Report of US Forces European Theater, 1942–6, Study No. 1, loc.cit.

an open flank now taking place.[1] There was certainly no debate about what was to happen:

> The new broad Allied strategy that had emerged concentrated on the possibility of swinging the Allied right flank around toward Paris. The sweeping turn would force the Germans back against the lower reaches of the Seine River, where all the bridges had been destroyed by air bombardment.[2] Pushed against the river and unable to cross with sufficient speed to escape, the Germans west of the Seine would face potential destruction.[3]

The mission of spearheading the drive east fell to Haislip's XV Corps which held, on the night of 2 August, a line running from north of Fougères with the 79th Division, northeast to Juvigny with the 90th Division. The recently arrived 5th Armored Division was ordered to halt on the Sée River outside Avranches and was assigned by Patton as the cutting edge of XV Corps. Even before Bradley had formalized his decision it was evident that Patton had an exploitation to the east in mind.[4]

The first week of August was the most decisive period of the Normandy campaign: not only were the Allies poised to deliver a killing blow, but it was the week in which Hitler personally sealed the fate of the German Army in Normandy by committing an incredible blunder.

After the Allied breakthrough at Avranches Hitler had dictated a new strategy designed to stabilize the German front until reinforcements could be marshalled and steps taken to establish new defences along the Marne and the Somme. To accomplish this, Hitler reckoned he needed from six to ten weeks; to buy this time he ordered that each of the Atlantic ports be defended to the death and a scorched earth policy for all transportation facilities in France be implemented by German forces as they withdrew.[5]

---

[1] This point is emphasized by Bradley who comments: 'A key assumption in the Overlord plan was that after we had achieved overwhelming strength in Normandy the German armies facing us would make a gradual withdrawal to the Seine River, a natural defensive barrier.' A General's Life, p. 289.

[2] See Chapter 26.

[3] Blumenson, Breakout and Pursuit, p. 432.

[4] Patton's order to Haislip was given late in the morning of 2 August. As the US official history states, it was ostensibly for the purpose of protecting the exposed flank of VIII Corps, but it would also position three divisions to the southeast in exactly the right spot from which to launch a drive toward Laval and Le Mans.

[5] Blumenson, Breakout and Pursuit, p. 340.

Hitler had never placed great trust in his military commanders and the attempt to kill him on 20 July had further warped his confidence in the army to the point where he decided to assume personal charge of the Western Front. Suspicion had not yet fallen upon von Kluge but within days he was linked with the suspected traitors to the Reich who were being arrested. Although the number of plotters was small, Hitler used the plot as an excuse to dispose of his enemies; untold numbers were executed in a series of savage reprisals. Hitler was certain that the outcome of the Normandy campaign would decide the destiny of Germany, which only he could save. During a conference on 31 July at the Wolf's Lair he had raged against the moral bankruptcy which he claimed, was rampant within the high command of the army. 'He insisted that Germany's problem was a moral and not a material one. . . He lashed out at those who felt that it was possible to come to some sort of arrangement with the Reich's enemies, saying that this was not a struggle which would be settled by negotiation or some clever tactical manoeuver, but rather a Hunnish war in which one or the other of the antagonists had to perish.'[1] Hitler had also refused to disclose his full plans to von Kluge but would only tell him enough so that his orders could be carried out. He despatched General Walter Warlimont to brief von Kluge with this admonition: 'Tell Field-Marshal von Kluge that he should keep his eyes riveted to the front and on the enemy without ever looking backward.'[2]

On 2 August Hitler sent OB West a directive which changed the course of the campaign. He ordered von Kluge to launch a strong armoured counterthrust by Hausser's Seventh Army between Mortain and Avranches, to recapture the neck of the Cotentin Peninsula and to cut off all US forces in Brittany and south of Avranches, where, without resupply, he believed they could no longer function. Hitler demanded that 'All available panzer units, regardless of their present commitment, are to be taken from the other parts of the Normandy front, joined together under one specially qualified panzer operations staff, and sent into a concentrated attack as soon as possible. The outcome of the whole campaign in France depends on the success

---

[1] Pogue, *The Supreme Command*, p. 202. The minutes of this conference were taken by Jodl.
[2] Quoted by Warlimont, ibid, p. 203.

of this attack.'[1] It was, argued Hitler, 'a unique, never recurring opportunity for a complete reversal of the situation'.[2]

There were three qualifications to the German plan. Hitler insisted that: 'Von Kluge must believe in it. He must be able to detach enough armour from the main front in Normandy to create an effective striking force. And he must achieve surprise.[3] None of these necessities was attained, and the third of Kluge's failures was disastrous.'

According to the OB West Operations Officer, General Leutnant Bodo Zimmermann, Hitler's order reached von Kluge as he was visiting the front and 'struck him like a thunderbolt'. 'He knew very well that carrying out this order meant the collapse of the Normandy front and probably catastrophe.' As Zimmermann later remembered it, von Kluge cabled his misgivings to OKW, pointing out that 'Tanks are the backbone of our defense, where they are withdrawn, our front will give way... If, as I foresee, this plan does not succeed, catastrophe is inevitable.'[4] Nevertheless, von Kluge's doubts were ignored by Hitler, who renewed his insistence that the order be carried out, although he did give some latitude in the timing of the offensive. What later came to be known as the Mortain counterattack was indeed a unique opportunity – but not for Hitler.

There has been some dispute over the role played by ULTRA in the Mortain affair. Two recent British accounts have advanced the notion that the Allies were aware of Hitler's order of 2 August to von Kluge and that as a result Bradley baited a trap for the Germans. The first to reveal the existence of ULTRA was RAF Group Captain F. W. Winterbotham in a book called *The Ultra Secret*: he recalls receiving an ULTRA intercept of Hitler's intentions on 2 August. Ronald Lewin's excellent account, *Ultra Goes to War*, also dates the first Allied intercept to the early morning hours of 3 August. Lewin's version is based on Winterbotham's account which was written from memory and without access to the ULTRA records, still classified at that time. The truth is that neither ULTRA nor any other source revealed Hitler's intentions of

---

[1] 'OB West, A Study in Command', MS No. B–308, German Report Series, US Army Military History Institute.
[2] Quoted in Pogue, *The Supreme Command*, p. 207.
[3] Ronald Lewin, *Ultra Goes to War*, London, 1978, p. 338.
[4] Zimmermann in MS No. B–308, loc.cit.

2 August. Ralph Bennett points out in his authoritative account, which is based on messages from Bletchley Park giving the sense of the actual ULTRA decrypts: 'There appears to be no Ultra warrant for a number of his [Winterbotham's] statements, in spite of the circumstantial detail with which he surrounds some of them. Several can, however, be approximately reconciled with the signals by a change in dating.'[1]

The British never revealed the existence of ULTRA to the official US historians during the preparation of their accounts. As Dr Pogue recently commented: 'I was not truly aware of the source of ULTRA. I knew there were items classified 'ULTRA'. I thought the material was from spies. I knew it was a British source. The term is used in more than one interview I had in 1946 and 1947. Someone asked [US historian] Maurice Matloff the other day if he was aware of the source and he said no . . . The British official historians never warned us because they assumed – I imagine – that we knew nothing.'[2] Thus neither the British nor American official history of the Normandy campaign provides any clue that ULTRA even existed.[3] In the case of the Mortain counterattack, ULTRA does seem to have played a role even though, as will be seen, Bradley downgrades its importance, noting that he was made aware of an imminent German

---

[1] Bennett, *Ultra in the West*, op.cit., p. 119. Bennett notes 'There were three stages in the Mortain attack: (1) Hitler's order of 2 August, of which Ultra knew nothing, (2) the attack order of 6 August and (3) von Kluge's renewal order of 9 August, both of which Ultra reported in time. It seems possible Group-Captain Winterbotham confused stages (2) and (3) with (1).' *Ultra in the West*, p. 119.

[2] Letter to the author, 15 April 1983. Dr Maurice Matloff was author of several volumes of the US official history of the Second World War.

[3] ULTRA was undoubtedly the best kept secret of the Second World War. Several thousand people were connected with ULTRA in some capacity during the war yet, until Group Captain Winterbotham became the first person permitted to reveal what ULTRA was and that it had been pilfering German signals since 1940, no one had ever heard of it. Even though the advent of modern computer codebreaking technology of the sort employed by the US National Security Agency, its top-secret British counterpart at Cheltenham, the KGB and others, has long since rendered the Enigma machine a relic, the secrecy of ULTRA was such that its story was not told until 1974. Nevertheless, there are some in Britain today who believe Winterbotham was quite wrong to have revealed the secret. Ronald Lewin notes that up to this time there had been no leaks. 'Perhaps never before has there been such a prolonged corporate act of silence.' One of those privy to the ULTRA secret told the author that there had never been any official restraint imposed upon him by the British government, such as the Official Secrets Act. When asked if he had ever discussed it with anyone, he replied 'no'; it simply had never occurred to him to reveal its existence to anyone. During the war even the use of the codename ULTRA was forbidden in order to prevent further possible compromise. The Lewin quote is from *Ultra Goes to War*, op.cit., p. 17.

attack only on the night of 6 August, some four hours before the Seventh Army struck American positions around Mortain. The ULTRA secret stopped at Bradley, thus no commander subordinate to him was aware that there was a source of secret intelligence.

The great masterstroke that Hitler thought might cut off the Third Army and all other American units below Avranches may have been brilliant in its conception but it overlooked the problem of what might happen if it failed. In fact he had ordered von Kluge to send Seventh Army into the jaws of what Omar Bradley would turn into a great Allied trap. Within days the German Army in France would be crushed and the Normandy campaign decided.

CHAPTER 25

The Great Encirclement

In a few days' time we were to gain a victory which
was to be acclaimed as the greatest achievement in
military history.

Montgomery, *Memoirs*

To hell with compromises.

George S. Patton, *The Patton Papers,*
1939–1945

The German counterattack came on the night of 6–7 August when
47 Panzer Corps, newly formed under General Hans von Funck,
slammed into the 30th Division east of Mortain. Von Kluge had
cobbled together a panzer force consisting of the 2nd Panzer,
1st and 2nd SS Panzer and 116th Panzer Divisions. Of these units,
only the 116th Panzer Division was fresh; it had been committed
earlier to the north but was able to disengage quickly enough to
shift to its new positions in the south. His attack achieved tactical surprise – the Germans frequently avoided compromising their
intentions by omitting a preparatory barrage. Several hours
after the 2nd SS Panzer thrust at the 30th Division, which had
taken over their positions around Mortain only a few hours earlier, the 2nd Panzer launched an attack to the north, parallel to
the River Sée.[1]

The German attack against Mortain was prevented from
driving through to Avranches only by the Americans' stout
defence of Hill 317, which provided a commanding view of the
German route of attack and was the key terrain feature in the
area. Nonetheless, the 2nd SS Panzer managed to penetrate
several miles southwest of Mortain before being stalled by the
arrival of Allied reinforcements in the form of the 35th Division,

---

[1] At midnight, 6 August, VII Corps warned all units that a counterattack might come
near Mortain sometime within the next twelve hours. About twenty minutes later the first
attack by the 2nd SS Panzer hit the 30th Division. Cf, Martin Blumenson, *Breakout and
Pursuit,* Chapter XXIV.

which Bradley had ordered moved to Mortain from the vicinity of Fougères only hours before the German attack.

The following morning Quesada's IX TAF, with support from the RAF, smashed at the German panzers – it was the first time in Normandy that they had become exposed targets for Allied airpower. The Luftwaffe had promised but again failed to put in an appearance over the battlefield. As one German account later bitingly stated, 'The air situation in the forenoon of 7 August stopped the whole counterattack against Avranches – not even one of the announced 300 German fighters appeared. Afterwards the Air Force declared that the fighters had started but had either been contained by the enemy air force at their airports or during the approach flight to the operations area . . . any movement in the combat area was made impossible.'[1]

That afternoon the 1st SS Panzer and 116th Panzer also attacked, but by this time 47 Panzer Corps was receiving a very hostile reception, not just from the Allied air but on the ground. Once the flanks were sealed off, VII Corps was able to contain the German advance while inflicting heavy losses from north and south. American determination was never more evident than around Hill 317 which was surrounded and isolated until 12 August. Of the 700 men of the 2nd Battalion, 120 Infantry Regiment (30th Division), nearly 300 were killed or wounded. General Collins has called the defence of Hill 317 'one of the outstanding small-unit actions of World War II. The battalion was given a presidential unit citation and each of the four company commanders received the DSC . . . According to German reports they had been a "thorn in the flesh" that helped paralyze enemy movement in the area.'[2]

Nearly two weeks earlier, during the disastrous start of COBRA, Major General Leland S. Hobbs's 30th Division had absorbed heavy casualties from the 'short' bombing by American aircraft. Now it bore the brunt of the Mortain counterattack: the

---

[1] Major General Rudolph von Gersdorff, Manuscript No. A-921, German Report Series, US Army Military History Institute. Von Gersdorff had replaced Pemsel as Seventh Army Chief of Staff. After the war von Gersdorff earned the respect and admiration of the US historians for his many contributions to the German Report Series which has enabled us to gain an excellent picture of events taking place on 'the other side of the hill'.

[2] Collins, *Lightning Joe*, op.cit., p. 255. The Distinguished Service Cross (DSC) is the second highest US award for gallantry after the Medal of Honor.

warning from ULTRA had come too late for them to prepare for the attack by the 2nd SS Panzer on 7 August, during which more than six hundred men were lost and a number of units isolated. After the initial shock of the attack the division showed its mettle by standing firm against repeated German attacks across its front. Bradley later called the gallant 30th Division the 'Rock of Mortain'. Now he reasoned that if he could swing Patton's XV Corps behind the Germans in the direction of Alençon and Argentan in a 'short hook', the Allies might be able to trap the enemy.

Bradley had considerable reservations about ULTRA and, as we now know, was alerted to the impending counterattack only on the night of 6 August. Of Winterbotham's account, he notes: 'My recollection is in sharp variance. In this instance Ultra was of little or no value. Ultra alerted us to the attack only a few hours before it came, and that was too late to make any major defensive preparations. . .'[1] Bradley always tended to treat ULTRA rather cautiously. He had seen for himself how Eisenhower's G–2 in Algiers, Brigadier Mockler-Ferryman, had erred in February 1943 by predicting an attack at Fondouk by von Arnim's Fifth Panzer Army (Pz Aok 5) as Panzer Group West had been redesignated, based on ULTRA intercepts. Eisenhower had been furious, believing that Mockler-Ferryman had placed too much trust in ULTRA, and within days had replaced him.[2] It had been about this time that Bradley arrived in North Africa and was admitted to the small, select circle of those privy to the ULTRA secret. The lesson of Mockler-Ferryman's unfortunate mistake was not lost upon him: 'I did not then or later embrace Ultra as the Oracle of Delphi, but rather as a marvelous source of intelligence to be evaluated and used tactically with utmost care.'[3] Later, in Northwest Europe, Bradley concluded that Allied intelligence had come to rely too heavily on ULTRA, which

[1] Bradley, *A General's Life*, p. 291.
[2] Butcher Diary, Eisenhower Library. Mockler-Ferryman was replaced by Major General Kenneth Strong who remained as Eisenhower's G–2 for the remainder of the war. The case of Mockler-Ferryman was not quite as straightforward as generally portrayed. What no one knew at the time was that the Germans were indeed planning to attack at Fondouk until Rommel ordered the objective changed to Sidi bou Zid. At that time Mockler-Ferryman had no other source of intelligence to rely on except ULTRA. Cf., F. H. Hinsley, *British Intelligence in the Second World War*, Vol II, London, 1981, Appendix 21, which provides a detailed examination of this incident.
[3] Bradley, *A General's Life*, p. 132.

by this time had come to be regarded as 'infallible'.[1]

Both Bradley and Collins were alert to the fact that the VII Corps sector – especially Mortain – was the most vulnerable place in the event of a German counterattack. In particular, Collins had warned of the necessity of controlling Hill 317, but beyond this all he remembers is that 'I – and General Bradley I am sure – foresaw the possibility of a German counter-attack from the Mortain area to capture Avranches. . .'[2] The warning of 6 August did not specify that Mortain was the German point of attack, nor did ULTRA at that time pinpoint von Kluge's troop concentrations. But, according to Bennett, there was evidence he had shifted three panzer divisions into the area north of Mortain around Sourdeval.[3]

Moreover, there was other evidence provided by ULTRA that Bradley either forgot or which was ignored in the preparation of his recent autobiography. In addition to the strong evidence that the Germans were massing their armour near Mortain, suspicion must have been aroused in the Allied High Command by an ULTRA warning early on 6 August that, partly in response to a request from 2nd SS Panzer Division, the Luftwaffe had announced on 5 August that it intended night bombing operations against St Hilaire and Mortain, night fighter attacks against the Pontorson area and concentrated fighter operations on 6 August in the area Mortain-Fougères. The connection between the Luftwaffe message and the panzer divisions reported by ULTRA in the Mortain area would have been clear to Bradley.[4] Thus, while Bradley was quite right to dismiss Winterbotham's account as irrelevant, he should have credited ULTRA's warnings – however short – as playing a role in the repulse of the German counterattack at Mortain.

[1] A specific example was the Ardennes counteroffensive in December 1944 when, as he did at Mortain, Hitler launched a surprise attack. In this instance there were certain clues, but not from ULTRA. Hitler had ordered a total communications blackout, thus eliminating ULTRA traffic. Bradley comments: 'It apparently did not occur to our intelligence community that the Germans could – or might – plan and launch an operation with complete radio and telephone silence imposed. The fallacy that crept into our thinking was that since Ultra had not specifically forecast or suggested a major strategic counterattack, there was no possibility of one.' *A General's Life*, p. 351. Bradley's remarks are somewhat oversimplified and, as Ralph Bennett's account shows, while there was indeed too much reliance on Bletchley Park, clues were not altogether lacking.

[2] Collins op. cit. p. 251.   [3] Bennett, op.cit., p. 115.

[4] Edward E. Thomas, letter to author, 19 April 1983. Thomas also points out that 'According to the Third Army's ULTRA officer, it was the Mortain incident that first alerted Third Army to the great potential value of ULTRA and made them care for it from then on.'

That same day – 7 August – Montgomery was launching the First Canadian Army in a major offensive, codenamed TOTALIZE, to capture Falaise. Montgomery's strategy for TOTALIZE was for the Canadians to pass down the corridor of the Caen-Falaise Plain to Falaise itself, while the Second Army swept the bocage to their right. Together the two armies would pivot to their left and, while the First and Third Armies drove east through southern Normandy, they would trap the Germans in a double envelopment along the River Seine by taking advantage of the open south flank. This was the so-called long envelopment. After GOOD-WOOD Montgomery had finally activated Crerar's First Canadian Army which now had room to operate in the newly expanded Orne bridgehead.[1] Dempsey's Second Army was shifted to the right flank of the British sector to support COBRA and on 30 July Dempsey initiated Operation BLUECOAT, with six divisions and two independent tank brigades, in a powerful attack along a front running from Caumont to the inter-army group boundary, some ten miles to the west where the US V Corps was operating.

When COBRA had begun to show signs of being decisive, Montgomery speeded up his plans for BLUECOAT, signalling Eisenhower: 'I have ordered Dempsey to throw all caution overboard and to take any risks he likes, and to accept any casualties, and to step on the gas for Vire.'[2]

In what has recently been termed 'the British breakout', Dempsey thrust O'Connor's 8 Corps down the right flank in a drive on Le Bény Bocage and Vire with the object of collapsing the increasingly vulnerable flanks of Seventh Army and forcing a withdrawal. On the left flank, 30 Corps was to press south and capture Mont Pinçon to prevent the Germans from using the protection of this hill mass during any withdrawal to the east, but their attack quickly showed the same lethargy that had been long evident to Dempsey. The 7th Armoured Division had been ordered to capture Aunay sur Odon and when, after two days, they were still nearly five miles short of their objective despite light resistance, Dempsey had had enough. 'I decided to sack

[1] There were numerous problems between Montgomery and Crerar, whom Monty considered totally unsuited for army command. One of Crerar's first actions was to quarrel with Crocker, whom he demanded be sacked. It took the firm intervention of Montgomery to restore peace between his generals.
[2] Quoted in memorandum by Lieutenant General W. B. Smith, 22 February 1945, Eisenhower Papers.

Bucknall very early – as far as I remember it was on the evening of the first day that I rang him and warned him that he had better get on or else. The following morning I rang Monty and told him that I was tired of Bucknall and that evening when 30 Corps' progress was still unsatisfactory I told Bucknall he would have to go. The next day or the day after, I decided that Erskine and Hinde would have to follow.'[1] Montgomery immediately summoned the veteran Sir Brian Horrocks from England to replace Bucknall, and he assumed command of 30 Corps on 4 August. Thereafter the performance of the corps improved significantly.[2]

O'Connor had better success with the 11th Armoured Division; they captured the important high ground around Le Bény Bocage and threw the Germans into a crisis when they penetrated the boundary separating Panzer Group West from the Seventh Army. A recent British account of this operation charges that Montgomery let an exceptional opportunity to elude him:

> The town of Vire, key road junction in the rear of the German Seventh Army was seven miles further on, undefended and at the mercy of the British armour. General Montgomery . . . chose just that moment to change the army boundary by placing Vire inside the American sector. The advance of the British [11th Armoured] division was directed south-east, with a warning not to trespass beyond the boundary two miles north of town. Montgomery had allowed a great opportunity to pass him by.[3]

This was the opportunity:

> Had the British taken Vire on 2nd August, then the Seventh Army would have been forced to retreat. The next day troops from the American First Army were to widen the Avranches gap at Brécy and push on south-east to enter Juvigny. They were fifteen miles south of the town of Vire. With the British in the town and the Americans in Mortain the retreat of the Seventh Army would have been turned into a rout. The less mobile of the German troops would have been trapped. It was only Patton of the Allied generals who at this early stage saw the possibility of such a development. . . Seven more days were to pass before the Allied command saw the great opportunity that was passing them by.[4]

[1] Dempsey interview with Wilmot, loc.cit.
[2] Within days Montgomery noted that 'a great change and impetus took place very quickly'.
[3] Major J. J. How, *Normandy: The British Breakout*, London, 1981, p. 219.
[4] How, op.cit. There is no discussion in the British official history about the impact on operations of the change of boundary by Montgomery.

Major How charges that 'Montgomery's account of the offensive in his book, *Normandy to the Baltic*, seems to be written to mislead rather than to inform. It is full of half-truths and inaccuracies. There is no word of a British breakout. The impression is given that Vire was strongly held by the enemy, and he makes no mention of the change in army boundary that placed the town out of bounds to the British. . . Had the British reinforced success with the same energy and speed the Germans had moved to forestall disaster there would have been a different end to the Normandy campaign.'[1] This action, How suggests, brought confusion at the time and has managed to defy accurate reporting ever since. If Montgomery recognized the importance of his action in changing the boundary or of the opportunity passing him by, he never acknowledged it. After nearly two months of painful slogging in the bocage, the Allied commanders were required to reassess their strategy on virtually a daily basis. The action at Vire appears to have been one of those situations that was not properly understood at the time.

Mortain, however, changed the thinking of Eisenhower, Bradley and Montgomery. On the morning of 8 August Eisenhower met Bradley who now outlined his new concept of a shorter envelopment – a left hook – to trap the Seventh Army between the Canadians advancing toward Falaise and Patton swinging north toward Argentan with XV Corps. If Bradley could contain the Seventh Army around Mortain for another two days it would give XV Corps – which was then driving towards Le Mans – time to complete the swing to the north. The result would be to trap the entire Seventh Army in the jaws of a pocket from which there could be no escape. It was, Bradley told visiting US Secretary of the Treasury, Henry Morgenthau, later that morning, 'an opportunity that comes to a commander not more than once in a century. . . We're about to destroy an entire hostile army.'[2] 'While Morgenthau looked on skeptically, I pointed to the German bulge at Mortain and outlined my reasons for that statement. "If the other fellow will only press his attack here at Mortain for another 48 hours, he'll give us time to close at Argentan and there completely destroy him. And when he loses his Seventh Army in this bag, he'll have nothing left with which

[1] How, *Normandy: The British Breakout*, pp. 220–1.
[2] Bradley, *A Soldier's Story*, p. 375.

to oppose us. We'll go all the way from here to the German border.'"[1]

Eisenhower enthusiastically endorsed Bradley's change of plan. Bradley telephoned Montgomery, who agreed to the idea. Bradley's objective – Argentan – lay some twelve miles inside the 21st Army Group boundary but, as he later remarked, 'Monty happily forgave us our trespasses and welcomed the penetration.'[2] Montgomery's later claims that this was all part of his overall plan were misleading:

> I have shown that up to this period my plan was to make a wide enveloping movement from the southern American flank up to the Seine about Paris, and at the same time to drive the centre and northern sectors of the Allied line straight for the river. In view of the Mortain counter stroke, I decided to attempt *concurrently* a shorter envelopment with the object of bottling up the bulk of the German forces deployed between Falaise and Mortain. It was obvious that if we could bring off both these movements we could virtually annihilate the enemy in Normandy.[3]

There are two serious misrepresentations in Montgomery's version. First, Bradley's proposal for the short hook towards Falaise was endorsed by Montgomery, but the idea originated solely with Bradley, with the firm backing of Eisenhower. If Montgomery had misgivings about this new strategy he apparently kept them to himself, at least at that time. Second, there is no evidence to support the notion of *concurrent* long and short envelopment at that moment. There were two options open for the utilization of XV Corps – to continue the long envelopment toward the Seine, or to move Haislip's corps north in a short hook. The remainder of the First Army was bottled up round Mortain, clearing up the Mortain bulge, and in no position to drive to the Seine until approximately 17 August. Patton's VIII Corps was tied up clearing Brittany, and his other two corps – XX and XII – were likewise too far to the west to participate in such a man-oeuvre until some days later. On 8 August the immediate choices open to Montgomery were either to make the long or the short envelopment, but not both. The decision to attempt both did

[1] Bradley, *A Soldier's Story*: pp. 375–6.
[2] Ibid, p. 375. That evening Eisenhower met Montgomery and this subject was undoubtedly a point of discussion between the two commanders.
[3] Montgomery, *El Alamein to the River Sangro and Normandy to the Baltic*, p. 267.

eventually come about, but not until 14 August, and for far different reasons.

Thus, on 8 August the decision was made to turn XV Corps to the north, initially toward Alençon, then on to Argentan, while the Canadians continued to drive hard for Falaise. Montgomery was confident (excessively so) of his ability to secure Argentan with the Canadians before XV Corps. The Germans, as usual, had a good deal to say, but by 11 August Montgomery was expressing an optimistic outlook. Led by Simonds's 2 Canadian Corps, Crerar had launched TOTALIZE on the night of 7–8 August. Dispensing with the traditional artillery bombardment, Simonds attacked in typically German fashion out of the darkness in order to circumvent the threat posed by the German artillery and anti-tank guns still ringing Bourguébus Ridge. Concurrently, RAF night bombers struck at the German flanks in an effort t⸱ seal them off while two divisions penetrated the German lines.[1]

The Canadians enjoyed good success initially but, as a recent account points out, 'Unfortunately, Simonds's exploitation divisions, the Canadian 4th Armoured and the Polish 1st Armoured, were inexperienced and fell into the usual consequent errors; particularly that of pausing to deal with strongpoints rather than bypassing them.'[2] By 9 August the Canadians were nearly half-way to Falaise, but German resistance proved savage and the offensive slowed to a crawl. Aware of the urgency of pushing through to Falaise quickly, Crerar and Simonds renewed their attacks in an effort to punch through to this key town. They were unsuccessful.

At that moment Montgomery had an opportunity to influence the course of TOTALIZE by reinforcing Crerar with units from the Second Army, which was progressing through the bocage with relative ease in a series of secondary attacks. Privately, some have wondered why Montgomery did not act at such a critical moment. It has been suggested, for example, that he could easily have detached 7th Armoured from Dempsey and shifted it to Crerar's front. That he did not do so may well have stemmed from the fact that he did not trust the Desert Rats because of their

---

[1] Simonds was successful – where O'Connor had not been – in turning some of his self-propelled artillery into makeshift armoured personnel carriers for the infantry, called 'Kangeroos', to permit them to keep up with the leading tanks. Cf., Weigley, p. 204.

[2] Weigley, op.cit., p. 204.

consistently poor performance in Normandy. This was not, however, his only option. As we shall see, the battle of the Falaise gap generated enormous controversy and criticism of both Montgomery and Bradley, but whatever mistakes may have been committed during this series of battles, the most serious by Montgomery was failing to take advantage of the opportunity to reinforce the Canadians and thus bolster the advance on Falaise.[1] Time was critical if the trap were to be sprung successfully and it was obvious the Canadians were in serious trouble; consequently, there was hardly a basis for Montgomery's false optimism that they would push on to Argentan before Patton got there. In the next chapter we shall examine in detail Montgomery's actions at this critical time.

Crerar and Simonds did their best with what they had but it was not enough; Falaise, like Caen weeks before, lay several miles away, a prize necessary for the success of the northern pincer movement. As early as 12 August, Bradley's staff were grumbling that 'the British effort . . . appears to have logged itself in timidity and succumbed to the legendary Montgomery vice of overcaution.'[2] That evening XV Corps was in Alençon and Sées, prepared to drive north with four divisions to close the southern portion of the gap, which was now eighteen miles wide.[3]

Montgomery was presented with the problem of deciding whether or not to adjust the inter-Army group boundary which lay south of Argentan:

> As the gap between the Canadians and Americans narrowed, he estimated, the Germans could bring up additional divisions from the east, or, more probably, could move their armored and mobile forces eastward out of the pocket toward ammunition and gasoline supplies. If the Germans chose the latter

---

[1] Montgomery's Operations Officer, General Belchem, has admitted that his C-in-C 'had forces available to reinforce them but did not do so'. Cf., Belchem, *All in the Day's March*, p. 208. One possible explanation is that Montgomery considered such a move would be interpreted by the sensitive Canadians as a loss of confidence in their first real test of battle under the command of the First Canadian Army. Other than Lieutenant General Simonds's 2nd Canadian Corps which had participated in GOODWOOD, the Canadian units were inexperienced. This is precisely why Bradley could never understand why Montgomery failed to make the obvious move of reinforcing the Canadians with the more battle-seasoned British troops of the Second Army.

[2] Quoted in Weigley, p. 205.

[3] Major General Jacques Leclerc's 2nd French Armoured Division, the 5th Armored Division and the 79th and 90th Infantry Divisions. Haislip's drive was led by the two armoured divisions with an infantry division following: 2nd French Armoured/90th Division on the left and the 5th Armored/79th Division on the right.

course of action, they would probably operate in the Argentan – Alençon area 'to have the benefit of the difficult "bocage" country' there. Their purpose would be to hold off the Americans while they used the more advantageous terrain in that region to cover their withdrawal. Expecting, then, the Germans to mass stronger forces in defense of Alençon than of Falaise, Montgomery concluded that it would be easier for the Canadians to make rapid progress. The Canadians could probably reach Argentan from the north before the XV Corps could attain Argentan from the south. General Montgomery therefore ordered the Canadians to continue their efforts to capture Falaise and proceed from there to Argentan.[1]

Unfortunately, Montgomery's assessment was quite wrong and the reason stems at least in part from the repeated failure of the British commanders to perceive the ability of the US Army to move rapidly and decisively under conditions of mobile warfare. Colonel Bonesteel, among others, has commented that the British and SHAEF 'never comprehended the mobility and striking power of American troops. The British tended to come along more slowly. Fantastic the way our people could move.'[2]* Since the entry of American forces into the war against Germany in 1942 the British had too often tended to underestimate American fighting ability. Many of the US units that had started in Normandy inexperienced and untested in battle were now effective and veteran fighting units. Patton's ability, too, was disparaged and even the Third Army's exploits in Normandy later failed to convince them that the strongest assets of the American Army were a mastery of mobile warfare and the ability to improvise under the most difficult conditions. Both Montgomery and SHAEF reacted with disbelief during the opening days of the Ardennes counteroffensive in December 1944, when Patton said he could shift his Third Army from Lorraine, move nearly a

[1] Martin Blumenson, 'General Bradley's Decision at Argentan', in *Command Decisions*, Kent Roberts Greenfield, (Ed.), London, 1960, p. 309.
[2] Bonesteel interview, loc.cit.
* The ability of American troops to move with astonishing rapidity owed much to Patton, who drove his commanders hard and refused to accept the slightest lack of dash. During the Third Army drive toward Chartres, Patton went to see one of his division commanders and asked when he was going to take Chartres. The commander replied that there were a number of Germans in the town, and it would take some time. Patton replied there were no Germans there: "It is now 3 o'clock. I want Chartres at 5, or there will be a new commander..." Patton's instincts proved correct and the division had Chartres by 5 p.m.

hundred miles to·the north, in some of the bitterest winter weather of this century, and attack within forty-eight hours. He did, and the veteran 4th Armored Division was the first unit to liberate the 101st Airborne Division which had been trapped in Bastogne. It was Patton's greatest triumph and a classic example of American mobility.

Montgomery's decision not to reinforce the Canadians was made on 11 August, the same date on which von Kluge was arguing with Hitler that continuation of the Mortain counter-offensive was hopeless. Hitler had ordered that the Fifth Panzer Army be stripped of three more panzer divisions to assist in a renewal of the offensive. His insistence on pressing the offensive against Mortain played directly into the hands of Bradley, whose plan for the short hook was working out exactly as he had hoped. Although the Germans began to shorten their line round Mortain on this date, there was no retreat eastward. On 13 August the Germans had begun to build up the shoulders of the gap but it was not until the next day that Hitler reluctantly accepted the urgent necessity for withdrawal before his forces were annihilated in the pocket. It was two more days before the Germans began organizing their withdrawal to the east in a desperate attempt to escape the Allied trap.[1]

As XV Corps drove north toward Argentan, Haislip reported to Patton that he was close to capturing his final assigned objective, leaving it up to the Third Army commander to provide him with further guidance. He also suggested that with additional forces he could effectively block the east-west roads in his sector north of Alençon.[2] The Canadians were still stalled well north of Falaise and making bitterly slow progress.

Patton was aware that it was unlikely the Canadians could close the gap quickly, and with this in mind sent the following message to XV Corps at 2000 hours, 12 August:

UPON CAPTURE OF ARGENTAN PUSH ON SLOWLY DIRECTION OF FALAISE ALLOWING YOUR REAR ELEMENTS TO CLOSE. ROAD ARGENTAN-FALAISE YOUR LEFT BOUNDARY INCLUSIVE. UPON ARRIVAL FALAISE CONTINUE TO PUSH ON SLOWLY UNTIL YOU CONTACT OUR ALLIES.[3]

[1] Blumenson, 'General Bradley's Decision at Argentan', pp. 314–5.
[2] Ibid. p. 310.
[3] Message Third Army to XV Corps, 12 August 1944, from the diary of Major General Hobart R. Gay, Chief of Staff, Third Army, US Army Military History Institute.

When Bradley learned of Patton's intentions he made what was to become the most controversial decision of the campaign – he ordered Patton not to proceed north of Argentan, later arguing that he was fearful of colliding with the Canadians, 'For any head-on juncture becomes a dangerous and uncontrollable manoeuvre unless each of the advancing forces is halted by pre-arranged plan on a terrain objective. To have driven pell-mell into Montgomery's line of advance could easily have resulted in a disastrous error in recognition. In halting Patton at Argentan, however, I did not consult with Montgomery. The decision to stop Patton was mine alone; it never went beyond my CP.'[1]

During this conversation with Bradley, Patton had begged to be allowed to continue north, saying in half-jest: 'We now have elements in Argentan. Shall we continue and drive the British into the sea for another Dunkirk?'[2] Unhappily, Patton's flip remark got back to the British, whose sensitivities over Dunkirk were still raw. They were not amused. The controversy resulting from Bradley's decision has yet to be resolved and he has defended it by contending that he preferred 'a solid shoulder at Argentan to a broken neck at Falaise'. Bradley has maintained, correctly, as we shall see, that Montgomery never prohibited his closing the gap nor had he ever proposed such a course of action. 'I was quite content with our original objective and reluctant to take on another.'[3]

The Canadians did not capture Falaise until late on 16 August, which still left some fifteen miles between the American and Canadian armies – the now famous Argentan-Falaise gap. The Germans began a massive withdrawal from the east and it was not until 19 August, when the Polish 1st Armoured and the US 90th Division joined forces at Chambois, that the gap was finally sealed. In that time the Germans absorbed terrible punishment[4] as the units of the Seventh Army and the Fifth Panzer Army tried with great desperation to fight their way out of the pocket till the Allies slowly but inevitably closed the trap.

Some 10,000 German soldiers perished in the Falaise pocket and an estimated 50,000 were taken prisoner. There were thought to be nearly 80,000 Germans trapped, and though it later proved impossible to make an accurate accounting of how

[1] Bradley, *A Soldier's Story*, p. 377.   [2] Hansen Diary, 12 August 1944.
[3] Bradley, *A Soldier's Story*, p. 377.
[4] In one instance a column of some 3,000 vehicles was caught head to tail and destroyed.

many escaped, the figure is thought to be about 20,000.[1] Most German units simply disappeared as troops fled individually and in small groups toward the Seine. Of the fifty divisions in action in June, only ten were left as fighting units.[2]

Hitler's blunder at Mortain and the inspired decision to envelop and trap the forces of von Kluge at Argentan-Falaise had destroyed German resistance in Normandy and turned near-stalemate into one of the most crushing and decisive victories ever attained by the Allies during the entire war. As the remnants of Army Group B fled east with four Allied armies in hot pursuit, France was left wide open and undefended all the way to west wall of the German Reich.

Several brief descriptions will provide an idea of the magnitude of the German defeat. The area of the final battles around Trun, St Lambert and Chambois was littered with unburied dead, thousands of dead horses which had served as one of the principal means of transport for the Germans,[3] dead cattle and everywhere, broken and burning vehicles. In their excellent account of the battle, James Lucas and James Barker have described the scene:

> The smell was all-pervading and overpowering. So strong in fact that pilots of light artillery observation aircraft flying over the area reported that the stench affected them even hundreds of feet in the air. Above the battlefield shimmered a miasma of decay and putrefaction; everything was covered with flies and blue-bottles. In the hot August sun the cattle which had been killed only days before were masses of crawling maggots, and the unburied Germans, swollen to elephantine grossness by the hot sun inflating the gases in the stomach, lay with blackened faces in grotesque positions. Here there was no dignity of death. In the worst bombarded areas fragments of bodies festooned the trees. . . Some roads were impassable due to the congestion caused by burnt-out trucks, dead horses, smashed tanks and destruction on a scale which the Western Allies had never seen.[4]

[1] James Lucas and James Barker, *The Killing Ground*, London, 1977, p. 160.
[2] Ibid.
[3] The Germans had lost so many vehicles to Allied air that for much of the campaign the use of horses became the only feasible means of transport, hauling guns, etc. In the age of the blitzkrieg it was a measure of the seriousness of the German situation in Normandy that what was once the most modern army in the world was reduced to the use of horsepower.
[4] Lucas and Barker, p. 158. Montgomery described the carnage in the Trun area as 'almost unbelievable'. The German disarray was typified by the example of 12 Corps which took prisoners from *thirteen* different divisions southeast of Falaise. M103, Montgomery to Brooke, 19 August 1944, Alanbrooke Papers.

Eisenhower described it as unquestionably one of the greatest 'killing grounds' of any of the war areas. 'Forty-eight hours after the closing of the gap I was conducted through it on foot, to encounter scenes that could be described only by Dante. It was literally possible to walk for hundreds of yards at a time, stepping on nothing but dead and decaying flesh.'[1]

The fate which befell Kurt Meyer's once proud Hitler Jugend Division was typical. His division, or rather what was left of it, was a shambles. Meyer escaped by himself, led out of the pocket by a French civilian, undoubtedly at gunpoint. He reckoned his division had lost 80% of its tanks and men, 70% of his reconnaissance and personnel carriers, 60% of his artillery and half the vehicles.[2] Allied investigating teams later found a staggering array of equipment. In the US portion of the battlefield were recorded: 220 tanks, 160 self-propelled guns, over 700 artillery pieces and 5,000 vehicles. The British tally was equally high: 187 armoured vehicles and self-propelled guns, 157 armoured cars or personnel carriers, 1,800 lorries, 669 civilian cars and staff vehicles and 252 other pieces of ordnance[3] – making the total over 9,000 items of equipment. The retreating Germans were able to take only a fraction of their vehicles with them and it has been estimated that fewer than 120 armoured fighting vehicles managed to escape across the Seine.[4]

By 19 August the first Allied units of Patton's Third Army had reached the Seine, and by the 25th the four Allied armies had closed in to the river. The first unit to cross the Seine was the US 79th Division on the night of 19 August. Within days the Seine was crossed en masse by these armies from Elbeuf near the mouth of the river to the area of Fontainebleau below Paris. On 25 August Paris was liberated by Leclerc's 2nd French Armoured Division and the City of Light was again free.

The Normandy campaign can be said to have ended then on 25 August – the day the four Allied armies established themselves along the Seine – on D+80.[5] Montgomery, despite severe and

[1] Dwight D. Eisenhower, *Crusade in Europe*, London, 1948, p. 306.
[2] Lucas and Barker, p. 160, and post-war interrogation of Brigadefuehrer Kurt Meyer, Liddell Hart Papers.
[3] Lucas and Barker, p. 160.
[4] Ibid.
[5] The selection of D+80 is arbitrary and based on the original concept of OVERLORD which called for the Allied armies to establish a lodgement area in France as far east as the Seine, when a new phase was to begin. Montgomery suggests that the campaign ended the

unexpected difficulties, had attained his objective of the Seine River line ten days earlier than originally envisioned in the pre-D-Day planning. Bradley had proved his mettle as an army and later, an army group commander. Patton had redeemed himself and written the first chapter in the splendid history of the Third Army: ahead lay a pursuit of the Germans across central France into Lorraine until his army literally ran out of petrol. On 1 September 1944 the BBC announced that the victorious commander (pro tem) of Allied ground forces in Normandy had been promoted to Field Marshal. Churchill's decision to promote Montgomery was seen as a sop to the 21st Army Group commander for his apparent demotion when Eisenhower assumed the role of Allied ground C-in-C the same day. The promotion infuriated Patton, who noted: 'The Field Marshal thing made us sick, that is Bradley and me.'[1] Bradley shrugged it off with the comment, 'The commander always gets credit for the operation.'[2] Always the diplomat, Eisenhower praised Montgomery 'and said that anyone who misinterpreted the transition of command as a demotion for General Montgomery simply did not look facts in the face... Montgomery is one of the great soldiers of this or any other war...'[3]

Although the Normandy campaign ended on a note of triumph for the Allies, it was also the beginning of the worst quarrels and greatest controversies of the war in Europe. Until he was nearly relieved of command in January 1945, Montgomery would squabble with Eisenhower over Allied strategy and command; Patton would rage at Eisenhower for denying him supplies, ammunition and petrol with which he believed he could have won the war; what had been merely disapprobation and resentment of Montgomery by Bradley would erupt into an irreparable split during the German counteroffensive in the Ardennes in December.[4]

day the first Allied unit crossed the Seine – D+75. Eisenhower's official report gives no date but his statistics on enemy losses are as of 25 August. Bradley dates the end of the campaign as D+80.

[1] *The Patton Papers*, II, p. 535.

[2] Hansen Diary, 5 September 1944.

[3] Butcher, op. cit., p. 560. On 22 August Churchill told Eisenhower that Montgomery's promotion would be announced when the Supreme Commander took over control of the ground forces. This promotion was at least partly, as Churchill related, an obligatory concession to British public opinion. Cf., Pogue, *The Supreme Command*, p. 253, fn. 22. Churchill's remarks were contained in a note to Eisenhower.

[4] Eisenhower gave command of all American forces in the northern half of the

The crushing Allied victory in Normandy also fostered a false and dangerous sense of optimism and euphoria that Germany was beaten and that the war would soon end. This understandable but mistaken delusion appears repeatedly in the public and private comments of senior British and American officers. Arnhem, Metz, St Vith, Bastogne, the Reichswald and the Huertgen Forest were some of the shocking illustrations to come that the war in fact was far from over.[1] In September the overconfident Allies suffered a sharp reverse at the Dutch town of Arnhem during Operation MARKET-GARDEN when the British were unable to hold 'a bridge too far', and lost the 1st Airborne Division. Checked at the borders of Germany by winter weather and Hitler's last desperate gamble – 'Wacht am Rhein', the great Ardennes counteroffensive – the war dragged on into the spring of 1945 until the Russian and American armies finally met on the Elbe River in early May. On 4 May 1945 Montgomery accepted the surrender of all German forces in northwest Germany in a tent on Luneburg Heath. Three days later, Eisenhower accepted the unconditional surrender of the Third Reich at Rheims from Field Marshal Jodl, representing Grand Admiral Doenitz, who had inherited what was left of the thousand-year Reich after Hitler's suicide only days before.

The campaign in Normandy succeeded far beyond the expectations of its architects, but with success came a legacy of controversy and unanswered questions; as usual, the debate focused mainly on Bernard Law Montgomery. When the Normandy campaign passed into history, so too did the unresolved questions, the first of which was about the battle of the Argentan-Falaise pocket.

Ardennes to Montgomery, mainly because the massive German thrust had severed communications between the First Army and Bradley's 12th Army Group located in the south. Bradley never forgave Eisenhower for making the decision to place Montgomery over his troops and the event, more than any other in his career, galled Bradley to the end of his life.

[1] As was Brest, which held out against repeated Allied sieges until 19 September. The further east the Allies drove, the less the need for the Brittany ports, and even had Brest fallen quickly, by the time the damage could be repaired it is doubtful it would have been utilized as a major port. Instead of isolating the large German garrison in the city, Bradley, for reasons he has admitted had more to do with prestige than military value, left VIII Corps behind to deal with the 38,000 tough German troops who inflicted nearly 10,000 casualties on Middleton's troops. In hindsight it was, said Bradley, 'far too high a price to pay to maintain illusions of invincibility'. Bradley also said that German tenacity at Brest kept him from being infected with the general euphoria that Germany was beaten. 'If she could hold out so stubbornly in a lost cause like Brest, what would happen when we reached her own borders or the Rhine River?' *A General's Life*, p. 306.

PART IV

Aftermath

In war more than anywhere else in the world things happen differently from what we had expected, and look differently when near from what they did at a distance.

Von Clausewitz

CHAPTER 26

The Falaise Controversy

More recently, Omar Bradley took a swing at
Monty on a point where he was dead wrong –
failure to close the Falaise pocket. . . But in the end
it was impossible to assign blame accurately.

S. L. A. Marshall[1]

As the Normandy campaign drew to a close, Winston Churchill
cabled Montgomery to question the figures of German losses
submitted to him the previous day. 'In your last [message] you say
that the preceding two days have yielded 25,000 German prisoners in the pocket, but how many have in fact been taken since the
Americans broke through at Avranches? . . . I should like to
know the two numbers respectively. I had, of course, rather
hoped we should be in the region of hundreds of thousands when
sixteen divisions were mentioned but with the dead the figures
will be more impressive.'[2] In his reply the following day, Montgomery told the Prime Minister: 'Since 25th July figures are:
prisoners, 133,000; enemy dead, 23,000; enemy wounded,
100,000, making total 256,000 enemy written off. . .'[3] It was, of
course, far too early to gain even an approximation of German
losses in the pocket until Allied investigation teams could complete a rough count, but Montgomery's figures appeared wildly
optimistic, especially his claim that the Allies had taken 133,000
prisoners since COBRA. It is doubtful whether 83,000 prisoners
could have been taken between 25 July and the beginning of the
Falaise battles. Both the American and British official histories
candidly admit that the final figures are only an approximation,
but both came to the same conclusion: that the Allies had

---

[1] Quoted in letter, S. L. A. Marshall to Liddell Hart, 10 February 1965, Liddell Hart
Papers. Unfortunately, throughout his long time correspondence with Liddell Hart,
Marshall never again mentioned Falaise.
[2] Churchill, cable to Montgomery, 23 August 1944, PRO (CAB 120/421).
[3] Montgomery, cable to Churchill, 24 August 1944, ibid.

captured 50,000 Germans. There is little dispute over the figure of 10,000 German dead. The greatest uncertainty remains the actual number of German troops who escaped the pocket. As the US official history points out, even before the Germans began their retreat from the pocket some nonessential personnel and equipment had been moved towards the Seine. 'Later estimates of the total number of Germans escaping varied between 20,000 and 40,000 men, but combat troops formed by far the smaller portion of these troops. The average combat strength of divisions was no more than a few hundred men, even though the overall strength of some divisions came close to 3,000.'[1]

Whatever the figures, the aftermath of the battles around Falaise has left lingering doubts that despite their great victory the Allies had let slip from their grasp an even greater opportunity, not only of bagging the whole of Army Group B, but the greater psychological victory of forcing a formal surrender and perhaps of ending the war sooner. The question of assigning responsibility for the failure to have closed the pocket has been the subject of innumerable debates, charges and countercharges, and has never been satisfactorily resolved. In fact, it may never be, but what can be established is that the reasons given for the actions and decisions of Bradley and Montgomery during mid-August are incomplete and frequently inconsistent.

The first to raise questions was Churchill, who was suspicious of what he considered to be the excessively low number of prisoners, and he first expressed his disappointment in a note to his Foreign Secretary, Anthony Eden, on 22 August. Although he took pains not to question Montgomery's victory, Churchill obviously believed that something was amiss. His doubts were based upon the figures of sixteen divisions trapped in the pocket, but in fact he had failed to understand that these units were severely understrength: many had been lost in the gruelling battles fought since D-Day and few of those losses had been replaced. Kurt Meyer's elite 12th SS Panzer had at one time numbered over ten thousand men, but by the final battles around Trun it was estimated there may have been fewer than a hundred men – the division had virtually dissolved as a fighting force.

---

[1] Blumenson, *Breakout and Pursuit*, pp. 555–6.

Before examining the actions of Montgomery and Bradley during this crucial period we must first review the sequence of events which led to the eventual closing of the trap on the German Army:

8 August: Bradley proposes a short envelopment with Patton's XV Corps to trap the Seventh Army between Mortain and Argentan-Falaise. Montgomery concurs and Bradley is given permission to move beyond the inter-army group boundary line between 21st Army Group and 12th Army Group, located some twelve miles south of Argentan. Bradley elects to move only as far as Argentan to meet the Canadians driving south from Falaise to close the trap.

11 August: With the Canadians stalled north of Falaise, Montgomery orders Crerar and Dempsey to press their offensives. Dempsey is instructed to advance his left flank to Falaise to join up with the Canadians. 'This is a first priority and a vital one. Sufficient forces will be allotted to the left corps to ensure that it can fight its way forward to FALAISE, and quickly.'[1] On this date Montgomery's intention was quite clear: 'We will now concentrate our energies on closing the gap behind the main enemy forces, so that we can possibly destroy them where they are now.'[2] Montgomery does not, however, elect to reinforce the Canadians with units from the Second Army.

During the afternoon, 21st Army Group orders Dempsey and Crerar to exchange artillery liaison officers with 12th Army Group in preparation for their eventual linkup with the Third US Army. 'Closest possible liaison now essential between your arty and arty of Third U.S. Army. One arty liaison offr from First Cdn Army and one arty liaison offr from Second Army NOT below rank of Maj will report to HQ 12 Army Group by 1700 hours today. . . These parties will be attached for all purposes to Third U.S. Army. Arty offr from 12 Army Gp has agreed to provide similar liaison parties.'[3] These instructions included a requirement for radios mounted in halftracks, netted to the frequency of the Royal Artillery command post of both armies.

12 August: In response to telephone notification from 21st

[1] 21st Army Group Directive M-518, 11 August 1944, PRO (WO 205/5G).
[2] Ibid.
[3] War Diary, First Canadian Army, 1330 hours, 11 August 1944, PRO (WO 179/2596).

Army Group, an exuberant watchkeeper at the First Canadian Army reports: '1930 – FLASH: The Yanks are 4 kms south of Argentan and fighting against Pz Div believed to be 9 Pz Div.'[1]

2000 hours: Patton orders IV Corps to push north of Argentan to Falaise. Shortly afterwards, Bradley learns of Patton's order and cancels it; XV Corps is to remain where it is outside Argentan.

13 August: 1215 hours – Dempsey records in his diary:

> Flew to 21 Army Group and there met C-in-C and General Bradley. We discussed future operations – particularly as regards Army Group and Army boundaries; and the bringing up by Third Army of another corps directed on Laigle. So long as the northward move of Third Army meets little opposition, the two leading Corps will disregard inter-Army boundaries. The whole aim is to establish forces across the enemy's lines of communication so as to impede – if not to prevent entirely – his withdrawal.[2]

The First Canadian Army sends an 'immediate' message to all subordinate units reminding them that 'the converging move-[ment] of the Twelfth U.S. Army Group and 21 Army Gp and the partial enclosure of the enemy in a restricted area between these forces is increasing the importance of ground/air recognition.' All forward units were *urgently* reminded of the necessity for using yellow ground recognition strips and yellow smoke, to ensure that there were no more accidental bombings of friendly forces by the Allied air forces.[3]

14 August: 0950 hours: Air Vice Marshal Strafford of the Advanced AEAF records the following during a conference between Bradley and Leigh-Mallory:

> AVM joined Air C-in-C for conference with General Bradley in latter's mobile office. General Bradley explained on the map his general intentions. He stated that immediately the Germans were pinned in the area west of ARGENTAN/FALAISE, he wished to detach a minimum force necessary to complete the tidying up of the BRITTANY peninsula and the opening of the BRITTANY ports and then to drive East from ALENCON in an encircling

[1] War Diary, First Canadian Army, 12 August 1944, loc.cit.
[2] Dempsey Diary, 12 August 1944, PRO (WO 285/9).
[3] Message, GSO 2 OPS, First Canadian Army, 13 August 1944, PRO (WO 179/2596). During TOTALIZE there had been further incidents of mistaken bombings by tactical air of 2nd TAF. Allied ground troops were beginning to fear their own air as much as the Germans did.

movement against PARIS through the gap as early as possible. He states that the American forces had little opposition between ALENCON and ARGENTAN and had started toward FALAISE, but had been instructed by the C-in-C, 21 Army Group to halt on the inter-army group boundary. There had been few German troops in the area when the Third Army forward elements had arrived there, and he was confident that the Third Army now held a firm front on the arc to the north of FALAISE.[1]

Bradley confers with Patton and directs him to detach two divisions of XV Corps for a long envelopment toward Dreux, and thence to swing northeast towards Mantes Gassicourt where a bridgehead was to be seized across the Seine. Patton's XX Corps was to move in the direction of Chartres and XII Corps towards Orleans. The remaining two divisions of XV Corps holding the southern shoulder of the gap around Argentan were to be reinforced by an additional division and supported by VII Corps, which was now moving east from the Mortain sector.

ULTRA decrypts reveal German intention to launch Panzer Group Eberbach in a counterattack aimed at Haislip's exposed left flank round Argentan. By the early hours of 15 August the complete text of General Eberbach's intentions is in the hands of the Allied field HQs.

Hitler awakes to the peril of entrapment and desires an attack 'in the Alençon-Carrouges area' for the purpose of destroying the greater part of XV Corps. This action is, says Hitler, to be the immediate task of OB West and that all further directives 'would depend on the course of the battle there'.[2]

The Canadians are six miles north of Falaise. In addition to capturing Falaise, Crerar is ordered to swing part of 2 Canadian Corps to the southeast to seize Trun as rapidly as possible.

16 August: The Canadians capture Falaise. The gap is reduced to approximately twelve miles. XX Corps liberates Chartres and XII Corps captures Dreux.

The Germans are beginning a fullscale retreat to the east; Montgomery recognizes that the gap between Falaise and Argentan cannot possibly be closed in time. Instead, he decides to close the trap on the Germans farther to the east along the River Dives,

[1] War Diary of Air Vice Marshal Stephen C. Strafford, Chief of Operations and Plans, AEAF, 14 August 1944, PRO (AIR 37/574).
[2] Blumenson, *Breakout and Pursuit*, pp. 516–7.

between Trun and Chambois. Bradley is asked to move a force northeast to Chambois, there to link up with the Canadians and Poles driving from Falaise and Trun to close the trap. Crerar is once again told by Montgomery of the necessity to seize and hold Trun quickly.

Despite their heavy pressure on XV Corps, Panzer Group Eberbach is too weak to initiate the kind of attack envisioned by Hitler, a point made clear to his Chief-of-Staff, Jodl, by von Kluge at midday. Later this day, OKW authorizes the withdrawal of all German forces in the pocket to new positions behind the River Dives. Panzer Group Eberbach is to cover the withdrawal by enlarging the Argentan-Falaise gap by an attack to the southeast.

17 August: XV Corps begins to swing northeast from Dreux towards the Seine. Late that night the 90th US Division captures the important ridge overlooking Le Bourg-St Leonard from elements of the 2nd SS and 116 Panzer Division, who are holding open the gap in the south. The gap extends from Trun in the north to Le Bourg-St Leonard in the south.

18 August: The Canadians capture Trun and advance near St Lambert sur Dives (midway between Trun and Chambois) until they are held up. Elements of the Polish Armoured Division move east toward Mount Ormel. The 90th US Division halts about three miles south of Chambois. The gap is now approximately six miles wide.

19 August: The area around Mount Ormel lies astride the main German escape route to the east. At noon the Poles capture the northern part of Mount Ormel, called the Mace, and promptly attack a German column massed on the ground below. Violent battles rage until 21 August as elements of 1 SS Panzer Corps launch successive counterattacks in a desperate attempt to keep their escape route open. While the struggle for the Mace continues to the east, elements of the 10th Polish Mounted Rifle Regiment join the US 90th Division at Chambois. The Trun-Chambois gap is closed. The Falaise pocket is strewn with the carnage of war from Mortain to Mount Ormel.

XV Corps reaches the Seine at Mantes Gassicourt and the 79th Division seizes the first Allied bridgehead over the Seine.

For reasons that we shall examine, the pocket was eventually closed at Trun-Chambois rather than at Argentan-Falaise. Bradley accepted personal responsibility for halting Patton on his own initiative at Argentan, but in *A Soldier's Story* he blames Montgomery for failing to close the gap:

> ... As we waited impatiently for Monty at Argentan, the enemy reinforced that gap. Already the vanguard of panzers and SS troops were sluicing back through it toward the Seine. But instead of redoubling his push to close that leak, Monty shifted his main effort against the pocket farther west. Rather than close the trap by capping the leak at Falaise, Monty proceeded to squeeze the enemy out toward the Seine. If Monty's tactics mystified me, they dismayed Eisenhower even more. And at Lucky Forward where a shocked Third Army looked on helplessly as its quarry fled, Patton raged at Montgomery's blunder.[1]

Bradley's version of events is inconsistent with the facts. In a lucid analysis of General Bradley's decision, Martin Blumenson has carefully and thoroughly demolished the main thrust of his argument that a meeting of American and Canadian forces would have been tactically disruptive because it would impede plans to 'get the US and British forces lined up and started together going east'.[2] Blumenson correctly dismisses this rationale as patently weak and as inventing a cause that conveniently fits the results.[3]

Inasmuch as up until at least 14 August both Montgomery and Bradley were committed to the plan to close the trap between Argentan and Falaise, the notion that the US and Canadian forces should not meet is illogical, as is another suggestion that XV Corps had been halted because the Allied air forces had sown the highways in the area with time bombs, thus making movement northward risky. It is not known if this action in any way influenced Bradley's decision, but the bombs, dropped over a three-day period, had been fused only with a twelve-hour delay, a fact which the airmen could easily have confirmed. Equally

---

[1] Bradley, *A Soldier's Story*, pp. 376–7.
* In *A General's Life*, Bradley called this news 'a shattering disappointment – one of my greatest of the war. A golden opportunity had truly been lost. I boiled inside, blaming Monty for the blunder.' (p. 299).
[2] Blumenson, 'General Bradley's Decision at Argentan', p. 313.
[3] Ibid.

suspect is Bradley's argument that he was reluctant 'to chance a head-on meeting between two converging armies as we might have done had Patton continued on to Falaise.'[1] What Bradley did not reveal was the precautions which were taken to prevent exactly what he claimed to fear most, as the Canadian war diary confirms. He also ignored the fact that if the Falaise gap were ever to be closed, then the Third Army and the First Canadian Army had to meet eventually – where they met was immaterial.

So much for Bradley's argument that the manoeuvre was too dangerous; it was evident that neither of the armies was going to permit an unfortunate collision. The most controversial aspect of the entire question is Bradley's statement that he lacked authority to send XV Corps north of Argentan. Not only was XV Corps already well beyond the inter-army group boundary but, as Bradley himself pointed out, Montgomery had already given permission to advance to Argentan. 'Bradley needed Montgomery's permission to go farther to the north. Though it is true that Montgomery did not sanction an American advance beyond Argentan, neither did Bradley propose it.'[2]

General Dempsey's recently released diary suggests a far different course of events. The critical day was Sunday, 13 August, when something had to be done quickly before the opportunity was lost. When Dempsey met Bradley and Montgomery there was apparently no restraint placed on further northward movement by XV Corps. Certainly, there was no question of Bradley violating the inter-army group boundary, for XV Corps was already beyond the now rather meaningless demarcation line. If Dempsey's version is correct – and there is no reason to believe it is not – then the fact that the Third Army did not move north of Argentan appears to have been Bradley's *choice* rather than a prohibition by Montgomery.[3]

By this date it was obvious that the Canadian advance on Falaise was in very serious trouble; in fact, it was not even renewed with any prospect of success until 14 August. Less easy to discern are Montgomery's motives for not reinforcing Crerar

---

[1] Bradley, *A Soldier's Story*, p. 377.

[2] Blumenson, 'General Bradley's Decision at Argentan', p. 314.

[3] In 1946 Montgomery told Chester Wilmot that the Third Army was never ordered to stop at Argentan. 'It was ordered to strike north on the axis Alençon–Argentan and to close the gap. If Patton stopped he must have been stopped by opposition.' Interview 18 May 1946, Liddell Hart Papers, King's College, London.

from the Second Army, which was not as heavily opposed as the Canadians. As Belchem admits, Montgomery could easily have done so; but he offers no reason for this strange omission. Whether Montgomery was not disposed to make an adjustment on grounds that it would have been too late to affect operations, or whether his dislike of the short envelopment was so great that he refused to consider the idea, is unknown. Another option – dropping two British airborne divisions behind the German lines near Falaise to break the screen of 88s holding up the Canadian advance – was rejected. This idea originated with an officer in Bradley's G–2 (Intelligence) section and was enthusiastically endorsed by Bradley himself. Colonel Bonesteel was chosen to carry the idea to 21st Army Group and, as he has related, he sold the idea to Richardson and Belchem in twenty minutes. 'They sold it to de Guingand in another twenty. Word came back after several hours that Master had turned it down.'[1]

Although Montgomery was still committed to closing the gap, he was never happy with the plan. It was more likely that he viewed the problem in greater terms of reference; that is, to prevent the Germans from escaping en masse if the gap continued to remain open, which looked more and more certain with each passing day. This meant deploying a suitably strong blocking force along the Seine to prevent a German escape across the river, something which could be accomplished only by dint of a long envelopment by Bradley. The choice had existed since 8 August and it represented his preferred strategy. However, with both Bradley and the Supreme Commander favouring the short envelopment, Montgomery was in an awkward position. Refusal would have created yet another storm of controversy; since after GOODWOOD he was quite conscious of the pressures from above and since there was every possibility of the manoeuvre succeeding at this early date, Montgomery appears to have cast aside his misgivings and concurred. Bradley notes: 'To his credit, Monty was flexible in his thinking. Ike wrote in his memoirs that Monty "agreed the prospective prize was great and left the entire responsibility for the matter in Bradley's hands"'.[2]

To argue in hindsight that Montgomery had missed a spectacular opportunity is to disregard the problem that there was no

---

[1] Bonesteel interview, loc.cit.
[2] Bradley, A General's Life, p. 295.

certainty he could trap and destroy the German Army in the pocket, and that without a blocking force somewhere to the east – either at Trun-Chambois or along the Seine – he was taking an enormous gamble, one he could not, realistically, afford to take at that moment. What he could and apparently did do was to authorize Bradley to move as far north as he thought safe. As will be seen, it was evident that Bradley likewise shared the same concern and elected the 'solid shoulder at Argentan to the possibility of a broken neck at Falaise'.[1]

Bradley never wavered in his original declaration that Montgomery had nothing to do with his decision to halt Patton at Argentan. In his opinion, these were sound orders and '[I] believe so to this day'.[2] Bradley also disputes the allegation that Montgomery refused to move the boundary north at his behest:

> Patton, in his diary, blamed Montgomery: 'I believe that the order . . . emanated from the 21st Army Group, and was either due to [British] jealousy of the Americans or to utter ignorance of the situation or to a combination of the two.' *But, in fact, Montgomery had no part in the decision; it was mine and mine alone.* Some writers have suggested that I appealed to Monty to move the boundary north to Falaise and he refused, but, of course, that is not true. For all the reasons I have stated, I was determined to hold Patton at Argentan and had no cause to ask Monty to shift the boundary. Ike, as he wrote in his memoirs, 'completely supported' me in this decision.[3]* (Author's italics.)

Thus, by the morning of 14 August both commanders felt that a long envelopment still held promise.[4] That being so, there were three alternatives open to Bradley. He could elect to move beyond Argentan toward Falaise (an option he firmly ruled out); he could sit tight where he was until reinforced by units of the Third and First Armies moving east from the Avranches-Mortain sector (never seriously considered); or he could strike quickly east towards the Seine, while continuing to hold the Argentan shoulder temporarily with a smaller force. Bradley briefly toyed with the idea of attempting to block the German retreat by a

---

[1] Bradley, *A Soldier's Story*, p. 377.
[2] Bradley, *A General's Life*, p. 301.
[3] Ibid.
* Eisenhower was present at Bradley's CP on 12 and 13 August.
[4] Montgomery had in fact ordered Bradley on 12 August to hold a fresh corps in readiness at Le Mans to press quickly towards Chartres if ordered. M97, Montgomery to Brooke, Alanbrooke Papers.

slight swing to the northeast towards Chambois, but with the Canadians still stalled north of Falaise and his intelligence officers telling him that the Germans had already begun to break-out to the east, this choice did not seem to him to improve the chances of closing the pocket.

It is possible that the ULTRA decrypts about Panzer Group Eberbach, which came in later that day, served to reinforce Bradley's determination to shift Patton east rather than to make any attempt to pursue the closing of the gap. With an uncovered opening of some fifty to seventy-five miles between XV Corps and Collins's VII Corps, any further movement in the direction of Falaise would be fraught with danger to Haislip's forces. Bradley has related that the choice was not as simple as hindsight might suggest:

> Of all three [options], the dash to the Seine offered the greatest tactical promise. For if Patton were to secure a bridgehead there, he would have thwarted the enemy's last bright chance for defense of the Seine River line. But by the same token, we would also be taking a chance. For in striking out for the Seine in preference to the Chambois attack, we might make it easier for the enemy to escape that Falaise trap. Normally, destruction of the enemy's army is the first objective of any force. Was a Seine River bridgehead important enough to warrant our rejecting that military tenet?[1]

Bradley thought so, for he records: 'George helped settle my doubts when on August 14 he called to ask that two of Haislip's four divisions on the Argentan shoulder be freed for a dash to the Seine. With that, I brushed aside the first two alternatives and sided with Patton on the third. If Montgomery wants help in closing the gap, I thought, then let him ask for it. Since there was little likelihood of his asking, we would push on to the east.'[2]

Bradley's decision obviously suited Montgomery, who noted after the war that 'The battle of the Falaise pocket never should have taken place and was not meant to take place.'[3] Montgomery's point was that the short envelopment was not his idea nor did it fit in with his concept of the battle. 'Monty as stated, did

---

[1] Bradley, *A Soldier's Story*, p. 378.
[2] Ibid, pp. 378–9.
[3] Papers of John North, King's College, London. North was a journalist selected by the British government to write an informal history of 21st Army Group (*Northwest Europe, 1944–5*, published in 1953 by Her Majesty's Stationery Office). North interviewed Montgomery on several occasions during his research for the book.

originally envisage the rolling up of the German left flank [at Caen] – not [the] right, of course. He did not envisage – and could never have envisaged – the double envelopment battle that resulted in the dissolution of the German armies in Normandy. It is to this battle, the battle of the Gap [that I refer].'[1]

Montgomery began to develop his options on 14 August by ordering Crerar to capture Trun as well as Falaise. This decision signalled his growing belief that the gap could still be plugged farther east in the Trun-Chambois sector while Patton was making his end run to the east. Did this modification to the scheme mean that Montgomery had abandoned the short envelopment? According to Dempsey, the answer is 'no'. His orders to 12 and 30 Corps on 15 August were quite explicit: 'Both Corps have made considerable progress during the day. Their tasks are quite clear – to get forward on the line FALAISE-ARGENTAN.' Earlier that day Dempsey had again met Bradley and Montgomery. 'We discussed future operations – in particular as regards closing the gap between FALAISE and ARGENTAN, neither of which we hold yet.'[2]

The assertion that Montgomery made no effort to close the gap is without foundation. What Bradley seems to have misconstrued as Montgomery's blunder in his use of the Second Army, which gave the illusion of pushing the Germans out of the pocket instead of bottling them up, was in reality a serious attempt to plug the gap. The previous afternoon, 14 August, Montgomery had again reminded Crerar of the urgency of capturing Falaise, but it was clear that he placed a somewhat higher priority on the securing of Trun. 'Falaise is to be captured with least possible delay by First Cdn Army. This is not to interfere with our drive on Trun.'[3] On 16 August, when Falaise finally fell, the priority of effort was in fact shifted to closing the Trun-Chambois gap.

In fact, Montgomery showed evidence of using Trun-Chambois as a back-stop in the event that the trap could not be closed near Falaise. His determination is quite evident in his communications with General Crerar during this time. For example, on 13 August Crerar recorded the following: 'When 2 Cdn Corps has firmly established itself to the NORTH and EAST

---

[1] North, letter to Liddell Hart, 27 January 1954, loc.cit.
[2] Dempsey Diary, 15 August 1944, PRO (W) 285/9).
[3] War Diary, First Canadian Army, 1715 hours, 14 August 1944, loc.cit.

of FALAISE, and action by Second British Army to take over the town itself, has been sufficiently advanced, 2 Cdn Corps will exploit SE and capture or dominate TRUN . . . It is the intention of C-in-C, 21 Army Group, that Second British Army will take over all territory within its army boundaries . . . (a portion of which will have been secured by First Cdn Army in this operation) and complete the firm juncture with Third US Army, as soon as this can be arranged.'[1]

On 16 August, 'At 1530 hours C-in-C, 21 Army Group spoke to me on the telephone. He stated that 15 Corps of Third US Army, holding the SEES–ARGENTAN–CARROUGES sector and salient, was being heavily attacked today by what was estimated to be elements of five panzer divisions . . . this group of Pz and SS formations trying to break through to the EAST. He was convinced that General Patton would hold them. C-in-C appreciated that when the group of Pz divisions WEST of ARGENTAN found their outlet decisively blocked, they would swing NE and attempt to get out by the small gap now remaining between ARGENTAN and FALAISE. He emphasized the necessity of capturing TRUN early and holding it strongly'.[2]

Montgomery remained outwardly confident of the outcome, writing optimistically to his friend and confidant, Sir James Grigg:

> These are great days; and this week may well see great events. We have the great bulk of the German forces partially surrounded; some will of course escape, but I do not see how they can stand and fight seriously again this side of the Seine. At the best we shall round up many divisions.[3]

In recent years suspicion has still fallen upon Montgomery as the culprit who failed to close the Argentan-Falaise gap. A recent Canadian account cites Dr Pogue's interview with Brigadier Williams in 1947, during which the following notes were taken:

> Remember [he] was in Freddie's [de Guingand] truck near Bayeux when 2nd French Armored made its swing up and crossed the road towards Falaise. Monty said tell Bradley they

[1] War Diary, Lieutenant General H. D. G. Crerar, 13 August 1944, PRO (CAB 106/1064).

[2] Ibid, 16 August 1944. Within the hour Crerar had ordered General Simonds to commence a thrust with 2nd Canadian Corps in force against Trun that day.

[3] Montgomery, letter to Sir James Grigg, 14 August 1944, Grigg Papers, Churchill College, Cambridge.

ought to get back. Bradley was indignant. We were indignant on Bradley's behalf. De Guingand said 'Monty is too tidy.' Freddie thought Bradley should have been allowed to join the Poles at Trun. Monty missed closing the sack. Bradley couldn't understand. Thought we were missing our opportunities over inter-Army rights. However, it should be pointed out that Monty regarded Bradley was under his command; therefore his decision was not made on the basis of inter-Army considerations. . . Master of tidiness. He was fundamentally more interested in full envelopment than this inner envelopment. We fell between two stools. He [Montgomery] missed his chance of closing at the Seine by doing the envelopment at Falaise.[1]

Williams ascribes Montgomery's decision to his dislike of the short envelopment plan:

Monty didn't want to do the short hook. Freddie, using my information and his own ideas, persuaded Monty into that with Bradley arguing for it from his angle. Monty didn't want to do it, but saw a chance to pull it off after he had pushed Bradley back. In the first stage he was looking toward a grander basis, and he thought 'Hell, those guys are excited, they are spoiling the way we are going.' Then Freddie and Bradley favor the short hook. He agrees, but it's already too late. So he misses both opportunities.[2]

Air Vice Marshal Strafford's war diary also suggests that Bradley had not been permitted to move north of Argentan, as does Chester Hansen's, whose entry for 13 August reads: 'It is suggested in G–3 that we were ordered to hold at Argentan rather than to continue the drive to Falaise since our capture of that objective would infringe on the prestige value in closing the trap. Accordingly, our forces were held at the Argentan line and subsequently refueled while the British were still short of their objective; permitted much of the strength of the pocket to escape eastward toward the Seine.'[3]

Unfortunately the passage of time has dimmed Williams's recollection[4] of what transpired at 21st Army Group over the

---

[1] Williams interview, loc.cit. Also quoted in *Patton's Gap* by Major General Richard Rohmer, London 1981, pp. 226–7.

[2] Williams interview, loc. cit.

[3] Hansen Diary, 13 August 1944.

[4] It must be remembered that Williams's comments about Falaise were fragmentary and part of a lengthy interview with Dr Pogue about military operations throughout Northwest Europe, a point emphasized to Rohmer by Pogue when the quotation was given to him over the telephone. As Dr Pogue reiterated in a recent conversation with the

boundary question, but even so it appears possible to draw several conclusions. Even though Air Vice Marshal Strafford's war diary leaves the impression that Montgomery ordered Bradley not to attempt to close the Falaise gap from the south, Dempsey's diary reflects no such dispute over boundary rights; nor does Bradley's posthumous account: rather than a dispute over boundary rights, there was general agreement that Bradley could move north if he so chose.

Too much emphasis has been placed on this subject of boundary lines. The so-called inter-army group boundary was established *two days before* the decision was made to initiate the short hook – that is, on 6 August. Bradley mistakenly says that the boundary line was established on 8 August at the time of the decision: 'We drew a "boundary line" through Argentan where we would close the trap.'[1] Montgomery's directive M-517 of 6 August delineated in no uncertain terms the boundary lines which were to be used in the advance to the Seine: the boundary between the Canadians and the Second Army was Falaise and swung due east to Vimoutiers – Bernay and Les Andelys on the Seine; the boundary between the Second Army and 12th Army Group ran from Tinchebray to Argentan, then due east to Laigle and Dreux, before swinging northeast to Mantes Gassicourt.[2]

This boundary line had been conceived by Montgomery at a time when a more deliberate advance to the Seine was still planned.[3] Moreover it had lost much of its significance during this period when no one really knew what was going on inside the pocket. Tampering with the boundary in such conditions would not have been sound tactics, inasmuch as there was no method of determining where a new line ought to be set. For example, moving it north to Falaise would have obliged Bradley not only to gain this new line but to *hold* it, and this he was not willing to do. The boundary line controversy is thus a tempest in a teapot.

There is no doubt that Montgomery did compromise by

author, it was made clear to Rohmer that these remarks formed only a small portion of a lengthy interview with Brigadier Williams, and were not a verbatim transcription. Dr. Pogue argues that he may have missed Williams's distinction between Argentan–Falaise and Trun–Chambois.

[1] Bradley, *A General's Life*, op.cit., p. 295.

[2] 21st Army Group Directive M-517, 6 August 1944, PRO (WO 205/5G).

[3] Montgomery's order was issued sometime on 6 August *before* ULTRA detected von Kluge's counterattack, which was launched at Mortain late that same night.

attempting both the long and short envelopments and, as we have already seen, his post-war account stating that both had been initiated concurrently is misleading, since there was a lapse of six days (from 8 to 14 August) before Bradley, on his own initiative, sent Patton on to the Seine when it was clear that there was little likelihood of the Canadians closing the gap. In *Operation Victory*, de Guingand confirms this.[1] Thus it can be concluded that at no time did Montgomery order Bradley to halt at Argentan, nor is there any evidence to support undue concern by Bradley at this alleged order. Had this been the case, Bradley would most certainly have complained to Eisenhower, yet neither his personal papers nor those of Eisenhower refer to the matter. Hansen's diary entry of 13 August was evidently written *after* the conclusion of the Falaise battles, as it would have been impossible for him to have known any Germans would escape on that date. More probably, it reflected the opinion of officers in Bradley's operations staff, where there was considerable dislike of Montgomery. Hansen, too, who frequently quoted Bradley's remarks in his diary, is strangely quiet on the subject of any anger by his chief against Montgomery.

Montgomery's liaison officer to Bradley was Major Tom Bigland, RA. During mid-August Bigland was in daily contact with Bradley and kept a detailed diary of these events. What he has to say about Falaise is revealing. 'It is important to understand that at this time, it was not called the battle of the "Falaise Gap". It was only one of the matters which were being considered at the time.' Nor was there any unusual activity at Bradley's HQ to indicate that anyone was greatly upset by the situation. 'You must remember that there was a great deal of the "fog of battle" at that time... There was definitely no question of Bradley's being annoyed or upset at that time.'[2]

Dr Pogue's notes refer to both the Argentan-Falaise and the Trun-Chambois gaps. The dissent at Montgomery's compromise appears to be a reference (at least in part) to the Trun-Chambois gap, when Pogue records Williams saying: 'Freddie [de Guin-

---

[1] De Guingand, *Operation Victory*, p. 407.
[2] Bigland, letter to the author, 18 February 1982. Bigland was never considered an outsider at Bradley's HQ because he represented Montgomery. Before making his daily reports to Montgomery, Bigland would frequently discuss the current situation and what he was going to report with Bradley, who was always courteous and cooperative.

gand] thought Bradley should have been allowed to join the Poles at *Trun*.' (Author's italics.) It may well be that in view of his dislike of the short hook Montgomery's initial reaction to Bradley driving on to Argentan was negative but, as we have seen, what scant evidence there is that such an order was given to Bradley is thoroughly contradicted by Dempsey. Nor was there an opportunity for American units to have closed the second gap at Trun rather than at Chambois – unknown at that time was the fact that the American drive toward Chambois was delayed by a change of corps command in the Argentan sector,[1] and there was never an opportunity for the 90th Division to have driven beyond Chambois before the first Polish units arrived on 19 August.

During the series of battles to close the Trun-Chambois gap there was another problem with the inter-army group boundary which still lay below Chambois at Sées. Again, Montgomery declined making an adjustment to the boundary, preferring instead to issue another verbal order authorizing Bradley to violate the line in his thrust toward Chambois. The matter was of some concern to the air force, who complained on 19 August that the boundary was causing confusion over where British and American tactical air should be operating; but the problem was eventually resolved and was not a factor as the Allied air forces constantly bombed and strafed the hapless Germans trapped in the pocket.

As S. L. A. Marshall has suggested, instead of being left with neat pieces to support one view or another, we have a series of contradictory and confusing scraps which tantalize but fail to solve the dilemma. The battle of the Falaise gap was one of the most dramatic events of the war and the fact that a large number of Germans did manage to elude the Allied trap has resulted in the idea of some great Allied blunder. This idea is mostly the result of accounts written for their sensational value rather than for historical accuracy.

One such account, already quoted here, was Rohmer's *Patton's Gap*. He used an extract from Dr Pogue's notes of the Williams interview, which, by his own admission, he obtained over the telephone, as a basis for drawing a sweeping and highly

---

[1] Bradley ordered V Corps to take over this sector from the provisional corps HQ left behind by Patton when XV Corps was split on 14 August.

inaccurate conclusion that Montgomery bore sole responsibility for failing to close the Falaise gap. Far worse, however, is the motive which he ascribes to Montgomery – that he wished to deprive the Americans of publicity and credit for their contributions to the great Allied victory at Falaise. General Rohmer pictures Montgomery as a vengeful and spiteful commander concerned only with his own reputation. He cites Montgomery's anger and dismay over Eisenhower's criticism to Churchill on 26 and 27 July and his conviction that the Supreme Commander and SHAEF were continuing to misunderstand his Normandy strategy. While the British and Canadians were struggling in the bocage, Bradley and Patton were reaping all the publicity and credit:

> For the sake of face, for the sake of his job, and in order to deprive the Americans of the undeserved ultimate credit and glory th_ would receive if it was they who completed the encirclement by driving north to Falaise; and in order to avoid the avalanche of criticism he would be subjected to for again not moving and having to let the Americans do it for him – for all these reasons something had to be done. What could he do? Or not do?[1]

On the unproven basis that Montgomery was acting from personal spite and self-seeking egoism, General Rohmer concludes that:

> The answer is that Montgomery would deny the Americans the opportunity to go north of Argentan, to drive forward to Falaise to complete the encirclement. He would hope by some miracle that his own forces might finally break through the German wall still standing between his troops and Falaise. But even if they did not, his attitude toward the Americans was so antagonistic and vengeful that he would not move that Argentan boundary line.[2]

Rohmer's misreading of Montgomery's intentions does a grave disservice to useful discussion of a very serious and complicated question to which there are no glib solutions. There were certainly flaws in Montgomery's character, as his biographer Nigel Hamilton has demonstrated, but that he would needlessly sacrifice lives or deliberately allow his enemy to escape in order to enhance his own self-glorification is a preposterous claim and Rohmer fails to offer a single shred of evidence to substantiate his

[1] Major General Richard Rohmer, *Patton's Gap*, op. cit., p. 225.   [2] Ibid, p. 226.

absurd conclusion. Montgomery was at times deceitful, boastful and infuriating, to friend and foe alike; as has been and will be seen, he was quite capable of creating and helping to sustain a myth about his role in Normandy. But whatever dark side there was to his character he was, above all, an intensely dedicated and honourable professional soldier, something no amount of fanciful innuendo can disguise. No other Allied commander in the Second World War was more committed to the task of defeating the German Army in battle than Montgomery. Having endured the humiliation of Dunkirk and the virtual disintegration of the British Army in 1940, it is beyond belief to suggest that he would jeopardize the defeat of the Germans in Normandy over a point of vanity.

General Rohmer's transparent dislike of Montgomery caused him to construe the criticism of Williams, de Guingand and Bradley as a basis for concluding that Montgomery's motives were personal. Rohmer also concludes that Montgomery's alleged decision to deny Bradley authority to move north of Argentan was made on 12 August; his authority for this comes from Pogue's notes of the Williams interview – but the truth is that no dates are given in connection with the Falaise battle, thus this is nothing more than conjecture.

Rohmer also misjudges the results of the battles by suggesting that the so-called 'Patton's Gap' permitted 'the escape of tens of thousands of troops, and tanks, vehicles, guns and material from the pocket to fight again another day.'[1]* In fact those troops who did manage to escape took little more than their personal weapons and the clothes on their back. As Martin Blumenson's impartial account reveals, little in the way of materiel got away: '. . . 7 armored divisions managed to get the infinitesimal total of 1300 men, 24 tanks, and 60 artillery pieces of varying caliber across the Seine. The German remnants east of the Seine, lacking armament, equipment, even demolitions to destroy bridges be-

---

[1] Rohmer, op.cit., p. 227.

* The total number of German troops alleged by Rohmer to have escaped is placed at 200,000 – 250,000. 'With them went enormous numbers of tanks, vehicles and huge volumes of war material.' (Patton's Gap, p. 214). If so, it would certainly have been news to the Germans. Moreover, on 13 August Monty made it quite clear that 'our great object will be to see that whatever part of enemy forces escapes us here does not (repeat not) get back over the Seine without being so mangled that it is incapable of further action for many days to come'. M89, Montgomery to Brooke, 13 August 1944, Alanbrooke Papers.

hind them, could do nothing more than retreat toward Germany.'[1]

The view of many senior German officers substantiates the American version. Speidel asserts: 'There were barely a hundred tanks left out of six panzer divisions.'[2] Von Kluge's successor, Model, reported: 'Five decimated divisions returned to Germany. The remains of 11 Infantry Divisions allowed us to regroup 4 units, each with a handful of field guns and other minor equipment. All that remained of eleven armoured divisions when replenished with personnel and materiel amounted to eleven regiments, each with 5 or 6 tanks and a few artillery batteries.'[3] *

Perhaps just as important is the fact that the Argentan-Falaise gap was not necessarily a bad thing, as Blumenson reminds us: 'What critics of Bradley's decision sometimes overlook is the fact that by escaping through the Argentan-Falaise gap, the Germans ran a gaunt:t of fire that stretched virtually from Mortain to the Seine. Artillery and air attacks took a fearful toll of the withdrawing enemy troops. . . Radios, vehicles, tanks, supplies were lost; "even the number of rescued machine-guns was insignificant". All that remained were fragments of two field armies, the Fifth Panzer and Seventh, which had effectively bottled up the Allies in Normandy during June and July, before the American breakout.'[4]

What Rohmer and other critics of Montgomery and Bradley have failed to grasp is that the ability of Haislip's XV Corps to hold the gap shut north of Argentan was, as Blumenson believes, questionable. Without doubt it could have been closed, but if the furious German reaction at Mount Ormel when the SS found the Poles blocking their escape east of Trun is any example, then the answer is certainly open to doubt. Moreover, whatever opportunity may have been lost by the decisions of Bradley and Montgomery applied equally to the Trun-Chambois gap. In

---

[1] Blumenson, 'General Bradley's Decision at Argentan', op.cit., p. 319.

[2] Speidel, op.cit., p. 149.

[3] Quoted in Eddy Florentin, *The Battle of the Falaise Gap*, New York, 1967, p. 335.

* After the war Lieutenant General Edgar Feuchtinger noted that on D-Day, the 21st Panzer Division had 127 Mark IV tanks and 40 assault guns. 'Of this formidable force not a single armed vehicle was left when the Div crossed the SEINE, 10 weeks after D-Day.' By 31 August the 21st Panzer had lost approximately 12,000 men and 350 officers. The remnants of the division that managed to escape behind the Seine consisted only of about 300 men. Cf., Feuchtinger interrogation, Liddell Hart Papers.

[4] Blumenson, 'General Bradley's Decision at Argentan', pp. 318–19.

1951, Bradley wrote: 'To this day I am not yet certain that we should not have postponed our advance to the Seine and gone on to Chambois instead. For although the bridgehead accelerated our advance, Chambois would have yielded more prisoners.'[1]

More recently, Bradley candidly admitted this 'was not only a poor decision but a distinctly dangerous one'.[2] It had been made on the basis of intelligence which estimated that a fullscale German retreat to the east had already begun and that a number of German divisions had escaped:[3]

> Unknown to us, the major share of German forces were still inside the pocket, still vulnerable to encirclement. Had we known this – had we not been misled by intelligence – we would have held Haislip solidly in place on the Argentan shoulder and most likely would have sent Walker [XX Corps] directly north on Haislip's right flank toward Chambois, to help close the gap.[4]

Bradley believes – with some justification – that Collins's VII Corps, Haislip's XV Corps and Walker's XX Corps, totalling eleven divisions, would have formed a firm front on an east-west line to hold the southern edge of the sack. 'We would probably have then requested that Monty pull the boundary back so that our forces could advance on Falaise to link up with Crerar and Dempsey, probably on August 16. Had this been done, we would have trapped most of the German force inside the pocket.'[5] Instead, Bradley notes, he left behind a gravely weakened southern shoulder at a moment when it was the most vulnerable.[6]

There were also other factors which contributed to the slowness in closing the two gaps, the most important of which was the inability of the Canadians to develop their operations more quickly. As the official Canadian history points out: 'It is not difficult to put one's finger upon occasions in the Normandy campaign when Canadian formations failed to make the most of their opportunities. In particular, the capture of Falaise was long delayed, and it was necessary to mount not one but two set-piece operations for the purpose at a time when an early closing of the Falaise gap would have inflicted most grievous harm upon the

---

[1] Bradley, *A Soldier's Story*, p. 379.
[2] Bradley, *A General's Life*, p. 302.
[3] Ibid, p. 299.
[4] Ibid, p. 302.
[5] Ibid.
[6] Ibid.

enemy and might even, conceivably, have enabled us to end the war some months sooner than was actually the case.'[1] Both the Canadian 4th Armoured and the 1st Polish Armoured Division were fighting in their first battles and two of the infantry divisions had met problems with the veteran German formations.[2] The experience of battle soon corrected this, but not without its price.

If Bradley and Montgomery both played for safety by initiating the long envelopment, they also ensured the dismemberment of two German armies. Montgomery's responsibility went well beyond merely worrying about the Falaise gap: it was to ensure that victory in this final, decisive engagement in Normandy was not forfeited by any untimely or foolish decision that would have allowed the Germans to escape en masse from the trap. While this necessitated what some would interpret as excessive caution, it also ensured that the Allies would enjoy an extraordinary success. Without doubt more Germans escaped the pocket than anyone would have preferred, but it would have been unrealistic to expect that they would all be trapped. That a large number eventually escaped across the Seine may be due to other reasons. For example, the 1 SS Panzer Corps Chief-of-Staff has revealed that their retreat across the Seine was made easier by the absence of Allied air forces at a critical moment. 'Contrary to their lively activity heretofore, enemy air forces temporarily became comparatively inactive. Only a few enemy fighter and reconnaissance planes were in the air. Crossing of the Seine would have been impossible if the enemy's air forces had kept the ferrying sites under constant observation.'[3] Eddy Florentin, a former officer in the French Resistance who spent eleven years researching the Falaise battles, points out that Allied air forces failed to destroy the important bridge across the Seine at Putanges. '"This bridge," writes the Chief of Intelligence of the 58 Corps, Major Hayn, "was the only one still available to the Army Korps on the 17th August. It is incredible that the enemy planes did not destroy it. This river crossing was the last life line remaining to be cut, before forcing the German traffic to use small, narrow bridges unable to support heavy vehicles."'[4]

---

[1] Stacey, *The Victory Campaign*, pp. 275–6.
[2] Ibid, p. 276.
[3] Generalmajor Fritz Kraemer, '1 SS Panzer Corps in the West (1944)', loc.cit.
[4] Quoted in Florentin, op.cit., p. 331.

Among the German dead near Falaise was the hero of Villers-Bocage, Michael Wittmann, who perished during the opening day of TOTALIZE. 'During the battle at Cintheaux he had attacked a group of Sherman tanks head on and had smashed two of them. The remaining five opened fire upon him and at point blank range. No crew members were seen to leave the Tiger.'[1] With the Third Reich now being slowly but inevitably strangled by the advancing Allied and Russian armies, Germany could ill afford to lose soldiers of Wittmann's calibre who could never adequately be replaced from a dwindling manpower reserve soon to be conscripting young boys and old men.

In the last hours of his life a despairing von Kluge – now stripped of his command and replaced by another fanatical Nazi, Field Marshal Walter Model – wrote his final words to Hitler before committing suicide, attempting to convey the futility of further resistance by the German Army in the west:

> Both Rommel and I, and probably all the leaders here in the West, who have experienced the struggle with the English and Americans and [witnessed] their wealth in materiel, foresaw the development that has now appeared . . . our views were *not* dictated by pessimism but by sober recognition of the facts. . . You have made an honorable and tremendous fight. History will testify this for you. Show now that greatness that will be necessary if it comes to the point of ending a struggle which has become hopeless.[2]

The Argentan-Falaise gap was an important factor in the final battle in Normandy but, without further evidence, it does not appear to have been the great tactical misjudgement that some have claimed. Undoubtedly decisions were taken which, in the comfort of hindsight, appear to have been unsound. The end, however, certainly seems to have been justified by the means. Despite crushing Allied superiority the Germans in the pocket still comprised a dangerous fighting force which could not be taken lightly. Montgomery and Bradley were faced with a constantly changing situation demanding that decisions of enormous importance be made often and with increasing frequency.

---

[1] Lucas and Barker, op.cit., p. 110.
[2] Quoted in Blumenson, *Breakout and Pursuit*, p. 536. Unlike Rommel, who was accorded a state funeral after his suicide, von Kluge was buried in obscurity and without honour.

Tempting as it may be for the armchair strategist to argue that they ought to have done better, we can best judge the results by the opinions of the defeated German commanders. Perhaps one day more conclusive evidence will emerge, although S. L. A. Marshall, the senior American military historian of the European theatre of operations, doubts this. Whatever failure there may have been to close the noose sooner had less to do with lapses in Allied generalship and more to do with the German will to survive, as US forces were to have conclusively proved to them during the Battle of the Bulge.[1] As far as the Germans were concerned, two representative comments summed up their frustration and anger over this final, decisive battle of Normandy. Said Kurt Meyer twenty years later: 'It was all useless. What crass folly.' That most ardent of Nazis, SS General 'Sepp' Dietrich declared: 'There was only one person to blame for this stupid, impossible operation. That madman Adolf Hitler.'[2]

[1] Lieutenant General Walter Bedell Smith told Dr Pogue after the war that: 'The matter of closing the Falaise Gap was not Monty's fault.' According to Smith, the principal reason was German determination to keep the escape corridor to the east open. Cf., Interview with Lieutenant General Walter Bedell Smith by Dr Forrest C. Pogue, 9 May 1947, loc.cit.

[2] Both quoted in Florentin, op.cit., p. 340.

CHAPTER 27

The Legacy of Normandy

The proper development of Allied strategy north of the Seine will become one of the great controversies of military history.

                Field Marshal Bernard Montgomery

. . . I knew that any pencil-like thrust into the heart of Germany would meet nothing but certain destruction. . . I would not consider it.

         General of the Army Dwight D. Eisenhower

Falaise was by no means the only bone of contention between the Allies during the final month of the Normandy campaign. While the battles raged there, two other major controversies surfaced.

The first, ANVIL/DRAGOON, had been simmering for months as Churchill argued, pleaded and cajoled with Eisenhower and Roosevelt to call off the operation and leave the British-American invasion force in Italy where, he argued, it would be more useful under Alexander. Flexible as Eisenhower proved to be in military and political matters, he absolutely refused to compromise over the invasion of southern France.[1] The long and warm relationship between Eisenhower and Churchill, fostered in 1942 between the crusty Prime Minister and the then junior American general, nurtured during the battles in the Mediterranean, and brought to fruition during OVERLORD, was never more sternly taxed than in the period leading up to DRAGOON, which took place virtually unopposed off the Riviera on 15 August.

Churchill's bulldog qualities were never more evident than during the debates over the controversial landings in southern France. He nagged at Eisenhower like an old fishwife but in this,

---

[1] Eisenhower had called off the simultaneous landings in Normandy and the Riviera under Churchill's prodding and as a consequence of the need to give priority for landing craft to OVERLORD. He was determined not to give in to Churchill a second time.

as in other British-American political matters, it was increasingly apparent that his influence had waned. When General Ismay visited Eisenhower on 15 August, the Supreme Commander told him of Churchill's last-ditch effort to persuade him to cancel the operation. 'Ike said that at his last meeting on Friday [11 August] the PM had practically wept and, in fact, actually had rolled tears down his cheeks in arguing that the Americans were adopting a "bullying" attitude against the British in failing to adopt their, meaning primarily his, ideas as to grand strategy. Both love the Prime as they frequently speak of him, and their comment about him is like that of two admiring sons discussing a cantankerous yet adorable father.'[1]

The question of strategic necessity for operation DRAGOON was never resolved. Critics (and there were many) maintained that it was never a viable operation of war and that events in Normandy had by 15 August rendered it unnecessary. Fundamentally, ANVIL/DRAGOON represented the diverse opinions which existed over grand strategy. Protagonists on both sides of the question had valid arguments. Churchill and Brooke considered it a foolish waste of valuable manpower which ought to have been kept in Italy. Eisenhower's reasons were based on the same rationale he had used since early 1944: that the Allies required additional ports, particularly Marseilles, and the second invasion force would serve to protect the right flank of the broad Allied advance towards Germany.[2] In retrospect, neither of his arguments seems valid but Eisenhower's reasons may have been more compelling than he admitted. He was all too well acquainted with the myriad problems leading up to the final approval for OVERLORD and the difficulty of obtaining priority of effort, and this was no time to forfeit that advantage by permitting Churchill and Brooke to siphon off troops and supplies to Italy and the pursuance of a strategy which was disavowed by both Marshall and Roosevelt. Sir Edgar Williams is probably correct when he notes, 'Ike insisted on carrying on with ANVIL simply because he realized it was the only way of absolutely guaranteeing the priority of that campaign. Otherwise, there would have been a push-pull sort of thing. I don't think ANVIL

---

[1] Butcher, op.cit., p. 553.
[2] Eisenhower had Marshall's backing over ANVIL for much the same reasons.

was really necessary except to make it quite clear which was your *Schwerpunkt.*'[1]*

The issue of ANVIL was thus both political and military, and it was the former aspect that Eisenhower wished to avoid. During his debates with Churchill he later recalled attempting to compel the Prime Minister to accept the distinction: 'The only reasonable ground for argument concerning ANVIL . . . was the posing of political against largely military objectives. This I tried to make perfectly clear in my own book.[2] In our intimate discussions in the summer of 1944, I told Winston that I thought he was probably right as to the political problem, but he paid no attention to my urging that he take the subject to President Roosevelt and his political advisors rather than come to me as an individual who was necessarily required to make decisions on the *military basis only* . . . I now understand that he *had already*, before talking to me, made strong representations to President Roosevelt, without success.'[3]

Unwittingly, Hitler's insistence in early August on the destruction of the Brittany ports and holding out to the end had reinforced Eisenhower's belief in the necessity for capturing Marseilles, which had the best port facilities in France; and it hardened his insistence on ANVIL taking place as scheduled.

When Eisenhower presented Churchill with a *fait accompli* the matter died. Unfortunately, the other controversy emanating from Normandy was not disposed of so easily. This was the argument over future Allied strategy after Normandy; it gradually grew to such proportions that it threatened not only Allied harmony but Montgomery's future as commander of 21st Army Group.

The original Allied plan had included a pause at the Seine while the armies regrouped, advanced their logistical base farther forward and made plans to resume offensive operations north and east of the Seine. It was predicated upon an orderly German retreat across Normandy and a solid defence of the Seine river line, not a rout such as had occurred as a result of the American

---

[1] Interview with Sir Edgar Williams, 28 July 1981.
* It is believed by some that Eisenhower's insistence on ANVIL inevitably committed him to the broad-front strategy.
[2] Eisenhower, *Crusade in Europe*, op.cit.
[3] Eisenhower, letter to Lord Ismay, 3 December 1960, Eisenhower Presidential Papers.

breakout and the entrapment of Army Group B in the Argentan-Falaise pocket. Obviously, this pleasant turn of events left no time for the luxury of a pause, and with the remnants of the German Army in full retreat toward the German border it was a time for pursuit, not consolidation. Unfortunately, however, SHAEF had failed to propose plans for dealing with success on such an enormous scale..

Eisenhower stoutly maintained and the papers of his HQ-SHAEF support this – that the strategy he intended to employ was a broad advance against Germany, one which would see Montgomery's Army Group push through Belgium towards the Ruhr industrial complex, while Bradley's 12th Army Group advanced to the south, covering the British right flank.[1] The sudden collapse of German resistance in mid-August gave rise to a different proposal from Montgomery, for what he called a single, 'full-blooded' thrust towards the Ruhr with the two Army Groups abreast. This force, reasoned Montgomery, would consist of some forty divisions 'which would be so strong that it need fear nothing'.[2] Pivoting on Paris, 'The basic object of the movement would be to establish a powerful air force in Belgium, to secure bridgeheads over the Rhine before winter began, and to seize the Ruhr quickly.'[3]

It is difficult to understand why Eisenhower refused to acknowledge that Montgomery's proposal was no mere 'pencil-like' thrust. It may well have been that Eisenhower's growing annoyance with his obstinate subordinate led him deliberately to belittle the plan. There is evidence that in the days immediately following the great victory in Normandy he had begun privately to question Montgomery's loyalty. Eisenhower and Admiral Sir

---

[1] For example, a May 1944 SHAEF planning paper entitled 'Post-Neptune Courses of Action After Capture of Lodgement Area' (PRO, (WO 219/2506), stated: 'Our main chance of success would appear to lie in advancing astride the Ardennes with two mutually supporting forces extending the enemy forces and, by surprise and deception, achieving superiority of force in one or the other of the groups and defeating the enemy in detail. Such a course of action would enable us to exploit the flexibility of our superior air power by concentrating air support in one sector or another in accordance with need.' The proposed axes of advance were: (1) Main axis of advance along the line AMIENS–MAUBERGE–LIEGE–THE RUHR (2) A subsidiary axis of advance on the line VERDUN–METZ. Copies of this document were sent to 21st Army Group and a copy is to be found in the PRO (WO 205/660), thus making it clear that Montgomery and his staff must have known well before the invasion of SHAEF's proposed broadfront strategy for the post-Normandy period.

[2] Montgomery, Memoirs, op.cit., p. 266.

[3] Ibid.

Bertram Ramsay had become close friends and in a conversation on 11 September the Supreme Commander finally admitted just how frustrated he was at Montgomery's persistence in questioning his broad-front strategy. Ramsay recorded the essence of their conversation in his diary:

> Went on to see Ike and found him in pyjamas with his knee bad again. Stayed to tea and he let himself go on the subject of Monty, command and his difficulties over strategy, etc. He is clearly worried and the cause is undisputedly Monty who is behaving badly. Does not trust his loyalty and probably with good reason. He has never let himself go like this before. Discussed possible alternative Supreme Commanders and what they would have done in his place.[1]

Eisenhower rejected Montgomery's proposal out of hand, arguing that there were inadequate sources of logistical support to give priority to 21st Army Group.[2] Nor was he ever convinced of the merit of Montgomery's plan to seize the Ruhr and drive on quickly to Berlin and end the war. 'I pointed out that, without railway bridges over the Rhine and ample stockages of supplies on hand, there was no possibility of maintaining a force in Germany capable of penetrating to its capital. There was still a considerable reserve in the middle of the enemy country and I knew that any pencil-like thrust into the heart of Germany such as he proposed would meet nothing but certain destruction. This was true, no matter on what part of the front it might be attempted. I would not consider it.'[3]

The legacy of the great Allied victory in Normandy was not harmony based upon the successful attainment of a common goal, but rancour and controversy. So powerful were the differences between Eisenhower and Montgomery then that their disagreements over strategy have since been the focus of more debate than any other single aspect of the war in Europe. Generally, this debate focused along national lines, with proponents on each side marshalling arguments to bolster their point of view. The one notable exception was General de Guingand, who

---

[1] Diary of Admiral Sir Bertram Ramsay, 11 September 1944.

[2] The great Allied breakout was a triumph except for the logisticians, for whom it was a nightmare. They were faced with the immense task of attempting to keep up with supply lines that were being stretched to hundreds of miles, as the four Allied armies dashed across France and into Belgium.

[3] Eisenhower, *Crusade in Europe*, op.cit., p. 335.

sided with Eisenhower on the grounds that the logistical system could not support Montgomery's thrust.[1]

During the battle of the Falaise pocket one of Montgomery's most pressing problems had been to determine what strategy the Allied armies ought to employ when the Normandy campaign ended, as it most certainly would in the very near future. On 19 August he met three of the other army commanders, Dempsey, Crerar, Hodges, and Bradley. Montgomery was aware that his tenure as temporary ground forces C-in-C would soon come to an end, and he was certain that Eisenhower and SHAEF were not prepared for the task. SHAEF Forward had recently – and quite inexplicably – moved from England to the seacoast resort town of Granville, north of Avranches, on the Cotentin Peninsula. Why SHAEF picked this remote spot is one of the great mysteries of the war: not only was Granville remote and inaccessible, but it lacked adequate communications – as the Allied pursuit operations developed, it might as well have been on the moon. During the great Allied airborne operation at Arnhem in mid-September the absurdity of SHAEF's location was demonstrated when Montgomery's liaison officer to the AEAF, Lieutenant Colonel C. E. Carrington, recalled receiving a frantic telephone call from Leigh-Mallory at Granville, pleading for information about the operation. SHAEF was uninformed about what was happening in Holland and was completely without ability to exercise any form of command and control. Towards the end of September SHAEF moved to the Trianon Palace Hotel in the Paris suburb of Versailles.

What Montgomery hoped to accomplish at this 19 August meeting was to obtain the consensus of the field commanders and to present their joint recommendations to Eisenhower in the hope that he would accept their views over those of the SHAEF staff. Dempsey's diary records in some detail the plans the commanders agreed at the conference. German intentions were thought to be the abandonment of western and southwestern France, with Army Group G sending two divisions to Kesselring in Italy and the remainder joining Army Group B to protect its left flank. Ultimately Army Group B would attempt to hold on some

---

[1] Cf., de Guingand, *Operation Victory*.

unspecified front.[1] In the short term, 12th Army Group would pivot northwards, prepared to take Paris whenever the moment was opportune. Two series of stop-lines would be established, the first by the Canadian Army at Trun-Chambois, and the second by Bradley at the River Seine. Dempsey's task with the Second Army was 'to drive the birds into the stop lines'.[2] The long-term objective was for the Canadian Army to capture the Havre Peninsula while the Second Army drove northeast toward Calais and into Belgium with its right flank on the line Beauvais-Amiens. The US forces were to be established in the area Troyes-Chalons, Rheims-Laon-Beauvais, prepared to move either east, northeast or in both directions.

Montgomery claimed that he had met privately with Bradley on 17 August and that the latter had agreed with him, but by 23 August had changed his mind and was in favour of a 12th Army Group drive to the east toward Metz and the Saar. On 23 August, Montgomery met Eisenhower in a final effort to persuade the Supreme Commander to adopt his plan.[3] Eisenhower refused and elected to proceed with a broad-front advance by which Bradley would thrust 12th Army Group eastward towards the Saar and the Frankfurt gap. Montgomery would be allowed to thrust northeast towards the Ruhr, but first he must capture the port of Antwerp which Eisenhower correctly considered the vital key to support the Allied advance. Antwerp was the largest and best equipped port in Europe, and with the Normandy ports becoming more and more incapable of handling Allied logistic requirements as well as being too far from the front lines, Antwerp was the obvious alternative.

In principle the British would advance north of the Ardennes while the Americans advanced to the south. To protect his right flank Montgomery asked for and got Hodges's US First Army over the strenuous objections of Bradley. Because there were inadequate supplies particularly of gasoline to support both thrusts fully, Eisenhower allocated priority to Montgomery,

[1] Dempsey Diary, 19 August 1944, loc.cit.
[2] Ibid.
[3] Montgomery also sent de Guingand to plead his case with Eisenhower – to no avail. Bradley says that he agreed with only *part* of Montgomery's outline plan: that 21st Army Group wheel northeast to capture Antwerp and the V-rocket sites. Terming Montgomery's claims as deceitful, Bradley maintains that he never wavered in his support for a 'two-thrust' strategy. A General's Life, pp. 312–3.

much to the annoyance of Bradley and Patton, whose role was reduced to that of a minor thrust in the south. Moreover, Patton was convinced that the fabled Siegfried Line was an empty shell capable of being easily breached if only the Third Army were given permission to move rapidly east before the Germans could reinforce it. Patton persuaded a sympathetic Bradley to permit the Third Army to thrust toward Metz in the belief that if he became deeply involved in the Saar Eisenhower would be presented with a *fait accompli* which he could not ignore. By the end of August the Third Army was camped outside the gates of Metz.

Patton used every subterfuge in his bag of tricks to keep the Third Army moving, including diversion of gasoline and ammunition destined for the First Army: on more than one occasion the Third Army troops obtained vital supplies by purporting to be from the First Army; trucks of the Red Ball Express were mysteriously diverted to Third Army supply dumps. Aware that Eisenhower would sooner or later put a stop to his advance, Patton employed what he called the 'rock soup' method of advance into Lorraine. As he later explained it:

> A tramp once went to a house and asked for some boiling water to make rock soup. The lady was interested and gave him the water, in which he placed two polished stones. He then asked if he might have some potatoes and carrots to put in the soup to flavor it a little, and finally ended up with some meat. In other words, in order to attack, we had first to pretend to reconnoitre, then reinforce the reconnaissance, and finally put on an attack – all depending on what gasoline and ammunition we could secure.[1]

Montgomery was incensed when he learned of these actions and complained loudly to Eisenhower; but the charade soon ended when the Third Army literally ran out of fuel outside Metz, where they remained for much of the autumn of 1944 while the Germans scraped together a strong defence which cost Patton his first bloody nose.[1] Many have argued that in failing to reinforce

---

[1] Patton, op.cit., p. 125.

[2] The setback at Metz caused Patton to write with tongue in cheek to his friend Lieutenant General Jimmy Doolittle: 'This is to inform you that those low bastards, the Germans, gave me my first bloody nose when they compelled us to abandon our attack on Fort Driant in the Metz area. I have requested a revenge bombardment from the air to teach those sons-of-bitches that they cannot fool with Americans. I believe that this request will eventually get to you, and I am therefore asking that you see that the

Patton, Eisenhower squandered the greatest opportunity prsented to the Allies to end the war in 1944. Others argue that even if Patton had penetrated the Siegfried Line and driven to the Rhine River, the Third Army, with its flanks unprotected, would have faced destruction. The argument continues to this day and will doubtless never be resolved to anyone's satisfaction.

The wrangling over the advance against Germany was not the only problem nettling Eisenhower. Montgomery was convinced that now was not the time to change the Allied command structure, contending that Eisenhower was too preoccupied with the problems of politics and other matters to assume the burden of directing the ground campaign as well. Montgomery therefore proposed that he continue as the ground C-in-C. 'Someone must run the land battle for him. We had won a great victory in Normandy because of *unified* land control and not *in spite of it*. I said this point was so important that, if public opinion in America was involved he should let Bradley control the battle and I would gladly serve under him. . .'[1]

Public opinion was indeed an important factor in Eisenhower's reasoning but most important of all was the Supreme Commander's continued insistence there not be another layer of command created in the form of a land-force commander.[2] His original plan had always been to assume control of the land battle once two army groups had been created by the activation of 12th Army Group. He postponed taking control until the Normandy campaign was resolved, much to the disgust of Marshall, who was convinced that Eisenhower had already delayed too long.

The fact was that the British were now politically and militarily in the position Churchill had long feared. The preponderance of military forces were American and had he elected to concur in Montgomery's proposals – either the single thrust to the Ruhr or his formal elevation to permanent ground commander – Eisenhower could not have survived as Supreme

Patton-Doolittle combination is not shamed in the eyes of the world, and that you provide large bombs of the nastiest type, and as many as you can spare, to blow up this damn fort so that it becomes nothing but a hole. With warm regards, I am as ever, Devotedly yours, G. S. Patton, Jr. Letter of 19 October 1944, Doolittle Papers, Manuscript Division, Library of Congress.

[1] Montgomery, *Memoirs*, pp. 268–9.

[2] The fact which Eisenhower ignored was that 21st Army Group would have continued to perform two roles as it had in Normandy, thus eliminating the need for another level of command.

Commander. Public opinion should not dictate military strategy but it is hard to ignore the suggestion that Eisenhower's broad-front strategy had as much to do with politics as it did with logistical considerations and military philosophy. Martin Blumenson points out: 'The whole broad-front versus narrow-front controversy can, I think, be understood in light of Eisenhower's point of view – he could not let either a British or an American general win the war singlehandedly; both British and Americans had to win together.'[1]

The broad-front/narrow-front controversy was also a power-ful example of the fundamental disparity between British and American military doctrine. That the clash over strategy should come along national lines is no coincidence. Just as British tactics on the battlefield called for a concentration of force to be applied against an enemy, so too did their philosophy of command call for a separate commander to carry out each aspect of the battle – on land, sea and in the air. American doctrine rejected this approach in favour of the single commander concept, and the broad-front idea likewise reflected an American approach. These differences were so deeply ingrained in each side that it was inevitable they would quarrel over fundamental issues. Eisenhower was aware of this problem and commented in his unpublished memoirs:

> On this subject both Mr Churchill and General Marshall, holding diametrically opposed views, were obviously in-fluenced by the military doctrines of the two governments. Americans believed in one commander for one mission or theater, no matter what the composition of the forces. The British believed in a committe comprising a Commander-in-Chief for each service – ground, air, navy represented in the region. They seemed to make the method work. I should here remark that so far as I know the two governments never exchanged philosophic views or arguments on the subject. I was at times the target of insistent advice, directly or indirectly given, but I was, of course, from the days of Fox Connor, fully committed to the single commander theory. I still am.[2]

The problem was that, having been firmly rejected by Eisen-hower, Montgomery continued to argue, complain, and at times insist (as Churchill had done with ANVIL) that the Supreme

---

[1] Blumenson, letter to the author, 23 February 1983.
[2] Eisenhower, unpublished manuscript, loc.cit.

Commander change his mind. Montgomery could not abide 'bellyaching', yet his actions after Normandy completely contradicted this attitude, one he refused to accept in others. He managed to lose the sympathy and goodwill not only of Eisenhower but the other American commanders. However justified his proposed strategy may have been, it was seen by the Americans as one more example of his vanity and his inability to accept Eisenhower's authority. Still, as Sir Edgar Williams has pointed out, there was one beneficial side effect to Montgomery's boastfulness and vanity: it provided the perfect cover for ULTRA.[1] For the remainder of 1944 a steady stream of letters and personal complaints from Montgomery finally drove Eisenhower, during the dark and uncertain days of the Ardennes counteroffensive, to draft a cable to the US Joint Chiefs-of-Staff saying he could no longer tolerate the problem. As Eisenhower later recalled, their differences had become so acute 'that I decided to make an issue of it. He [Montgomery] sent me such an urgent expression of his belief – which I had to assume, at the time, expressed the Prime Minister's ideas also – that the war could not be won unless we adopted his ideas on this matter, that I prepared a cable to the Joint Chiefs-of-Staff saying the rift between Montgomery's thinking and mine had become so deep that one of us would have to be removed from duty. My message suggested that a decision be made at once by the Combined Chiefs of Staff.'[2]

Had this cable been sent Montgomery would undoubtedly have been dismissed at once. Whatever his own personal views, Churchill was totally committed to the concept of full authority vested in a Supreme Commander. Brooke, much as he sympathized with Montgomery – and he was scornful of Eisenhower's strategy, firmly believing it unsound and strategically a breach of the principles of war, particularly the plan for the advance beyond the Rhine in early 1945[3] – was dismayed at Montgomery's failure to heed several warnings to stop criticizing Eisenhower. Instead, his lack of tact and inability to learn when to keep his mouth shut had led to a showdown. No matter what his personal beliefs, had Eisenhower pressed the issue of command Brooke could not have saved Montgomery; it would have

[1] Interview with Sir Edgar Williams, 8 April 1983.
[2] Eisenhower, loc.cit.
[3] David Fraser, *Alanbrooke*, London, 1982, pp. 466–7.

been a dispute beyond his influence to resolve. Had de Guingand not heard of the problem and flown to SHAEF to make a last-ditch plea on behalf of his chief, Montgomery's future would have been very different. Publicly, the matter of Montgomery's near-removal has been downplayed as an exaggeration but the story told by de Guingand reveals what a near-run thing it really was: 'I got a report from the liaison officer I'd sent to 12th Army Group which confirmed my worst fears.' Upon arriving at SHAEF de Guingand went directly to see Eisenhower and in the subdued light of his office found him studying a document:

> Eisenhower looked up very surprised and he said 'What are you doing here, Freddie?' I said, 'Well, I've come on a very important mission,' and I then explained my fears, saying that I hoped I could help. And Eisenhower said, 'At the moment we've just agreed upon a signal we're sending to General Marshall. . .' He said, 'I think you'd better read it'. . . So I read it; I was absolutely shattered. This more or less said that he'd come to the end of his tether, and it was now a question of deciding who should stay as Supreme Commander, Eisenhower, or Montgomery, Commander of the 21st Army Group, as they simply couldn't go on in the present way. And the decision was that Montgomery should go and he would nominate General Alexander for the post. . . But if, on the other hand, they felt that Montgomery must stay, then he would accept the decision.[1]

De Guingand was forced to employ every argument at his disposal to head off what was certain to be the sack for his C-in-C:

> That really shook me, and I virtually went down on my bended knees and asked him whether he wouldn't hold it up. . . I tried to explain that really I'm sure that Montgomery didn't realise the seriousness of the situation and I was perfectly certain if I got back to him and explained it all I could resolve the matter. I said give me 24 hours . . . and Tedder stepped in and said, 'No, we've decided on the signal, it must go.' And I said, 'Oh, please, give me 24 hours,' and then Beetle Smith magnificently came to my support and I eventually persuaded Eisenhower to give me that 24 hours.[2]

---

[1] Quoted in Thames Television Interview, 'The World at War, 1939–1945', IWM.
[2] De Guingand, loc.cit.

As might be expected, Montgomery's reaction was disbelief
when told of the situation the following afternoon:[1]

> He said, 'Well, who will take my place? Who? The British
> government would never allow this.' I said the signal said that
> Eisenhower would nominate Alexander; he'd forgotten about
> that, I think, and that did it. He said: 'What shall I do?' I had
> drafted out a signal which I thought he ought to send to
> Eisenhower and he read it through, and he made a couple of
> small alterations, rang his bell, got his ADC up. 'Send this up by
> my special link to Supreme Headquarters.'[2]

At long last a chastened and sober Montgomery had awoken
to the fact that he had very nearly dug his own grave.[3] His signal
to the Supreme Commander was apologetic and he promised
Eisenhower that he would hear no more on the subject of
command. Sir Edgar Williams believes that the problems between the two might never have grown so acute had Eisenhower
in the beginning said, 'Shut up, Monty!' His failure to do so led
Montgomery to overstep himself, as he was prone to do in such
situations. 'In the matter of the thrust to the Rhine, Ike showed
his difference from Monty. The latter could think only as a
soldier. He thought he saw a chance to win on his front. He could
see only that. Ike looked over the whole scene, saw the necessity
of doing something for the whole front. Gave a military states-

---

[1] De Guingand had flown from SHAEF to Montgomery's HQ at great personal risk
during a snowstorm in weather totally unfit for flying.

[2] De Guingand, loc. cit. In an interview with journalist Alan Moorehead, Dr Pogue's
notes confirm de Guingand's version. According to Pogue's notes: 'He [de Guingand] said
to Monty, I must see you at once. Then when he got Monty alone he turned loose on him
and finally broke through the tough exterior. He said if you keep on, one of you will have
to go, and it won't be Ike. Monty broke down; went to pieces. Finally said what shall I do?
De Guingand wrote a cable saying that Monty gave way to Ike and asked Monty if he
would sign it. To his amazement Monty signed it as it was written and called for an
orderly to send it off.' Alan Moorehead, interview with Dr Pogue, 21 January 1947,
US Army Military History Institute.

[3] British historian Ronald Lewin notes that Montgomery's inability to understand the
political ramifications of the British-American alliance was a grave disadvantage. Montgomery was never able to grasp the fact that American public opinion, the United States
Congress and ultimately President Roosevelt would not stand still for what might have
been the final battle of the war being led by a British general. Lewin might have added that
not only was this impossible on political grounds but even more so due to Montgomery's
extreme unpopularity in the United States. What Eisenhower seems to have understood
perfectly, Montgomery did not. 'Thus we were brought to that dreadful day when the
Alliance very nearly was cracked asunder, the day when Montgomery was really within a
pen-stroke of being removed by Eisenhower, the consequences of which I dread to think.'
Extracted from Ronald Lewin, 'World War II: A Tangled Web', Lecture given at the
Royal United Services Institute for Defence Studies, *RUSI Journal*, December 1982, p. 18.

man's answer of closing up on the whole front. However, he didn't hold strictly to his answer. He let part of it get away. Ike tended to let the boys have their way a little – "Have a go, Joe." Let Patton edge forward towards Frankfurt when that was not part of the immediate plan. Let Monty go by himself at Arnhem.'[1]

These unfortunate disputes engendered all sorts of unpleasant side effects. Patton's dismay over Montgomery receiving priority of supplies was equalled only by his disgust with Eisenhower for giving it to him. A stunned and disbelieving Patton, who in early September had boasted, 'I hope to go through the Siegfried Line like shit through a goose', found himself mired in the mud of Lorraine and unable to advance, bringing him to the conclusion that his long-time friend and benefactor had sold out to the British. Although not quite so vocal about the issue, Bradley too was unhappy with Montgomery being favoured over his Army Group. During the Battle of the Bulge relations between Bradley and Montgomery soured irreparably after the latter's press conference in January 1945, which appeared to patronize and belittle the American effort.

There was one other, less well known unfortunate legacy of Normandy – this time between Bradley and Dempsey. The decision in mid-August to swing US forces to the Seine to block the German escape route had resulted in priority being given to American movement. Although this meant cutting across the route of the British advance, both Dempsey and Montgomery had willingly given Bradley permission. By 25 August the First Army had cleared the area between Mantes Gassicourt and Rouen for the Second Army. Hodges and Dempsey then agreed to a system of two-hour clearances round all major crossroads, so that the First Army could withdraw and allow the Second Army to assume control of this sector. At a press conference several days later Dempsey complained that he had been unnecessarily obstructed by American traffic across his front.[2] The normally mild-mannered Bradley was incensed and said privately that Dempsey's charge was 'one of the greatest injustices ever done to the American Army'.[3] He protested strongly to Montgomery

[1] Williams interview, loc.cit.
[2] Bradley, *A Soldier's Story*, pp. 381–3.
[3] Bradley oral history, loc.cit.

who apologized for Dempsey's remarks, 'adding that he was sure Dempsey was misquoted, or that he didn't mean the statement the way it sounded.'[1] This was the only time Dempsey ever publicly criticized another commander and it got him in considerable trouble with Montgomery, who gave him a severe 'rocket' for his loose tongue.

This legacy of disenchantment between the top Allied generals in the post-Normandy period continued after the war, when various personal memoirs and accounts appeared. As will be seen, relations between Eisenhower and Montgomery were eventually damaged beyond repair.[2] However, during the period of good feeling which followed immediately after the end of the war, Eisenhower did nothing to prevent the creation of a myth about Montgomery's role in Normandy.

[1] Bradley oral history, loc.cit.

[2] As were relations between Bradley and Dempsey. The bad feeling between the two generals over the incident at the Seine surfaced again in 1951 when Bradley criticized Dempsey in A Soldier's Story. Dempsey was incensed and wrote the following caustic letter on 25 May 1951: 'Dear Brad: No doubt you have very good reason for the attacks on me which are now being quoted in the English press. They are interesting in that they show what a great difference in outlook there is between American and British generals. We over here place great store on Loyalty, and those of us who had the good fortune to fight alongside such men as Bradley, Hodges, Simpson, Ridgway, Taylor and so on, would hesitate a long time before attacking them in print: they were our friends. I understand there is a lot of money in the sort of stuff you have written, so perhaps that is the reason. But I feel it is letting Ike down very badly for you may remember he was rather keen on Anglo-American cooperation and friendship, and I am sure still is. Yours Ever, Bimbo Dempsey.'

Montgomery sent a copy of Dempsey's letter to Eisenhower with the comment: 'Bimbo Dempsey is extremely angry with Brad and has written to him. He sent me the enclosed copy of the letter and asked me to show it to you. So I send it to you. What a pity this all is.' Letter of 31 May 1951. Eisenhower attempted to smooth over the matter by writing to Dempsey: 'I assure you of my very deep regret that anything should have been published by any American general that was unnecessarily embarrassing to any of my old friends. . . I must fully agree with you that there is no point in giving dissention and mutual resentment among old friends. Of all times when we should be working in complete accord this is the most important.' Letter of 2 June 1951; all letters in Eisenhower Presidential Papers, Eisenhower Library.

CHAPTER 28

The Normandy Myth

The Caen fight was a failure. Monty thought up
excuses later... We would be at Caen yet but for
the American advance on the right. The truth will
probably never be told. Will Ike think he can afford
to print all the facts? Will the airmen think they can
afford a split with Monty? So we will have a legend.

Air Vice Marshall Sir Philip Wigglesworth[1]
Senior Air Staff Officer, AEAF

Nearly forty years later the debate over Normandy continues
unabated, even though all of the principals are dead. In fact it
seems that this passage of time has served only to harden
long-held beliefs, as recently demonstrated with the publication
of General Omar Bradley's posthumous autobiography, which
renews old questions about Montgomery. Since his death in
1976, Montgomery remains as controversial as he was when
alive. The Montgomery master plan is as much of an enigma now
as it was in 1944.

There has been considerable doubt in the minds of a great
many people, including officers closely associated with Montgomery at the time, whether the master plan evolved as originally
intended. Out of the mass of confusing detail, claim and coun-
terclaim there emerges one overriding question: to what extent
did the master plan effect the outcome of the battle of Normandy? The answer hinges upon what the plan was actually
designed to achieve. In Volume II of his monumental life of the
Field Marshal,[2] authorized biographer Nigel Hamilton aims
to show that its prime purpose was for the British Second Army
(and later the First Canadian Army) to act as a strong shield,
driven deep into the interior of the Allied eastern flank in order to

---

[1] Air Vice Marshal Sir Philip Wigglesworth: interview with Dr Forrest C. Pogue,
1947.
[2] Nigel Hamilton, *Monty: Master of the Battlefield, 1942–44*, London, 1983.

hold off German reserves and reinforcments, while Bradley was both to cut off the Cherbourg Peninsula and to drive south to stretch the German defences to breaking point. From there Bradley would drive east with the certain knowledge of ample logistical backup via the Brittany ports, which Patton's Third Army would capture.

However, as Hamilton admits, neither the shield nor the American advance lived up to expectations, and for this reason Montgomery ought to have been franker. In relating Montgomery's view of the campaign he points out how the master plan was characteristically Montgomery in both form and substance, spelling out in advance the method by which he would mount and conduct the battles in Normandy, just as he had done previously in other battles, beginning at Alamein. He did so in order to instil a sense of clarity and purpose into his armies, and his plan was thus a general framework within which he would orchestrate the day-to-day battles.

Despite the fact that these battles did not go according to plan, Hamilton suggests that by providing this larger framework Montgomery was able to tolerate the local setbacks which occurred and to demonstrate a confidence that infected all who met him. It was only when this confidence visibly waned after the frustrating lack of progress during the first month of the campaign, that others began openly to express doubts at the lack of results. Nevertheless, Hamilton maintains that Montgomery retained sufficient flexibility to alter his day-to-day tactics according to success or failure.

Of his attempt to paper over the obvious cracks in the execution of the master plan, Hamilton writes: 'Monty should have been franker in admitting this – but such an admission was neither in his character nor would it have suited his relentless drive to simplify: to see things in broad strokes.'[1]

Certainly, there is no dispute over Montgomery's intention to provide a solid shield for Bradley, nor did he contemplate using 21st Army Group to exploit a breakout as far as Paris. However, there are other aspects of the master plan which require examination before any conclusions can be drawn. No matter how well intentioned the master plan it was nevertheless a strategic failure

---

[1] Nigel Hamilton, letter to the author, 17 March 1983.

at Caen, and the consequences of this were far too grave for it to be dismissed as merely a 'local setback'. To attain the protective shield Montgomery considered so vital, the capture of Caen and its surrounding key terrain was not merely *desirable*, as has been suggested by Montgomery himself – it was *vital*. In the period after D-Day reverse followed upon reverse as the Second Army either failed to take advantage of priceless opportunities like Villers-Bocage or was forced to engage in debilitating battles such as EPSOM and CHARNWOOD. The keys to achieving the goals of the master plan were retention of the initiative and flexibility, and it was at Caen that Montgomery lost both.

Rommel's admittedly often crude defensive measures certainly succeeded in denying Montgomery the flexibility he sought. As Dempsey's papers consistently reveal, the object of the Second Army was to keep the initiative so as to *prevent* the British front from congealing around Caen; but congeal it did, forcing Montgomery into a head-on and costly confrontation in order for the Second Army to gain more favourable terrain and the space for 21st Army Group to manoeuvre. Without adequate manpower reserves, the British Army was ill-prepared to fight a series of wasting battles at Caen, something Montgomery took pains to point out after the war when he told Chester Wilmot that had he adopted a strategy of pressing these infantry battles 'it would have crippled the British Army'. However, in the end such battles could not be avoided, and the cost was indeed high.

The confidence Montgomery attempted to instil soon waned as Bradley, Eisenhower, the airmen and senior officers at SHAEF became increasingly disillusioned, not only by what he was doing but by what he said. Moreover, even his own troops, who were at their peak of enthusiasm for D-Day, soon became overcautious and weary of repeated exhortations and reassurance that they were doing their job despite the obvious lack of progress.

Before D-Day neither Montgomery nor Bradley had ever planned a breakout on the scale of COBRA: the Germans would, it was believed, resist all the way to the Seine in a series of delaying actions. The Allied advance, on the other hand, was never seen in terms of the mobile warfare which developed in August, when Patton's armour broke the last German defences at Avranches, but rather in terms of a more deliberate, strongly contested sweep to the east.

Whether or not these events can be considered as falling within the framework of the master plan is something which is, finally, a matter of interpretation. What is indisputable, however, is that by early July Eisenhower was losing faith both in Montgomery and in the master plan, which clearly was not succeeding as intended. As the need for the British Army to act as a shield for Bradley gradually diminished, the need for expansion in the east became more and more obvious to Eisenhower: as a consequence, he enjoined Montgomery to take a stronger offensive attitude round Caen.

Eisenhower's role in Normandy was undoubtedly played down by Montgomery. That he was irritated by Eisenhower's complaints to Churchill and Brooke is understandable, but what he never grasped was that his superior – despite his growing dissatisfaction with Montgomery – refused to meddle in operational matters or to undercut his authority with Bradley, a temptation to which another Supreme Commander might well have succumbed. In his desire to take credit for winning the battle of Normandy, Montgomery was unfair in his criticism of Eisenhower's alleged 'misunderstanding' of his strategy and his contributions to the defeat of the German Army.

According to his biographer, Montgomery never lost his belief that he was indeed still conforming to the overall framework of his plan, but his refusal to acknowledge the obvious setbacks to his aims not only failed to reassure others, but left the distinct impression – however false – that he was covering up the entire matter. His unwillingness to be candid about Normandy, and a series of events connected with the writing of the official British history of the campaign, eventually resulted in the creation of a myth that has managed to escape serious challenge since the war.

Why was Montgomery so insistent that the campaign had 'gone according to plan' when the evidence clearly suggests otherwise? A brief investigation of the man and his military philosophy may offer some insight.

It was Monty's habit to spell out in advance, both in his personal notes and in addresses to his senior subordinates, the plans of every major battle that he undertook. The plan for OVERLORD was no exception, and certainly no mystery within the Allied high command. Those present at the two D-Day expositions – and this included virtually every senior commander involved in Normandy – had heard the plan explained in great detail by Montgomery himself on the large terrain model of Normandy. Eisenhower and others had copies of his notes which clearly outlined the genesis of his strategy. He was followed by Dempsey, whose fifteen typewritten pages of notes[1] set out with equal clarity the planned operations of the Second Army, leaving no possibility of misinterpretation.

The final revision in December 1943 to Morgan's original COSSAC plan called for the Second Army to capture Caen while Bradley cut off the Cotentin and took Cherbourg. After an administrative pause, British and Canadian forces would break out toward the Seine ports, the Seine River line and Paris. While 21st Army Group fought the great battle around the Seine, the Americans would press down the Cotentin and proceed to capture the Brittany ports. What Montgomery did was to recast the Morgan plan by widening the frontage of the invasion force and adding two divisions, thus providing a more secure and cohesive basis for the operations to follow. Once Bradley captured the Brittany ports, American forces would sweep to the east to line up with British and Canadian forces along the Seine. Although he has left the impression there was no relation between his master plan and the COSSAC plan, Montgomery, in reality, changed only the logic of carrying out the objectives of the COSSAC plan. In so doing, he removed not only the weakness inherent in the COSSAC plan but also the defeatist attitude which had existed in the HQ of 21st Army Group over the Morgan concept.

Contrary to the popular misconception fostered by Montgomery himself, he did know and understand that no battle ever goes completely according to plan[2] – Alamein, Mareth and Sicily had been recent examples. However, what Montgomery knew to be the truth and what he was prepared publicly to admit were two entirely different things.

In Normandy, Montgomery was convinced that he had developed the outlines of a plan which would eventually succeed.

[1] Personal notes, 15 May 1944, Dempsey Papers, PRO (WO 285/1).
[2] Nigel Hamilton, letter to the author, 13 April 1983.

He knew that the Germans were sensitive to the threat in the east where the British army was expected to break out with the object of liberating Paris. Having failed to take the original objectives of Caen and the high ground beyond, Montgomery quickly realized that it was vital to convince the Germans that the main Allied effort would come from the eastern flank.

The great storm before EPSOM was more significant than has previously been thought: it prevented Bradley from taking Cherbourg and simultaneously driving south in the Cotentin as had originally been planned. Instead, he was forced to concentrate on Cherbourg and delay his great offensive until early July, by which time the Germans had strengthened their defences in the west.

The problem, according to Hamilton, was that Montgomery held so closely to the plan in his mind that he inhibited his troops since it produced no visible results.[1] The very confidence the plan was designed to achieve failed to materialize, as we have seen.

Montgomery followed a pattern in Normandy similar to that of Alamein where there had also been a fundamental change of plan. Nigel Hamilton offers some penetrating reasons for his behaviour. There were two sides to Montgomery's character. On the positive side were his traits of clarity, simplicity, an uncanny ability to inspire his troops to carry out a coherent battle plan, and his unblemished record of never having lost a battle. The unpleasant side of Montgomery's personality revealed traits of conceit, boastfulness, and a deeply rooted belief that he had earned a place alongside the other great figures of British military history. As Hamilton has pointed out, Montgomery viewed himself as the natural twentieth-century heir-apparent to the legacy of Marlborough and Wellington.[2] Montgomery also seems instinctively to have understood that fame is frequently as fleeting as yesterday's headlines, and that his many enemies might eventually attempt to rob him of credit he deemed rightfully his. After Alamein there had been displayed what his biographer called 'a quasi-paranoid streak of subsequent self-justification', and it was this trait which resulted in his ability to be more candid about Normandy. It was this 'noxious insistence that his battles and campaigns were fought exactly according to plan – claims so obviously untrue that some historians and

---

[1] Hamilton letter, 13 April 1983.
[2] Hamilton, *Monty: The Making of a General, 1887–1942*, p. 606.

critical contemporaries were bound to see him as a boastful and profoundly suspect figure, and seized every opportunity to denigrate him. Montgomery himself remained unrepentant, and went to his grave declaring that, in more ways than one, "the rats will get at me".[1]

That he was fallible like others and occasionally forced to improvise in order to achieve success was not something he liked to admit. Improvisation and flexibility had, in his own past experience, resulted not in victory but in defeat. By contrast, the United States Army taught that flexibility and the ability to improvise were essential traits in any successful commander. Bradley, for example, had learned his craft under the tutelage of Marshall and Stilwell at Fort Benning, where a war of movement was stressed. As he noted: 'Such perceived warfare demanded simplicity, improvisation, ingenuity and speed... If an unexpected advantage arose, an officer was to instantly seize the prize. If an unexpected setback occurred, he was to work his way out of it by his own resourcefulness.'[2]

The dramatic ending to the Normandy campaign was a personal triumph for Montgomery; he had thereby played an important role in avenging the British humiliation of Dunkirk. For many years he had experienced first-hand the grievous results of poor training and unsound planning, and this experience had helped to shape his philosophy of command, based on the doctrine of concentration of forces at a decisive point, and the absolute necessity for clear, well-defined strategic and tactical plans. When once asked the secret to successful high command, he replied without hesitation: 'To produce a simple plan out of a mass of confusing detail.'[3]

Montgomery had seen for himself the mindless waste of good men in the trenches of the Western Front in 1914–18, and the blundering at Dunkirk had served only to convince him that the British Army had learned nothing during the inter-war period. He had vowed that such a calamity would never again occur as long as he possessed the means to prevent it. The master plan for Normandy was a classic example of the Montgomery philosophy in action: the plan was clear, simple and designed to save the

[1] Hamilton, *Monty: The Making of a General, 1887–1942*, p. 606.
[2] Bradley, *A General's Life*, p. 66.
[3] The papers of John North, loc.cit.

lives of his men. Unfortunately, it also contained two major flaws.

The first of these was the assumption that there would be a rapid penetration beyond Caen to give him space from which future operations could develop with more flexibility. Bradley was critical of what he identified as 'a grave weakness in the invasion plan', observing: 'A great amount of work, thought and intelligence gathering had gone into the assault phase – getting a toehold on the beach. But not nearly enough planning and intelligence gathering had been devoted to the immediate *problems* of exploitation of the beachhead.'[1] (Author's italics.) As Bradley also admits, too little thought was given to exploitation in the American sector of the bocage, but of equal importance was the failure of Montgomery's operations staff to perceive and plan an alternative course of action if the Second Army bogged down in the early going in the restrictive terrain round Caen. It is true that Dempsey had studied alternative plans for exploitation beyond the Odon and Orne Rivers using O'Connors's 8 Corps and the 1st Airborne Division; but there seems to have been no study of Allied alternatives in the event that the Second Army failed to penetrate these barriers. The problem was that under the Montgomery system such plans were not made, nor, apparently, were they desired: when a plan was drawn up it was on the basis of expected success. The rigidity and inflexibility of British planning can be seen repeatedly in Montgomery's battles, and it produced serious consequences on the eastern flank.

The second flaw was gross underestimation of his opponent. Montgomery had accurately predicted Rommel's tactics in response to the invasion, but he should have examined more seriously the possibility that Rommel might actually succeed in blunting a rapid advance inland; the last thing Montgomery wanted was to be fly-trapped in terrain favouring Rommel. When the Germans managed to hold Caen in the first few days after the invasion, a series of battles for position ensued whereby Montgomery lost much of his initiative. This left him in a 'no-win' situation: his front was too lengthy and yet too shallow to mount a major offensive with the limited combat strength at his disposal; by the time the necessary forces were available

[1] Bradley, *A General's Life*, p. 234.

(when 8 Corps landed), the Germans had strongly reinforced the Caen sector. The only alternative was for Montgomery to revise his strategy to one of limited operations in order to keep Rommel fully occupied around Caen until Bradley had completed the capture of Cherbourg and was able to enlarge the American bridgehead further south in the Cotentin. Patton would undoubtedly have argued that Caen was a prime example of unsound planning: 'One does not plan and then try to make circumstances fit those plans. One tries to make plans fit circumstances. I think the difference between success and failure in high command depends upon the ability, or lack of it, to do just that.'[1]

The most consistent mistake made by the Allied commanders in Northwest Europe was a failure to realize – despite repeated examples – the will and tenacity of the German Army to resist against overwhelming odds and in the most appalling conditions. The Allies had superiority of air, sea, logistics and troops, while the Germans were devoid of air support, lacked reinforcements and material, were handicapped by a clumsy and unworkable command structure, and constantly overruled by Hitler, who refused to permit his commanders tactical freedom. Although they never knew it, Rommel and later von Kluge, were further thwarted by the masterly conceived and enormously successful FORTITUDE deception plan and by ULTRA, which kept the Allied commanders informed of German problems, troop strengths, dispositions and intentions. By the time the Allied commanders had recognized that defeating the German Army would not come about without unrelenting pressure and much bloodshed, the die had been cast. Plans and tactics were thus altered in an attempt to break the German cordon blocking the Allied advance out of the bocage into terrain favouring their superiority, in particular the US armoured divisions under Patton.

In more favourable circumstances the outcome in Normandy might well have been far different. It is worth remembering that the immense Allied military machine was, in the later stages of the campaign, fighting an enemy who was reduced to the pitiful necessity of utilizing horses as a major means of transport. Yet, astonishingly, the German Army still battled to the bitter end at

[1] Patton, *War As I Knew It*, p. 116.

Falaise. Once the Allies had firmly established themselves on the soil of Normandy there was never any chance of a German victory. Hitler and OKW may have lived in a fool's paradise, but for the commanders forced to continue a hand-to-mouth existence at the sharp end there were no such illusions.

Despite his arguments to the contrary, Montgomery recognized from the beginning that the eastern flank offered the best prospects for success in the early stages of the campaign: it was, as he repeatedly emphasized, a bastion for the side controlling it. A rapid seizure of the vital Caen-Falaise Plain would not only have eliminated the dreadful battles of attrition during the first six weeks, but might well have shortened the campaign. Bradley has shown that he well understood Montgomery's need for Caen, noting that the city was much more important than mere possession of it. 'Its quick capture was essential to provide a bridgehead across the Orne, provide room for manoeuver and avoid the difficult seize of a stone city . . . Monty knew the value of Caen. Look at his order about June 20 when he says "Caen is the key to Cherbourg."'[1]

The eventual strategy of holding on the left and breaking out on the right proved so successful because Bradley and Eisenhower belatedly recognized that the campaign could end in stalemate unless the American thrust towards Brittany was mounted with the application of *decisive* strength, in giving rise to a breakthrough in the Cotentin. Lord Scarman[2] has described what happened: 'It is true that there was a plan which showed the Americans coming up on the right towards the Seine while they [the British] swung at Caen. But that is far different from the decision to strike out on the right and pull quickly around. Monty undoubtedly intended to start the breakout on his front, and then let the Americans come around as they could. He intended at first for Patton to spend his time cleaning up the few Germans left in Brittany.'[3] Although this was a trifle exaggerated it illustrates the difference between Monty's concept, and the breakthrough as it developed.

As for Eisenhower's role, Scarman 'thinks Eisenhower decided to work with Bradley on the deal, and by-pass Monty after

[1] Bradley interview with Dr Forrest C. Pogue, 14 October 1946, loc.cit.
[2] Then Wing Commander Scarman and Tedder's personal assistant.
[3] Scarman interview with Dr Forrest C. Pogue, 25 February 1947.

Monty failed to get going. [This] shows the great sacrifice General Eisenhower is willing to make for Anglo-American relations that he is willing to sacrifice his reputation as a strategist and give backing in his Report to Monty's argument.'[1] Eisenhower was fearful that Montgomery would lead the Allies into stalemate and his frequent exhortations to Montgomery to attack were not so much examples of his 'football coach' mentality as they were of the clear recognition that constant pressure must be kept on Rommel. After repeated setbacks in the east, Eisenhower was no longer willing to accept Montgomery's declarations that all was going 'according to plan', and quietly shifted his backing to Bradley without undercutting the British commander's authority.

The eventual myth which has evolved about Montgomery's role in Norman y had its roots in the first official document to emerge from the war: Eisenhower's SHAEF despatch, completed shortly after V-E Day.[2] Eisenhower made no attempt to dispute Montgomery's change of plan, saying only that 'In the east we had been unable to breakout towards the Seine, and the enemy's concentration of his main power in the Caen sector had prevented us from securing ground in that area we so badly needed. Our plans were sufficiently flexible that we could take advantage of this enemy reaction that the American forces smash out of the Lodgement area in the west while the British and Canadians kept the Germans occupied in the east.'[3] Montgomery's handling of the campaign was termed 'masterful'. 'From the beginning of the campaign in Normandy, I agreed with the Field-Marshal Montgomery and General Bradley that our basic policy should be so to maneuver and attack as to pin down and destroy substantial portions of the enemy in our immediate front in order later to have full freedom of action. . . The enemy's reaction had con-

---

[1] Scarman interview with Dr Forrest C. Pogue, 25 February 1947.

[2] 'Report by the Supreme Commander to the Combined Chiefs of Staff on the Operations in Europe of the Allied Expeditionary Force, 6 June 1944 to 8 May 1945.' The report was dated 13 July 1945, but was not formally published until 1946.

[3] Supreme Commander's Report, op.cit. In *A General's Life* Bradley's collaborator criticizes Eisenhower and Smith for fostering what he calls this erroneous impression. However, Bradley's collaborator appears not to have known about the British appreciation of 7 May 1944 in which one of the options discussed was a breakout to the east. A copy of this document was furnished to the First Army by 21st Army Group BGS (Plans), but its present whereabouts are unknown. Cf., Chapter 6.

vinced us that we should strike hard with our left and then follow through promptly with a right-hand blow.'[1] For reasons we shall explore, Eisenhower saw no purpose then or later in a public disagreement with his former subordinate.

Montgomery's first public pronouncement about Normandy came on 3 October 1945 when, with Brooke in the chair, he addressed the members of the Royal United Service Institution.[2] The text of his speech was soon obtained by Eisenhower's post-war headquarters in Frankfurt, where an irritated Bedell Smith ordered the preparation of a detailed analysis of the decisions made in Normandy.[3] Among the points in his speech which rankled the Americans was this one: 'The Battle of Normandy had conformed to the pattern decided upon before D-Day. There was nothing the enemy had been able to do which ever upset this plan, and there was never a moment in which we had not firmly held the initiative.'[4]

> Once ashore and firmly established my plan was to threaten to break out on the eastern flank – that is in the Caen sector; by this threat to draw the main enemy reserves into that sector, to fight them there and keep them there, using the British and Canadian armies for the purpose. Having got the main enemy reserves committed on the *eastern* flank, my plan was to make the break-out on the *western flank*, using for this task the American armies under General Bradley, and pivoting on Caen; this attack was to be delivered southwards down to the Loire and then to proceed eastwards in a wide sweep up to the Seine about Paris. . . The operations developed in June, July and August exactly as planned.[5]

Montgomery also took credit for ordering the short envelopment at Falaise, declaring: 'I ordered the right flank of the Twelfth U.S. Army Group to swing North towards Argentan, and intensified

---

[1] Supreme Commander's Report, op.cit.
[2] Now called the Royal United Services Institute for Defence Studies.
[3] On 23 October 1945 the G–3 (Operations) Division of US Forces European Theater submitted to General Smith a detailed appreciation, sharply disputing Montgomery's RUSI lecture. It stated that 'A review of planning papers and other documents fails to substantiate the accuracy of Field-Marshal Montgomery's claim that actual operations followed exactly the pattern of planned operations.' Included in this appreciation was an earlier memorandum prepared by General Smith which similarly disputed these claims. The American paper was never made public but copies of both documents are in the Eisenhower Papers, Abilene.
[4] *RUSI Journal*, November 1945, pp. 431–54.
[5] Ibid.

the British and Canadian thrusts southwards to the capture of Falaise.'[1] This idea was, of course, Bradley's brainchild, a point stressed in *A General's Life*: 'Let me put it very plainly: it was my idea. Official army historian Martin Blumenson credits me as the author. So does Ike, in a private memorandum he dictated that day, August 8.'[2]

In 1945–6, while Montgomery served as the British occupation commander in Germany, his unofficial account of 21st Army Group operations, *Normandy to the Baltic*, was prepared, ghosted from Montgomery's documents by Brigadier Belchem. In his summary, Montgomery maintained that 'The outstanding point about the Battle of Normandy is that it was fought exactly as planned before the invasion. This plan had been relentlessly followed in spite of the inevitable delays and *minor setbacks* which the changing course of the battle had imposed upon us, and had fir.. lly brought us to overwhelming victory.'[3] (Author's italics.) This was, to say the least, a gross exaggeration.

The Normandy controversies were brought into sharp focus during the post-war years when many of the principals published their versions and when the first of the official histories appeared. The great disparity between these accounts, no matter how well intentioned, served only thoroughly to blur and exacerbate these unresolved questions. Admirers and critics of Montgomery tended to use these accounts to prove either that Montgomery was correct or that he was not telling the whole truth. As will be seen, Montgomery was not a liar but neither was he even remotely objective.

The most controversial account to appear about Normandy was not written by Montgomery, but by the British government.[4]

[1] *RUSI Journal*, November 1945, pp. 451–54.

[2] Bradley, *A General's Life*, p. 295. The Eisenhower memo reads: 'The American right wing should swing in closer in an effort to destroy the enemy by attacking him in the rear. On a visit to Bradley today I found that he had already acted on this idea, and had secured Montgomery's agreement to a sharp change in direction toward the Northeast instead of continuing directly toward the East. . .' Cf., *The Eisenhower Papers*, IV, p. 2057.

[3] Montgomery, *El Alamein to the River Sangro and Normandy to the Baltic*, p. 383.

[4] Another controversial unofficial account by a former member of Bradley's staff appeared in 1946: Ralph Ingersoll's *Top Secret* shattered post-war Allied harmony by its attack on the generalship of both Montgomery and Eisenhower. Although Ingersoll's account was an honest if bitter memoir of what he believed to be the truth about the mishandling of the war in Europe by the Allied commanders, it generated enormous controversy and ill-feeling in Britain, where it was interpreted as an outrageously unfair and vicious smear on the Allied leadership. The book created more public and private

After the war a team of British historians began preparing a two-volume account of the campaign in Northwest Europe in 1944–5, entitled *Victory in the West*. Under the direction of the principal author, Major L. F. Ellis, they had access to most of the official papers of the OVERLORD planners and 21st Army Group. There was also mutual cooperation with the US historians in Washington, who freely furnished American documents to the British whenever requested. However, during the seventeen-year period between 1945 and the appearance of the Normandy account in 1962,[1] no effort was made to interview the senior British or American commanders involved.[2] Unlike their American and Canadian counterparts, the British historians did not believe in the use of interviews or oral history, and consequently forfeited an exceptional opportunity to add an important new dimension to their account. Instead the official history relied on incomplete documentary evidence.[3]

---

reaction than any other single account of the war: numerous documents in British and American archives attest to the anger felt on both sides of the Atlantic. Lieutenant General Sir Ian Jacob promptly published a series of articles in *The Economist*, while Bedell Smith wrote: 'My comments on *Top Secret* are unprintable.' Eisenhower referred to *Top Secret* in a post-war letter to Montgomery as a 'trashy book'.

Nevertheless, Ingersoll has insisted in a letter to the author that his book represented the views of a number of senior officers on Bradley's 12th Army Group staff, but that the manuscript was deliberately kept away from the general to avoid any embarrassment or compromise.

[1] Vol. I covered Normandy, and Vol. II (1968) the remainder of the campaign in Northwest Europe. The source notes and references for Volume I remained classified and were not printed until a revised edition was published in 1974. None of the war documents was available to the public until Prime Minister Sir Harold Wilson in 1969 reduced the fifty-year closure rule on the release of official government documents to thirty years. The first war documents were made available for public inspection by the Public Record Office in 1972. However, any document considered sensitive can still be withheld by the agency responsible. Despite repeated attempts in recent years to pass an Act of Parliament similar to the US Freedom of Information Act, there is no right of public access to any document HM Government chooses to withhold, nor is a reason required to be given for such withholding. By contrast, the official US and Canadian histories fully document all unpublished sources utilized in their preparation. Vol. II was published without source notes and a revised edition has never been issued.

[2] The lone exception was General Dempsey, who was interviewed about his role in Operation GOODWOOD, but only *after* it was learned that he had discussed this subject with Liddell Hart in 1952. Cf., 'Operation Goodwood, 18 July 1944', Liddell Hart Papers loc.cit., in Chapters 20 and 21.

[3] For example, Ellis does not seem to have had access to Montgomery's notes for the 15 May 1944 St Paul's School final OVERLORD briefing. ULTRA, of course, could not be discussed in any of the official histories. At the request of the British government, the official historians in Britain, the United States and Canada were not made aware of ULTRA's existence and no reference to it appeared in their accounts. The source listing of unpublished sources in Volume I of *Victory in the West* contains no reference to 15 May 1944 notes by Montgomery.

The most serious defects of Ellis's *Victory in the West* were a clear lack of objectivity and a failure to address a number of important questions, among them: manpower; morale; leadership; the failure of the campaign to develop 'exactly as planned' along the lines of Montgomery's master plan; the poor performance of the veteran divisions (including the 7th Armoured which Ellis made the scapegoat for Villers-Bocage); and the abysmal British tank-infantry cooperation. Brigadier Richardson's outline of the master plan is dismissed by Ellis with a brief reference only to the covering note, which stated that the development of operations could not be predicted accurately at that moment – in complete disregard for the fact that this document set out Montgomery's post-D-day intentions in specific detail.[1]

The British account had been eagerly awaited but proved to be a grave disappointment. American reaction in 1963 when the book appe. red in the US was immediately critical. Martin Blumenson spoke for the American official historians when he wrote:

> Major Ellis has seized the opportunity to present an account of the campaign from the British commander's point of view. This is perfectly justifiable, for there is a legitimate and valid Montgomery viewpoint. What is objectionable is the vehemence with which Major Ellis identifies himself with that viewpoint. Basic questions that are still controversial today have been omitted from discussion or dismissed lightly. And points considered by Ellis to be particularly telling in defense of Montgomery's course of action have been italicized for the benefit of less discerning readers. As a result the book is an apologia, and the effect is quite opposite from the one desired by the author... What bothers Ellis is "ill-informed criticism". What may bother the reader is the author's certainty that all criticism of Montgomery is ill-informed.[2]

Privately, Blumenson was disturbed by a feeling that Ellis had done his fellow official historians and the historical profession as a whole a disservice by sweeping controversy and unpleasantness under the rug, and by providing ammunition for those sceptics who believed that all official history was the same as court history and that the official historians were 'kept', i.e.

---

[1] *Victory in the West*, p. 81 and PRO (WO 205/118).
[2] Martin Blumenson, review of *Victory in the West*, Vol I, in *Army*, April 1963, p. 82.

practising discretion in order to avoid government censorship.[1]

Blumenson's irritation was directed at Ellis's conclusion in which he wrote: 'General Montgomery had kept firmly to the general plan he intended to follow, undeterred by incidental disappointments and unperturbed by ill-informed criticism. He can fairly be criticized for what at times he said or wrote, but not easily for what he did.'[2] This is a reference to the airmen and many of the senior officers in SHAEF, but the principal culprit singled out by Ellis is Eisenhower who, he charged, wholly misunderstood Montgomery's conduct of the campaign, citing the Supreme Commander's official report as evidence.[3]

Why did the British official historians so readily accept Montgomery's version, and were they aware it was less than forthright? The answer is suggested by Dr Pogue who wrote the official US account of SHAEF – *The Supreme Command* (1954). Armed with a letter from Eisenhower, Dr Pogue interviewed well over a hundred of the senior military and political figures involved with the campaigns in Europe.[4] Notably absent from Pogue's list of interviewees was Montgomery, who declined to see him unless Eisenhower asked him personally.[5] 'I later saw Montgomery when working on the Marshall book. Montgomery said: "I decided I had better see you. I wouldn't see you or Correlli Barnett[6] and you both were rather harsh with me."' As Pogue notes: 'I got full cooperation from the British Historical Office. I sent my first draft of *The Supreme Command* to them

[1] Draft review of *Victory in the West*, 1963, Liddell Hart Papers.

[2] Ellis, *Victory in the West*, p. 493.

[3] Ellis, p.494.

[4] Those interviewed included: Eisenhower, Bradley, Dempsey, de Gaulle, Mountbatten, Brooke, Cunningham, Portal, Ismay, Bedell Smith, Morgan and Tedder. A full list is contained in the biographical note at the conclusion of his book. Some, notes Dr Pogue, were interviewed as many as ten times. These important documents formed what is known as the Pogue interviews, most of which are preserved in the US Army Military History Institute at Carlisle, Pennsylvania.

[5] As Dr Pogue notes: 'Montgomery was one of the first people I tried to see in 1947. His aide told me that he was sure the Master would want to see me and asked me to come back the next day.' Later Pogue was told by the aide in some embarrassment of Montgomery's refusal: 'You know, many people try to see him. He feels he must have a request from the principal.' Eisenhower's letter which served to enable Pogue to interview all the British Chiefs of Staff and many others proved unsatisfactory to Montgomery.

[6] Correlli Barnett's *The Desert Generals*, London, 1960, was highly critical of Montgomery and caused great controversy over what Barnett alleged was Mongomery's failure at Alam Halfa to acknowledge that the plan had originally been Auchinleck's. A revised edition, published in 1983, reiterates this criticism and attacks what is called Nigel Hamilton's attempt to rehabilitate Montgomery's reputation.

and suggested they show it to Montgomery and former members of his staff. I also sent it direct to Brigadier E. T. Williams, who wrote detailed comments from Oxford. Montgomery did not look at it, but Miles Dempsey did and I was told went to Montgomery and said he should do something about it. He suggested the book be dropped in the interest of Allied unity.'[1]

After Dempsey's complaint, Montgomery approached Eisenhower, who asked Dr Pogue if he would let the Field Marshal see the revised draft. Pogue agreed to let Montgomery see it on the same basis as he had done with Eisenhower: for correction of errors but not for censorship. Pogue heard nothing further and the book was eventually published without Montgomery seeing it. The important point is that Montgomery only asked to see the draft manuscript *after* learning that it was critical.

In Dr Pogue's opinion the official British historians were fully aware that operations in Normandy had differed from Montgomery's version. According to Pogue: 'The people I knew best in the British Historical Office – Brigadier Latham and Colonel Warhurst – were critical of Monty. Ellis, however, followed the straight Montgomery line. Latham and Warhurst tended to agree with the views of many Americans that Montgomery had indicated in his St Paul's School briefing before D-Day a much more vigorous campaign than he later laid on. They also believed that he intended to break out quickly on the Caen front. Then, when he was stopped, they believed that he began to say that he had always planned to let the Americans wheel on the right.'[2] Recently Dr Pogue reiterated that both the Cabinet Office Historical Section and Brigadier Williams had approved of his original draft. Williams wrote to Dr Pogue: 'I thought at first that you had been too rough on the Master. But then I realized you had it right.'[3]

Montgomery had also declined to cooperate with the official British historians who had approached him with a request for missing copies of some of his wartime correspondence with Eisenhower. In frustration the historians turned to Eisenhower, who was by this time president of Columbia University. At

[1] Dr Pogue, letter to the author, 21 October 1980.
[2] Ibid.
[3] Quoted by Dr Pogue in letter to the author, 3 March 1983.

Eisenhower's direction Dr Pogue furnished the missing letters.[1]

The appearance of Ellis's *Victory in the West* in 1962 legitimized what had begun as far back as June 1944 when Montgomery insisted for the first of many times that the master plan had been strictly followed. The lone dissenting voice was that of Martin Blumenson in the United States, who disputed both Montgomery's claims and the official history.[2] Montgomery himself took full advantage of the British official history by appearing on BBC television with a copy of Ellis's book in his hand to defend his version of the campaign.

In view of the strong evidence to the contrary, why then was the British official history so one-sided? Obviously, to have disputed Montgomery's claims would have raised enormous controversy and publicly embarrassed Britain's best known war hero who had already published both his unofficial account and, by then, his *Memoirs*, which had a worldwide sale.[3] Moreover, Montgomery was still a very influential figure in post-war Britain and until his retirement in 1958 had served as CIGS and Deputy Supreme Commander of NATO's military arm, Supreme Headquarters, Allied Powers Europe (SHAPE). Had Ellis elected to tell the whole truth about the Normandy campaign an unpleasant public quarrel between Montgomery and his own government could have resulted.

Victory in the West was a strong example of the fundamental differences in philosophy between the American and British official historians. Simply put, the American approach was expressed by S. L. A. Marshall: 'I had made up my mind that come hell or high water, we would some way come to the point where no commander in U.S. uniform would be considered to have the right to hold out on the people of the country. We got that

---

[1] Dr Pogue, letter to the author, 3 March 1983. Montgomery's reluctance to release his private correspondence may have stemmed partly from an article by British journalist, Alan Moorehead, in *Collier's Magazine* in October 1946, called 'Montgomery's Quarrel with Eisenhower'. Montgomery was disturbed by the article and wrote to Eisenhower that he was 'very sorry': 'I want to assure you that no one has at any time seen the correspondence that used to pass between us privately . . . I do wish they would leave the past alone and devote their attention to easing the present and building a worth-while future.' Cf., *The Eisenhower Papers*, VII, p. 1364.

[2] Cf., Martin Blumenson, 'The Genesis of Monty's Master Plan in *Army*, January 1959; 'The Most Overrated General of World War II', in *Armor*, May/June 1962; and 'Some Reflections on the Immediate Post-Assault Strategy', in *D-Day: The Normandy Invasion in Retrospect*, University of Kansas, 1971.

[3] *Normandy to the Baltic* (1947) and *Memoirs* (1958).

principle accepted in the E[uropean] T[heater of] O[perations], that what happens in war is national property, and there must be a full and accurate accounting of it. It provides a sharp contrast to the Pershing attitude, and I might say the Montgomery attitude.'[1]

Eisenhower was not pleased by some of the things said in Pogue's *The Supreme Command* but refused to interfere in any way. On several occasions Dr Pogue recalls him saying: 'I would have hoped that I was smarter than to say such and such but if that is the way Dr Pogue found it, let it stand.'[2]

The American system was to involve the principals fully by soliciting their views but to tolerate no interference in what was finally published. The British method never subscribed to this notion and the results have dismayed many, among them Lord Tedder, who wrote to Liddell Hart in 1963: 'I wonder if it has struck you that there is a remarkable likeness between Monty and Winston in their respective attitudes towards history. In other words, each of them determined, so far as lay within his own power, to make sure that his story should record his own version of events rather than history. . . Indeed, while it is evident that Winston's story will in due course be disentangled, on the other hand as regards Monty the record was so skilfully adjusted at the time that I see little, if any, prospects of the truth being disentangled from the story.'[3]

Why then did others not attempt to counter the Montgomery version? Both Tedder and Coningham were disturbed, but their public quarrels with Montgomery were well known and their views would effectively have been dismissed out of hand as uninformed criticism by meddlesome airmen. Coningham, in particular, was so emotional in his criticism of Montgomery that he could not have made a coherent or believable argument, especially as his venomous official despatch had been suppressed by the Air Ministry. Like Leigh-Mallory and Ramsay before him, Coningham died in a plane crash not long after the war and was thus removed from the scene.

Montgomery's subordinates were certainly not prepared to

---

[1] Letter, S. L. A. Marshall to Liddell Hart, 12 April 1950, Liddell Hart Papers.
[2] Dr Pogue, letter to the author March 1983.
[3] Letter, Tedder to Liddell Hart, 7 March 1963, copy furnished by Lord Tedder. In this instance Tedder is referring mainly to North Africa; however his remarks apply equally to the campaign in Northwest Europe.

question his wartime strategy publicly[1]. Dr Pogue found Dempsey evasive when interviewed and Liddell Hart noted in 1954 that
he carefully avoided contradicting Montgomery.[2] This left only
the American commanders. Patton was long dead and Bradley
had never forgiven Montgomery for his role in the Battle of the
Bulge. His war memoirs, A Soldier's Story, clearly stamped him
as anti-Montgomery, although his account of the Normandy
campaign was genuinely respectful.[3] Eisenhower in 1948 published his intentionally bland version, Crusade in Europe. Nevertheless, even he managed to ruffle feathers in some circles in
Britain, as his personal correspondence during this period
affirms. In addition, as Pogue points out: 'Without any question,
Eisenhower and Bradley [deliberately] weaken their case against
Montgomery. You must remember both of the accounts were
written, certainly Eisenhower's report was, in a period of good
feeling. The Americans knew that many of the British were aware
of the truth so they thought, "why stir up trouble?" Bradley
probably toned down his account because a former member of
his staff, Ralph Ingersoll, had written a savage attack on Montgomery's slowness and Ike's failure to exercise leadership. To a
degree Eisenhower was trying to dampen some of the criticism of
his own leadership by pointing to Montgomery's successes.
Patton's diary and Bob Allen's Lucky Forward[4] were as much
anti-Ike as anti-Monty. Eisenhower, in his desire to give equal
credit, wrote the SHAEF report as Supreme Commander and
played up the positive side. His Crusade in Europe kept the same
tone.'[5]

[1] De Guingand had mixed emotions and was the only one mildly to dispute some of his
chief's actions in Operation Victory. He remained loyal to Montgomery but he also had
formed a deep friendship with Eisenhower. De Guingand was too much the pragmatist
not to recognize Montgomery's shortcomings, and as he wrote to Eisenhower in
December 1949: 'I'm afraid Monty, in his endeavour to justify his every action, forgot
that some of us could tell a very damaging story. It is a pity he is so sensitive. . .' Letter of
1 December 1949, Eisenhower Presidential Papers, Eisenhower Library.
[2] Liddell Hart Papers, King's College, London.
[3] A General's Life is exceptionally critical of Montgomery, and his dislike and distrust
of the Field Marshal are far more evident than in A Soldier's Story which, despite its
criticism, was more evenly balanced. Among Bradley's comments: 'There was no "chemis-
try"; our personalities simply did not mesh. He left me with the feeling that I was a poor
country cousin whom he had to tolerate.' p. 232.
[4] Colonel Robert S. Allen, Lucky Forward: The History of Patton's Third U.S. Army,
New York, 1947. Allen was a journalist and syndicated columnist who had served in
Lucky Forward, the codename for Patton's forward command post. Unofficially, the Third
Army had the code pseudonym 'cocky bastards'.
[5] Dr Pogue, letter to the author, 21 October 1980.

There was another reason for the pro-Monty line taken by Ellis. According to Pogue: 'At the time I was writing, Eisenhower was the great hero in Britain and there was considerable anti-Monty feeling. In the presidential years, Eisenhower sank to some extent in the estimation of the British. There also seemed to be the feeling that Montgomery was their best general and should be given great credit. This involved in some circles, a writing down of Ike and, of course, his very fair accounts played into their hands.'[1]

Thus, Eisenhower's refusal to criticize Montgomery and the publication of the British official history left no one else to dispute Montgomery's version of the Normandy campaign. Eisenhower kept silent because he placed Allied unity above personal consideration, including his own reputation: his fondness for the British people and his near-obsession with preserving British-American rapport came first.[2] Eisenhower abhorred unnecessary controversy and not once in the post-war years, when criticism was sometimes rampant in various books and magazines, did he ever attempt to defend himself publicly. He did not, however, discourage Lord Ismay or de Guingand, who frequently worked behind the scenes, from speaking on his behalf.[3] No officer in the Second World War was more deeply committed to the concept of coalition warfare than Eisenhower, and the price he paid was frequent criticism from both sides. He not only enraged Anglophobes like Patton, who once remarked: 'Ike is the best general the British ever had,' but many senior officers in the American War Department were also disturbed including, on occasion, Marshall, who believed he was too lenient with Mont-

[1] Dr Pogue, letter to the author, 21 October 1980.
[2] In a colourful and dramatic ceremony in June 1945, Eisenhower had been given the Freedom of the City of London, a rare honour for a foreigner. He had been cheered by thousands of admiring British, and had addressed his hosts from London's famous Guildhall. He always considered it one of the greatest honours ever bestowed upon him.
[3] During the writing of his *Memoirs* Montgomery frequently summoned Sir Edgar Williams to Isington Mill to look over and comment on his first drafts. Williams recalls how he would often challenge Montgomery over certain statements and demand to see documents to substantiate a claim. Sometimes Montgomery would flatly refuse and adamantly insist that a certain passage remain as written. On other occasions he would capitulate and agree to Williams's suggestions. Sir Edgar Williams, interview of 8 April 1983. After the *Memoirs* were published there arose a question of what was believed to be a clear libel of Auchinleck. Through his solicitor Auchinleck declined to sue but demanded that his honour be satisfied by an apology from Montgomery. A compromise was eventually reached in the form of an inserted acknowledgement, in reprints of the *Memoirs*, of Auchinleck's role at El Alamein.

gomery. A letter to General Thomas Handy in early 1943 was representative of Eisenhower's attitude: 'I am not British and I am not ambidextrous in attitude. But I have got a very wholesome regard for the terrific tasks facing the United Nations in this war, and I am not going to let national prejudice or any of its related evils prevent me from getting the best out of the means that you fellows struggle so hard to make available to us. . . It is never out of my mind for a second.[1]

Eisenhower's success in the Mediterranean and Northwest Europe lay in his powerful belief that Hitler could be defeated only through a strong and healthy British-American alliance. Nevertheless, he was quite capable of taking a firm stand against Churchill and the British Chiefs-of-Staff as he proved with ANVIL and his broad-front strategy.[2]

The allegation that Eisenhower misunderstood the intent of Montgomery's Normandy strategy is a demonstrably false part of the myth, as a 1946 letter establishes. Montgomery had written to Eisenhower to say that in view of 'a great deal of nonsense being written in the press on both sides of the Atlantic about the strategy of the Normandy battle', he proposed to write his despatch so that it would be 'in tune with yours on that subject'. The implication of his remarks had questioned Eisenhower's statement in the official SHAEF despatch about a British breakout to the east. In his reply, Eisenhower laid to rest the myth of his supposed ignorance by writing: 'The operations immediately following the landing diverged quite considerably, in a tactical sense, from what we had hoped to execute. Specifically, one of our earliest objectives was the open ground to the south and southeast of Caen and Falaise, which areas we wanted to seize quickly in order to establish airfields and to bring into

---

[1] Eisenhower, letter to Handy, 28 January 1943, *Eisenhower Papers*, II, p. 928. Eisenhower's letter succeeded only in further disturbing Handy and others, who could not appreciate his problems.

[2] Eisenhower's obstinacy was not confined to military matters as he was to prove on more than one occasion. Lord Scarman provides a graphic example when, during a visit to Paris: 'Ike refused to leave the field until Tedder arrived. As they were ready to leave the bands played the Star-Spangled Banner and La Marseillaise. Then they started forward but General Eisenhower didn't budge. The French generals waved him to his car, and still he didn't move. Then someone whispered to him, and he sent an aide to the Frenchman in charge of the ceremonies. He turned red and gave a signal to the orchestra, which thereupon played God Save the King. It was in little things like this that General Eisenhower won the love and gratitude of the British.' Quoted from interview with Dr Pogue, 25 February 1947.

play our superiority in armor. The idea was clearly expressed as an objective by Bimbo Dempsey in his 21st Army Group presentation as his first important task following upon the landing. . . You will recall also that we felt before the invasion that the capture of the open ground south of Caen would assist the Americans on the west to get through the difficult Bocage country following the capture of Cherbourg. Thus we expected to have a Dog (D) plus seventeen line including Granville on the west, and including the line of the Orne on the east. From there we expected a break out largely according to the actual subsequent pattern of the operations, and depending upon developments to give such direction to troop masses as would most quickly accomplish the destruction of the enemy.'[1]*

Not until his later years and after the publication of Montgomery's *Memoirs* did Eisenhower's reveal his frustration with Montgomery in confidential letters to close friends; with these few exceptions he continued to keep his views to himself. Furthermore, he was always mindful of the damage such a revelation might have on post-war British-American relations at a time when harmony was far more important than needless controversy. When NATO was created in the hostile climate of the Cold War which had seen a Russian blockade of Berlin and the life-saving Berlin airlift, Eisenhower became its first Supreme Commander and Montgomery once again his subordinate. The timing would not have been suitable then for recriminations and would have reopened issues best left forgotten at a moment when it was vital to focus on the threat from Russia and the newly created Warsaw Pact Alliance.

Several recent studies of Eisenhower have revealed that his approach to military command carried over to his presidency, where he would frequently and deliberately accept responsibility for the actions of others, fostering the impression that they were manipulating him when, in fact, the exact opposite was occur-

---

[1] Eisenhower, letter to Montgomery, 23 May 1946, *Eisenhower Papers*, VII, pp. 1068–9.

* The significant point about Eisenhower's letter is how closely it conforms both to Brigadier Richardson's appreciation of 7 May 1944, which outlined in writing the strategy Montgomery intended to follow after seizing the initial Allied bridgehead, and to Dempsey's notes of his 15 May 1944 presentation. These were clearly not the remarks of a man who had 'misunderstood' Montgomery. The relevant portion of this important letter is reproduced in Appendix C.

ring. A case in point was his relationship with Secretary of State John Foster Dulles, who was always thought to have dominated Eisenhower on foreign policy matters. This has lately been seriously questioned in the light of new evidence available in the Eisenhower presidential papers. One political scientist has dubbed Eisenhower the master of 'hidden-hand leadership'.[1]

Eisenhower's relations with Montgomery were in this same vein: rather than openly contradict Montgomery, Eisenhower was quite satisfied to correct the picture by informal means through his long-time friends. Publicly, however, the picture remained unaltered – helped until the 1970s by the lack of access to secret British documents. Their fragile relationship took a sad turn for the worse, though, after the appearance of the famous Montgomery *Memoirs*.[2] For Eisenhower they were the last straw, and henceforth relations soured beyond hope of repair. That same year the two old soldiers toured the Gettysburg battlefield during a visit by Montgomery to the United States. With a corps of newsmen following them, Eisenhower finally wearied of Montgomery deliberately raising his voice for their benefit and walked away, only to hear the Field Marshal exclaim: 'Both Lee and Meade should have been sacked!' Eisenhower remembered: 'I think he added something about incompetence, and then he called to me, "Don't you agree, Ike?" Frankly I was resentful of his obvious purpose and his lack of good taste in his public familiarity, so I merely replied, "Listen, Monty, I live here. I have nothing to say about the matter. You have to make your own comment."'[3]

The *Memoirs* were archetypical Monty: clear, straightforward, self-serving, selective and frequently critical of others.[4] One of his strongest criticisms was in fact reserved for Eisenhower, whom he still accused of failing to understand his strategy and of complaining to Churchill in July 1944 about his slowness around Caen. Eisenhower was not amused; nor were many others including Lord Ismay, who wrote to Eisenhower that he

---

[1] Cf., Fred I. Greenstein, *The Hidden-Hand Presidency*, 1982.
[2] Published in 1958.
[3] Eisenhower, letter to General Leonard T. Gerow, 15 November 1958, Eisenhower Presidential Papers, Eisenhower Library.
[4] Montgomery's *Memoirs* are still controversial because of his claims, but by today's standards his remarks about the other Allied commanders are relatively mild, especially when compared with Bradley's recent *A General's Life*.

deplored Montgomery's book. 'I had always hoped that he would go down in history as one of the great British captains of war and that his less attractive personal qualities would be forgotten. But alas he has now insured by his own hand that posterity will know all about them.'[1] A thoroughly disgusted and angry Eisenhower replied to Ismay and finally unburdened himself, saying that his opinion was probably so much lower that he did not care to discuss it even in a letter. 'Do you remember,' wrote Eisenhower, 'the great promises that he made during the planning for OVERLORD about moving quickly to the southward beyond Caen and Bayeux to get ground fit for airfields and his post-war assertions that such a movement was never included in the plan?' His strongest criticism was reserved not for Montgomery's military actions but his traits of character. 'I cannot forget his readiness to belittle associates in those critical moments when the cooperation of all of us was needed. So, I personally believe that, on his record, historians could never be tempted to gild his status too heavily, even if his *Memoirs* had not reflected traits far from admirable.'[2]

That these two should have ended their long relationship in such bitterness was disheartening.[3] For all his public arrogance, Montgomery seems to have had a genuine affection for Eisenhower, despite the latter's never concealed preference for Alexander. Similarly, over and above the bitterness evident in his later years, Eisenhower's opinion of Montgomery was never as scornful as his letter to Ismay would suggest: even though he was frequently annoyed by Montgomery's lack of tact, Eisenhower tended to view his one-time subordinate as one would a naughty, spoiled child. An incident typical of their relations occurred shortly after the conclusion of the Normandy campaign when Eisenhower emerged from a meeting with the new Field Marshal and was seen to shake his head and grumble: 'Monty again.' After Eisenhower's death in 1969 Montgomery was quoted as

---

[1] Ismay, letter to Eisenhower, 9 January 1959, Ismay Papers.
[2] Eisenhower, letter to Ismay, 14 January 1959, ibid.
[3] Nigel Hamilton has written: 'Montgomery could never understand why his *Memoirs* so offended Eisenhower. He believed that he had paid high tribute to Eisenhower's great qualities as an Allied leader and could not accept that his portrait of Eisenhower's battlefield ignorance would be deeply disturbing to a professional soldier, which Eisenhower had been almost all of his life.' Letter to the author, 13 April 1983.

saying: 'He had only to smile at you and there was nothing you would not do for him.'[1]

Montgomery had not intended to create a myth when he vigorously defended his actions in Normandy, and there is no reason to doubt that he firmly believed his plan provided the firm framework of the Allied victory. Despite his public image of disdain and aloofness from these quarrels, Montgomery was deeply distressed by the criticism of Ingersoll, Correlli Barnett, R. W. Thompson, Tedder, Bradley and others. Without question it led to a hardening of his attitude that his reputation would suffer considerably unless he resolutely defended himself. Nevertheless, his refusal ever to admit that the campaign had not gone 'exactly according to plan' was paid for at the cost of his credibility.

The most unfortunate legacy of Normandy is that Air Vice Marshal Wigglesworth's astute prediction that 'we will have a legend' has long since come true and the legend is now inseparable from the history of one of the most dramatic episodes of the Second World War.

---

[1] Quoted in *National Geographic*, July 1969, p. 40. Typical of Montgomery's mixed emotions towards Eisenhower was this comment to Brooke during the Falaise battle: 'Ike is apt to get very excited and to talk wildly – at the top of his voice!!! He is now over here; which is a very great pity. His ignorance as to how to run a war is absolute and complete; he has all the popular cries, but nothing else . . . He is such a decent chap that it is difficult to be angry with him for long.' Letter, Montgomery to Brooke, 14 August 1944, Alanbrooke Papers.

Epilogue

The many accounts written about Normandy have not been particularly kind to Eisenhower: he has frequently been depicted as a superb coordinator and diplomat but a poor battlefield strategist and commander. It would seem that even his long-term friend and West Point classmate, Omar Bradley, gave him low marks for generalship.[1] The disparaging opinions of Alanbrooke[2] and Montgomery[3] are, of course, well known.

In the United States where he had always been highly unpopular, Montgomery fared far worse, in no small part due to his performance in Normandy. Assessments of his generalship, particularly in that theatre,[4] have frequently lacked balance and objectivity: failure to probe deeply enough into his campaigns has resulted in superficial judgements based more upon the personality of the man than the effectiveness of the commander. Montgomery was probably difficult to like in the best of circumstances, a maverick who did not conform to the image of a British officer and gentleman yet who became one of Britain's most successful generals. Eisenhower's warm personality earned him admiration and respect on both sides of the Atlantic, even if his generalship was felt to be somewhat suspect. By contrast Montgomery seemed guilty of an overweening conceit and arrogance and his boorish behaviour towards his superior – no matter how well intentioned or militarily sound – dismayed and infuriated even his supporters. American opinion of him has, over the years, evolved into a stereotyped image of a pretentious,

---

[1] In *A General's Life*, Eisenhower is castigated for being too pro-British, and Bradley's assessment of him as a commander would seem to be as harsh as Montgomery's: 'Ike was clearly a political general of rare and valuable gifts, but as his African record clearly demonstrates, he did not know how to manage a battlefield.' p. 130.
[2] Arthur Bryant, *The Turn of the Tide* and *Triumph in the West*.
[3] Montgomery, *Memoirs*.
[4] Notable exceptions are the three American official histories: *Cross-Channel Attack*, *Breakout and Pursuit* and *The Supreme Command*; and the Canadian account, *The Victory Campaign*.

egotistical general whose achievements never matched an inflated reputation.

Montgomery has frequently, if unfairly, been compared with Alexander, whose generalship was never more than respectable but whose charm and warmth endeared him to many Americans – a point well demonstrated by Bradley in his autobiography. Moreover, the public image of Montgomery as one who would do anything (if necessary at the expense of others) to enhance his own reputation as the master of every military situation has not been helped by his many public pronouncements in his own defence. On the contrary, such statements have generally served to raise fresh doubts about his credibility. Unwilling to entrust his place in history to the judgement of others, Montgomery's attempts to rewrite history to agree with his own preconceptions have not only failed, but have denied him credit he properly deserved.[1]

As infuriating as he frequently was, there was much to admire in Montgomery, not least his determination to stick to his principles. The occasions when he was dead wrong in doing so, such as the quarrel with Eisenhower over the 'broad-front, narrow-front' strategy, were more than offset by the many times when he was correct. The public Monty who gave the appearance of imperturbability in the face of heavy criticism was not the same Monty who wrote to Liddell Hart in 1946: 'I have come to realize in the last few years that the way to fame is a hard one. You must suffer and be the butt of jealousy and ill-informed criticism; it is a lonely matter. One just has to go on doing what you think is right, and doing your duty: whatever others may say or think; and this is what I try to do!'[2]

To isolate the truth from the mythology of Normandy has been the major task of this account, for unless the veneer of myth and conjecture can be stripped away, it becomes impossible to assess Montgomery's achievements with any degree of balance.

---

[1] Colonel C. P. Stacey has written of Montgomery: 'For some reason, commanders seem to consider it the supreme form of military achievement to plan an operation in advance and subsequently carry it out precisely as planned, though surely it might be considered a higher attribute of generalship to maintain and profit by the degree of flexibility which enables the commander to adjust his operations to events and to alter his plans to take advantage of fleeting opportunities.' *The Victory Campaign*, p. 273.

[2] Montgomery, letter to Liddell Hart, 14 May 1946, Liddell Hart Papers, King's College, London.

The Montgomery who emerges is a man who was, as his biographer has observed, 'his own worst enemy'.[1]

No better example exists than Normandy. Montgomery's pretensions dismayed his admirers and encouraged his enemies to question the fiction he helped to create. Lost in all this dissent have been Montgomery's outstanding qualities as the foremost trainer of troops produced by Britain during the war, to whom (along with Brooke and Paget) belongs a good deal of the credit for the successful rebirth of the British Army after Dunkirk. In Normandy he masterminded the most successful invasion in the history of warfare, aided by the exceptional contributions from the Allied air and naval forces in what will probably stand as a classic example of three-dimensional battle on a large scale.

The notion that Montgomery's campaign in Normandy was the product of a grand design executed exactly as planned is, of course, a misconception which has failed the test of careful scrutiny. Montgomery kept his nerve in trying circumstances and Eisenhower was correct when he credited Montgomery with flexibility in adapting quickly to the situation he encountered after the Germans refused to concede Caen. His shift to a strategy of containment had many adverse side effects, but in defiance of the circumstances arising from the failure of the original plan, Montgomery's perseverence, in the face of harsh criticism, eventually enabled Bradley to grasp the initiative and to stage a breakthrough which turned into the great breakout in the West.[2] The battle of Normandy may not have been a model operation of war but its very unorthodoxy was necessitated by the terrain and by the fact that the British Army faced an exceptionally serious manpower problem. Also, at the campaign's commencement most of the Allied troops in Normandy were untested in battle and it took more time than Montgomery would have liked for them to adjust to fighting a battle-experienced enemy; then again, Montgomery's own veteran divisions never lived up to

[1] Hamilton, *Monty*, p. 606. In 1946 Liddell Hart wrote candidly to Montgomery, saying: 'Your manner has always been your own worst handicap.' Letter, 17 March 1946, Liddell Hart Papers.

[2] In early August Montgomery acknowledged the crucial importance of Brooke's support: 'It makes a great difference to me to know that you stand like a firm rock behind us, and your faith in what we are trying to achieve is constant.' Letter of 6 August 1944, Alanbrooke Papers.

their reputations and the result was an endless morale and leadership problem.

The commander whose reputation soared in Normandy was Omar Bradley: he proved his worth as an enormously successful battlefield strategist who made the transition from junior corps commander in North Africa and Sicily to army and later army group command in Normandy with extraordinary ease. Towards the end of the war Eisenhower said of him that his 'brains, selflessness and outstanding ability as a battlefield commander are unexcelled anywhere in the world today'.[1]

Rommel was an exceptionally worthy opponent; moreover there can be no doubt that his strategy for defeating the invasion was correct. That it was doomed to fail was a direct result of the absence of the Luftwaffe and the inefficient command set-up which denied him control of the only force capable of repelling the invasion: the panzer divisions. S. L. A. Marshall has observed: 'Rommel had the right idea; it might not have succeeded, but when it is silhouetted against what eventuated during the battle, it should become clear that it was the only thing which had a chance to succeed. Unfortunately, some of our bright boys over here have swallowed whole the ex-post facto statements of Rundstedt, Blumentritt, et.al. and come up with conclusions which take into account *everything except the development of the battle*.'[2] The task for Rommel's forces was, however, hopeless. Not long before his death Rommel told his young son, Manfred,[3] the grim truth: 'All the courage didn't help . . . Sometimes we had as many casualties on one day as during the whole of the summer fighting in Africa in 1942. My nerves are pretty good, but sometimes I was near collapse. It was casualty reports, casualty reports, casualty reports, wherever you went. I have never fought with such losses. If I hadn't gone to the front nearly every day, I couldn't have stood it, having to write off literally one more regiment every day . . . And the worst of it is that it was all without sense or purpose. There is no longer anything we can do. Every shot we fire now is harming ourselves, for it will be returned a hundred-fold. The sooner it finishes the better for all of us.'[4]

[1] Quoted in Ambrose, *The Supreme Commander*, p. 659.
[2] Letter, S. L. A. Marshall to Liddell Hart, 8 February 1950, Liddell Hart Papers.
[3] Now Oberbürgermeister (Lord Mayor) of Stuttgart.
[4] *The Rommel Papers*, p. 496.

Normandy was primarily an infantryman's battle with little quarter given by either side. The tone of the campaign was established in the earliest days when the Canadian 3rd Division tangled with the elite 12th SS Panzer Division near Bayeux. It has not been established how, but word soon spread that 'the other side' was shooting prisoners of war. In the hamlets of Le Mesnil Patry and Audrieu several miles northeast of Tilly sur Seulles, atrocities were committed against the Canadians by 12th SS. In mid-June the worst such incident occurred at the Chateau Audrieu, where a unit of the 12th SS summarily executed nearly forty Canadian and British prisoners against a stone wall in the garden of the chateau, reputedly on the orders of Kurt Meyer.[1] From that time forward engagements between these two units took on a note of unparalleled savagery[2] – a savagery which thereafter characterized the entire battle of Normandy.

It has been said that 'After a battle is over people talk a lot about how decisions were reached, but actually there's always a hell of a lot of groping around.'[3] Such was the case, too, in Normandy until Montgomery and Bradley finally found the right way to defeat the German Army.

The enduring memory of Normandy is that of the dramatic and heroic invasion of 6 June and the great breakout and pursuit emanating from COBRA at the end of July. Yet most of the campaign was a grim struggle and those who fought there are more likely to remember the dreadful bocage; the heat, mud and dust; the terror of unseen mortar and sniper fire; the incessant artillery and aerial bombardments; and the loss of many com-

[1] The Normandy atrocities are recorded in a series of reports prepared by SHAEF Courts of Inquiry convened on the orders of Eisenhower. The Canadian government was outraged and after the war SS Major General Kurt Meyer was convicted of war crimes by a Canadian court and sentenced to death. His sentence was later commuted to life imprisonment on the grounds that there was no proof that he had actually ordered the shooting of prisoners of war. Some years later he was unconditionally released due to ill health; he died not long after. See SHAEF Papers, National Archives and C. P. Stacey's *The Victory Campaign*. The records of the SHAEF Courts of Inquiry are also in the PRO but are closed to the public. In 1979, the story of the atrocity was related to the author by members of the family who own the chateau, now a small luxury hotel and a one-star Michelin restaurant. Few who take their leisure in its lovely surroundings are aware of the awful scene which took place in June 1944 a few yards away from the wall by the swimming pool.
[2] Stacey's *The Victory Campaign* provides a vivid picture of the numerous brutal engagements between Canadian units and 12th SS Panzer Division.
[3] US Admiral Frank Jack Fletcher, quoted by Walter Lord in *Incredible Victory*, 1968.

rades to an enemy that was rarely seen. Certainly few who fought there in the hot summer of 1944 would dispute Rommel, who gave the campaign its epitaph: 'It was one terrible blood-letting.'[1]

[1] *The Rommel Papers*, p. 496.

Postscript

The Normandy campaign brought together many of the greatest political and military figures of the twentieth century in the decisive battle of the war in the west. After the war each went his own way: some into obscurity, others, like Eisenhower, to even greater fame. Eisenhower's ascendancy to the Presidency of the United States was nearly as rapid as Churchill's fall from grace which saw his Conservative Party turned out of office shortly after the surrender of the Third Reich.

The Second World War took a heavy toll of Field Marshal Sir Alan Brooke. At its end he was anxious to give up the enormously heavy burden he had carried as the Chief of the Imperial General Staff and as Chairman of the British Chiefs of Staff Committee. Brooke was, as his biographer has noted, 'without peer'. 'He was the best Chief of the Imperial General Staff ever produced by the army and he was produced at the vital hour. Britain was fortunate indeed.'[1] A weary Brooke retired in 1946 into relative obscurity, virtually unknown outside Britain until immortalized in Arthur Bryant's two epic volumes in 1957 and 1959.[2] In 1946 he was elevated to the peerage and became Field Marshal Viscount Alanbrooke. He died in 1963 a few weeks before his eightieth birthday.

Brooke, arguably the greatest CIGS ever, handed over the mantle of leadership of the British Army to his friend and protégé, the newly created Knight of the Garter, Field Marshal Viscount Montgomery of Alamein, just as arguably one of the most undistinguished CIGS in memory. During his two-year tenure, from 1946–8, Montgomery squabbled endlessly with his war-time nemesis, Tedder, who was now the Chief of the Air Staff, succeeding Portal. Relations between them were so sour that the two men would rarely appear together at the same meeting or function. In the political maze of Whitehall, Montgomery found

---

[1] Fraser, *Alanbrooke*, op.cit., p. 539.
[2] *The Turn of the Tide* (1957) and *Triumph in the West* (1959).

to his dismay that he was unable to order about the politicians and his counterparts in the RAF and the Royal Navy as he had during the war.

Montgomery fared better as Deputy Supreme Commander of NATO under his former wartime chief, Eisenhower. In 1958 he retired and spent his remaining years writing and travelling. To the end he remained the Monty of old: complex, vain, irrascible, opinionated, frequently controversial and occasionally capable of generating great hilarity. His long association with the *Sunday Times*, through his friend, Sir Denis Hamilton, brought him into contact with some of the *Times* journalists. In typical Monty fashion he was never above dispensing advice. *Times* columnist Godfrey Smith recently revealed one such example:

> When we ran his history of war we needed a picture showing a group of the great soldiers Monty admired most – the Tommy, the poilu, the doughboy and so on. A platoon of guardsmen were detailed to dress in the parts for the photographer. The photocall was on the manicured lawn of his house at Isington Mill. Monty came out resplendent in his Field Marshal's uniform and gave his first order of the day. 'Tell the guardsmen,' he said, 'that if they want to pee they can do it in the river. I won't have them doing it on my lawn.'[1]

When he died at the age of eighty-eight in 1976 he was honoured for the last time in Britain, but in the United States his passing was barely noticed. A personal memoir by Sir Denis Hamilton appeared in the *Sunday Times* on 28 March 1976 under the caption 'The Last Great Captain'. Montgomery was undoubtedly the most controversial Allied general of the Second World War, and he was certainly a far greater commander than most Americans were willing to admit or to comprehend. Montgomery's place in history will be long debated, but as Michael Howard has written: 'No British commander in the War showed a better grasp of the intricacies of his appallingly difficult profession, and none showed a better understanding of the men that he led.'[2] Whatever one's opinion of Monty, he was one of a kind and it is doubtful if we shall see his like again.

The other two commanders-in-chief on D-Day met tragic deaths. The AEAF had from the outset been the unwanted

---

[1] *Sunday Times*, 8 June 1980.
[2] Michael Howard, *The Causes of Wars*, London, 1983, p. 223.

stepchild of the Allies, caught as it was between SHAEF and the senior RAF and USAAF air chiefs. It was abolished soon after the Normandy campaign ended and its chief, Leigh-Mallory, was reassigned to Mountbatten's new Southeast Asia Supreme Command as Air C-in-C. En route to his new post in November 1944 his plane disappeared over southern France and was not found until the following spring, when a French shepherd discovered the aircraft remains in the mountains near Grenoble. Leigh-Mallory, his wife and all aboard had died.[1]

Admiral Sir Bertram 'Bertie' Ramsay also died after Normandy, when his plane crashed on takeoff from a Paris airfield on 5 January 1945. His untimely death was a grievous loss, for his contributions during the war had been immense. With great skill he had marshalled the naval force which extricated the BEF from the beaches of Dunkirk; and with equal skill he had masterminded the naval plan for OVERLORD, which eventually brought over a million men to the shores of France in 1944. He and Montgomery had not always seen eye to eye on military matters but they had liked and respected one another. Montgomery lost a friend and the Allies a brilliant naval commander.

Bradley attained the exalted five-star rank of General of the Army, an honour given to only four other American army officers.[2] Immediately after the conclusion of the war in Europe in 1945 he was summoned home to take charge of the Veterans' Administration: he successfully managed the transition of several million veterans back to civilian life. In 1948 he succeeded Eisenhower as Chief of Staff of the Army and in 1949 was promoted to become the first Chairman of the Joint Chiefs of Staff, a post he held throughout the Korean War until his retirement in 1953. His 1951 war memoirs, *A Soldier's Story*, became a bestseller and were serialized in *Life* magazine. In later years his health deteriorated; nevertheless he often returned to Normandy to attend the annual D-Day ceremony at the American military cemetery at OMAHA beach. His last visit to honour

---

[1] His brother, the mountaineer George Leigh-Mallory, and Andrew Irvine, disappeared on the upper slopes of the then unconquered Mount Everest in 1926 and were never found.

[2] Eisenhower, Marshall, MacArthur and 'Hap' Arnold. Pershing was the only five-star officer ever to hold the title General of the Armies. Four naval officers also attained five-star rank: Admirals King, Leahy, Nimitz and Halsey. Five-star rank has since been abolished in the armed forces of the United States.

his fallen comrades was in 1979. In 1981 he died suddenly, moments after being honoured at a ceremony in New York. To his death, Bradley remained one of the most respected figures of the war, both in Britain and the United States.

General Sir Miles Dempsey served in Southeast Asia after the armistice in Europe and concluded his long military career as C-in-C, Middle East from where he retired in 1946. Until his death in 1969 Dempsey lived the life of a country gentleman in rural Hampshire, a largely forgotten figure.

Lieutenant General Sir Richard O'Connor remained in command of 8 Corps until November 1944 when he was suddenly transferred to India at Montgomery's instigation. The reason stemmed primarily from O'Connor's refusal to prepare an adverse efficiency report on the commander of the US 7th Armoured Division, Major General Lindsay McD. Silvester, during a short period when the American division was under the control of 8 Corps. After holding several command appointments under his former C-in-C, Wavell, O'Connor was promoted to full general in 1945 and in 1946–7 served in the War Office as Adjutant General under Montgomery until his retirement. The post-war years were spent mainly in Scotland, where he served as the Lord Lieutenant of the County of Ross and Cromarty. When he died in 1981, aged ninety-two, he was hailed by Correlli Barnett in the *Sunday Times* for his exploits in the Western Desert as the 'Lost Leader of the Desert War'. Had O'Connor not been captured in 1941 he would undoubtedly have become the commander of Eighth Army; how differently the desert war in 1941 and 1942 might have turned out with O'Connor in command we can only speculate.

General Sir John Crocker continued in a variety of important post-war assignments and was widely considered a leading candidate to succeed Montgomery as CIGS, a post which in the event went to Field Marshal Slim. Crocker was the first officer of the Royal Tank Regiment to command a corps in combat, the first to become a C-in-C (Middle East), and the first to become a member of the Army Council. He died in 1963.

Lieutenant General Neil Ritchie likewise went on to the rank of full general and several key post-war appointments, including C-in-C, Far East Land Forces, 1947–9. General Ritchie retired in 1951 and now lives in Toronto.

Lieutenant General G. C. Bucknall became GOC, Northern Ireland 1945–7, prior to his retirement. He died in 1981. His successor, Lieutenant General Sir Brian Horrocks, served as GOC, 30 Corps until the end of the war and, after commanding the British Army of the Rhine, was invalided out of the army in 1949. He became a well known public figure as a result of a popular BBC television series about the war, and wrote two books about his military career. He now lives in retirement in Sussex.

Major General J. Lawton Collins's brilliant performance did not end with Normandy. He went on to earn plaudits for his role during the Battle of the Bulge, and after the war quickly rose to the position of Chief of Staff of the US Army in 1949, succeeding Omar Bradley. After ending his tour as Chief-of-Staff, Collins remained on active duty, at the request of President Eisenhower, as the US Representative on the Military Committee and Standing Group of NATO 1953–6, with time out for a special assignment as Eisenhower's personal representative to Vietnam with the rank of ambassador. General Collins retired in 1956 and now lives in Washington, D.C.

Like Montgomery, General George S. Patton has remained as controversial since his death as he was in life. Patton was a soldier born to fight and he found no joy in peace. His famous Third US Army became the Allied occupational force in Bavaria and within a short time he was in serious trouble for ignoring Eisenhower's decree which forbade the employment of Nazis in official occupational positions. By early October 1945 Patton had tried Eisenhower's patience for the last time and he was summarily relieved of command of the Third Army and relegated to the command of a 'paper' army whose sole task was to prepare a history of the war in Europe.

In early December 1945 his staff car collided with a US army lorry near Mannheim. Patton was critically injured and immediately rushed to a US Army hospital in nearby Heidelberg. Patton, who had always wanted to die a hero's death in action instead died quietly of his injuries twelve days later. He was buried with full military honours in the American military cemetery at Hamm, Luxembourg; he would undoubtedly have taken comfort in the knowledge that he was eternally in the company of many of the soldiers he had led so well.

APPENDIX A

Exact photocopy from PRO (WO 285/2) of Montgomery's letter of 4 May 1944 to Dempsey about the importance of air-ground cooperation during the forthcoming battle of Normandy.

SECRET AND PERSONAL.

21 A.Gp/1001/C-in-C.

WO 205/1B

TAC HEADQUARTERS,
21 ARMY GROUP,
No.1 A.P.D.C,
LONDON W.1.

4 May 1944

My Dear Dempsey

During the last four months, i.e, since I got back from Italy, it has been gradually brought home to me that there is a definite gulf in England between the Armies and their supporting air forces.   Of course I naturally compare the situation in England with that which obtained in the Allied Armies overseas. There the Army concerned and its Air Force were welded into one entity; the two HQ were always adjacent; and the spirit of unity went right down to the individual soldier and airman.   These fine results were achieved only by a great deal of "give and take" on both sides; gradually mutual confidence and trust grew up, and the Army and its supporting Air Force became one fighting machine.

2.   In England to-day the problem is somewhat different, since Armies are not actually fighting and being supported by their Air Forces.   It is therefore not so easy to link them up into one entity - as one fighting machine.

But they can at least get to know each other, and get that understanding of each others problems which will be the firm foundation of mutual confidence and trust when we begin fighting.

3.   From my own experience I am convinced that the following points are important if real unity is to be achieved between an Army and its supporting Air Force or Group:

(a) The two HQ, Army and Air, must be side by side, or adjacent.

(b) Army HQ may on occasions throw off a Tac HQ; but Main Army must always be with Air HQ.

(c) Army HQ must never plan a move of HQ without first consulting Air HQ.   The deciding factor in the location of Main Army will be whether it will suit Air HQ.   There must be give and take on both sides; but the Army staff must realise that Air HQ requires to have telephone communication to airfields, and this is often the ruling factor in the location of the combined HQ.

(d) Before the Army staff initiates or takes any action the first question must always be:

"How will this affect the air?"

The appropriate branch of the staff at Air HQ must be consulted especially on administrative matters.

The Chief of Staff at Army HQ, and the SASO at Air HQ, must be in constant touch at all times.

Similarly for the heads of the operations and intelligence staffs.

/(e)

(c) This integration must be carried right down the scale to the regimental officers and men.   At the lower end, the traffic policeman must recognise at once a flagged Air Force car, and accord it the usual facilities.

Formation and unit commanders, and the regimental officers and men, must be taught to realise that without the help of the air they cannot win the land battle; and they must understand the repercussions that follow from this statement of fact.

(f) On the air side, every pilot in air forces allotted specifically for the support of an Army, must realise that his sole job is to help the Army win the land battle; sometimes this involves fighting in the sky; at other times it involves <u>coming right down</u> and participating in the land battle by shooting up ground targets.   This side of the problem is I know being tackled energetically by the air commanders.

4.   I feel very strongly on the whole matter, and I know that we can achieve no real success unless each Army and its accompanying Air Force can weld itself into one entity.

Visiting each other occasionally, and having the odd meal together, will never achieve what is wanted; there is far more to it than that.   The two HQ have got to set themselves down side by side, and work together as one team; that is the only way.

5.   I wish Army Commanders to give this matter their personal attention.   There is much to be done and not too much time in which to do it.   We must not merely pay lip service to a principle we must put into practice the actual methods that will achieve success.

ys ever

B. L. Montgomery.

Lt-Gen. M.C. Dempsey, DSO, MC.,
Commander,
Second Army.

Battle Casualties
6 June to 29 August 1944

The visitor to Normandy today will find little evidence of the great battles fought there in 1944. Caen has been rebuilt and is once again a busy centre of commerce for the region. The villages and hamlets destroyed in the fighting have been restored to their previous drabness and time has once again weathered them to the point where scant evidence of combat can be found. Hill 112, once a ghastly deathtrap, is being cultivated by the plough rather than the cannon. The Falaise pocket is again a quiet backwater where occasionally one can observe a restored vehicle of evident German, British or American origin on the road.

The most visible evidence of the war are the many national cemeteries which dot the landscape, twenty-seven of them: six German: 77,866 graves; one American, located on the bluffs overlooking OMAHA beach: 9,386 graves; sixteen British: 17,769 graves; two Canadian: 5,002 graves, and one Polish: 650 graves.[1]

Some 637,000 combatants on both sides perished or were wounded in Normandy during the eighty days of the campaign:

	Killed	Wounded	Missing	Total
21st Army Group (British/Canadian/Polish)	15,995	57,996	9,054	83,045[2]
United States	20,838	94,881	10,128	125,847[3]
Allied Air Forces:				
Royal Air Force	8,178	killed and missing		8,178[4]
US Army Air Force	8,536	killed and missing		8,536
Estimated Allied losses in pre-OVERLORD opns.	12,000	killed and missing		12,000
German	200,000	killed and wounded		200,000
	200,000	prisoners-of-war		200,000[5]
			TOTAL	637,606

Notes overleaf.

German equipment losses:

Tanks: 1,300; vehicles: 20,000; assault guns: 500; field guns: 5,500; aircraft: 3,545. Troop units: equivalent of five panzer divisions destroyed, six severely mauled. Equivalent of twenty infantry divisions eliminated, and twelve more (including three parachute divisions) severely reduced. One parachute and two infantry divisions trapped in Brittany, and one infantry division left isolated in the Channel Islands.[6]

---

[1] Source: Belchem, *Victory in Normandy*, pp. 186–7.

[2] War Diary, 21st Army Group, 'A' Section, SITREP, 29 August 1944, PRO (WO 171/140).

[3] Ellis, *Victory in the West*, I, p. 493.

[4] Ibid, p. 488. The majority of the airmen lost were from Bomber Command (6,761). Losses from 2nd Tactical Air Force were 1,035.

[5] Source: Supreme Commander's Report, p. 62. Figures are an approximation inasmuch as an exact count was impossible to obtain. Of the 200,000 Germans captured, 135,000 were taken between 25 July and 25 August. SHAEF estimated Luftwaffe losses as another 270 probable and 1,028 damaged in the air.

[6] Ibid.

APPENDIX C

Extract from
Eisenhower's letter
of 23 May, 1946
to Field Marshal Montgomery[1]

Dear Monty:

I thank you for your long telegram which I received while I was enjoying a couple days vacation. Although I do not have my records with me, I think I can fully answer the questions you have raised. In the first place, I believe you are overemphasizing the possibilities of misunderstanding due to somewhat varying accounts of plans and operations following our invasion of Normandy.

I thoroughly agree with you that the line we had established as our dog (that is, D) plus ninety objective was not only attained at an earlier date, but the operations bringing us to that line generally followed the conceptions we had held before the invasion was launched.

On the other hand, the operations immediately following the landing diverged quite considerably, in a tactical sense, from what we had hoped to execute. Specifically, one of our earliest objectives was the open ground to the south and southeast of Caen and Falaise, which areas we wanted to seize quickly in order to establish airfields and to bring into play our superiority in armor. This idea was clearly expressed as an objective by Bimbo Dempsey in his 21st Army Group presentation as his first important task following upon the landing. The fact that we were long delayed in obtaining this particular area, because of the intensive concentration of enemy forces in the Caen district, is some justification for those people that claim our early tactics had to adjust to enemy reaction. This I regard as normal in war and I would be the very last to subscribe to any plan or theory of operations that was compelled to depend for its success on an exact sequence in the attainment of tactical objectives. You will recall also that we felt before the invasion that the capture of the open ground south of Caen would assist the Americans on the west to get through the difficult Bocage country following upon the capture of Cherbourg. Thus we expected to have a dog (D) plus seventeen line including Granville on the west, and including the line of the Orne on the east. From there we expected to break out largely according to the actual subsequent pattern of the operations, and depending upon developments to give such direction to

[1] From *The Eisenhower Papers*, Volume VII, pp. 1068–9.

troop masses as would most quickly accomplish the destruction of the enemy.

I repeat that while the intensive concentration and resistance of the enemy on the east compelled divergence from our anticipated tactical progress during the first thirty or forty days, the instant adaptation of our own tactics to each day's requirements eventually enabled us to carry out a broad strategic program for the conquest of France that had been visualized long before dog (D) day.

Sources

1. Unpublished Sources:

In recent years a wealth of new material about the Second World War has become available in British and American archives and these sources have been extensively used in the preparation of *Decision in Normandy*. In addition to official documents and war diaries, use has been made of other unpublished sources which include personal diaries, letters, private papers, oral histories and, where possible, interviews with surviving participants. Although it was forbidden for British or American personnel to maintain personal diaries, most of the senior participants did, and these provide valuable insight into the inner workings of the various Allied commands involved in the planning for OVERLORD and operations in Normandy. Several are included in private collections which I have been privileged to use: the personal desk diary of Marshal of the Royal Air Force, Lord Tedder, maintained by his personal assistant, Wing Commander Scarman; the personal diary of Admiral Sir Bertram Ramsay; and extracts from the personal diary and papers of Major Tom Bigland, RA.

Principal collections used in public and private institutions are:

The Imperial War Museum, London:

The papers of Major General L. O. Lyne; the papers of Lieutenant General G. C. Bucknall; the papers of Air Vice Marshal E. J. Kingston-McCloughry; the papers of Major General G. H. A. MacMillan; the papers of General Sir George Erskine; and oral history transcripts from the Thames Television series 'The World at War, 1939–1945'.

The Public Record Office, Kew, London:

The Churchill papers (PREM 3); SHAEF papers WO 219); 21st Army Group papers (WO 205); AEAF papers, including the personal diary of Air Chief Marshal Sir Trafford Leigh-Mallory (AIR 37); Cabinet Office Historical Section records and papers (CAB series); the Dempsey Papers (WO 285); unit war diaries: British (WO 171) and Canadian (WO 179); and other official government papers.

Royal United Services Institute for Defence Studies, London:

Montgomery's speech to the RUSI, November 1945.

Churchill College, Cambridge:

The papers of Sir James Grigg; the papers of Air Vice Marshal Sir Thomas Walker Elmhirst.

Liddell Hart Centre for Military Archives, King's College, London:

The papers of Sir Basil Liddell Hart, including the papers of Chester Wilmot and post-war interrogation of German generals; the papers and diary of Field Marshal Lord Alanbrooke; the papers of General Sir Ronald Adam; the papers of General the Lord Ismay; the papers of Major General Sir Francis de Guingand; the papers of General Sir Miles Dempsey; the papers and diary of Lieutenant General Sir Humfrey Gale; the papers of General Sir Richard O'Connor; the papers of John North; and the papers of General Sir Harold Pyman.

Royal Air Force Museum, Hendon, London:

Various air papers and collections.

The University of East Anglia, Norwich:

The papers of Lord Zuckerman.

United States Military Academy Library, West Point, New York:

The papers of General of the Army Omar N. Bradley.

Manuscript Division, Library of Congress:

The papers of General Carl A. Spaatz; the papers of General James Doolittle.

Modern Military Branch, National Archives, Washington, D.C.:

US War Department records and papers; operational records of the First and Third US Armies and 12th Army Group.

United States Army Military History Institute, Carlisle Barracks, Pennsylvania:

The papers of General of the Army Omar N. Bradley,[1] including the papers and diary of Lieutenant Colonel Chester A. Hansen; the Pogue interviews, German Report Series, US Army Europe; the diary of Major General Hobart R. Gay; various oral histories.

The Dwight D. Eisenhower Library, Abilene, Kansas:

The papers of Dwight D. Eisenhower (pre-presidential and presidential); the diary of Captain Harry C. Butcher, USN; The papers of Lieutenant General Walter Bedell Smith; the papers of Major General H. R. Bull, various official documents, oral histories.

Hoover Institution on War, Revolution and Peace, Stanford University, Palo Alto:

German Report Series, US Army Europe; various miscellaneous collections.

Sterling Memorial Library, Yale University, New Haven, Connecticut:

The papers of Henry L. Stimson.

---

[1] The Bradley papers are deposited both at Carlisle and West Point. As collaborator Clay Blair notes in *A General's Life*, there is some duplication but those at Carlisle deal mainly with the Second World War, while those at West Point are personal.

II. *Published Sources*

Ambrose, Stephen E. *The Supreme Commander*, London 1970 and *Rise to Globalism*, London 1980.

Belchem, David *All in the Day's March*, London 1978 and *Victory in Normandy*, London 1981

Belfield, Eversley & Essame, H. *The Battle for Normandy*, London 1975

Bennett, Ralph *Ultra in the West*, London 1979

Bidwell S. and Graham D. *Fire-Power: British Army Weapons and Theories of War, 1904–1945*, London 1982

Blumenson, Martin *Breakout and Pursuit*, Washington 1961 and *The Patton Papers*, Vol II, Boston 1974.

Blumentritt, Gunther *Von Rundstedt*, London 1952

Bradley, Omar N. *A Soldier's Story*, New York 1951 and *A General's Life*, with Clay Blair, New York 1983

Bryant, Arthur *The Turn of the Tide*, London 1957 and *Triumph in the West*, London 1959

Butcher, Harry C. *Three Years with Eisenhower*, London 1946

Carell, Paul *Invasion – They're Coming!*, London 1962

Chandler, Alfred D. (Ed.) *The Papers of Dwight David Eisenhower: The War Years*, 5 vols, Baltimore, 1970; and *Chief of Staff*, 3 Vols, Baltimore, 1979, Louis Galambos (Ed.).

Churchill, Winston S. *The Second World War*, 6 vols, Boston 1953

Collins, J. Lawton *Lightning Joe*, Baton Rouge 1979

Colville, John *The Churchillians*, London 1981

Cooper, Matthew *The German Army 1939–1945*, London 1978

Cooper, Matthew and Lucas, James *Panzer*, London 1976

Crookendon, Napier *Dropzone Normandy*, New York 1976

Cruickshank, Charles *Deception in World War II*, London 1979

Davies, W. J. K. *German Army Handbook, 1939–1945*, London 1973

D-Day: The Normandy Campaign in Retrospect, Kansas 1971

De Guingand, Francis *Operation Victory*, London 1947 and *Generals at War*, London 1964

Ehrman, John *Grand Strategy*, Vol V, London 1956

Eisenhower, Dwight D. *Crusade in Europe*, London 1948 and *At Ease*, London 1958

Ellis, L. F. *Victory in the West*, 2 Vols, London 1962 and 1968

Farago, Ladislas, *Patton: Ordeal and Triumph*, New York 1965

Ferrell, Robert H. (Ed.) *The Eisenhower Diaries* New York 1981

Florentin, Eddy *The Battle of the Falaise Gap*, New York 1967

Forty, George *Desert Rats at War*, London 1980

Fraser, David *Alanbrooke*, London 1982

Gale, Richard *With the 6th Airborne Division in Normandy*, London 1948

Gavin, James M. *On to Berlin*, New York 1978

Greenfield, Kent Roberts (Ed.) *Command Decisions*, London 1959

Grigg, P. J. *Prejudice and Judgment*, London 1948

Hamilton, Nigel *Monty: The Making of a General 1887–1942*, London 1981

Harrison, Gordon A. *Cross-Channel Attack*, Washington 1950

Hastings, Max *Bomber Command*, London 1979 and *Das Reich*, New York 1982

Hastings, R. H. W. S. *The Rifle Brigade in the Second World War, 1939–1945*, Aldershot 1950

Hinsley, F. H., *British Intelligence in the Second World War*, Vol. 2, London 1981.

Horrocks, Sir Brian *Corps Commander*, London 1977

Hough, Richard *Mountbatten*, London 1980

How, J. J. *Normandy: The British Breakout*, London 1981

Irving, David *The Trail of the Fox*, London 1977

Ismay, Lord *Memoirs*, London 1960

Jackson, W. G. F. *Overlord: Normandy 1944*, London 1978

Keegan, John *Six Armies in Normandy*, New York 1982

Kingston-McCloughry, E. J. *The Direction of War*, London 1955

Lewin, Ronald *Montgomery as Military Commander*, London 1968; *Rommel as Military Commander*, New York 1977; *Ultra Goes to War*, London 1978 and *The Chief*, London 1980

Liddell Hart, Sir Basil *The Rommel Papers*, (Ed.), London 1953; *The Tanks*, Vol II, London 1959 and *History of the Second World War*, London 1970

Lovat, Lord *March Past*, London 1978

Lucas, James and Barker, James *The Killing Ground*, London 1978

Maule, Henry G. *Caen* London 1976

McKee, Alexander *Caen: Anvil of Victory*, London 1965

McNish, Robin *Iron Division: The History of the 3rd Division*, London 1978

Montgomery, Field Marshal Viscount *Memoirs*, London 1958; *The Path to Leadership*, London 1963 and *El Alamein to the River Sangro and Normandy to the Baltic*, (one volume) London, 1973

Morgan, Sir Frederick *Overture to Overlord*, London 1950

Mosley, Leonard *Marshal*, New York 1982

Nicolson, Nigel *Alex*, London 1973

North, John *North-West Europe, 1944–45*, London 1977

Patton, George S. *War As I Knew It*, London n.d.

Pogue, Forrest C. *The Supreme Command*, Washington 1954 and *George C. Marshall: Organizer of Victory, 1943–1945*, New York 1973

Public Record Office *The Second World War*: A Guide to Documents in the Public Record Office, London 1972

Pyman, General Sir Harold E. *Call to Arms*, London 1971

Report by the Supreme Commander to the Combined Chiefs of Staff on the Operations in Europe of the Allied Expeditionary Force, 6 June 1944 to 8 May 1945, London 1946

Rees, Goronwy *A Bundle of Sensations*, London 1960

Richards, Denis *Portal of Hungerford*, London 1979

Rohmer, Richard *Patton's Gap*, London 1981

Ruge, Friedrich *Rommel in Normandy*, San Rafael 1979

Ruppenthal, Roland G. *Logistical Support of the Armies*, Vol I, Washington 1953

Ryan, Cornelius *The Longest Day*, London 1961

Salmond, J. B. *The History of the 51st Highland Division*, Edinburgh 1953

Scarfe, Norman *Assault Division*, London 1947

Shirer, William L. *The Rise and Fall of the Third Reich*, New York 1960

Speidel, Hans *We Defended Normandy*, London 1951

Stacey, C. P. *The Victory Campaign*, Ottawa 1960 and *Arms, Men and Governments: The War Policies of Canada 1939–1945*, Ottawa 1970

Stagg, J. M. *Forecast for Overlord*, London 1971

Strong, Kenneth *Intelligence at the Top*, London 1968

Tedder, Lord *With Prejudice*, London 1966

Van Creveld, Martin *Supplying War*, Cambridge 1977

Weigley, Russell F. *Eisenhower's Lieutenants*, Bloomington, Indiana 1981

Wheeler-Bennett, Sir John, (Ed.) *Action This Day*, London 1968

Wilmot, Chester *The Struggle for Europe*, London 1952

Winterbotham, F. W. *The Ultra Secret*, London 1974

Zuckerman, Solly *From Apes to Warlords*, London 1978

Acknowledgements

No work of contemporary history can be written without the cooperation and assistance of others, and this book is no exception. A great
many people have given freely and graciously of their time to share their
recollections of OVERLORD, the battle of Normandy, and to provide
invaluable background information about the armies and the men who
fought there. With many there has been extensive correspondence; with
others a combination of correspondence and interviews, always with
honesty and candour. Indeed, the most rewarding aspect of five years of
research and writing has been not only the courtesy and hospitality
shown to me but a genuine eagerness to be of help in any way possible.
To each I express by deep gratitude: Major General G. T. A. Armitage;
Ralph Bennett; Major Tom Bigland; Air Chief Marshal Sir Harry
Broadhurst; C. E. Carrington; General J. Lawton Collins, USA Ret.; Sir
John Colville; Commander Rupert Curtis; General Sir Richard Gale;
Lieutenant General James M. Gavin, USA Ret.; Major General G. P.
Gregson; Rear Admiral E. F. Gueritz; Professor F. H. Hinsley; Ralph
Ingersoll; Lieutenant General Sir Ian Jacob; Dr Robert C. Larson;
Lieutenant Colonel S. F. T. B. Lever; The Rt. Hon. The Lord Lovat;
Alexander McKee; Major Christopher Milner; the late General Sir
Richard O'Connor; Brigadier C. A. Ramsay; David Ramsay; General
Sir Charles Richardson; Major General G. P. B. Roberts; Professor Vice
Admiral Friedrich Ruge; Major W. H. J. Sale; Peter Selerie; General Sir
Frank Simpson; Major General E. K. G. Sixsmith; Brigadier K. Pearce
Smith; Colonel C. P. Stacey; Major General Sir Nigel Tapp; the Rt. Hon.
the Lord Tedder, who kindly provided me a copy of his father's desk
diary; Major Peter Verney, who provided extracts from the diary of his
father, the late Major General G. L. Verney; the Rt. Hon. the Lord
Zuckerman, who took time to answer my questions and provided
access to his superb collection of personal papers.

A number of people deserve special mention for their contributions:
Martin Blumenson and Dr Forrest C. Pogue provided invaluable
counsel which led to the writing of this book. In addition to providing
considerable encouragement, each has made thoughtful and important
comments on the draft manuscript, for which I am sincerely grateful. Dr
Pogue also took time from his own hectic schedule to provide an
illuminating background of the post-war events surrounding the writing of the official histories. Brigadier Shelford Bidwell who, in my
opinion, understands the inner workings of the British Army in the
Second World War better than any living historian, cast a professional
eye over several parts of the manuscript and offered numerous sugges-

tions. He has also obtained on my behalf some of the manpower data from the Ministry of Defence. The Rt. Hon. the Lord Scarman took considerable time from his duties as a Law Lord to discuss the Normandy campaign with me and to read a portion of the manuscript. Sir Edgar Williams not only submitted to two lengthy interviews but took considerable time to read the final proofs of the manuscript and made numerous constructive suggestions. John S. D. Eisenhower provided a copy of his father's unpublished manuscript and graciously permitted me to quote from relevant portions. My gratitude to Norman Scarfe, who was indefatigable in providing background information about the 3rd (Br.) Division, putting me in contact with former members of the Division and reading the D-Day chapters. My thanks, too, to Manfred Rommel, Lord Mayor of Stuttgart for providing the photograph of his father.

I am sincerely grateful to the British official intelligence historian Edward E. Thomas, who painstakingly guided me through the labyrinth of ULTRA and secret intelligence data and provided many of the missing links necessary to round out the intelligence picture, as well as reading those portions of the manuscript dealing with ULTRA.

I gratefully record my deep appreciation and indebtedness to Montgomery's official biographer, Nigel Hamilton, whose encouragement, perceptive advice and thoughtful criticism have been exceptional. His unflagging conviction that I should write about Normandy was unselfishly demonstrated throughout innumerable hours of illuminating conversation, supplemented by an extensive correspondence over a period of more than four years during which he placed at my disposal his unique knowledge of Montgomery for the sole purpose of ensuring that I gained the fullest possible understanding of the Field Marshal's complex character. As my sternest and most demanding critic he reviewed both the early and final drafts of the manuscript and offered countless useful suggestions and criticisms at a time when fully engaged in researching and writing the second volume of the Montgomery biography. My appreciation goes also to his father, Sir Denis Hamilton, for permission to quote several brief passages from the Montgomery collection.

No historian can function without the assistance of the librarian and archivist, whose professional knowledge of sources and collections can spell the difference between orderly research and chaos. To those at the many institutions and archives visited during the research for this book, I wish to express my appreciation for making the task so rewarding: the Librarian and staff of the Liddell Hart Centre for Military Archives, King's College, London, particularly Miss Patricia Methven, the archivist and her able assistant Mrs Brigit Malcolm; Dr G. H. Martin and his hard-working and efficient staff of the Public Record Office, Kew; the Director and staff of the Imperial War Museum: Department of Documents, Department of Printed Books and Department of Photographs; the staff of the Air Historical Branch, Royal Air Force, London; the Cabinet Office Historical Section; the Commonwealth War Graves Commission, who kindly provided the photograph of Jerusalem Cemetery; Mr Gordon Phillips, archivist, at *The Times*; the staff of the Royal United Services Institute for Defence Studies; Brigadier M. G. Harvey of the Directorate of Army Training, Ministry of Defence, for arranging a special viewing of the film about Operation GOODWOOD; Miss Alexandra Ward and the staff of the Army Historical Office; the staff of the Royal Air Force Museum, Hendon; Correlli Barnett, Keeper of the Archives, and the Master, Fellows and Scholars of Churchill College, Cambridge; Mrs Deirdre Sharp, Lord Zuckerman's archivist at the University of East Anglia, Norwich, was invaluable in providing leads to various air documents and in my research of the Zuckerman papers, and Mrs Gillian Booth, Lord Zuckerman's personal assistant; Mrs Marie T. Capps and Robert E. Schnare, Jr, of the United States Military Academy Library, West Point, New York, who were of considerable help in my search for information about General Omar Bradley and other US officers; the staff of the Manuscript Division, Library of Congress, who were likewise extremely helpful, as were the archivists at the Modern Military Branch, National Archives, Washington, D.C.; Dr Richard J. Sommers, archivist–historian of the US Army Military History Institute, Carlisle Barracks, Pennsylvania; John E. Wickman and his superb staff of the Eisenhower Library, who helped make my stay at Abilene exceptionally useful; and the staff of the Hoover Institution on War, Revolution and Peace, Stanford University.

Grateful acknowledgement is made to Her Majesty's Stationery Office for permission to reproduce extracts from documents in the Public Record Office. My thanks go also to the Johns Hopkins Press for permission to reprint extracts from *The Papers of Dwight David Eisenhower*; to Simon and Schuster, a Division of Gulf and Western Corporation and to Sidgwick & Jackson, Ltd., for permission to quote from Omar N. Bradley and Clair Blair, *A General's Life*; to B. T. Batsford Ltd., for permission to quote from Eversley Belfield and H. Essame, *The Battle for Normandy*; to Houghton Mifflin Co. for permission to quote from Martin Blumenson, *The Patton Papers*, Vol II; to Chatto & Windus Ltd., for permission to quote from Major General David Belchem's *Victory in Normandy*, and to Mrs David Belchem for permission to quote from *All in the Day's March*; to my publishers, William Collins Sons & Co. Ltd., for permisson to quote from Arthur Bryant's *Triumph in the West and The Memoirs of Field Marshal the Viscount Montgomery of Alamein*; to Thames Television for permission to quote from oral history transcripts used in the television series the *World at War*, 1939–1945; to Mr Ronald Henderson for permission to quote from the diary and papers of Major General L. O. Lyne; to Mrs Sheila Harvey for permission to quote from the papers of her father, Air Vice Marshal E. J. Kingston-McCloughry;

to R. C. Bucknall for permission to quote from the papers of his father, Lieutenant General G. C. Bucknall; to Field Marshal Lord Carver, for permission to quote from his letter of 8 May 1952 to Liddell Hart; to Field Marshal Montgomery's son, Viscount Montgomery of Alamein, for permission to quote from his father's personal correspondence; and to the Trustees of King's College, University of London, for permission to quote from various collections in the Liddell Hart Centre for Military Archives.

I conclude on a note of very special thanks to those who have contributed so much in a personal way during the journey this book has taken from conception to reality: Robin Baird-Smith of Collins, who believed so strongly in the book; Gillian Gibbins of Collins, for her masterful job of editing the typescript; Tom Stalker-Miller, who drew the maps; my daughter Liane Rippingale and her husband, David, who provided a safe haven for me during several research trips to England in 1982 and 1983; Colonel John D. O'Donohue and his wife, Jan, who gave me the warm hospitality of their home during a lengthy research trip to Washington, D.C. in 1980; Mrs Marcia Ducharme, who typed the final chapters of the book; Eleanore Clark and my son, Christopher, for help in checking the manuscript; my agent, Anne Harrel to whom I owe the debt of friendship and encouragement at the time it was needed most; and finally to my wife, Shirley Ann, not only for her help in checking the manuscript but for her love and unflagging support during the writing of *Decision in Normandy*.

CARLO D'ESTE
Cape Cod, Massachusetts

INDEX

Adair, Major General A. H. S. 377, 389

Adam, General Sir Ronald 49, 253, 260, 354–5

Advanced AEAF 313; *see also* Allied Expeditionary Air Force

Afrika Korps 355

Air Commanders' Conferences 223

air forces and actions: Allied superiority in 95, 116, 146–7, 153, 327; pre-invasion bombing 112; and bombing of German transport 147, 213–14, 216n, 223; and bocage 155; command 212–13; dispute over operation use of 213–17; relations with ground forces 221–3, 225–6, 228–9; need for Normandy airfields 222–3; at Caen 226–8, 297, 309–18, 343, 354; casualties and losses 258; support in GOODWOOD 261–4, 358, 369–72, 379, 381, 391; in Bradley's COBRA breakthrough 343–4, 384, 390, 400–3, 406; attacks in German Mortain counterattack 419; use of time-bombs in Falaise battle 443; support in Falaise battle 453, 458

Air Ministry 213–14

airborne forces 65, 109, 111, 117, 169, 445; *see also* individual formations under countries

airfields 222–3

Alamein, El, Battle of 30, 65, 79, 206, 355, 480–1

Alanbrooke, Viscount *see* Brooke, Field Marshal Sir Alan

Alençon 299, 349, 420, 426, 427, 429, 440–1

Alexander, General the Hon. Sir Harold 27, 45, 47–53, 54, 301, 472–3, 501

Allen, Colonel Robert S. 495

Allied Expeditionary Air Force (AEAF): and OVERLORD briefing 82–3; records 82n; supports Montgomery 212; command 212–13, 217, 219; OVERLORD bombing plan 214; overlooked in honours list 221n; Eisenhower attends HQ meeting 310; and Caen bombing 310, 313; controlled from Stanmore 313; and GOODWOOD 362–3, 370; and Falaise battle 440

Allied Force HQ, Algiers 59

Amaye-sur-Seulles 184, 190–1, 195

Amiens 468

ammunition: expenditure and shortages 201n, 225

Anderson, Lieutenant General Kenneth 60

ANISEED, Operation 188–9

Anisy 121

Antwerp 34, 468

ANVIL, Operation (*later called* DRAGOON) 57, 65, 69–70, 264n, 301, 305, 326, 461–3

Anzio 69, 78–81, 84, 88, 168, 302

Arcadia Conference, Washington 1942 23–4

Ardennes 17, 276, 428, 433–4, 459, 465n, 468

Argences 78, 362

Argentan: in Montgomery's master plan 93–5, 101; in Falaise battle 420, 424–7, 429–30, 434, 439–46, 448–52, 454–7, 459, 488

Armed Forces High Command (OKW: German): and first landings 111, 115; on use of panzer forces 116–18, 141, 147–8; reserves 157; refuses withdrawal from Caen 251; and Hitler's orders 414–15; *see also* Hitler, Adolf

Armitage, Major General G. T. A.
185, 190, 193
armour *see* panzer forces; tanks
armoured brigades: composition
146
armoured divisions: composition
360
armies (and formations) *see under*
individual countries
Arnhem 128, 264, 287–8, 434, 466
Arnold, General H. H. ('Hap') 215,
224, 313
Arromanches 229
Atlantic Wall 116, 153, 158
atrocities 507
Attlee, Clement (*later* Earl) 52, 254
Auchinleck, General Sir Claude
26–7, 61, 496n
Audrieu 163, 507
Aunay sur Odon 357, 422
Aure, River 172, 176, 187, 198
Avranches: in Montgomery's plan
100; in revised plan 231, 348; and
Bradley's offensive 299, 324, 328,
339, 343, 351, 405–7, 409, 410,
412n, 478; and Hitler's strategy
414; and Mortain counterattack
418, 421
AXEHEAD, Operation 77

Babcock, Captain Chuck 189
Barber, Major General C. M. 239n
Barker, Major General Ray W. 87n
Barnett, Correlli 491, 501, 512
Bastogne 177, 428
Battle of Britain 20
Bayerlein, Lieutenant General Fritz
162–3, 188–9, 402–3
Bayeux 64–5, 85, 150, 162, 205,
227, 507
Beauvais 468
Beaverbrook, William Maxwell
Aitken, 1st Baron 53
Beda Fomm (Cyrenaica) 61
Belchem, Major General David: on
Montgomery's phase lines 92–4,
97–8, 222; on Montgomery's
presentation of master plan 95–6;
on 3rd Division failure 120, 145;
on airfields 223; and relations of
army with air forces 229;
planning meetings with Bonesteel

Belchem – *cont.*
345, 349; and Montgomery's 10
July directive 349; on
GOODWOOD 392; and US
eastward drive 411; on
Montgomery's not aiding
Canadians in TOTALIZE 427n,
445; and airborne troops at
Falaise 445; ghosts Mongomery's
Normandy to the Baltic 488; *All
in the Day's March* 92; *Victory in
Normandy* 93
Belgium 464, 467
Bennett, Air Vice Marshal Donald
363–4
Bennett, Ralph 416
Bénouville 119n
Bernay 451
Beuville 137
Bidwell, Brigadier Shelford 283, 292
Bieville 136–8
Bigland, Major Tom 452
Blainville-sur-Orne 137
BLUECOAT, Operation 197n, 274n,
421–2
Blumenson, Martin 337–8, 350–1,
443, 455–6, 470, 488, 490–1, 493
Blumentritt, General Gunther 407
bocage: in Montgomery's master
plan 85; Brooke's pessimism over
fighting in 87, 206; difficulty of
103, 153–6, 172, 193, 279, 291,
296–7, 341–2, 507; and Odon
offensive 239–40; and casualties
256, 267; effect on experienced
troops 270, 277; tank
vulnerability in 291–331; and
Bradley's operations 306, 319,
337, 341, 350–1, 411–12, 483
BOLERO, Operation 24, 28, 34
Bomber Command (Royal Air Force)
see under Britain
Bonesteel, Colonel Charles III
345–7, 349, 428, 445
Bourguébus (and Ridge) 298, 318,
349; and GOODWOOD 357–60,
364–7, 375–83, 388; bombed
370–2, 381; and TOTALIZE 426
Bradley, Lieutenant General Omar
N.: commands First US Army
44–5, 60n; and capture of
Cherbourg 63, 73, 200–2, 230,

Bradley – *cont.*
240; and planned use of airborne
forces 65; and Montgomery's
master plan 71, 75, 80, 98,
199–201, 250, 305, 322–3, 477,
480, 483; at Montgomery's
briefing 82; and phase lines 93,
96; planned advance 100, 102;
and OMAHA setback 114; on UTAH
landing 115; and Orne
bridgehead 148, 160; criticises
Montgomery 149, 321, 478; and
revised Caen plans 164, 230, 250,
484; and cooperation with air
forces 221; delayed by weather
230, 390, 400, 480; faces 2nd SS
Panzer Division 232, 246; and
Odon offensive 234; Montgomery
shields 238, 247, 322–3; delays
breakout 247–8; and British
manpower shortage 259;
casualties and replacement
problems 267; use of experienced
troops 271; offensive for Cotentin
Peninsula 299–300, 306, 331,
340, 484; and Montgomery's
concern over panzers 299;
relations with Montgomery
306–8, 328; and bocage 306,
320, 331, 341–2, 483; and Patton
308, 404–5; and stalemate danger
321; and 21st Army Group's
inaction 324,328; commands
12th Army Group 330, 408;
meets Montgomery and Dempsey
for breakout plan 332–4; and
COBRA (breakout plan) 337,
339–46, 350–1, 387; working
method 338–9; tactics 340–1,
344; use of air bombing 343–4;
anger at Eisenhower over single
command 346–7; Montgomery's
10 July directive to 349; and
Brittany ports 351; and
GOODWOOD 361, 365, 384; and
press 393; and COBRA bombing
errors 401–2, 403n; and COBRA
advance 403–5; exploits eastward
drive 410, 412–13; foils Mortain
counterattack 415–17, 419–21,
429; praises 30th Division 420;
and ULTRA 416, 420; traps

Bradley – *cont.*
German Seventh Army in Falaise
gap 424–6, 429, 439–42, 445–7,
449–53, 457, 459, 488; restrains
Patton's advance on Falaise 429,
440; success 432; on
Montgomery's promotion to Field
Marshal 433; split with
Montgomery 433, 495, 501;
resentment at Montgomery's
command 433n; criticises
Montgomery for not closing
Falaise gap 437, 443–6, 456;
favours using airborne troops at
Falaise 445; receives publicity and
credit 453; strategic advance 464;
and Montgomery's strategic
advance 466–9; and ground
command 469; on Montgomery's
preferential treatment 474;
differences with Dempsey 474–5;
flexibility 482, 485; on
Montgomery's need to take Caen
486; and Eisenhower 502;
reputation and achievements
506–7; honours and death
511–12; *A General's Life* 475,
488, 504; *A Soldier's Story* 495,
511
Bras 359, 383
Brécy 423
Brereton, General Lewis 218
Brest 63, 347, 408–10, 434n
Bretteville-sur-Laize 78, 235, 362,
364, 383
Bretteville-sur-Odon 318–19
Bréville 167, 357
Britain: forces and formation
    AIR
    83rd Group, RAF 219, 239n
    Bomber Command: in command
        structure 213; operational use
        of 213–14, 216; opposes
        Leigh-Mallory's Caen bombing
        plan 228; casualties 258;
        requested to bomb Caen
        309–11; bombs Caen 313–15,
        317–18, 354; and GOODWOOD
        bombing 354, 361, 370–1
    2nd Tactical Air Force 162, 212,
        218–19, 235
    ARMY (general) training 19,

Britain: Army – *cont.*
283–7; regimental composition
128*n*; casualties and manpower
249–50, 252–5, 259–62,
264–9; composition 263–4;
battle performance 271–97;
officers and NCOs 279–81,
287–9; lack of cooperation
between units 284–91;
leadership 287–9; weak field
tactics 289–91
21st **Army Group:** formed 38–9;
command 52, 53, 54; staff
58–9; coordinates OVERLORD
59, 75; and phase lines 90,
96–7; intelligence 203; and air
bombing 228; manpower and
casualties 252–3, 256, 258–9,
262, 265, 267–8; uncommitted
reserves 268–9; troops'
experience and performance
271–2; relations with SHAEF
302; calls for Caen bombing
313–14; stalemate 324, 326;
planned drive east 346; and
GOODWOOD 364, 368, 378;
and Falaise trap 439–41, 450;
strategic advance 464; in
Montgomery's master plan
477–8
First Army 60
Second Army: staff and command
59, 60*n*; in master plan 74,
76–8, 95, 199, 323, 476, 478;
landings 112; intelligence
warning on German armour
123–4, 127; in Orne
bridgehead 148, 160; at Caen
164, 166, 192, 202, 204, 207,
210, 246, 248, 250, 289; aided
by airborne forces 169;
manpower shortages 230, 239;
and EPSOM 235, German
opposition to 239; strength
247, 325; disbandments 269;
officer shortage 279; defensive
role 297, 349; stalemate 322,
325, 345; proposed breakout to
east 334, 362; Montgomery's
10 July directive to 348; and
Bradley's COBRA 358; and
GOODWOOD 364, 367, 382,

Britain: Army – *cont.*
386; casualties 384; and
TOTALIZE 421, 444; and Falaise
gap 448; boundary line 451;
strategic advance 467; early
failures 478
Eighth Army 27, 30, 39–40, 46,
58, 355
Corps
1: command 60; landings 112; in
Orne bridgehead 115, 120, 143,
148, 160, 162*n*, 163; cautioned
on panzers 123, 127; in revised
Caen plans 170*n*, 191, 231,
250; in Odon offensive (EPSOM)
235, 237; assault on Caen 305;
in taking of Caen 314–15; and
GOODWOOD 357; casualties
384, 388
2 17
8: command 61; and 1st Airborne
Division 169; and Caen 211,
231, 250; in battle for Odon
(EPSOM) 232–7, 239, 241–2,
245, 248, 299, 483; casualties
242, 244, 384–5, 388; lack of
cooperation with 30 Corps 285;
renewed Odon offensive
(CHARNWOOD) 305; in
GOODWOOD 357, 359–60,
364–7, 372, 380, 382, 384,
388, 391, 396
12 61, 246, 249, 298, 357, 384,
448
13 60, 219
30: command 62, 193–4, 276,
423; landings 112; in Orne
bridgehead 148, 159, 162; in
revised Caen attack 165,
170–1, 197; and 1st Airborne
Division support 170–1; and
battle for Villers-Bocage
174–5, 185, 191–2, 195–6; as
offensive unit 192, 198; in
Odon offensive (EPSOM)
234–5, 237, 239–40; lack of
cooperation with 8 Corps 285;
in GOODWOOD 357; casualties
384; in BLUECOAT 422–3, 448
Airborne Divisions
1st 165–6, 169–71, 192, 200,
212, 224–5, 264, 434, 483

Britain: Army – *cont.*
  6th: Orne landings 111, 112*n*,
    118–19, 136, 138; panzers
    attack 138–9, 167; awaits
    reinforcements 161;
    bridgehead 233, 357; detached
    for rest 263*n*; casualties 263*n*;
    in master plan 323
  Armoured Divisions
  7th: in North Africa 61; and
    Caen 121, 165, 170–1; in
    Seulles Valley 172; casualties
    172; in drive for Villers-Bocage
    173–5, 178, 183–8, 190,
    192–3, 195–7, 224, 490;
    withdrawn east of Caumont
    188–90, 197, 200, 234;
    Bucknall and 194–5; as threat to
    12th SS Panzer Division 200;
    experience and performance
    271–3, 286; command changes
    272–3, 286; lack of cooperation
    with infantry 295; Bradley
    takes over Caumont front from
    299; and GOODWOOD 354,
    360, 372, 379–80, 381*n*,
    382–3; and BLUECOAT 422; and
    aid for Canadians in TOTALIZE
    426
  11th: and capture of Falaise 170*n*;
    in Odon offensive (EPSOM) 235,
    239–42; casualties and losses
    244, 381; in GOODWOOD 354,
    360, 366, 372–3, 376–8, 381,
    382, 389; success in BLUECOAT
    423
  79th 263*n*
  Guards: 354, 360, 372, 374–7,
    381–2, 386, 389; losses 381
  Infantry Divisions
  3rd: 46; in Orne bridgehead
    119–21, 132, 134, 141–3,
    145–6, 149, 161, 162*n*;
    landing 125; and Allied
    intelligence 128; leadership and
    conduct criticised 132–4, 145,
    149; opposed by panzers 136,
    139–40; casualties 137*n*;
    advance halted 198; in assault
    on Caen 305; and Caen
    bombing 315; in GOODWOOD
    374, 381

Britain: Army – *cont.*
  15th (Scottish) 235, 239–40, 242,
    244, 282
  43rd (Wessex): 235, 237;
    casualties 244, 281*n*
  49th 188, 191, 239, 263, 278,
    282*n*, 284–5
  50th: and Caen 121; links up with
    US forces 161; opposes Panzer
    Lehr Division 172, 195–6; and
    drive for Villers-Bocage 174–5,
    184–91, 195–6; Bucknall and
    194; disbanded 263; experience
    and performance 271, 277–81;
    casualties 278, 280; in master
    plan 323
  51st (Highland): Rennie
    commands 133, 274–6;
    reinforces Orne bridgehead
    161, 357; arrival delayed 163,
    166; in revised Caen attack
    164, 171–2, 230; aids Gale
    167; experience and
    performance 271, 273–6; lays
    minefields 365; in GOODWOOD
    373–4
  52nd (Lowland) 264
  59th 262–3, 305
  Armoured Brigades
  3rd 18*n*
  4th 161, 163–4, 166, 197*n*, 289
  8th 124*n*, 146, 159, 172, 296*n*
  22nd: in drive for Villers-Bocage
    175–6, 183–5, 188–9;
    engagement with Wittmann
    179–82; in bocage 342*n*; in
    North Africa 373; in
    GOODWOOD 379
  27th 128, 141, 145–6, 159, 262,
    263*n*
  28th 242*n*
  29th 372–3, 375–7, 379–81
  33rd 190, 195, 263
  8th Tank 263
  34th Tank 262
  Infantry Brigades
  8th 121, 128, 130, 138*n*, 141,
    144
  9th 121, 141–2, 145
  70th 263
  56th 172*n*, 262–3
  131st 295, 380

Britain: Army – *cont.*
   151st 191
   159th 379–80
   185th 121, 128–32, 136, 141, 144, 316
   1st Air landing 39
   1st Commando 112*n*, 161, 286
   5th Parachute 119*n*
   Armoured and Infantry Regiments
   4th County of London Yeomanry: 175*n*, 176, 179, 193, 194*n*, 197*n*; casualties 182; in Royal Armoured Corps 293
   6th Battalion, Duke of Wellington's Regiment 282*n*
   8th Battalion, Durham Light Infantry 280–1
   5th Battalion, East Yorkshire Regiment 281*n*
   2nd Battalion, Essex Regiment 172*n*
   2nd Fife and Forfar Yeomanry 375
   2nd Battalion, Glasgow Highlanders 244
   Grenadier Guards 287–8
   13/18 Hussars 131
   Inns of Court Regiment, R.A.C. (armoured car) 145*n*
   2nd Battalion, King's Shropshire Light Infantry 128–31, 136–8, 144
   24th Lancers 159
   1st Battalion, Leicestershire Regiment 282*n*
   Reconnaissance Regiment 294
   Rifle Brigade:
   1st Battalion 176–7, 179, 182
   8th Battalion 376
   1st Battalion, Royal Norfolk Regiment 128–9, 134
   2nd Battalion, Royal Warwickshire Regiment 128–9, 136
   Staffordshire Yeomanry 128–31, 139, 144–5
   1st Battalion, Suffolk Regiment 130–3
   Royal Armoured Corps 259, 293–4, 296
   Royal Artillery: in Orne bridgehead 128–9, 143*n*;

Britain: Army – *cont.*
   excellence 240*n*, 281, 295; manpower 253; casualties 259; composition 293; in Falaise battle 439
   Royal Horse Artillery 175, 294
   Royal Tank Regiment (*formerly* Corps) 19, 175*n*, 292–4, 296, 375, 379–80
   see also Royal Navy
British Expeditionary Force 17–19, 63
Brittany: as invasion site 33; in plans 36, 62, 72, 77, 100, 102, 247, 344, 412*n*, 480; ports 70, 78, 305; Patton's campaign in 305, 324, 328, 350, 408–10; Montgomery's focus on 344–5, 347–8; and Bradley's breakout 350; and COBRA 406–7; campaign maintained 434*n*, 440
Broad, General C. M. F. 292
Broadhurst, Air Vice Marshal (*later* Air Chief Marshal) Sir Harry 219–23, 227, 313–14, 318, 354, 393
Brooke, Field Marshal Sir Alan (*later* Viscount Alanbrooke): and Dunkirk evacuation 17–18; on Chiefs of Staff Committee 22; grand strategy 25; relations with US Chiefs of Staff 25*n*; attitude to OVERLORD 29; on planning of OVERLORD 32; and Mediterranean strategy 33, 39, 65, 70; organizes British force for OVERLORD 38–9; and appointment of Supreme Commander 43–4; relations with Churchill 45, 261, 303–4, 397; favours Montgomery's appointment 46–50, 52–4; supports Ritchie 61; and ANVIL 64, 70, 462; and Montogomery's master plan 78, 82; pessimism on bocage fighting 87, 206, 341*n*; supports OVERLORD 87*n*; meets Montgomery in France 105; D-Day anxieties 107–9; and Simpson 164*n*; and Bucknall 193; quarrel with Churchill over delays 261, 303–4; and

Brooke – *cont.*
manpower shortages 262; and
inadequacy of 51st Division 274;
opposes Churchill's reprisals for
V-1's 310*n*; and removal of
commanders 303; and threat of
Montgomery dismissal 311, 471;
Montgomery misleads over results
of GOODWOOD 381–2, 391; and
Churchill's anger over
Montgomery's ban 397; on
personal clashes 398; criticises
Eisenhower's grasp of strategy
398, 471; and eastward drive from
Brittany 410; influence on British
army 505; retirement, peerage and
death 509; 'Notes on My Life',
47–9, 52–3, 193, 397
Browning, Lieutenant General Sir
Frederick ('Boy') 60*n*, 171, 288
Bryant, Sir Arthur 509
Bucknall, Lieutenant General G.C.:
commands 30 Corps 61, 112,
193–4; advances 162; and
conduct of battle for
Villers-Bocage 172–5, 185–93,
195–6; assessed 192–5; relieved
of command 197*n*, 274*n*, 277,
289, 353*n*, 423; post-war career
513
Bulge, Battle of the 459; *see also*
Ardennes
Bullen-Smith, Major General D.C.
274–5
Burt, Lieutenant Colonel 313
Butcher, Captain Harry C., USN 69,
110, 394, 398

Cabourg 154
Caen: landings proposed near 35,
66–7; in master plan 35–6, 64*n*,
65–8, 73–8, 81, 85, 93–5, 119,
128, 160, 203–7, 246, 322–3;
Dempsey and 60, 164, 168–72,
192, 197; not planned as holding
operation 77; German defences
94, 119, 122–5, 127–8, 140–1,
144, 151, 155, 208, 233, 246, 323,
483–4; first airborne landings
111; I Corps attacks 112; and
Orne bridgehead 121–2, 128,

Caen – *cont.*
132; British stalemate 128–31,
137, 143–5, 150, 155, 160–5,
210–11, 297, 321, 483–4; terrain
154, 156–7; bombing of 155,
226–8, 297, 309–18, 343, 354;
revised (encirclement) plan
164–5, 200–11, 230, 234, 250,
298–9, 306; Second British Army
role at 199–200; enlargement of
bridgehead 200–1; German
troops committed 201–2;
Williams on 203–5; air
commanders' views on 224–5;
and EPSOM 231, 233–4, 245–6;
British manpower shortage affects
259; expected counterattack 298,
338; casualties 317–19;
part-capture 317–18, 331; and
British line 325; and breakout
plans 333, 348–50; in
Montgomery's 10 July directive
348; and GOODWOOD 357–60,
365, 382, 385; completely
captured 385; Montgomery's
failure at 476–8, 483
Caen-Falaise Plain: terrain 154; and
Odon offensive (EPSOM) 233, 235,
239; and major offensive 305,
349, 485; Germans retain after
loss of Caen 320; in GOODWOOD
354, 376, 381, 382; *see also*
Falaise
Cagny 165, 370–7, 381–2, 388
Canada 253, 255–7, 267
ARMY (general) 263–4
First Army: command 60*n*; in
master plan 76, 475; on left flank
238; delayed by EPSOM 246–7;
casualties 257; landing delays
299, 324, 328; in TOTALIZE 422,
426–30, 439–40, 448, 451, 457;
and trap for Seventh German
Army 424, 439–42; junction with
US army 444, 451; in strategic
advance 467
Corps
1 264
2 246, 275, 357, 384, 426, 448
Armoured Divisions
4th 426, 457
5th 264

Canada: Army – *cont.*
  Infantry Divisions
  1st 264
  2nd 383
  3rd: at JUNO beach 112; in Orne
    bridgehead 121, 124; link-up with
    3rd British Division 138; panzer
    attacks on 161, 507; advance
    stops 198; as threat to 12th SS
    Division 200; in Odon offensive
    (EPSOM) 237; in CHARNWOOD
    assault on Caen 305–6; in master
    plan 323; German atrocities
    against 507
  Armoured Brigades
  2nd 124, 143, 146, 165*n*
  Infantry Brigades
  9th 145*n*
Canadian Military Headquarters
  (CMHQ), London 256–7
Canal de Caen 372
Carentan, River (and estuary) 75,
  85, 111
Carentan (town) 160
Carpiquet Airfield 141–3, 145*n*,
  154, 163, 235, 306, 318–19
Carr, Major 180
Carrington, Lieutenant Colonel
  C. E. 466
Carrouges 441
Carver, Field Marshal Michael, 1st
  Baron 289–91, 294, 296–7
Casablanca Conference 1943 33
Cass, Brigadier E. E. 130, 132–3
casualties: in D-Day landings 115;
  KSLI 137; Gale's parachute
  battalion 167*n*; 7th Armoured
  Division 172; Villers-Bocage
  (British) 182; 8 Corps 242, 244;
  4th US Infantry Division 248;
  Montgomery's concern over
  249–50, 252, 278; and manpower
  shortages 252–68, 278; German
  260, 378, 517; Allied figures 261,
  517; 6th Airborne Division 263*n*;
  1st Airborne Division 264;
  calculation of 265, 267*n*; 50th
  Division 278, 280; officers 280;
  Duke of Wellington's Regiment
  282*n*; at Caen 317; in Bradley's
  offensive 332*n*, 340*n*; in
  GOODWOOD 383–4, 388; Second

casualties – *cont.*
  British Army totals 384; US 30th
  Division 401–2, 419; in Falaise
  killing ground (German) 431–2,
  437–8, 457; US VIII Corps in
  Brittany 434*n*; totals summarised
  517
Caumont 78, 171–2, 184, 188, 201,
  273, 299, 332, 421
Chambers, General S. P. 55
Chambois 430–1, 442, 446–8,
  452–3, 456–7, 467
CHARNWOOD, Operation 305, 315,
  317, 319, 325, 343, 354, 358, 361,
  478
Chartres 428, 441
Cherbourg: as invasion port 33; in
  master plan 35–6, 62–3, 66–8,
  73, 75, 78, 200, 202, 347; German
  defence 99, 167, 201; isolated
  160; Bradley advances on 200–2,
  230, 481, 484; falls 240–1, 300,
  331
Cherbourg Peninsula 477
Cherwell, Frederick A. Lindemann,
  Viscount 214*n*
Cheux 240, 242, 244, 285
Chevasse, Captain Noel 397–8
Chicheboville Woods 139
Chiefs of Staff Committee (British)
  22–3, 27, 32, 38
Churchill, Clementine, Lady 397–8
Churchill, (*later* Sir) Winston: on
  Dunkirk 17; and US aid 19–20;
  view of Second Front 19–22,
  27–31, 33, 37, 80, 87–9, 108;
  letter to Roosevelt 23; mistrusts
  USSR 23–4; strategy 23–9, 38;
  and OVERLORD plans 37, 39,
  56–7, 75, 79–84, 86–7; and Italy
  39–40, 65; on Montgomery's
  appointment 41, 51–2; and Allied
  Supreme Commander 41–4;
  relations with commanders 45–6,
  53, 58*n*; favours Alexander 45–7,
  51, 53; health 51; and ANVIL 66,
  69–70, 301, 305, 461–3; and
  capture of Vienna 70; and Anzio
  81, 84, 88, 168, 302; Eisenhower's
  attitude to 87–90, 108;
  announces D-Day landings to
  Commons 149–50; bombing

Churchill – *cont.*
  policy 214n; quarrel with Brooke
  over British delays 261, 303–4;
  on manpower difficulties 263,
  265–6, 269; and declining British
  influence 264–5; and Caen
  stalemate 302–4; and removal of
  senior commanders 303, 394,
  471; supports bombing of Caen
  310, 317; forces Montgomery's
  hand over Caen 311–12; on
  Bradley's breakout 335; relations
  with Montgomery 396–7;
  promotes Montgomery 433;
  questions figures of German
  Falaise losses 437–8; Eisenhower
  criticises Montgomery to 453;
  strategy of advance 470; version
  of history 494; loses office 509
Cintheaux 459
COBRA, Operation: Bradley's plans
  337–46, 350, 411, 478;
  background (LUCKY STRIKE) 346;
  aims 351; and GOODWOOD 358,
  364, 384, 387; and ULTRA 377; air
  support 384, 390, 400–3, 406;
  delayed by weather 390, 400;
  advance 403–5, 507; effect on
  later operations 411–12
Collins, Major General (*later*
  General) J. Lawton: and
  Montgomery's master plan 78;
  and phase lines 96–7; and naming
  of UTAH 98n; and UTAH landings
  113; captures Cherbourg 240; on
  Bradley and Montgmery 307n; as
  Bradley's operations chief 339; in
  COBRA breakthrough 343, 351,
  404; on defence of Hill 317 419,
  421; in Falaise battle 457;
  subsequent career 514
Colombelles (Caen) 318, 359–60,
  382
Colville, Sir John 90, 312
Combined Chiefs of Staff
  (US-British) 33–7, 65–7, 69
Combined Commanders 33n
Combined Operations Staff 20–1
COMPASS, Operation 61
Condé-sur-Noireau 170n
Coningham, Air Marshal Sir Arthur:
  commands Desert Air Force 79n;

Coningham – *cont.*
  harries panzers 162; criticises
  army progress 212, 223;
  command 212, 218–19, 313;
  presents flowers to Spaatz 218;
  hostility to Montgomery 218,
  220–2, 248, 313, 393, 494–5;
  moves to Normandy 223;
  criticises Montgomery on Caen
  224; and Leigh-Mallory's Caen
  bombing plan 227–8, 316; and
  air support for GOODWOOD 362,
  371; death 494
Connor, General Fox 470
Corlett, Major General Charles H.
  400
COSSAC (organization): and planning
  of OVERLORD 34–8, 47, 480;
  Eisenhower discusses 55–7;
  dissolved 58; staff transferred to
  OVERLORD 59, 65n; and phase
  lines 90n; intelligence sources
  124n
Cota, Brigadier General Norman D.
  114
Contentin Peninsula: in OVERLORD
  plans 35–6, 63, 66–8, 73, 160,
  200, 347; US airborne drop in
  127, 166; terrain 154, 326n, 339,
  342; Germans reinforce 167;
  Bradley's campaign in 201, 299,
  324; Rommel's defensive tactics in
  328; and Bradley's breakout
  (COBRA) 331–2, 337, 339, 342,
  405–6
Coutances 230, 337, 343, 347, 405
Cranley, Lieutenant Colonel W. A. B.
  Onslow, Viscount 177, 178,
  181–2, 197n
Crerar, Lieutenant General H. D. G.:
  command 60n; at OVERLORD
  briefing 82; and cooperation with
  air forces 221; and Montgomery's
  review of position 238; delayed by
  EPSOM 246; concern over
  casualites 257; in TOTALIZE 421,
  426–7, 439, 441–2, 444, 448, 457;
  criticizes Crocker 422n; and Montgomery's strategic advance 466
Crocker, Lieutenant General John: at
  Dunkirk 18; commands I Corps
  60, 112, 132, 357; at Orne

Crocker – *cont.*
  bridgehead 120, 128, 141–3, 145,
    160; and panzer opposition 128;
    and Gale's position 161; and
    attack on Caen 162n, 305; and
    proposed Caen bombing 226–7;
    and 51st Division's failings 274;
    in GOODWOOD 357, 365;
    post-war career 513
CROSSBOW, Operation 301n
Cunningham, Admiral of the Fleet Sir
    Andrew 49n, 64n, 79, 108
Cunningham, Brigadier J. C. 141–2
Cuverville 171, 373–4, 376, 378,
    389

D-Day 71, 107–11, 120, 148, 163,
    258
Daily Mail 298
Deauville 77
de Guingand, Major General Sir
    Francis ('Freddie'): appointed
    Chief of Staff, 21st Army Group
    58; and Montgomery's phase lines
    97; and Leigh-Mallory's
    non-cooperation over 1st Airborne
    Division drop 165, 224; and
    Montgomery's Caen attack and
    delays 166; relations with
    Montgomery 203; and strategic
    bombing 228–9; liaises with
    Eisenhower 302; and Patton 308;
    planning meetings with Bonesteel
    345–6; witnesses GOODWOOD
    bombing 371; and GOODWOOD
    outcome 382, 398; favours
    airborne troops at Falaise 445;
    and Falaise gap 449–50, 452,
    455; on Montgomery 495n;
    speaks for Eisenhower 496;
    Operation Victory 452
de Lattre de Tassigny, General Jean
    264n
Demouville 172, 373–4, 376, 379,
    389
Dempsey, Lieutenant General Sir
    Miles: at Dunkirk 18; GOC
    Second Army 59; and
    Montgomery's OVERLORD plans
    71, 80, 98; on Caen 74, 160;
    issues operational orders 78; at
    OVERLORD briefing 82, 322; on

Dempsey – *cont.*
  British-Canadian deep thrust 95;
    in Orne bridgehead 128, 148; and
    revised Caen plans 164, 168–72,
    192, 207, 230, 483; and 1st
    Airborne Division 169–70; and
    Villers-Bocage battle 174–5, 188,
    190–2, 196–7, 200, 272; and
    congealed front 197–8, 247;
    relations with Broadhurst 219,
    220n; and cooperation with air
    forces 221; and proposed Caen
    bombing 226–8; and Odon
    offensive (EPSOM) 223–4, 241–2;
    talk with Adam on casualties 260;
    and dissolution of 59th Division
    262; and manpower shortages
    265, 267, 354–5, 370; and 51st
    Division failings 274; tolerance of
    leadership weaknesses 289; and
    assault on Caen 305; and Caen
    bombing 314, 318, 354; and
    GOODWOOD 320, 332, 348, 351,
    354–60, 365–6, 374, 389; notes
    on Montgomery's master plan
    322–3, 480, 498n; at meeting with
    Montgomery and Bradley on
    breakout 332–4, 337; knighted in
    field 352; role under
    Montgomery 352–4; qualities
    353–4; issues GOODWOOD
    operational order 362, 364; and
    Montgomery's GOODWOOD
    directive 364–5, 374, 388, 391;
    moves up TAC HQ 367; on
    GOODWOOD attack and outcome
    370, 372, 381–4, 387–8, 389,
    395–6; and BLUECOAT 421–3,
    439–40; and Falaise gap 444,
    448, 451, 457; and Montgomery's
    strategic advance 466–7, 498;
    differences with Bradley 474–5;
    on role of Second Army 478;
    interviewed on GOODWOOD 489n;
    and Pogue's *Supreme Command*
    492; and controversy over
    Montgomery 492, 495; retirement
    and death 512
Devers, General Jacob L. 264n
Dickson, Colonel B. A. ('Monk')
    113n
Dieppe 30–1

Dietrich, General Joseph ('Sepp')
118, 141, 168, 241, 378, 392, 460
Dill, Field Marshal Sir John 25n, 45
discipline 283–4
Dives, River, 154, 441
Dodigny 171
Doenitz, Grand Admiral Karl 434
Dollmann, General Friedrich 111,
118, 163, 241–2
Doolittle, Lieutenant General James
H. ('Jimmy') 469
Dowding, Air Chief Marshal Hugh
213n
DRAGOON, Operation see ANVIL,
Operation
Dreux 441–2, 451
Dreux-Evreux 205
Dulles, John Foster 499
Dunkirk 17–18, 454, 482
Dyas, Captain Pat 176, 180–1

Eadie, Lieutenant Colonel J. A. 13
Eberbach, General Heinrich 215n,
368, 377, 386, 441–2, 446–7
Eden, Anthony (later 1st Earl of
Avon) 438
Eisenhower, General Dwight D.: as
US chief planner 24; opposes
SLEDGEHAMMER 27n; on
Churchill and Second Front 29n;
C-in-C Allied Forces in N. Africa
30; appointed Supreme
Commander 41, 44–5, 52; and
Marshall 42–3; Churchill's
fondness for 44; and field
commanders 45; favours
Alexander for command 49–51;
personality 50; relations with
Montgomery 50–1, 217n, 301–2,
393–5, 398–9, 464–5, 471–5,
478, 495, 498–501; discusses
COSSAC plan 55–7; on
Montgomery as initial assault
commander 59; staff and
commanders 59; and planning
62; and ANVIL 64, 69–70, 461–3;
and Montgomery's master plan
65–6, 68, 75, 247–8, 309; at
OVERLORD briefing 82, 84, 86–7;
on Churchill's attitude to
OVERLORD 87–90; and phase
lines 92; and landings 107;

Eisenhower – cont.
D-Day anxieties 108–9;
postpones landings 109–10;
overrules Leigh-Mallory on air
drop 166; and use of air forces
213–14, 216; frustration over
Montgomery's delays 220,
247–8, 261, 300–2, 308–9, 345,
398, 453; on Montgomery-
Coningham feud 248, 308–9; and
British casualties and manpower
261, 264–6; on breakout to west
302–3; powers over commanders
303, 394; and Patton 307–8;
urges Montgomery forward 309,
312, 479; broad-front strategy
309, 464, 466, 468–70, 497–8;
attends AEAF meeting 310,
312–13; Montgomery disregards
322; and 21st Army Group
inaction 324, 345; US criticisms
of 328–30; pressed to take field
command 330–1; and large
SHAEF staff 331; and bocage
difficulties 342; and Bradley's
breakout 345; and GOODWOOD
361–2; reaction to GOODWOOD
failure 391–5; letters to
Montgomery 395; on heavy
bombers 403; and COBRA
advance 405; and US eastward
drive 412, 425; assumes ground
command 433, 469; Montgomery
squabbles with over strategy 433;
gives Montgomery command in
Ardennes 433n; accepts German
surrender 434; and Falaise gap
443, 452, 488n; rejects thrust into
Germany 461, 464; distrusts
Montgomery 464–6, 471–3; and
squabbles between generals
474–5; loses faith in
Montgomery's master plan 479,
486–7; and drive for Brittany
485; VE-Day despatch on
Montgomery's plan 486; Ellis
criticises 491; and Pogue's
Supreme Command 492, 494; and
historians 493; reputation in
Britain 496, 497n; belief in
US-British alliance 496–7; as
NATO Supreme Commander

Eisenhower – *cont.*
499; generalship 503; US
President 509; letter to
Montgomery of 23 May 1946
(text) 519–20; *Crusade in
Europe* 495–6
Elbe, River 434
Ellis, Major L. F. 196, 210, 489–94,
496
Emiéville 371, 380–1, 383
Enigma (cypher machines) 122*n*
EPSOM, Operation 231–43, 298–9;
Montgomery ends 242, 244;
casualties 242–4, 249, 259;
assessed 244–8, 478, 480; and
GOODWOOD 357, 370
Erskine, Major General G. W. E. J.
(*later* General) Sir George
('Bobby'): and Villers-Bocage
battle 172–5, 183–8, 190, 192,
196–7; on Point 213 disaster 193;
relieved of command 197*n*,
272–3, 274*n*, 289, 423; fails to
use infantry 295; in GOODWOOD
379, 381*n*
Essame, Major General H. 285
Evrecy 143, 146, 148, 164–5, 170,
200, 323, 325
Evreux 365

Falaise: in Montgomery's plans 73,
94–5, 101, 164, 348, 425; and
revised Caen plan 170*n*; Germans
block advance to 318; armoured
thrust for (GOODWOOD) 332, 359,
362, 364–6; Canadian offensive
against (TOTALIZE) 421, 426,
426–30; Haislip's advance on
429; battle of gap 429–31,
437–60; German casualties and
losses 431–2, 437–8; proposed
use of airborne troops at 445
Faubourg de Vaucelles 348, 367,
373
Feuchtinger, Lieutenant General
Edgar 122, 124–5, 138–40
'Fireflies' (Sherman tanks with
17-pounders) 140
Florentin, Eddy 458
Fondouk (N. Africa) 420
Fontenay 285
Foord, Brigadier E. J. 208

Forêt de Cinglais 332
FORTITUDE, Operation 107, 118*n*,
158*n*, 201, 326, 365, 484
'Fortress Europa' 37
Fougères 348, 413, 419
Four 383
France, French:
First Army 264*n*
  Armoured Division
  2nd 427*n*, 432
Frankfurt 468
Frénouville 383–4
Freyberg, General Sir Bernard 206
Fuller, Major General J. F. C. 19,
292

Gale, Lieutenant General Sir
Humfrey 267
Gale, General Sir Richard 142, 161,
167, 171
Gavin, Lieutenant General James M.
39, 287–9, 342
George, VI, King 82–3, 86, 352
Germany: surrender 434; advance
on 464–5
  Luftwaffe 116, 146–7, 153, 158,
  328, 506
  ARMY (general): early strength
  17, 19; command in west
  115–19; D-Day mistakes 141,
  147, 151; tactics and weapons in
  Normandy 155–7; casualties
  260, 378, 431–2, 437–8, 457;
  fighting qualities 283*n*, 485;
  defence tactics 289–92; use of
  armour 292–3
  Army Group B: deployment and
  command 115, 118, 138;
  panzer forces 116, 138; D-Day
  weakness 147; warns on
  pre-invasion buildup 158*n*;
  weakened 337; Rommel leaves
  after injury 368; intelligence
  378; weakness after
  GOODWOOD 386; eastward
  flight 431; in Falaise pocket
  438, 464; strategic deployment
  466
  Army Group G 115, 466
  Seventh Army: and first landings
  111, 114–15; intelligence on
  124; and command of panzers

Germany: Army – *cont.*
138; Hitler's orders to 152; and
Odon defence 241; in Cotentin
365, 400; defends against
COBRA 400, 407; Mortain
counterthrust 414, 416–17;
O'Connor attacks flank 422–3;
trapped in Falaise pocket 424,
430–1, 439, 456
Fifteenth Army 111, 115, 117,
158*n*, 201, 319
Corps
XXV 111*n*
LXXIV 111*n*
LXXXIV 111, 139, 178, 198,
400, 458
LXXXVI 377
Infantry Divisions
346th 167
352nd 113, 123, 161
716th 113, 121, 126, 129, 141,
145
Luftwaffe Field 318, 375
Panzer Forces:
Panzer Group Eberbach 441–2,
447
Panzer Group West: command
115–16, 368, 377; at Caen
166; bombed 167, 370;
strategic hopelessness 386;
GOODWOOD defence 387;
separated from Seventh German
Army 423
Fifth Panzer Army (*formerly*
Panzer Group West) 420, 429,
430
Corps
1SS 123, 141, 178, 197–8, 232,
242, 377, 458
2SS 237, 241–2, 250
47 418–19
II Parachute 400
Divisions
1st SS 232, 237, 378–9, 418–19,
442
2nd SS ('Das Reich') 232, 233*n*,
234, 246, 306*n*, 406, 418, 420,
442
2nd 178, 182, 184, 187–8, 191,
195–7, 200, 418
7th 17, 18*n*
9th SS 232, 241*n*, 242, 325

Germany: Army – *cont.*
10th SS 232, 241*n*, 242
12th SS ('Hitler Jugend'):
deployment 118, 123, 137, 140,
147–8; early counterattacks
160; holds ground 163;
threatened 200; in position
against Second Army 202;
opposes O'Connor on Odon
237, 240; defends Carpiquet
Airfield 306; losses at Caen
318; Rommel deploys 328;
opposes GOODWOOD 377–8,
383; losses and fate 432, 438
21st: at Caen 74, 111*n*, 117–19,
125–6, 128, 140–1, 144, 151,
155; intelligence on 122–5,
127; trained in counterattack
126; opposes 3rd Division
136–40, 143; withdraws from
6th Airlanding Brigade 140;
tank losses 140; repulses 51st
Division attack 172; in position
against Second Army 202, 204,
237, 375; in GOODWOOD
assault 377; losses in Falaise
gap 457*n*
Panzer Lehr: 118, 157; losses
162–3; in Seulles valley 172;
defence of Villers-Bocage
175–6, 178–9, 181, 184,
187–8, 190, 195–6; in position
against 2nd Army 202, 234,
237; defends Rauray 239;
defends St Lô 306*n*; bombed
before COBRA 402; opposes
COBRA 403
17th SS Grenadier 123, 157*n*,
204, 406
116th 418–19, 442
Regiments
22nd 139
125th Grenadier 375
192nd Grenadier 136
Gerow, Major General L. T. 98*n*,
113
Gleave, Group Captain T. P. 208–9
gliders 38
Goering, Field Marshal Hermann
158
GOLD beach 72, 112, 159
GOODWOOD, Operation: casualties

Goodwood – *cont.*
   and losses 259, 383–5, 388;
   lessons of 297; use of tanks in
   332, 354, 360, 372, 374–81, 384,
   388–9; Dempsey plans 334, 351,
   354–60, 367; operational
   directive 349; preliminary
   bombing 358, 360, 363–4,
   370–2, 381, 388, 391;
   Montgomery's directive (Notes)
   on 364–5, 374, 388, 391–2;
   British minefield obstructs 365;
   aims 366; intelligence failures on
   defences 367–8, 376–8; attack
   and battles 370, 372–81; further
   bombing denied 379; outcome
   and assessment 381–90;
   demonstrates German defence
   genius 387; Allied reactions to
   391–9; air chiefs on 391–4; film
   on 396
Gort, Field Marshal J. S. S. P.
   Vereker, 1st Viscount 46
Gott, Lieutenant General W. H. E.
   53
Granville 231, 466, 498
Graziani, Marshal Rudolfo 61
Gregson, Colonel (*later* Major
   General) G. P. 185, 188
Grentheville 379
Grigg, Sir James 52, 54, 206, 254,
   261, 449
Guderian, General Heinz 292
GYMNAST, Operation 25

Haislip, Major General Wade 409,
   413, 425, 429, 441, 447, 456–7
Hamilton, Sir Denis 510
Hamilton, Nigel 454, 476–7, 481
Handy, General Thomas 497
Hansen, Chester 307n, 341, 400,
   402–3, 450, 452
Harding, Major General (*later* Field
   Marshal Lord) Sir John 49n, 289
Hargest, Brigadier James 279–84,
   295–6
Harris, Air Chief Marshal Sir Arthur:
   heads Bomber Command 48n,
   213; bombing policy 213, 371;
   opposes OVERLORD plans
   213–14; and Caen bombing plan
   228–310; on casualties 258; and

Harris – *cont.*
   GOODWOOD 361, 363–4, 369,
   371
Hausser, General Paul 241–2, 245,
   251, 400, 414
Hayn, Major Friedrich 458
Hermanville 128–30, 140, 143n
Hill 112 154, 231, 235, 242, 517
Hill 174 184, 187
Hill 317 418–19, 421
'Hillman' (German fortress, D-Day)
   130–4, 136, 141, 144
Hinde, Brigadier Robert 175–7,
   183–5, 187, 189, 193, 197, 423
Hitler, Adolf: and blitzkrieg 17, 19;
   and first landings 111–12; and
   use of panzers 116, 118; Rommel
   visits 147; interference in
   Normandy campaign 151–2,
   157–9, 200, 208, 251, 321, 484;
   Geyr von Schweppenburg
   criticises 158; meets Rommel and
   von Rundstedt 241; and stand at
   Caen 318–19; deceived over Pas
   de Calais landing 318–19; critical
   of Rommel 327–8; intransigence
   338, 369, 386–7; and July plot
   369, 399, 414; scorched earth and
   defence policy 413–14; orders
   Mortain counterattack 414–16,
   428–9, 431; suicide 434; and
   Falaise battle 441–2, 459; blamed
   by Dietrich 460; and illusion of
   victory 485
Hobart, Major General Sir Percy
   C. S. ('Hobo') 292, 366, 373,
   381n
Hobbs, Major General Leland S.
   402, 419
Hodges, Lieutenant General
   Courtney H. 60n, 82, 408, 466,
   468, 474
Hopkins, Harry 42–3
Horrocks, Lieutenant General Sir
   Brian 18, 62, 240n, 277, 353,
   423, 513
Hottot 187–8
How, Major J. J. 423–4
Howard, Michael 510
Hubert Folie 359, 379, 383
Huebner, Major General Clarence
   402

Huertgen Forest 341
Hughes-Hallett, Captain J. 206
HUSKY, Operation 32, 39, 91, 307, 329, 404

infantry: in bocage 153, 155; casualties and manpower shortage (British) 252–60, 266, 283; UK reserves 268–9; morale and performance 282–5; cooperation with tanks 291–2, 294, 296, 389–90, 490
Ingersoll, Ralph 488n, 495, 501
intelligence 122–5, 127, 157, 167; see also ULTRA
Irving, David 158n
Isigny 160
Ismay, General Sir Hastings (later Baron): on Churchill's post-Dunkirk optimism 20n; on Churchill's strategy 28; letters from Eisenhower 27n, 29n, 500–1; and COSSAC planning 34, 37; on Montgomery's OVERLORD plan 57; at OVERLORD briefing 82, 84, 87; on Churchill's words on OVERLORD 87; on D-Day 108; and ANVIL 462; speaks for Eisenhower 496; deplores Montgomery's Memoirs 499–500
Italy 20, 40, 65, 68–70, 257, 301, 305, 461
Tenth Army 61

Jacob, Lieutenant General Sir Ian 311, 489n
Jodl, General Alfred 111, 117, 158, 327, 434
JUNO beach 72, 112
Juvigny 413

Keitel, Field Marshal Wilhelm 251, 327
Keyes, Admiral Sir Roger 21
King, Admiral Ernest J. 25n, 42
Kingston-McCloughry, Air Commodore E. J. 221n, 226–7, 310–12, 316–17, 343
Kippenberger, Major General Sir Howard 280
Knox, Frank 42

'Knutsford incident' 307
Kraemer, Generalmajor Fritz 178n, 197

La Haye du Puits 160, 230
La Hogue 380, 383
Laigle 440, 451
La Roche-Guyon 368
Latham, Brigadier H. B. 492
Laval 299, 349
Lawson, Corporal R. L. 131
leadership 288–9
Leahy, Admiral William D. 42
Le Bény Bocage 348, 422–3
Lebisey (and Wood) 136–8, 145, 161, 316
Le Bourg-St Leonard 442
Leese, Lieutenant General Sir Oliver 53, 194
Leclerc, Major General Jacques 428, 432
Le Havre 33, 63, 77, 101, 207, 467
Leigh-Mallory, Air Chief Marshal Sir Trafford: command 53, 212–13, 216–19; at OVERLORD briefing 82, 84, 86; D-Day air support in poor weather 100; opposes 1st Airborne Division drop 165–6, 170, 212, 224–5; and Dempsey's Caen plan 192; and Montgomery's Caen strategy 211, 297, 299–300; and OVERLORD bombing plan 214–15; opposition from strategic bombing chiefs 215–17; frustration over delays 220; urges early capture of airfields 222; proposes strategic bombing of Caen 224–8, 297; praises O'Connor 236; criticises Montgomery's redirection of US forces 299–300; Caen bombing plan revived 309, 313, 317; and Bradley's pre-COBRA bombing 343; on Coningham and GOODWOOD 362; Montgomery deals with 392–4; and COBRA 400, 403; and Falaise battle 440; and Arnhem 466; death 495, 510–11
Le Mans 77, 101, 209, 299, 349, 446n
Le Mesnil Patry 507
Les Andelys 451

Lever, Major (*later* Lieutenant Colonel) S. F. T. B. 177, 183, 189, 194*n*, 277*n*, 342*n*

Lewin, Ronald 91, 415, 416*n*, 474*n*

Liddell Hart, Sir Basil: and use of tanks 19, 115*n*, 117*n*, 118*n*, 208, 292; on training 284, 287; on battle performance 286–7, 289; on Normandy results 297; on von Kluge's attitude to Rommel 327; and GOODWOOD 381*n*; letter from Montgomery on fame 504

Linklater, Eric 286

Lion-sur-Mer 35, 138, 140

Lisieux 118, 141, 148, 209, 365

Lloyd, Selwyn (*later* Baron Selwyn-Lloyd) 353

Lockwood, Sergeant (22nd Armoured Brigade) 181

Loire, River and Valley 72, 74, 100–2, 345–6, 349, 411

Lorraine 428, 432, 474

Lovat, Simon Christopher Joseph Fraser, 17th Baron 112*n*, 161, 281*n*

Lovett, Robert A. 329

Lucas, James and Barker, James, cit. 431

Lucky Forward 443

LUCKY STRIKE, Operation 345–6, 349, 412

Lumsden, General Sir Herbert 355

Lyne, Major General L. O. 262, 286

MacArthur, General Douglas 44

McCreery, Lieutenant General Richard 49*n*, 206

McLean, Brigadier (*later* Lieutenant General) Kenneth R. 37, 89*n*, 247, 304

MacMillan, Major General G. H. A. 239*n*, 244

McNair, Lieutenant General Lesley J. 401

MAGIC (decrypt) 122*n*

Mantes Gassicourt 441–2, 451, 474

Marcks, General Erich 139*n*

MARKET-GARDEN, Operation 264, 287, 434; *see also* Arnhem

Marne, River 413

Marrakesh 56–7

Marseilles 462–3

Marshal, General George C.: as US Chief of Staff 23; grand strategy 23–8, 32, 42; appoints Eisenhower 24, 29; relations with Brooke and Dill 25*n*; and Mediterranean operations 33, 65; proposed as Supreme Commander 41–4, 52; and field commanders 45; rests Eisenhower 57; and ANVIL 64, 462; supports Leigh-Mallory's Caen bombing plan 228*n*; and Patton 307–8; poor opinion of Montgomery 329; anxiety at stalemate 330; presses Eisenhower to take command 330–1, 469; and drive to east 412*n*; strategy of advance 470; and Eisenhower's relations with Montgomery 472, 496–7; teaches Bradley 482

Marshall, S. L. A. 437, 453, 460, 493, 506

MARTIAN reports 124*n*

Matloff, Maurice 416

Maurice, Lieutenant Colonel F. J. 130, 136

Mayenne 299, 349

Mediterranean 33; *see also* ANVIL; Italy

Merderet, River 201

Messina (Sicily) 404–5

Metz 468–9

Meyer, Major General Kurt 147–8, 306, 432, 438, 460, 507

Middleton, Major General Troy 405, 408–9, 434*n*

Milner, Captain Christopher 182

Miteiriya Ridge (N. Africa) 355

Mockler-Ferryman, Brigadier Eric E. 420

Model, Field Marshal Walter 456, 459

Montgomery, Field Marshal Bernard Law (*later* Viscount Montgomery of Alamein): on 1940 inadequacies 17; at Dunkirk 18, 46, 454, 482; on Mountbatten 21*n*; commands Eighth Army 27, 30, 39, 46; Normandy command 41, 45–7, 50, 52–4; relations with Churchill 46; relations with Eisenhower 50–1, 217*n*, 301–2, 393–5, 398–9, 464–5, 471–5, 478, 495, 498–501; discusses

Montgomery – *cont.*
  COSSAC plan 55–7; St Paul's School HQ 58; staff and commanders 58–62; OVERLORD master plan 62–70, 71–85, 90, 99–104, 120, 149, 169, 199, 202–3, 321–2, 411, 476–91; opposes ANVIL 69, 463; anticipates Rommel's defences 72, 76, 79, 82, 84–5, 94, 99–101, 149; briefings on plan 75, 77–8, 81–4, 96, 194, 209, 490*n*, 492; letter emphasising offensive action 80–2; phase lines 90–9, 222; oral orders 102–3, 163; advises Eisenhower to launch invasion 110; plan for Caen as pivot 94–5, 160, 164; and Orne bridgehead 120–1, 127, 145, 148–9, 160–7, 200; and 3rd Division 121; hindered by panzers 151, 155; and German defensive tactics 157; favours simple plans 163; revises Caen plans 164, 170–2, 200–11, 230–1, 234, 246, 248–50, 298, 305; and Villers-Bocage failure 191–2, 195, 197, 199; appoints Bucknall 193–5; Williams on 203–5, 352, 391–2; relations with air chiefs 212, 218–21, 248, 308–9, 391, 393; and use of air forces 222, 229; and bombing of Caen 224–6, 310–13, 315, 317; and battle of Odon (EPSOM) 232, 235–7, 242, 244–6; 23 June review 238–9; admits Caen shortcomings to Wilmot 249; concern over casualties and manpower 249–50, 252, 257–9, 261–2, 264–7, 278, 299, 334; and army performance and experience 271–4, 278; tolerance of leadership weaknesses 289; use of armour 294, 355–6; caution 297; redirects US force 299; Churchill criticises for delay 303–4; removal from command considered 303, 311–12, 394, 471–4; relations with Bradley 306–7; Eisenhower exhorts 309; and capture of Caen 318; breakout plan 320; Tedder

Montgomery – *cont.*
  criticises 321; reputation and defence of plan 321–4, 328; numerical superiority 325–6; US criticisms of 329–30, 356; meeting with Bradley and Dempsey on breakout operation 332–3, 340; interest in Brittany 344–5, 347; proposes no breakthrough operation 347; 10 July directive on strategic aims 347–50; and COBRA 351; and Dempsey's GOODWOOD plans 354–6, 360–3, 366–7; tactics 356; written notice revising GOODWOOD 364, 372, 374, 388, 391–2; and GOODWOOD outcome 381–2, 387, 391; terminates GOODWOOD 384; criticised by colleagues for GOODWOOD failure 391–6; and press 392–3; letters from Eisenhower 395; communications with Churchill's wife 396–8; letter to Brooke about GOODWOOD objectives 399*n*; and revised eastward plan after COBRA 410, 412; fails to reinforce Canadians in TOTALIZE 421, 426–8, 439, 444; and BLUECOAT 421–3; claims two enveloping moves 425–6; and Falaise gap 426–7, 429, 437, 439–44, 446–54, 457–9, 487–8; disbelieves Patton's mobility 428; reaches Seine 432; promoted Field Marshal 433; squabbles with Eisenhower over strategy 433, 461; given command in Ardennes 433*n*; accepts German surrender 434; on German prisoners and losses 437; accused of anti-US motives 453–5; dedication 454; on strategy north of Seine 461; strategy of advance 464–6, 471, 473–4, 498, 504; Eisenhower mistrusts 464–5; and Patton's supply deceptions 468; resists Eisenhower's ground command 469; controversy over plan, and Normandy 'myth' 476–88, 501; lack of candour 479–80, 487–8; address to RUSI 487; as British

Montgomery – *cont.*
occupation commander in
Germany 488; declines to
cooperate with historians 491–4;
at NATO 499, 510; generalship
503–5, 507; as CIGS 509; death
510; letter to Dempsey on air
cooperation 515; letter from
Eisenhower of 23 May 1946 (text)
519–20; ; *El Alamein to the River
Sangro and Normandy to the
Baltic* 92, 97, 200, 202, 349, 423,
488; *Memoirs* 202, 392, 399,
411–12, 418, 496n, 498–500
Moorehead, Alan 492n
morale 282–4
Moran, C. M. W., 1st Baron 51
Morgan, Lieutenant General Sir
Frederick E.: and COSSAC planning
of OVERLORD 32, 34–8, 56, 58,
62, 68, 480; appointed Chief of
Staff to Supreme Allied
Commander 34; urges
appointment of Supreme
Commander 42, 44; as critic of
Montgomery 322; on bocage
fighting 341n; *Overture to
Overlord* 36, 38
Morgenthau, Henry 424
'Morris' (German fortress) 130–1,
133, 144
Mortain 348; German
counterattack 414–16, 418–21,
424–5, 428–9, 431; Americans in
423, 425
Mountbatten, Admiral Lord Louis
(*later* Earl Mountbatten of
Burma) 21–2, 25n, 26, 29–30,
32–3, 44, 49n, 68
Mudgett, Colonel Gilman C.
(*miscalled* Muggeridge) 92–3, 96,
96n
Mulberry 63, 229
Mussolini, Benito 20

NEPTUNE Initial Joint Plan 68, 75,
83, 85
Nicolson Nigel 49n
Nijmegen Bridge 287
Normandy: as invasion site 32–3,
35; defences strengthened 37,
108; terrain 99, 153–6; 19 June

Normandy – *cont.*
storm 229–30; Allied strength in
230, 298n; *see also* bocage
North Africa 26–9, 39
North Atlantic Treaty Organization
499
Noyers 165, 170, 200, 237, 357

OB West (Oberbefehlshaber West)
111, 115, 116, 141
O'Connor, Lieutenant General (*later*
General) Sir Richard: command
61, 236; and use of 1st Airborne
Division 169–70; Odon offensive
(EPSOM) 233, 235–7, 240, 483;
relations with Montgomery 235,
352; capture and escape 235–6,
279; renewed Odon offensive
(CHARNWOOD) 305; in
GOODWOOD 360–1, 364–6,
372–4, 375–80, 384, 388–92,
396; and Roberts 373–4; and
tank-infantry cooperation
389–90; breakout to Vire 422–3;
post-war career 512
Odon, River and Valley 141; in
German defence 156; airborne
operation in 170; and
Villers-Bocage battle 177, 179,
190; in Montgomery strategy
199; battle for (EPSOM) 232–4,
242, 245; expected counterattack
298; renewed assault on
(CHARNWOOD) 305; salient and
British line 325–6; and
GOODWOOD 385
officers (British) 279–82, 285, 287
OKW *see* Armed Forces High
Command
Oliver, Major General Lunsford 428
OMAHA beach: landings 72, 113–15,
121, 146, 148, 205; naming of
98n; bridgehead 161; Mulberry
destroyed 229; Bradley returns to
512
Oradour-sur-Glane 233n
Orleans 441
Orleans gap 204, 410, 412
Ormel, Mount 442, 456
Orne, River: in OVERLORD plans 35,
64, 73, 75, 78; airborne landings
111, 118; bridgehead 119,

Orne – *cont.*
    120–50, 160–7, 230, 233–4, 326,
    357; crossings 119*n*, 146, 237,
    241, 367; panzer forces at 123,
    125–6, 139–41; German blunders
    at 140–1; strength of German
    defences 143–4, 156, 318; salient
    and British line 325–6; in
    Montgomery's 10 July directive
    348; and GOODWOOD 357–60,
    362, 367, 372, 377–80, 385
Ouistreham 112*n*, 119*n*, 209
OVERLORD, Operation: British
    attitude to 28–9; COSSAC
    planning of 34–40, 55–7;
    commanders 41–54;
    Montgomery's master plan for
    63–85; briefings on 75, 77–8,
    82–4, 95–8, 194, 209, 490*n*, 492;
    Churchill doubts on 87–90;
    phase lines 90–9; Richardson's
    appreciation 99–104;
    pre-invasion anxieties 108; and
    air forces 212–14; and British
    manpower 253–4, 256; plan
    abandoned after COBRA 410

Paget, General Sir Bernard 32,
    38–9, 53, 58, 505
panzer forces: deployment after
    landings 115–18, 122–7, 158;
    strength 123–5, 202;
    reinforcements 232–3; German
    employment of 292–3, 322;
    Hitler unites for Mortain
    counterattack 414, 419; *see also*
    forces and formations under
    Germany
parachute troops 79; *see also*
    airborne forces
Paris 77, 411, 413, 425, 432, 467,
    481
Pas de Calais: as invasion site 32,
    35; defences 37; Allied deception
    plan 107, 111, 115, 118*n*, 146,
    157, 201, 319, 365; in bombing
    plan 216*n*; *see also* FORTITUDE,
    Operation
Patton, Lieutenant General (*later*
    General) George S.: use of tanks
    19; in Sicily 39, 404–5;
    commands Third US Army 59, 73,

Patton – *cont.*
    408; at OVERLORD briefing 82–3;
    and Pas de Calais deception 107,
    319; leadership 288, 408; and
    infantry-armour cooperation 291;
    moves to Normandy 307–8, 401;
    rivalry with Montgomery 307–8,
    404; impetuosity and manner
    307–8, 404–5; Brittany
    campaign 305, 324, 328, 350,
    408–10, 425, 477; planned
    breakout 343, 351, 484; and
    Loire Valley scheme 345–6, 349;
    commands VIII Corps in COBRA
    404, 407, 478; Bradley and
    404–5; exploits eastward drive
    410, 413; refuses compromises
    418; and British hesitancy at Vire
    423; and trap for Seventh German
    Army in Falaise battle 424, 427,
    429–30, 439–41, 444, 445*n*,
    446–7, 449; mobility and speed
    428; success in Normandy 432;
    on Montgomery's promotion 433;
    rages at Eisenhower for 'neglect'
    433; and Montgomery's failure to
    close Falaise gap 443–4, 446;
    drive for Seine 451; receives
    publicity and credit 453; and
    strategic advance 469–70, 474;
    on Montgomery's preferential
    treatment 474; on Caen planning
    484; diary 495; criticises
    Eisenhower 496; subsequent
    career and death 513–14
Pearl Harbour (1941) 22
Pegasus Bridge 142
Pemsel, Generalmajor Max 111
Périers 339–41, 343, 401–2; Ridge
    125, 128, 130, 136, 139
Pershing, General of the Armies John
    J. 42
phase lines 90–9, 101–2, 222, 356
Pinçon, Mont 154, 171, 175, 177,
    348, 422
Pogue, Dr Forrest C: interviews
    203–5, 208, 220, 304, 347, 416,
    449, 452–3; supplies Montgomery
    letters to Eisenhower 493; on
    Eisenhower's reputation in Britain
    496; *The Supreme Command*
    491–2, 494

Point 213 (Villers-Bocage) 177, 178, 179, 181–3, 187, 192, 193
POINTBLANK (directive) 213, 214*n*
POLAND, Operation 121
Poland:
  Armoured Divisions
  1st 426, 430, 442, 449, 452–3, 456–7
  Brigades
  Parachute 169
  Regiments
  10th Mounted Rifle 442
Pontaubault 406–7, 409
Portal, Marshal of the RAF Sir Charles (*later* Viscount) 22, 29, 48, 214, 216, 222, 313, 394
Port-en-Bessin 161, 164
Pound, Admiral Sir Dudley 22
prisoners-of-war 259
Putanges 458
Pyman, Brigadier Harold E. ('Pete') 194, 353

Quebec Conference, 1943 ('Quadrant') 36, 41, 43, 47
QUEEN beach 129–30
Quesada, Major General Elwood ('Pete') 86, 343, 406, 419
Quiberon Bay 102, 409–10

railways: bombing of French ('Transportation Plan') 107, 147, 213–14, 216*n*, 223
Ralston, Colonel J. L. 253
Ramsay, Admiral Sir Bertram: command appointment 53; at OVERLORD briefing 82, 87*n*; and D-Day timing 110; bombardment 112; and 1st Airborne Division drop 165; on Eisenhower's relations with Montgomery 464–5; death 495, 511; assessed 511
Ranville 119*n*, 138–9
Rauray 235, 237, 239–40
Red Army 24, 25*n*
Rees, Goronwy 83
Rennes 102, 405, 408–9
Rennie, Major General T. G. 128, 130, 132–3, 141, 145, 274–6; killed 276*n*
Rhine, River 469
Richardson, Brigadier (*later* General Sir) Charles: appreciation of

Richardson – *cont.*
  OVERLORD 99–100, 498*n*; air force criticism of 223; appreciation on British stalemate 325–6; recommends armoured operations 331–2, 334, 348; and Montgomery's 10 July directive 349; on Dempsey 353; and GOODWOOD air support 363–4; and airborne troops for Falaise battle 445
Ritchie, Lieutenant General Neil M. 18, 61, 246, 249, 262, 357, 513
Roberts, Major General G. P. B. ('Pip') 239, 272*n*, 280, 296, 366, 372–5, 379, 380*n*, 382, 388–9
Rocquancourt 376
Rohmer, Major General Richard 449, 453–6
Rommel, Field Marshal Erwin: commands 7th Panzer Division in 1940 17; N. African advance 26; and TORCH 27; Montgomery defeats in N. Africa 30, 65, 355; in charge of defences in western Europe 37, 116; and Auchinleck 61; Montgomery anticipates defensive strategy 72–6, 79, 82, 84–5, 94, 99–101, 149; reserves and defence of Caen 78, 88, 164, 191, 202, 207, 210–11, 232–3; Churchill on use of reserves 88; strengthens Normandy defences 108–9; absence during first landings 111, 112*n*, 115, 118–19, 147; commands Army Group B 115; and panzer forces 115–17, 126–7, 139, 147, 153, 158, 232–3, 241, 293; and first (coastal) line of defence 116–17, 126, 153, 154; resumes command 141; on air weakness 147; and Hitler's interference 151–2, 157–8, 386; defensive tactics 155–9, 200–1, 320, 323, 478, 483, 506; deceived over Pas de Calais 157, 484; Geyr von Schweppenburg criticises 158–9; expected Caen counterattack and defence 164, 210–11, 232–3, 245; mistrusts Dietrich 168; Montgomery on use of strategic

Rommel – *cont.*
  reserves 191, 202, 207; fails to
  bypass in N. Africa 209; absence
  in Germany 241; and Odon
  battle 241, 245; recommends
  withdrawal from Caen 251; use of
  armour 293; relations with von
  Kluge 327–8; injury, retirement
  and death 368–9; builds defensive
  network 386; von Kluge on 459;
  on severity of fighting 507
Rommel, Manfred 506
Roosevelt, Franklin D. 22, 25–7,
  37–8, 41–2, 65, 329, 462–3
Rouen 34, 77, 101, 474
ROUNDUP, Operation 25–6, 28, 30,
  33–4
Royal Air Force 20, 31, 167, 189,
  229; *see also* forces and formations
  under Britain
Royal Navy 20, 112, 131, 235
Royal United Services for Defence
  Studies Institution (RUSI) 487
Ruge, Admiral Friedrich 139*n*, 152,
  158*n*
Ruhr 464–5
Russia 23, 29–30, 43; *see also* Red
  Army

Saar 468–9
St Aubin d'Arquenay 134, 140
St Denis-le-Gast 406
St Gilles 404
Ste Honorine 171
St Lambert sur Dives 431, 442
St Lô 76, 232, 306, 337, 339–41,
  343, 347, 400–2
St Malo 409
St Martin de Fontenay 383
St Mauvieu 240
St Paul's School, London 58, 75, 82–3
Saint Pierre 281
Sale, Major W. H. J. 199
Salerno 40, 81
Scarfe, Norman 133*n*
Scarman, Wing Commander (*later*
  Lord) Leslie 393, 485, 497*n*
Scheldt Estuary 257
Sées 427, 453
Seine, River: crossing planned 72,
  77, 92, 101; ports 100–1;
  German defence of 100, 102, 157;

Seine – *cont.*
  and British offensive 305; US
  Third Army's drive for 411, 413;
  Montgomery on move for 425;
  Allies reach and cross 432, 442; as
  trap for German army 445, 450;
  Bradley heads for 447; in original
  plan 463
Seulles Valley 163, 165, 172, 177
SHAEF *see* Supreme Headquarters
  Allied Expeditionary Force
SHELLBURST (tactical HQ) 330*n*
shipping: storm losses 229–30
Sicily 33, 39–40, 307
Siegfried Line 266, 468–9, 474
Silvester, Major General Lindsay
  McD. 512
Simonds, Lieutenant General Guy
  290, 357, 426–7, 449*n*
Simpson, Major General (*later*
  General) Frank ('Simbo') 164, 233
Simpson, General William H. 82
SLEDGEHAMMER, Operation 24–7,
  30
Slim, Field Marshal William, 1st
  Viscount 513
Smith, Godfrey 510
Smith, Brigadier K. Pearce 128–30,
  137, 143–4
Smith, Lieutenant General Walter
  Bedell: and appointment of
  Supreme Commander 43;
  discusses COSSAC plan 55–7; and
  OVERLORD staff 59; and
  Montgomery's master plan 62,
  67; opposes ANVIL 64*n*; on
  allocation of forces to landings
  72; reassures Churchill 88; on
  Montgomery and Caen 205, 300,
  309; on Leigh-Mallory 217*n*; and
  SHAEF staff 331; and bocage
  341*n*; and Bradley's breakout
  345; and army's slow progress
  394; defends Montgomery against
  dismissal threat 472; orders
  analysis of Normandy decisions
  487; on Ingersoll's *Top Secret*
  489*n*
Smuts, Field Marshal Jan Christian
  82, 86–7, 304
Soliers 359, 383
Somme, River 413

Spaatz, Lieutenant General Carl A.
    47–8, 213–15, 218, 227–8, 363,
    401
Speidel, Lieutenant General Hans
    126, 139, 147, 158, 327, 369n,
    456
Sperrle, Field Marshal Hugo 368,
    377
Stacey, Colonel C. P. 262, 504n
Stagg, Group Captain J. M. 109–10
Stalin, Joseph 24, 41, 43
Stilwell, General Joseph 482
Stimson, Henry L. 25, 41–2, 328
storm (19 June 1944) 229–30,
    232–3, 237, 238n, 239
Strafford, Air Vice Marshal Stephen
    C. 227n, 313, 440, 451
Strategic Air Force 213, 228
Strong, Major General Kenneth
    W. D. 420n
Suisse Normande, La (region) 154
Supreme Headquarters Allied
    Expeditionary Force (SHAEF):
    formed 37n, 58, 213; intelligence
    on 21st Panzer Division 122–3,
    124n, 127; and air forces 213,
    217n; and British manpower
    difficulties 264–5, 267; and Caen
    stalemate 300; relations with 21st
    Army Group 302; advance HQ
    (Portsmouth) 330; LUCKY STRIKE
    studies 345; and Montgomery's
    caution 362; and GOODWOOD
    364–5, 367, 382, 391–2; and
    scale of Falaise success 464;
    strategic advance plans 465n,
    466; forward HQ in France 466;
    Pogue's book on 491–2
SWORD beach 72, 111–12, 120–1,
    138, 159

tanks and armour: British neglect of
    19; German superiority in 71–2;
    comparison between Allied and
    German 124n; cooperation with
    infantry 291–2, 294, 296,
    389–90, 490; British tactics
    290–4; Montgomery's use of 294,
    355–6; in Montgomery's master
    plan 323; in advance towards
    Falaise 354, 360, 372, 374–84,
    388–9; losses 385; see also panzer

tanks and armour – cont.
    forces; and individual formations
    under names of countries
Tapp, Lieutenant Colonel (later
    Major General Sir) Nigel 128,
    133, 136–7, 140, 143n, 144,
    316–17
Taylor, Colonel George A. 114
Tedder, Air Chief Marshal Sir
    Arthur: as Deputy Supreme
    Commander 47–8, 52, 213, 217;
    relations with Churchill 53; on
    Montgomery's master plan 78,
    82; relations with Montgomery
    79, 220–2, 509; and phase lines
    91; D-Day air support in poor
    weather 110; and Zuckerman
    214; and OVERLORD bombing
    plan 214–17; relations with
    Leigh-Mallory 216, 217n;
    appoints Coningham 218;
    frustrations over stalemate 220,
    222–3; career 222; cancels
    Leigh-Mallory's bombing plan for
    Caen 227–8, 311, 316; on
    Montgomery-Coningham feud
    248; and Montgomery's delays
    309, 321; at AEAF meeting on
    Caen bombing 310, 313;
    suppresses report 317; supports
    GOODWOOD 361–3; on
    GOODWOOD aims 392–3; and
    V-1 threat 394; criticises
    Montgomery 394–6, 398, 501;
    and Montgomery dismissal threat
    472; on Montgomery's and
    Churchill's attitudes to history
    494; as Chief of Air Staff 509
Teheran Conference 43
Templer, Field Marshal Sir Gerald
    289
Tessel Wood 285
Thetford (Suffolk training area)
    277n, 342n
Thomas, Edward E. 124n, 125
Thompson, R. W. 501
Thucydides 105
THUNDERCLAP, Exercise 75, 77–8,
    82, 84, 127
Thury-Harcourt 73, 205, 348,
    357
Tilly la Campagne 382n

Tilly-sur-Seulles 172, 176, 178–9, 184, 187, 295
Tinchebray 451
Tobruk 26
TORCH, Operation 26–9, 39
TOTALIZE, Operation 422, 426, 458
Touffreville 381
Tracy-Bocage 183–5, 190, 195
'Transportation Plan' *see under* railways
Troarn 154, 377
Trun 431, 438, 442, 445, 448–9, 452–3, 456, 467

ULTRA 122–4, 167, 203, 233, 237, 241, 365, 368, 376–7; and Mortain affair 415–16, 419–21; and Eberbach's counterattack 441, 446–7; and Montgomery 471; gives advantage to Allies 484; secrecy 489n
United States of America: alliance with Britain 19–20; enters war 22; war policy and strategy 23–7; criticism of Normandy stalemate 328–9
forces and formations:
AIR
8th Air Force 223, 363, 370, 400–1, 403n
9th Air Force 218, 370, 400–1
Tactical Air Command IX 86
Tactical Air Force IX 406, 419
ARMY (general): casualties 261, 265, 267; composition and strength 263–4; battle performance 276, 287–8; dismissal of commanders 278–9; mobility 428
1st Army Group 365
6th Army Group 264n
12th Army Group (formerly 1st): formed 45; command 60n, 330, 408; operational 408, 469; and Falaise trap 439–40, 451, 487–8; strategic advance 464, 467–8
First Army: Bristol HQ 45; command 60n; planned strategy 73, 76–8, 202, 322, 411; and phase lines 93–4; and

United States of America – *cont.*
Orne bridgehead 148; and 17th SS Panzer Division 204; Montgomery eases pressure on 238, 247, 322; takes Cherbourg 300; St Lô offensive 306; advance to Avranches 324; strength 325; planned breakout from Cotentin 332, 334, 349, 351; Hodges commands 408; eastward swing 411, 421; widens Avranches gap 423; and Falaise battle 446; in Montgomery's strategic advance 468
Third Army: Patton commands 59, 307; drive for Brittany 73, 77, 324, 347; planned landing and operations 77; success 291, 410; in Normandy 307–8; breakout from Cotentin 332, 351; and Loire Valley scheme 345; becomes operational 408; drive to east 411, 421; and Mortain counterattack 416; mobility and speed 428; reaches Seine 432; in Falaise battle 439–41, 443, 445n; junction with Canadians 444; supply 468; and Siegfried Line 468–9; in occupation of Bavaria 512
Seventh Army 39
Corps
IV 440
V 113, 115, 160–1, 171, 175, 190, 201, 421
VII: in landings 113; link-up with V Corps 160; Bradley commits 201; takes Cherbourg 240; in Brittany 299; in COBRA breakthrough 306–7, 339, 341, 400, 403–4; foils Mortain counterattack 419; in Falaise battle 441, 447, 457
VIII: in Montgomery's master plan 77, 160; Bradley commits 201–2; delayed arrival in Normandy 247; Montgomery's directive to 348; and COBRA breakthrough 351, 404, 405–7; Brittany campaign 409, 425, 434n; casualties 434n

United States of America – *cont.*
 XII 441
 XV 409, 413, 420, 424–6, 427,
  439–40, 442–4, 447, 456–7
 XIX 201, 400
 XX 428, 441, 457
 Airborne Divisions
 82nd 38, 111
 101st 111, 428
 Armored Divisions
 2nd 404, 406
 3rd 259
 4th 406–7, 409, 428
 5th 413, 427*n*, 428
 6th 409–10
 Infantry Divisions
 1st ('Big Red One') 113, 161, 173,
  188, 271
 4th 65, 113, 115, 248
 9th 401
 29th 113–14
 30th 401–3, 418–20
 35th 418
 36th 40
 79th 413, 427*n*, 432, 442
 90th 413, 427*n*, 430, 442, 453
 Infantry Brigades
 504th Parachute 287
 505th Parachute Regimental
  Combat Team 39
 Infantry Regiments
 120th 419
Urquhart, Major General R. E. 169
UTAH beach, 65, 72, 98*n*, 111, 113,
 115, 127, 205

V-1 weapons 301
Verney, Major General G. L. 272–3,
 286
Verrières 376
Versailles 466
Vienna 70, 301
Vierville-sur-Mer 36
Villers-Bocage 146, 148, 159, 163,
 164–5, 170–2; advance on
 173–6, 179; British enter 176–7;
 British lose battle for 182–93,
 195–7, 224, 230, 289, 297, 490;
 effect of failure 199–200, 234,
 478; Montgomery holds line at
 299; in master plan 323; bulge
 323, 331–2; and GOODWOOD 358

Vimont 362, 364, 374, 375, 381,
 383
Vimoutiers 451
Vire 78, 100, 153–5, 231, 348,
 422–4
von Blaskowitz, General Johannes
 115
von Clausewitz, Karl 435
von Falkenhausen, General
 Alexander 159
von Funck, General Hans 418
von Gersdorff, Generalmajor
 Rudolph 419*n*
von Kesselring, Field Marshal
 Albert, 40, 466
von Kluge, Field Marshal Gunther:
 replaces von Rundstedt 251, 326;
 and shift of forces to US sector
 323; tactics 326–7; relations with
 Rommel 327–8; appraisals of
 situation 328, 338, 391, 407; and
 outcome of GOODWOOD 386–7;
 and Bradley's COBRA 402, 407;
 and Hitler's orders for Mortain
 counterattack 414–15, 418, 428,
 459; forces trapped in Falaise
 pocket 431, 459; suicide 459;
 deceived by FORTITUDE 484
von Luck, Oberst Hans 375, 380*n*
von Rosen, Leutnant Freiherr 370
von Runstedt, Field Marshal Gerd:
 command and relations with
 Rommel 76, 158, 369; and first
 landings 111; forms Panzer Group
 West 115; and us of panzer forces
 116–18, 141, 151–2, 162; and
 defence of Caen 141; and Hitler's
 interference 151–2; mistrusts
 Dietrich 168; absence in Germany
 241; dismissed for recommending
 Caen withdrawal 250, 326;
 proposes suing for peace 251; gives
 Rommel's funeral eulogy 369*n*
von Schlieben, General Karl 240
von Schweppenburg, General Geyr
 115–16, 126*n*, 158–9, 166–8,
 251, 369
von Stauffenberg, Colonel Claus,
 Count 399

WAKE, Exercise 169
Walker, Major General Walton H. 447

Warhurst, Lieutenant Colonel A. E.
  492
War Office 252–6, 260, 262
Warlimont, General Walter 414
Washington Post 329–30
Wavell, General Sir Archibald (*later*
  1st Earl) 20, 26, 45, 108
Weeks, Lieutenant General Sir
  Ronald 278
Weigley, Russell F. 342
West, Major General Charles A. 65
Westphal, General Siegfried 147
Whistler, Major General L. G. 133*n*
Wigglesworth, Air Vice Marshal Sir
  Philip 310, 476, 501
WILD OATS, Operation 170–1
Williams, Brigadier (*later* Sir) Edgar
  T.: 345, 349; intelligence on
  352nd Division 113*n*; on
  Montgomery's detachment
  127–8; observations on
  Montgomery 203–5, 352, 391–2;
  and Foord 208; and Falaise gap
  449–50, 452, 455; on ANVIL 462;
  and Montgomery's boastfulness

Williams – *cont.*
  471; and threats of Montgomery's
  dismissal 473; and Pogue's
  Supreme Command 492; helps
  Montgomery with *Memoirs* 496*n*
Wilmot, Chester 132–3, 144, 148,
  173–4, 188, 197*n*, 200, 207–8,
  249, 445*n*, 478
Wilson, General Sir Henry Maitland
  ('Jumbo') 48, 49*n*, 52
Winterbotham, Group Captain F.
  W. 415–6, 420
Wittman, Obersturmführer Michael
  178–83, 197; death 197, 459
Wood, Major General John S. 409

Zimmermann, General-Leutnant
  Bodo 415
Zuckerman, Solly, Baron: bombing
  policy 214, 216; on
  Leigh-Mallory 217; on Caen
  bombing 226, 310*n*, 312–13,
  315–17; advises Montgomery
  312; advises Bradley 343; studies
  GOODWOOD bombing 372*n*

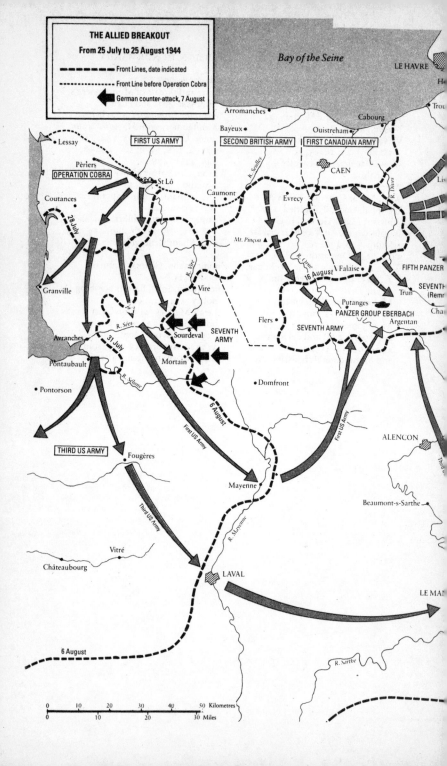

THE ALLIED BREAKOUT

From 25 July to 25 August 1944

▬ ▬ ▬ Front Lines, date indicated

- - - - Front Line before Operation Cobra

◄ German counter-attack, 7 August

Bay of the Seine

LE HAVRE

He—

Trou—

Arromanches •

Cabourg •

Bayeux • Ouistreham •

Lessay •

FIRST US ARMY SECOND BRITISH ARMY FIRST CANADIAN ARMY

Périers • CAEN Lis—

OPERATION COBRA St Lô •

R. Seulles

R. Dives

Coutances • Caumont • Evrecy •

28 July

Mt. Pinçon ▲ FIFTH PANZER

R. Vire

R. Orne

Granville • Vire • Falaise • SEVENTH (Remn—

16 August

Trun • Cha—

R. Sées Putanges

Avranches • SEVENTH Flers • PANZER GROUP EBERBACH

31 July Sourdeval ARMY Argentan

Pontaubault • Mortain SEVENTH ARMY

R. Sélune

• Pontorson • Domfront

ALENCON

6 August

First US Army

THIRD US ARMY Fougères •

First US Army

Mayenne • Beaumont-s-Sarthe •

Third US Army

Vitré •

Châteaubourg • LAVAL LE MAN—

6 August

R. Sarthe

0   10   20   30   40   50 Kilometres
0   10   20   30 Miles

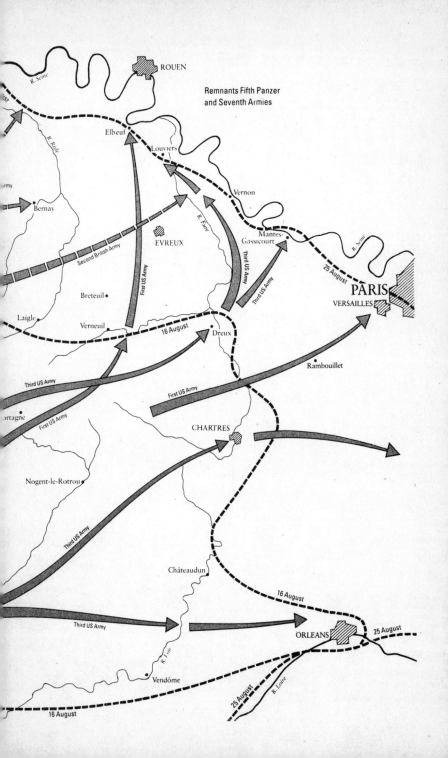

ROUEN

Remnants Fifth Panzer
and Seventh Armies

R. Seine

Elbeuf

Louviers

R. Risle

Vernon

R. Eure

Bernay

Second British Army

EVREUX

Mantes-
Gassicourt

Third US Army

Third US Army

25 August

PARIS

VERSAILLES

Breteuil

First US Army

Laigle

Verneuil

16 August

Dreux

Rambouillet

Third US Army

First US Army

First US Army

ortagne

First US Army

CHARTRES

Nogent-le-Rotrou

Châteaudun

16 August

Third US Army

ORLEANS

25 August

Vendôme

25 August

R. Loire

R. Loir

16 August